THE
ALASTAIR CAMPBELL
DIARIES

Praise for *Volume Three, Power & Responsibility*

'The great challenge of history is to recapture things as they really were, when the outcome of wars was unknown, deaths were not foretold and things that "everyone knows" were known only to Time Lords ... Campbell's four-volume monsterwork is the best record of what it was like at the centre of politics at the time.'
Independent

'Campbell had a Manichaean single-mindedness and the most extraordinary energy. After working similar hours to him, I would read a book and go to sleep. Campbell, who was ever accompanied by a thick A4 daybook in which he constantly scribbled his contemporaneous record of the day's events, would then write up his diaries at length, fail to sleep properly, and then rise early to deal with the next day's events ... This is a serious work, lightened occasionally by hilarious episodes ... instructive as both an example to follow and a sign of the pitfalls to avoid.'
Jack Straw, *Guardian*

'As with earlier volumes, the pace is relentless. This is a warts and all account. Campbell spares no one, not even himself ... One can't help admiring Blair and Campbell for their extraordinary resilience, somehow managing to keep their eyes on the big picture while all around them mayhem reigns.'
Observer

Praise for *Volume Two, Power & the People*

'A fascinating, candid account of recent history' *Financial Times*

'*Power and the People* retains the capacity to shock ... it should be required reading for coalition MPs because, despite a sometimes exhausting level of detail, there is still no better minute-by-minute account of what life is like in No. 10.' *Guardian*

'Plunging into the second volume of Alastair Campbell's diaries is like opening a Samuel Richardson novel. The tone is breathless and excitable and the dramatic world of backstabbing, tittle-tattle and palace intrigue is instantly captivating. Historians will scour the book for valuable new information. Practitioners of media management will regard it as a classic.' *Spectator*

'Fascinating stuff' *Daily Express*

'Explosive ... a warts-and-all account of the feuds, friendships and fall-outs of the first days of the New Labour government' *Daily Mirror*

'Like the Bloomsbury Group of the Twenties, the New Labour clique is churning out an apparently inexhaustible number of memoirs, diaries and memorabilia. Alastair Campbell's diaries are by far the most important record to have emerged. Nothing like them exists in British political writing. They are the product of an almost monastic self-discipline. No matter how gruelling the circumstances, Campbell found time to settle down and make a daily record of events, which at the most frenetic times could extend to several thousand words ... The account of Blair's wise and agile handling of the crisis that followed the death of Princess Diana is powerful and authentic.' *Daily Telegraph*

'The real value of the "complete" diaries lies in their total immersion in the fierce urgency of the present tense ... The diaries capture what seemed important at the time, without knowing where it would lead or what was coming next. So, huge issues creep up without historical fanfare, as the author, at the end of a long day, has no idea how important they will seem the next day ... Campbell is a great diarist, and precisely because he is not a stylist. His is spare, Orwellian prose, compelling by virtue of his position and his narrative "grip" – a favourite Campbell word. Whatever you think of Blair and the Blair years, this is what it was like at the time.' *Independent on Sunday*

'Although there has been no shortage of memoirs from the New Labour era, this is without doubt the most authoritative. Campbell is no ordinary spin doctor. He enjoyed total access not only to Tony Blair and the New Labour court but also to just about every mover and shaker in the global power elite up to and including the US President.' *The Times*

Praise for *Volume One, Prelude to Power*

'Hugely gripping … all of human life is here. It makes *The Thick of It* look tame. And sane.' *Sunday Times*

'Campbell is a compelling diarist … *The Campbell Diaries* provide the fullest insider account so far of New Labour's ascent to power.' *The Times*

'Campbell's world is the brutal, angry, hard-driven, jokey, football-crazed and intensely male world of tabloid journalism. He is a fluent and industrious reporter, with amazing stamina.' *Daily Telegraph*

'There are plenty of nuggets here that are fascinating, some passages that make you wince and others that are gripping. It has historical value.' *Observer*

'Campbell's great strength is that he tells it like it is … This is as near as we are ever likely to get to the definitive account of the Blair governments up to the moment of Campbell's departure in August 2003. A brutally honest, relentless roller-coaster by a man who enjoyed total access.' *Spectator*

THE
ALASTAIR
CAMPBELL
DIARIES

Volume 3

POWER & RESPONSIBILITY
1999–2001

Edited by
ALASTAIR CAMPBELL
and
BILL HAGERTY

arrow books

Published by Arrow Books 2012

1 3 5 7 9 10 8 6 4 2

First published in Great Britain in 2011 by
Hutchinson
Random House, 20 Vauxhall Bridge Road,
London SW1V 2SA

www.randomhouse.co.uk

Addresses for companies within The Random House Group Limited can be found at:
www.randomhouse.co.uk/offices.htm

The Random House Group Limited Reg. No. 954009

A CIP catalogue record for this book is available from the British Library

ISBN 978 0 09 949347 1

The Random House Group Limited supports The Forest Stewardship Council (FSC®),
the leading international forest certification organisation. Our books carrying the
FSC label are printed on FSC® certified paper. FSC is the only forest certification
scheme endorsed by the leading environmental organisations, including Greenpeace.
Our paper procurement policy can be found at www.randomhouse.co.uk/environment

Typeset in Palatino by Palimpsest Book Production Limited,
Falkirk, Stirlingshire

Printed and bound in Great Britain by
CPI Group (UK) Ltd, Croydon CR0 4YY

To Joe Hemani, for his friendship, and his generous
support of the political and charitable causes I believe in

Contents

Acknowledgements

Many thanks once more to Bill Hagerty, who took over the task of editing these diaries after the sad death of our friend and colleague Richard Stott, and to Mark Bennett, who was with me in Downing Street and has also been with me on the long and sometimes tortuous road to publication.

Both through my diaries, and the two novels I have published, I have come to appreciate the professionalism and kindness of many people at Random House. I would like to thank Gail Rebuck, Susan Sandon, Caroline Gascoigne, Joanna Taylor, Charlotte Bush, Emma Mitchell and the team of 'spin doctors', Martin Soames for his legal advice, David Milner, Mark Handsley, Vicki Robinson, Helen Judd, Sue Cavanagh, and Jeanette Slinger in reception for always ensuring one of my books is at the front of the display cabinet downstairs – at least when I am visiting the building. My thanks, as ever, to my literary agent Ed Victor, to his PA Linda Van and to his excellent team.

I want to thank Tony Blair for giving me the opportunity he did, and thank the many friends and colleagues who have helped me in good times and bad.

Finally, thanks to my family. As these diaries show, the pressures of the job I did also fell on Fiona and the children, and I thank them for their love and support.

Introduction

Volume 3 of my full diaries begins on May 1, 1999, and ends on September 11, 2001. The first of these dates, the anniversary of Labour's election win under Tony Blair two years earlier, was another over-busy Saturday in the life of the government, dominated by a horrific and deadly nail bombing at home, and overseas by continuing difficulties in the conflict in Kosovo. The second was a day, and a date, that immediately wrote itself into the history books: 9/11. The terrorist attacks on the twin towers in New York and the Pentagon in Washington DC would alter the course of George Bush's presidency: 9/11 would herald war in Afghanistan, still going on today, and be part of the thinking that led to war in Iraq, perhaps the most difficult decision Blair had to take, and certainly the most controversial.

Looking back, Kosovo might seem straightforward, an obvious cause, a one-sided war – NATO vs Belgrade – easily won; these diaries make clear it was anything but. It was, however, seen – and not just by his closest supporters – as one of TB's finest moments, an episode in which he showed real leadership and moral courage in his determination to reverse the ethnic cleansing of Kosovar Albanians ordered by the Milosevic regime. The Iraq War, for many reasons, remains more divisive and less clear-cut. The full story, at least as seen from the perspective of these diaries, comes in Volume 4, *The Burden of Power*, to be published early next year. But that September 11 is an important milestone in that story is beyond doubt. It was a remarkable day, among the most remarkable of the many I spent in TB's company, and provides a dramatic close to this book.

There can be few if any graver responsibilities upon a prime minister than sending troops to fight, knowing that some will not return alive. So with war acting as bookends to this volume, Kosovo in the opening pages and what George Bush defined as the war on terror at the end, *Power & Responsibility* seemed an appropriate title, following on from

Prelude to Power, the story of our journey from opposition to government, and *Power & the People*, in which despite all the problems we faced we did at least have the wind of public opinion blowing most of the time behind us.

It is often said that we enjoyed the longest honeymoon in British political history. Perhaps we did, but it didn't always feel like that. Though I lived through all the events described here, and lived them at times with a ferocious intensity, often I cannot exactly recollect either the events or how I felt. I have to rely on my own record more than my memory. But reading it all now, it certainly feels as though things were getting tougher. Though I was still able to work long hours and with huge energy, my own moods seem to be darker more frequently. Rows with my partner Fiona are more frequent too. TB and I appear to be at odds, not least on a strategy for dealing with the increasingly difficult and negative media, far more than I remember from the time.

The problems we had in opposition and in the early stages of government in seeking to make a well-functioning team out of strong egos and fractious personalities appear to be greater, and our handling of them if anything less sure. For the third volume running, TB's frustration at his inability to get me, Gordon Brown and Peter Mandelson working together cohesively is a part of the story. He says at one point that he believes all three of us had touches of genius but also touches of madness. In my case, I have the certificates for the latter, but certainly TB's basic optimism about the good nature of his colleagues is regularly tested. He seems to be moving towards the position of many of his staff, that Gordon's ambitions to be prime minister are getting in the way of a productive relationship. I did not often see TB lose his temper. But the day when he took GB to one side, after the Chancellor had been rude and obstructive in a meeting attended by senior ministers and civil servants, was one of them. 'Don't ever speak to me like that again ...' The anger was real. GB seemed to feel it, and went away chastened. But there were times when he did, alas, speak to him like that again. Yet most of the time, TB continues to hold to the view that on the balance between 'brilliant but impossible' – the description he used of GB in his own memoir, *A Journey* – the brilliance manages, just about, to keep the upper hand. Peter – 'a fighter not a quitter' – and Gordon appear at times to be at war, and Europe and the euro often give a policy backdrop to rows that often were as much about personality and an inability to put the team effort first. We have the second Mandelson resignation which, I have subsequently realised, did irreparable damage to his relationship with me, despite occasional bouts of seeming to work together well, not least at the 2010 election. I fear he will always believe that I, not he, nor even TB, was responsible for what he calls his 'defenestration'. He's wrong, but there we are.

My worries about my own profile seem to be greater in this volume, not least because pressures from Fiona to cut the workload or, preferably, get out of the job, are growing. I had forgotten how early I had been thinking about moving on, and how much this seemed to 'discombobulate' TB. I had also forgotten the scale of the coverage I was attracting during this phase; not just the incessant press attention, but a play based on me, a website dedicated to me, books, my own impersonator on Rory Bremner's comedy show – and perhaps I didn't help myself in agreeing to a documentary about our media operations. I was hoping that if people saw genuinely behind the scenes, they would realise the whole thing about 'spin' was overblown. But BBC documentary maker Michael Cockerell later told me the film got more publicity than all other films he had made combined – including several on prime ministers – so perhaps that both made the point whilst also suggesting I had defeated the object of the exercise. It was deemed to be 'news' if I missed a briefing. One of my best-known – and most regretted – phrases, the 'bog-standard comprehensive', came to be uttered, and caused an enormous frenzy. It still regularly appears in print, probably beaten only by 'we don't do God' and 'the People's Princess' as the most quoted mini sound bites of the era. In fact I was trying to defend comprehensives but it came out wrong. Less well-known than the phrase is the fact that the reason it was in my mind was because TB himself had used it in an interview a few days earlier, without a stir. When the spokesman saying something gets more attention than when the principal says it, clearly something is wrong.

But whatever the personality issues, and the media management problems, we got through a lot, and at the end of it we won another landslide victory. Reading the account of the pre-campaign period and the election campaign itself, I am left wondering how on earth we managed a second successive three-figure majority. We have a lot to be grateful to our Tory opponents for. First we had to postpone the date because of a serious outbreak of foot-and-mouth disease which did considerable damage to agriculture and tourism, and to our reputation for competence. The launch of the manifesto, when finally it happened, was one of the most accident-prone days in the history of elections – first TB was harangued by a hospital patient, wiping out coverage of the launch; then Jack Straw was slow-handclapped by the Police Federation – not great for a Home Secretary; and finally Deputy Prime Minister John Prescott lamped a voter with a mullet haircut. It was also a period of real tension between TB and GB, even though Peter Mandelson was not around, but somehow we won and we won big. Yet far from our election victory ushering in a sense of new drive and energy, MPs appeared sullen after the event and Number 10 went into a time of real anger and division.

This period saw another campaign, for London Mayor, and the diary records our failed efforts to get Frank Dobson elected ahead of Ken Livingstone, who eventually won as an independent. The fallout, alongside a similar misfortune in Wales, taught TB the lesson that if you were going to devolve power you had to be serious about it. It is an interesting episode too for what it said about our failure properly to harness the talents and popularity of Mo Mowlam, who became convinced – wrongly – that we had been seeking to undermine her.

Power & the People made me feel we did not adapt nearly as well as we or others thought to the advent of the 24-hour media age, and *Power & Responsibility* confirms me in that view. Media pressures are all to be tactical, to respond to the agenda of others. That should force policymakers always to seek to be more strategic. I'm not sure we always did that. It is also possibly the case that my own role, and the dominant position I came to adopt within Number 10 and the government more broadly, contributed to that. Getting the balance right between the urgent and the important is not easy. The media make it harder. The focus on Cherie and the family was also becoming more intense. I suppose that was inevitable when Cherie became pregnant, and even more so when Leo was born and hard-headed political hacks for a day or two became baby correspondents. Cherie forgetting to buy a rail ticket was a major front-page story. And when the family's former nanny sought to write a book about her time with them, they felt their privacy so invaded that we sought one of the few injunctions of the Blair era.

As with previous volumes, the planned and the expected are constantly clashing with the unplanned and the unexpected. There was plenty of time to plan for the arrival of a new millennium – it was not as if the date was a secret. But if the fears about the so-called Millennium Bug that was going to devour our computers came and went without incident, the birth of the Millennium Dome and the celebrations on the night itself were not quite so pain-free. Pretty much anything that could go wrong appeared to do so. Likewise more preparation went into TB's speech to the Women's Institute than any speech outside a party conference. It turned out to be a disaster, with thousands of WI members slow-handclapping the Prime Minister, an event which brought to a head an internal debate about what TB was all about in this period. Then there was the phase when we appeared to be having memos leaked left, right and centre, and amid all the paranoia and the security service worries, it emerged they were being stolen from Philip Gould's bins. A visit to the UK by heavyweight boxer Mike Tyson became a huge issue because of his previous convictions for attacks on women. Fox hunting continued to bedevil us, with the two sides of the campaign passionately engaged and TB constantly wondering why we had got into it, and trying to work out how to get out of it. Food seemed to play a bigger role in this period, with Prince Charles a leading figure in the campaign against the government's position on genetic modification, and a problem over beef on the bone. Prince Charles crops up again after TB's party conference speech themed around the need for Labour to take on the 'forces of conservatism'. In my view, it was among his best ever speeches. But he became unsettled by the vehement reaction against it – not least by the forces of conservatism – and to some extent the energy and momentum it gave us were quickly lost. GB pursued a similar theme when he took up the case of Laura Spence, a young student denied access to Oxford University but who made it to Harvard and became something of a symbol of the conflict between class and opportunity for all. Again, TB was quickly unsettled, feeling we were getting perilously close to class war, and an undermining of the New Labour 'big tent'. He was also constantly worrying about whether the civil service really had the desire or the capacity for the pace and scope of reform he wanted in the public services. His speech on the 'scars on my back' gathered in pursuit of reform was seen as an attack on the trade unions. I think it was just a reflection of the frustrations he felt at being able to see so clearly how he wanted to change the public services, and how hard that was in practice.

Those frustrations were as nothing, however, compared with those he felt when dealing with the two biggest domestic crises not just of this volume, but perhaps the whole period of the Blair premiership. Crisis is an overused word. There were hundreds, possibly thousands of events and situations we dealt with that were described by the media as crises. I think that during my entire time with TB, we had five that I would describe as full-blown, 24-carat crises. Three were international: Iraq, at several points; Kosovo, because at times it did appear that we might not be able to see the action through to its conclusion; September 11 and the events which flowed from it. The two domestic crises, in some ways the worst of all we had to deal with, because both gave a sense of the country lurching out of control, or even reason, were the fuel protests and foot-and-mouth disease. Both fall within the period of this volume and in both, the responsibility to lead the country through the crisis, unsurprisingly, fell largely on TB. This was also the period when I think a little iron entered our souls about much of the modern media. For in both there was a strong feeling that they were not really covering these events as such, but using their coverage to make a bad situation even worse, operating in a way that we came to call '*Pravda* in reverse'.

If those episodes contained some of the low points, one of the highest was the day that power was devolved to Northern Ireland. To see Unionist and Sinn Fein leaders sharing power was the culmination of a lot of hard work. But that first day of devolution was not the end of the story, and even if Northern Ireland is less dominant in this volume than in *Power & the People*, its ups and downs continue to consume enormous amounts of TB's time and energy. With Northern Ireland such a dominant theme of *Power & the People*, I spent almost a week in Ireland north and south when the book was published earlier this year, including a visit to Stormont to see the Northern Ireland Assembly at work. The mood was very different from when we were there trying to bring the parties together. To see Martin McGuinness of Sinn Fein as Deputy First Minister alongside First Minister Peter Robinson of the DUP, once sworn enemies, is confirmation of the remarkable journey they have made, and the remarkable success so far of the peace process itself. This volume also contains one of the odder testimonies I have ever had: 'You scare the life out of me' – this from Gerry Adams, no less.

Another high point was the fall of Milosevic. When people talk about spin, it is usually in a negative light. But with regard to both Northern Ireland and Kosovo, I think that communications played an important role in the meeting of our objectives. In military terms, Kosovo was a fight that could not be lost: NATO vs Belgrade. NATO includes several major military powers. But we were a collection of democracies, in some of which the military action was deeply unpopular. He was a dictator with total control of his media. We could, and at times we did, lose the public-relations fights in our democracies. So I was both privileged and proud to have been asked by Bill Clinton, Tony Blair and NATO general secretary Javier Solana to oversee a revamp of the communications of the conflict, and I know that we made a difference for the better.

Whilst my obsessiveness may be part of the madness that TB

referred to, I hope that historians of the future will appreciate it. The diary paints a detailed picture of what we tried to do, and of what went wrong alongside what went right. I do think it shows TB at what I sometimes refer to as his 'infuriating best': determined, driven, and totally focused on meeting tough objectives. He was genuinely moved by the cause, and further fired up when we visited some of the refugee camps filled with people fleeing Milosevic. His zeal took him to some difficult political territory, not least in his dealings with President Bill Clinton, who at times felt we were building up TB at his expense. We weren't, and we would have been pretty stupid if we had, but that didn't stop the president showing some 'red-hot anger' in a late-night phone call to TB. The issue of ground troops was always difficult, not just because of a difference of emphasis between TB and Clinton, but also because of clear differences within the US Administration. General Wes Clark, NATO's Supreme Allied Commander in Europe, was moved to warn us of just how isolated TB might turn out to be. But I am in no doubt TB's determination to force the issue of ground troops lay in large part behind Milosevic's collapse, without ground troops actually being needed. But if victory in Kosovo was clear, the aftermath was not, as the Russians moved in and at one point the concept of 'World War 3' entered the diplomatic lexicon. Life was never dull with Boris Yeltsin around, nor with Vladimir Putin when he followed. It was never dull with Bill Clinton, nor with George W Bush. It was never dull with Tony Blair. Challenging. Difficult. But never dull.

Ronald Reagan's speechwriter Peggy Noonan once wrote that being president is like painting a portrait made up of thousands of tiny actions and decisions that collectively make up the final picture. This diary is part of that story so far as it relates to a British prime minister. I think history will be kinder to TB than the judgement much of the media passes on him now. Even when my diaries of the whole period have been published, they will still only be telling part of the story. But I am confident this is as close as it gets to recording what life was like close to Tony Blair during a pretty remarkable period in British history. I'm not sure a diary can do much more than that. It can never be a full account of history, but hopefully it is a contribution to it, and I am pleased now to be able to share it with others.

Who's Who

May 1999–September 2001

The Cabinet

Tony Blair	Prime Minister (TB)
John Prescott	Deputy Prime Minister and Secretary of State for the Environment, Transport and the Regions to June 2001 (JP)
Gordon Brown	Chancellor of the Exchequer (GB)
Robin Cook	Foreign Secretary to June 2001, then Leader of the Commons (RC)
Jack Straw	Home Secretary to June 2001, then Foreign Secretary (JS)
David Blunkett	Education and Employment Secretary to June 2001, then Home Secretary (DB)
Margaret Beckett	Leader of the Commons to June 2001, then Environment, Food and Rural Affairs Secretary (MB)
George Robertson	Defence Secretary to October 1999, then NATO Secretary-General (GR)
Mo Mowlam	Northern Ireland Secretary to October 1999, then Chancellor of the Duchy of Lancaster to June 2001
Lord (Derry) Irvine	Lord Chancellor
Clare Short	International Development Secretary
Chris Smith	Culture Secretary to June 2001
Frank Dobson	Health Secretary to October 1999 (FD, Dobbo)
Alistair Darling	Social Security Secretary to June 2001, then Work and Pensions Secretary
Jack Cunningham	Chancellor of the Duchy of Lancaster to October 1999 (JC)
Donald Dewar	Scottish Secretary to 17 May 1999, First

	Minister of Scotland May 1999 to October 2000 (DD)
Nick Brown	Minister of Agriculture, Fisheries and Food to June 2001
Stephen Byers	Trade and Industry Secretary to June 2001, then Transport, Local Government and the Regions Secretary
Alan Milburn	Chief Secretary to the Treasury to October 1999, then Health Secretary
Alun Michael	Welsh Secretary to July 1999, First Secretary of Wales May 1999 to February 2000
Baroness (Margaret) Jay	Leader of the Lords to June 2001

Also attending Cabinet

Lord (Denis) Carter	Lords Chief Whip
John Morris	Attorney General to July 1999
Ann Taylor	Commons Chief Whip to June 2001

Additional Cabinet changes 1999–2001

Hilary Armstrong	Commons Chief Whip from June 2001
Charles Clarke	Minister without Portfolio and Labour Party Chairman from June 2001
Lord (Peter) Goldsmith	Attorney General from June 2001
Patricia Hewitt	Trade and Industry Secretary from June 2001
Geoff Hoon	Defence Secretary from October 1999
Tessa Jowell	Culture Secretary from June 2001
Helen Liddell	Scottish Secretary from January 2001
Lord (Gus) Macdonald	Minister of Transport to June 2001, then Chancellor of the Duchy of Lancaster
Peter Mandelson	Northern Ireland Secretary, October 1999 to January 2001 (PM in index only)
Estelle Morris	Education and Skills Secretary from June 2001
Paul Murphy	Welsh Secretary from July 1999
John Reid	Minister of Transport, then Scottish Secretary May 1999 to January 2001, Northern Ireland Secretary from January 2001
Andrew Smith	Chief Secretary to the Treasury from October 1999

Lord (Gareth) Williams	Attorney General July 1999 to June 2001, then Leader of the Lords

10 Downing Street

Andrew Adonis	Policy adviser, head of Policy Unit from June 2001
Phil Bassett	Special adviser, Strategic Communications Unit
Mark Bennett	AC's researcher
Alison Blackshaw	AC's senior personal assistant
Cherie Blair	Wife of TB (CB)
Julian Braithwaite	Press officer, Foreign Affairs
Bill Bush	Special adviser, Research and Information Unit
Alastair Campbell	Chief press secretary and Prime Minister's official spokesman (AC)
Hilary Coffman	Special adviser, Press Office
Kate Garvey	Diary secretary
Bruce Grocott MP	Parliamentary private secretary
David Hanson MP	Parliamentary private secretary from June 2001
Jeremy Heywood	Principal private secretary
Robert Hill	Policy adviser, political secretary from June 2001
Anji Hunter	Presentation and planning
Peter Hyman	Strategist and speechwriter (PH)
Tom Kelly	Northern Ireland Office spokesman, later Prime Minister's official spokesman
Liz Lloyd	Special adviser, Policy Unit
Pat McFadden	Special adviser, Policy Unit
Lucie McNeil	Press officer
David Miliband	Head of Policy Unit to 2001 (DM)
Fiona Millar	AC's partner, aide to CB (FM)
Sally Morgan	Political secretary
Jonathan Powell	Chief of staff
Lance Price	Special adviser, Press Office
John Sawers	Foreign Affairs adviser to 2001
Martin Sheehan	Press officer
Godric Smith	Deputy press secretary
Sir Richard Wilson	Cabinet secretary

HM Treasury

Ian Austin, Ed Balls, Ed Miliband, Sue Nye	Special advisers
Bob Shrum	Political adviser

Northern Ireland

Gerry Adams	President, Sinn Fein. NI Assembly member (GA)
Bertie Ahern	Prime Minister of Ireland (BA)
General John de Chastelain	Chair, Independent International Commission on Decommissioning
Sir Ronnie Flanagan	Chief Constable, Royal Ulster Constabulary
John Hume	Leader, SDLP. NI Assembly member
Joe Lennon	Bertie Ahern's press secretary
Seamus Mallon	Deputy First Minister. Deputy Leader, SDLP
Martin McGuinness	Minister of Education. NI Assembly member (Sinn Fein) (McG)
Senator George Mitchell	US special envoy for Northern Ireland
Ian Paisley	Leader, Democratic Unionist Party
Chris Patten	Tory peer, chair of NI policing review
John Taylor	NI Assembly member. Deputy Leader, Ulster Unionists
David Trimble	First Minister. Leader, Ulster Unionists

The White House

Sandy Berger	National security advisor
George W. Bush	43rd President of the United States (from January 2001)
Bill Clinton	42nd President of the United States (BC)
Hillary Clinton	First Lady (HC)
Al Gore	Vice President

Europe

Jose-Maria Aznar	Prime Minister of Spain
Jacques Chirac	President of France
Lionel Jospin	Prime Minister of France
Romano Prodi	President, European Commission
Vladimir Putin	President of Russia (from August 1999)
Gerhard Schroeder	Chancellor of Germany
Boris Yeltsin	President of Russia (to August 1999)

Kosovo

Martti Ahtisaari	UN special envoy
General Wesley Clark	SACEUR (Supreme Allied Commander – Europe)
General Sir Charles Guthrie	Chief of the (UK) Defence Staff (CDS)
General Sir Mike Jackson	Commander, KFOR
Slobodan Milosevic	President of Yugoslavia
Jonathan Prince	US official seconded to NATO
Jamie Rubin	US state department spokesman
Jamie Shea	NATO spokesman
Javier Solana	NATO secretary-general to October 1999

The Labour Party

Lord (Charlie) Falconer	Cabinet Office minister, 'Dome Secretary'
Stan Greenberg	US pollster
David Hill	Labour Party spokesman
Glenys Kinnock MEP	Wife of Neil Kinnock
Neil Kinnock	Labour Leader 1983–92, European commissioner
Michael Levy	Businessman, Labour Party fundraiser
Margaret McDonagh	General secretary
TBWA	Labour's advertising agency

Parliament

Paddy Ashdown	Liberal Democrat Leader to August 1999
Betty Boothroyd	Speaker of the House of Commons to October 2000
Kenneth Clarke	Former Chancellor of the Exchequer
William Hague	Leader of the Opposition 1997–2001
Michael Heseltine	Former Deputy Prime Minister (Hezza)
Charles Kennedy	Liberal Democrat Leader from August 1999
Ken Livingstone	Successful independent candidate for London mayoralty
John Major	Former Prime Minister
Shaun Woodward	Conservative MP for Witney, Labour MP from 1999

The Media

Tony Bevins	*Express* political editor
Rory Bremner	Impersonator and satirist
Michael Brunson	ITN political editor to 2000
Michael Cockerell	BBC documentary maker
Paul Dacre	*Daily Mail*
Sir David Frost	Broadcaster, *Breakfast with Frost* presenter
Trevor Kavanagh	*Sun* political editor
Donald Macintyre	*Independent* political commentator
Andrew Marr	BBC political editor from 2000
Piers Morgan	Editor, *Daily Mirror*
Rupert Murdoch	Chairman, News Corporation
Robin Oakley	BBC political editor to 2000
Peter Oborne	*Daily Express* and biographer of AC
Andrew Rawnsley	*Observer* columnist
John Sergeant	BBC chief political correspondent to 2000, then ITN political editor
Rebekah Wade	Editor, *News of the World* from 2000
Philip Webster	*Times* political editor
Michael White	*Guardian* political editor
David Yelland	Editor, *Sun*

Family and Friends

Donald and Betty Campbell	Parents of AC
Rory, Calum and Grace Campbell	Children of Alastair Campbell and Fiona Millar
Alex Ferguson	Friend of AC, manager of Manchester United
Philip Gould	Political pollster and strategist, adviser to TB (PG)
Audrey Millar	Mother of Fiona
Gail Rebuck	Publisher, wife of Philip Gould

The Diaries

Saturday, May 1, 1999

I said to Fiona [Millar, AC's partner] – two years to the day since the election. It feels a lot longer, she said. Things were certainly feeling different to how they were two years ago. Wall-to-wall bomb coverage this morning.[1] TB sounded very fed up and was beginning to think there might be a Serb connection. We had had another good night on the military front [in Kosovo]. [General Wesley] Clark [Supreme Allied Commander Europe – SACEUR] specifically asked for JB [Julian Braithwaite, Downing Street press officer, foreign affairs] to attend the EUCOM VTC [United States European Command video teleconference]. Jonathan Prince [US official seconded to AC's team at NATO] activated a conference call on news that NATO bombs had hit a bus whilst attacking a bridge. I said to [NATO spokesman Air Commodore David] Wilby we should have two scripts prepared straight away – one for it being true, one for it being Serb propaganda. The immediate hunch was it was true. The Serbs were playing it up for all it was worth and we were struggling to get the info quickly. Wilby called me at 10pm to say we would have it soon, but it didn't look good. I said if we could get a clear factual statement out tonight it would help. If we had to wait till the morning it would dominate a whole news cycle.

PJ Crowley [US National Security Council spokesman] called me at 2am with an agreed statement admitting there had been an unfortunate accident. We stressed we did not target civilians and were able to deny categorically the Serb claim we had hit an ambulance. The other fast-moving story was [US Baptist minister and former candidate

[1] A nail bomb had been exploded the previous evening in the Admiral Duncan pub in London's Soho, killing three people and wounding seventy. Perpetrator David Copeland had previously detonated similar bombs in Brick Lane and Brixton.

for the Democratic presidential nomination] Jesse Jackson's visit to see Slobodan Milosevic [President of Yugoslavia]. He was clearly winning the battle for the release of three PoWs.[1] I was feeling very uneasy about the whole thing. Jackson was starting to call for an end to the bombing, and the US media would go wall-to-wall schmaltz with this stuff. In the conference calls I said we had to stay focused on a tough message and not get driven down that route. We had three situations pushing us potentially off course – Jackson, the bus, and a downed F-16. We agreed, and circulated, a cautious response re Jackson that we would welcome any release but it made no difference to the vigour with which we would pursue our objectives. We had dealt with the bus and we had to turn the F-16 situation into a story of heroism and bravery. TB was doing his speech on the 300th anniversary of the Sikh religion. He emphasised the battle of values, and there were clips in it to fit both Kosovo and the Soho bomb. We were trying to get more focus on refugees.

Sunday, May 2

TB called after his Sikh event, pleased with the speech and with the warm reception he got there. We were both worried that the PoWs were going to take the Americans overboard on the schmaltz front, weakening resolve. We already had all this Jesse Jackson stuff, which Milosevic was exploiting. [Major General] Walter Jertz [NATO's new military spokesman] did a good murder board [role-playing panel firing questions] and people seemed to think he was up to it. The conference call was low-key but OK. We were about to hit the power stations and hopefully plunge Belgrade into darkness, which we had been pressing for for some time. Catherine Colonna [spokeswoman for French President Jacques Chirac] called me after the call to tell me in confidence that Chirac was going to go to Moscow and he would like to speak to TB tomorrow.

I did a bit of planning with the MoD and Anji [Hunter, head of Downing Street presentation and planning] re the plan for TB to announce more help for Macedonia, and for the refugee situation, tomorrow, and to sort TB's visits programme. We wanted the story to be one of TB tying in the front-line states but it would be very hard for it to be anything other than refugees. David [Miliband, head of TB's policy unit] and Louise [Shackelton, Miliband's wife]

[1] Three American soldiers had been captured along the Yugoslav–Macedonian border on March 31. Having embraced and prayed with the three men, Jackson successfully appealed directly to Milosevic for their release.

came round for dinner but as ever it was constantly interrupted. David Wilby called to say he and his SHAPE [Supreme Headquarters Allied Powers, Europe] colleagues felt they were seen as a bunch of no-hopers by the Brussels lot and they were getting fed up with it. He was sure Jonathan Prince was bad-mouthing him. We were trying to get Julian B through all the security clearances to get him properly installed in there and I said to both they just had to keep plugging away.

Monday, May 3

PoWs was not as bad as I feared. The arrest [of neo-fascist David Copeland] re the nail bombing plus darkness hitting Belgrade over-night were the main media focus. On the way out to Northolt, I sent over a note to the MoD re their press conference, setting the line on the extra money for refugees and the defence of electricity as a military target. TB arrived half an hour later. He had sent another note to [US President Bill] Clinton pressing on the setting up of a US–UK nerve centre in London, having received no real response to the last one. He said he was getting frustrated with them, felt the US system still wasn't responding with the urgency we needed.

Chris Meyer [Sir Christopher, British ambassador to Washington] had sent a telegram saying Bill had disengaged a bit from the Kosovo situation. He went through the military side of things with [Chief of the Defence Staff – CDS – General Sir Charles] Guthrie, and then the humanitarian with John Vereker from DFID [Department for International Development]. He is a nice, kindly man, but his compassion is also matched by a hard-headedness. He told me he was fed up with the Home Office, who were being very slow and difficult about deciding on taking more refugees. But I could see TB's eyebrows arch upwards when John said he wanted the UK to be getting up to 1,000 a week. He warned TB/CB [Cherie Blair, TB's wife] how awful the camps were going to be. John S [Sawers, TB's foreign affairs adviser] and I were working on the speech for Romania, which was fine. We landed and drove to 4 Armoured Brigade where [British General] Mike Jackson and Brigadier [Hamish] Rollo briefed TB inside what from the outside looked like a very ordinary tent but which inside was a major and very sophisticated military operations centre. The logistical skills of these guys is something else. Cherie had brought a hideous Nicole Farhi jumper for TB to wear, which would have been a hideous fashion statement to make touring a refugee camp. I was wearing a Gap T-shirt Fiona had bought in Washington and was going to suggest we swap.

TB wandered round talking to some of the troops in their tanks and minesweepers and then went down into the middle of a field, they gathered round and he did a very good rallying speech. I met a couple of Burnley fans and chatted a bit about football. We then had a private session with CDS and Jackson, who was another one who had soldier written all over him. He has a rich whisky-coated voice, bags under his eyes you could carry your boots in, and a wonderful clarity of view. He said there was no way in the world we would win without a build-up of ground troops. He was unimpressed by the way the war was being waged and we had to keep pressing them [the Allies] to get tougher and quickly.

Then news came through from Macedonian intelligence that they had picked up a threat, which was being taken seriously, that TB would be attacked if we went to Kumanovo[1] so instead we organised for him to speak to some of the people there by phone. I was briefed on Jertz's first briefing, which went well. But Julian still wasn't being listened to enough, e.g. he wanted to put out a strategic briefing re SACEUR's visit to Bulgaria and Albania but they couldn't see the point. We drove to the Stenkovec refugee camp [accommodating some 23,000 refugees]. Anji had done a great job advancing it, with TV corralled properly. It was a vast sprawling place. Kids were swimming in what looked like pretty dodgy water. As soon as we arrived, TB was virtually mobbed, and the kids were shouting 'Ton-ee, Ton-ee,' smiling and really generous of spirit in pretty grim conditions. It was hard to walk around with the crowds following, and both he and Cherie were clearly moved by the whole thing.

Anji had organised for him to talk to smaller groups inside some of the tents. They told heart-rending stories of relatives dead or missing, the long journey to escape, their worries about the future. But they were totally supportive of what we were doing. He then went up to the mike that had been set up to speak to them and announce the doubling of money for refugees and the plan for the UK to take more. He met the UNHCR [United Nations High Commission for Refugees] and the NGOs [non-governmental organisations giving aid] to ask what more they needed and try to get a proper fix on things. We then left for Blace [refugee camp on the Kosovo–Albanian border], where even though the refugees were standing in queues, many exhausted and emotional, eyes glazed, clearly hungry, they started to applaud as he arrived, first a ripple, then louder as people realised he was there.

[1] Third largest city in the Republic of Macedonia, north-east of the capital, Skopje.

It was close to thirty degrees. In the queue I spotted a little girl who could have been [AC's daughter] Grace's double. She had a huge great smile, yet next to her, her mother was crying, and looked as though she had been crying for days on end. An old man tried to press his papers into Tony's hands and asked us to take him to Britain. Then we walked across no-man's-land to the top of the queue, where there was a more palpable sense of fear, no crying, no talking, silence apart from the voices of the people from the NGOs explaining the process by which they were taken in. We did a doorstep with the silent queues as the backdrop. We got into the car. It is a total obscenity, I said. It just makes me so angry, he said, that we have been so slow and still we are not going fast enough. He said it had confirmed him in his view there was no way in the world of doing a deal with Milosevic, whatever the deal they thought could be cooked up. It was hard to understand why Clinton, the ultimate empathetic politician, did not seem to get this in the same way as we did.

We got back to the embassy where I briefed the lobby by phone and then to a meeting with Prime Minister [Ljubčo] Georgievski. He was young, just thirty-three, and told us Macedonia had the youngest PM and the oldest president in the world. They were grateful for what we were doing but there was a fair bit of edge there. Ten per cent of their two million population was now made up of refugees. It had been like an earthquake. We were trying to persuade them to have another transit camp, which would be temporary, but they had heard that before. We also wanted more troops stationed here. TB spoke of the prospects of EU and NATO membership.

Then with President [Kiro] Gligorov, the one with two bullet holes in his head [Gligorov had survived an assassination attempt in 1995], we went over the same ground, then left for the airport. On the conference call we discussed the need for better systems to deal with the Serb claims about civilian targets being hit. We had to do a better job of publicising the false ones, which again depended on being able to get the military info straight away. We were getting very good coverage for TB's visit, and the speech for tomorrow was well set up. We arrived in Romania, worked on the speech over dinner, with TB again complaining re the US, who were about to lose a vote in Congress. He said he wondered if we didn't need to tweak their tails a bit in public.

Tuesday, May 4

We got an amazing press out of yesterday, in some ways too amazing, in that it was all a bit Messianic, but we could hardly complain. I had a swim first thing, then in to finish the speech with TB. I wrote in a very powerful passage re the refugee camps. He was writing in a bit about pushing for Romania's EU and NATO membership. Clinton had talked about a 'bombing pause', which though consistent with the Washington communiqué was going to give us one or two problems. The *Independent* led on Serb claims of twenty dead in the bus attack. I sent them a letter pointing out that even where mistakes were admitted, that does not mean they should take at face value Serb accounts of the consequences.

TB met the PM [Radu Vasile], then the president [Emil Constantinescu], in what they told us was one of [former President Nicolae] Ceauşescu's smaller palaces. It was vile, a really ghastly place. TB was being very warm and friendly to them, really pushing the hand of friendship whilst trying to bind them in to the campaign. They were not exactly jumping for joy, but clear we had to win. He did two separate doorsteps hitting the main points again, with no questions. We then left for the enormous and equally ghastly parliament building. There were a few anti-NATO protesters around but generally the reaction was warm. I did the eleven o'clock [lobby] briefing down the line to Number 10, pushing on the visit and the speech. They pushed hard on refugees, and by the end of the day we were up to 1,000 a week.

I peeled off to get a flight to Brussels via Frankfurt. Wes [Clark] had asked for me to go to the chateau again and have dinner with him and Gert [Clark's wife]. Julian briefed me on the way from the airport on what we wanted out of it – basically an acceptance that JB was in there, drafting all the scripts and with proper access to the info that would shape them. Wes had been to Bulgaria and Albania and like TB had been more fired up by the urgency of the whole thing. He wanted to know every last detail of our trip, particularly the state of the refugees and the views of our military on the ground. I said what TB most feared was a wounded Milosevic still in power, and Wes was equally of the view he had to go, there could be no deal.

He couldn't understand why Clinton wasn't more engaged. He felt he was getting bad advice – that [Sandy] Berger [National Security Adviser] is an accountant type, [Jim] Steinberg [Berger's deputy] a wuss, [Bill] Cohen [US Defense Secretary] can't make tough decisions. The politics are screwed up. He also felt too many people in the Administration were either worrying about their position with [Al] Gore [Vice President and potential presidential candidate in 2000], or looking around in the private sector. Public opinion was not being led. If it was, he was sure it would follow. He felt we were showing that in the UK. I was sure if Clinton went to the camps, it would transform his attitude and get the urgency injected. It was a chance to redefine this period of his presidency.

Wes felt TB was going to have to take on a lot of the leadership here, because he was the only one who could persuade the Europeans to provide the kind of numbers for a ground invasion – 100,000 maybe – that would persuade the US they would not have to provide them all. His wife said America would tolerate forty per cent max. He said the US and UK troops were the only ones he really trusted, but he hoped if the UK provided 40,000 so would Germany, we could get maybe 8,000, then we would need more from the smaller countries and TB would have to get them.

Ed Burba [retired general, adviser to SACEUR] was there, and had been quietly working on ground invasion plans in his tiny office at SHAPE. Julian had clearly been working on him, because he said JB had been a breath of fresh air, brought a new energy and rigour to the place. I could see Wes taking note. He signed up totally to Julian taking charge of his scripts for press events etc. He had a briefing tomorrow with Cohen and [US General Hugh] Shelton [chairman of the US Joint Chiefs of Staff] so I got Julian working on that. Over dinner – cheese, chicken and rice; he ate really simple food – we had an interesting discussion on the Serbs. He understood why we had to separate Milosevic from the people. He didn't like the Serbs one bit. His wife did a fair amount of the talking. Burba was quiet but astute. Clark told me we were about to hit Arkan's palace [headquarters of paramilitary warlord Zeljko Raznatovic, known as Arkan], and more power stations, then he went to bed. I finished various scripts and then headed back to Brussels.

Wednesday, May 5

I had about four hours' sleep and was beginning to feel a bit tired, but Clinton's visit would hopefully perk everyone up a bit. The usual crowd were with him, and I peeled off for a chat with [Jonathan] Prince and Jamie Rubin [chief spokesman for the US State Department]. JR had a real downer on [Jamie] Shea [NATO spokesman]. I got down on him from time to time, but from the perspective that he was unsupported. I did a fair bit of schmoozing of the non-Brit, non-Yank members of the new media team. We'd had to involve them, but the French and the Germans were causing difficulties. The Germans were constantly stressing peace moves, and signalling a desire to do a deal, whilst the French were demanding we clear all scripts through the French Embassy. I had to tell them, as politely as possible, to fuck off. It would slow everything down and it would kill the flexibility and rapid response we needed. They were trying to write everything by committee. I got them all together and said it just wouldn't work. There had to be one guiding hand on scripts, others could feed in views and comment on drafts, but we could not have writing by committee, and everyone thinking they had a veto.

Clinton came down after his meeting with [NATO Secretary General Javier] Solana and wanted to see the new media operations. He came over, was very warm and friendly, and said thanks for what you're doing. He wanted me to show him around, so I introduced him to a few people. He was working his usual magic on them all. I suggested he go to one of the camps. He said he would love to, but his people wouldn't let him because of the security. I met Clark and he and Berger had a very difficult conversation. He said the most important thing the president had said to the briefing was that we were going to do what it took to win, but we had to see that through, it was not happening. I could see both of them losing their tempers, and there were plenty of people around to witness it. Berger eventually took Wes to one side and calmed him down a bit, but it was not a good scene.

They headed off to Germany and I went back to the media room to get a proper fix on how it was working. I sensed a bit of drift. I wasn't convinced that things were being seen through properly when work was commissioned. The French were OK, but didn't really seem to get it. There was far too much focus on the day-to-day and not enough on the strategic. I instigated an 8am meeting and wanted outcomes sent to me, and updates through the day. I had a good meeting with Jertz, who still felt Julian should be better plugged in.

I met Solana at 4, said it was better but there was still obstruction going on, that his office didn't really get what we were trying to achieve and he had to instruct them to leave the communications to people who knew what they were doing. He accepted he had been getting a better press himself since we started organising his visits better. But overall I was a bit alarmed by the day's events. BC had been on form on one level, but lacking that focus he normally has. Solana talked the talk but his people were still pissing around, and as the numbers had grown in the media operation, so the drift had crept in.

I called everyone together for a pep talk, was a bit rougher than the last time, emphasised how important this was, that Clinton would not have bothered coming to see us if it hadn't been important, but

May '99: Wes Clark and Berger lose their tempers

we had to raise the game, integrate better, be more strategic and more creative too. I felt a bit down about it on the train back home.

Thursday, May 6

I woke up exhausted and with Rory [AC's elder son] ill, I decided to have a day at home. We had the security people in putting in the new security stuff on the house. Clinton got an OK press out of yesterday but there was a lot of 'wobble' talk, and with the G8 [group of eight influential countries] about to meet in Bonn, we had to be careful. TB was worried. Jonathan [Powell, Downing Street chief of staff] said he wanted a press blitz, including articles from him, with the basic no-compromise message. I got the Brussels team to draft three different pieces, rewrote them, cleared them with TB, and got them placed. RC [Robin Cook, Foreign Secretary] called around midday and said he had had very difficult talks at the G8. There was a lot of talk of deals. He had tried to strengthen the language on the international force and succeeded up to a point, but he believed there had been a deal with the Americans not to change the language. He sensed a desire to stampede to the exit and he felt no help from the Americans at all. They sat on their hands whenever he tried to push harder.

Julian called, said he had finally cracked it, and Wes had said at his desk-side meeting that JB did the best scripts and he wanted him doing them for his briefings. TB was doing a stack of Northern Ireland meetings, and felt we were making progress, that he was beginning to think we could get decommissioning. I had to go in later for a secure call with Clark who wanted to discuss a few things, including some of the targets for Friday night, including Arkan's palace and another command and control bunker and a hotel used by troops.

I saw TB who was worried re the G8 that we would be seen as weak. We also had Bill saying 'Yes' in answer to the question whether Milosevic could survive. It was in one way a statement of the obvious but it was taken by e.g. John Simpson [BBC world affairs editor] in Belgrade as a signal that Milosevic could in those circumstances be said to win – rebutted by Mark Laity [BBC defence correspondent] who said Milosevic wanted a greater Serbia. I stayed up for the local election results, which were not great for us.[1]

[1] In local authority elections in England, Scotland and Wales, Labour suffered a net loss of thirty-two councils and 1,150 council seats. The Conservatives gained forty-eight councils and 1,348 council seats.

The Scotland [Scottish Parliament] results were good, Wales [Welsh Assembly] and the locals indifferent, though it was the first time this century the party of government polled ahead in local elections.[1] Plaid [Cymru, Welsh nationalist party] did better than expected [with seventeen seats] and there was a long wait before it was clear Alun Michael [Labour's prospective First Secretary of Wales, standing in the Mid and West Wales constituency] was safe. TB did a doorstep in the garden which was fine.

I went in for a TB meeting on office structures. He still wasn't happy. He was also arguing that Jonathan and John Sawers should be in proper offices, with proper support, not stuck outside in the crowded private office. Truth is they prefer it there, whatever the inconvenience. Siobhan Kenny [press officer], who was doing a great job for me, was leaving because we couldn't match the money she was being offered by the private sector. I tried to talk her out of it but I couldn't really blame her. It made my blood boil that we lost good people while people thought not to be up to the mark got promoted. The Kosovo conference call was at 7pm, largely about the G8, and we agreed to do a concerted G8 push, including a Chirac/Schroeder press conference, that we were all demanding all five NATO conditions be met in full.[2] No compromise. No going back on any of them. Catherine [Colonna] called to say Chirac was totally firm.

The Serbs put out a claim that we had hit a hospital and we had the usual teeth-drawing exercise trying to find out from SHAPE exactly what had happened, if anything. We had a long and difficult conference call beating up Wilby to get a quicker response. It was more than ten hours before we had a useable response. I got so exasperated I called Wes Clark at 11pm and he said he thought we'd already put the line out. But worse was to come. Julian warned me there were suggestions we had hit the Chinese Embassy in Belgrade.

I went to bed, was asleep, when the phone went and it was Switch [the Downing Street switchboard] with someone from SHAPE. An

[1] Labour won fifty-six out 129 seats in the Scottish Parliament, forming a coalition with seventeen Liberal Democrats. With a total of twenty-eight out of sixty seats in the Welsh Assembly, Labour would form a minority government.

[2] The five conditions demanded of Milosevic were: he must stop the killing; he must allow all refugees to return to their homes; he must agree to the deployment of an international security force; he must withdraw all of his forces from Kosovo; and there must be a political process that would lead to a permanent solution based on the proposed Rambouillet Agreement.

American, very clipped and precise. 'Mr Campbell, General Clark asked me to call you and let you know that we have hit the Chinese Embassy in Belgrade.' He said it in exactly the same tone as he might have said 'General Clark has had his breakfast and is on his way to work.' Speaking quietly because I didn't want to wake up Fiona, I asked him to repeat that, which he did, word for word. I assume it wasn't deliberate, I said. No sir, came back this robot voice, it was an accident. Fucking hell. Twenty-four-carat disaster time. First a convoy, then a bus, then a hospital, and now we hit the Chinese fucking Embassy.

I got out of bed, and started ringing round the other capitals, and working up a response with Julian. There was nothing to do but admit to a terrible error. Depending on how the Chinese react, it could be absolutely disastrous. I was on the phone for several hours during the night and when I did get back to bed knew that I wouldn't sleep.

Saturday, May 8

PJ Crowley called and said he felt Wes should do the briefing today, as this was going to be heavy. I worked up a script for him based on the lines agreed last night and got Julian working on him, but he wasn't at all keen. So the script went to Jertz instead. Meanwhile we were pumping out 'regret' in briefings in all the main capitals. TB called as I was listening to [John] Humphrys trying to pummel RC on [BBC Radio 4's] *Today*, Humphrys doing his usual anti-war stuff, saying we had done nothing for the Kosovar Albanians. TB heard it too, was furious, said what would that man have been like during the Second World War? Robin though was excellent.

On the conference call the Germans thought we should be expressing 'deep regret', and I said fine but we also say these accidents happen from time to time and we have to move on; also emphasise the five conditions again. We should rule out an investigation, say we know it was an accident, and this was the worst time to go weak on Milosevic.

Jamie Shea said he would be 'funereal' at the briefing. I said don't overdo it. We have to make sure this does not dominate the agenda for days. We regret it, we move on. Julian said to me he was trying to think of what target wrongly hit could be worse than this, yet I think by being open but robust about the big picture we helped contain the fallout. RC was strong on it, so was Catherine [Colonna], so was I, so were the US. There was a lot of black humour flying around, Chinese takeaways etc., someone suggesting we have a sweepstake on what target we wrongly hit next. Berger called John S though and said Clinton was a bit shaky. We then got a message BC wanted to speak to TB from Air Force One at 8pm. He had done media and had done an apology, plus move on, the air campaign is working, core message. We were all starting to get angrier and angrier re the media lack of balance, all focused on our mistakes, no account of progress elsewhere and Milosevic getting treated if anything better than we were in terms of analysis and pressure.

TB said we had to hold our nerve. BC said that's right, this thing will turn soon. It is going to work. He sounded a lot better than in the last call. I called Clark and said both had said on the call how well he was doing. It wasn't strictly true, TB had talked him up and Bill had said he needed supporting, but I thought it important to bolster when I could, and I know he worried what the leaders thought of him. He said the embassy bombing was the result of an intelligence error. We agreed it was important to get all the facts out straight away, not have them dragged out. The papers weren't brilliant of course but quite a few of the editorials were on the line that this was not the time to stop, far from it.

Sunday, May 9

The first call of the day was from [General] Dieter Stockman [chief of staff] at SHAPE, wanting to dispute the notion running in the Western media that we were running out of ammunition; then from JB who had been asked by Clark to go with him on his visit to the troops at Aviano, where he was also doing an interview for ABC. I did a note for him on the interview re tone, message and specifics. It was an opportunity to stabilise the campaign, show progress, draw a line definitively post-Chinese Embassy, contrast our regret with the cruelty of the Serbs. I also suggested he tweak the media's tail, say of course they should cover the embassy bombing, but what about the suffering of people inside Kosovo, which was just as newsworthy – but there were no pictures.

On the conference call, we agreed to pressure the media into putting as much energy into coverage of atrocities inside Kosovo, e.g. through refugees, as to NATO mistakes. Catherine was against the approach, and maybe in France it was different, but I felt for us the only way we would turn things a bit was to make it an issue. Arkan was doing clips saying none of his people were at the bombed Hotel Jugoslavija. Don't say we hit the wrong building again. Julian seemed to be well in now, was pleased to be going with Wes to Aviano.

I worked on TB's speech for tomorrow for a couple of hours, very powerful, but not sure he would deliver it. I felt we, and Wes today, had to get over the difference between accident and deliberate atrocity. There were protests going on around the world but considering what they might have done, the Chinese were not being too bad. TB felt the press could be worse. He called re the Liberals, said he was getting tired of them leaking the detail of their discussions, e.g. now on tuition fees. He intended to tell Paddy [Ashdown, Liberal Democrat Party leader] if this was an indication of what they were like at this level, it was hard to see how it would work if they moved up a few levels. I'm not sure they're serious people, he said. I went through the speech I'd drafted which he liked, even with the whacks at the media. Peter M was of the view that the media was not nearly as bad as it might be. My problem was the equivalence they were applying – Milosevic word as good as ours; our mistakes getting enormous coverage, his atrocities taken for granted, refugees' stories no longer news. As tomorrow's speech was to a press audience, I thought it was worth doing. The DoD [US Department of Defense] had a very good map showing the scale of what was happening inside Kosovo, which I got turned into a backdrop for the speech. TB and I both felt we should put a bit of heat on here. Julian called, the visit having gone well. I got to bed, then was woken with a call that Derek Fatchett [Labour MP and Foreign Office minister] was dead. Fifty-three. Really sad, and not easy to replace.

Monday, May 10

The Chinese were being a lot trickier now. Hypocritically, given their own position on demos, they were now encouraging the demos to go on, and their media had still not reported NATO's apology and admission of error. So to the Chinese we had just decided to take out their embassy. TB was even more pissed off with the Russians, found their basic attitude that what happened inside other people's countries was 'their own business' disgusting when you thought what Milosevic was actually doing, added to which they were perpetually on the lookout for money out of it.

I was in early and up to see him in the flat to finalise the speech. He knew he was out on a limb, now more than ever, but he still felt we could get the US into a better place. That was not what Charles Guthrie told me when I saw him later. He said General Shelton was getting a bit desperate. He couldn't even get them to contemplate ground forces. TB felt we had to stay out front, that even if we ended with some kind of fudge, we should be in the position of everyone knowing we wanted to go further. TB still felt Clinton would come round. CDS felt we were getting too late. I rewrote the speech to keep the content but lower the temperature a bit and get the tone right. There was no point it being seen just as a whinge or a whack at them, more a description of what was happening inside Kosovo, and the need for our media to try to reflect that when they had no access to pictures.

TB's speech couldn't have gone better. Though the audience was mainly regional newspaper people and guests, there was prolonged applause at the end, and several people came over to say they had found it moving and compelling. Both BBC and ITN did major packages on refugees as a result. TB liked it, felt it had real muscle. Just before the four o'clock, Tanjug [Belgrade-based Serbian news agency] ran a line that Milosevic had ordered a partial pull-out. I called the media operations people and said we must circulate a line that he cannot be believed and we wait to see if anything happens, meanwhile the conditions must be met and the attacks continue.

Clark was very pleased with the GR [George Robertson, Defence Secretary] headline in the *Telegraph*, 'Wesley Clark is the man to beat Milosevic', which would also get shown around Washington and hopefully bolster him a little. But CDS came to see me, said he knew I had to build him up, but the truth was a lot of the military weren't happy with him. Cohen had tried to sack him twice but Clinton or Shelton talked him out of it. He said ground forces were the only option but the Americans were terrified. I liked Charles, who had been one hundred per cent solid throughout all this. He was also clearly a bit of a mover. He had just had lunch with Michael Levy [businessman, Labour peer and party fund-raiser] who described himself as 'Tony's Kissinger' [Henry Kissinger, Secretary of State to presidents Nixon and Ford]. Good meeting with Solana. He was almost Levy-like though in his hand-grabbing, back-stroking tactile ways. But he was definitely buying into what we are trying to do.

Tuesday, May 11

I was heading for Brussels again. The Chinese Embassy protests were dying down, and we had been hugely helped by Milosevic's troop withdrawal ploy. He was panned all round. Bill C was also getting a bit of a mauling in the US press. [Clinton's wife] Hillary's trip would be important and I put through a note to Melanne Verveer, her chief of staff, to suggest a few ideas on the refugee visit front, including maybe something with CB. I felt it was important we get mega-coverage out of HC. I was sure that Bill's natural instincts were being curbed by the system. I felt she would end up genuinely moved and go back and fire him up. I enjoyed these train journeys, had a bit of time to think and also time to do proper notes on forward planning and strategy.

Michael Howard [Shadow Foreign Secretary] did his second attack in two days on Kosovo. They were doing what they did re NI, saying they were bipartisan but acting very differently. I did the eleven o'clock briefing down the phone from the train, hit Milosevic re the ploy, had a go at Howard, said when things get tough is not the time to show lack of resolve and determination. I was met by Jamie Paver [UK official at NATO], who was excellent and filled me in on what had been happening. Tim Livesey [press officer] had made a difference, was very good at chivvying along. Lucie McNeil [Downing Street press officer] was doing a great job on visits in particular. I wrote to Catherine and Uwe [Karsten Heye, German Chancellor Gerhard Schroeder's spokesman] to say thanks for the people they had sent but they were a bit prone to working by committee the whole time and slowing things down. I also said to Uwe it was important he came on the calls, as most of the other Number 1 people did, and we needed the output from these calls to be accepted all round.

At 1.45 I had another meeting with Solana. He was talking again about what kind of offer we could make to Milosevic that we knew he would have to reject. We talked about his visits and I said again I felt there was insufficient planning on the media side. There was no thought re pictures. Him in a suit talking to politicians or officials would never make much. Him in a tent talking to refugees would. His officials seemed more interested in whether they would get into meetings to take notes than in the outcome of the meetings and how to communicate to the wider world. He seemed OK, and capable and reasonably strategic, so it was odd he hadn't gripped his own operation. It was the layer around him that was the problem.

There was a big piece in one of the German papers today saying we were trying to influence opinion rather than just give information. Oh really. I was due to see Clark for dinner again and hung around waiting for him to finish his presentation to the NAC [North Atlantic Council] ambassadors. He looked weary, said that it was crazy that they had to have everything cleared in this way. 'They would keep me there for days if they could.' We got into the car and headed for the chateau. His leg was jiggling more than usual and he had the start of deeper bags under his eyes. He said Italy was flaky, so was Germany. I suggested he did visits there too, if he had the time. But he said he'd had a good day, and Julian had been a great help on the visits, which generated positive coverage all over the place. On the war more generally, he asked me not to pass on, but his view was that Milosevic would not back down. He was throwing out bait, e.g. troop withdrawal, just to test resolve, but he felt his own position was strong. He was desperate to break the alliance and the longer we took, the more chance he had to do that.

Wes and I discussed Hillary's visit. Over dinner at the castle he said it was important she become a kind of spokeswoman for the refugees. He said don't forget New York has more Kosovar Albanians than anywhere outside the Balkans. Hillary had agreed to do an event with CB on the way through which we were planning. He felt Hillary had deep moral convictions. He had mixed feelings about Clinton. He liked him, but he said the reason most Republicans – and that meant a lot of soldiers – hated him was that when he became president he did gays in the military, and he used to say Wes was a friend of his as a way of trying to buy some cred with the military. But it did Wes a lot of damage inside the military. He thought he would have been a runner for the top job [i.e. chief of staff] but for that. 'Also, if you are an Oxford and Rhodes scholar, you are marked.' He was in a fairly mellow, reflective mood. He believed in the end the US would do the right thing, but they really wanted to test whether the air campaign could do it. He reckoned we had till about June 1. Over dinner – chicken and rice again – Wes said TB must be tearing his hair out. 'He seems to see it all clearly but it isn't happening.' But he seemed more confident the Americans would move to the right place, without indicating where the new confidence was coming from. He said it was hard for the US because they'd had a disaster in Somalia, added to which the Russian situation was difficult because the Russians still saw the US as a real sparring partner and they were messing around. He said the Americans had illusions about both Russia and China, thought they were changing faster than they were, but in truth couldn't make up their minds how to handle them. What he knew was they would never really be our partners. He had received a letter from someone saying 'Don't worry about the criticism – [General William] Westmoreland got lots of abuse re Vietnam too.' Great. I felt he had far more qualities than his critics, e.g. Charles, suggested. The politics attached to the job were hard, and he handled them pretty well. He was bright, had a really lively mind and was engaging, but he needed constant reassurance that he was a good leader.

Wednesday, May 12

I had breakfast with General Burba. Like Clark, he did not believe Milosevic would quit, and that ground forces would be needed. He was doing a lot of work on it but wasn't supposed to say so, because

parts of Washington were 'paranoid'. He felt the Serbs were just drag-
ging things out, playing around with a few 'peace moves' in the hope
we would reach winter and ground troops became harder and harder
as an option. He was sure we would win but felt it may be a longer
haul than it ought to be. He couldn't understand Clinton and the
people around him. There was a piece by [Paul] Routledge in the
Mirror saying I couldn't stand Jamie Shea, not true, and I called Jamie
to say so. These fuckers just made it up. Burba and I travelled in
together. I spoke to TB from the car pre his GMTV interview, which
went fine, strong on general message again. I went to Clark's desk-
side meeting and for the first time, the seat to Clark's right was
reserved for me, but I felt a bit odd going right in there like that, with
these military guys maybe feeling squeezed, but he – or his office –
was clearly sending a signal.

There had been some major hits overnight which would form the
basis of a strong briefing by Jertz. He was OK, but I said we had to find
ways of improving the co-ordination on scripts between Brussels and
here. He was blaming 'the clever new boys from America'. There was
clearly still tension unresolved. Stockman asked me what I thought of
Jertz. I thought he was OK, but needed to display more confidence in
what he was saying. I liked Stockman. I'd thought initially he was so
diffident as to be ineffectual but actually he didn't miss much and once
he wanted something to happen, he quietly made it happen. I saw
[Deputy SACEUR, General Sir] Rupert Smith for a chat. The Brits were
far and away the best in here. Smith felt the campaign wasn't really
working, and we should have done much more damage by now. He
felt we lacked a clear approach to the KLA [Kosovo Liberation Army].

I did the eleven o'clock down the line from his office, basic message
on overnight hits, defend Clinton, defend [Italian Prime Minister
Massimo] D'Alema as strong. I travelled to Brussels with Jertz,
working on his briefing script. At NATO I had a meeting with Burba
who took me through some of his planning. He said we had about
two weeks to decide whether we were serious on ground troops, and
if we were we had to get on with it. Winter was October 15 and
everything would need to be in place before that. He had a little camp
bed in there, and said he had now cancelled six air tickets home.
[Russian President Boris] Yeltsin sacking [Yevgeny] Primakov [Russian
Prime Minister] was the main story, and we agreed on the conference
call not to get drawn into it. PJ was doing a good job with Solana
and we got him beamed in from Macedonia. I met Jertz and Shea to
agree better co-ordination on scripts and briefings. I told Jamie that
today he should just introduce Solana and let that be the focus, but

he kept being drawn on different questions. Jonathan Prince and I had a meeting with him afterwards and said he allowed them to set the agenda again. He looked very hurt. I said he was a huge asset. The press trusted him. His briefings were getting big play, but we had to make them work better for us, not just for the media.

I set off for Aachen to wait for TB's arrival in advance of his speech tomorrow.[1] I did a section on Kosovo, and another on 'the vision thing' re Europe. He wanted the big message to be about Britain needing to overcome its ambivalence re Europe. He was worried I was become 'obsessed' re Kosovo, to which I replied he was the one who asked me to get on top of it. I told TB of Clark's and Smith's view that the air campaign was not working as effectively as it should. He was not sure the US would do ground forces. Like us, Wes was banking on Hillary to move Bill, but it was a pretty hopeless position to be in.

Thursday, May 13

TB, Jonathan [Powell] and I were up at 6 to finish the speech. I worked on a new ending while TB drove the argument through the rest of it and basically it was done, but lacked the real hard edge I thought it needed re Europe. TB went off to the Mass, which needless to say he took. We were in the week of the [German] Green Party conference, and there were big anti-war demos. I stayed for [French Prime Minister Lionel] Jospin's introduction and then went off to brief the lobby down the line. TB's speech went fine, fairly clear lines even if it was not one of the really big ones.

TB and Jospin travelled together to the airport. Jospin was against ground troops but accepted we had to win, and that we had to plan. [Spanish Prime Minister José María] Aznar called TB, and was pretty strong. TB was showing off his [Charlemagne] medal and going into a great parody about how it would be possible to travel the world just picking up prizes and medals. Re Kosovo, he said the choice was victory, which brought its own difficulties but which had to be secured, or defeat in the form of a fudge, in which we would have to be clear we were not happy, which had its own consequences for the US relationship.

We got back and waited for Hillary C to arrive. She was very friendly, said half jokingly that she was going to the Balkans for me. We had got together some refugee families who gathered in the White Room, and both she and CB were terrific with them. Once the cameras

[1] Blair was also to receive the annual Charlemagne Prize, awarded to the statesman, of any nationality, who had contributed most to European unity.

were out, Hillary and Cherie got them all to tell their stories in more detail. She was a good listener, let them talk, didn't mind the occasional silence and the stories they told of their own escapes and family losses were genuinely moving.

What was also moving was their clear gratitude that we were trying to do something. We are the lucky ones, we want to help the others was their basic position. TB felt Hillary's visit to the region was really important, because we were running out of time on ground troops, and Bill was going to have to shift things quickly. If we failed on this, Bill was dead meat, which is why he couldn't understand why he was not more seized of this. Fiona and I had dinner with Melanne [Verveer, Hillary Clinton's chief of staff]. She felt Bill was really up for it, so was [US Secretary of State Madeleine] Albright but others were not and they were holding him back. She said HC was almost certain to go for the Senate.

Friday, May 14

I had been ignoring toothache for ages, and today it was really bad. We'd had another good night on the military front but then came news that journalists were on their way to Korisa to see the results of a NATO cluster bomb attack that had allegedly killed one hundred civilians. Fuck, not another one. Julian called me and said there was an extra dimension – the White House had put a call through last night saying no more cluster bombs after a previous incident, so there was a chance this was British. UK Harriers had flown in the area yesterday. But JB's bigger point was that Clark was feeling undermined. He still hadn't got the go-ahead for the use of Apaches [attack helicopters], and there was no movement on ground troops. TB was holding another round of NI talks and by the time I got in with my tooth sorted, he was having lunch with Bertie [Ahern, Irish Prime Minister]. They had obviously been talking about me because at one point, when I asked Bertie what Mary Robinson [former Irish President, now UN high commissioner for human rights] was up to in her criticisms of NATO, TB laughed and said 'Told you, he is obsessed with Kosovo.' I said that was because he told me to be. NI seemed to be going a bit better. The current plan was to reaffirm commitment to the GFA [Good Friday Agreement of 1998], set a deadline for June 30 for full devolution, run D'Hondt[1] and let [John]

[1] A method of proportional representation voting named after Belgian mathematician Victor D'Hondt. The D'Hondt system, electing candidates in constituencies as well as party lists, had been used in the Scottish Parliament and Welsh Assembly elections.

de Chastelain [Canadian chairman of the Independent International Commission on Decommissioning] decide if decommissioning was taking place. The meetings went well, much better mood than of late, and then ran late into the evening, with some decent food being served, to sort it out. By the end we were close to a line that said we had a process all of them would support, which would be seen as a breakthrough of sorts.

Jamie Shea was doing a presentation on atrocities inside Kosovo and pushing back on the Korisa incident as best he could, given we didn't have the full picture yet. I wrote to the BBC, ITN and Sky warning them against taking at face value the pictures from these Serb outings organised for the Western media. On the 8pm call, we agreed we had to keep pressing the media on this, but also keep pushing for the facts and get them out ASAP.

Julian called me at 3am to say they had established it was a NATO dumb bomb, that it was a legitimate military target because it had been used as a Serb command post. However, that dated from intelligence imagery dated April 23 so it was not impossible that it HAD been a command post but now the KLA had gone back, and we were in a human-shield situation. We had to make the best of the facts as they were. We then fixed a conference call for 4.20am. Joe Lockhart [White House press secretary] was keen we say nothing that we could not prove. I felt we had to go with what we had, and emphasise this was what we believed to be the case but we were still seeking etc.

Julian took everyone through the facts as we knew them. We could categorically deny it was a cluster bomb. We could defend it as a military target. We could refute Serb claims of the impact. We agreed Jamie would do interviews on it. Fiona had woken up with the phone going and when I explained what it was about said most people would assume they had put people in there deliberately for this kind of eventuality. Certainly it did not go as badly as it might have done. We were always helped when the Serbs lied and exaggerated on a specific point we could categorically refute.

Hillary C got terrific coverage for her trip to Macedonia. But our main problem remained an air campaign not doing the job as predicted, and being underpinned by the realistic threat of ground troops. TB felt Cohen and US public opinion were the biggest obstacles at the moment. Jonathan thought Berger and Cohen were the problem. But if they were not careful they – and we – were heading for a military vs politician briefing war that the politicians would never win. I was feeling tired and depressed again.

Saturday, May 15

I got next to no sleep and was exhausted. The Korisa incident was wall to wall, though the overnight stuff reshaped the morning broadcasts. TB said that even though Milosevic could have scripted the BBC reports, most real people would assume we were dealing with a human-shield situation here. He was more optimistic, believed Clinton would end in the right place. But there was a growing sense in the media of us being in very different positions, that TB was way out in front and BC was stopping him doing what he wanted. TB felt ground forces were now the only moral option left, that we could not bomb forever and we could not do a deal if he just sat there.

I picked TB's brains on NI before doing a Sunday lobby briefing by phone to try to get the NI statement when it came in the right place. They were straight on to the right questions though – namely if we were running D'Hondt and appointing ministers designate, it was clear what Sinn Fein were getting, but what about the Ulster Unionists? During the day, the UUs started to move to reserve their position, so it was looking tricky again. Scotland was settling down, with the Lib-Lab coalition coming together. In Wales Alun Michael had decided against a deal. DD [Donald Dewar, now First Minister of Scotland] was looking more the part though I was still hearing there was zero news management up there. I took Grace and her friends to the cinema, but was in and out dealing with the NATO people.

Sunday, May 16

Der Spiegel ran a nasty piece about the [NATO] Media Operations Room. The Germans really had a problem with it. Also the *Sunday Telegraph* ran a piece saying media was taking precedence over military. I spoke to RC after the first conference call to get him to do the NATO briefing tomorrow at 11, and tie in to the MoD at 11.30. He jumped at the chance. Robin was very onside at the moment and really motoring. He said he was very happy with things but the sense of a rift with the US over ground forces was becoming difficult to deal with. I got Jamie to trail TB's speech in Bulgaria tomorrow. His briefing was OK in that you knew what he wanted to say but he just went on and on today.

On the call, Ken Bacon [US Department of Defense spokesman] said the White House and the Pentagon both felt our tone had been too apologetic re Korisa, a point echoed by Clark when I spoke to him later. I had done him a note on how to reshape the military briefings, which he signed up to and said he would activate first thing. He wanted me out there but I said I was going with TB to Bulgaria. He was going to Washington later in the week to get them to do some 'proper thinking' re ground forces, but he sounded down about it. I said we would be rooting for him and if he needed help at any time, we were there to help. TB sent through a note which was not one of his best. Rambling and repetitive and not clear.

Monday, May 17

The news led this morning on a *Newsweek* article saying the military were warning the Defence Secretary we could not win without ground troops. Throw in yesterday's *Sunday Times* saying we were at odds over ground troops, and you had the media fix for the day. I drove in with Jonathan and TB called to go through the reshuffle. He had agreed with GB [Gordon Brown, Chancellor of the Exchequer], and Pat McFadden [policy adviser], that John Reid [transport minister] should get [Secretary of State for] Scotland, Helen Liddell [Deputy Secretary of State for Scotland and education minister] pissed off. At the office meeting, TB said there was little point talking about Kosovo as it was so obvious what we had to do, but out of our hands as to whether we would do it. This was crunch week and the media knew it, and we would get pushed harder and harder. TB was worrying re the domestic scene, felt that schools, health and crime were in danger of moving backwards, that when there was a big international thing going on, ministers and departments relaxed. Charlie [Lord Falconer, Minister of State, Cabinet Office] had been to the Home Office in his delivery capacity [he was touring departments to assess delivery] and had found them pretty down about things. They said the best that could be done was to slow the rise in crime. They couldn't cut it, he was told. It had nothing to do with the economy and everything to do with the numbers and nature of young men. TB just sat and shook his head. Today we had the vote on incapacity benefit and I wrote a strong line for the eleven o'clock re people wanting welfare reform in general but always baulking at the individual changes that had to be made.

We left for the airport and on the flight worked on his speech for Bulgaria. I did a 'whatever it takes to win' passage, which would be seen as a signal on ground troops. TB wrote in a tribute to the US, and a section on this having the potential to be a turning point for the region. By the time we arrived, TB was seized of the fact we had a public problem with the US.

Berger made clear to John S that they had been picking up on the different signals re ground troops, and also some of the briefing re Cohen and him being the obstacles, and they were unsurprisingly pissed off. If they imagined it was a deliberate briefing operation, they were wrong. But the atmospherics had a way of getting out because so many people spoke to so many people. If anything, the media were understating the differences, and the frustrations TB felt. We tried our best to assure them this wasn't being briefed, but I don't think they believed us.

TB and Bill had not spoken for more than a week, which was bad. This was going to have to get cleared up. I was asked about when they last spoke and just dodged it, said they kept in touch the whole time. We got a message that the UUP [Ulster Unionist Party] had rejected the Friday proposal, so TB dictated a letter to DT [David Trimble, UUP leader and First Minister of Northern Ireland] urging him to think again. Bulgaria went fine. Both [Bulgarian Prime Minister Ivan] Kostov and [President Petar] Stoyanov, not to mention their very attractive foreign minister [Nadezhda Mihailova], were supportive, said whatever doubts earlier they knew we had to win, while the speech was well received, particularly the long-term commitment to the region. Stoyanov said they had waited 120 years for a British PM to visit, but it was worth it. I couldn't believe that – 120 years!

They were now terrified of a Milosevic who survived and was stronger and able to threaten his neighbours even more. TB did an OK doorstep but the interpreters interrupted so often to make it virtually unusable in packages. Mum was getting inundated with calls after a story in Nigel Dempster's [*Daily Mail*] column that she plays bridge with [Conservative leader William] Hague's aunt Mary. Ridiculous that was deemed to be a story. I told her to get someone to answer the phone for her and tell them all to get lost.

Tuesday, May 18

A combination of TB's and Robin's words of yesterday, while they said nothing new, was being seen, especially in the US, as a hardening of the position on ground troops. Added to which the Germans were briefing that they could not understand why the UK was pushing this out further than before. BC was getting a hard time and there was bound to be some blowback in our direction. Then it got worse when we heard Schroeder, visiting Italy, had said ground troops were unthinkable. Even before that, over breakfast, TB said he didn't mind admitting he was 'really worried now', and that he couldn't see a way out of this. He felt Robin had not shown enough finesse yesterday.

I said Schroeder's remarks were the equivalent of his 'fuck off' at Berlin – it was deliberate and divisive.[1]

The US meanwhile clearly believed we were briefing against them. I tried to explain to Jonathan Prince, and get him to persuade the White House that it just was not in our interests to brief against the president, but that people knew there were differences. The thing was to resolve the differences, not fret and frazzle over who was saying what to whom. I said for us to brief against them would be dumb and counterproductive because they can always hit back harder. TB was really worked up by now, feeling the US had pretty much given up on the idea of ground troops and the Europeans, sensing no lead, just fell into the same position. He was half attracted to Massimo D'Alema's idea of a 48-hour bombing pause while the UNSCR [UN Security Council resolution] was put together, calling on him to withdraw. TB planned to add to that that if he didn't then the bombing would resume and ground troops would be on the table. I was worried this would just allow Milosevic to go into a protracted negotiation and string out even further towards winter.

On the flight down to Tirana he kept asking how do we get out of this? I said his original position was right, we had to stand firm and if it ended in failure, better that people understood we had wanted to take a tougher line. We were in the morally right position and had to stay there. He said he couldn't understand the other eighteen. We were all saying we had to win, yet they were stopping themselves from doing what was required to ensure it happened. CDS said he felt the French were moving our way, but TB was not convinced. We flew in past the seemingly redundant Apaches parked on the airfield, which kind of summed up the campaign being fought at half-throttle. [UK General John] Reith was impressive, very calm and measured, and told me at one point it was great to have the PM there but they were getting too many VIP visits. We were briefed on two big demonstrations inside Serbia.

TB was convinced we had at least to threaten ground forces, and make the preparations, otherwise Milosevic would think he could just sit there until our resolve weakened. I said he must speak to Schroeder tonight because he was due to be at NATO tomorrow and would be the main media focus for the day, and we had to get him in a different position. In Tirana, we visited the refugee camp, and an old couple

[1] At an EU conference in Berlin the previous March, Gerhard Schroeder, then holding the EU presidency, had become frustrated over Blair's defence of the UK's rebate on its contribution to the EU budget, and demands for support for UK regions, and had sworn (in German) at him.

May '99: Blair concern re Kosovo strategy

who had survived their escape and were very matter-of-fact but also very moving about how they did it. The kids were suntanned and cheerful and seemed to be getting enough to eat, though inside the tents it was unbelievably hot and clammy. Mothers seemed to be the ones finding the going toughest. One woman stopped us and said her husband came out with four broken ribs. They had all their money taken off them, and had left behind relatives they knew had been murdered or raped. TB did a little 'you will go home' message to them, and spoke of the basic need for humanity to prevail.

We were flown by helicopter into Tirana stadium and then taken to the various political meetings. There was a massive supportive crowd in Tirana Square outside the PM's office and people waving banners obviously prepared for them to hold. One said 'Tony, you lead, we die,' which I took as being critical but was told it meant they would die for him. The PM was very supportive and the meetings went fine. I couldn't say the same for the conference call. The Americans were clearly pissed off and my efforts through Prince had failed. I said we could not possibly say we would only send in troops if there was a peace agreement because that effectively gave Milosevic a veto. But of course timing was everything, and I knew why they were pissed off. I said we had to set this in the context of Milosevic trying to divide us. We should talk up the US leadership and the massive contribution they were making. They should talk up the strength of the alliance as a whole.

Then off to the president's office. [Albanian President Rexhep] Meidani was pretty strong, indeed the front-line states as a whole were getting stronger and stronger for us, strengthened by their fear of Milosevic surviving after they had helped try to get rid of him. I liked the Albanian leadership. They were clear and had less of a victim mentality than some of the others. Meidani said he was a keen follower of the Third Way debate. TB did a few local interviews and just danced around the ground forces question, and was clearly not comfortable. Meidani picked up on it, said there were some questions best answered by not answering them. We were flown by helicopter from the stadium to the flight home, during which again we discussed ground troops.

TB was minded to try again with BC, to say he was now genuinely worried we were to be left with no strategy but air power, and Milosevic would just sit it out until we ran out of options. He knew that the more we bombed the more civilians we would kill and over time the resolve of some of our partners would break. The refugees were not going to go back if he was still there, and we were unlikely to get rid of him without at least the realistic threat of ground troops.

TB drafted two different notes, one to POTUS [President of the United States], the other to Chirac, Schroeder and D'Alema. I suggested we add Solana and Aznar to the list. He felt the majority was moving to a position of some kind of negotiated deal and wanted us to remain on the tough end of the market. I got home and did the evening conference call, where the Yanks were again very tense and difficult, and there had been more stuff in the US press re TB having to stiffen up Bill.

Just before midnight, John Sawers woke me up to fill me in on a 'very difficult' BC/TB phone call. They had spoken for over an hour, and the first five to ten minutes were taken up with Bill in a total rage. He had seen the UK reports and the stuff in the US and he 'knew what was going on, it was deliberate and it had to stop'. He said it may play well with the UK media and public but 'there is a price to pay and you will pay it'. John said he was clearly suggesting I had been briefing deliberately to build up TB at his expense. TB protested as best he could, said he was appalled they would think we would undermine him when he was leading the whole thing, to which BC said in which case it is happening without you knowing – the implied notion being that was even worse. John said he didn't name names but it was obvious who he meant. He had never heard him so angry and TB was taken aback. On the substance, however, BC appeared to be moving. He shared TB's view that the D'Alema option could be a way of getting the ground force option out there. TB put it in terms – we have a 48-hour pause while we agree a new UNSCR, then if Milosevic does not comply, based on the five NATO demands, we bomb again and plan for ground forces. Bill leapt at it.

Wednesday, May 19

TB said BC's outburst was 'real, red-hot anger'. He felt he was just getting a lot out of his system, and TB was the only one he could really let rip with. He claimed that he had always been basically in favour of ground troops, but it had to be understood he could not be briefed against like this. All that was happening was that people were picking up the obvious differences of tone and emphasis. Our right wing of course, which hates a Labour government and a Democrat White House running a military situation, was stirring as best they could. Boris Johnson [*Telegraph*] had a piece today suggesting we had a deliberate strategy to make TB look good alongside BC. They would be getting all this played back to them. Joe Lockhart called and said they were getting sick and tired of reading that Robin Cook was flying out to stiffen their resolve. I said these things happened, we understood why they were pissed off, but I would be very pissed off too if I thought they thought we had done this deliberately.

I talked up the US leadership constantly and had been trying to get RC/Albright words agreed that got us back on the same pitch. He said it may not be you, but there is someone in your system doing it and we are sick of it. I sent him a copy of the email I had circulated internally warning people not to play into the desire to divide us when talking to the media, and also the letters I had sent for publication on the same subject. I said I was convinced nobody with TB's authority was at it. TB said they didn't really like the fact we got so much press in the States of such a positive nature because even if the comparison was unstated, it was there.

Schroeder had another pop when he did the NATO briefing. Mark Laity [BBC] asked him where he stood on ground troops and he said he didn't want to take part in this exclusive British debate. It was a deliberate and pretty stupid statement. TB said there was a total illogicality to the German position – they said we had to do what it took to win, but ruled out one of the means. Schroeder could not publicly state the true position – his coalition made it impossible. I watched the press conference and he went right down in my estimation. It wasn't just that he was putting a different position, but doing it in a fairly glib way.

I got into a bit of a mess at the morning briefing. An Italian journalist asked me about the D'Alema plan,[1] and I engaged too much as a way of trying to be non-dismissive, and ended up giving the impression we supported the idea of a bombing pause, which led the 12.30 news. I was furious with myself. I had opened a flank when I could easily have batted it off. Thankfully the BBC ignored it and instead went on my line that all the demands must be met. I had tried both to be tough and uncompromising whilst not dumping on D'Alema, and I had fucked up. I had to do a lot of ringing round one-on-one to try to wrestle it back.

Joe called after the call, and said I should understand that though they were angry, it was a sign of how close they were that BC could lose it with TB like that. He asked me to get RC on to CNN to try to calm things and get us on the same pitch, which I did. PMQs preparation was mainly Kosovo, disability and NI. We had another round of talks today, as if Kosovo wasn't enough to be dealing with. At one

[1] The Italian prime minister had proposed a 48-hour ceasefire on condition that Russia and China support a UN Security Council resolution imposing the G8 terms on Milosevic.

point, TB's kids were trying to show [Sinn Fein president Gerry] Adams and [chief negotiator Martin] McGuinness how to use a skateboard.

Julian called to say there was intelligence that around 1,000 Serb leaders had deserted to join demonstrations because they had heard on Radio Free Europe that their families were being punished for being in the demos. The Serbs put out a statement which was a confirmation of sorts so we cranked it up big time and it was leading the news by early evening. Clark had left for Washington and his warning a couple of weeks ago about us being out on a limb, with the US willing to sacrifice us, was looking pretty prescient. We had an Italian on the conference call for the first time, with D'Alema the big story tomorrow. He was fine but clearly saw no problem in saying we could have a bombing pause to get the Russians on board, without Milosevic having to do anything in return. I said that would cause real difficulties for us, and the US and French came in on pretty much the same line.

Catherine Colonna was proving to be an absolute trooper on these calls. I think she and some of the others could sense that I had felt some wind go out of my sails – a combination of a whack from Clinton plus, in my own mind at least, fucking up this morning, plus tiredness. I felt she and Jamie Rubin were the ones who most came in where I would likely be. Joe L said there was a CBS report contrasting Blair out front with the wimps in the White House. I got home, and Fiona said tell them to do it all on their own then. It was BC who had wanted me to sort out NATO and that was still what I was trying to do.

Thursday, May 20

D'Alema in Brussels, like Schroeder refusing to be drawn on ground troops, so we had another anti-UK situation. The crazy thing was that we were being seen as the people trying to change to a policy of invasion, yet people were constantly saying we had to do whatever it took to win (as long as we don't have to talk about ground troops). The main story overnight was a bomb hitting a hospital, with three dead, though this time it was devoid of the hysteria. Openness was definitely the best policy here, added to which the line that the Serbs' exaggerations had to be treated with caution had been getting through. It was a bad news day all round – D'Alema plus the hospital, NI going nowhere, another welfare revolt.

Cabinet was NI, Kosovo, plus GB on the economy. TB and Mo [Mowlam, Northern Ireland Secretary] both said they had never known a situation where there was such a desire for progress, yet they couldn't take the last vital steps. The UUs won't form an executive without IRA decommissioning. SF say they will work for it but it cannot be a precondition. On Kosovo, TB said the demonstrations were real and a positive sign. The air campaign was doing a lot of damage but the worry was Milosevic was stringing us out to a time it would be too late, because of winter, to mount a ground force invasion. D'Alema offered opportunities as well as difficulties. It was a way of getting the ground force option on the table. GB warned that the cost of the military operation, and the refugee crisis, meant there could be no room for anything else from the Reserve, and it all underlined the need for stability to be maintained, welfare-to-work programmes to be improved, other departments to ensure money is well spent. AD [Alistair Darling, Social Security Secretary] gave a very tough message on seeing the welfare changes through. The *New York Times* had an account of the TB/BC call, clearly briefed, saying Clinton had told TB to get control of his people. I was worried it would get picked up and run here and in Europe, and form a new backdrop.

I worked with Mark Bennett [AC's researcher] on my speech to [Cabinet Secretary Sir] Richard Wilson's Sunningdale conference for top civil servants and leading business people tonight, and I was planning to deliver a pretty hard message about how they still didn't get why communication mattered, and still saw it as a dirty word. I drove down with Richard Wilson and we had a frank discussion about how, in my view, the Civil Service systems did not encourage innovators, idea entrepreneurs, or strategists. I said I had seen how bad people were promoted and good people pushed out. He disagreed of course. I had put a lot of work into the speech and it sparked a very lively debate. My main argument was that people had failed to understand the pace of change in the media, and the impact that had on decision-making processes, and the need for strategy to be stronger and clearer. Andrew Turnbull [permanent secretary, HM Treasury] felt we needed to do something about the [Rupert] Murdoch [head of News Corp] press. Wilson took me aside afterwards and said he really appreciated the obvious effort I put into it, and that he understood better now what I was driving at the whole time. It could have been bullshit but he seemed genuine enough. Turnbull was also pretty effusive, said it had been a revelation to some of the ones who didn't know me that I thought things through and had a plan. Several of the business guys asked for a text of what I said, and said some of the lessons can apply equally to their own businesses.

Friday, May 21

The *Guardian* led on a rewrite of the *New York Times* account of the TB/BC call, which was clearly going to run big through the day. 'There's the revenge,' said TB. 'It's silly because the people rubbing their hands at this are the Europeans and in the end the people the US will need to stand by them are us.' He asked me to call Joe, which I did. I said once more that it would be stupid to get into a briefing war, and if we did we knew we could not win it. He said he had discussed it with the president yesterday and everyone had moved on. TB, on his way to the North-East, said he sensed BC knew he was in the wrong position and took it out on his friends. Maybe, maybe not. The RC/Madeleine double act was going fine, and we did need to work to get back on the same songsheet.

Godric [Smith, AC's deputy] did the 11, and got a lot of questioning on the Clinton call, as did I when I did the Sundays. We stuck to the line that we were in constant touch, that we were able to discuss all the issues clearly, but denied falling-out. Of course it had been bad-tempered but it was important not to let them flare it up. And what was interesting was that on the policy, they did seem to be shifting. Wilson had said to Jonathan [Powell] that bad management was responsible for Siobhan [Kenny] leaving, which was bullshit and I wrote to him to protest. I went up to see TB and he was pretty downcast about things and was minded to take a low profile in the next few days and just see where the others took it to.

He couldn't understand why they didn't see the need for a threat of ground forces as clearly as we did. He said people are going to die as a result of our failure here. I said their argument was more would die if we use ground forces and lots of them will be US soldiers. But the drift was reprehensible. He was also fed up with Schroeder, said he would have more respect if he just admitted he had coalition realities to deal with, not try to blame us for fracturing the alliance. Chirac was waiting to see where the wind blew.

Saturday, May 22

Another bombing error. We hit a Serb command post which had been taken over by the KLA, and which had even been visited by Western media to be shown how the KLA were doing. There had also been some major hits overnight though, and again, the scale of coverage of the mistake was not as large as earlier. I did the Sundays by phone and they were pushing mainly on NATO divisions. I pushed the unity of the alliance as one of the great success stories. Ken Bacon had talked last night of an expanded KFOR [NATO-led

Kosovo Force] and our press was seeing that as another step towards ground forces.

It was FA Cup Final day, and I took Rory and Calum [AC's sons] into Number 10, and went upstairs to see TB. He was wearing a Real Madrid tracksuit and doing lots of different impersonations, much to the boys' amusement. We got an escort up to Wembley and on the way he had a couple of difficult calls with Trimble and Adams. I had fixed an interview with Jim Rosenthal [sports commentator] on the live coverage with both Bertie [Ahern] (Man U) and TB (Newcastle). He got a pretty good reception from the Newcastle fans, apart from one in a wheelchair who yelled out 'Tony is a Tory.'

TB and Bertie did a bit of NI in the margins, but they were pretty much on show here at events like this and expected to mingle etc. We were taken up to the wives' section beforehand and TB chatted to Posh Spice [Victoria Beckham] and her dad, while I chatted to Bertie and Celia [Larkin, Ahern's then partner]. It was an OK match, without being storming, and I was chuffed for Alex [Ferguson, Manchester United manager] that he won. He was loving it at the end and when I spoke to him later, he said he had a feeling about the treble. TB called on his way home and said Newcastle just weren't at the races.

Sunday, May 23

A group of male Kosovan refugees, until recently in prison, had been released and were suddenly on the media. I was slow to react, not having seen the pictures when we did the first conference call. But by the second one, I had seen them, gaunt, frail and with stories of abuse and torture, and said we should really try to generate massive coverage, and try to get some of them for our press conferences. I suggested our war crimes co-ordinator go out and interview them. Far better we hear their own stories than the public simply hear our version of them. GR said we would send our war crimes expert to interview them in the region, so we would have a decent start to the week media-wise. There was also a feeling the NATO briefings were becoming dull. One or two of the papers had told me they were losing sales every time they led on Kosovo, so we were going to have to be more imaginative about how we retained their interest and support.

TB spoke to Bill at 9.45pm. Bill was free of the rancour of last week, and was definitely hardening his position towards ground troops. He said as much to TB, but said we would have to set it up very carefully with our public opinion. TB felt he should be out there signalling a change. Whether it had been deliberate or not, Ken Bacon's comments on KFOR being extended were helpful in that regard. TB was worried that with me almost totally focused on Kosovo, we were losing some of our drive and crunch on domestic policy issues, e.g. we were being run ragged on GM [genetically modified foods], and on welfare reform, and Scotland had not settled down. The problem was that though Godric could do the briefings well, as a civil servant he couldn't do the politics, and Lance [Price, special adviser, press office] didn't really fill the gap.

Monday, May 24

I went in late after Grace's school concert and briefly saw Godric and Lance. Neither of them were really filling in and it meant that on a whole stack of issues we were not really focused. Anji and Philip [Gould, pollster, strategist and adviser to TB] both sent me notes on it, Anji saying there were lots of people with opinions but nobody driving through decisions. Identical to NATO. The conference calls today were a bit depressing, just focusing on day-to-day news and not enough on forward strategy. There was a big strategic gap and I felt the pressure to fill it fell too much on me. Milosevic was still winning the media war. That being said, today we had a refugee up there which led to more complaints that I was using the briefings to spin rather than give them what they wanted. We were far too defensive about this as it was basic snobbery. But we definitely needed to shake things up again. Bruce Mann [MoD secondee] was doing a good job getting stuff out of the military. Lucie McNeil was doing well getting a bit of life into visits.

Tuesday, May 25

I was up at 6am local time and off to SHAPE with Julian. I went to see Stockman and explained that the media were bored and restless and the briefings becoming very formulaic. There was little or no imagination, added to which I felt Jertz's confidence was low. At the desk-side meeting, Clark looked tired and fed up. He wanted to go to the NAC this evening and say it was time to get real, either we really go for the air campaign and stop whining about there being more collateral damage, or we go for ground forces. His leg was jiggling more than ever, and he was snappy with some of his advisers. As we walked to the video-conference room, he said he was getting fed up with the mood of apology surrounding everything. Did people really think you could run a sustained air campaign without civilian deaths?

I then met Wilby and Jertz. I was frank about the problem, and at the end of it felt they didn't really understand what I meant by strategic communication. Jertz complained that Jamie strayed too much into the military situation and also that there were too many last-minute changes to scripts. They claimed that PJ [Crowley] got on to the Pentagon and got things pulled if he wanted the Pentagon rather than NATO to be in the driving seat. Wilby must have seen the writing on the wall because he volunteered that if we wanted Julian to do all the scripts he was happy with that, but it would mean him basing himself there. Julian's worry was being swallowed up in the system. It all got a bit too heated, with me saying this was no more than a personality clash and Wilby saying Julian just wandered around doing what he wanted and going behind their backs, Julian saying there was no real system in place to do a proper job. I said I feared they still believed there was something a bit wrong and dirty about communications. They really had to buy into this, not grudgingly. We finally agreed to agreeing Julian should be in charge of strategic direction there, which included scripts.

Wednesday, May 26

I went in, largely to show my face after almost a week of barely speaking to the lobby. On the Kosovo front, we were on to the fact that tomorrow ICTY [International Criminal Tribunal for the former Yugoslavia] would indict Milosevic as a war criminal. It wasn't straightforward. The obvious question was whether we would actually deal with him later when he was still president. I was really looking forward to getting away with Rory to Barcelona for the Champions League Final [Manchester United vs Bayern Munich]. The atmosphere at the start was terrific but it was actually a poor game, though nobody will ever remember that given the unbelievable ending.[1] United didn't really click and Alex was looking more and more anxious towards the end. Bayern should have buried them in the second half. Then United scored in injury time and suddenly, all round the ground, people were saying they were going to do it again. And they did. The place went absolutely ballistic. Amid the celebrations, which seemed to go on forever, I suddenly remembered that Richard Wilson had told me if they won the treble, they would rush Alex into the Honours List with a knighthood, but they would need to know tomorrow that he was up for it.

We were needing to leave for the plane, so I jumped into the VIP section, found Cathy [Ferguson], explained the situation, and she said

[1] Manchester United beat Bayern Munich 2–1 with two goals scored in rapid succession in the closing moments of the game.

'I'm against all that. And don't you think he's won enough already?'
To be on the safe side I also told Mark [their son], who was clearly
keener than she was. I left a message on Alex's mobile and he called
later, said he had been numb most of the night. He said he wanted
to think overnight about the knighthood, talk to Cathy and one or
two others. The question that mattered for him was whether his
parents would be proud of it or not, and he thought they probably
would. TB had pretty much missed the whole thing because he had
been stuck at a reception for the official opening of the Welsh Assembly.
He said when the result was brought in, the Queen literally said, no
joke, that she was 'over the moon'. It had definitely been a special
night, one of those when you wanted to try to retain every moment.
The Germans lying shattered on the pitch, one of them barely able to
walk, totally devastated. And then the walk out of the ground,
complete strangers hugging and kissing, grown men stopping Rory
and telling him to remember everything because life would never get
better than this. We got home at about 4am. Rory was fast asleep. A
brilliant, brilliant night.

Thursday, May 27
Up at 7 telling Fiona everything about last night. I got in to see TB,
who was doing another note to Clinton about how we would explain
the ground force option. There was a real buzz around the place and
everyone wanted to know every last detail about last night. Cabinet
was mainly Kosovo, Robin more pompous than ever. He went through
the whole process, which was not straightforward, and centred on
the fact that we could not exclude the possibility of having to deal
with Milosevic in the future. TB said there had been a mood shift,
and that the resolve, including the possibility of ground forces, had
strengthened. GB chipped in again with a warning about costs saying
it could go to billions and have implications for every department's
budget. TB spoke to Clinton again. He said Bill basically felt we had
shafted him and we now had to help him get back to the position he
wanted to be in.

To Paris for a socialist leaders' meeting. We had a bilateral with
Jospin at the Matignon [French Prime Minister's office]. He is a real
football fan, and we spent the first few minutes talking about the
Man U game. He was very strong on Milosevic, said he did not
believe there were any circumstances in which he could stay as leader
in Serbia. He thought it was good that [Martti] Ahtisaari [President
of Finland] was speaking to him, but we should be cautious and
again, he indicated French military were very cautious about ground

forces. We left for the utterly ghastly event, speech after speech to an audience that spent most of the time muttering. Schroeder, in shirtsleeves, was totally dismissive of the whole event and was absolutely crap. Jospin spoke really well on Kosovo but then waffled on for half an hour, meandering from one issue to the next without clear argument.

TB sat there with a fixed grin throughout, clearly hating it. He said on the flight back that if ever he agreed to such an event again, we had to overrule him, no matter how forceful he was, on pain of death or dismissal. He had not been impressed by Schroeder again. He had seen in Clinton's posture the chance to do us in a bit and he went for it. I said the problem was that within NATO, the truth was we really were more like the Americans and we were not like the Europeans in the final analysis. 'That is exactly what [Margaret] Thatcher [former Conservative Prime Minister] said when I saw her on Tuesday,' said TB. Her view was the Germans try to be disciplined and so become inflexible. The French can't be trusted. The Italians are too weak and the Spanish don't count. The only people like us are the Dutch and they are too small. TB said he didn't necessarily agree with it all but there was something in it.

Meanwhile, I received an unbelievably grovelling letter from Wilson thanking me for my speech at Sunningdale, saying he agreed totally with what I said, though how much of this was bullshit I couldn't work out. I was home after midnight, totally knackered. I was travelling too much and it just never stops at the moment. I was also getting stacks of calls and letters from people saying they were being contacted by the various authors of biographies about me. They were clearly trying to give the impression I was co-operating and I needed a strategy to deal with that.

Friday, May 28

I did a TB piece for the *Sun* on the war, which [editor David] Yelland wanted to splash on as an interview. I said no. An article was one thing, but not an interview. Alex F called to discuss the logistics re his knighthood, and agreed to do a clip for our PEB [party election broadcast] on leadership.

Saturday, May 29

Philip G called, and said he was really worried about our operation. He said if TB and I were not engaged in something, it just didn't happen. There were lots of good people with good ideas but if we were not there, there was drift. He thought I had done a brilliant job on the war, not just in improving media relations, but in getting us in the right position, but there was a price to pay. We were losing drive and direction on domestic issues. We left Saturday early pm to go to Charlie Falconer's in Nottinghamshire. He was always good fun. He too though was worried about my absences. He said I have unchallenged authority on the communications front and if I wasn't there nobody assumed that authority. The Clark/Solana briefing [at Aviano airbase, Italy] went OK but the sound was dire and the camerawork poor, which annoyed me.

Sunday, May 30

Some of the Sundays did stories on Alex F campaigning for us, and he was due to record something tomorrow, so we talked that through. Some of the papers were already into him. He said some of them honestly would have preferred United to have lost.

Monday, May 31

There had been a few more collateral damage incidents over the weekend, including one that injured some journalists. The Germans as ever were pushing for big apologies and expressions of regret. The Americans and I were saying we should simply say we do not target civilians, that we recognise the difficulties of working there as journalists but this is a military campaign.

Prince Charles' office sent through the article he was doing for the *Mail* tomorrow on GM food, which would be a huge hit. He was basically saying we didn't need this stuff at all, and would no doubt have all the pressure groups out saying how marvellous he was. I tried to contact TB but he was playing tennis. I formulated a line that they had sent us the article, we have been calling for a sensible, rational debate and it should be seen in that context. When I finally got round to reading the article in full, it was dreadful. It could easily have been written by the *Mail*. It was clearly going to lead the news tomorrow and I would have to pretend that we were totally unbothered by it. Re-reading it, I felt that it was over the top and it might backfire on Charles. There was a sense of it being gratuitously anti science from someone whose locus in the debate wasn't clear.

Tuesday, June 1

TB called early and his view [of Prince Charles' GM article] was the same, but he said I mustn't engage in any way that suggests we are being critical. But in the end this country is going to have to decide whether we are serious, or whether we want a whole new area of science and technology to be taken away from us to let the rest of the world take it over. He was pretty wound up about it, said it was a straightforward anti-science position, the same argument that says if God intended us to fly he would have given us wings. It certainly had a feel of grandstanding. It was also, I said, a cheap shot because it was an issue on which Charles said he was open-minded, but in fact had a settled opinion, and he knew we couldn't actually answer back. Through the day [Sir] Stephen Lamport [private secretary to Prince Charles] was asking John Sawers what the informal view was. I gave John our emollient words to fax over but said he may as well make clear the informal view was not at all favourable.

TB's other beef at the moment was the Germans. He felt they were just desperate to get any kind of deal on Kosovo. They had also had a difficult call yesterday re who should be the EU's first 'Mr Foreign Policy' on CFSP [EU high representative for common foreign and security policy]. TB agreed it should be Solana. Then, when they discussed David Hannay [UK diplomat] as Number 2, Schroeder said there was a two to one majority for a Frenchman because Solana, being from NATO, effectively represented the transatlantic relationship and the Number 2 should represent the continent of Europe.

I spent lunchtime with Mark B working up my script for the 3pm briefing on Cologne. The main focus was Ahtisaari in Bonn. The briefing went fine, though needless to say there was more interest in GM foods and they could see I was determined not to give them any sense of division. They pointed out, rightly, that if Friends of the Earth had said the same thing, we would attack it. There you go. TB saw the Queen and seemingly didn't push too hard re Charles but he was very pissed off, especially once it became clear from their briefings that they were emphasising he had thought through the consequences.

Wednesday, June 2

There was lots of toing and froing all day re Ahtisaari, who was in Bonn with [acting Russian Prime Minister Viktor] Chernomyrdin. The day started with their visit to Belgrade very much on, then off after some more US demands, then on again. Jamie Rubin made it very clear on the conference call that he didn't want Jamie Shea briefing on it. He called me later to say that his powers that be were fed up with Shea's briefing on diplomacy. Hague was getting fairly big coverage on Europe and it was time to take on the Tories over it, to draw the line as 'leading Europe, or leaving Europe'. The feeling was we were heading for pretty bad results in the European elections and we had to build up to the last few days painting the Tories as wanting to take us out of Europe. GB was worried that was not credible, but I felt Hague's recent line about renegotiating the Treaty of Rome – which needs unanimity – could get us there.

TB saw Hague yesterday re Kosovo and they were now busy briefing that we had asked them to stiffen the spine of other right-wing parties in Europe. On the conference call, the Germans didn't seem to know what was happening re Ahtisaari. Rubin was very clear that Brussels had to stay out of it. On the flight to Cologne, John Sawers said the Russians had agreed a paper that met NATO's demands but there were real difficulties over the configuration of forces, with virtually separate command and control. On arrival we went straight to the PES [Party of European Socialists] dinner, TB still fulminating about Charles, having just read a clearly briefed account in the *Independent*. By the time I got back for the conference call, we had a text of the agreement and I emphasised we shouldn't let the Russians, not to mention the Serbs, get away with all their positive spinning on it. But the US wanted the Russians to seem happy with it, and then when people saw the text they could see our demands were met.

But at the end of the call I was concerned and spoke to TB, who agreed we have to have a line out that the demands were the same as ever, Milosevic had to accept them, and if there was progress with the Russians, it was only because there was diplomacy backed by force. But we had to be careful. It would not take too much to tip the apple cart. Clinton was talking up ground troops, which was helpful, TB was still nervous that the US were capable of hanging us out to dry, and conceding on the NATO core demands. Back at the hotel, we had a bilateral with Bertie Ahern, which was extremely gloomy. They agreed that without real decommissioning, it wasn't going to work. I caught Sky News which was dreadful, the agreement text being presented pretty much as a win for Milosevic.

Thursday, June 3

TB's education speech did fine. I had an early meeting with Robin, who was doing media, emphasising no compromise, real pressure still on, keep hitting them hard. Through the morning, news came that the Serb parliament had voted to accept the plan. I did a briefing and there was a real buzz in the media, an excitement building up that it was over and moving our way. I did a briefing saying Milosevic seemed to be getting the message, but we were absolutely clear all the conditions had to be met, nothing else would do. I called John

Simpson, who surprised me by saying 'Congratulations, it looks like game, set and match.'

TB did a very tough pooled clip – 'We hope it's true, if so, it's progress and now must be implemented.' On the conference call, the Americans were urging caution. It was going to be tricky for a while yet. I got a message from Wes Clark that he didn't want the Italian general to brief, so we pulled him, and also that he was worried about the idea of not pinning down all the details of the Russian force before the deal was done. TB was pretty buoyant but determined to keep it low-key, and use this period to hammer home the advantage. TB was convinced that it was the fear of ground troops, and the apparent shift by the Americans, that moved Milosevic to where he was. There was an irony in the fact that this was all happening on Schroeder's watch, when had he been in charge of the overall strategy, the threats would not have been there in the first place. Although the afternoon session [in Cologne] went ahead re economic reform, they were really just waiting for Ahtisaari. TB did an extended CNN interview, partly for news, partly for the profile they were doing. Everyone seemed to be presenting it now as a great victory. Jonathan [Powell] said that Simpson's report had been superb for us, that it was all one way. We had to resist any triumphalism, but it was clear they were already on to 'anatomy of a victory' pieces.

Ahtisaari finally arrived, looked tired but pretty exhilarated for a Finn, limped in to loud applause and again I thought Schroeder misread the mood by doing a great bear hug. It sent all the wrong signals. The Germans were telling us to lighten up, but I agreed with the Americans that we should be cautious, not least because of Milosevic's record. Indeed, Ahtisaari was foremost in urging us to take nothing for granted. He and Schroeder went off to do a press conference. TB did some TV interviews before we left for the hotel and then later to the [Grandhotel] Schloss for dinner. It had all come pretty suddenly. There didn't seem any doubt that we had won, though there was no jubilation. Chirac, who did a broadcast to the nation, complained that the Americans could have done this earlier if they had involved the Russians properly. TB was totally on the line that this only happened because of our resolve and determination. He was getting a great press.

Friday, June 4

Both the *Sun* and the *Mirror* did 'who Blairs wins' headlines. I met Robin, who said that TB and I should be more upbeat, that this was a huge success. But we felt that if the mood of celebration was overdone it would send Milosevic the signal that we had given up on further negotiation. The military-to-military paper had been worked up overnight, with various drafts flying around through the day and the final version sent to the Serbs at 4am Saturday. RC felt we had to be saying this was our victory but TB was still cautious.

We toyed with the idea of a prime ministerial broadcast but John Sawers and others felt it was premature, and in any event would be difficult to organise. So we decided instead to go for a proper measured statement at the start of the press conference. We persuaded the French to give us their lectern on the grounds that Chirac and Jospin should sit together. I drafted a very strong script for TB which he played around with during the meeting. On the conference call, we started to focus on the job that we would need to do in the region itself once we got in there. In the meantime, stay cautious and the bombing continues until there is verifiable withdrawal of his troops.

We flew to Rotterdam with [Dutch Prime Minister Wim] Kok for a joint campaign effort that turned out to be typical Dutch chaos. What we thought was going to be a public meeting turned out to be a rambling TV discussion. We seemed to be there an age. I was getting very tired and grumpy about everything. It reminded me of how I felt when we won the election, not celebrating because there was a whole stack of new stuff to focus on. The main story of the day was the announcement that Mike Jackson was meeting the Serb general tomorrow.

Saturday, June 5

Julian called early, having travelled to Macedonia with the SHAPE team for the Blace talks. There was a problem. The Serbs did not want to come to the venue we had chosen. The talks were due to start at 9. The Serbs came up with another venue and after a lot of toing and froing, NATO agreed we may have to move. This might be the start of all his usual pissing around. Last night SIS [Secret Intelligence Service, 'MI6'] had called to ask if it was sensible to get out the intelligence that Milosevic was looking to get family out. My immediate reaction was to stay quiet but overnight I changed my mind. It would be a useful cover for them causing trouble, a reason for him trying to buy more time, rather than because we were facing problems.

Julian's next call said not to expect any progress today because the Serbs claimed they didn't get the text till late, and because they were only authorised to negotiate the verifiable withdrawal. In other words, they would negotiate the start, get the bombing suspended, and then negotiate the rest. I did a phone briefing, again stressing caution. TB said it didn't bode well and was trying to speak to Yeltsin to get them on board for some of the diplomatic stuff that would now be necessary. We also had the usual Sunday rubbish to sort out.

I had to get [the Queen's press secretary] Geoff Crawford from the Palace to rubbish a *Mail on Sunday* story that the Queen was fed up with TB missing audiences when in fact the majority of those missed were because she was away. There was also a story doing the rounds that Prince Charles had said Cherie was against GM. When I mentioned it to TB, he said maybe there was an upside in that at least it showed her to be on the side of the argument most people seemed to be on. I felt it showed he couldn't even persuade his wife. It was also a bad story for Charles. The Sundays were far more upbeat than they ought to have been. We were now dealing with classic Milosevic. He did the deal on the principle, then screwed around on the detail in a way that made it look like he was winning on the narrow points he was defining.

Sunday, June 6

We had a real conundrum. The Serbs would not withdraw without a UNSCR. The Russians would not negotiate a UNSCR until we stopped the bombing. And we would not stop the bombing until they withdrew. Julian called regularly through the day, getting more and more of a sense of the Serbs buggering us about. He said the Serb delegation was saying they didn't have authority to negotiate on anything other than withdrawal. TB was starting to get anxious and spoke a couple of times to Ahtisaari, to Clinton and to Mike Jackson. Jackson told TB that he didn't believe they were serious and we should tell them to get lost. Ahtisaari suggested he went there and in the final analysis said he would call Milosevic, say KFOR would have to go in and we get a UNSCR afterwards. After the Clinton call, we had a conference call – TB, Jonathan, John S, AC – re whether Ahtisaari should go to Belgrade. Jackson felt it would make Milosevic feel he was able to negotiate, which was just what he wanted. At 9pm Julian called, said Jackson was getting very tired and ratty and wanted to tell them to take it or leave it. We had changed the text to take on board at least one of their points and as far as he was concerned, that was more than enough.

TB said he feared Jackson was a great soldier but less good as a negotiator. He thought it was crazy these negotiations were carried out by soldiers not expert negotiators. Clark also wanted to pull the plug. Jackson basically believed we shouldn't be negotiating with them at all, and we hadn't hit them hard enough. I called Jackson, said it looked ragged and it would be good if he went out and said there were a number of important technical issues to be addressed, they had asked for clarification, they had got it, they were going back to Belgrade, meanwhile the bombing had to go on. He said he did not believe they were yet willing to concede, at least not on NATO terms, and there is a bloody great hole in the document that gives them the opportunity to bugger about endlessly. He said he felt the governments were expecting him to do something that was not appropriate, namely deliver a political solution. I liked him, and he is a tough character, but prickly and impatient, and not necessarily aware of the difference between what was going on in reality and what it made sense to brief. What had to be clear was that the buggering about all came from the Serb side and meantime we had to carry on bombing. We were also going to need a major media operation down there. The news tonight was a mess, with two not very convincing people, one a Brit and the other an American, who looked like they didn't really know what was hitting them.

Monday, June 7

I had gone to bed after my calls with Jackson, then woke to find he had gone out in the early hours and was now leading the news saying pretty much what we had agreed, plus a bit about intensifying the bombing. The story, though, was collapse in the talks. TB called at 6.50 – he was worried whether there was enough subtlety to these negotiations. TB spoke to Ahtisaari for the fifth or sixth time in twenty-four hours, at one point asking what is Schroeder doing and why are we having to do this? I put together a line for the 11 basically saying it was a test of how serious he was about implementing the agreement.

The other story was GM, a farmer destroying his trial crops because of pressure from farm trustees. CB was furious with Prince Charles re the *IoS* story, which was clearly briefed, and said she wasn't going to reply to his recent missive on the subject. At the office meeting, as ever TB was worrying about delivery. He also felt we had no real message out for the European elections. I got Anji [Hunter] to plan on going down to Macedonia/Albania to set up new media systems and also to schmooze Jackson a bit. When I spoke to SACEUR, he said Julian had been very important at the talks. I asked in what way? When I see you, I'll tell you. TB found it hard to believe that Milosevic could really hold out now and assumed he was just trying to move the ground so he could claim some kind of success. TB, GR, CDS, Clare [Short, International Development Secretary] and lots of officials met to take stock. Clare asked about reports showing that the Kosovar Albanians were Marxist drug dealers. What have you got against Marxists? I asked. She paused then after a while, very defensively, said 'I was never a Trot.' Clearly struck a nerve.

I called Clark about 10 and, parodying the line we had been using for days now, said 'You're winning, he's losing and he knows it.' He said he still believed it was only 50–50. Milosevic was perfectly capable of playing several moves ahead of us. He was looking for a new game to play and we had to work out what it was. He said we were 'bombing the Dickens out of them' and doing real damage but Milosevic was just sending in more and more replacements. He just didn't care how many men he lost.

Tuesday, June 8

Having spoken to Clark, and got his agreement to beef up the media operation in the region, I sent a note, copied to various generals, saying that Anji was there with his and our blessing. Anji went off to Skopje and called me after her meeting with Jackson. He basically blew a gasket, said he was sick of spin doctors and media manipulation, there was nothing wrong with his operation and he was not going to take orders from anyone, so get lost. She said she got pretty much no help from anyone but gave as good as she got, and said we were trying to assist not supplant. Later she took him a bottle of whisky and he calmed down. She said he was a bit of a powder keg and it would be wrong to send Jonathan Prince, who would drive him up the wall. Prince was really upset about it but I think between us we persuaded him it was the right thing to do. The G8 meeting in Bonn finally led to a draft SCR and we were also finally getting the Schroeder declaration. By 2 the G8 ministers were doing a very strong press conference, we were united and the writing was on the wall for Milosevic. There was again a real sense of progress, the draft SCR leading to the military agreement talks opening again with Jackson. TB said we had to get the message to Jackson that he was not to disturb the negotiations but get it through.

At the eleven o'clock, there was a lot of interest in the Schroeder stuff and I pushed hard on the shared commitment to economic reform. The Commons statement on Kosovo went fine, the main story being the outcome of the G8, the continued bombing, ending with the meeting back on. TB felt it had gone fine in the Commons but said he couldn't believe [Labour MP] Tony Benn's contribution, saying we could have done this deal weeks ago.

We went back to greet Schroeder, who was far friendlier than in

Cologne. He asked how we would do in the elections. TB said badly because of the new system and GS said but 'Der Doktor Campbell will get the press to hail it as a triumph.' I said no, because I didn't believe in the system. TB said there was a drawback with his press secretary – he wouldn't defend policies he didn't believe in. They did an OK doorstep in the garden and then we left for Millbank [Labour Party HQ] for the political side of things and people were seeing it as significant that Schroeder wanted to be on our political territory. TB's speech was OK but without passion. Schroeder spoke off the cuff. He said he was impressed by the operation. I was impressed that Jackie Stacey [Labour Party staff] spoke German. Schroeder said all his key people spoke English. I said 'You can't play football though,' to which he replied 'We can, for eighty-nine minutes.'

Wednesday, June 9

The military-to-military talks resumed. I had two further long chats with Jonathan Prince who claimed he had to stop Clinton from calling TB to say he wanted Prince to go to Macedonia. He thought this was us trying to make it a British thing, but it was just about making sure we handled Jackson properly and proceeded with care. We were still waiting for progress on the talks. Berger had been bad-mouthing Clark who in turn, when TB spoke to him, was bad-mouthing the US and telling TB he was the one who had given indispensable political leadership. [KFOR spokesman Lt Col Robin] Clifford seemed pretty well plugged in. It was a real up and down kind of day but as I left the four o'clock briefing, Sawers called, and then Julian to say that the top Serb was leaving for Belgrade to see Milosevic. I called Clifford who said they were getting messed around the whole time and had lost the initiative. But within an hour, he and then Julian called to say the Serbs were on their way back, not having gone to Belgrade at all, and it was all on again.

Just before 8 John S called to say the US had given the go-ahead to sign the agreement, with one final change demanded by Milosevic agreed to, and Jackson would sign it shortly, and then it would go to the North Atlantic Council. Julian called to say Clifford didn't want to announce it and I said don't be ridiculous we had to get out there on the front foot. Jackson came out not long after and though he looked pretty dreadful he spoke well, got the tone right and did fine. I laid Julian a bet that in a future conflict Jackson would come back as an armchair general, the kind Guthrie was always raging at. GR called and we agreed he should do a statement while I put out TB words on the need to be just as determined and resolute now as we were during the air campaign. More than last Thursday, I felt this was the day when we won it. And I felt very moved watching the news at the end of the day. I remembered something Anne Edwards [US official] said – find your moral star and follow it – and felt we had done that. I also told TB I'd been getting very tired and fed up and wanted to leave, and he said I couldn't.

Thursday, June 10

There was mega-coverage of yesterday's events and we were getting a pretty good press. I went up to see TB and we agreed he should do a statement to the media after Solana. I gave [David] Bradshaw [special adviser, Strategic Communications Unit] an outline which he worked up into a script focusing on this being a victory for good over evil and now we prepare for the difficulties ahead. At DOP [Defence and Overseas Policy committee], CDS said Jackson was dealing with horrible people who would continue to be horrible throughout. SACEUR had spoken to the Serb chief of staff who had indicated they would move at midday. TB said we had to deny Milosevic any credibility at all, and remain very tough in seeing it all through.

At Cabinet, TB said we were hoping for the withdrawal to start soon but there would be enormous problems in building the peace. Refugees. A new civil administration. What to do about Milosevic? But at least we weren't facing the problems of fighting a ground war. He paid tribute to the troops, said they were magnificent. GR went over the same ground, and also said the UK's role in holding the alliance together was remarkable. He said at the risk of sounding sycophantic, it would not have happened without TB. TB was not remotely triumphalist but pretty much everyone was saying he had done an amazing job. After Cabinet, TB took me, RW, GR and CDS aside and said he wanted to set up a small team to review the lessons to be learned. He said he would never have gone into this in the way we did if he had known how weak our allies would become. It was noticeable, in one of the conference calls today, the higher than usual proportion of British voices.

The story wasn't here but out in theatre and in Brussels, where we were waiting for Clark to tell Solana that withdrawal had begun. Clark spoke to a Serb general who said it would begin at noon. On the conference call, Prince said Solana wanted to announce it alone. We all agreed it would be better with Clark there too. More hanging around and then half an hour later, he was out.

TB meanwhile was on the phone to Clinton and I was listening in and responsible for a near disaster. I didn't realise that whenever I pulled out of the call I cut off. Twice. Also, even though I had hit the mute button, for some reason they could hear me, for example saying 'God this is fucking bollocks' as they were talking about AIDS. The first time I cut them off was when I went through with a note saying that Solana was about to go out and they should go out soon after. TB was full of praise re Bill and Bill, I felt, less so in return. But even those who hated to give us anything were acknowledging it was a good win. As soon as Solana was done, we got TB's script finished and did a briefing mainly for TV plus a few foreigners, which pissed off the lobby and led to a great row with them at 4. They were totally obsessed with themselves. TB did fine, though some felt he was too sombre. We fixed for him to do some lives, including Jon Snow [*Channel 4 News*], and it was only when I was watching the news reports before the interview that I realised why they were expecting a tone of triumphalism.

Friday, June 11

What should have been an amazingly positive day for everyone was close to being a total fucking fiasco. We had been told last night that the Paras and the Gurkhas would lead the way in today. We woke up to reports that there had been a delay. The suggestion being made was that we had to wait for the Marines so that the US could go in too. This was clearly being said by people out there but was potentially very damaging. Lucie [McNeil] was due to go in with the first wave to help Jackson set up his press conference in Priština. The delay became the story. And, mid-morning, the news that a small convoy of Russian tanks was on its way to Kosovo from Bosnia. This electrified the place. The truth was nobody was aware in advance. CDS and George R came over for a meeting with TB and we agreed to try to put out a calm line, namely we had always envisaged working closely with the Russians. Everyone seemed to think they may go into Priština before us. Charles said the only way to beat them, and secure the airport, was to send in forces by air – helicopter – but it was by no means a risk-free operation. TB was very nervous about it, said he couldn't really send in troops at such a risk and we didn't even know what the situation would be, what the Russians were up to, where they would be going. So we tried to calm it.

Then at 1.05, Wes Clark called me and said that Russian troops were moving and now he had learned they had asked for airspace for six planes through Hungary. Either we go for a very risky military operation, or we risk partition, with the Russians just taking over. This is now a political-military operation. He said the Serbs were one hundred per cent in cahoots with the Russians. His instinct was that we should go in and take the airport. But Jackson was concerned. I said TB's instincts when Guthrie raised it were cautious but I would speak to him again. He said this was the result of diplomatic ambiguity at the heart of the agreement. We have to ask political leaders to give us clear cover. This is grand strategy stuff. He said he didn't want it known that he had called me, it was an offline call.

I went to see TB, who was doing his policy unit awayday upstairs, took him out and just relayed what Wes had said. Don't shoot the messenger, I said. He said 'You are suggesting that I lose some of our soldiers in fighting with the Russians. That is World War Three. I could just about stand up in the Commons and say there's a bit of a mess about who controls the airport. But I cannot defend starting World War Three. Tell him we have to wait and see what their plans are and in the meantime they have to get rolling into Kosovo. I wish to God these generals would calm down a bit.' It was a year on from Ellie's funeral [Ellie Merritt, daughter of AC's late friend John, had died of leukaemia] and I promised to take the kids to the cemetery. It was upsetting but equally I was glad just to get out for an hour or so. I got back in to a meeting with TB and CDS, who said he had spoken to Jackson and said he had to take our advice on media. On the conference call, we had nobody on from down there today, which was ridiculous and they looked ragged again. The reporters were doing endless two-ways [broadcast conservations between journalist and studio anchor] saying different things because they weren't being guided.

The story was becoming a shambles, the sense of a race to get in, and it was all about the ego of politicians. I put out a statement that they should stop talking rubbish. I did the Sundays, who as ever just wanted bits of colour to slot into whatever fiction they were planning. I couldn't stand their cynicism, their pettiness and their lack of political nous. Patrick Wintour [*Observer*] was about the only one there I had time for at all. GB called to say he was appointing Ian Austin [Labour press officer] as a special adviser. The Russians were moving towards Kosovo and the Paras were on standby to head them off at the airport so by the end of the day we could be fighting the fucking Russians. On the 8pm call, I really laid it on, said today had been a total shambles in communications terms and there had to be better co-ordination.

CDS spoke to Jackson's chief of staff, General [Andrew] Ridgeway, and suggested we discuss things. I went through my spiel that we were trying to take a load off them, that the 24-hour media was a real problem and only if you kept it busy on your terms could you actually get on and do the things that needed to be done. The aim was to take the burden off Jackson, not add to it. Turnout at the European elections was low and there was a chance the Tories would be ahead of us in share of the vote. TB said he wanted me back focused on the domestic agenda but I couldn't quite see how.

I got to bed fairly late and then at 1.05, Robin Clifford called and said they had got an order down from SACEUR that they were to be put on hold for another twenty-four hours while the US continued to work on the integration of the Russians. This was unbelievable. We had looked ragged enough as it was, but this was ridiculous. I called John Sawers and also put in a call to Clark. John was asleep, unaware, and said he couldn't believe it and would call Berger. He called back, Berger having said they were trying to tie down the arrangements with the Russians to be part of the US sector. CNN was showing Russians already in Priština. Strobe Talbott [US Deputy Secretary of State] was asking the Russians what was going on and they claimed they had been deployed in error. Some error. Clifford, watching on CNN, said they were being greeted by Serbs as liberators.

Wes Clark called and said he was told they were going to apologise and withdraw. The White House had asked for a 24-hour pause to talk to the Russians and sort out the integration question. He had one hour, maybe one and a half hours, to call off the deployment. The Russians will not talk to NATO, only to the US. We agreed that not only would it look dreadful if we didn't go, with all the media already lined up, but it would send the signal the Serbs most wanted – that the Russians could call the shots. The whole thing was dreadful.

I called TB, who said that if we didn't deploy he would have to speak to Clinton. He said what earthly reason is there not to deploy? We can resolve the Russian question later. If we run into the Russians in Priština, so what? Either we overwhelm them or we can embrace them. And if they really are leaving, we won't meet them anyway. Everyone agreed we had to deploy KFOR for real reasons of substance as well as for presentation. John spoke to Berger again to say TB wanted to speak to Bill if there was no deployment. I spoke to Wes to say TB was fully behind the decision to deploy. Berger wanted a few more minutes to pin down the Russians. Wes said the plan was to send a couple of guys from SHAPE to Moscow, collect some Russians, get to Macedonia, meet Jackson, then discuss with the US if the Russians would deploy as part of the US force. That takes another eighteen hours. John came up with another very good idea which Wes leapt at. Deploy the French and the Brits and say to the Russians that we will hold back on the Americans – who were not due to go in yet anyway – and let the Russians discuss that. While I was on to Wes, CNN broadcast Igor Ivanov [Russian foreign minister] saying that the Russians arriving in Priština was an unfortunate error. Unbelievable.

Clark said this was not about NATO, but about US–Russia relationships. I spoke twice to Clark, who wanted TB to speak to Clinton. John S spoke three times to Berger. Fiona was getting fed up with the phone ringing the whole time now that we were in the middle of the night. Wes said 'My instinct says go now, but there are other things going on. This is all coming from the White House.' He was due to speak to General Shelton again. Clifford came on asking for the line. I said say that this as an episode may make good theatre but has nothing to do with the real operation. He wanted to say we were delighted Russians were involved. I said better to say we always expected them to be part of the operation, those who are there are there in error but we welcome the fact that we will be working with them. By now, with forty-five minutes to go before they were due to deploy, Jackson had not sent the decision to the Brigades because it would get straight to the press, but it looked now to be moving our way again.

Clark said this could be a tempest in a teapot but if they go from the town to the airport we have a problem. Just after 3am, Charles Guthrie came on. The US had finally agreed to go, delaying their own troops till later. He had spoken to Clark and Shelton, told them both they were a shambles and they would come out of it dreadfully if they didn't go now. This was crazy stuff.

Saturday, June 12
I got a couple of hours' sleep, up to see the news, pictures of the troops and tanks inside Kosovo and then to the [Hampstead Heath] lido for a swim. Wes asked me to do a script for his press conference later. I spoke to TB before he left for Trooping the Colour. He said it would sort itself out diplomatically. On the conference call, we agreed to play it all down, however serious it actually might be. Wes did fine and I called him afterwards to say so. He said either there was a government within a government in Russia, or there was a good cop/bad cop routine going on, but either way it was worrying. TB felt it was settling down, that the Russians were just trying to take the gloss off NATO's triumph by being first into Priština. Ivanov having claimed deployment was a mistake, Yeltsin now promoted the

general who took the troops into Priština. There were still Russian tanks driving around the airfield, and some of the TV reporters described it as a farce.

Sunday, June 13

Lucie McNeil called at 7 to say she was stuck in a convoy hemmed in at either end by Russian tanks. However much we said that the Russians were just trying to be noticed, there were real problems of substance here which would have to be addressed diplomatically. Later John S called to say Wes was suggesting we actually seize the airport, despite the risks of a firefight with the Russians, which would be a disaster. I put round a line that their understandable frustrations were not significant compared with the job our military had to do and the importance of getting the refugees back home. The Russians were making us look silly and we were unable to give a clear sense of who was in charge. TB found the Russians outrageous on this. They are party to the agreement and now they try to screw us up.

Berger called Sawers to say they weren't happy with some of the things our military were saying out there, for example that we were happy to concede the airport to the Russians. It was true that a line went out from the MoD to senior Brits out there to say that we were not to take part in any Clark plan for an attack on the airport. It was a national red-card job. Jackson, according to Sawers, had threatened to resign because he was being asked to do something he believed would involve shooting at Russians and he was not prepared to do it. George R confirmed to TB Jackson was adamant that if the Russians were supposed to be part of KFOR, we could hardly start shooting at them. Clark, via US ventriloquising, was saying we had to take the runway with Apaches and paratroopers. Our public line was still that we were working it out but it was becoming near untenable. The worry about Clark was that years of pent-up feeling about the Russians was boiling up and he was spoiling for a fight.

Clark and Guthrie both thought I should go out there to set up another MOR [Media Operations Room] type operation and the office was fixing flights to Macedonia. By the later conference call, things were looking more ragged, a journalist shot dead, German troops killing Serbs, Albanians stoning withdrawing Serbs and making it very difficult to police the two sides, plus the Russian problem was still there. TB spoke to Clinton, who said Yeltsin was out of it at the moment and causing real bother. Philip G called, worried we were going to come second in the European elections. I stayed up to watch

June '99: Jackson not prepared to shoot at Russians

the pretty disastrous results come in.[1] Wes Clark called at 1am, wanting to discuss the Russians. He wanted to send in air force to take it, including Brits. He was being overruled but said 'A beautiful victory is in danger of being lost because we were resolute for seventy-eight days but we're being irresolute now.' The Russians would see us as weak and take advantage. They were ready to send 20,000 troops in because they wanted to screw up the whole operation and if we let them, it would be a real problem for the long term. They had raced to Berlin in '45 and that was what this was about. The problem for Clark was that Clinton had made clear he thought any notion of a battle with the Russians was crazy.

Monday, June 14

The Euro elections disaster was leading the news as I was driven off at 6 to [RAF] Brize Norton to join a military flight to Skopje. TB called at 7 and said 'You're not still going are you?' I said I was but he called me back so, pissed off, having got myself psyched up to go, I headed back to Number 10. The results were certainly worse than we had feared and the Tories would certainly get a lift. As we walked round the garden, he said too many people think that because the public hated the Tories, they would automatically stay with us and it's not necessarily so. Meanwhile, I had Fiona on in tears saying she couldn't cope with our lifestyle, me being away, constantly being disturbed at night. We put together a script for TB, disappointment, low turnout, Tory vote in perspective, no going back, positive European policy. Jackson was meeting the Russians but the truth was this was a critical situation. I felt these next few days were key. It was a beautiful hot day and TB and I had a long chat out in the garden about some of the changes we needed to make. Jackson did extremely well at his briefing, despite their efforts to make it all about the Russians.

Richard Wilson chaired a meeting – CDS, Kevin Tebbit [MoD permanent secretary], John Sawers, John Kerr [FCO permanent secretary], Michael Pakenham [Cabinet Office], AC and Sebastian Wood [Wilson's private secretary]. It got a bit rambling but the basic feeling was that we had been pretty lucky. Richard asked why we won and Charles said 'Because Milosevic caved in.' There was a fair bit of covering of

[1] The European elections saw Labour MEPs reduced from sixty-two to twenty-nine. Conservative MEPs increased from eighteen to thirty-six, and Liberal Democrats from two to ten. It was the first time proportional representation had been used for a nationwide poll, and saw the UK Independence Party and Green Party gain seats for the first time. The voting turnout in the UK was 23.3 per cent. The average turnout across Europe was 49.5 per cent.

tracks going on. Both John S and I felt there were times when we had just been stumbling, that we didn't have the fullest range of advice for TB. We didn't have a clear assessment of the politics of NATO, or of the politics of the US administration. But in fact it was only when the US engaged that things really moved, and at times it felt like we had been carrying the whole show. TB had been exposed at times and we had had to fly by the seat of our pants.

There was a general feeling that after a dreadful start we had worked wonders in presentation but Charles and I got into a rare shouting match when I said there had been too many soldiers doing interviews with potential policy ramifications. He said it was easy to sit watching television and criticise but it's very hard not to do interviews. I said that was rubbish. There was some talk about doing a White Paper on lessons learned, but I doubted TB would want to go that far. Clark called at 10 still worried about the Russians. He still wanted to go in and was confident it could be done without any deaths.

I said I would speak to TB again but knew his view already, that he thought the whole idea was mad. If we suddenly sent UK troops to attack the Russians, he would have Clinton, Chirac and everyone else against him. It would be inexplicable. He hated what the Russians were doing, and was troubled by Clark's perseverance, but believed it would resolve itself. Wes believed the Russians were planning to get more troops in again tonight and it was important we stopped people giving them airspace. Yeltsin had told Clinton there would be no more Russian troops into Kosovo without agreement. Then again, he had also asked Bill for a US–Russian summit on board a submarine. TB said I needed to keep talking to Wes. He quite liked him and he felt there was something in what he said but it was politically impossible. I asked Wes to write a private note which I would give to TB tomorrow.

Tuesday, June 15

I was off at 5 to Brize Norton again. The election coverage was grim, with a bad picture of TB going under a tree which made him look like he was walking away dejected. They clearly felt they had us on the run a bit. We were getting it from the antis for being pro and from the pros by not being pro enough. Nobody really had a good word to say for us and the danger of being popular abroad and unpopular at home, and the two possibly linked, was very clear. TB had been fairly relaxed yesterday but would be unrelaxed if this mood developed. He felt we had too few people who were really up to the mark.

I was not really copping much of the blame, partly because of Kosovo, but also they knew I had avoided being too political. I felt I needed to get my role reinterpreted so that I could be more political but it was difficult.

TB, on his way to Ireland, agreed to speak to Wes after seeing his note. He was in agreement that we had to be tough, but could see no course of action that wouldn't risk a real confrontation with the Russians, and/or a huge diplomatic rift. The plane was full of soldiers heading out there, some of them looking not much older than Rory. I sat at the back and worked on a note to TB on the lessons of the elections. I also did TB a private note on yesterday's Kosovo-lessons-learned meeting. His own view was that NATO had been exposed as ineffective and he had been shocked at the Americans. The way NATO worked was that the US basically ran it, sometimes we managed to get our hands up their back and sometimes the others managed to screw them over. Kerr had said TB's standing was so high he could probably get [Paddy] Ashdown as the UN civil authority person.[1]

We landed and to my amazement at the bottom of the steps was Julian, wearing the most extraordinary square-pointed shoes. I thought you would need some local knowledge, he said. We walked across the tarmac to a waiting Puma helicopter complete with machine-gun protection guys hanging out of the doors and off we went, the sides open and the wind howling through. We were flying through some extraordinarily beautiful scenery, but so close to the ground that when we went through valleys, you could almost touch the trees on either side, and suddenly we would swoop up and be able to see for miles and miles. Through the headset I could hear the voice of the pilot spotting potential dangers, like Serb troop movements as they withdrew. We flew over some of the ethnically cleansed villages, homes that were shells of themselves, animals scavenging, lots of rough-and-ready graves.

Ten minutes into Kosovo and there were people clearly walking home who were waving up at the helicopter. I was really excited to be there. I felt that I had been part of something important and powerful and deeply moving. What I couldn't see was much sign of beaten-up tanks or Serb military, and the Serb liaison officer at the talks apparently told Jackson that we only hit fourteen out of 400. We arrived at the military base and met Clifford, who looked thunderstruck when he saw Julian. I'm not sure exactly what he had done to

[1] UN special representative in Kosovo. The post would be given to French politician Bernard Kouchner.

upset them but clearly he had. Clifford told me later there was a time and a place for clever people with briefcases but Kumanovo in the last few days was not one of them. He had just been too clever and pushy in constantly talking about his conversations to 'important people in London'.

Then left with a French driver, a very pretty woman soldier named Aude. We overtook a column of tanks and vehicles going over a bridge, then a line of Serb cars and lorries and the bandana brigade staring at us, giving us the finger, making obscene and threatening gestures. It was eerie. They had guns and were pointing them at us, finger on the trigger. Whenever they clocked Aude, they went into a kind of weird group grunt. I had never understood why stories of invasion and victory are always accompanied by stories of rape. But I could see the rapist in their eyes. They were among the most disgusting people I had ever seen and I felt all the more satisfied at what we had done. We got to Priština. We parked the car by their old HQ, now occupied by the British Army. There was an over-whelming stench of burning of evidence.

Jackson was excellent with the Serbs, very calm, polite, even-handed. As he finished, he came over and said what are you doing here? He was both gruff and friendly at the same time. He said who are you working for, the prime minister or Clark? I said I was working for him. He said good, he needed real help, not lots of bright boys. As we chatted, and I explained how I thought we could help him, the aggression disappeared and he became quite friendly. I went to the early evening operational update. The logistical skills of these guys was second to none. They had set up a proper, well-functioning base in no time at all. Jackson was very jolly but also very strict with his men, telling them to shut up if they went on too long. A pressing issue was whether we removed weapons from the Serbs. He said the troops needed something clear not legalistic. If they are threatening, take them. If not, don't.

Jackson was growing on me. He had a great booming voice, took no crap from anybody and struck me as having done a pretty extra-ordinary job. I tried to get to the bottom of just why Julian caused him such offence. When I mentioned to Clifford that Clark had really taken to Julian, he said 'That says it all.' Jackson was even more dismissive, said that on Sunday when he wanted to hit the airport, 'I said Wes, you're fucking barking. I'm just not doing it.' Prince later told me that Jackson had told his people he felt I did have something to offer them. Rupert Smith called with a message for Julian that not all the military had taken against him, which was nice of him.

Julian told me that on the day Milosevic caved in, Wes said that the Americans believed he was too close to the Brits. Berger had another of his media-inspired rants at John Sawers over a piece in the *Herald Tribune* which said we and the French were critical of the way the US handled the airport issue. They reminded me a bit of GB's people in how closely they read everything and how unprepared they were to think things could appear in newspapers without being inspired. I had no idea who the source was and promised to write a letter of rebuttal, which I did. Clifford and I had a real heart-to-heart. I said he was a natural military briefer. We had to put in place the infrastructure that allowed him to do the job properly. A bit like Jamie [Shea] when we first went to Brussels, he was worried about being overloaded with people he didn't need, and I tried to persuade him that he needed a good team around him to give him the time and space to do his job well. Once you got through the slightly brittle exterior, the nerves, and his obvious irritation with Julian, he was perfectly likeable. He also had Jackson's backing.

Wednesday, June 16

I woke up at 5.30, tired and my bones aching. I had not slept in a tent for God knows how long. The helicopter flight to Skopje was even more extraordinary than yesterday. The scenery was stunning but then every few minutes we would fly over either a scene of joy, kids jumping and waving and giving victory signs, or scenes of desolation and devastation, communities totally wiped out, bodies, graves. I did the eleven o'clock down the line after talking to TB. He said Ireland had gone well though at the Orange Order meeting some guy was literally foaming at the mouth. He said I had to get back on the domestic agenda, which was right, but I was glad I had gone to Kosovo. I felt it was without doubt one of the most worthwhile things we had done since the election and I was proud of the job I had done. I had brought together a disparate group of people from different parts of the world and from Clinton and Clark down, I think they acknowledged that we had used communications strategically to make a difference on the military side too.

Thursday, June 17

The only story about my visit yesterday was a snide piece in the *Telegraph*. Guthrie called and said he was more than happy for me to say that he had asked me to go, and that SACEUR had asked me to. He said he had spoken to Jackson and felt things would work out fine. Lucie felt Clifford was being pretty two-faced, saying yes to me, but then being difficult after I had gone. Both she and Jonathan Prince called after their evening meeting because 'Campbell accused of meddling' was one of their media PowerPoint items. And Jackson had apparently muttered 'Bloody right.' I said there was no point making a fuss. The media coverage was focused on wall-to-wall atrocities now. The media having been sceptical when we talked about them now realise if anything we had understated. As Robin C told Cabinet, it was amazing how many people who had been against the air campaign were now suddenly in favour of it, and how many people who had felt we had exaggerated the atrocities were now asking why we hadn't made more of them.

Cabinet was mainly Kosovo plus a run round the table on the European elections. TB felt the Tories had made a mistake in over-claiming success. Jack Straw [Home Secretary] felt the problem was general cynicism about politics. Robin and JC [Jack Cunningham, Minister for the Cabinet Office and Chancellor of the Duchy of Lancaster] felt we had to make it easier for people to vote. JC felt the problem was as much with Europe as with the government and also that we had in fact become complacent. Meeting with TB, GB, Ed Balls [special adviser to GB], Jonathan, Jeremy [Heywood, principal private secretary], re EMU [EU economic and monetary union]. They agreed we had lost votes because we were seen as pro EMU yet we were being attacked by the pro-Europeans for not being pro enough. We had to get the situation moved to a place where we could kill the issue for the next election by saying that ultimately it would be decided in a referendum. GB felt there may be a case for doing an assessment of how we were doing on the five conditions, which currently would almost certainly make clear we were not joining before such and such a date. He wasn't keen but felt it might be possible. He felt the language we had agreed for the changeover plan had been too forward. We were moving to a position that wasn't that far off where John Major [former Conservative Prime Minister] had been, and we were some years down the track. TB wasn't saying much but he clearly wanted us back towards a more neutral position that accurately reflected the policy rather than the politics. There was a huge flurry late on about a story about [*Telegraph* owner and Canadian citizen] Conrad Black's peerage and we had to quickly agree a line with the Canadians, who had to back the idea of a peerage and were refusing.[1]

[1] Despite Black holding dual British and Canadian nationality, the Canadian government had raised objections to a peerage, citing Canada's 1919 Nickle Resolution which restricts British titles and honours for Canadian citizens.

Friday, June 18

We headed to Northolt and on the plane TB was trying to get his head round all the G8 briefing. I was working with Mark Bennett on an article/speech re the media in Kosovo. We arrived in Cologne and went straight to the bilateral with Clinton. On Kosovo, there was still a bit of tension there and TB really went to town on Clinton's leadership and the fact that nothing would have happened without the US military. They were worried there was nobody obvious to put in to run Kosovo for the UN. Berger said it always comes down to former foreign ministers or defeated prime ministers. TB talked up Paddy Ashdown and Clinton said he wasn't averse but said it was going to require somebody with remarkable skills, maybe someone who had run a big business. He said if he was retiring and had millions in the bank, he would just love that job. TB was pretty scathing about the UN refugee operation.

Clinton said we had to look beyond short-term relief towards a stability pact with south-east Europe and the Balkans but we have to get rid of Milosevic, get the people there to define their own vision of the Balkans and then work for it. TB was clear that we should be pushing money to the neighbouring countries while Serbia was getting none. They had to know Milosevic had totally screwed up. They were both worried about Yeltsin, who clearly felt the Americans were trying to extend their influence through the whole region. The talks with the Russians were continuing all day at Helsinki and they reached agreement late on, pretty much on our terms. We had a bilateral with [Jean] Chrétien [Canadian Prime Minister]. Ludicrously, they were having to deal with Conrad Black's peerage. Chrétien said he was once asked, as a Quebecois in British Columbia, what did he think about the monarchy. 'I said I am neither strongly for, nor strongly against. My worry is what we would do if the Brits abolished her first.'

Saturday, June 19

The *Herald Tribune* now carried a story that was basically the opposite of Tuesday's story, said that we blocked the US from taking the airport, which of course was true. I got John S to call Berger who was pretty tough with him, said the story was dead and why did they get it up again? There was a trust problem and we had to sort it out. I went in on the call, said I wasn't stupid and what earthly reason could there be in me having briefed as they thought I had? He said Cook had done stuff in the past and there was no smoke without fire. I asked again why I would have briefed a story I knew to be wrong. He accepted it wasn't in our interests. Had breakfast with TB and a pretty circular conversation about the domestic agenda. He was worried about the health department. I said he had to reconnect with the domestic agenda with the same zeal he showed for the war and Northern Ireland. He did a pre-record for Adam Boulton [Sky News political editor] mainly focused on Europe. Adam somewhat tendentiously compared me to Goebbels. I did a briefing and said there could be no possibility of any financial help while Milosevic was still there. If the Serbian people were prepared to tolerate him, there could be no question of us trying to help them, none whatsoever.

I went out for lunch with Catherine Colonna, who had been brilliant in the last few weeks. She was very open about Chirac. She liked him, but he was not like he seemed. He was much more insecure than people imagined. Sometimes he lashed out and then regretted it. He found it hard to change a position or a view. He tended to develop an opinion of someone and not let experience change it, which meant he could be very black/white. He found it hard to get on with Jospin. He had noticed, and didn't like, TB's quote on page 1 of *Le Monde* saying we must never let the right back in Europe. TB came back from the session and we went for a walk by the river. He was worrying about the quality of the Cabinet. GB is good but flawed. Peter M [Mandelson, former Trade and Industry Secretary] is good but not there. Derry [Irvine, Lord Chancellor] and Charlie are clever but not sufficiently political. So I have to rely too much on a very small group of people. We went back for a meeting with Bono and [Bob] Geldof [musicians campaigning to cut Third World debt]. First we had to get them there, because Bono for some reason told Boulton he wasn't going. I called Geldof and got him to persuade him that it would be seen as total grandstanding not to turn up when the media were already there waiting. In the event, we had a very good meeting. I liked them both. They were really funny but also incredibly committed, and they knew what they were on about. They had facts at their fingertips. There was no way this was just a spray-on cause to help their rock-star image. TB said at one point that we were pushing as hard as we could but there was a lot of politics, different countries with different agendas, and it was like climbing Everest. Bono said 'When you see Everest, Tony, you don't look at it, you fucking climb it.' We got the cameras in and they went a little bit rock star-ish but it was impossible not to like them.

Sunday, June 20

The Cologne summit was big on TV but pretty low-key in the papers. TB said he'd had a fascinating chat with Chirac, not dissimilar to my conversation with Catherine. He'd said he was impetuous and impulsive but we must never take it too seriously when he has one of his storms. He said he wanted to come to London to go to a nice Japanese restaurant that TB had mentioned, and he would take TB to one of his favourite Paris bistros in return. He was clearly, in general, in a fairly musing and whimsical mode. We bumped into him and he went off on a tirade about the music from last night, and then about nouvelle cuisine. 'I hate it when a big plate is brought ceremoniously to the table, and a huge silver thing on top, then the waiter lifts the silver thing and you are staring at three haricots vert.'

He then told us a story about how Claude, his daughter, was called by someone she thought was Mike Jackson the soldier and it turned out to be Michael Jackson the singer. Yeltsin finally arrived with Schroeder. He was looking pretty unstable with an enormous fixed smile. It was painful watching him try to hold the smile together. He went round giving everyone enormous bear hugs. He and TB had a brief chat. Yeltsin said 'Anthony, I told you it would be a dangerous course and you should have got off it before. But now we must work together.' Clinton was laughing and joking with him, saying he prayed for him every night. Close up, Yeltsin looked really quite ill. TB's press conference went fine, though they were obsessing a bit about the fact he had used the word 'daft' to describe the idea of going into EMU now. I had been polishing and repolishing my media speech with Mark B and on the flight home, TB read the draft. He thought it was basically OK though he toned it down a bit. He was raving about how friendly and funny Chirac had been. He was on much better form now, though I sensed Cherie had not had a great time.

Monday, June 21

TB's 'daft' EMU outburst was the main story in several of the broadsheets so we were on the back foot again. Some idiot had briefed that TB would be steadying nerves at the PLP [Parliamentary Labour Party] on Wednesday so the eleven o'clock was all about Europe again and domestic politics being difficult for us. The daft episode showed again how the BBC had its agenda run by the press. It came from an interview with Robin Oakley [BBC political editor]. But that part of the interview wasn't even broadcast. The papers picked up on it, ran it big, and the BBC ran it big and their reporters were leading the questioning at the eleven o'clock. I wrote to Tony Hall [BBC director of news] pointing out this absurdity

At the office meeting, TB was obsessing about the euro, wanted to get the dividing lines moved, make a strength of our wait-and-decide policy. Hague at least had a clear line and was enjoying pushing it. TB still couldn't decide whether to attend the Britain in Europe [pro-euro campaign] meeting. He felt they should become a campaign focused on the broader question of Britain in Europe, not just EMU. As ever he felt delivery was a problem and he was getting more and more frustrated with the main departments. Wes Clark called, furious about a *Herald Tribune* piece on him and Jackson.

Tuesday, June 22

The overnight briefing on the New Deal went well, though it played into the Old/New Labour argument. But at least it meant the New Deal was getting some decent coverage, several splashes in the broadsheets, big build-up to the speech. TB worked on it on the train to Birmingham [to launch the Transco Green Futures youth employment scheme] and did a very good clip about never again allowing Britain to choose between a Labour Party that was not interested in ambition and enterprise and a Conservative Party that saw no need for justice or compassion. It was a strong speech and went fine. But he was still mainly exercised about Europe. He wanted to build strength into our position but it was difficult to make indecision a strength. He felt we had to get the dividing lines in a better place. He believed eventually that the Heseltine/Clarke axis [Europhile Conservatives Michael Heseltine, former Deputy Prime Minister, and Kenneth Clarke, former Chancellor] would move against the Tory leadership. I was not so sure. They might help re Britain in Europe because they passionately believe it, but ultimately they are pretty tribal.

I sent my draft speech on Kosovo and the media to Wes Clark, who called back and said 'I love it. I think you and Jamie Shea should fly the press down to Kosovo, visit the mass graves and rub their noses in the dirt.' Charles Guthrie liked it and wanted me to deliver it as a speech to his commanders. Oona [Muirhead, director of information strategy and news at the MoD] and Jamie Shea had a few good comments to make, and Oona suggested and then fixed that I should do it at RUSI [Royal United Services Institute]. Jonathan thought it was self-indulgent. Peter M liked it but wanted to tone down the attacks on the media. We flew back by helicopter, TB working on a note on the euro. Northern Ireland suddenly flared up. Trimble had an article in *The Times* and later he called on Mo to quit, which put TB in a total rage. Jonathan and I had tried to calm TB down but he was really pissed off. Jonathan felt it probably wasn't worth going there on Thursday as there was no give or take on either side but we had to push on.

Wednesday, June 23

Suddenly there was a sense across the media that NI had become very gloomy. TB was tired, and really pissed off at the Trimble situation, and generally downcast. He hated it when he couldn't see a way forward. Normally, no matter how bad everyone else was saying it was, he would always find some ray of hope somewhere, but today he was as down as any of us. On the way in I drafted some lines he might want to use at the PLP, and also a note re PMQs, with Hague likely to do NI, but he was disinclined to take any help today. The eleven o'clock was all about the PLP and I was on form. Hilary [Coffman, special adviser, Downing Street press office] said afterwards that it was the best exposition of the New Labour case she had ever heard, though delivered with such contempt for the media's inability to get it, that they were unlikely to cover much of it. TB was dreading the PLP because he feared it would be the usual whingeing but in the end he went down well and only Tam [Dalyell, Labour MP], who compared TB to Napoleon, had a real go.

TB was good at PMQs, didn't let his mood show, and was a lot more political than of late. He did say he would 'listen to the debate' on PR [proportional representation], which was a bit weak, was defensive on NI but he was definitely back on form on Europe and the domestic agenda. Mo came in to tell me she believed GB was really stirring at the moment. Anji, who was not normally paranoid about GB, also thought he was up to no good just now. I chaired a meeting of all the various departments involved in the GM debate, where the lack of a communications strategy had been woeful. Stories were popping up all over the place. The rebuttal was dreadful and there was no proper strategy for getting the debate out there on our terms. We needed a cross-departmental group who would drive it from the centre. One or two whinged about being understaffed and not being able to spare people – what the fuck do they all do? Number 10 and the Treasury drive more media than any other department on a tiny staff compared to these departments.

Thursday, June 24

Trimble came in to see TB, TB still in a bit of a rage with him. He wanted to do a piece for *The Times* which took up a bit of the morning. SACEUR and Solana were visiting Kosovo and on the morning call, based on what Mark Laity had said, I told Jamie he would get mobbed, and indeed he was. He looked really touched by it, and said later he had found it incredibly humbling. He was actually a really nice guy who had handled himself well in the last few weeks. To go from being the head of a fairly sleepy media bureaucracy to being a high-profile part of one of the most difficult comms jobs going, it wasn't easy and he did pretty well. He could easily have put up more barriers to me than he did, but we just about made it work. At DOP [Defence and Overseas Policy Committee] TB was saying we needed a far more aggressive approach to Milosevic, that reconstruction of the Balkans was virtually impossible with him still there. We needed the French and the Germans more involved in trying to isolate him. Cabinet was Kosovo and NI mainly, and TB seemed tired again. Mo was quite chirpy re Trimble, said it was the tenth time her resignation had been called for this year – slightly down on a year ago.

PG had done a couple of dreadful groups – no sense of delivery and re the war what a waste of fucking money. It made you wonder why we bothered sometimes. Philip said he wanted to hit some of them. He said the *Mail* was a real problem, just poisoned some of these people against any understanding at all. They had no idea of anything we had done. On Kosovo, they thought Clinton carried TB as a poodle. It was ludicrous. TB worked on the NI draft [article] and really put a lot into it. It was going to land with a big hit, a small nuclear device into NI politics, basically spelling out the reality and the reasonableness of the deal which they had all conspired to fuck up.

Friday, June 25

The [*Times*] NI article, though rushed, had the immediate effect of putting the story up in lights and at least with the sense of a plan, even if all it did was state the blindingly obvious in a very direct way. I called Joe Lennon [Bertie Ahern's press secretary] to make sure the Irish didn't go offside on it. TB now wanted to push hard on a statement of general principles – 1. an inclusive executive; 2. decommissioning by May 2000; 3. de Chastelain judging. It was ridiculous, given that it was all pretty much agreed at the time of the GFA, that we were having to portray this as progress. Jonathan and I saw TB to go through PG's latest, unbelievably gloomy note. TB thought he was overstating it, that the problem was really lack of progress in public services. He looked tired and drawn though and I think felt that having done as much as he had to win a war people had said they supported, it was odd not to get at least some credit for it. Equally, they did not seem to want to give us credit on the economy.

Bertie came in around 9 to take stock. They were both wearing black ties for the [Cardinal Basil] Hume funeral at Westminster

Cathedral. The Irish seemed OK with TB's article, though the UUs were already out attacking it on the grounds that it conceded to SF on the question of prior decommissioning, and SF were attacking us because it made it look like they, not the IRA, were responsible for arms. TB said 'If you ask me, I think we are pretty fucked on this. I can normally see a way forward but at the moment I can't.' He said the UUs were fighting like ferrets in a sack. Also we sometimes underestimated just how important the Drumcree march was to them. He felt if we could get a breakthrough on the march, the door would open on the bigger picture.

He even wondered if Clinton shouldn't call Brendan McKenna [Garvaghy Road residents' spokesman] which on one level was absurd but if it shifted it, it would be worth it. I could just see McKenna pocketing a call from the most powerful man in the world and then carrying on buggering us about. There was actually a simple enough formula, easily put-downable on a postcard, and all his article did was make the obvious explicit – there would have to be an inclusive executive and there would have to be decommissioning – but getting there would be hard.

The other issue I was dealing with was Man Utd. David Davies [Football Association] called for help because he was worried about how to get through the FA the idea of Man U coming out of the FA Cup to be able to play in the Club World Championship in Brazil, which they thought was important to the World Cup bid. As a bit of cover, they wanted to say the government had asked for this, which would have been bad for us. It would be seen as inappropriate interference, added to which I didn't fancy the government copping it for Man Utd not being in the Cup, which would weaken it hugely. I called Alex F who said they had looked at every way round it, like an extension to the season, giving them a bye through the early rounds, no Utd players for friendly internationals, but they couldn't get agreement on any of it. Martin Edwards [Manchester United chairman] had committed them to the Brazil tournament so he felt they had no option but to pull out. The fans would hate it, he said, and we should watch out for the FA trying to put the blame on us.

I met Ian Austin [GB's newly appointed spokesman] to discuss how best to avoid a repeat of the Whelan situation, and how best to politicise the GB operation. He said he was determined to work with us and GB did not want divisiveness of any sort. *On verra*. Anne Edwards [US official] called from Albania and horrified me with a story that the UNHCR were thinking of running 'dress rehearsal' refugee returns, where they would get refugees back, testing whether they could deal with the collapsed infrastructure etc., and then bring them back to Albania! Get a grip. I said make sure it just does not happen.

We headed to Northolt, on the plane with Bertie. We arrived at [RAF] Aldergrove, jumped on a helicopter and headed straight for a quick round of talks, TB and BA together, with first SDLP [Social Democratic and Labour Party], then UUs, then SF. TB felt there was room for some progress, and suggested I brief the same message as the morning, but more upbeat. Things were made more difficult though with [Jeffrey] Donaldson [Ulster Unionist MP] in the Trimble team, as he was constantly second-guessing, and throwing in unhelpful observations. He was clearly having none of the TB stuff in *The Times* on prior decommissioning. Donaldson looked to me to be taking Trimble close to the edge. TB could barely bring himself to be civil. Joe Lennon and I worked up a press statement around the three principles and then briefed that the last-minute changes were because DT would not agree on the timings or sequencing.

TB said on the flight home he had started out in government determined to like the Unionists, and always to try to understand their point of view, but they made it bloody hard. 'The other side may kill people but at least you can have rational conversations. When the UUs are like this, they are so ridiculously unreasonable. They are too stupid to realise they have won and SF are too clever to admit they've lost.' It had been a beautiful day but we were potentially a day away from political disaster.

Saturday, June 26

TB called just the once. He was back totally focused on Northern Ireland. He was feeling a bit more hopeful but thought there would have been a more positive response re them seeming to sign up to decommissioning. On Kosovo, we needed a major plan of repatriation.

Sunday, June 27

Trimble was putting out a less grudging line re SF/decommissioning, but when TB called, he said he was really worried about him, felt the others were getting to him big time. He was also worried Jonathan was getting too emotional about it, which I felt was a good thing. But TB was alarmed last week, e.g. when the Orangemen were attacking TB and Jonathan really went for them, saying you cannot talk to a prime minister like that. I don't know why but I felt we should be more confident. The engine was in place, the carriages were waiting, and it was just a question of getting the carriages in the right order.

TB was also worrying re JP [John Prescott, Deputy Prime Minister and Secretary of State for the Environment, Transport and the Regions], who he felt was working too hard to not much effect, and worried he was being thought by his department to be out of his depth. I got to bed and then around midnight JP called. He had been faxed a load of cuttings that were bad about him and about transport. He sounded pretty desperate and was looking for help on the media side. He said he was fed up of Number 10, felt they didn't engage with him properly, I was the only one who took him seriously etc., and he and TB needed to get on a better keel.

Monday, June 28

With NI, Britain in Europe, welfare to work, we were at least back dominating the agenda, even if not all on our terms. The press were picking up on the JP situation. Heaven knows how but there were several stories out there of TB critical of JP. I spoke to JP who sounded very down. I got TB to speak to him, and he was better after that, though TB was worried he was on the edge. Part of the problem was he never really rested. I put together a big positive pro-JP briefing for the 11.

I left with TB for Northolt just after 8. He said he had slept really badly, didn't get to sleep till 3 and then was waking up on and off after that. NI was occupying his mind, along with delivery, and someone was definitely getting at him re GB. It was true there was stuff in the papers today we didn't know was coming, but it wasn't really stuff we could object to. TB was also wondering whether he could send Peter M to NIO [Northern Ireland Office]. On the plane he mapped out the various approaches to take with the different parties. He was pretty fed up having to go through it all again. Jonathan had spent the whole weekend out there, poor sod, talking to the Garvaghy Rd residents' association and the Orange Order.[1] On arrival we worked through a plan for the day with Bertie. We wanted SF to agree that they would say they would persuade the IRA to decommission, whilst the UUs would accept a statement that the war was over. But a lot of his time was taken up with the residents and the Orange Order re Drumcree, which was dire. Whenever we got on to these marches, even TB's patience wore thin after a while. Both sides just lectured from their different takes on it. He told them this

[1] The Parades Commission that day ordered the Orange Order's annual Drumcree march to be re-routed away from the Garvaghy Road. In the end, despite an Orange Order protest meeting, the march passed off relatively peaceably.

was never going to change until at least they tried to see the other point of view, but he might as well have asked them to dive into a vat of burning oil. They were not listening let alone changing their minds. As Paul Murphy [NIO minister] said, fighting for this was all some of these people felt they had, and they were not prepared to lose it.

After doing various meetings at Stormont we left for Hillsborough [Castle, official residence of the Northern Ireland Secretary] by chopper to meet Bertie and have lunch with de Chastelain. He too seemed pretty downbeat, was not confident of getting anything out of SF. Bertie was fairly quiet but when he did speak was constantly trying to come up with practical suggestions. Joe Lockhart called as Clinton was about to do a BBC interview and I sent through a note on the lines we had been pushing over the past twenty-four hours. BC did fine, as ever, and gave it a bit of impetus media-wise. We flew back to Castle Buildings [Stormont] for a long session with GA/McG and then Trimble. We were waiting for the Parades Commission announcement on Drumcree and DT was really on edge. TB suggested all I could do was put the best face on this, and keep talking up DT and at least give the sense of progress. But Drumcree was taking the meat out of the negotiations. Bertie came in at one point and told me he felt Adams and McG were ready to say they would act as persuaders for decommissioning. But even that was probably not going to be enough for Trimble.

TB and I went for a walk round the gardens after dinner. He said he felt if we had nothing else to deal with, he could sort this. But it needed even more time than we were giving it. At times, he said he felt like we were dealing with madmen. He was also fretting still re lack of strength in depth in ministerial ranks. 'I am a bit of a fluke. So is Gordon. We are both a cut above your average politician. But we are exceptions.' That was why we needed Peter back. He gives us problems, but he gives us extra intelligence.

Tuesday, June 29

We needed to keep up at least some sense of momentum so after a long meeting on the way forward, I went out to brief a mix of atmospherics and an outline plan about how to move on. Gerry Adams was already there, planning to brief, and said he intended to be positive, which he was, saying some progress had been made. Trimble said the opposite not long after. The problem on the talks was that we were getting vague agreements but whenever we looked like getting closer to pinning them down, something would get in the way. DT was saying we had to have decommissioning in two weeks, SF that we might be able to see something by December.

We kept going, and TB and BA just went from one round of meetings to another. I did three full briefings through the day and by the third, there seemed to be an acceptance of progress, created largely by the fact we were still persevering, and people thinking there must be a reason for that. TB and Bertie did a five-sider, with SF, UUP, SDLP, then we left for Hillsborough. TB gave instructions that overnight we had to get words from all three signalling the direction of travel on decommissioning. De Chastelain called, and I briefed him on what we had been saying publicly, and also the mood inside the talks.

Wednesday, June 30

Over breakfast with Bertie, TB said he feared real problems with the UUs today. They were imagining that by the end of the day, there would be a commitment to acts of decommissioning but of course even if we got decent words, there would have to be an IRA convention to get it agreed. SF were going to make a historic statement of intent of their commitment to decommission, without any guarantee of how it could be delivered. Overnight we had worked on a single text – 'Essential elements for an understanding' – based on the various drafts and statements. TB was going to use it as a speaking note first before seeing whether we could bind the parties to it. First he went over it in detail with Bertie at Castle Buildings. The Irish were getting pretty impatient.

TB said we had to lower the bar for SF and we had to lower it for Trimble. We got DT in and he was pretty nervy. We tried to persuade him that the media was actually worse for SF than for him, and the pressure was still on them more than him. If they were to make a commitment as historic as the one we were working on, he had to seize that as major progress won by his side. We knew it didn't mean for sure all the weapons would go but it signalled a direction of travel that was surely worth seizing on. He didn't look so sure. We were now into a round of long, long meetings, and with little to brief of any substance, there was a bit of a vacuum developing. I was trying to put out the mood that we were in for a long haul, but we wouldn't be doing it if we didn't think we had a chance of real progress. SF presented to us their own version of what they could do – the overall commitment was there but it was clear there would be no product before October at the earliest.

A while back that would have been seen as real progress, but in the current mood it would be difficult. On the one hand it was remarkable that they were prepared to say 'total disarmament' but on the other, if that was the case, it would merely confirm and strengthen suspicion on the other side if they could not go further and talk about how, when, etc. It would be hard to take the UUs forward on the basis of what they were saying. DT saw TB alone at 2pm, and left looking really downcast. I went in to see TB, who was now just sitting there looking out of the window. He looked up, shook his head, and he said he could scarcely believe it – the UUs were about to turn the victory of the IRA handing in weapons into a defeat because psychologically they were incapable of getting out of defeat mode. If they see a Republican with a smile on his face, they assume they have lost something. They were incapable of seeing a bigger picture.

At 2.20 Trimble came in, and alongside him John Taylor, Reg Empey, Donaldson and Ken Maginnis [Ulster Unionists]. TB was very curt with them, less of the small talk and the bonhomie he usually doles out. He said he was trying to get a statement from SF, and from the IRA, effectively that de Chastelain was the means of decommissioning, the process, and the failsafe. But it was clear from their faces, barely reacting as he spoke, that they would not be able to go with anything other than a 'jump together' – the executive set up at the same time as arms were handed over. Trimble said that with Drumcree rerouted, and with the [Chris] Patten [former Conservative Cabinet minister, now a European commissioner] review on policing due, and bound to be terrible for them, they could not hold their own people with this. If we push too far, we risk the UUP falling to the extremists. Whether Donaldson, smirking a bit throughout, was the target of that one I wasn't sure.

Maginnis said the release of prisoners 'cost us 45,000 votes and we have bugger all to show for it'. 'With all due respect,' TB said – which he tended like me to say when he meant to indicate a lack of respect on a particular point – 'I think you have a tendency to snatch defeat from the jaws of victory and you are in danger of doing that now. In the GFA, you got a good deal – especially the principle of consent re constitutional change. Now you have the IRA making a commitment to decommission and you are saying it is not significant. Empey said it may be, but they were being asked to accept a post-dated cheque. 'We give them a whole load of cash now, but we have to wait to get anything in return.' Also they hated the failsafe idea because it suggested SF/IRA had a veto on the whole thing. Trimble said the people who were trying to make it work would be the ones who end up punished. TB said if we fail to reach agreement he could not defend spending days and days of his time trying again. 'People will not understand if we pull the plug at this point. There is a Rubicon to be crossed and you have to lead the way.' If we could get an agreement around this, and sort Drumcree, we are back on track. If we don't, we will never get it done. Empey said nobody doubted his commitment or seriousness of intent but it had to be a good deal.

So off we went again, trying to recalibrate the atmospherics to benefit the UUs. I put together a briefing note based on some of the intelligence re key IRA figures moving, which we put on hold pending another round of TB/Bertie meetings, the most important of which was with Adams and McGuinness at 4 to 5.10. TB was saying we could transform the whole picture if we could get a deal here, and they responded with a magnanimous gesture re Drumcree. They said it was impossible. TB said it wasn't. It was essential. If we didn't get progress on Drumcree, Trimble's position was very difficult. Adams gave a picture of how horrible life was for the people they wanted to march through. They could not countenance a march this year. Joe Lennon came in, very flustered because Donaldson and Taylor had been out briefing that actual guns and explosives had to be handed over before they could sit on the executive. Joe said if SF went out and reacted badly to that, we were dead in the water. I went out with Tom Kelly [NIO spokesman] and did a massive briefing – massive re the numbers present rather than the content – to the effect that we had the makings of a deal, that the two sides were testing the quality of the other's commitment before going snap. They pointed out I said the same at Hillsborough and at Downing St. I pointed out I said the same not long before we secured the GFA and we were hopeful again. So based on nothing, we somehow managed to inject a sense of forward momentum, enough for us to keep going into the next few hours. I got back in to find TB with the Orange Order, the usual barrel of laughs – not – with him trying to calm them down re Drumcree. Then into another round of talks and the gap was getting closer.

We were in a TB/Bertie stocktaking session when Jonathan came over to me and said two of my best friends were at the door wanting to see me. I went over and it was Adams and McGuinness, with some of their other key guys behind them. 'Here's the guilty man,' said Jonathan in that wonderfully flip way he has. They claimed I had briefed they were going to get an IRA statement. I had done nothing of the sort and I explained they were confusing two things. I had briefed that there were SF/IRA meetings going on (which they later denied). I wasn't convinced they believed me, and there was something pretty heavy about seeing them lined up demanding explanations. They were jovial, but there was a real hint of menace. 'Look Alastair,' said Adams. 'We live here. We know what is going on.' I said I wished to fuck I did, because so far as I could see, we were going nowhere. Back inside, TB was looking downcast again, but we decided to keep going through 9, then 10, then 11, when Adams did a pretty positive briefing, followed by Trimble being very negative, prompting me to go out and say de Chastelain was putting forward his report shortly, and that both GA and TB were keen to see the UU Assembly members. It was time to put the pressure on Trimble. I briefed [BBC journalist] Mark Mardell and [ITN political editor] Mike Brunson that there was real movement from Adams and the pressure was all on Trimble now. TB had talked to both the Queen and the president by now. We regrouped with the Irish after 11, TB having done another sweep of the smaller parties to stop them getting too fed up. It was all getting a bit high-wire again, but we had rediscovered a third wind and we were determined to sort something.

The problem was that the UUs were feeling a real blow – Drumcree – and it kept them in a very negative mindset. I played the bagpipes out on the terrace at one point – the acoustics were terrific and it seemed to cheer people up a bit, but we were drifting a bit. We got a helicopter to Castle Buildings. TB saw Trimble while Bertie saw Adams. TB called me in to say David felt all the public pressure was on him, and we needed to balance up by getting some pressure on SF. I said we should say there was still the chance of progress and that on the question of decommissioning, TB and Bertie were 'one hundred per cent' behind DT's demand for a clear and unequivocal commitment. DT was pretty calm by the usual standards. I briefed as agreed, both in person in Belfast and down the line to London. Bertie felt we could get 'the war is over' from SF, and a commitment to try to persuade the IRA re decommissioning but we were still a long way off. Then we discovered de Chastelain was about to publish a gloomy report making clear there had been no real progress on the decommissioning front. There was no way we could let him publish as things stood. We got TB to speak to him and they agreed to meet at 1. The only defensible line was to say that we had asked him to postpone because we believed we were making progress on decommissioning. De Chastelain was happy to delay publication for a day. We now had to pin them down.

McGuinness had called de Chastelain to say they would be making a statement making clear their commitment to decommission, though not speaking for the IRA. He accepted it at least as a step in the right direction. They then went into a more detailed discussion on the modalities, and a plan for a timetable. I was intending to go out and brief a sense of progress but both Joe Lennon and Paddy Teahon [Ahern's adviser] nobbled me to say we could not mention the commitment to decommission as it would send SF off the deep end. We retreated to Tom Kelly's office, where we agreed a toned-down briefing. At 3.15 TB/BA met Adams and McGuinness for one and a quarter hours, after which TB said we were moving in the right direction. They didn't like the idea of a named person dealing with de Chastelain. They wanted to be more flexible about things. We were still a huge way apart on the timetable for the establishment of the executive. TB thought it significant they had themselves put forward new ideas, e.g. a South African to verify decommissioning.

We were now working on a paper with a variety of options. We told them what we needed by way of amendments. We needed an IRA statement. They had to accept the executive will only come into being once the process starts. The process must start, then the timetable will want weapons a few months later. TB said they will want to see if it beds down. Bertie said they still feared if they did this, nothing would change. Trimble would still not speak to them. McGuinness came to see TB. Their problem was going out and saying decommissioning will happen. In some ways it would be easier to do if they didn't have to say they were doing it. De Chastelain is the key to determining any progress. The Irish were seeing Donaldson who was seemingly being more reasonable.

As midnight approached, TB called me in and said what do we do by way of fallback? What do we say if we make no real progress? He was really tired and tetchy. 'I can't understand them. I am really scared about it this time because I don't have a clue what I would say to the country and I don't have a clue what the consequences will be if we have to walk away without real progress.' DT was seeing GA at midnight but was unable to get real detail on what they planned. TB set out for DT what we saw as a best-case scenario for him but even that wasn't good enough. He said to him he (DT) was the leader who was getting the IRA to commit to decommission, and he was walking away from it as though it were a defeat. All we could really do was let them sweat – put out details of the kind of deal on offer and let them consult. I worked on a draft failure statement, with the key line 'I believe the parties are sincere, but the parties do not believe each other.' Trimble took TB's best-case list to his people and reported back that not one of them supported it.

He came back with Seamus Mallon [deputy leader, SDLP] at 1.05am for an unbearably gloomy meeting. Even Jonathan and I had given up on the black humour for now. Trimble said he had no support for what was being proposed. They did not believe we would kick SF off the executive once they were on, and they did not believe decommissioning would happen. TB was tired and saying little for once. Mallon quizzed Trimble, said there was never a good time but real opinion out there supported him more than he thought. Trimble said that didn't matter, because the Unionist Council would not support it. TB was getting close to the view that deep down they just didn't want to share power with Catholics. Mallon felt DT lived in permanent fear of political crucifixion by [Ian] Paisley [leader of the Democratic Unionist Party] and [Bob] McCartney [leader of the UK Unionist Party].

Bertie was patient as ever, trying to coax out DT into a more positive position. TB said 'If I get them to agree to decommission within a month, would that do?' He said 'I wouldn't be there. They only need two weeks to get me out.' He was clear his Assembly people just wouldn't wear it. Mallon said 'David, think the worst the whole time, and we all go down, but Adams goes out smelling of roses, while you are there with your party intact but you'll be wrecked.' 'I'm wrecked whatever,' he said. Mallon: 'Who dares wins.' Trimble: 'I'm always wary when others are urging me on to what I know will be my own destruction.' TB: 'At least give me a counter-proposal.' Silence. TB turned to me and said what do we say? I said all we can do is say we have failed and you give an honest assessment of where we got to, what was on offer, and let people make their own judgement. TB said if we go out there and offer no hope at all, we have a bloodbath on our hands. But he also said he wasn't prepared to keep coming again and again to put in day after day on negotiations going nowhere.

Then at 1.55am, Adams came in and made clear there was no way he was going to sign up to a deal that had decommissioning prior to the executive, or to a shadow executive going nowhere. I had now drafted a three-page statement setting the context for failure but TB was for now determined to keep going. We cannot go out of here having failed, he said. Adams and Trimble had another meeting but as ever came out with totally different interpretations of what had been said. The problem was DT kept going back to his own people and instead of offering leadership around a position secured by him, he took all their criticisms like a sponge. We had another round, then TB spoke to Clinton around 3.45, gave him his assessment and got him to speak to both GA and DT to urge them on.

DT was in our office when the call came through from the US and he was almost embarrassed, looking away from us, whispering and mumbling, humming like he did when he was nervous, then turned to us, wiped his mobile on his sleeve and said 'It's President Clinton.' BC took the line that the world would not understand if we failed to take this step forward now. As we left TB was pretty apocalyptic, could see it going nowhere fast, and then with dreadful consequences on the street as the blame games and the retreats started. In the car, he said he felt the Irish were not putting enough pressure on SF, whose position was a mirror of the UUs, and they were both as unreasonable as each other but because SF were cleverer negotiators and media operators, they got away with more. I reckoned he had about eighty meetings long and short behind him, and he was looking really tired. 'I have to find some verve and energy from somewhere. Otherwise this is going down.'

Thursday, July 1

Willie Whitelaw [former Conservative Deputy Prime Minister] died. The other big event was the official opening of the Scottish Parliament and TB's absence was going noted without being too much of a story. The press was full of the knife-edge stuff re NI. At breakfast, he said it was time to put real pressure on them. He intended to say it was now or never, that the civilised world would not understand if we did not do this now, and that we agree the co-ordination of two historic steps. The IRA will disarm. The UUs will share power with Catholics. No sane person outside of this place would remotely understand how you can turn your backs on that. He intended to do a round-table talk and say all that on arrival. We had the full-cholesterol Hillsborough breakfast, which was one of the delights of NI, and then flew off by helicopter. He was fired up by the time we landed. We linked up with Bertie and they did the last bit of the journey by car together, TB spelling out his plan of action. We got inside, then they went out again to do a brief doorstep, during which Adams came down, very wired for him, close to hyperventilating, saying TB had to meet them because Republicans did not understand why the deadline passed, why they had made this huge shift on a commitment to decommission and they were still waiting for a proper response.

TB spoke to Clinton, who had had another go at Adams, but felt he had pushed him as far as he would go. TB was just as angry with Trimble because the reason he had been negotiating on the basis of no prior decommissioning was because at one point DT had signalled he could live with that. The media were just about buying the line that we could make it, but there was not a lot of optimism. At 4.40 we got Bertie and co back in, TB briefed them on Trimble's position. Bertie was really down now, said he thought we were pissing about, that the UUs were not serious about sharing power, but he would give it a go. When Paddy and Dermot [Gallagher, Irish diplomat] came back and said they had to be clear that if they went for this, that was it so far as further demands were concerned, we were a bit more hopeful again. But then TB was downcast again, struck by the logic of what we were saying, set against the seeming near impossibility of making it happen. But Trimble and Taylor were still hanging out for the IRA statement, which made us think it was still worth persevering. Taylor definitely seemed to have shifted gear. He said at one point 'I agree with the prime minister that if the IRA stuck to their word, we could ride out a storm, but it would depend how quickly.'

TB to DT: 'I need to know you can back me on this.' DT: 'Sorry, I can't.' It seemed we had Taylor in a better position than Trimble. TB explained, as if they didn't know, that it took the IRA six to eight weeks to get round all their people. To which Trimble replied – OK, let's wait a few weeks then. But he also knew that they needed to be able to take with them the power sharing. TB said that if they signed up to the 'possible sequencing' paper, that was an enormous step for them, and he couldn't ignore that. We went round and round in circles, having hit the absolute nub of the problem – they wanted decommissioning prior to the executive being established. SF wanted it the other way round. And neither trusted the other to deliver if they were meant to go second.

Trimble went off to see Bertie while we worked on Sinn Fein, just to see if changing the mix might produce something. One-hour-plus TB meeting with Adams and McGuinness who was in full flow about how he and Gerry were being ripped apart for their 'peace strategy', their people feeling they were giving all and getting nothing. Decommissioning in days was not a runner, he said, it just was not possible. It was hard enough to get an IRA statement on the general commitment. They felt I had been pushing too far in briefings on the seeming progress they were making with the IRA. They lived in fear, he said. I said I know sometimes they thought I pushed too far, but they needed to understand I did nothing without TB wanting it done, so if he wanted the pressure shifted one way or the other, that's what we did. 'Alastair, that stuff (IRA statements re decommissioning is what I think he meant) is sacrosanct. Youse cannot get involved like that, and sometimes you scare the life out of me.' He said he would decommission 'the day before yesterday' if he could, but we had to deal with the realities we had before us. We pressed on and they finally agreed to put a proposal to the UUs. BA gloomy again. Trimble in again. TB said he was going to speak to Clinton and together the three leaders would put the deal to Gerry.

Trimble was talking about not making a specific comment on the specific proposal. Unbelievable. Adams had talked of this being the beginning of the end of the IRA, but Trimble would not seize it. We were now going round in circles and getting very ragged again. Sinn Fein were more nervous than usual, e.g. at one point before a bilateral with Trimble coming to ask TB for advice. We briefed on TB's meeting with the UUs and agreed after tortuous meetings with the Irish that Joe [Lennon] and I would go out with a package of 1. SF/UUP bilateral led to 2. round-table talks, led to 3. de Chastelain report in the morning, led to 4. the joint paper. We gave out the text, absolutely mobbed. There were dozens of journalists, God knows what kind of life they are leading in this crazy media village. But at least we had a process story to keep going.

Friday, July 2

Breakfast was pretty gloomy. Jonathan reported that de Chastelain was getting restless and feeling messed around. TB was worried it was all going down the pan again. Bertie was equally gloomy. The date of an IRA statement and lack of certainty about decommissioning were holding us back. Trimble seemed on for it early on but Donaldson could see his moment and was trying to undo the whole thing. The good news was that Taylor and Maginnis seemed better than before. But TB was exasperated that they could not grasp the fact they were about to deliver the death of the IRA, if only they would seize it. SF were being difficult. McGuinness and Gerry Kelly [Sinn Fein] came in while I was talking to TB and Jonathan. 'We're here about him,' said McGuinness, pointing to me. He said I was currently spinning the line that we were about to announce there would be legislation to exclude them if there was no decommissioning. I said it would be far better if he focused more on the talks inside and less what was said out there by the press. Kelly, sharp-eyed and sharp-suited as ever, flashed one of his looks. People still said McGuinness and [Martin] Ferris [Sinn Fein] were the real hardnuts, but Kelly could be pretty disconcerting.

De Chastelain came over with his report and had half an hour with TB while we waited for Bertie to come back from Sinn Fein.

He was effectively talking to the Provisional Army Council, pushing for a statement. De Chastelain, and perhaps more importantly Ambassador Don Johnson,[1] clearly did believe the IRA would decommission and that SF had moved. At 4.10 Trimble came in on his own and said he could not go for it. Then exactly half an hour later he came back and said he would go for it. He may not survive but he was willing to give it a go. TB said it was the right thing to do. It was better than the Hillsborough deal and there would be the legislative failsafe. By 5 I was telling the broadcasters we were on for a deal, that Trimble was hanging tough. Trimble came back in again and I gave him the line which he seemed OK with, 'Are we really not prepared to test for thirty days a process that could end thirty years of violence?'

At 5.20 Paddy Teahon came in saying SF were having big trouble with anything that suggested days and weeks. Joe Lennon was pissed off I was briefing on the deal at all. But TB, who was now seeing the smaller parties, was keen to press the button. We gave the thing the title 'The Way Forward' and some new lines to inject forward process. Then at 7, Trimble came back in with Taylor and Reg Empey, said sorry but he couldn't do it. His party could not support it, they would split and he would be gone. TB said let me go and speak to them. They didn't want that. He said it was an own goal of potentially historic proportions. They could be the people to end the IRA and see off violence for good but for the sake of a few days' uncertainty they weren't prepared to take a risk. He looked pretty close to despair. They all went over to shake TB by the hand, Trimble said nothing, Taylor said thank you for everything you have tried to do. TB said 'I fear you will deliver public opinion to the nationalists at a time they don't deserve it. It is a real error and you will take time to recover from it.' TB had to go through another session with the Garvaghy Road residents' association. Then finally we were off, and on the car radio on *The World Tonight* [BBC radio] the reporter said he had a sinking feeling. So did we. On the plane Jonathan and I tried to keep up TB's spirits but he was as fed up as I've seen him, veering from silently looking out of the window to looking back and muttering about the UUs' zero strategy. In the car he called Clinton, who was also amazed they rejected the deal. TB said only the Unionists could throw that chance away.

[1] US ambassador Donald C. Johnson, one of three members, with General John de Chastelain and Brigadier Tauno Nieminen of Finland, of the Independent International Commission on Decommissioning.

Saturday, July 3

TB was desperate to breathe some life into the NI process. We wrote a piece for the *Sunday Times* and for Monday's *Belfast Telegraph*. He called several times to ask how it was going and all I could say was it wasn't dead yet but it felt fairly close to it. He was now being accused of having misled them by giving the impression that only Sinn Fein could be excluded. So as well as failure, he was getting blame. The *Sunday Times* piece was designed to meet Unionist concerns, but TB felt let down by Trimble, first because he had agreed to the plan and second because some of the changes had been his ideas. We have given up a week and got nowhere, he said.

Sunday, July 4

The press were pretty much writing the deal off. TB said there was real malice in the way some of the papers wanted us to fail on this. It made him more determined, but there was a danger of him being continually distracted from domestic policy. If we were able to put the same kind of energy into health and education, we might make more progress. Trimble was doing *On the Record* [BBC television] and, speaking to TB, said he was worried he wouldn't get a word in edgeways with [presenter John] Humphrys. I spoke to Humphrys to say Trimble wanted to get himself to a position where he could at least not totally reject it and he said he would help, but they would need to explain the thinking behind the failsafe and the need for the IRA statement. Trimble was pretty negative, saying it was a con job and Adams duped him.

Monday, July 5

I was feeling Northern Ireland was pretty much all over but TB wanted to press on. There was another bad story in the *Telegraph*, Sinn Fein people telling their members there would be no decommissioning. But Drumcree went OK and TB was not too downhearted when I went in to brief him for the *Today* programme and *Good Morning Ulster*. He did well on both. The problem now was that in trying to please the Unionists we risk pushing Sinn Fein off the deep end. We went over to the House for the statement on Ireland. TB had seen Hague and Andrew MacKay [Conservative Northern Ireland spokesman] at 9, but at 3, Trimble was pretty clear with TB that he was being wound up by the Tories to press for more. The statement was fine but at the four o'clock I was pressed on prisoners, was unsure of my ground, and ended up with them filing stories about us reviewing prisoner legislation if they didn't decommission. This was a real problem area for Sinn Fein. Throwing a prison review into the mix had the potential for disaster. What I had said was factually right but politically difficult.

Tuesday, July 6

I slept badly. Even though I had been factually right on the prisoners, it was a fuck-up to get drawn, and provoke Sinn Fein. They were livid. Joe Lennon said Bertie also felt we were doing too much for the UUs now. TB could tell I was worried and he said it was fine but I hated messing up. I was speaking at an awayday for ministers where I did the usual script about strategy and co-ordination, and a fairly good Q&A before going back to work on TB's speech [to the British Venture Capital Association]. It was fairly strong, but the bit that made the news was when he departed from the script, said the public sector was more rooted in its ways than anywhere else and that he had the scars on his back to show for it. People thought it was an odd thing to say and it was quickly whipped up into a 'storm', with people being dragged out to attack it as having been an attack on anyone who wanted to see it that way. He was genuinely nonplussed when I told him it would be a big thing. I had a meeting with Colin Byrne, Danny Alexander [Britain in Europe campaigners] and Roger Liddle [policy adviser] to go over the Britain in Europe launch plans and then saw Ricci Levi, [former Prime Minister of Italy, and soon to be President of the European Commission, Romano] Prodi's spokesman, and Geoffrey Martin from the [European] Commission. I told them I thought they had a real problem in that there was an arrogance about the way the European debate was being framed, that anyone who questioned one part of the project was somehow against it all. I felt myself, as someone basically pro-European, that whenever we went to a major EU event, the distance between the political class and the public seemed to be growing, whilst all the time the politicians spoke about getting closer to the people. Philip called from Eddisbury[1] and said he had done another worrying set of focus groups. They had no sense of anything we were doing. TB was looking really tired but Christ knows when he would get a rest before the holiday.

[1] Former Conservative chief whip Sir Alastair Goodlad had resigned from the House of Commons on June 28 to become high commissioner to Australia. A by-election would be held on July 22 in his former constituency, Eddisbury in Cheshire.

Wednesday, July 7

TB was amazed his 'scars on my back' speech had sparked off such a big debate. He was due to see GB who was going to try to persuade him to delay once more the Britain in Europe launch. TB felt we needed to crack on with it. GB was worried we were allowing strategy out of our hands, to an organisation none of us really felt was up to it, and to one that had a lot of Tories involved. He felt they had done no proper polling, had no really interesting endorsements, no central message and that there was a real arrogance to the way they went about the debate. I found myself more in agreement with him than not. He was worried we were going to make it an election issue. We decided to cancel Poland and Kosovo visits because of Northern Ireland. We got back and heard JP had had a little dig in his speech in Harrogate, with a big salvo of praise for the public sector, rounded off with 'I'm glad I got that off my chest.'

Thursday, July 8

JP was in recanting mode, called and said what should he do to get out of it? Cabinet had quite a good discussion on the difference between making policy and driving delivery. We then had a meeting on TB's [BBC] *Question Time* appearance. He was tired but we worked through briefs on all the obvious stuff and he did pretty well. But for some reason he dropped in a pretty clear pledge to ban fox hunting, which was the obvious story out of it and would be big news for the next day's papers. He was exhausted on the way but bucked up during the programme. However, he didn't realise he had been so unequivocal about a ban when I asked him in the car why he had gone as hard as he did.

Friday, July 9

Hunting was going big on the news, and everyone in the office was surprised both that he had made the commitment and at how big it was now going. On one level, it was helpful for him to be seen to be pushing what was a fairly popular and populist cause. On the other hand, he had always had big doubts about how practical this would be. He was making out he had done it deliberately, but I wasn't so sure.

Walked across Whitehall with Alison [Blackshaw, AC's PA] and Mark [Bennett] to do my speech [on the media coverage of Kosovo] to RUSI, which, needless to say, was seen as a scathing attack on the media, which is how they see anything I say about them, but in fact was much more rounded than that. Guthrie was in good form and paid a very nice tribute to me at the end. I enjoyed the Q&A. John Keegan [military historian] said he agreed with everything I said. The audience was mainly diplomatic, foreign media and defence experts. Iain Duncan Smith [Conservative Shadow Defence Secretary] was there. I'm not sure I would have advised him to go. The broadcasters wanted interviews, but I felt best to leave it to text. *Channel 4 News* did a snide package but would have done anyway. I got back to work on TB's speech for tomorrow. The good thing about his 'scars on my back' was that it had generated renewed interest in modernisation and the domestic agenda. His stuff on nurses was going really well. Earlier, TB and GB saw [Lord] Colin Marshall and explained we didn't think Britain in Europe [which Marshall was chairing] were yet in the right shape to do the launch and in particular needed more polling. They must have thought we were total plonkers.

Saturday, July 10
The coverage for my speech was totally predictable, dominated by John Simpson's self-serving attack. As Guthrie said, they showed themselves to be the thin-skinned wankers that they are. They only ever wanted to present one side of an argument, the side that fitted their agenda or prism. Lucie [McNeil] felt we should have organised supportive statements, but in the end I felt the argument got through. I was speaking at an Irish press ball in Dublin and [UK ambassador Sir] Ivor Roberts, our man in Dublin, had invited the whole family out for the weekend. The dinner itself was a pretty drunken affair. It reminded me of Fleet Street in the 80s. We auctioned me playing the pipes and raised £3,500 out of a total of £75,000 for Kosovo charities.

Sunday, July 11
The Sunday papers were really quiet, though full on inventive reshuffle rubbish. After breakfast we went off to the beach and after a while I realised I had left my phone behind. Once I got used to not having it, I rather enjoyed it. But by the time we got back, there were stacks of messages to deal with, most of them Northern Ireland related.

Monday, July 12
Northern Ireland was the main story all day. The bill on the Northern Ireland Executive suspension [allowing devolved government to be suspended in certain circumstances] was being published. John Sawers

had been in late last night for final bit of drafting. It was due to be published at 3.30 but it quickly became clear we would have to wait. The Irish weren't happy because it was obvious we were talking about Sinn Fein exclusion. But the UUs weren't happy either. I went through it with John to work up an idiot's guide for the eleven o'clock. The four o'clock briefing must have been the longest ever, taking them through the details of the bill whilst saying I was not able to give it to them yet. This stuff was never easy. But it was very difficult to sell it properly when we weren't in a position to publish it. They got a sense of how difficult when Mo called halfway through and said the Irish had effectively rejected the bit about Assembly meetings. I did OK I think, but God was it long.

TB wondered if we shouldn't get out that the Irish weren't happy. I called Mo, who was very opposed on the grounds it would provoke a big-split story, and she was right, though they would probably brief it themselves anyway. I didn't think there was much intellectual coherence to their position but they were genuinely pissed off at the moment. Trimble and Maginnis for once did a fairly helpful doorstep and didn't get drawn into questions and it wasn't running too badly on the news. Also the marches were going off fairly peacefully so perhaps we were going somewhere.

Tuesday, July 13

Ireland was the main story again with the bill due in the House today. Jonathan, John S and I were called up to the flat first thing. There was a sense of political crisis out of yesterday but the marches going well is a bonus. TB was worried that we were stumbling towards the end of the road and we had no real strategy. The eleven o'clock was again totally dominated by Ireland. We were pressing for a statement from the IRA but we didn't even have one at the moment from the SDLP. TB felt we were going to have to give even more to the UUs. Mo came over at 12. [John] Hume [SDLP leader], Mallon and [Eddie] McGrady [SDLP] came in and they were very unkeen on saying they would sit on the executive without Sinn Fein. Both they and TB were pretty vitriolic about the Tories, who were deliberately making things more difficult for the Unionists.

Went over to the House. The Tories abstained, Trimble voted against but without going over the top. Mo was pretty poor. Hume was dreadful, Trimble not as bad as he might have been. TB saw Robin afterwards to see whether he was interested in the NATO job. RC said he would go for it if he felt TB would dispense with him in the next year. TB said he wasn't able to give guarantees. He felt Robin would do a good job at NATO, and it would appeal to him because of the salary and the status of being the top man. We were pretty confident the US would back the British candidate to replace Solana. TB was in two minds about losing Robin from the Cabinet but he did need some space for a reshuffle. He had a private meeting with Trimble and said afterwards he felt DT really wanted to help, and TB was the only person he trusted to deal with, but it was difficult for him. He felt we might need to park the whole thing for the summer, which would be a big disappointment.

Wednesday, July 14

Northern Ireland was still dominant. John Sawers had put together a number of amendments to the bill. There was a lot of excitement at the amendments plan though I was careful to say we didn't know if it would be enough and by now Adams and McGuinness were spitting fury. The briefing went on for an eternity. Now we were just waiting for the outcome of Trimble's meeting. Elinor Goodman [*Channel 4 News* political editor] called to say they had rejected the deal. It also meant there was no longer a need to rush through emergency legislation. TB agreed with Bertie there was no point doing the legislation now. But Sinn Fein and SDLP were livid. Mallon sounded close to quitting. TB spoke to an as ever graceless DT who sometimes spoke as though he wasn't actually involved in the process at all, as if his party was some kind of distant entity. The rollercoaster was rolling in the wrong direction again. Denis Murray [BBC Ireland correspondent] said to me even you cannot persuade me this is anything but bad news.

Thursday, July 15

It was descending into farce and chaos. Trimble didn't go to the Assembly meeting. Mallon resigned despite TB personally calling him on his mobile and urging him not to. Recriminations were beginning, with some of the blame going towards TB, but Trimble taking the bulk of it. Cabinet was pretty downbeat. TB said neither side was really ready for this. He said we would put those limited issues into a review process and the Assembly would effectively be in recess. But he believed there was something to come back to. He asked me to speak to Trimble and urge him to be more positive, at least give the sense there was some hope there. TB's view was that provided we could limit the recriminations, and give the sense there was something to come back to, it would not be so bad.

Friday, July 16

I took a day off. TB called a couple of times re Ireland and the Eddisbury by-election. The polls there were looking pretty good and we needed to decide whether we should go.

Saturday, July 17

Work-wise it was fairly quiet all weekend and I was starting to think about what we needed to do to start planning the next election. The party machine did not feel to be in very good shape. There was loads in the papers about Peter M going to Northern Ireland.

Sunday, July 18

The Sundays were totally crap. There was loads of reshuffle stuff. Peter M called, said he was worried he was being set up for a job he wouldn't get and that he would get mauled if he didn't get it. We had a problem with Bertie who was quoted as saying decommissioning may go beyond the May 2000 deadline.

Monday, July 19

I was finding it hard to get the SCU [Strategic Communications Unit] to gel. Philip came to the 8.30 meeting for the first time, which was helpful. He said the problem was that most of the people there were in awe of me and scared to say anything. It was ridiculous, because I was constantly asking people their views, and urging them to take responsibility. We were umming and ahhing all day about whether TB should go to Eddisbury. There was a danger we were setting up a Tory win as an enormous success for Hague. Peter M and GB thought he should go. At a meeting with GB on Europe, Gordon was clearly going cold on the euro. He felt we had to reposition Britain in Europe as a campaign on membership, and economic reform. But TB felt we had to give them a launch of some sort. We have to drive the strategy, not leave it to a small group of euro fanatics in the business community. I felt we had to show some balls on it. The meeting was barely over when I took a call from Mike White [*Guardian*] saying he had heard we were thinking of putting off the euro campaign until after the second election. That can only have been briefed out of the meeting.

Tuesday, July 20

Another Northern Ireland day with both Bertie and [Senator George] Mitchell [chairman, all-party peace negotiations, Northern Ireland] coming in at 4. The Anglo–Italian summit was a total bore. Thankfully I had avoided the dinner that TB said was just as dull. He said that apart from Aznar, Europe was pretty weak on the leadership front. After all the dithering, under more pressure from the party, we finally decided to go to Eddisbury.[1] Nobody was saying we were going to win but they were saying we could come close and the TB visit might tip it. Mo had made some comments about wanting to stay at the NIO. I was asked about it at the 11 and stressed only TB decided and we never talked about reshuffles. Mo called to apologise, and yet she was saying that in the US she would say the same thing. Later, she was behaving a bit oddly, e.g. walking out with TB to meet Bertie, interrupting and contradicting TB during the meeting and overdoing the touchy-feely stuff with some of the officials, who looked a bit taken aback. I stayed away from TB's Britain in Europe meeting as [Kenneth] Clarke and [Michael] Heseltine were there. TB said he had bumped into an old friend who had said to him 'Alastair really hates Tories doesn't he?' And after Bertie's doorstep with Mitchell, I had a meeting of [Civil Service] heads of information which was as depressing as ever. No matter what I did, they seemed either cowed and intimidated, or they just didn't get it.

Wednesday, July 21

TB was seeing [Israeli Prime Minister Ehud] Barak, who was much more confident, and likeable, than the last time he saw him. He was pretty positive about the role he could play. He had met all the key players and was clearly more comfortable talking about their different positions. He was full of praise for TB re Kosovo, said it was good to end this century and begin the next one with despots around the world getting the message that Milosevic got. TB said he wanted to help in any way he could re the Middle East and Barak seemed keen on some kind of European role. TB said he was constantly saying to EU leaders that if we just lecture the Israelis the whole time it makes it harder for them to move. Barak felt he would be able to develop a certain level of trust with [Palestinian leader Yasser] Arafat, but he had to understand every Israeli leader's commitment to security. He was also clearly pretty wound up by Iran, their use of proxies for technology and international terror. He felt their weapons development was a threat to civilisation. Robin said Iran is not Iraq.

After he left, we went to Northolt for the flight to Eddisbury. We went straight to a shopping-centre walkabout in Winsford, which got pretty riotous. There were lots of supporters, but also people who were very aggressive, and made it very difficult for TB to be heard.

[1] Blair's appearance in Eddisbury would break the convention that prime ministers did not actively campaign in parliamentary by-elections.

The police weren't terribly helpful. Jonathan called to say the IRA were putting out a statement. For one great moment, I thought it was going to be the statement we had been working for but in fact it was deeply gloomy, critical of the government and with a clear veiled threat to return to violence. Denis Murray did a pretty breathless two-way. TB, who was seeing the Sultan of Oman, was pretty fed up.

Thursday, July 22

The IRA statement was leading the news. TB was due to see Trimble and Adams, and TB, John Sawers and I felt there was a case for cancelling the meeting but Jonathan was strongly against. TB saw George Robertson re the NATO job. He was clearly keen but worried Sandra [his wife] was totally against. As well as it being a good thing to get a Brit there, TB was limited in his room for manoeuvre on the reshuffle. He later asked me whether he could send Peter M straight to the DTI [Department of Trade and Industry]. John Sawers was pretty desperate. He said the NIO were for a move there but if Mo was the only move that was a problem. Mo was worried that the Cabinet Office job was all spin not substance. Cabinet was a very political discussion on dividing lines.

Meeting with Adams, McGuinness and Ferris. John Sawers thought Adams and McGuinness had asked Ferris to be there to show they weren't patsies and could be really tough with TB. TB was pretty tough back and there was a fair amount of mutual fed-upness. TB said, re the IRA statement, 'Well I get the message, and it's a pretty heavy message too.' McGuinness said 'Nothing to do with me. Not guilty.' In a different context, it would have raised a smile but on both sides, there wasn't much humour. Adams said, rather patronisingly, we think you are trying your best but the Unionists have no interest in sharing power. The Mitchell review is a waste of time. We have been sitting on the Agreement for fifteen months and getting nowhere. He said that TB was the best guarantor of not going back to violence, but as an organisation they were not as disciplined as sometimes we thought. 'I know you may have doubts about us but we are the best you've got. We have our own reasons to do this and the main one is a better future for our young people, and the only person that can make it work is you. They have to know change is coming.'

TB said both sides operated according to norms that they couldn't imagine changing. He believed the Unionists did want to make it work, but they had people capable of talking themselves into despondency greater than any people he has ever met. 'That doesn't mean they don't want to share power. You have a real understanding. I can put pressure on them as the Irish put pressure on you. I also know that if you go back to violence then I see none of you again. I'm a pragmatist but I feel things deeply. I felt Kosovo. I feel this peace process and if I get an IRA statement like that on the day Gerry Adams and Martin McGuinness are coming in, I don't like that. I don't like the threat. I don't operate like that. And just understand if you go back to violence, I see none of you again.'

McGuinness said their only strategy was to stop power sharing. TB was having none of it. 'The problem with you is that both sides have absolute clarity about the wrongness of the position of the other side. They say to me the IRA will never do it and I say, you're wrong. Just as I'm telling you you're wrong about Trimble.' They seemed a bit taken aback by how heavy he was with them and Adams tried to soften it, said he accepted part of Trimble wanted it to happen. TB said so what the hell do you want me to do? Adams: Implement the Agreement. TB: What the hell do you think I am trying to do? I am implementing the damn Agreement. McGuinness: The only person that can sort this is you, by making them do it. TB: You still can't see it from both sides, as I have to. He said the relationship between Britain and Ireland would change when we joined EMU, 'which we will'. At last there was a bit of laughter, and TB said that's about the only story that can knock the IRA off the front pages. I said I'd be grateful if they didn't brief that historic commitment. Adams said they couldn't believe it when TB had talked about there being decommissioning within days and weeks. All that pressure piled on them, all the compromise going the UUs way, didn't we read the barometer of opinion on Seamus Mallon's resignation? If we had behaved the same as they [the UUs] did, would you have been so benign? TB: Yes I would. McGuinness: But would Alastair? He was obsessed with this idea that I somehow had a different agenda to TB when in fact if anything instinctively I was much more on their side than TB. Adams had a go as well. He said this is going to be bad long after me and Alastair have gone. It's a life-and-death situation. Jonathan made a joke about that being a direct threat to me, which again lightened the mood, and I said to McGuinness 'You're obsessed with this media stuff.'

TB joked he would tell me to be nice and gentle with them, but then went back to being serious bordering on heavy. 'If there is a return to violence, just be clear I will have absolutely nothing to do with any of you. I will pursue the justice and equality agenda because I said I would and because it's right. But do not lose your patience so quickly. I will keep mine and get it done. I regard Unionist supremacy as an intolerable historical relic. But it won't go just because you will it to go. And it certainly won't go through more intimidation.

My doubt about you is not that you don't want to do it but that if you do not get what you want, you can revert to a situation where you become an enemy when you don't really want to be. I don't want to sound like some kind of Relate counsellor but you should work harder at finding out what the other side is thinking and why. Retreat into your boxes and you will squander it all.' McGuinness said TB and Trimble have to come to terms with the fact that they have more influence on the IRA than him or Gerry. They hung around for a fair bit, obviously trying to work out how best to deal with it.

Over at the House, I bumped into [Conservative MP Nicholas] Soames by the cash dispenser. He was raging at me about hunting. 'How would you feel if we got back into power and passed a law banning Burnley fucking Football Club?' He said he had told 'that fucking halfwit Grocott' [Bruce Grocott MP, Blair's parliamentary private secretary] it was war. To add to the lively scene, Trimble and his wife wandered by, Trimble saying he wished he had his camera, then Andrew Lansley [Conservative MP] who gave us a quizzical look, provoking Soames to yell at him 'Well you can fuck off for starters!' He said he was desperate for ten minutes with TB to talk him out of 'the worst decision he's ever made' re hunting. I stayed up late for the by-election which came through at 2am. 1,606 [Conservative] majority.

Friday, July 23

The by-election wasn't coming over nearly as well as it should have done early on, but through the day it seemed to dawn on people that the results were pretty dreadful for the Tories even if they had the word win in the headlines. Hunting was still running as a bit of a problem. I had briefed yesterday that we might not bring forward hunting plans before the recess and some of them saw it as a U-turn. I briefed the Sundays, largely on the [government] Annual Report as well as batting off endless different reshuffle stories. The best today was the *Telegraph* saying Ashdown was in line to be Northern Ireland Secretary. Vincent Moss [*Mail on Sunday*] asked if they would look stupid if they said the reshuffle was next week. I said they looked foolish every Sunday so why should I help them look any different? Julian called to say that the Tories had briefed Iain Duncan Smith saying I risked lives by over-briefing military success in south Serbia. I called Wes Clark in Arkansas, who agreed to speak to a British journalist to put a more positive line. I linked him up with Patrick Wintour.

Saturday, July 24

Wes spoke to Patrick and tried to ingratiate himself by saying he had read his stuff on Kosovo and it was reasonably accurate, to which Patrick replied 'Like your bombing campaign.'

Sunday, July 25

Out for dinner with Peter M and Reinaldo [da Silva, Mandelson's partner], Philip and Gail [Rebuck, publisher, Gould's wife]. Philip felt we were in quite poor shape at the moment. TB called, not knowing till I told him that I was with Peter. He said he had spoken to Mo and was wondering if he could put Peter in as Mo's Number 2. I said it was sellable but was it the right thing to do? I spoke to Mo who was about to go on holiday to Turkey and we needed to agree a line in case he went ahead and did it. She sounded pretty mad about the whole thing, saying it was all about Tony and why did he need Peter back at all blah blah blah? I raised it with Peter at the end of the evening and he went into ultra-haughty mode, said it was a total non-starter, he could not possibly work with her. I said I wondered if that was the wrong approach and whether he shouldn't give it a little bit more thought.

Monday, July 26

Annual Report day. TB was bad-tempered about it, feeling it just set us up for trouble. In fact the coverage so far wasn't bad, and it led the broadcasts for most of the day with the tone far less cynical than last year because it was much more factual and less glossy. We had a meeting with Stan Greenberg [US Democratic pollster] which showed the surface figures quite good but discontent beneath, thermometer ratings for TB and the party were falling and there were problems on trust and delivery. He said one quarter to a third of Labour supporters did not feel warm towards us. With Clinton, even at the bad times, it never went below fourteen per cent. And while Kosovo was seen as a success, it didn't necessarily lead to political dividends. On the contrary, it begged in their minds the question why he seemed to fight harder for that than for them. PG said he and Stan [they worked in association] also had a meeting with GB on the poll and Bob Shrum, another American pollster effectively working for GB, was there. Philip's sense was there was something fairly close to a total rival operation going on. He said Ed Balls had come out and said that New Labour was the problem because it wasn't popular.

We were working on tomorrow's speech on Europe. TB didn't want it to go big, because we hadn't really had time to do a proper job, but there was no way they were not going to make it go big. Julian had volunteered a draft which was pretty good and which TB used as the base. But on our general position he felt we were being identified as too unquestioningly pro and we needed more caveats. I had a meeting with [Sir] Richard Dearlove, the head of SIS, who was pretty media-savvy, and felt we could increase and improve co-operation with them. He thought I should go over there and meet all his key people. We had an interesting chat on Iraq and Milosevic, who was apparently trying to get money to China.

Tuesday, July 27

Julian had been working most of the night on TB's speech and TB himself was up at 5 to work on it. TB had done a pretty major rewrite and we were still working on it right up to moment when we left for the London Business School. The process never got better, but it was quite a good speech, an attack on anti-Europeanism, took on the sceptic press, restated the position on EMU but in a way that would make news. He had discussed it on the phone with GB who was claiming that Peter was behind the little rash of irritating stories on Europe, e.g. the *Mail* saying Balls was making GB more sceptic and pushing him away from a referendum, or [Andy] Grice [political editor, *Independent*] who was saying that not having a referendum early was a change of policy. Nick Jones [BBC journalist] gave the first public airing to the word 'garbagic' which I had been using to describe reshuffle stories and which I hoped to get into a dictionary within a few years. We went back and into a round of reshuffle meetings, the first time we had really gone into it in any detail. Dobbo [Frank Dobson, Health Secretary] and Jack [Cunningham] were close to the chop but we agreed there wasn't much point at the moment. We went through the list to identify junior and middle-ranking ministers. TB was pretty clinical about it. He told JP that if he didn't sort out transport in eighteen months he would be dead politically. TB said at one point 'We are not exactly greatly blessed with talent.' TB was wondering whether twelve to fifteen ministers going was enough. He still wasn't sure about what to do with Peter M. Truth be told, he didn't like the personnel side of stuff and was not looking forward to it.

Wednesday, July 28

David Miliband and I did one of our double acts at the *Express* and it was a far more mature discussion than before. Then into the office for the reshuffle day. As last year, it was TB, Jonathan, Anji, Sally Morgan [political secretary], David M, Bruce and I, later with Richard Wilson and Ann Taylor [chief whip]. We had sheets of paper both with current names and blank, Jonathan in charge of a master copy as names were moved around. [Scottish Office minister Lord] Gus

Macdonald was agreed early on for transport, which would be bad for Helen [Liddell, serving minister for transport] but there we were. The sackings were agreed fairly early and then most of the day just trying to fit different people into different bits of the operation, like a jigsaw. We had some new, good women, a few surprises. At 2, TB said he wanted the main list out by 5. JP said we had to avoid it looking like his wings were being clipped, this on the day [Labour MP] Gwyneth Dunwoody's [transport] select committee put out its report saying he was crap. TB was convinced she did it on purpose to inflict maximum damage on him. TB believed JP was a mix of clever instinct, guile and insecurity and he was clever enough to know things weren't working out at the department, but didn't know what to do about it.

By now we were just going over the whole thing again and again, moving different pieces of the jigsaw while I was still maintaining a news blackout on the whole thing and being as unhelpful as we could so that nobody could say the ministers weren't hearing first. Just before 6 I got TV reporters and a few others in from the street to say he was beginning the reshuffle this evening but it did not involve the Cabinet. Having spent all day telling their viewers he was already reshuffling them, they went straight out and said he had bottled out. And so began lots of self-indulgent rubbish that we could have stopped all the speculation whenever we chose. At 7, we left for the House. Saw Helen, who looked and sounded shafted. Anji had squared Gus who agreed he would move to London to do the job. He then did a series of sackings, John Morris [Attorney General], John Gilbert [junior defence], Glenda Jackson [junior transport], who looked absolutely thunderstruck. I agreed she could say she was resigning to stand for mayor [of London]. [Sports minister Tony] Banks and I had spoken earlier and had agreed he would stand down to focus on the [2006] World Cup bid.

TB hated doing this and it brought out the worst in him. We were getting a bad press mainly because the feeling was out there that he had wanted to make more changes but his colleagues had hemmed him in. But we couldn't afford an offside Mo plus an offside Frank [Dobson] let alone JP. They knew he was in charge but there was no point picking too many fights at once. JP was grateful TB was consulting him the whole way through but he was definitely feeling bruised. It was impossible not to have something of the feeling of an undertaker hanging around waiting for people to come out and then discuss how we handled their demise. It was definitely better doing this in the Commons but it was going on far too long. Bits of the jigsaw kept changing. At one point we had both [Peter] Kilfoyle and

[George] Howarth [Merseyside Labour MPs] going to NIO, which would have been like a scouse outing, so [Adam] Ingram stayed despite wanting to go to MoD.

Thursday, July 29

I was in at the crack of dawn again. We were being savaged by the press for alleged weakness because he hadn't moved the Cabinet. I spoke to Jack C before his *Today* programme interview to get over that TB ran the government for the country not for the media. Margaret Beckett [Leader of the Commons] did the same thing brilliantly on *The World at One*. TB called and said we have a problem. He had also had a difficult call with Peter M to tell him he wasn't coming back in but he would be putting him in a party role later. He was very down on Peter at the moment, felt he had been diddling through the media to try to put himself in line for a recall. GB was being very onside, as was often the case when Peter was down. There was a real sense of payback in the vehemence of the media attacks over this. In the end we just had to take a hit and get it sorted. TB loathed the whole thing. He hated doing the sackings, didn't like pressures being put on by ministers looking after their friends, or the desperate pleas from individuals, Joyce Quin [Europe minister] last night for example who was desperate not to move. Others like Jeff Rooker [agriculture minister], about whom he had sometimes had doubts, but who totally bowled him over with his passion and his commitment.

I had a meeting with Joe Irvin [special adviser to Prescott] and JP's communications people to go over the strategic issues and how we use Gus' arrival to get to a better place. The news was running better once we had the likes of Charles Clarke, Pat Hewitt, Nick Raynsford, Rooker etc. coming in and out.[1] We finally settled on Kate Hoey [junior Home Office minister] for sport, though both TB and I had our doubts, and Anji wasn't sure she would take it. I called Hoey to see that she would and it was true she didn't sound keen, fearing it would lead to a sidelining. I fed that in to TB who said he was fed up with these people. I thought it was the job she had always wanted. We got Anji to call her and she said she had been shocked when I had called and she really did want it. I felt instinctively she was going to be a problem because she had a touch of the Frank Field [maverick Labour MP,

[1] Charles Clarke, a junior education minister, became Minister of State at the Home Office; Patricia Hewitt, Economic Secretary to the Treasury, became Minister of State for Small Business. Nick Raynsford was promoted to Minister of State at the Department of the Environment, Transport and the Regions (DETR). Jeff Rooker became Minister of State for Social Security.

former minister] about her. TB disagreed, felt she was basically loyal and would be fine. She came in and after she had seen TB I said the most important thing was to focus on policy and not just become a commentator, e.g. watch out for the Man U/FA Cup situation. She immediately fucked that one up.

We got out a few more names for the lunchtimes and finally got it together for 4.30. I had a copy of a CD someone had sent me by a group called Garbage and I gave out prizes for the biggest and most garbagic reshuffle stories. George Jones [*Telegraph*] won for his Ashdown to Northern Ireland story. Robert Peston [*Financial Times*] was second with Dobson to Leader of the House and third prize to the *Independent* for saying John Reid should be promoted to the Cabinet when he was already in it. They took it reasonably well but I also made the serious point that nobody ever went back to them and asked them to explain how they got so many stories wrong. Meanwhile, George Robertson had agreed to go for the NATO job and we were busy phoning round to get support for him. Schroeder was on for it. Chirac had to be squared. I left early to go out for Calum's birthday but by now we were in better shape, with a sense of more women, the first black woman [Patricia Scotland, Foreign Office], [Chris] Mullin [junior environment minister] showing we were taking from left as well as right. And when George R became public, we would at least have post-facto rationalisation for the rather roundabout way we did the reshuffle.

Friday, July 30

Needless to say, Kate Hoey was the splash in the *Mirror*. I had feared she would be a liability. She was claiming that the line she deployed was the one I had suggested she deploy. In fact I had said that if we could sort it fine, but in the end it was not for us to do. Instead she said Man United had treated their fans shabbily, no doubt as a way of getting the *Mirror* to be nice to her. Alex F called at 7.15 because we were on the way to Northolt. 'Who is this silly woman?' He said it was a dumb thing to do because it gave them licence to attack us and the FA. He said that both he and [Sir] Bobby Charlton [former player for, now director of, Manchester United] had been trying to get [chairman Martin] Edwards to pull out of Brazil but had failed.

The papers were full of the idea that the reshuffle had been a presentational disaster. I felt it was fine, that all that had happened was that the media were stupid and now were casting around to find a justification for their uselessness. TB was OK on the reshuffle, felt that the media coverage of it would be quickly forgotten and that what mattered was that we had a stronger government. John Sawers had done a good job setting up support for George as NATO Secretary General so that by the time we got to the Kosovo reconstruction summit, TB quickly squared Clinton, pinned down Schroeder and D'Alema and in a ten-minute bilateral, got Chirac lined up too. Chirac was in very jolly form. We got to Banja Luka [second largest city in Bosnia and Herzegovina] and were then transferred for a horrible flight to Sarajevo. I had a long chat with Wes Clark, who was very down. He said he had been totally shafted in a very deliberate plan. He had been told to wait for a call at 10pm. He had got the call at 10.10 whilst at a dinner. At 10.40 he had got a call from the *Washington Post* saying they had got an official leak – he was going and how did he react to that? He was amazingly relaxed on one level but clearly hurt. Clinton called him and said that he never knew, which was surely doubtful, and he was sorry. TB made a point of being very nice to Wes, who said that TB's visit to NATO had been a key moment in the campaign and in his life. He appreciated all the support we had given him but there had been a plan to get him, and they got him.

By the time we got to Kosovo we only had PA [Press Association] and Reuters on the written press side and one phone, so I got those to agree I would put out the story on George R to their agencies in their name. TB was worried we were jumping the gun re Chirac, but he had seemed pretty signed up. We flew to Skopje, then out to KFOR HQ where we were met by Jackson. TB did a not very good doorstep, though he was good with the troops. We had dinner with Jackson, Cohen and [Bernard] Kouchner [now UN special representative in Kosovo]. They were pretty gloomy about the politics because [Kosovan Prime Minister Hashim] Thaci was relatively immature. Both Jackson and Kouchner were pretty fed up with him and they were not really sure he wanted elections. TB said they needed political strategic help. The food, though cooked up and served in a tent, was superb.

Saturday, July 31

The Robertson story was going well and the sense was it would definitely happen. TB did a brief doorstep then flew by Chinook to Priština, landing at the stadium, met by Kouchner, with crowds beginning to gather on hearing TB was there. We had an OK meeting with Thaci but there was an air of petulance and also fear about him. He gave the right answers, e.g. on elections, but without a great deal of conviction. The scale of the challenge was huge – policing, rebuilding the infrastructure, let alone trying to put together a political structure people would buy into. When [President of Kosovo Ibrahim] Rugova arrived, the crowds went far more wild than they did for Thaci. TB felt that maybe they wanted a moderate, because they feared Thaci could easily slip back to KLA ways. Rugova was making all the right noises but with much more conviction, re elections, Serbs, multi-ethnicity. He had real confidence and was effusive about the UK role.

As word had spread, crowds had grown and the cops were a bit worried. As we left he was given a hero's welcome as warm and powerful as any I had ever seen. They were chanting his name: Tony, Tony, in a rhythm that got stronger as he walked through, kids waving flags and running up to him with flowers. One man went to shake his hand, took TB's hand in both of his, and wouldn't let go, just smiling and saying thank you. We then went to the military centre, which was well organised, and I introduced him to some of the Brits I had met when I came out earlier. We went out to the main piazza, where he did an off-the-cuff speech relayed to the crowd through an interpreter, and what with the translations and the cheering, it seemed to go on an awful long time, but the mood was terrific.

Jackson was totally unsentimental about Clark's dismissal. It may have been shitty but it couldn't have happened to a nicer man, he said. It had been a terrific visit, and right that TB had gone there. We got a helicopter out to Banja Luka and then flew home. TB was thinking he wouldn't put [John] Reid into MoD but who else? I slept most of the way home, called JP on landing. He was very down. He felt that TB had clipped his wings in the reshuffle. I said he had to be really careful not to be portrayed as a victim. The press would be looking for one of two things, his head dropping or snapping back at TB. He had to be a big figure again, not a wounded animal. He said he would try.

Monday, August 2

We were due to leave on the Tuesday, so I went in for a few hours, to clear the desk and get everything sorted before leaving. TB was at Chequers, first seeing GB, a few journalists, and most important, JP. After the reshuffle fallout, we were worried about him. Their meeting seemed to go fine and at lunchtime JP called me, said he had to get his act together and was there any chance of him seeing me before I went away? It was a good sign, so I suggested he come round for dinner. Typically of JP, there then followed endless phone calls both to me and to Fiona about whether it wasn't too intrusive on us the night before we left to go away. He and Pauline [JP's wife] came just after 7, with Joan [Hammell, special adviser]. He was pretty relaxed, but limping because he had a septic toe. We had been planning to order an Indian takeaway but Pauline preferred Chinese so JP, Rory and I went down to the Chinese at the end of the road and while they prepared our order, to the bemusement of passers-by, we went and sat on the railings outside, talking things over. 'I know I've got to get my act together. I'm deputy prime minister, the Labour Party gave me everything. Tony backed me when plenty of people would have been telling him not to and he gave me that job and I won't forget that. I've got five to six years left at this level of politics and I don't want to be remembered as the man who always stood for Old Labour. I want to be remembered as someone who got things done.'

When we spoke at the weekend, I had said that the press would wind him up over the summer and try to put him in his Old Labour box but he mustn't play into it. He had far more clout than sometimes I thought he realised. He should be more confident of his position, be less defensive, less sensitive, less prone to going round looking like a victim. He said a lot of it was about constantly needing to prove himself to the people he defined as snobs, the ones who took the piss out of the way he spoke. I said they didn't matter a damn. I had noticed that sometimes in interviews he was answering questions that weren't even asked, because he was seeing a hidden motive behind the question, someone out to get him, out to show he didn't cut it brain-wise. Yet he had real power, real support in the party, TB's backing and ministers who were respectfully wary of him. That was quite a strong position to be in. Because the takeaway people took so long, we must have had half an hour to forty minutes talking fairly intensely, in between the odd chat with passers-by, so by the time we got back I think we both felt the heavy stuff was done and we were able to unwind a bit. All in all, it turned out to be a nice evening and a good way to set up tomorrow's departure.

August Holiday 99

The only little drama on the way down through France was another little bout of Jackson vs Clark. TB said he continued to have confidence in Jackson, but Jackson rarely missed an opportunity to make a snide remark about Clark, and his general view was out there in the ether. TB's holiday [in Tuscany] was coming in for the usual attention, and he wasn't helped by the police shutting down a beach for eight miles either side, to local uproar. TB ordered its reopening, but it meant parts of the press now felt the holiday was generally fair game. It was virtually impossible for him to have a normal holiday. George Robertson was endorsed at NATO. Neil [Kinnock, former Labour leader] and Glenys [his wife] arrived on the Monday for what turned out to be a bit of a tense visit so I think there was part of me that just wanted to cut off from the whole political thing. Neil talked of little else, especially the European stuff. He also had a few complaints about the reshuffle, but must have known from his own days as leader that often appointments were made purely for jigsaw-fitting reasons, not because such and such a person is absolutely right for such and such a job. We had taken a newer house near Puyméras [Provence] and though it was a bit more remote than usual, the kids seemed to take to it straight away.

The *Sun* had been on asking if TB had a new marble bathroom. The press office had checked out the facts, which were that £43,000 was being spent on a rolling programme of refurbishment, £15k on the bathroom, of which £4k was marble bits. These stories were a total nightmare. Security meant only certain companies could do the work. It was a Grade 1 listed building, which meant all kinds of different considerations, but in the end everything that happened there was seen as their decision and there was something about the word marble that took it to a different problem level. Brian Bender [Cabinet Office permanent secretary] had had to authorise £8,000 beyond what [Sir Richard] Wilson thought was reasonable. I felt it was a real problem that the companies and licensing agents knew they had us over a barrel, because of security and because they knew that this kind of detail was lapped up by the press. They later did a conference call with TB and he insisted that they didn't bother me with it. But then Lance called and said TB just wanted out of it, cancel it, and if need be he would pay any cancellation costs. Jeremy said it was not beyond the realms of possibility that the PAC [Public Accounts Committee] would look into something like this, he having been a veteran of the inquiry into [former Conservative Chancellor] Norman Lamont using public money for legal fees.

TB was immediately seized of what was going on, called me, said our opponents are struggling to get us on policy so will go for lifestyle and personality, knowing that's the stuff the press prefer anyway. He said neither he nor Cherie were aware of the cost involved, he had talked to her and we should just cancel it. There was no way he was having a four-figure sum spent on a few bits of marble. TB said at one point 'Last year it was the Omagh bombing, this year it's a piece of marble. It is crazy the time and energy we have to waste because of the media we have got.' We had both been pissed off to be bothered about it, but at least we had groped our way to the right decision. Marble apart, it was fairly quiet on the work front.

Saturday August 28

Back to earth with a bit of a bang. The *Mail on Sunday* had a really nasty piece about Mo, with a 'source' claiming she would be 'left to twist in the wind'. I assured her it was nothing to do with us. I genuinely believed the bulk of anonymous quotes particularly in the Sundays were routinely made up. But Mo was very gloomy. The IRA had threatened four kids with death over local crimes and the 'ceasefire intact' line was looking a bit shaky. I put together a line defending Mo to the hilt.

Sunday, August 29

TB called and sounded pretty rested though the panning he had had in parts of the media over his holiday was a pain. He felt that the Tories were hopeless, unable to bridge divides on policy and so their only plan was to use the press to portray him as remote and out of touch. The focus on me and spin was part of that, it was about eroding trust but we just had to be robust and see it through. He had spent part of the summer trying to work out where the next wave of talent was going to come from. There were still a number of ministers in big jobs giving him real cause for concern.

Monday, August 30

There was a terrific leader in the *Sun* which said I was brilliant and should be left alone. Both the Tories and the SNP [Scottish National Party] had piled in but it was all inside page and reasonably light-hearted. The main story on our watch was Ken Maginnis calling for Mo to go and I put out a very strong line in her defence, saying TB is fully behind her. In truth, he felt she should have moved on when the going was good. I took Calum to Bristol Rovers vs Burnley and on the train down, a young black family sat opposite and told first me, and then the whole carriage, that this was the best government we had ever had.

Tuesday, August 31

Trimble was demanding a meeting and TB, Jonathan and I all felt we needed to push them back a bit. TB felt the UUs were using what was happening as an excuse not to go into further discussion with Sinn Fein. Peter Hyman [strategist and speech-writer] had done a very good note on the need to focus on the domestic agenda. It didn't bode well when TB said he wanted to go to Chequers when everyone else felt he should be in Number 10. I had a good meeting with Philip. He felt that spin was not yet a real problem, as it was confined to being a chattering-class obsession. I had thought a lot about this on holiday, and felt we had to make the nature of the modern media part of the debate about modern politics, because they were setting themselves up as a kind of alternative Opposition and becoming a barrier to any communication of political progress at all. I had several conversations with TB who was zoning in on the basic problems of definition and delivery. He had done one of his stream-of-consciousness notes, covering anything and everything but nothing in much depth, just trying to spark a conversation. Peter H said it was a classic of its kind but it had nothing to match his favourite line from a previous note – 'Foreign policy? AC speak to me.' Peter H said if that is not a chapter heading, I don't know what is.

Wednesday, September 1

We had spent part of yesterday dithering about whether and when to do an interview with *The Times* and had finally fixed it for today, Peter Riddell [*Times* assistant editor] having to delay his holiday. I left at 7.30 to travel down to Chequers with Pat McFadden and Peter Hyman. TB said he was not happy about internal processes in Number 10 and said the key to that was me freeing up more time to be strategic. He was not yet in a position to bring back Peter M, e.g. to Millbank, and felt it better to make him part of a committee under GB. We had a private session where he asked me if I thought I could cope with more work and I said only with real difficulty. Then I had to free myself up. In which case, I said, he had to stop expecting me to sort the day-to-day and be on top of the media. TB felt that the conference speech had to be about us being on the side of ordinary people and against the forces that held them back. He also felt we had to get better integrated into Gordon's agenda and modus operandi. Sally said he was kidding himself if he thought that wasn't all deliberate. On public services, he didn't yet know whether the remit of government was slowly and incrementally to manage change, or whether real, radical change could happen, but he was sure there had to be a sense of struggle and modernisation. He felt we were making progress on education but he was worried about health, transport and crime. Peter H said he had to understand that Dobson was not nearly on the same wavelength and therefore there was a constant tension in the direction of policy. I felt we had to use the perceived success in education as the foundation, first base met and now we would push with the same vigour on the other public services. Margaret McDonagh [Labour Party general secretary] warned us the party was in pretty severe financial straits. On [Ken] Livingstone [Labour MP and former leader of the Greater London Council], TB was clear that we had to block Ken [from the mayoralty of London], and make it a New vs Old Labour fight. He felt [Conservative Lord Jeffrey] Archer vs Ken risked making London a laughing stock. As we left, he asked me to turn today's discussion into a three-month forward strategy paper, one which preferably we could circulate widely. He accepted that he and GB were in different places, but they had to be brought together. He was desperate as ever for GB and Peter M to work together.

Thursday, September 2

The *Times* interview went well but thankfully they changed the first-edition headline 'My mission to spend' to 'My reforms go on'. We stuck to health on his visit to Central Middlesex Hospital which got OK coverage, but ITN talked of it being a fight back after 'the summer from hell'. It was comic stuff. I did a meeting with ten of the new ministers to go through the media operation. Charles Clarke and Brian Wilson [Scottish Office minister] were both absolutely scathing about the GICS [Government Information and Communication Service]. The more I saw of Gus Macdonald, the more I thought he would be good for JP and good for the transport brief. He was very calm and on top of things. I think they found it useful, and so did I. I was urging them to seize control of things, to find the people who have got it, and give them responsibility and don't let the machine grind them down. They also needed, some of them, to get Cabinet ministers more engaged on this front. I had lunch with Max Hastings [editor, London *Evening Standard*] at Wiltons, who was desperate for the mayoral contest not to be Livingstone vs Archer, he felt we had to put our heads above the parapet to stop it happening.

I went home to work on the strategy paper TB wanted, but Peter M came round with Reinaldo, to go over some of the ground from yesterday's meetings, but also to discuss how he was going to handle conference. He felt our problem was that although Jonathan was chief of staff, people inside and outside the government felt I was the bigger figure, and yet I didn't really have deputies that e.g. ministers felt they could go to. So I was expected to do management, strategy and brief the day-to-day. He obviously saw a role for himself in there somewhere but my sense was at the moment TB was stalling even on him going to Millbank. TB was effectively asking me to do both the job I had always done, plus the job Peter had done, standing back a little. I wasn't sure it was possible.

Friday, September 3

I got up at 6 to finish the draft of the forward strategy which I revised on the plane to Scotland and sent round to Peter M, PG and PH. It began by setting out what we wanted the government to have done by Christmas, how we wanted it viewed by the public, and how we might get there. We had worked up a strong drugs initiative for the Scotland visit but the plane crash in Glasgow[1] pretty much wiped it out. We were met by Donald [Dewar] who had a session with TB. Donald was very Donaldish, very downcast about the press, feeling there was no desire properly to explain what they were trying to do. And he also felt John Reid was doing him in. TB didn't do much to hide his irritation, felt that he had the leadership position and had to show more leadership. The whole visit felt a little bit ragged. The *Record* had splashed a total non-story about us trying to avoid Margaret Cook [ex-wife of Robin]. We had the launch of Diana nurses [for children], the by-election [in Hamilton South, the seat vacated by George Robertson], a drugs seminar, a dodgy walkabout and then back to Edinburgh.

What was interesting though was that when TB sat down with the Scottish editors, there was no real heat in any of the arguments they put against the parliament. It reinforced my view that if Donald and co could be more strategic and proactive, there would be a lot more buy-in for what they were doing. TB did an interview with Andrew Rawnsley [*Observer* columnist] back at the Caledonian Hotel, which was fine, very strong on the family, but it lacked an obvious story. The focus was on moral purpose after the story about a twelve-year-old mother [in Rotherham, South Yorkshire], but TB was worried that without policy, it was just a bit of a whinge. But the grit was in the fact councils were not using [youth] curfew orders, antisocial behaviour orders, and we intended to send reminders to local authorities and police. We got little on the news out of the visit apart from his clip on the plane crash. Over dinner, he said we had a short period in which to make a mark and make real change, and we had to go for it. He was also getting worried re 'Haguery' which had become our shorthand for the possibility of Hague being replaced. He could not believe that they would go for [Shadow Home Secretary Ann] Widdecombe but he did believe there may come a point when they decided the only way to cut into the majority was to get rid of him, and anyone would do.

[1] A twelve-seater Cessna aircraft had crashed and burned in a field shortly after taking off from Glasgow airport. The pilot and seven passengers were killed.

Saturday, September 4

I got very little sleep because it was so hot still. I checked on the *Observer* who were totally overdoing the curfew stuff, saying TB was calling for a national curfew, which we got changed later to him calling on councils to use them on antisocial teenagers. There was a lot of interest re George Mitchell [commencing a review of the Northern Ireland peace process] on Monday and Chris Patten [delivering his report on policing in Northern Ireland] and Mitchell would ensure it was a big Northern Ireland week but we really had to try to stay focused on the domestic policy issues. Joe Lennon and I agreed we should try to stay out of it and see whether we couldn't keep the meeting with Bertie on Monday a secret. Once the *Observer* stuff on moral purpose was up and running, I felt we had to make the most of it so I called Jack Straw to get him engaged. TB had headed up to Balmoral and was now at the Braemar Games with some of the papers saying he had 'muscled in'. Stories on him and the Royals were clearly going to be part of the effort to make him look presidential, disrespectful, out of touch.

Sunday, September 5

Jack was out there expressing his 'irritation' at councils and police not using powers they had been given. He was keen to take on civil liberties too. [New Liberal Democrat leader Charles] Kennedy attacked TB, saying we should leave the moralising to the bishops. So we got Jack out on that as well, saying the Libs put their head in the sand on the big questions. The interview was a good example of how talking points as much as policy could generate coverage and debate. TB was a bit worried that we were going to get into a Back to Basics[1] problem, but I felt it was clear enough what we were talking about, and Jack was doing a good job, though Rawnsley had overwritten it to a fair degree.

Nick Soames called, worried about [Conservative MP and mutual friend] Alan Clark's health. When I mentioned TB was up north, he said there would be civil war in Scotland if we banned hunting. 'Why are you picking these fights? Tony's great strength is that he makes change without fighting anybody. Don't get a fight going on this.' He said he had been out defending me in the little flurry last weekend. He said somebody had asked him if I was more powerful

[1] Back to Basics, a 1993 campaign by the Major government aimed at seizing the moral high ground by focusing on law and order and responsible behaviour, had been almost immediately undermined by a string of sex and sleaze scandals involving various Conservative politicians.

than Charles Powell [former adviser to prime ministers Thatcher and Major] had been. He said it was like asking if the Pope was more powerful than the parish priest, and went off on one about some of Thatcher's people. He was never less than colourful. I didn't realise that John Williams [deputy head of news, Foreign Office] had briefed up Robin's euro speech in Japan. When I queried it on Monday he said it came from the TB/RC meeting last week. Needless to say, GB was livid and convinced it was a plan to throw his plans off course. At the end of the weekend, I realised I hadn't spoken to a single journalist.

Monday, September 6

There were mixed feelings in the office about the moral-purpose interview but I felt we had successfully got up a theme which would strike a chord with some of the people we had been becoming detached from. We were certainly back on domestic policy. I had a little brainstorm with Godric [Smith] and we worked up a plan on the CSA [Child Support Agency] tracking teenage fathers once they were earning. The *Standard* splashed on it, the lunchtimes ran it. I felt the eleven o'clock was how a lobby briefing ought to be – it was about real-people issues, policy changes and where they fitted in an overall strategy. I was also talking round the office about whether I could pull out of doing the briefings.

I had a meeting with Keith Hellawell [former senior police officer now Labour-appointed 'Drug Czar'], who complained that the system was keeping him in his box, that he had very little freedom, that any ideas were just sat on. Jack Cunningham said he was a nightmare, a real egomaniac whose real interest was self-promotion. It had a very bad feeling to it. Bill Clare [press officer seconded from FCO] had told me during the holiday he was leaving and now came to tell me he was going to work for Liam Fox [Shadow Health Secretary] at Tory Central Office. 'Fuck off then,' I said, but actually made a big joke of it, and wished him well. But during the day, several colleagues were getting very angry about it, the fact he had the grids going into the future, some even wondering whether he had been a plant. I wrote to Richard Wilson and John Kerr just to make sure Bill got the message about confidentiality, etc.

I had a meeting with GB and his team on the WFTC [Working Families Tax Credit] campaign which we were trying to get up tomorrow. I was keen for it to play into the rights and responsibilities agenda, but GB was very stuck on it being about working families and targeting children raised in poverty. Hilary [Coffman] was setting up the Richard and Judy [Richard Madeley and Judy Finnigan, presenters of ITV chat show *This Morning*] interview [with TB and GB] tomorrow. It was bound to be attacked by the papers but their viewers were a prime target for a campaign that was costing quite a lot of money. We had a separate session, TB, GB, Ed Miliband [Treasury special adviser] and I, to go over the difficulties we were having managing the relationship between party and government. Ministers were less engaged politically and I felt there must be structural changes to make but GB felt it was much more about the way we presented the government thematically. He was also still of the view that we must hold back on presenting the government as an economic success story. TB saw Patten about his report on policing with Mo who was looking pretty stressed out. He had done a really serious piece of work but as he was also giving it to the Irish and to Trimble today the chances are it would get into the press. There wasn't much we could do about that. But I felt uncomfortable, as I think did he, not really being in charge of how this thing landed.

Tuesday, September 7

We were still generating pretty decent coverage on the moral-purpose debate. TB wanted to write a piece explaining what he meant and positioning it so that it didn't become Back to Basics, and I got Andrew Adonis [policy adviser] to draft. TB was worried about East Timor and keen that we do something.[1] WFTC was going fine. GB did *Today*, hit all the buttons, though he couldn't quite bring himself to agree with Robin on the benefits of the euro to euroland economies. They did a joint visit and doorstep which went fine. And then to Richard and Judy. Hilary and Ed Miliband had done a good job laying the ground and the interview went fine. GB was the more animated of the two of them, and better on the detail. As an interview, it was strong. Richard and Judy seemed to have a bit of a spat at the end because Richard asked GB when he was going to get married.

Alan Clark's death was announced. He had died on Sunday and the family had buried him without announcing it. [Nicholas] Soames called, said he probably just could not face coming back and being seen as old and crippled so 'He turned his face to the wall'. Piers [Morgan, editor] asked me to write a piece for the *Mirror* which I did, though I didn't have that much time and I wasn't totally happy with

[1] Widespread violence had broken out in East Timor after a referendum result in favour of independence from Indonesia. Anti-independence militants attacked civilians and some 1,400 people died. An Australian-led UN peacekeeping force would be deployed to end the violence.

it. His death took over from GB as the main political story. It also started lots of speculation about a [by-election] comeback for [former Conservative Cabinet minister Michael] Portillo. Peter M felt Portillo would be a liability for them, extreme and divisive, whereas I felt a reinvented Portillo would give them freshness, get some of the press moving back to them, e.g. the *Sun* leader tonight urging him to go for it. I got home reasonably early, but for the second night running I had a huge row with Fiona. I called Jane [Clark] to chat about Alan.

Wednesday, September 8

We had a longer than usual office meeting, TB was quiet, didn't seem confident. He was warning against creating too many enemies. He was banging on at me again about freeing up time. It was a deeply unsatisfying meeting, unstructured, no clear purpose. Peter M suddenly launched into a big defence of fox hunting. Charlie [Falconer, responsible for the Millennium Dome] went through the marketing strategy for the Dome, but didn't sound convinced. Afterwards I had a brainstorm with Peter M, Philip G and Peter Hyman re TB's conference speech. As per my note, I thought the key to the speech and to the next few months was for the government in general and TB in particular to be seen to be in a struggle against the forces that held people back.

I had sent the note to GB for his views and went over to the Treasury to discuss. He said he agreed with it, but he warned that it meant taking on a lot of people, which risked creating a lot of enemies, and he was not sure how we did that successfully. He felt we should plan these challenges one by one, and bind in the Cabinet. He also felt our approach was too presidential, that too much of the focus was on TB. He was very good on one level, and unlike most of them at least thought strategically, but he could also be maddening, fixing on one point that wasn't that important and going on and on about it. He was still going on about Cook and [David] Blunkett [Education and Employment Secretary] doing what he called 'freelance initiatives'. He still didn't want to move on the economy, felt it was premature, not least with interest rates up today. Jonathan and Anji joined us later to discuss structures. We basically wanted GB to take more of the load day to day, and to improve links into the political operation. He said we needed a government committee which because of the people on it would effectively be a party committee too, but which civil servants were able to attend and service. I said I felt Wilson would go crazy at that, but he was not so sure. It is simply about ensuring the party knows what the government is doing, and nobody

September '99: Brown says too much focus on Blair

is asking civil servants to do things for the party. He was going through one of his open, engaged and engaging phases. He said he was OK with Peter M being involved, and with Peter chairing election planning. We agreed to try to set up those structures, though I felt it could be difficult. But he was clearly wanting to be more involved, saying he would give whatever help he could, and we had to seize that. TB called after Poland vs England [Euro 2000 qualifier, 0–0], still worried about Haguery but felt Portillo was not an easy option for them either. Julian called about 11 to say that Portillo had admitted homosexuality in the past in an interview with *The Times*. He had done the interview for publication at the time of their conference but they had brought it forward. It was clearly part of a strategy and the initial reaction suggested it may work. Both TB and I felt instinctively that it wouldn't.

Thursday, September 9

TB seemed a bit lost at the moment. He said he had hated yesterday's meeting. It was too frivolous and not structured enough. I said it was up to him to drive those meetings. I had found the whole thing depressing and a waste of time. It was just a random group of people throwing in random points of view on random subjects. He said I seemed very down on him and I said no, but I found these circular conversations in meetings a real waste of time. We went for a walk in the garden and he admitted he had lost confidence for some reason, thought he would regain it with the break, but he hadn't. He felt there was something missing in the operation and that we would benefit if we could find the right outsider with a big brain. I felt what we lacked was people able to implement change, grip and drive the system.

Richard Wilson came to see me, very exercised re Bill Clare, felt it was wrong and that he had let the side down and he would be reminding him of his duty of confidentiality. He said permanent secretaries were convinced that we were briefing against the Civil Service and that TB's 'scars on my back' crack [speech to venture capitalists in July] had caused real problems across the public service. He wanted to get the Civil Service reform plan seen as his, rather than TB's. And he felt he had a good story to tell. I recommended he did a big interview on it, and then have discrete campaigns running on the main areas of reform, and possibly at some point get cameras in to show him doing a presentation to TB on change. Philip called from Hamilton [by-election] having done a few groups and said TB was not popular there but we would win.

Friday, September 10

Portillo was definitely destabilising TB. He said that if he came in there was a good chance we would be facing him at the election, that Hague would just do a deal because deep down he must know he was not cutting it with the public. He said we had to make sure Portillo didn't succeed in reinventing himself and was stuck out on the right wing. He was sounding very unconfident and Philip was convinced that Peter M was destabilising him by constantly undermining the people around him. I had certainly been on the receiving end of Peter on Jonathan, as no doubt was TB, and he wasn't averse to giving not wholly favourable assessments of me, even though ultimately he basically wanted us to work together.

I went in late and took quite a useful meeting on spin. Philip and I both felt it was becoming a real problem, with potential to affect the public, rather than just a media thing, but I wasn't sure how we addressed it without stopping operating effectively. Peter M said I must not stop doing the things that need to be done to get a grip of the government machine and put our case effectively and aggressively, because not to do so would be to gift a win to the Tories and to the press. They were running a campaign to stop me from being effective and we had to see it off. Godric and Ian Austin felt that the basic problem lay in over-claiming, when we should be under-claiming and over-delivering. GB was very much now wanting to understate economic success until others started to claim it for us. Hilary felt I made it too obvious in briefings that I despised the vast bulk of journalists. She felt I was perfectly capable of charming them and ought to do so.

Saturday, September 11

The Times had a huge story on an old spy, Melita Norwood.[1] Nobody at the Home Office had alerted us and it was running as Jack ruling out prosecution, or that she should be interviewed. I spoke to TB, who felt we should just let it go, and to Jack, who put out a statement denying that he had said don't prosecute as it wasn't his decision. Widdecombe was enjoying something close to a free hit.

---

[1] It had become publicly known that Melita Norwood, a retired British civil servant, had for years been supplying the KGB with secret information on metallurgy research and, in 1945, schematics of the atomic bomb. The authorities had known of her activities for some time, but had considered her prosecution might compromise other investigations.

Sunday, September 12

TB called a couple of times to discuss both TUC [Trades Union Congress] and conference speeches. He had done a note on the basic argument, and I felt we were getting there. It was about doing what was necessary to take down the barriers that held people back. He spoke to Robin and they agreed we should suspend arms sales to Indonesia re East Timor. Jack called me and said he had had no idea the *Times* story on the spy was coming until the paper was out. It was yet another example of the general operation simply not being up to scratch at weekends. Unless TB and/or I really leapt on these things, they seemed to turn from problems into disasters.

Monday, September 13

Wall-to-wall spies. Jack was due to see [Sir] Stephen Lander [director general of the Security Service] to get a report. Word came out that ministers in the last government weren't told. Jack only knew a few months ago, or so we were saying. But then, after I told the lobby that the first TB knew was as *The Times* published it, Wilson sent through a paper which showed 1. TB and RC were made aware of the book project [*The Mitrokhin Archive*] just after the general election, and 2. a note was sent through to us in Castle Buildings [Stormont] during the five-day marathon. Both Jonathan and I could only vaguely remember a secret paper but neither of us recalled reading it. TB emphasised that the only question that mattered was whether to prosecute Norwood and we were guided by the fact we were told she could not be prosecuted. I didn't prepare well enough for the eleven o'clock, hadn't taken the story seriously enough over the weekend, and stumbled into it. Poor. I told Godric I felt like the Alan Shearer [Newcastle United and England footballer] of the government, past his best, but with no clear replacement.

I left for the Horticultural Hall for a supposedly special four-hour session with heads of information. I did my opening spiel, Philip did a polling presentation, then four of them did presentations. It was OK up to a point but most of them really didn't get it. John Kingman [Treasury] was the best, gave a very good account of their slow burn strategy, but was also good on our weaknesses. Philip felt I was pretty tough on them, but he had no idea how much effort I had already put in with them. The overriding theme that came up was that we did better by under-claiming, and also that the more events were planned with the centre, usually the bigger hit they got. I hoped some good came of it, but I doubted it. It did coalesce in my own mind the need for downspin.

Jack's statement [on the Melita Norwood case] was hopeless, left too many questions unanswered and we had had to redraft it. It didn't go terribly well. TB and CB were doing a picture for the Christmas card with Terry O'Neill [celebrity photographer] and Carole Caplin [friend and adviser to CB] was there causing trouble, along with some twat who wanted to create a digital picture of them on the Dome. Fiona was telling Carole to stop trying to tell Terry what to do, and Cherie was upset about that. I told TB I found it unfathomable that she still had anything to do with her. He said she did lots of good for Cherie. He was finally getting worried about Melita. It was now being defined as something of a shambles and we had to get it back on track. The press would now be chundering on endlessly about it, with large dollops of hindsight, as if we hadn't had enough to focus on in Northern Ireland.

Philip said the last few groups had been dire. In one of them the only good thing that anyone could remember about the government was TB on Diana. PG said to TB and me that if we went to one of his groups at the moment, we would probably kill ourselves.

Tuesday, September 14

TB worked all morning on the TUC speech which he basically wrote from scratch. He felt that since the holiday the combination of the row over moral purpose and his reference to a new economy had got us back with some domestic traction. The papers were grim on spies. I went to see Richard Wilson and said there had to be a way of bringing MI5 and MI6 media operations more into the centre. They couldn't handle these things in isolation. He accepted that they operated in a different way, that the media was largely alien and it meant they weren't at their best when a media frenzy blew up. My bottom line was that ministers were kept in the dark and that what was potentially a perfectly good story – the coup of uncovering a spy – was turned into a PR disaster that was now pretty much non-recoverable. John Sawers said he had no recollection whatever of showing a memo to TB in Northern Ireland, and TB had no recollection of seeing it. Looking at it again, John Sawers said there was no reason for him to see it because it didn't require a decision.

We set off by train for Brighton and with the Poet Laureate due there later [Andrew Motion had written a poem for the TUC called 'In a Perfect World'], I drafted a few limericks and poems for TB to try, but they didn't really work. The speech went reasonably well, if a bit dull and with the audience flat, but TB then went off script and

September '99: Carole Caplin causing trouble

was good. The press liked it. Steve Evans [BBC reporter] told me he thought it was brilliant and for a moment or two I assumed he was taking the piss, but actually even the old hands round the press room had to acknowledge it had been pretty powerful. TB saw the main brothers [leading trade unionists] and we then did a reception. Bill Morris [general secretary, Transport and General Workers' Union] was saying TB had said we were going to loosen the purse strings – which he hadn't, and which we won't. Philip called from Milton Keynes, said he had done two very good groups. The news was fine, a bit of conflict and drama in the speech and a sense that we were into the second half of the first term and moving towards a general election. TB had found the argument again but I was still feeling a bit like Shearer. The poem was a truly dreadful idea.[1]

Wednesday, September 15

Things were getting very tricky re East Timor. The issue, the arms question, and its relation to an ethical foreign policy all a bit of a mess. But my first problem of the day was a pretty extraordinary item in the *Guardian* diary to the effect that I had said I had been having an affair with [murdered TV presenter] Jill Dando. I spoke to [*Guardian* editor Alan] Rusbridger to demand letter space. Lots of people were saying I could easily sue and win. I didn't particularly want to but I got Roy [Greenslade, *Guardian* media commentator] to warn Rusbridger I might. What was depressing though was that pretty much nothing I said or did might not end up in the press, usually distorted to suit the agenda of those writing it.

I left a bit later for Chequers where he was chairing the pre-conference Cabinet meeting. Only TB and GB really made contributions of any strategic worth. There was one very funny moment when TB was drinking from a Monty Python mug and said he had got it from John Cleese [Monty Python comedian]. Ann Taylor asked who was the dead parrot, and Nick Brown [agriculture minister] said 'That's agriculture.' If there was one point coming through the majority, it was the need for a more collegiate approach. JP said TB's speech yesterday went down well and we had to get over more sense of what we had achieved and why. Margaret B said she thought we weren't good at post-legislative enquiry and analysis. Jack C said people were too departmentalised. Chris Smith [Culture Secretary] talked of the levels of ignorance amongst the public at what we were

[1] Tony Blair had delivered a poem, written by Campbell, to play along with the presence of the Poet Laureate at the TUC.

doing. Alistair Darling defined the public as content but not enthusiastic. George R started by saying, to much nervous laughter, that he was in the luxurious position of being able to say with certainty that it was his last Cabinet meeting. He felt we should show more confidence and be more collective. He had a tear in his eye when Tony said he was one of the nicest and most decent people he had ever worked with.

Robin ran through the facts and figures on poverty and unemployment and said 'There is a real Old Labour speech in me struggling to get out.' Straw said 'Do you want some pills?' GB came in at the end and simply made bigger points – about how we got back on the side of hard-working families, how we communicated steady change, what was actually happening in the economy and how we turned that to the best political advantage, how we prepared ourselves if they tried to shift to so-called compassionate conservatism. At lunch, I sat next to Jack Straw who said he thought it was a real problem that I was being built up in the way that I was. But like me, he wasn't exactly full of ideas about how to deal with it. Richard Wilson did a presentation on his great Civil Service reform plans but in the discussion, apart from Jack C, people really pulled punches. Meanwhile we were having to deal with Nick Raynsford who had told the *Standard* he was going to launch [a London mayoral campaign] tomorrow and do an interview with them today, but JP was adamant that he couldn't stay as a London minister whilst also running to be mayoral candidate. I called Nick and, with some difficulty, persuaded him to wait till [Jeffrey] Archer was selected, do it then, present himself as the serious candidate against Archer as a joke. He was very reluctant but agreed. TB was more confident we had the argument right for the conference speech but we needed really strong lines and that was what I needed to work on.

Thursday, September 16

GB was doing a speech in New York, pretty upbeat. He had a good line in his *Times* interview – we have never had it so prudent. The *Mail* ran a page of poems on the government. Peter H and I were working on the conference speech when TB phoned and asked us to go down to Chequers for lunch. He had taken his own outline and written dozens of pages of draft material, some of it pretty good. We were all being drawn to the line about the forces of conservatism, which not only gave the grit and edge we were looking for, but also was a good vehicle for on-your-side language and message. His main argument was that we existed to give everyone the chance to fulfil their true potential, and the forces of conservatism existed to prevent that happening. They had to be taken on and defeated. As David M said, we needed policy specifics to bring it alive, but that could be done.

TB was even being attracted, though not for long, to the idea of taking away titles in the Lords. He had been reading about [former Labour Prime Minister Harold] Wilson's government and said that by comparison, ours was amazingly united. Those people just could not stand each other. He said one thing Wilson always did well was have single lines to sum up whole speeches, and we needed that. I said we were taking on the forces of conservatism so that power, wealth and opportunity go to the many and not just the few. That felt pretty strong. It also allowed us to fight back better against the right-wing commentariat who still basically dominated the media. He was very up today, felt that moral purpose and new economy were strong ground for us, and his off-the-cuff bit at the TUC speech had got his confidence coming back. It was a useful meeting and we left with plenty more material to work on. He agreed that we should do the first picture of him in glasses for *Woman's Own*.[1]

Friday, September 17

I worked on the speech all day, though not as well as yesterday. Between us, though, we had just about got together a complete draft. TB was still basically honing the argument while Peter H and I were now just trying to strengthen the lines. Forces of conservatism allowed us to go into a lot of policy areas with a coherent theme. We were getting into bother on Indonesia. The *Sunday Times* were on to the story of three Hawks [combat aircraft] waiting at Bangkok airport to go to Jakarta, and there was a lot of buck-passing between MoD, FCO and DTI. *Channel 4 News* did a big number on landmines for sale at a British defence event. There was a real desire to do over anything that conflicted with the so-called ethical foreign policy.

Saturday, September 18

I tried to work on the speech but I was word blind, and just couldn't get going. Despite Burnley winning 3-0 [against Colchester United] to go top of the league, I was suddenly feeling depressed, unable to engage, and just went to bed.

[1] 46-year-old Blair, having been diagnosed as long-sighted, had begun to wear glasses. He later told *Woman's Own* 'I have been feeling self-conscious just because it's a change. The trouble is you're in the public eye and all your changes have to be made in public.'

Sunday, September 19

Without knowing why, I had got into a real deep gloom, and we were due to go out to [director] Hugh Hudson's film premiere [of *My Life So Far*], and lunch with him and the Kinnocks later. I really didn't feel like it. I could never work out whether these moods were cyclical, caused by tiredness, or just the way things were, but I was glad to get out of there.

Monday, September 20

The serialisation of [journalist Peter] Oborne's book on me started in the *Express*, and the day started with Fiona in tears because the *Mail* spoiler by Geoffrey Levy was very unpleasant, not just about me, as expected, but her and the kids. It also said that Dad died when I was ten. For once, we had them absolutely bang to rights. I sent over a letter to [*Mail* editor Paul] Dacre who replied in the most grovelling fashion imaginable, and when I spoke to him said he felt dreadful, terrible mistake, blah blah blah. He agreed to run the apology I drafted word for word, with a cheque for the kids' school.

Tuesday, September 21

The *Mail* ran the apology word for word. TB was at the NEC [National Executive Committee of the Labour Party] when news came through that [Cabinet Office minister] Ian McCartney's son [Hugh] had been found dead [from a heroin overdose]. TB spoke to him, then I did and he was in a pretty bad way. We agreed, after speaking to his ex-wife, to put out a short statement including an appeal for privacy, which needless to say fell on deaf ears. He called at one point to say his parents were being harassed by the *Mail* who were refusing to go until they had a picture. When TB got back, he did the *Mirror* interview with Piers Morgan and Paul Routledge [columnist], who ended up asking for TB's autograph for his grandchildren. TB was fine on the big picture, but a bit vague and waffly on some of the stuff I tried to brief him on, e.g. Diana, FA Cup – where he talked total rubbish. He backed the idea of a Diana memorial, which GB had been trying to shut down for ages. So when Piers went out and the first person he bumped into was GB and he told him what TB had said, GB came in with steam coming out of his ears. 'You can't do this,' he said to Tony. I'm afraid he has, I said. He said the [royal] family didn't really want it. But it was too late, and it was surely the right thing to do anyway.

I got together with Ian Austin to agree a line to give to Piers that it was a joint TB/GB effort rather than TB bouncing GB. There were plenty of stories in the interview, though whether it would change the *Mirror*'s general approach, I had my doubts. Piers was basically a Tory, but more relevant he saw politics as just another form of showbiz or entertainment. We had a meeting with GB who, what with the Libs committing themselves to more and more spending, was all the more keen that we sit tight for a while longer. We needed to maintain very tough messages on the economy and avoid the argument developing that it was all a choice between tax cuts and spending. Jeremy [Heywood] said that because of the underspend on welfare, there was the possibility of TB announcing we had freed up £1bn we could put to schools and hospitals. GB was of course opposed to the idea. TB was also asking whether there was any other argument currently in the speech that would overpower forces of conservatism. Not really. Someone was clearly undermining his confidence in it, but the basic argument was strong, and terrific for a progressive speech. I took Peter Hyman home for dinner and we worked till gone midnight on the forces of conservatism section of the conference speech.

Wednesday, September 22

Ian McCartney called in tears after identifying Hugh's body and also went through some of the stuff he and his family have had to endure with the press. I drafted for him a letter to [Press Complaints Commission chairman Lord] Wakeham highlighting some of the incidents and asking what the rights of his family were. It was a pretty dreadful business, added to which there were the editorials saying it was time to act on drugs. JP called me, said Ian was really in a bad way, blaming himself. Ian called, several times during the day, getting really worked up about the press. The Diana memorial went OK, and the *Sun* picked up and splashed in later editions. Piers and I negotiated different Man United words for Friday's paper because the real words were dreadful. I had a stack of calls with TB, a bit all over the place because he was still wrestling with the central argument. We had forces of conservatism and we had nothing really to overwhelm it, or even balance it, on the other side. He thought maybe bonds of connection as a way of talking about community and society, but it was weak. Equality was what he meant, but it was something politicians had been saying forever. Maybe equal worth was better. PH and I worked on a section on belief and conviction, which had a hint of God in it. By the end of the day, the sections on conviction, forces of conservatism and the potential of children were strong. We definitely had the makings of a decent speech and schedule-wise we were definitely ahead of ourselves.

Philip called, having done some groups in Oxford, said the cynicism was dreadful beyond belief and the kind of concepts we were talking about were way over their heads. Peter Oborne had got on to my breakdown in the serialisation and I thought was quite perceptive. I talked to Kim Fletcher [journalist] who was reviewing the book and said Oborne was clearly a bit in love with me. In one of TB's seemingly endless circular conversations during the day, I told him the book was saying that he had left me to deal directly with Clinton over Kosovo. He said he found it incredible how they just made things up the whole time. Fiona and I were barely speaking and she was going on about having to hold everything together while I just worried about work and nothing else.

Thursday, September 23

Alex [Ferguson] called, said I must be feeling stripped bare by the Oborne serialisation and we had a good whinge about the press. He said [David] Beckham [Manchester United and England footballer] was losing the plot, his wife pushing him around, and he was about to fine him for being away on Monday at some fashion event. Peter H and I were working on a section for the speech about TB, his worries, how HE had his potential liberated. I tried it out on Philip, Sally M, Anji, who all thought it worked. TB asked me to go down to Chequers in the evening but as I left, at 7pm, Godric mentioned *The Times* had a story about the [London] Oratory [school attended by Euan and Nicholas Blair] appealing for cash from parents. Alarm bells rang, but not loudly enough and it was only when I got to Chequers and saw the letter – which Andrew Adonis had had for thirty-six hours – that I realised just how awful it was. [Oratory headteacher John] McIntosh was basically saying that government policy had put the school's success at risk and parents had to pay a voluntary levy. TB was livid. It meant that instead of working on the speech we were having to spend the next few hours sorting this. TB didn't want me to speak to McIntosh, rightly thinking I would lose it with him. We got Godric to tell him that we would have to respond if he went up and did interviews. TB said if he had known this would be as bad as it was turning out to be, he would never have sent the children there. It was going to make it harder to do the equality stuff in the speech.

Over dinner, we went through the speech, which was coming on. We also discussed GB and whether he would make a good prime minister. TB said he believed he was one of the top five politicians this century, that he was a Lloyd George figure, had massive qualities but was flawed and he worried whether the flaws would harm his judgement. His biggest worry was whether his general take on the world – that you were either for him or against him – would lead him to promote bad people at the expense of good. Charlie Whelan [Brown's former spokesman] had done an interview saying TB had apologised to GB re psychological flaws. TB said to me he had never done that because although he believed somebody did say something that made them feel justified in running that story, he was not prepared to say as much to GB. I think TB was as surprised as I was about just how much publicity these books about me were getting, and it was all a bit too much. The speech was definitely getting there, though as ever we couldn't quite work out how to get the policy bits in there. On the reshuffle, we were thinking of doing it during the Tory conference week. Godric couldn't get hold of McIntosh and none of us could find Adonis, who had failed to see what a big story this would be. McIntosh was a total menace.

Friday, September 24

I didn't sleep well. I got to bed about 1 and was up before 6. The *Guardian* splashed on Whelan re psychological flaws. The *Indy* page 1 said I removed the word socialist from next week's PPB [party political broadcast]. Oborne was now in the *Telegraph* on me courting Murdoch and had a front-cover piece in the *Spectator* about me and the Tories. I was getting far too much publicity. The Oratory was going big and running on the broadcasts, added to which he [McIntosh] had put the letter on the internet. TB said he could happily kill him, wrote a letter saying he thought the way he did it was a disgrace which showed no regard whatever for the likely impact on the boys. We won the Hamilton and Wigan by-elections, though the results weren't brilliant.[1] TB did an interview with Mike White and Polly Toynbee for the *Guardian*. I did the Sundays, who didn't really bite on economic message and instead they tried to get something going about whether TB would stay through the next parliament, obviously trying to work up some kind of phony row with GB.

Briefing TB I mentioned a story that was running about the menopause and he suddenly looked pained and said Cherie might be

[1] The Wigan by-election had been caused by the death from liver cancer of Labour MP Roger Stott, who had achieved a 22,643 majority in 1997. His successor, Neil Turner, was elected with a 6,729 majority on a much lower turnout. In Hamilton South, Labour's Bill Tynan won the seat vacated by George Robertson by 556 votes after a strong campaign by SNP candidate Annabelle Ewing.

pregnant. I laughed out loud, then said I could not imagine having a baby at my age, let alone his. Added to which, there would be the whole business of the media management of it, wanting to know every detail, and promulgating theories as to why, what significance, etc. It would also make the planning of trips involving Cherie even crazier. Nobody can complain you don't make news, I said. We worked some more on the speech, and felt the attempts to run the equality argument alongside forces of conservatism was cluttering it up. We headed back to Number 10 for a meeting with the Policy Unit. The local council [Labour-run Hammersmith and Fulham] had got involved in the Oratory situation, saying the school had got a good deal and the sense was definitely out there that McIntosh was politically motivated.

Saturday, September 25

There was yet another profile of me, this time by Steve Crawshaw in the *Independent*, plus the Oborne reviews were beginning and it was all getting ridiculous. The main story out of my briefing yesterday was a bit of a disaster. I knew from the first question what the game was, had danced around it a bit but of course it was hard not to say that TB would fight the next election and stay the whole term if elected. But they were writing it up as TB slapping down GB which in turn was being seen as a reaction to the Whelan claims. GB was bound to think it was deliberate, which it wasn't, but it meant that the focus we had planned was lost. I went into the office first thing, then up to see TB.

He was now sure Cherie was pregnant. They worked out it happened at Balmoral. A royal baby. He said he felt a mix of pleasure and horror. Thank God I'm a Christian, he said. It allows me to assume there must be a reason. We discussed it on the train. At the moment, TB, CB, Fiona and I were the only people who knew, and I was winding them up as to how much money we could make by tipping off the press. There was a part of it that was just funny, but it was also clearly worrying him. Once we got to the hotel, any time the two of us were together, he would just want to talk about it, what impact it was going to have.

Once we had arrived at Bournemouth, we had a session on the speech and agreed to restructure it. We had a very good laugh when we imagined what it would be like to go out and deliver a truth speech – Conference, Gordon and Peter really do hate each other. It's true that Robin never stops diddling. Philip did a couple of groups down there and reckoned our problem was that we had this great majority and a useless Opposition and yet we appeared to be struggling to make change happen quickly. TB was doing the rounds [conference receptions] while PH and I were honing the speech. The Sundays were bad and it was all being built up around TB/GB and they twisted my briefing both to make it look like TB was taking power for granted, and also that it was putting Gordon in his place.

Sunday, September 26

The Sundays were full of my briefing and TB standing for a full term. I said we should bring forward the announcement planned for the speech re new laws on drugs, do it today, get it running on the bulletins, otherwise they would feel obliged to do this nonsense. TB did clips, saying the fight on drugs would be at the heart of the Queen's Speech. And on GB, he went into overdrive, said the papers were a joke, GB was terrific and would make a great prime minister. The whole operation went pretty well. TB/GB had been leading the news with Nick Jones just peddling the Sunday papers' line but that quickly went down the bulletins and drugs came up. Then later, at the Q&A, TB did a very tough message on spending. According to Ian Austin, GB was not too vexed about the briefing but Jonathan listened in to a GB/TB call and said he sounded very fed up. A combination of the Oborne reviews, the Whelan documentary [Channel 4's *Confessions of a Spin Doctor*] and McIntosh calling me a pig meant there was loads more in the press about me, far too much. My mum had an interesting take, felt it was all about trying to unnerve TB about me, make him resent the idea he wasn't really in control, and he would have to be a very big man to ignore it all.

Monday, September 27–Wednesday, September 29

Writing this at the end of a speech process which in the end seemed to work. It was touch and go. Philip captured the lowest point around 2am Tuesday when he did a note which began 'This speech has seriously lost the plot. The main argument is nowhere. What has happened?' What had happened, as ever, was that we had to go through the awful crisis of confidence that TB seems to need to go through before he can make a great speech. We had done it every year but this time, partly because he was struggling to settle on the central argument, and partly because I was struggling to find the words, it was worse than ever. We had spent two days with him repeatedly saying 'What is the argument? What is the main political point?'

We sat down and wrote out different versions, ending up where we started with the idea that Britain had been held back by forces of conservatism which had to be overwhelmed by modernisation and reform to liberate the potential of all the people. Only a modernised Labour Party could do that, because we believed in it, believed in the equal worth of all people and had found our voice and our mission. Peter H and I worked relentlessly trying to get him to take more colour in the speech and be more personal. But it was hard. He didn't like exposing himself too much, didn't like the personal sections which everybody else thought made the speech come alive. Monday had felt like a very long day, full of what seemed like the same conversation again and again. The drugs story had gone well though the *Mail* in particular was poisonous about the whole TB/GB business.

TB went over for the Gordon speech which went well, really well, and when TB came back he was totally discombobulated. I had been watching it with [David] Miliband and though both of us thought it was OK, neither of us thought it brilliant, so either there was an effect in the hall that didn't come over on TV, or this was just TB using everything and anything to wind himself up further to get him and the rest of us to dig deep and do better. He said it was the best conference speech by someone other than a leader he had ever seen. His worry now was that if we didn't do something special, the TB/GB mischief could get out of hand. There were also continuing arguments, e.g. GB refusing to let us say we would be switching spending from the DSS [Department of Social Security] budget to schools and hospitals. I had never really seen him like this. It wasn't quite panic. It was more like he was trying to convince himself it had been a great speech as a way of putting on pressure, almost like he wanted a moment of panic. He said the pressure on him had been building since the non-reshuffle.

He had all this to deal with and also the business of the pregnancy. Cherie and Fiona had gone back to London quietly so that she could have a proper pregnancy test, even though she knew in her heart there was no need. On Tuesday morning, Fiona called as they travelled back down and said the answer was yes. At this stage, only the four of us in Bournemouth knew though TB kept dropping hints, enough for both Sally and Anji to ask me if something was going on. For example at one point, when we were going through the section on childcare, he said he understood about children and then just stared into the middle distance. At times, my jokes about royal babies cheered him up, at other times he was saying he couldn't believe this had happened, added to which Cherie was actually a bit worried about the whole thing, though Fiona said the doctor had been pretty reassuring. What I dreaded was having to deal with all the guff that would come with it. The media would have a field day.

Monday and Tuesday the speech process was the usual, him working on it whenever he could, constantly saying he didn't have enough time, PH and I working on words, DM trying to square all the policy, PG working on notes tracking the different drafts, Jonathan organising and trying to keep up spirits. Lots of others coming and going, sometimes welcome sometimes not. GB came over after his speech before heading back to Washington and persuaded me it would actually send the wrong message to do the spending switch. He was convincing, though the others felt there were other motives there too. It was interesting that TB's plunging confidence came as we were trying to make confidence one of the key themes, possibly even the main concept. I loved it, felt it caught the moment, that we would get uplift through confidence and edge through forces of conservatism.

My overnight briefing was pretty low-key and I sensed the media weren't that impressed. We wanted the speech to carry an argument. They just wanted stories. I felt the same on the Tuesday when I did the regionals and it wasn't really until I sat down with Oakley, Brunson and Boulton [BBC, ITN and Sky political editors] that I felt it would work, but we were kidding ourselves if we thought anything other than forces of conservatism would be the main story. The Monday night was awful. TB got back from his final reception, read the draft, said this is truly hopeless, we are going to have to start again. It was a total overreaction but by now even Philip and I were starting to panic. Cherie was agitating for him to go to bed from 11, when the truth was we were hours off having anything like the finished item. GB had also undermined him, sold him the total pup that the story was economic efficiency and social justice. It was partly that but it was nowhere near big enough to carry the speech. We had to get back the central argument we had agreed ages ago when he came back from holiday, which was right.

We had the usual nightmare re jokes. Bruce and I worked away on that. TB was basically rewriting, trying to drive the argument through. I was doing lines and talking to him the whole time to try to get him in a better frame of mind, not chuck out the whole thing for the wrong reasons. He wanted a couple of purple-prose passages, which I worked on. We worked through till 3am, and he said he was in a total panic about it. But by then we were going round in circles and needed some rest. We were back working on it at 6am Tuesday and actually we had got the argument back in shape but we still needed more colour and drama in it. I realised we had too many endings and too many themes cluttering it up. It confirmed for me that we needed to strip it out again. I redid the ending and cleared out the clutter, as TB started to cut down the other parts.

We eventually had a text around 12 and when he went through the autocue rehearsal, everyone in the room felt we had the makings of a good speech. The [Countryside Alliance pro] hunt demo was going big and we agreed he should start the speech by saying tally-ho. We had got a couple of half-decent jokes but more important I felt we had a really good argument, good lines, policy that actually knitted into the speech as a whole. The reason the press hadn't liked the overnight briefing was because it lacked the forces of conservatism line that would give edge to the whole argument. It would fly because it was about him showing himself to be confident, in charge of the landscape, really going for it.

Once we had signed off the text we had a while just hanging around in the hotel. He was nervous. I said we had obliterated the Tories and he could now stand up and describe with confidence a new landscape. While he was getting dressed, I had a chat with CB who said she wanted to keep news of the pregnancy quiet for as long as possible because she was worried something would go wrong and she did not want to share it with the world. She looked really vulnerable. There was also an awful lot about children in the speech. We left for the conference centre, went over some of the trickier lines, agreed to put the TB personal stuff before the section on children. He was now worried there was too much purple prose, but it was too late.

The hall was gloomy. The set looked fantastic. For the first time, I watched it sitting down in the hall. Some of our best passages were brilliant, others not quite so good but as a whole it worked and I could feel the party connecting and going for it. The personal stuff worked, and forces of conservatism definitely gave it drama and definition. The first person I met afterwards was Peter Riddell who said it was too Richard and Judy for him. But the general feeling as I went around was good. Fiona and I went out for dinner with the *Independent*, where they were arguing we weren't doing enough to make the running on Europe. I didn't take at all to Janet Street-Porter [editor, *Independent on Sunday*]. She was totally self-obsessed and I hated the way she sprayed around gossip.

We went to the News International party where the talk was of the front page of the *Sun* – SURRENDER – which was pretty off the mark. I think [editor David] Yelland and [deputy editor Rebekah] Wade were just pissed off that the *Mirror* had got so much out of the

interview. I made a point of waiting till [*Sun* political editor] Trevor
Kavanagh was with [Murdoch adviser] Irwin Stelzer before going
over to say I thought his obsession with Europe was a madness. I
also thought they were doing it too often and it was losing effect. The
general immediate coverage was good but by Wednesday the feeling
was building that when we talked about the forces of conservatism,
TB meant anything that went before him. TB and I both felt, whilst
we needed to avoid any sense of a flip-flop, we needed to do something to recalibrate, so we organised a series of interviews to do a
direct pitch to One Nation Tories and also make clear there were
forces of conservatism on the left too. The danger was we had given
the Tories an easy platform for next week. The impact of the speech
provoked another round of circular conversations. I was pretty sure
Peter M was getting at him, felt the speech was a mistake.

JP set himself up for a total marmalisation by going to the conference from the hotel by car and losing it when he was asked about it
on ITN, claiming it was for security and also to stop [his wife] Pauline's
hair being blown about. He knew he was going to get a dreadful
pasting and both he and Pauline would feel dreadful. Fiona called to
say that Bloomberg agency had been on to Tanya [Joseph] in the press
office to ask if Cherie was pregnant. After we got back to the hotel,
the four of us sat down with Sally M and talked it through. CB just
didn't want it public yet. Tanya had pleaded ignorance, and I felt we
could just leave it at that for now. I think they were both, with the
speech out of the way, more clearly seized of the nightmare that was
about to be unleashed. It was perfectly possible that someone had
seen her visiting the doctor, or that the news had got out from us
talking on mobiles but it was not going to be easy to keep it quiet
for long. I went to the Sky party where Elisabeth Murdoch [business-
woman, daughter of Rupert] advised me not to worry about the books
and to take them as a bizarre form of flattery. Alex called to say he
loved the *Daily Record* headline, as did I. It was my favourite headline
of all of them – 21st Century Socialist. It was clear from TB's chats
with journalists and editors throughout the day that the right wing
were going to twist the speech into a kind of 'operation year zero',
as if everything pre-Blair added up to nothing.

Thursday, September 30

I had a decent sleep for the first time in ages. The fallout on the speech
was mixed. Fiona read Oborne's book, said she thought it was fine.
[Swedish Prime Minister] Göran Persson was in town to do the
[conference] overseas speaker slot and we persuaded him to do a line

re Sweden vs Poland, which was going to impact on England's chances. TB was seeing a number of journalists, including Trevor Kavanagh, and at the end of their chat I got Persson to go in and see him. After Kavanagh left, Persson said 'That is a very cold man.' Trevor had complained, as did others, that they didn't see TB enough. TB was on good form, had rediscovered his confidence. It was a fairly quiet day for me and I sloped off for a swim and a session in the sauna, where I fell asleep and woke up not knowing how long I had been in there but feeling pretty dehydrated. I had dinner with Fiona and Sally M and JP joined us for a while. He and Pauline were very down about things and we tried to cheer him up. TB had told him he should stop making it so obvious that the press get to him.

Friday, October 1

[Michael] Meacher [environment minister] caused a bit of a flurry overnight when he seemed to say we should ban second homes. TB was on *GMTV* and knocked it down. We had been hoping to use the interview to get a message about the need for new members and also about the CBI [Confederation of British Industry] backing the minimum wage, but he wasn't really on form. Jonathan called to warn the French FSA [food standards agency] had urged their government to reject British beef and we got TB to speak to Jospin. On the train back, TB was reading Oborne's book. He said he tended to agree with Fiona that it wasn't that bad. At the moment, most conversations seem to lead one way or another to the pregnancy. We were glad the week was over and it had actually gone quite well, with JP and Meacher's nonsense about two homes the only real glitches. My only worry was that we had given the Tories the script for the next few days and also got the press in the mood to give us another kicking. I took Rory and Calum to football and Alex called. He said there had been a [Manchester United] board meeting last Monday and Bobby Charlton tried to raise re-entry to the FA Cup and Edwards said no way. But then Edwards had asked Alex if it would be possible to play a youth team, which was a total about-turn.

Saturday, October 2

The papers were fairly quiet post-conference. Tory divisions were opening up and both John Major's and Norman Lamont's memoirs had started. On the way up to Burnley, I had to deal with a Meacher story over a charity he chaired which had been set up by his wife and which the *Sunday Times* was trying to cause trouble over, but all in all it was a quiet day.

Sunday, October 3

The *Sunday Telegraph* splashed on Dobson being ready to go for the [London] mayor's job. TB spoke to him and made encouraging noises, though he still remained unconvinced Frank would beat Ken in a ballot. He felt, as did [Tony] Banks when I saw him at Chelsea, that Ken would have to be blocked. Thatcher was doing a big piece in the *Telegraph* attacking TB so clearly people were falling out of the big tent but I was still pleased by the definition the forces of conservatism speech had given us. The football was pretty grim, Chelsea beating Man United 5-0 and Rory was pretty miserable by the end.

Monday, October 4

I had a really bad asthma attack overnight and [Tom] Bostock [AC's GP] came round at lunchtime. He said it was not possible to operate under the pressures I did without suffering illness. He said given my history there were three possible routes for that pressure – head, chest and stomach. There was a chance, if I was not careful, of me just dropping down dead and he didn't want to be responsible for the 'second most powerful man in the country' dropping down dead. He said he was only half joking. He put me on antibiotics and said I had to rest.

I missed it seems a lively office meeting where Peter M, Anji, Charlie [Falconer] and Pat [McFadden] all argued that we were in the wrong place on the speech. The *Mail, Sun* and *Telegraph* were all now reporting judgement as fact that it had been a bad and ill-judged speech, the *Mail* in particular, and Peter M was saying we had not thought it through and were in danger of losing part of our coalition.

TB defended it, said we finally had proper definition. Philip G, PH and DM all argued strongly that we finally had a sense of project back again. According to Jonathan, Anji had said we were in danger of alienating people who had been supportive up to now. Peter M said to PG that he spent too much time in big houses remote from people and press. Philip snapped back 'I don't think you would much enjoy a conversation about houses.' TB called a couple of times, worried that the Tories were getting a fair bit out of the new policy launches they were doing, but I felt that we had a fairly good operation on them, that they were seen as pushing further to the right. And Thatcher being out there against them was a good thing. It was nonetheless pretty clear the media wanted to give Hague a lift. On the speech fallout, he said I feel instinct telling me I am in the right place and reason tells me I'm in the wrong place. He said for the moment, he was sticking with instinct, but we also needed policy to take forward the central argument up to and through the Queen's Speech.

I still felt dreadful and took the day off at home. News came in of a rail crash [at Ladbroke Grove, close to Paddington station] and JP called to ask whether I thought he should go, which I did. TB wondered about going too, but we had to watch the precedent. The death toll rose steadily through the day. Hague [at the Tory Party conference] got a mixed press but there was no doubt the press were trying to give him a lift. Europe was up and running as a bad story for them again.

JP called as I got into the office and had a series of different things planned for the week ahead, starting by announcing a new inquiry into different [railway] warning systems. He was clearly thinking he should take away franchises, but when I mentioned this to TB, he said we had to be careful. People understood that accidents will happen, but I felt there was going to be a real wave of anger once the scale of this really sunk in. JP spoke to Derry [Irvine] and the Attorney General [Lord Gareth Williams] to agree the inquiry should take precedence over prosecutions, which is what slowed up Southall [rail crash in 1997]. TB seemed reasonably robust on the speech front, though the right-wing press was still at it and the left press as ever losing confidence. The Tories had gone right back into Thatcher's pocket. Hague had to grin and bear it as she dominated the whole show. As the day wore on, I got more and more worried about the rail crash and suggested to TB that we get JP over. He came over at 6.30, by which time we were trying to persuade Lord [William] Cullen to head the inquiry. He was reluctant but Derry later won him round. JP was pretty calm, had made the right decisions and it looked like we were dealing with human error, but we warned him flak would come his way, he just had to make sure he wasn't riled. I had done a script for TB on the crash which he was worried was over the top and would lead them [the media] to want to put the blame on the government. He felt if this all became political we had to be very robust in defence of ourselves. When it came to doing it, he was too emotional, but he was just about OK. The death toll could be as high as 170.

We had a meeting with GB and the Millbank people on the mayoral situation. We had very little by way of polling and we were going to need a pretty substantial campaign behind Frank [Dobson]. He was due to announce on Friday but we persuaded him to delay the launch till Tuesday to give us more time to plan it properly. TB was pretty brutal in his assessment, said he was basically Old Labour and he didn't really have on health a strong sense that he could deliver. He was going to have to resign from the Cabinet and it was far better that he said it was his choice to do that because he was going to have to persuade people that he was really up for this. I felt the best basis for a campaign built around him was trust and solidity. The problem was he looked and sounded very flat. TB said to him he could probably beat Ken in a ballot but it wasn't a risk worth taking and we would have to defend the decision very strongly.

I was up till 11.30 working on rail and it would help that we had the inquiry to announce tomorrow, but I sensed we were heading towards a very heavy period on this. John Redwood [Prescott's Conservative Shadow] had made an initially very political attack, which Bernard Jenkin [Shadow Transport Secretary] was calming down and adopting a more sensible position and I suggested to JP we get him in for a briefing. The *Sun* were really going for JP. Irwin [Stelzer] told Anji that Trevor Kavanagh felt he had the opportunity to turn the paper back to the Tories, but we shouldn't worry.

Thursday, October 7

JP did the *Today* programme pretty well, and we had Cullen coming down later. The Tories at their conference were getting marmalised, Thatcher taking over the show and Hague's speech was being briefed as a step further rightwards. We were getting a bit of heat on the crash but the enormity of it, and the scale of death, were such that overly political attacks were likely to backfire at this stage, but there was no doubt the heat would come on very powerfully as the full horror sunk in. The *Sun* ran a big piece on the mother of the Southall victim, Mrs [Maureen] Kavanagh, headlined 'I blame Prescott'. I got JP to meet her as a *Sun* exclusive. We had another meeting with GB and co re Britain in Europe. GB was circulating a very heavy paper to the Cabinet setting out the policy in stark terms, putting over a tough position and making clear we were not moving from the current line. He said RC and Peter M were trying to push us to a position that ultimately would be damaging. He denied having cooled on the euro but to move now would be a mistake. TB said 'Be honest – we both hate talking about it because we don't want it to be the defining issue.' He said we had to get Britain in Europe to be more about Europe rather than the euro, because otherwise we would be gifting the right the issue they wanted.

TB was adamant that the national changeover plan was always going to be a big thing. GB was equally adamant. We went round and round and ended up laughing because it slowly dawned on everyone it wasn't a real argument. But there were differences of shade, added to which we were giving [Michael] Heseltine, [Kenneth] Clarke and [Charles] Kennedy the chance to do us in if we didn't stay the strategic course. We agreed GB should circulate the paper and meet them in advance to try to get them squared. GB was constantly stressing that we had to stay in control of the campaign. He felt we had gone far enough and that Peter M wanted the fight now in part to reduce the power of the right-wing press. JP came in to see TB about the crash. The fast train was four minutes late. Bodies had just vaporised. Cullen came in with Gus [Macdonald] and Bill Callaghan of the HSE [Health and Safety Executive]. We were hoping he would do an interim report quickly but he wasn't keen. TB was doing an interview with children for the *News of the World*, at which he was asked which historical person he would want to be and he said Jesus!! Hilary [Coffman] almost collapsed, and TB claimed he thought they had asked which historical person he would like to meet. I watched Hague's speech and he did a pretty effective job but I felt the lurch to the right was a real problem for him. The right wing of his party would love it, but the public would be alarmed.

Philip's groups last night were barely aware of either [party] conference but they instinctively revolted against any sense of Thatcher dominating the Tories. TB's view was that Thatcherism without constraint was a real problem for them. He told me he had lost his confidence in the summer and got it back through the speech but was now worried that he had made a basic political error by not being balanced enough, allowing the speech to be misrepresented. Peter M was unsettling him, saying the speech was a mistake, and certainly Hague exploited it pretty well. I felt Hague was too strident and personal but he got his party going well. TB had to get out there, as soon as good taste allowed, post-Ladbroke Grove, to defend the speech properly.

Friday, October 8

The initial HSE report was bad for the driver but Bill Callaghan went out of his way not to blame the driver alone. We had a reshuffle meeting. TB was thinking of Peter M for NI, [Geoff] Hoon for defence, [Alan] Milburn for health. He didn't want to put out Jack C but he was looking to free up room and there was a lot of MoD lobbying of me, John Sawers and Jonathan for Jack C not to be sent to the MoD.

I was pretty horrified at the idea of Mo coming to the centre [as Minister for the Cabinet Office]. Jonathan was very funny describing what she would be like chairing meetings of the SCU and sorting out the Grid [news calendar designed to co-ordinate government announcements]. I had very bad vibes about it. Charlie was probably the best person for that job but with Peter coming back in, it would risk making the whole reshuffle about TB and his mates.

At the strategy meeting, we agreed the Tories had given us a big opportunity to pin them on lurch to the right. I wrote a script for briefing the commentariat, building in the forces of conservatism speech as an important strategic point. TB was still robust about it, but nervous, and now accepting of the view he had made a mistake for overexposing one flank. Philip did some London groups tonight and reported back that it was a disaster area. Ken [Livingstone] was very popular, Frank D was nowhere and Ken would be even more popular if he ran as an independent. I also had a meeting with Frank and Ann Keen [Labour MP and Dobson's parliamentary private secretary], who were pretty clueless. They had no strategy, no story, no top line, no forward plans. They didn't even have a line on Ken. It was a pretty depressing meeting. He was due to do *Frost* on Sunday and he didn't have a story for it at all, other than the event. I said his best bet was to say he had decided to leave the Cabinet to go full-time for this job. He said he needed more time to think about it. He was due to tell his CLP [Constituency Labour Party] tonight. Part of me felt we were just sleepwalking to defeat. I couldn't see Frank winning. Godric was doing an excellent job on rail and suggested that for the Sundays we should brief a legislative move related to the Transport Bill in the Queen's Speech. I spoke to JP who suggested we do something related to Railtrack [consortium owning rail infrastructure] responsibility for safety. He was due to go to Hull tonight but I suggested he stay down to meet TB tomorrow to show both of them were on the case.

Saturday, October 9

TB and JP were seeing the HSE and rail experts. JP was reporting on the HSE assessment of Railtrack's safety record, which supported the Sunday briefing on the threat to remove safety from Railtrack. The meeting was over fairly quickly but they took an hour to go through the line for JP's brief statement in the street, which in the end was not quite what we agreed, though near enough. TB had decided he wanted to do a piece for *The Times* re the speech, with some of the press still chuntering on about it. The first draft was far too defensive.

The *Mail on Sunday* had a story about Peter M not being happy with the speech, which was classic diddling.

Dobbo called and agreed to the idea of him announcing his own resignation. Philip's groups had been really dreadful for him, though politeness and a desire not to undermine his confidence even more stopped me telling him just how bad. As TB said, Frank just didn't inspire. I called [TV presenter Sir] David Frost to set him up for the interview with Frank and the story about him resigning. The Sundays weren't that bad. On the rail front, it certainly helped having the sense that TB was directly involved. And the general view was certainly there that the Tories had gone further to the right.

Sunday, October 10

Major was on *Frost* and tore into them [the Conservatives] pretty well. He was clearly going to fight back, which was good news for us. TB called a couple of times. He was thinking of seeing Jack C tonight to start the reshuffle. But every conversation at some point turned to the baby. 'Have you any idea what this is going to be like? Nappies. Toys everywhere. I'll have one child leaving university as another is starting school.' He was worried about Dobbo and said he was moving towards letting Ken run and we would have to go all out to win a ballot. I still felt that was difficult. His view was that Ken would win as an independent. He was happier about the Tory scene and felt we were now better placed for the Britain in Europe launch, which would further isolate Hague. TB saw Jack C at Number 10 late on. He said it was a difficult conversation and though he accepted it reluctantly, Jack was keen for serious projects outside government. I felt we were losing one of our few reliable communicators. But Cabinet changes were now settled.

Monday, October 11

The rail story was moving down the agenda with the death toll lower than predicted [the final figures were thirty-one dead and 520 injured] and there was definitely a sense we were on top of it. There was very little expectation of a reshuffle today, despite Frank's interview. I got in early to see TB and Jonathan. I was moaning about Mo, but his constant refrain was give me alternatives. I said Jack C, but that deed was done. We went over various possibilities for [minister for] Europe. RC rejected Kim Howells [education minister]. TB then overruled Ann Taylor and RC to go for Keith Vaz [a PPS]. At the office meeting, TB had still not decided re Ken, but we were all growing increasingly alarmed about Frank's lack of any campaign. TB was getting more and more frustrated about delivery. When I pointed out that at these Monday morning meetings, we seemed to be saying the same things week after week, he said 'What do I have to do to translate what we say into action?' TB then saw JP and GB and the reshuffle began. TB said GB was not happy with it and had warned him, 'with a hint of real menace' said TB, that there would be an avalanche of criticism. Well, make sure it's not from you, said TB. Jack C was in first and came through with a handwritten note that he intended to put out as his resignation letter suggesting he offered to resign some time ago. I told him that the press team would really miss him because he had been reliable and a team player and I hoped we could still call on him.

Then Mo came round after seeing TB, all lovey-dovey, burbling away about how she saw herself as a co-ordinator rather than an enforcer and she wanted to go to Belfast with Peter tomorrow. I had to persuade TB not to move Charlie F, who would be essential to making sure that Mo didn't run amok. Then [Alan] Milburn, then [Chris] Smith, and then Peter to Northern Ireland. I was glad he was back. He looked genuinely shocked and wasn't himself at all. He went to the loo and when after a few minutes he hadn't come back, I went looking for him and found him, still in there, saying he had never felt so anxious. I took him back through to my office and then got Mo round again and suggested they went out together and travelled off in the car together. He said he was due to see Gordon and then said, as if an aside to Mo, 'In this government I am appointed by two people not one.' TB claimed that when he saw him one-on-one he had been very hard on him, told him that if he didn't really behave, not diddle, just do the job properly, he would be finished. That may explain why he was so shell-shocked. I also wondered whether he might be worrying about needing round-the-clock protection.

GB was pushing for his usual people, Yvette [Cooper], Douglas [Alexander] and Michael Wills [Labour MPs]. Bruce [Grocott] at one point said can't we just have an hour put aside in the diary at every reshuffle for pointless discussions about Michael Wills. We needed resignation letters for the press, so I drafted TB's reply to Jack and liaised with Frank on his. Philip and Peter H were working with him on his launch tomorrow. At the briefing, most of the questions were about Peter and also whether Mo was pushed. I got Mo to do the media for tonight and Peter tomorrow. I had been pushing for promotion for Brian Wilson but TB had been unsure. Like all reshuffles, there had been difficulties but this one had probably been easier than most. Mo's interviews were pretty hopeless. The 'hiya babe' approach had a certain appeal I suppose, but she was incredibly loose with language. I spoke to Peter later, who was settling in. He was seeing his new protection team and said 'I've just introduced them to the concept of Reinaldo.' The general media comment was that TB had the modernising Cabinet he wanted, in his image. But Peter M would dominate the coverage and there would be a reaction at some point from GB at not having got what he wanted. We organised a series of baton-handover type pictures, Peter and Mo, Dobson and Milburn, Robertson and Hoon. Frank and team were round at Philip's house till late working on his script for tomorrow. I had very bad vibes and also, why was Frank planning his launch, and why were we letting him, on the day the NEC was putting together the process for the mayoral selection procedures?

Tuesday, October 12

We got a pretty good press for the reshuffle, and only a few really hostile remarks re Peter M. He did the *Today* programme fine and his visit with Mo was the main story until the coup in Pakistan.[1] TB was in a real rage about the crime figures. In a classic Jackesque kind of move, he had changed the system for recording crime so that although crime in fact was falling, the figures showed a twenty per cent rise. To be fair to him, through the day Jack did a pretty good job explaining it and TB did an OK clip at his seminar with chief constables. We had another Europe meeting with GB and his team. GB was madder than ever today and TB was getting irritable with him. He denied he had cooled on EMU but was the whole time setting out the dangers of the Britain in Europe campaign and of the EMU issue. He was still going on about how we had messed things up by our use of the word intention and that we were to blame for our current difficulties. It was almost comic. I said nobody out there in the world would be aware of what words exactly had been used. What they might be aware of was that we had a broadly pro-euro policy and if it was the policy that was the problem, we should say so.

TB said we were in trouble because we said we were in favour in principle, and the public by and large are not. It is not much more complicated than that. TB asked him if he still felt we were likely to be holding a referendum early in the next parliament. And GB went all defensive and said 'If you want someone else to give you better advice, go ahead and get them.' TB said what on earth are you talking

[1] The Pakistan Army, led by General Pervez Musharraf, overthrew the government headed by Prime Minister Nawaz Sharif.

October '99: Blair's rage at crime figures

about? GB said we had a settled policy and RC and Peter M had both been undermining it. We had been able to hold the line and they were trying to unravel by asking us to go further than we had to. He said he didn't think he would be able to make the Britain in Europe launch about in or out of Europe. I said I felt we could. He said he hoped so but he doubted it. He had also been agitating to keep Robin away from the Britain in Europe event, which would be ridiculous but Robin had virtually had to demand of TB that he be allowed to go.

GB also demanded that no questions be allowed at the launch, which was equally ridiculous. And he said TB would have to do the *Today* programme rather than him or Robin. TB said 'Wouldn't it just be easier if you admitted, in the privacy of these four walls, that you have gone a bit cooler?' 'I haven't,' said GB, 'but do you want to be held responsible for mass unemployment?' Tony shook his head, put on his best patronising look and said 'No Gordon, I don't.' Even in saying he hadn't cooled, GB was indicating the reasons why he had. TB was now talking to him like he was a child. 'Gordon, you are talking to me. Why not just be open about it?' It was all a bit pointless. I had a near comical meeting with Keith Vaz who asked me, literally, what is our line on EMU? Kim Howells called to say he had had a call from Robert Peston that he was going to get the Europe job and was really fed up that Vaz went ahead of him. How the fuck did Peston know that? It must have come from the FCO. I did a note for Jonathan. The *Standard* splashed on the story that the NEC electoral college was designed to stop Ken. TB was in a real flap, said we were going to get the worst of all worlds. It looks and feels like a stitch-up and yet we may still have to block him. I felt sure we would have to block him. Frank was doing OK but he wasn't a natural campaigner and Ken was hitting all the right buttons.

Wednesday, October 13

We didn't get mauled as much as I thought we would re Ken and the so-called fix. It was proving very hard to mobilise any kind of campaign against him. Dobbo's launch had rather been lost and he didn't have much of a press operation, and although the *Standard* was saying they were on board, they were actually being pretty critical. My main focus today was Britain in Europe. Julian had drafted TB's article for the *Independent* which was good. I was putting together a briefing note on Tampere [special European Council summit on justice and home affairs]. I was working on various Europe scripts, a joint TB/GB article and one joint with Clarke and Heseltine. We were helped today by Major and Patten both attacking

Hague's general position and we had to play our story into that. TB, Jonathan and I met up with Clarke, Hezza [Heseltine], Kennedy, GB, Simon Buckby [Britain in Europe]. Anji came in with Clarke and Heseltine through 70 Whitehall and they were both pretty nervy. Ken started by saying that there had to be an agreement that neither of us played party politics. 'We are in enough trouble as it is. They all think we are a pair of traitors.' Hezza said that the agreement would need to focus not just on TB's words but also the spin. 'Michael,' I said. 'After all we have been through together. As if . . .' He laughed, but looked and sounded nervous. His voice wasn't as strong as it normally is.

Clarke was doing that little 'Heh-heh-heh' laugh all the time, even when nothing funny was being said. Ken also said that it wasn't on for us only to talk about Europe and not the euro. Now it was GB's turn to look nervous, and he stirred uneasily, but Ken was adamant. They would stick to the line about economic conditions, but it simply wasn't credible to do a launch like this whilst avoiding the single most important issue. If we avoid EMU, we will be laughed at, he said. But TB said it was still important we make EMU part of the broader argument, because they want to make US the ideologues. He said to Ken 'If your concern is that we will slide away from this in due course, and we are just using you in the meantime, let me tell you we would not be doing this if we didn't think we would end up going the whole way. But we have to win the broader argument. I'm only interested in winning debates rather than just having them. It is also vital that you two stay and win the argument in your party.' Charlie Kennedy didn't have much to say and didn't seem to be in very good shape. TB was probing KC and MH gently about the Tory conference and Clarke said last week had been 'madness', that Hague had been bullied into it by Thatcher because the truth was she did ridicule him and he was trying to ingratiate himself.

Hezza was clearly wanting to do the big-vision thing and leave Ken to do the detail. The plan was for six speeches tomorrow, TB, GB, Kennedy, Hezza and Clarke, now plus RC, and I was thrilled when Clarke made the point it could make the event impossibly dull and wouldn't it be better just to have three, TB, MH and CK. Hezza then said he wanted Colin Marshall to sit in the middle, presumably because he didn't want to be photographed right next to TB. Buckby and I swatted that one away by saying Colin had to be near the lectern. Then he had another go, said wouldn't it be better if Colin chaired the press conference, and we said no, because TB would know the journalists. Clarke and Hezza both seemed like they wanted to hang around as if they couldn't bear to leave.

At 2.30 I did a briefing on Tampere, making it largely about Britain in Europe, but with justice and home affairs experts with me to help me through the trickier stuff. I had called Tony Bevins [*Express* political editor] and one or two others and suggested they ask lots of questions about the planning and the background. They loved the idea of pre-planning meetings with Tories like Clarke and Heseltine in advance of tomorrow's event. We had a strategy meeting on Europe at 6. Peter M was there too. I think the feeling was today had gone OK, but there was still a slight danger of mixed messages. We had our position and we should be confident in it.

Thursday, October 14

Yesterday went well, and in particular the stuff about Clarke and Hezza having been in for secret meetings at Number 10, etc. We were back to Tories in turmoil. We finished TB's words, then left with GB for the IMAX [cinema]. I really liked the venue, and the set looked terrific. At the pre-meeting, GB's body language was particularly awful. He really looked like he didn't want to be there. Charlie K seemed a bit out of it, very nervous. Clarke was last to arrive having done the interview round and was really chuffed up and raring to go.

We went through some of the questions we might get, but this was a roomful of pretty experienced people who didn't drop too many bollocks. There was a good video, then TB, then Hezza, then Charlie. The speeches were OK but I particularly enjoyed Hezza and Ken, for all their demands not to make it party political, getting stuck into the Tories. GB did a series of clips afterwards trying to get it more focused on in or out and saying very little re the euro. Ken tried to diddle a bit by saying we all agreed that one day we were likely to be saying yes, but the main point – that we were back to first principles – was not lost on anyone. To be fair to GB, he said to me as he came off the stage 'Go on then, tell me you told me so. I never believed we would be able to do that.' The truth was it was only because of the Tories' problems that we had been able to get it focused where we wanted. We told Ken and Hezza they had been terrific. I think Kennedy felt a bit out of his depth.

I drove back with TB and we had a wonderful moment crossing Westminster Bridge when the phone in TB's car went, he answered, and it was a phone company asking whose phone it was, saying that they had a bill and didn't know where to send it. He said try the

Cabinet Office in Whitehall. We got back for Cabinet. Afterwards TB saw Gerry Adams and Peter M privately and then we had a meeting with Dobbo and [Nick] Raynsford which was dispiriting. There was a bad poll in the *Standard*. I spoke to [editor Max] Hastings and complained about their coverage, saying it was all very well to be positive in the editorials, but the news stories and columns were pretty unrelentingly negative. Also, nobody was putting pressure on Ken over policy. But Dobbo was looking weak and tired. Raynsford said he was hopeless at making calls, or sticking to a plan.

I went for a walk with Jack Straw to try to get my head round the justice and home affairs stuff for Tampere. I then left with TB who had a phone call with [Chilean] President [Eduardo] Frei [Ruiz-Tagle]. They had put in fresh medical evidence re [Chilean ex-dictator General Augusto] Pinochet [under house arrest in the UK]. They were beginning to panic that he was going to die here. TB said that there was a judicial process to follow but also hinted that we would be able to do more now that Jack Straw had discretion. On the way out to Tampere, TB and Jack chatted about the Civil Service with [Stephen] Wall [UK permanent representative to the EU], [David] Bostock [European Secretariat, Cabinet Office] and Sawers. None of us could see the point of this trip at all. At Tampere, we met with Bertie [Ahern] just to take stock. Jonathan called to say the broadcast coverage of the Britain in Europe launch was broadly positive.

Friday, October 15

There was massive, and predictably mixed, coverage for the Britain in Europe launch. Great pictures, but the anti papers were very anti and the pro were pro but with their usual 'Blair should do more' line. TB was worried we had polarised it. He had GB in one ear saying we should not now push it, and PM saying we now had to build on this, distil the argument. I had breakfast with TB to brief him on all that and then go through the day. Beef [the unilateral French ban on British beef, the European ban having been lifted in August] was going to be the main focus for us, though we had Jack S with us on the justice and home affairs agenda. RC said at the foreign ministers' dinner the main focus of all the private discussion was TB, Chirac/ Jospin, Schroeder, and where instinctively people felt their support in the big arguments should go. Robin felt we were building support. Schroeder was looking a bit tired and drawn.

TB nabbed Jospin before the start of the meeting to press our case re the French not lifting the beef ban. We squared [Romano] Prodi [now European Commission President] to say they would prosecute if the French did not comply once the scientific committees had met on October 28. TB was bored out of his skull most of the time, could not understand why they had all been dragged there for this. He had a bilateral with Aznar, who was getting it in the neck from some of them because this whole thing had largely been his idea. I did a briefing with Jack which tided us over news-wise. I liked Jack, and we had a good laugh on the way back. He seemed to be loving the whole thing, being there and being the focus for a lot of it. TB met Jospin more formally and it was all beef. Schroeder was clearly not happy to be there at all. He didn't much like these summits at the best of times but at one point came up to me and just snorted 'This is bullshit.'

I had an interesting chat with [Chris] Patten re the Tories. He was a clever guy and clearly enjoying himself. He felt the Tories had to distance themselves from the whole *Mail/Telegraph* thing, get back in the real world. Major was absolutely seething at the rightward drift and what he felt was a dumping on him. To pass time as much as anything else, and also to get out where we were on beef, we did a TB, RC, JS press conference, which was low-key but fine. We had a meeting with Prodi who wanted advice on how to deal with the media, particularly the Brits. We had one or two ideas which we then took forward over dinner with Ricci Levi [Prodi's spokesman]. Prodi was being really helpful re beef, but the French were being pretty intransigent. The *Standard* had a dreadful poll for Frank. Hague had announced his 'flatbed lorry tour' [the Conservatives' 'Keep the Pound' campaign] which was worrying on one level, if it helped him connect, particularly on Europe, but also risked looking a bit desperate. TB was worrying about his seeming inability to get GB in the same place on Europe. The problem was that on some of these key issues, GB now wanted to be in a different place.

Saturday, October 16

We were hoping to get away early. There were one or two problems in the conclusions, e.g. harmonisation on asylum, but we got them ironed out OK. Robin was totally on top of the detail, and we were pretty much OK with things. The leaders were uniformly desperate to get away and at the little schmoozing session before the meeting itself all seemed to be saying what the hell are we all doing here? But the meeting started late, went on far longer than it needed to. It also meant my chances of getting back for the Burnley vs Millwall match were done. I showed Prodi the picture coverage of him and TB having a drink in the bar last night, trying to explain it is possible to get coverage through pictures if you do something a bit different. He just looked bemused.

I chatted to Schroeder's interpreter who said he was having a very hard time at the moment, and did I have any advice? I said he needed to make a virtue of conflict and show a bit more determination. The problem was their political system was very different, and weakened leaders. Why anyone backed PR for national government was beyond me. It is a recipe for weakness and every time I meet Schroeder that view is strengthened. We finally got away, most of the staff having been just sitting on the plane waiting. Patten flew back with us, and said re the Tories he could see nobody coming through and he was worried where Hague was taking them. The *Sun* had done a poll showing the Tories up six [points] at the expense of the Lib Dems, which they were doing as a big boost thanks to a tougher position on Europe. Hague was basically targeting the *Sun/Mail* agenda, and his tour was part of that. We had to pin it as a core vote strategy. But we were lacking confidence in our own pitch at the moment.

Sunday, October 17

The papers were a bit all over the place. Hague did a strong performance on *Frost*, and Robin didn't really do the business after him. Neil [Kinnock] did *On the Record* at my request, first on Europe, and then tore into Ken at the end. I had a fairly quiet day. TB called a couple of times, still a bit edgy re Europe, GB and the Tories. The *Sun* were asking if Prince Andrew had discussed remarriage with TB. I hated these Royal stories, because they were usually put out by someone in the Royal circles but if they became a problem they could always rely on the *Mail/Telegraph* lot to say we were at it. I watched Rory Bremner, who was pretty funny but potentially damaging.[1]

Monday, October 18

The papers were picking up on the lack of confidence we currently felt, added to which the *Mail* and the *Express* were running on the 'broken promise' line. Britain in Europe had not really got us into a better position, because we had a real long-term problem re Europe. We had bad stories re [new Health Secretary Alan] Milburn who had overspun his 'change of direction' line, plus GM [food] and police numbers were running as problems.

[1] Television impressionist Bremner had devised a series of sketches showing Blair and Campbell 'behind the scenes', with Campbell clearly the dominant character.

TB's morning meeting was pretty dispiriting, because he was the one lacking confidence at the moment, and there was a sense of drift. He was on at me again to free up more time for strategic thinking, but it was hard when he was also expecting me to be on top of everything day to day, hour to hour. He kept coming back to the same thing during the day – with GB disengaged, Peter M focusing rightly on NI, he was looking to me even more, and it meant I had to find more time for strategy; to which I said he had to stop pressing me re the day-to-day. Did he want me to stop doing the briefings, taking the morning meeting, overseeing the Grid, dealing with the commentators etc.? He felt I could cut down a bit. Well maybe.

I took a meeting of all my key people to take stock of where we were. I felt we had several problems coming together at once, which were undermining his confidence and therefore our operation – Europe, where the Tories at least had a clear and fairly popular position, even if long term we can win the argument; trust, where a lot of the focus inevitably was on him and us; delivery, where though there was progress to point to, it had not been as dramatic as we would have liked. I had lunch with Geoff Crawford [press secretary to the Queen] at Shepherd's. He was not exactly oozing with confidence re the future of the Royals, and they were clearly still worried about the longer-term problems and what to do about Charles' team freelancing, running a media operation separate from and sometimes at the expense of hers, etc. He asked me what I thought they should do, and whether TB might raise some of these things. I said I'm sure he would if they felt it right, but he was always very cagey re his discussions with her. Geoff was due to return to Australia next year and seemed happy to be doing so.

I asked if she would ever do an interview and he said they thought about it from time to time, and we went through the pros and cons. There was a danger it reduced her to any other talking head. There was also a danger, if it came over as just an extended Xmas broadcast with a few soft questions thrown in, that it would not live up to what would be massive hype. On the other hand, if they worked through a proper plan and decided what she wanted to say and she said it with real humanity, it could be very powerful. Geoff seemed to want me to say they were in a really bad way but I was keen not to overdo it, or seem like I was pushing to get involved. He said the Queen had valued the work I did post-Diana's death. But he said some of the hangers-on had been very edgy about it. Also [Prince] Andrew blamed me/Number 10 for some of the stories re Fergie/remarriage.

I got back for a round of internal meetings then went out for a stroll with TB. He was now saying I had to keep doing the briefings because they were the means by which I stayed on top of everything, exactly the point I had made earlier. But he was sure there must be a way of freeing up more of my time. He was really down about things at the moment, worried re Europe, re GB and also re Livingstone. I got home for Calum and Grace's parents' evening and was worrying I wasn't spending enough time with them. I was conscious of not being there as much as I should be.

Tuesday, October 19

TB was due to do an interview with the *Telegraph*, which was really about showing we were sticking to the forces of conservatism argument, and getting them to understand that while he preferred consensus to conflict, there were some things on which we and they would never agree. He had been very low in confidence when we briefed him, but he found his form, was clear and honest and straightforward and I think they left pretty impressed. The eleven o'clock was mainly about China, as we were beginning to get pressed harder on their human-rights record. We had a meeting with Britain in Europe, who needed help on repositioning. It wasn't focused on people and their lives enough. They also needed a sharper contrast to 'Keep the Pound' which wasn't just 'go for it'. TB did the Tampere [Commons] statement. The *Mirror* said TB walked it. The *Sun* said Hague walked it. Hague was really going for it, and they obviously felt they were on to something. TB pushed back hard with a line on extremism. I left afterwards with Godric for Cambridge vs Burnley [Cambridge 0, Burnley 1], discussing structures on the way. He was also of the view it was hard for me to give up the briefings, because when I did them, they felt they were talking to TB.

Wednesday, October 20

Geoffrey Robinson [Labour MP, former Paymaster General] was a problem in the press again, *The Times* and *Independent* both running stories that we were threatening him, and that he would 'name names' re people who solicited his money. PG told me GR meant me, which was bizarre. I went up to see TB in the flat. He said Geoffrey's anger was all about the DTI inquiry [into alleged irregularities around grants for failed engineering firm Transtec, which Robinson had founded and was chairman of until 1997]. At the eleven o'clock, again I got a lot of pretty tough questioning on China. They were going to make human rights the story of the visit. We had a Grid/diary meeting, back under Jonathan's chairmanship, and it was a bit meandering and all over the place. PG and I both argued that what we lacked was a big booming message that was understood inside and outside, and which we needed to give focus to the operation. We were too day-to-day at the moment.

The other problem we had coming through in focus groups was arrogance. Partly that was just longevity, but also there was a real problem in that people didn't think he [TB] understood their lives. I also felt that in listening to the right too closely, he sometimes got a distorted sense of what kind of things most people cared about, and what they did with their time. He had to get his own voice back, and start articulating it properly again. He wasn't himself at the moment. He admitted that partly it was the pregnancy, which had really thrown him. PG felt it was a post-Kosovo effect; that he had felt that because there was basic support for our position, there would be some kind of positive political spin-off. But actually what happened was that people reacted by thinking he had taken his eye off the domestic ball. In the car over for PMQs we were working on gags but the best one came spontaneously when TB challenged the Tories to name a country in the EU that supported Hague's policy. Hague appeared to say 'Norway' and TB was able to fire straight back 'NORWAY – it is not even in the European Union.' In fact, Hague claimed, he said 'No way', but there was no way back. It was just one of those total hit moments.

We had a strategy meeting later but TB was again lacking focus, and we just wandered around a few issues, NATS [National Air Traffic Services public-private partnership] and the Post Office [part-privatisation], but on the main message, we were floundering around. He was basically just back on enterprise and fairness. He called me later, said I seemed worried, and I said I was just frustrated that we were so lacking drive and momentum at the moment. The press were turning, and the public were starting to view him as arrogant. There was a danger they would just get fed up with us, and I didn't feel we were giving them enough reasons not to. Also, Anji had had a letter from Irwin Stelzer which was clearly hinting the *Sun* may go back to the Tories because of 1. forces of conservatism speech, on which they bought the right's line that it was an attack on anything pre-Blair; 2. his indication in the *Telegraph* interview that a referendum could be held soon after an election; 3. BBC and our continued protection and promotion of it; and 4. energy tax.

Thursday, October 21

We were really getting hit re the Chinese visit [of President Jiang Zemin], with big attacks on us for the policing of protests to ensure they were kept well away from the visitors, and loads of talk about us now being a police state blah blah. Jonathan and I reached the same view re [Geoffrey] Robinson – that we should just get the facts out there. We spoke to [Michael] Levy and [Baroness] Margaret Jay [Leader of the House of Lords] who agreed we could and should make it clear he gave no money to the Leader's Office fund. Also Stephen Byers [Trade and Industry Secretary] volunteered a letter from Michael Scholar [DTI permanent secretary] making clear he had no role in the DTI inquiry.

Peter H had done a good briefing note on TB's speech [to newly appointed headteachers], which was running well in advance, thanks to the line that we were revisiting forces of conservatism, and also the attack on a 'culture of excuses'. TB was worried it was going to be seen as teacher bashing, and that we were creating too many enemies on too many fronts. It ran big on the news all day though, and was fine. He was a bit discombobulated re Geoffrey R who, when Anji and I spoke to him separately later, denied ever having threatened to reveal anything. I always felt with GR that it was rather like talking to blancmange. He was clearly clever, but just wobbled at you, never clear, didn't really follow points through, occasionally made no sense at all.

For the third day running, I was given a really hard time on China, and pushed back with the same line, that human rights was part of the discussion but it didn't define the totality of our relations. Jiang Zemin arrived to his red-carpet welcome, TB and CB greeted him, and we went straight to the talks. Interestingly it was JZ who raised human rights, which allowed TB to touch on it perhaps more than he otherwise would have. They both did fairly long, more than usually guff-laden introductions, and JZ's people were nodding away happily. JZ also felt the need to give us a long spiel about why they dealt with the Falun Gong [banned spiritual movement in China] in the way they did, that they were a real threat, not a religion but a dangerous cult.

They did Hong Kong in a perfectly civil and reasonable way. He gave TB a bit of a lecture re Kosovo. I briefed the broadcasters before going into the lunch. The atmospherics were a lot better this time, partly because they had got more used to TB. I made a point of seeking out [Rupert] Murdoch for a chat to see if there was any warming to the Tories. There didn't seem to be. But he was so far off the radar on Europe there was never going to be a meeting of minds on it.

By the four o'clock, we had a proper rebuttal on Robinson, so the stories were beginning to fall down. Julian Lewis [Conservative MP] had named me in the Commons as having solicited cash from GR, so when George Jones [*Telegraph*] asked me to respond I was able to release the statement re GR never having given money to the Leader's Office fund and also the Scholar letter re the inquiry. So we were in a much better place on it. I was pushed hard again on China but was into my stride on that one. I went back for a meeting with Mo, who seemed very frustrated by the job. She was itching to get her hands on the SCU and the whole scheduling side of things, but I was not having that. She clearly wanted the Cabinet Office and Number 10 effectively to be one operation, but I was able to dissuade her I think. She seemed a bit lost really, didn't enjoy a lot of the committee work, and she was finding it was a hard department to run.

Anji spoke to GR again and he agreed I had never asked him for money, and that Anji had never pressured him re the book,[1] and he was happy to say so. I spoke to him and he said he had not been happy when I had said he was 'not a pariah' because it suggested some people might think he was. He said he had never intended to damage TB, that he was a great admirer, etc. He said several times he wasn't embittered, felt he had given money to the Leader's Office, but through the party. He was friendly again, but could not resist throwing in that 'Of course you have never really considered me to be honest or good.' He said he had read Oborne's book and thought I came out of it really well, but he was struck by the line at the end of the book that I had demons lurking in me that would come back to haunt me. 'You must be worried about that,' he said. Not really, I said, it's a line in a book. On the evening news TB was featuring big in the top three stories – his speech on education, China, and the visit of the World Cup bid inspection team. He was coming out fine though I didn't like the way some people were seeing his speech as an attack on teachers.

Friday, October 22

We had overspun the education speech in advance so a lot of the coverage today focused on the negative response, though the *Guardian* had a lot of positive teachers quoted. But it wasn't great, and was the result of us responding to the demands for advance briefing and not being clear about what we really wanted to be the central message. The other problem this morning was Prince Charles' people clearly briefed that he had deliberately snubbed one of the Jiang Zemin

[1] Robinson's book *An Unconventional Minister: My Life Inside New Labour* would be published in October 2000.

banquets. The TB/Charles strain was developing alongside the Buck House/St James's Palace tensions. I was in early for a meeting with TB, GB and PG. TB said afterwards it was his preferred forum for strategy discussions because he felt if we agreed on the overall strategy, we would be able to implement it through the government as a whole. If GB was offside on the overall strategy, it was hard.

It was a good meeting, one of the best we had had in a while. PG emphasised the problems re delivery and trust. GB was worrying about Milburn's strategy on health, felt he was pushing things too far, and lacked a clear stage-by-stage narrative or plan. He was also saying he was still unclear what we meant by forces of conservatism. TB had got over the hump on that one, said it was basically a means to give us definition as reformers and modernisers, and a way to show we were pushing for change against forces left and right that would hold us back. The Tories were trying to redefine themselves as the party of the people, and us as sleazy and arrogant. What had happened was that as we were branding them as extreme, others who felt they were being defined as forces of conservatism felt they were being put in the same box.

TB said we had three options – 1. give up on the argument – 'I have no pride of ownership'; 2. keep going, or 'dig a deeper hole' as the Tories would have it; or 3. find a different way of framing the same argument. For example, he talked of himself as a force of conservatism when it came to using computers. It was a shorthand for resistance to necessary change. We talked about London and GB shared our pessimistic view re Frank [Dobson]. 'No theme, no message, no campaign.' On Europe, we agreed the best antidote to 'Keep the Pound' was 'Save your Job', but it did mean getting Europe up on different terms. GB said nobody will ever love the euro, but as it becomes inevitable in their minds, so the argument will shift and if people have to choose economy vs sovereignty, they will choose economy. I asked what the main message for the PBR [Pre-Budget Report] was. Productivity. TB felt politically we were in the right place, but the media was turning and it would affect the mood. GB was much more engaged and though I knew it would be seen by some as a hit on me, I asked him to get more involved in the morning meetings. It was when we were hitting the same notes that we did best.

After GB left, PG and I stayed for a separate discussion with TB about himself. We said there was a feeling around that he was losing his touch a bit, in both senses, not on form and losing touch with people. He said he was not prepared to be something he wasn't. I said then we need to rediscover what he is, and get it out there again. PG said people wanted a competent government, but they also wanted him to care. As Stan Greenberg put it, when he was shaving in the morning, was he thinking about them, or about himself? They would sense that and at the moment it was him not them. He said he was always thinking about whether we were taking the right decisions to take the country in the right direction. We kept at him, said the feel of the government was too metropolitan.

We had a broader meeting with Jonathan, Anji, Sally, Pat, DM, PH. We had another gloomy discussion on London, this time backed by new polling. TB later got Dobbo in and said he really had to start landing a few blows on him [Ken Livingstone] or this was going to run away. There was plenty to go on – his past statements on the police, Sinn Fein, calling for GB to be sacked – but Frank didn't seem to have the fight. He lacked a killer instinct. I did him a note for his interviews but he couldn't punch a message through, so the overall impression was just 'I'm here'. A story broke about French beef being tainted with sewage and the Tories were out calling for a tit-for-tat ban. TB was adamant we do not overreact, and we simply said we obey the law and so should they. I locked myself away for three hours to work up a strategy note for the PBR and the Queen's Speech. We were going to have to get back on track.

Guthrie came in for a chat. He liked [new Defence Secretary Geoff] Hoon. Interestingly, he thought the forces of conservatism speech was pitched exactly right. I had a bit of an up-and-downer with Alan Milburn who systematically refused to do *Any Questions* and *Question Time* and who was now also saying he wouldn't do *Frost* this week. We went out for Rory's birthday, got back late, but I had another go at the strategy paper, which I wanted to get to GB over the weekend.

Saturday, October 23

TB was unfazed by the fuss the Tories were making on beef, and said there could be no question of us suggesting anything illegal. He felt that in general terms we were being tested classically à la mid term, and we just had to hold firm. For all the hoo-ha over the Chinese visit, he felt in the end we had taken the right position, and stuck to it and it would benefit us with the Chinese, as well as the public. He felt [Prince] Charles had been silly. The *Sunday Times* led on some cock and bull story about Robinson having a picture of a Cabinet minister in compromising circumstances, which would run big tomorrow and be a real pain in the arse. I told the press office to say we imagined it would turn out to be as true as all the other nonsense stories we had had to deal with on the GR front recently. Oborne had a good piece [in the *Express*] on TB the conviction politician and [*Observer* columnist and former editor of the *Independent* Andrew] Marr had a good piece on the press, saying they went OTT on politicians, particularly TB, so maybe sticking to our guns on forces of conservatism was having some effect for the better.

Sunday, October 24

The GR stuff was unleashing the usual rash of conspiracy stories – with [Charlie] Whelan and Peter M in most of them. The best way to deal with it was for Geoffrey to say the story was nonsense, and he said to Anji he would happily do that. Then he went to ground around 4pm and when Anji finally spoke to him at 8, he said he wanted to speak to his lawyer. It was hard to escape the impression he was letting this stuff run. The serious press thought this was getting very silly. Peter M felt there was a deliberate destabilisation campaign going on. Part of it was to say that now he was back, the government was full of division and divisiveness again. I finished my draft paper and got it to GB, Peter M, PG and PH for comments. It had the dividing lines in the right place and it would give us a new sense of momentum if we could get the whole government communicating from it. Peter M sent over some useful detail points. GB didn't get back in time before I sent it to TB, but he said he was OK with it.

Monday, October 25

Some, like *The Times*, ignored the Robinson stuff. Others, like the *Express*, splashed on it. For the eleven o'clock I took the line this was a story about modern political journalism rather than the government. Our big problem today was beef. Nick Brown had tried to get us back on track with the changes on labelling, but the French tainted meat had exposed their double standards and there was a real momentum behind trade-war ideas. TB was adamant we do not go down that route. We got Charlie [Falconer] to look into it and he recommended we get our scientists on to it. At the office meeting, TB was still expressing confidence re the forces of conservatism argument, broadly supported my note and felt we were getting proper definition on policy, which could only be increased through the Queen's Speech and PBR.

PG had done groups last night and said Hague was dead, but they were not very warm about us. They were pretty down on TB at the moment, and picking up on his lack of confidence a bit. Otherwise the meeting was the usual run around the block, him asking as ever why he asked for things to happen that didn't and then raging about departments. The 11 was mainly beef, with a bit of GR, and then I left with TB for the Internet interview he was doing for the *Sun*. It was a bit of a shambles but we were basically doing it for relations with the *Sun* rather than the content, which was a good job, not least because some of the answers he gave weren't even quoted accurately.

TB and I got stuck in dreadful traffic and got out to get the Tube from Monument. It was interesting to see the reactions of people. Most were just surprised to see him, and there was lots of nudging and nodding. Lots, this being the Tube, looked embarrassed to be looking. But the ones who came over and spoke were overwhelmingly friendly, though I think these days it is as much a celebrity thing as a leadership or political thing.

We had chaos out of the *Sun* interview. The stenographer had written a load of nonsense in parts. They had also put out a new line on EMU, which was not even discussed and on the monarchy they were going on about a referendum on the Queen! We were also apparently going to cut doctors' hours. Christ knows what had happened. They were embarrassed but as ever with papers not keen on just putting their hands up and saying they had screwed up somehow and quoted him wrongly. But it was so blatant they had very little choice. Alex [Ferguson] called after I went to bed, sounded a bit down. He was in a bit of a state re his goalkeeping situation. [Massimo] Taibi had lost confidence and [Mark] Bosnich didn't command the defence.

Tuesday, October 26

I was in for a Jonathan beef meeting with Charlie F and a stack of MAFF [Ministry of Agriculture, Fisheries and Food] people, trying to work out the best approach before Thursday. It was obvious that there were problems in our position and TB's call to Prodi suggested they were looking for compromise. It had a nasty smell to it. TB was adamant we do not change tack, but the press and the Tories were really winding up on the call for a ban on French products. I wanted at least to say he had spoken to Prodi to register our concerns, but he just wanted it played by the book, felt the furore would blow over and long term we would be in a better position. The last thing we needed was a trade war, or even talk of it.

Later he spoke to Jospin, who started with a real rant about my briefing of their conversation in Tampere. TB said he had never heard him so angry, that he felt they should have simply kept the whole chat private, which in the context of a summit is pretty unrealistic. TB felt he was probably under pressure to hold a tough line and this was the best way of letting his system know he was in tough mode. But it was a bit odd. Jospin said as a result of my briefing, all he got at his press conference was beef. Everything now depended on us getting the right result. Holding the line was fine provided we got to the right position in the end. [UK ambassador to France Sir] Michael Jay didn't seem overly optimistic. I said we would be fucked big time if this went wrong.

We had a meeting with TB on London to go over plans for tomorrow re Ken. It was clear that if TB really went for him, the assumption would be we were going to block him. We had to be clear about the outcome. But the way things were going there was no way Frank was going to be able to stop him. I had another problem with Mo. She'd told Richard Wilson that she wanted to make public she'd taken cannabis 'and inhaled'. Nigel Warner [Mowlam's special adviser] called to say the *Mail* had asked her and she was inclined to answer. Pure self-indulgence, which would put pressure on other ministers re all manner of personal life questions. Mo could get away with it, and she knew it, which was why she was keen to do it, but it was a bad idea. The problem was she had too much time on her hands, loved the image stuff and this kind of thing just appealed to her for all the wrong reasons. I raised it with TB after he got back from the Palace and he said he did not want anything done until he had spoken to her. He said we had to find ways of harnessing her popularity.

Wednesday, October 27

We were getting hit pretty hard on beef, but TB still felt we were in the right position. TB was clear that if we did not get a clear-cut decision our European strategy was pretty much in tatters. I kept going with the same line at the 11, and we were getting some marks for toughing it out but it all depended on the result. I said it was better to get a bad press for a good policy than a good press for a bad policy. TB was preparing for PMQs more and more on his own now, just asking for us, usually one-on-one, when he felt the need. The Tories thought they were on to something though and their tails were up, but again I felt TB was getting credit with serious people for holding his ground in tricky circumstances. If we didn't win tomorrow though, we were in deep shit. At the four o'clock, they were starting to press with some very difficult 'what if' questions. They had clearly worked out the scale of the problem if it went wrong. We left the Commons for Wood Green [London Labour Party event] and TB was fairly

October '99: Mo wants to come clean on cannabis

relaxed. The basic message was no going back to the 80s.[1] He also backed Dobbo pretty well. He was quite keen to get the news out re the baby but we were still holding the line. During the Q&A, a baby cried and he said 'Mmm, brings back memories.'

Thursday, October 28

I went up to the flat. TB was still worrying about yesterday. There was also another poll showing arrogance was becoming a bigger problem. I discussed it with Charlie F earlier who felt there was a problem, because TB simply believed he was right about everything. TB had a speech on health, though GB's relaunch of computers in schools was getting more coverage. But beef was the main thing.

Cabinet was meant to be a political discussion but it was pretty hopeless. TB didn't really give direction and he was vague about the overall political strategy. He didn't even mention forces of conservatism as a prong of the strategy. He said the three key issues were the economy, Europe and public service delivery. But there wasn't enough in what he said to generate anything remotely nearing a strategic discussion and so we had the usual round of rather unconnected interventions. Most of them were just justifying well-known positions. GB seemed to be in a sulk again. I got Robin to do the lunchtime media on beef to give Nick Brown a bit more support and cover. The 11.30 briefing was all about beef and they were trying to push me on hypotheticals, mainly what if the SSC [EU Scientific Steering Committee] didn't back us totally. Godric said afterwards that I got the tone right. We were having to rest on the science whilst not ruling out concessions.

I had a meeting with the Dome [communications] people, Jez Sagar and co plus Matthew Freud [PR expert] and a guy called Sholto [Douglas-Home, great-nephew of former Conservative Prime Minister Sir Alec]. I wasn't too impressed. I got back for a meeting with [Chelsea footballer] Frank Leboeuf who I was trying to get on board for the Europe campaign. He was OK in principle, but worried if it got out of hand, so we agreed he'd do an interview for the *Mirror* and see how that went. Man United finally announced they were not going back in the Cup. Alex called and said there were just too many fixtures.

[1] Blair told the audience of Labour members: 'This is nothing to do with me being arrogant or a control freak. We are in fact giving away power when we decentralise government in London. I never want the Labour Party to go back to the early 1980s, to become a byword for extremism or end up with Conservative MPs in parts of London because the Labour Party lost its way and ceased to be a force for good decent Labour values. I am never going back to those days.'

Friday, October 29

I was in early for a meeting on beef. It was not clear what we were going to get but the vibes were reasonably good. [EU health and consumer protection commissioner David] Byrne's press conference was due at 5 and we were to get the decision just before then. I slipped off to the dentist. Bad news. She reckoned I needed twelve to fourteen hours' work on my teeth. I was back for a meeting on the PBR which was OK up to a point. But I felt instinctively that Balls and co were holding something back. I had a meeting with Mo who was desperate to get out the line that she once took cannabis 'And unlike Clinton, I inhaled and didn't like it.' She felt there was no way of not answering it sometime and she wanted to tell the truth. I saw it as being no problem for her but a problem for others who would then be pinned down on the basis she had been upfront. She said it would connect with people and in particular young people. I wasn't sure about that either. Bizarrely, she said it would help her do her job properly.

Otherwise, we just ran round the usual issues in her brief, GM, 'regs' as she called deregulation, but she was really just casting around for things to do. She imagined she'd be having a big role in the election planning, but TB was unlikely to want to change personnel on that. I was doing the Sundays, dealing with the usual crap – Royals, Cabinet pay, background on beef – when Mark Bennett came through with a note from David North [private secretary, agriculture, food and home affairs] – the scientific committee meeting had gone totally according to plan, absolute vindication.[1] Thank God for that. I did a conference call with TB and agreed a line for him to do clips when his train got into Stevenage. We had to be reasonably measured but we really had to stick it to the Tories. It ran big and bold on the news and everyone was clear that it was a total vindication but the Tories were not put under much pressure on their stance. TB was talking about doing an open letter to the media on the whole Europe issue.

Saturday, October 30

OK coverage for beef though amazingly the *Mail* and *Sun* tried to claim it was because of their campaign. TB felt we needed to respond in some way to the arrogance attacks that had been led by the *Mail*. PM and I were both worried that it would just put arrogance up there as a theme. Godric came on saying we needed to keep the beef story

---

[1] The SSC concluded unanimously that it did not share the concern expressed by the French food safety agency about the safety of the meat and meat products exported by the UK.

going through the weekend and we came up with the idea of a big event to promote British beef to European markets.

Sunday, October 31

I spoke to Joe Irvin on a couple of JP stories – first, that he was intending to fight for a pay rise, later complaining he could see this was a classic TB/GB press operation to stop a rise from happening, and second, that he was not backing Frank but Glenda. We assumed that one was spun by Dan Hodges [son of Glenda Jackson]. The mayor situation was degenerating pretty badly. The big developing story was Prince Charles taking William out hunting. Again, it seemed pretty clear it was a political act coming so soon after GM and the 'boycotting' of the Chinese banquet. Then, news that *The Times* were splashing on Prince Charles becoming a 'beef ambassador'. What seemed to be happening was that he was following through a strategy to put himself at the head of the forces of conservatism. The speech had clearly really struck a nerve. Charles' people were briefing the Monday papers that his meeting with TB was basically about hunting. TB said I should say the meeting was long arranged, they got on very well, and it was no surprise to anyone that he hunted. But while publicly we stayed supportive, TB said Charles had to understand there were limits to the extent to which they could play politics with him. I agreed a line with [Sir] Stephen Lamport [private secretary to Prince Charles] to play it all down, but the fact of the meeting was out there and was going to be a big thing. When TB came back he was pretty shocked that the media had been staking it out. He said it was ninety minutes of pretty hard talk, not just about hunting.

Monday, November 1

Charles had given TB a long paper on hunting and why it was good for the environment. He had also set out his views on GM – 'I cannot stay silent' – and on China – 'I feel very strongly about it'. He said he was going to say nothing about us doing away with the hereditary peerage. TB said he bought the line that because we were modernising, that meant we were determined to do away with all traditions but he had to understand that some traditions that did not change and evolve would die. It all had the feel of a deliberate strategy, to win and strengthen media support by putting himself at arm's length from TB and a lot of the changes we were making. He was arguing for example how hereditary peers have so much to offer, or, a bit menacingly, saying 'We don't really want to be like the continentals, now do we?'

I talked Charles up in the briefings but some of the journalists thought Charles was overreaching himself. TB felt he had been really stung by the forces of conservatism speech. He said they felt much more vulnerable than in reality they are. We know they still have the power to 'keep us in our place' but they don't always see it like that. He had asked him whether he really thought we should have nothing to do with Jiang Zemin. He didn't really have an answer.

At the strategy meeting, Philip and I were arguing that we needed somehow to move the line on Europe. There needed to be more a sense that patriotism was driving our vision of Europe, not just a belief in Europe per se. TB seemed to be moving to my view that we needed to make the media and its coverage of Europe part of the narrative about Europe. On London, he still couldn't decide whether it was better to block Ken and have him win as an independent.

Tuesday, November 2
A truly dreadful meeting with Mo, Lance [Price], PH, Alun Evans [SCU], [Mike] Granatt [head of GICS] and others. She didn't have a clue what she wanted the meeting to be about. It was meant to be about message and co-ordination, and how she fitted into all that, but it just meandered all over the place. I said the problem was not our systems but the poor performance of ministers who still lacked the discipline of the Tories at their best. She also seemed to misunderstand what the various bits of the operation were meant to do, like the COI [Central Office of Information]. Meanwhile Elinor Goodman was doing the hunting 'solution' – accurately – on *Channel 4 News*.

I got home to a call from the *Sun* that Nick Brown seemed to have caved in to the French after his discussions on beef with [French agriculture minister Jean] Glavany. The French were now promising new tests in five different areas. Nick Brown was trying to say this was just about clarification but it was a presentational disaster. I was up till gone 12, talked to Nick a few times. You had to wonder what kind of discussion went on inside MAFF before they did something like that. Nick had really messed it up and lost all the gains of last week. I told TB as he got back from seeing the Queen. He had told her about Cherie being pregnant. The Tory line on beef was that we had snatched defeat from the jaws of victory. TB said he couldn't understand how Nick had managed to do this. Shambles time. Nick said he had simply agreed for our experts to meet to go through the five issues in relation to the science. But all the headlines, inevitably, were about us climbing down. I got Joyce Quin [now junior agriculture minister] on to *Newsnight* and she did fine. Nick apologised for the fiasco and agreed he would do the rounds on it. But what on earth was he thinking of? The whole strategy had been to go for the ban to be lifted, nothing else. We had succeeded, and then this. We really did have weak vessels.

Wednesday, November 3

Though TB was furious at the [beef] presentational fiasco, he felt we were probably doing the right thing. I put together a line that we were interested in getting the ban fully lifted, promoting UK sales and doing it without a long legal battle. TB felt we just had to stay calm, put the case, and highlight the Tories' opportunism. It was staggering that [Shadow agriculture minister Tim] Yeo was never challenged properly as he moved from one position to another. In substance, this would only become a real problem if the French tried to reopen the principle. Or were they just saving face?

The eleven o'clock was not that bad and I got the message up that the choice was between a few days to secure a clear win, or a long, drawn-out court case. I was trying to persuade TB to be more political at PMQs and really go for Hague. I felt he could make the argument that on Kosovo, Northern Ireland and beef, their various opportunistic positions displayed a lack of patriotism. But TB felt we had to handle beef very calmly. In the end, Hague stunned pretty much everyone by going on a tax measure that was being voted on tonight,[1] the welfare reform rebellion being the other issue we had to deal with. Though we hadn't really prepared for it, TB did fine, really hit them on tax and spend because they were clocking up so many commitments. George Mitchell came in to see TB [re Northern Ireland] and felt things were moving in the right direction. He said Peter M was a real help because he was not Mo and that helped on the Unionist side.

We had a meeting on London. To block or not to block [Ken Livingstone] was the only question. Peter M and I seemed to be the last two really to feel that the risk of him being a Labour mayor was greater than the wrath we would face for blocking him. But TB had definitely moved. He felt we would do real damage to ourselves if we blocked him now, that we would lose lots of [party] members, and not just on the hard left. He was not confident that JP, GB, Mo

---

[1] The Welfare Reform and Pensions Bill. A clause in the bill was designed to prevent IT specialists stating they were self-employed for tax purposes when in fact they were contracted by large companies. Hague claimed Labour would be levying a £500 million 'stealth tax' that would hit IT companies and drive them overseas.

would really support it in practice. They would just let us take the flak. Philip believed that if Ken stood as an independent and won, he would be in a position to show TB had allowed him to divide the Labour Party and the public would punish us for it. He was adamant that it was too late to block him. Margaret McDonagh felt the same.

TB felt the least worst option was to bind him in to a party platform. I said he would not sign up to it. Margaret said she believed Ken was so desperate to be mayor that he would do it. But it was pretty clear TB had made up his mind. We had to bind him into the manifesto, make sure he had a good deputy and chief executive. He said he had thought it through and he could see nothing but downside but the biggest downside of all would come if we blocked him. We now had to go out and fight for Frank. I said there was no way Frank was going to win and we were heading to a total humiliation. It was a total mess and I left the meeting rather fed up. Anji came round and tried to persuade me and Peter it was the right thing to do.

Thursday, November 4

[Tony] Bevins did a big page 1 'Where's the beef?' splash, putting together hunting, beef and London and said we were drifting. He wasn't far wrong. I told TB my fear was that the fundamentals had moved and we were not raising our game to match that. I knew that in part it was the baby that was discombobulating him, but the decision-making process seemed to be getting worse not better. We were more last minute on [preparing] speeches than ever, for example. He said none of that mattered. The question was were we actually doing the right things and whatever the media said, he felt we were. He was convinced the Tories had made big strategic errors that we would punish them for. Stan Greenberg did a very good note on the post-speech [Labour conference] terrain, felt we had a real opportunity to entrench definition if we kept going with the forces of conservatism argument with confidence. *The Times* splashed on an OECD [Organisation for Economic Co-operation and Development] report on tax, headlined 'Tax in UK rising faster than anywhere in Europe'. Bill Bush [Number 10 research unit] did an OK job on rebuttal. I tried to get GB involved but he wouldn't do it. Also, just before Cabinet I asked GB when he was going to get involved in the nine o'clock meetings, and oddly, he said he had to wait till he knew what we were doing re Ken Livingstone. He was clearly keen to block, as was I, but that was hardly a reason not to start proper involvement in day-to-day management of strategy.

At Cabinet, TB said we were unprecedentedly strong for a government at this time, not least because of economic management, and also because the Opposition was so badly perceived. But there was an impatience and frustration on public service delivery. Added to which the Tories were successfully labelling us as arrogant and out of touch and they were making inroads on Europe. GB said we had laid foundations. The Tories had gone too far on Europe. We can portray them as ideological. On the economy, there too they had gone to the right. They were also becoming incoherent, making inconsistent noises on tax cuts in general and spending commitments in particular. He felt we were able to put the case for compassion and prosperity together. But modernisation and reform was an important part of the argument. We have to be modernising public services and welfare and the Tory alternative is their dismantling. He also went through the argument for the PBR. The Tories would try and present us as arrogant and elitist which was why we had to be always on the side of hard-working families. I had a good meeting with Gus Macdonald, who is a real grown-up. I did the four o'clock with Margaret Beckett, mainly on the welfare rebellion.[1] She never put a foot wrong at these briefings.

Friday, November 5

I went in for GB's presentation on the PBR. It was fine on all the figures but I said I felt it was all a bit dry. Later he called me over to the Treasury to tell me some of the other things that would be in there. Free TV licences for over 75-year-olds. Changes to fuel duty. Big inquiry into the black economy. He was paranoid about me telling anyone else, but it was a pretty odd way to do business when even some of the departments concerned didn't know some of the plans. But as ever, he had the right mix of big economic message and individual measures that would connect big time.

Saturday, November 6

I don't know what triggered it but last night I plunged into depression which stayed pretty much through the weekend. Partly I think it was tiredness, but also the feeling that whilst Fiona gave me all the practical support I needed, emotional support was lacking because by and large she was against the fact I had to put so much into the job. I was definitely feeling under more pressure. Her basic take was that I just wanted everything on my terms and had to understand

[1] Some Labour MPs rebelled against proposed changes to incapacity benefit. In the end, the size of the rebellion – fifty-three – was not as big as expected and the changes were passed.

that it could be tough living with someone as driven as I was. TB called after watching the rugby with Jospin [Australia beat France 35-12 at the Millennium Stadium, Cardiff, in the World Cup Final]. I said the news had said he had been booed. He said it was barely noticeable, but I sensed it unsettled him. We went out for dinner with the Milibands [David and Louise]. David also felt we were slightly losing the plot at the moment.

Sunday, November 7

During the day, partly over lunch with Philip, I put together a briefing note bringing together forces of conservatism and some of GB's argument at Cabinet on enterprise and fairness. We had to use the PBR to get back on track. TB was working with GB on the PBR statement. He [TB] had cricked his neck really badly and was worried that it wouldn't clear up before Paris [Congress of the Socialist International] tomorrow. I was then working till gone 12 on his speech.

Monday, November 8

I was up early and straight out to the airport, and TB signed off the speech on the plane. Jospin and Schroeder both went on far too long and the main points of their speeches weren't very discernible. TB did OK but the more I did of these international speaking events, the less I liked them. TB did an interview with French TV and then a bilateral with Fernando de la Rua [President-elect of Argentina]. We got back for PBR meetings with GB, who didn't want to go too far in claiming improved standards of living, and wanted to promote productivity. Mo was still pressing me to do a statement on cannabis. She also had this mad idea that she sign up to do a book from which she, Nigel [Warner] and Jon [Norton, her husband] all take a third but Jon would get his third now. She said it wasn't an autobiography as such but it was all about 'how famous Mo coped with it all'. I said I couldn't see how a serving minister could do it and benefit financially from such a book. Added to which I thought the cannabis thing was just self-indulgence. She left by saying if she didn't hear from me tomorrow she would go ahead.

Tuesday, November 9

PBR day. I felt the series of meetings we had had got us in better shape. PBR Cabinet was fine. At the office meeting, TB and I were arguing about the extent to which we put our energies into the Tories. I felt we were getting definition through conflict and struggle and had to keep going on it. TB felt there was sometimes a benefit from him being above the fray. The PBR went well, both in the House and when we did the rounds later. I went back to Number 10 for a meeting with TB, Mo, Richard W and Jeremy H and we had to go through all the crap about drugs again. We got her to agree to say she was never into drugs and she wasn't going to go over her whole life. On the book idea, both TB and Richard felt there was a problem with it because she was earning money from it while in office. She then said 'Well, I hear what you say and I'll have to decide whether to go ahead and make a decision.' TB: What do you mean? Mo: Well you'd have to decide if you wanted me to stay in government. TB: There's no need to think like that, but it would not be sensible for you not to be in government but you would get badly hit if you went ahead with this, so I just say don't do anything without coming back to me. I said to her later if they had problems with money why doesn't Jon write a book himself, but even that had its own problems. Later she agreed she would not take any money.

Wednesday, November 10
GB got us a good press, though the *Sun* didn't splash on it and the *Express* just did a page 2 lead. The *Today* programme led on an interview with the French consumer affairs minister [Marylise Lebranchu] saying they weren't ready to lift the beef ban so that was the big story for the day. I went up to see TB. Peter M called TB to say the Unionists had come in with yet another list of demands, and it was dreadful. 'Boy, have we been here before?' TB said. He just had to keep going. On beef, he remained adamant we just had to stay reasonable. John Sawers felt we had claimed victory too soon. TB had a round of interviews, then GB came over to take stock post-PBR. We went off to do Nicky Campbell [BBC Radio talk show] and they [TB and GB] were OK, though the questioning was pretty tough. TB said he felt totally comfortable in the arguments on welfare and the economy. GB was a lot more relaxed at the moment. TB said he had come in like he always does and given us a sense of order and direction.

The eleven o'clock was all about beef and pretty grim. Then came news that the French Cabinet had met and decided they were not going to lift the ban, which was another hit for Hague at PMQs. We tried to fix a Jospin call but he cancelled at the last minute. TB felt Hague had to do the economy but I was sure he would go on beef, and he did.[1] TB hammered him in the end but I was given a pretty

[1] Hague told Blair: 'On Monday [in Paris] you gave the French the Third Way. On Wednesday they gave you two fingers.'

torrid time afterwards. TB saw Frank [Dobson] privately and later said he needed real help from me, Peter M, PG and GB.

Thursday, November 11

Beef was becoming a real disaster area in the media but TB was still of the view we were doing the right thing. I took the kids to school and listened in to a phone call with Jospin. There was a clear change of tone, no real warmth there at all. Jospin set out the reasons why it was difficult for him, and ended by saying he was fed up of being isolated and scapegoated by us. They agreed for the experts to meet tomorrow but all that was likely to lead to was a court case which would be seen as yet another failure. All this on the day Livingstone was allowed to go through. On that, before we left for South Africa [for the Commonwealth Heads of Government Meeting, 'CHOGM'], GB and I had another discussion with TB and tried one more time to say there was a case for blocking him, but TB was settled in his view. He intended to say publicly that he would have blocked him but it was clear the party wanted him to run. He felt there was a chance that the party would say yes to him being allowed to run, but no to him being the candidate. TB and I had a bit of a row. I said his interview with Nicky Campbell was crap and he disagreed. I said he failed at PMQs to do the basic enterprise and fairness message out of the PBR. I also felt he underestimated the damage being done to us on beef. He said he didn't, but he could see no other way of handling this. I said he made a better case for the French than they did.

Cabinet was Northern Ireland and beef, then TB and Hoon had to leave for the Cenotaph and JP chaired the rest of the meeting. GB did a bit post-PBR, and said he felt the Tories were really vulnerable on public spending, and he felt the economic dividing lines were becoming clearer – stability vs stop-go; employment vs unemployment; work vs poverty; support for public services vs privatisation. Alex F was in town and came in for lunch. We popped round for a quick chat with TB. Alex said afterwards he had that rare ability of making people feel special and optimistic. Peter M called, pretty exasperated, said Northern Ireland was looking really difficult and could even go belly-up today. There was a story in the *Mirror* that Mo hated her new job. She was going to become a real problem. GB called, said that [Shadow Chancellor Francis] Maude had been hopeless at Treasury questions, but he still felt we weren't getting the dividing lines with the Tories in the right place.

TB said the baby would be called Leo or Hazel [the names of his parents]. On the plane out [to South Africa] TB and I had another chat about what I felt was his, and our, loss of cutting edge. I felt he was becoming a bit too remote from the public, and did think he was listening less and becoming prone to thinking he was always right. There were always things we could do better. My only chat with the hacks on the plane had led to stories about CB having to spend lots of her own money on clothes. This had come out as I was defending myself over an untrue story in the Sundays that I earned more than the Cabinet.

Friday, November 12

I barely slept and as ever with these trips, there was always too much to do. I did a note on the Queen's Speech and the follow-through to try to get up dividing lines for next week. We arrived in Durban and TB went off to the opening ceremony. The French press had finally moved to covering beef big, really for the first time, and not all of it was pro-French. Back home, crisis time in Northern Ireland was running big. We went over to the Commonwealth Secretary General's party for the media, where TB was being quizzed by someone from Zimbabwe exactly as our press were quizzing [President of Zimbabwe Robert] Mugabe. Tom Kelly [NIO] called saying it would be helpful if TB did a calming clip on Northern Ireland. TB was reluctant but did it. [President of South Africa Thabo] Mbeki wasn't really pushing the summit agenda along and TB came out at one point and said he was bored rigid. Charles Reiss [*Evening Standard*] called to say that Mugabe had again said we organised Peter Tatchell's attack on him in London.[1] Mugabe's attack [on 'gay gangsters' in Blair's government plotting with gay activists to humiliate him] totally dominated my briefing at 3.30, with lots of Zimbabweans there who asked me what I thought the problem was between him and TB. God knows. The press loved the story.

[EU commissioner] David Byrne's office called me to say the *FT* was doing a story that TB was very gloomy about the chances of solving the beef dispute, that they had emphasised there was progress, but [Jean] Glavany was a problem, that they were dealing with Jospin's office who were being reasonable. TB spoke to Gerry Adams, said he really understood why they were so fed up with the UUs but just give us the weekend. There was a minor flap when nobody could

[1] The previous month, gay rights activist Tatchell and three others had approached Mugabe's car and attempted to perform a 'citizen's arrest' on charges of 'murder, torture, detention without trial, and the abuse of gay human rights'. Mugabe had five years earlier denounced male homosexuals as 'worse than dogs and pigs'.

find TB's black tie before he left for the banquet. Mugabe was running big, then Northern Ireland, then beef. England vs Scotland [Euro 2000 football qualifier] tomorrow was going to be massive.

Saturday, November 13

TB was pretty much focused on Ireland, though there were some tricky issues at the summit. Mugabe took up most of the press coverage though there were bits and pieces about a new role for the Commonwealth. Don McKinnon had been elected the new Secretary General and TB had the idea of him establishing a new committee specifically to work on the role of the Commonwealth in the next century. TB had done an interview with the *Mail on Sunday* on the flight out and they were leading on community service orders with CSA as second string, which would help us get up welfare reform when he did Boulton [Sky] tomorrow. I just did the one briefing then back to watch the football [Scotland 0, England 2]. TB was pretty tied up with official summitry through the day and he wasn't enjoying the event, though he was doing the main speech at the dinner. But as the leaders had all gone to the retreat, for me it was as near to a day off as I had had for ages.

Sunday, November 14

I was up early to go through the overnight cuttings and then down to a place near the retreat to do Boulton, who got through loads – football, CHOGM, Mugabe, beef, Europe, AIDS, pensions, Livingstone, welfare reform, Lords, Ireland. We were pushing the welfare issues. It was a good interview with lots for the press to get stuck into. TB briefed me on the dinner from last night before heading back to the retreat to play tennis. I worked on the Queen's Speech for a bit, then John Sawers and I went out to Victoria beach for a swim, then a long walk. TB called to say that they had agreed to the idea of a committee to review the Commonwealth's role, which was fine. It had been a rather odd event, and as we left I actually felt like I'd had a rest. We flew down to Cape Town. TB and CB arrived and for the first time I felt that I noticed a bump on Cherie. TB did a truly dreadful Prince Charles-style interview with [Robin] Oakley, not clear, drawling, long pauses. Really awful.

Monday, November 15

Over dinner on the plane, TB, CB and I talked about the baby. She was still keen to keep it all quiet but the bump was definitely beginning to show. We went through some lines for the Queen's Speech debate. I quite liked Hague-onomics. I took a sleeping pill, slept till we landed and we went straight to the office. The eleven o'clock was Ireland and beef. I was asked about a story about Peter waiting till he got the Ulster job before getting his flat refurbished, and I suggested he should sue over it. Both Mitchell and [John] de Chastelain made good statements suggesting progress and we got a broadly positive response from the parties.

TB met some of the party people when we went over to Millbank and he said he was going to come out against Ken tomorrow. He said it was important there was no chicanery and we had to play by the rules. But I could see no way Frank's campaign was going to beat Ken. We got back for a meeting with GB who still felt we should block him. He said better to have one week of hell than three months of hell. TB asked him would he feel the same if there were thousands of resignations and then we were challenged in the courts and lost. Also he believed a lot of people inside and outside the party no longer really bought the whole Red Ken image any more.

Tuesday, November 16

I went up to see CB to apologise for the wall-to-wall coverage of her clothes that had followed me trying to deal with the stories about my salary. She was very nice about it, even when the press coverage got so big the broadcasters felt obliged to follow it up. I had fallen for the oldest trick in the book and allowed myself to get verballed. She said 'To them, I'm just a picture.' As I left, she said she was on my side re Ken.

I was at the dentist for three hours, then back to more discussions on Ken. We had got the broadcasters lined up for 5pm but it was clear there was a problem. The transcript [of an interview with Labour's NEC] showed that Ken refused to say he would support a manifesto that included PPP [public-private partnership for the Tube]. There was a clear case for blocking him, but then Frank called me to say he did not make a habit of threatening prime ministers, but if Ken was blocked, we could not take it for granted that he would run as a 'lone ranger'. He said Ken had to stand. He called me again later to make the same point.

TB made the suggestion to Margaret [McDonagh] that we say they would call Ken back. It seemed that Clive Soley [chair of the PLP chairing the five-member NEC shortlisting panel] was for blocking him straight away whereas Ian McCartney [also on the NEC panel] wanted the party to see we were bending over backwards to be fair to him. But the hacks were all hanging around outside and it was beginning to look a bit farcical. TB felt though that he was slightly playing into our hands.

JP was pretty wound up about him refusing to sign up to our manifesto and he agreed to go up tomorrow on the *Today* programme. He was very bullish about it. 'You can't run on a separate manifesto.' About 8, Soley finally went out and said that Ken would have to come back on Thursday and that he had not been clear and straightforward. TB was pretty exasperated. Our famed so-called news management was looking pretty ropy. On *Newsnight*, Glenda [Jackson] and Ken united against the [selection] system. Ann Keen called me to say Dobbo was really angry, close to quitting, and she didn't trust the people in his camp. We had really fucked this from start to finish. The only good thing coming out of it was the sense of Livingstone as a totally divisive figure. But it was pretty hopeless. Mo told me she would support blocking if he didn't go for the manifesto. Margaret B was not so clear. But all in all, it was a dreadful day, the best part of which was probably the visit to the dentist.

Wednesday, November 17

Queen's Speech day, and Ken fucking Livingstone was leading the news. I think what I hated as much as anything was that we looked so incompetent. It was like something out of the 80s. Cherie's clothes was still running as a problem. It was all a pretty grim backdrop for the Queen's Speech. GB and I had another go at TB, said that whatever he signed up to, he would just shift afterwards. Clive [Soley] was excellent on the media. On PPP, GB felt Livingstone had to go for more than just saying he would support the manifesto. He would have to retract what he had said. JP was excellent on the *Today* programme, made clear he could not stand as an independent on a Labour ticket. Mo was doing the pre-Queen's Speech interview and was absolutely dreadful. She didn't even challenge their propositions on tax, class sizes, waiting lists going up. 'Can't do everything, it's cooking' seemed to be her line.

Meanwhile Frank D, or someone on his behalf, was busy briefing what Ann Keen had told me yesterday, mainly that he would pull out if Ken was not put forward. TB thought it was a pretty asinine move. Meanwhile Glenda J was sitting there thinking she would benefit from [the NEC] blocking Ken. I didn't feel we had prepared properly for the Queen's Speech debate. TB did OK, but it was all a bit flat and that was the mood of the briefing afterwards.

Dobbo's threat was the big story. TB felt that it was possible to block him [Livingstone] and he would go up and say why, but he had spent thirty minutes with Frank, who had said there was no way he would stand if Ken was blocked. But some of them felt there was some merit in that happening and getting both of them out. GB and I were the two most strongly arguing for him to be blocked. Lance [Price] came in with a statement from Ken which said he would support the manifesto and not withdraw halfway through if he was not happy with it. This felt like some of the nonsense Neil [Kinnock] had to put up with the whole time. TB was also worrying about possible legal challenges. At one point he said to me 'Would you mind refraining from just sitting there and shaking your head?' He felt the statement made it very difficult to block him.

GB said if he won, as Labour but effectively as an independent, our transport policy is dead. I got Neil to speak to Frank but he called halfway through the football to say that it was hopeless and he just wouldn't go for it if Ken was blocked. I saw Ian McCartney for a meeting on the COI, after which we chatted about Ken. Ian felt that he was capitulating and we had to let him go through. I said my worry was you couldn't believe a word he said, but Ian, like Frank, felt he could be beaten in argument.

Thursday, November 18

The Ken disaster was still rumbling on as he went back for his second [NEC] interview. Also, four of the papers led their Queen's Speech coverage on 'war on the motorist' which really annoyed TB. He was totally discombobulated by Ken. I said whose fault is it we're in such a mess and he said 'Mine.' I finished the political dividing lines speech with PH and then we set off for the Design Council. He did well in the Q&A and we planted a question on Ken which allowed him to get up 'no going back to the 80s'. Cabinet was Ireland, beef and the Queen's Speech. Peter M said part of the IRA statement was written by the UUs, which was a measure of how far we had come. Mitchell was due to make a statement at midday, that he believed it was possible for devolution and decommissioning to proceed. He said it was fragile but there had definitely been progress. I was back on form at the briefing, mainly on Ken.

At one o'clock, Piers Morgan called and said he had a story and if he told me what it was could he guarantee it would stay exclusive? I said I know what it is. He said 'How are your christening robes?' I said I would have to talk to TB. I had a meeting with Fiona and we agreed we would just let the *Mirror* run it and then confirm. But the *Sun* had heard something and Rebekah Wade was paging and calling both of us relentlessly. Eventually, after speaking to CB, Fiona gave the story to Rebekah around 8, which was clearly going to be disasterville with Piers. There was no way he would think the *Sun* got on to it themselves. I got TB to call him to try to mollify him a bit but later Piers was absolutely fuming. 'Why do those two women (Cherie and Fiona) have such a problem with me? I don't get it.'

CB was clear she didn't want her pregnancy to seem as somehow being owned as a *Mirror* story. Once the *Sun* were on to it, she wanted them to have the story. It was a one-fact story. Dealing with the *Sun* and the *Mirror* the whole time was like having two mistresses. It was a fucking nightmare. Both thought they were entitled to some kind of special treatment. It would probably have been better just to have announced it earlier, but Cherie had wanted to keep it quiet for as long as possible, which was fair enough. We had a statement out at 9.10, and it led Sky straight away. There was something amusing about seeing all these hard-nosed characters standing outside Number 10 going on about babies.

Friday, November 19

Philip sent me a message. Absolutely brilliant. He seemed to think the whole thing about the baby was a planned piece of news management to deal with Ken. I was able to disabuse him. News of the pregnancy led the *Today* programme, though Trevor Kavanagh [*Sun*] said later that Tony Hall [BBC director of news] had issued an edict that programmes and bulletins couldn't lead on it. Piers was out and about on TV trying to milk it. I was in just after 7 and went up to see TB and CB. She was perfectly happy with it. There was a fair old media crowd outside. Hague and GB were both being very nice about it, but TB had a slight concern people would think the whole thing had been designed for media purposes. What, I said, like we told you to have a baby because we had a few gaps in the Grid?

We had a meeting with GB at 9. He said we would regret letting Ken go through. We also had a bit of an up-and-downer about spending because GB didn't accept we should put more into schools and hospitals for now, but wait. TB said they needed it now. GB said 'You just want me to shovel in cash every time they ask. I can't do it. It's not on.' TB said 'No I'm not, but if we have the money what is the point in getting hit on it?' GB: 'I don't know what you're talking about.' I spoke to Dobbo to say he should get out and make a big thing about Ken having called for GB to be sacked [in June 1998].

At the eleven o'clock briefing, it was all about the baby and there was actually a very good mood and less cynicism than I thought there would be. Fiona had come to the briefing, said she really enjoyed it.

She was out and about with CB. TB had an interview with Patrick [Wintour] for the *Observer*, which we had planned to get up an attack on Ken, but even he was asking more about the baby than anything. Piers was very sore but said he managed to knock down the price [for the story] because it had been in other papers. We got TB out with CB for some pictures at 6.15 and he looked genuinely bemused, almost shy. Philip was convinced it would change the mood. He thought it would really help deal with the arrogance and out-of-touch attacks.

Saturday, November 20

Money could not buy the publicity we were getting. Even the *Mail* and the *Telegraph* were feeling they had to be nice-ish about it. There was a fair bit of speculation around about whether I had put the story out there, Roger Gale [Conservative MP] having said as much yesterday. The Piers/Yelland rubbish [*Mirror* vs *Sun* over the baby story] was still going on. I got Hilary C to go in and organise TB doing some words in the street as we left Number 10. Took Calum and Grace out to the Heath and then went into Number 10. The cabbie, who said Cherie's dad kissed him when he was pissed, said the country was loving it. TB said he couldn't believe the scale of the coverage. He did a little mingle with some kids in the street then we set off for the plane, working on the script for tomorrow [centre-left leaders' seminar in Florence]. He was reading the papers for once. A message came through that [Jeffrey] Archer had resigned.[1] I spoke to Frank to agree a line that now more than ever we needed a serious candidate. Frank sounded a lot more confident.

The [Florence seminar] dinner was in a fabulous setting but organisationally a total shambles. TB was worried that Frank had wanted to say [Steve] Norris [Conservative candidate defeated by Archer, now back in contention] was a more serious candidate. Our line should be that Hague's judgement was crap, and the Tories should reopen the whole contest. Pre-dinner drinks went on for ages and everyone, particularly Schroeder and Jospin, was getting more and more furious at the hanging around. I had a good chat with Jospin and made up re the [beef ban] briefing he had objected to. I had a good laugh with Schroeder re the baby. He said there is nothing you won't do to fill your damn newspapers. 'I'm going to have triplets.' TB asked me at

[1] Having won the Conservative candidacy for mayor of London, Archer was forced to withdraw after the *News of the World* reported that he had asked a friend, fellow novelist Ted Francis, to give him a false alibi to the court in a 1987 libel trial. Archer was subsequently tried and jailed for perjury. Francis was found not guilty of perverting the course of justice.

one point why we had given up a weekend for this event, but he perked up a bit when he and CB went off to see the Clintons. At least we were having a proper discussion about the continuing attacks on him for being aloof and arrogant. Clinton's speech showed once more how brilliant he was at connecting, not just through what he said, but how he said it, through the pictures he painted in words, and through body language, but above all through making the most of what he knew and what people told him.

You always had the feeling with Clinton that he was just hoovering up other people's stories and experiences, because they interested him, but also because he could use them. I discussed TB image problem with him. He said Hillary was being hit with exactly the same thing, that it's an obvious thing for the right-wing media to do, because it helps put up a barrier between the left in power and the people who elected them. All you could do was be aware of it and always strive to be in touch. Clinton was also asking TB to get more directly involved, given the success of his approach in Northern Ireland, in Cyprus and Kashmir. I was horrified at the prospect. I said I thought you were trying to help us get him back in touch, not find more reasons never to be at home.

Sunday, November 21

TB was moaning about the whole event now. He said he was all for a bit of political intellectual stimulation, but what a way to spend a weekend. There were stories in the press on the notion that GB would have to move out of the Number 10 flat, to make way for the baby.[1] Cherie sensed a bit of mischief and didn't want it denied. TB did, and said he was having none of that nonsense. Clinton turned up late, more than an hour late, for a breakfast that the Americans had asked for, and not surprisingly a lot of people were getting pissed off. When he arrived, he said he had been looking round Florence.

This was just summitry for a summit's sake. There was far too much ceremony. The speeches were better, especially TB and BC, though Jospin was far more New Labour than before. Schroeder was sitting next to Cherie at lunch and I tried to get him to repeat what he had said about having triplets. He said that I could quote him as saying that TB's performance in a stressful environment meant that other leaders were now being judged by very difficult standards. I did just one briefing, which was largely about the baby still, as they

[1] The Blairs were living in the bigger flat above 12 Downing Street, and the Browns living above Number 10.

were beginning to realise it was probably conceived at Balmoral. As ever, there was more interest from the foreign media on TB and the Third Way than from our own. We had a bit of a problem with the Elgin Marbles, because Clinton had seemingly told the Greeks he was happy to raise it with TB. He didn't and I was able to say 'We are not prepared to lose our marbles.' TB had made a couple of half-decent interventions in the Third Way discussions. D'Alema made yet another bad speech rounding things up. TB did a doorstep on Archer, beef, the baby, Third Way, then we were off to the [Prince Girolamo and Princess Irina] Strozzis' party. Absolutely ghastly. I just cannot for the life of me understand what he likes about this whole scene. I was just desperate to go now. But the plane was delayed for half an hour, apparently because of all the American security. I got home and we went out with the kids for dinner but I was absolutely shagged out. Archer was wall to wall.

Monday, November 22

TB had decided he should start this Friday with a visit that we billed as the first of a tour that showed he was determined to stay in touch, reconnect. I was worried that because of all the focus on spin/ strategy that it would just be seen as a piece of spinology. TB felt he would simply have to overrule GB on spending. GB had told him he was just a soft touch for spending ministers. At the eleven o'clock, I went into one of my occasional rants about the media not being interested in policy and of being obsessed with trivia. I went with TB for lunch at the *Express* and he did a doorstep on the way in about [the judgement of] Hague on Archer. The best line we were developing on Hague was definitely that he was good on jokes but bad on judgement. The *Express* lunch was pretty depressing. Neither [chief executive Lord Clive] Hollick nor [editor] Rosie Boycott seemed to have any real strategy for taking on the *Mail*.

I had a meeting with Frank Dobson and said the most important thing was to regain the initiative which would rebuild confidence in his people. 'I care about London. He cares about Ken.' But I doubted Frank's capacity. And his confidence was clearly low. There were already signals in the press that GB was backing Glenda [Jackson].

Wednesday, November 24

We had a meeting re PMQs. I felt we still weren't using them to promote and drive strategy. And because Hague was still coming up with good one-liners, TB wasn't getting the political plus points he ought to be. We were giving him good lines but he was very reluctant to use them in the House. He didn't like doing things that were over-rehearsed. It was fair enough. But he lacked a killer instinct in there. PMQs was a bit all over the place, debt, Chechnya, euro, slavery. Philip said later that he felt at the strategy meeting TB had been very low and I wondered whether it was because I put through a very tough note saying the operation today had been woeful. That there was no killer instinct from him and the MPs and we had missed opportunities. I left at 5 to go to Reading who were playing Burnley. Crap match. o-o. TB called, I think a bit hurt by my note. He said part of the problem was that some days he just felt ground down and his instincts weren't always so sharp.

Thursday, November 25

We had got the [Anglo-French] summit coverage [at Downing Street] in the right place, about three-quarters on defence and the rest on beef. The press gave TB a hard time on PMQs feeling that he had missed an open goal. I was livid at an extraordinary so-called strategy meeting. It was meant to be TB, GB, AC, PG and Douglas [Alexander], who looked nervous to me. GB arrived late with Ed Balls, despite Jonathan having told him TB just wanted the five of us there. They then had a kind of unreal non-conversation, first about London, then TB asking plaintively, almost pathetically, when GB was going to get involved in the morning meetings with me. Then about what our next strategic goals were, to which GB said that required a separate meeting. He was back in total sulk mode, possibly caused by the row they had about education spending, or maybe the baby and the stories about him having to move out of the flat, even though we denied them. TB was looking tired and dejected, and even I was flaking off a bit. If a fly on the wall had been in there, it would have flown out pretty shocked. TB said to me afterwards he felt exhausted and he really felt GB had actively decided not to co-operate.

At Cabinet, there was a good discussion on Anglo-French defence and then we waited for Chirac, and then Jospin upstairs in the White Room. Chirac was being helpful on beef but there were still problems in the text on the NATO-friendliness of the language. We were served Welsh wine at the lunch and Chirac did a brilliantly exaggerated approving tasting managing simultaneously to say it was marvellous while indicating through every part of his face that he didn't think much of it at all. TB told Chirac the Americans were very nervous about the defence initiative, and he had to understand NATO's centrality to it all. But he felt Europe had to improve its capability particularly re logistics and strategic lift. It wasn't on that Europe had to go for American help all the time. Chirac said the politics on this were very different. In Britain we were under pressure to be pro NATO. In France there are many anti-NATO forces. So the balance we had to find was between not being critical and not being submissive. But he never missed an opportunity to have a dig at the Americans, at one point saying Clinton was playing golf when he should have been focusing on some issue Chirac was badgering him about. There was a similarly tricksy mood in their discussions on Iraq.

With Jospin, they quickly went through beef and then on a long session on economic reform where again, it was a bit like listening to two speeches made by people who said they were agreeing but in fact weren't. It was also clear withholding tax was going to be a problem. He was asking us again how we put up with our press which he described as all opinion. He had a much easier time by comparison. He was trying to show us he was nearer our agenda than we thought and said *Le Monde* ran a headline recently 'Jospin – est-il socialiste?' The plenary session was pretty dull, the press conference went fine and defence was running pretty straight.

We went off to Mile End where TB was doing a [Labour Party] meeting with JP aimed at getting out the message about Ken. It went fine but got next to no coverage from the press. And then the tape went missing so there would be no TV coverage either. Fiona and I went out for dinner at Wingfield House [residence of the American ambassador], where Conrad Black [*Telegraph* proprietor] was telling me how Charles Moore [editor] almost resigned when Black tried to influence an editorial. I said editors were forever almost resigning. Maurice Saatchi [advertising executive and Conservative peer] came over and said he was lost in admiration for the way we had handled things so far. I don't think he was being ironic but you could never quite tell what was going on in there. At dinner itself, I was next to Andrew Lloyd-Webber's wife [Madeleine], and near [Sir] Angus Ogilvy [husband of the Queen's cousin Princess Alexandra of Kent] and Barbara Amiel [journalist wife of Conrad Black]. Ogilvy was [the Lord Chamberlain Lord] Airlie's brother and we had a good chat about the week of Diana's death. He told a very funny story, clearly at their expense, of when President John F. Kennedy died. He had been with the Queen and [Louis, Lord 'Dickie'] Mountbatten and they wondered whether to cancel their planned shooting party. No, said Dickie, the gamekeepers wouldn't understand. Interestingly, he also asked me if I thought [Prince] Charles could marry Camilla [Parker Bowles] and still be king, and what steps they needed to take in PR terms to get there. Fiona said if it required help from the government, Charles ought to stop briefing private conversations.

Friday, November 26

[Michael] Portillo was back, having won the by-election [Kensington and Chelsea, brought about by the death of Alan Clark] as expected. I took the kids to school before heading to [celebrity photographer] David Bailey's studio. The *Times* magazine were doing pictures of people doing the same thing in different generations and they wanted one with me and Joe Haines [former press secretary to Harold Wilson]. I don't know if the pictures worked at all but I quite liked Bailey. I don't think Joe did, because Bailey kept making jokes about us being homosexual. A group of kids from City of Leicester School [AC's old school] came in to do an interview. They were a really nice bunch and I quite enjoyed it, though I probably said one or two things that I shouldn't.

Saturday, November 27

We were in Norfolk for [special adviser] Tim Allan's wedding. The Ulster Unionist vote [backing the peace process plan and paving the way to devolution] went through. I did a conference call with Jonathan and John Sawers to agree a TB statement, but then we had to deal with the surprise move by David Trimble saying that he and his colleagues would issue pre-dated resignation letters by February if there was no decommissioning by then. We got our line agreed, playing it down, emphasising we were still moving forward together. Peter M was at the wedding so he and I were able to sort it. I played the pipes outside the church and they sounded fine considering how little I had played recently. As weddings go, it was quite a nice do and the speeches were pretty high quality.

Sunday, November 28

The *Sunday Telegraph* splashed on a Paddy Ashdown memo re a meeting with TB and a claim that they discussed Alan Beith [Lib Dem deputy leader] and Ming Campbell [Lib Dem foreign affairs spokesman] being given a Cabinet job. I spoke to TB who was reasonably relaxed. I said we should simply say it was wishful thinking.

Monday, November 29

At the morning meeting, I said we really had to push the line on jokes not judgement re Hague, get a paper done on it and get Margaret B to put her name to it. Partly, it was about trying to make Hague feel less comfortable using jokes, because he did it so well. We also agreed we should go for a big story about the North–South divide and regional variations of policy. At the office meeting, I said I was worried about rival GB and Peter M structures being started up on pre-election planning. For example, GB was having a meeting tomorrow which he knew AC, Philip G and Peter M couldn't be at. TB was on better form. He needed to get GB more onside re public services. I got Bill Bush and [the research] team working on a big North–South divide dossier. In the evening, TB hosted a dinner for Wes Clark. It was a perfectly pleasant do, lots of nice speeches. Both Charles [Guthrie] and Wes went right over the top re TB's leadership although to be fair he heard it all the time with regard to Kosovo. Guthrie told me that he told anyone who cared to listen that I was a real friend of the military, and that they should never believe anything they read about me. [Air Chief Marshal Sir] John Day [UK director of operations during Kosovo] said he told people that Guthrie and I were the people TB most leant on during that period, and [deputy SACEUR General Sir] Rupert Smith told me in his view I had been the 'man of the match' at NATO. [Javier] Solana [outgoing NATO Secretary General] was tactile as ever and enjoying himself. [General Sir Mike] Jackson and his wife [Sarah] were on great form and he was much more relaxed with us than he used to be. I chatted with Jamie Shea [NATO spokesman] who was as nice as ever and fascinated by the Livingstone affair. It was a nice evening but even though Kosovo was just a few months ago, it felt like years.

Tuesday, November 30
TB said of last night that he had formed a number of impressions. First, that Guthrie and the top brass genuinely liked us. Second, that there was a fair amount of preening and infighting between them. And third, that he imagined Wes could be quite eccentric. He was also feeling a bit guilty that he had made a joke at George Robertson's expense. He said he had been irritated because every time George came in all he seemed bothered about was getting Special Branch protection when he was in Scotland.

The news was still dominated by Northern Ireland with the devolution order to be laid soon and inevitably a lot of interest in Martin McGuinness as education minister. I couldn't go to GB's first strategy meeting but Lance and Peter H said it was fine and at least gave us the chance now to get him more engaged. There was a fair bit of coverage on my North–South [divide] stuff, and GB had been concerned it was opening us up to lots of questions we wouldn't want to answer – I presume he meant re the Barnett Formula.[1] I was purely interested in this as a big communications device to get coverage in all the regions for what the government was actually doing. I was sure we could do it without making the Barnett Formula or regional government the main focus.

Philip said the groups were better. The baby had definitely helped the atmospherics around TB and though there was a lot of whingeing about him, he was seen as a strong leader. The eleven o'clock was fine, not least because I was able to announce that Nick Brown was going to do a statement lifting the ban on beef on the bone after his meeting with chief medical officers, which led the bulletins all day. So that and Northern Ireland were strong delivery messages. JP was doing another rail safety meeting and planning later today to take Railtrack out of the [London] Tube plans because of [the train crash at] Paddington. It was tricky communications-wise and we had half an hour on the phone on the best way to handle it and make sure Livingstone didn't fill the vacuum. We agreed they should get it out for 7/8pm with a proper briefing around it. It could be a problem if it was just seen as a massive U-turn but it would at least shoot Livingstone's fox. The other story running was withholding tax with GB holding tough.

[Finnish Prime Minister Paavo] Lipponen came in for a pre-Helsinki [European Council] meeting – IGC [Intergovernmental Conference], Turkey, defence, withholding tax.[2] He said we were very isolated on tax. TB held out pretty strongly on it, said it was a German problem to do with their people going to Luxembourg and depositing their savings to avoid tax. But the measure being proposed would hit the City of London which has four times the business of New York. He said the City was pro Europe and many of them pro euro, and people will think it is crazy if they get hit in this way. He said it was not a piece of UK brinkmanship but it was madness to harm the City of London to allow Germany to deal with a few dentists avoiding tax.

Just as I was clearing my desk, one of the detectives came to see me to tell me the Jill Dando [murder] inquiry team wanted to interview me. I was absolutely horrified. It had the feel of a total set-up,

[1] A crude Treasury mechanism used since the late 1970s to allocate public expenditure in different parts of the United Kingdom, controversially according to population rather than need. It is said to be a convention without legislative status, and could be changed by the Treasury, hence Brown's possible concern at it becoming a talking point.
[2] As a measure to curb tax evasion, some EU member states were to introduce a withholding tax on bank and other interest paid to non-residents.

started by that silly *Guardian* diary piece, and which would end up in the papers. But I guessed there was nothing much I could do about it. Then when I got home, Kentish Town police said I had been upgraded further on security and they came round to look at the house again and check how the mail [deliveries] worked.

Wednesday, December 1

We got not bad coverage on beef on the bone which played straight into what Godric proudly called his beef summit breakfast. TB didn't want to be filmed eating and thought the whole thing a bit daft, so instead Godric got the cameras into the kitchens to film the sausages being cooked and through the day, every time the shots appeared on the TV, the office went into a round of applause for Godric. It was in fact a perfectly good idea that he had dreamed up at the weekend and we also had substance to underpin it. As ever, MAFF was not quite at the races.

Railtrack was not nearly as bad as it might be but such was the mood surrounding Ken that they all wanted to say it was a gift to him. In one way it was but I felt we had to have someone out there attacking Ken as dishonest. In the end, though I knew I might get tugged by RW, I did it. On the North–South stuff, there appeared to be a collective loss of nerve on it and someone, presumably GB, had got at TB over it. I said that he had asked me to find a way to generate more coverage around his regional visits and this was going to do it. He claimed I hadn't consulted him, which wasn't true. Within the office too, I had a string of people coming to ask me if I thought it was a good idea. I was convinced that it was. Demystifying the notion of the North–South divide as understood was a good talking point and the document would generate positive coverage in and about every region.

TB asked me why I was so fed up with him. I said because I was expected to do far too much, both by the politicians and by the press. He also expected me to do too much of the motivational stuff within the building, and not just with my own people. And it got very wearing when on the one hand he kept advising me to take more time off and on the other never stopped loading things upon me. Frank D had stood in for Jeffrey Archer at a media ball and I had a stack of calls from people telling me he had been absolutely dreadful. This thing felt worse by the day. The Northern Ireland order was laid after Peter M went to the Palace so we get devolution at midnight tonight. I took a meeting on the regional report to say it was happening and that was that and what needed to be done.

PMQs was OK though not brilliant. TB was probably attacking the Tories too much and later Bruce said Betty [Boothroyd, Speaker] had pulled him in and said TB was asking too many questions of them, and she would have to say so in the House if we didn't change tack. Hague had definitely cut down on the jokes so we were getting to him. We had a strategy meeting at the Commons, yet again trying to sort structures in the office, TB yet again saying we had to press GB on cash for health and education. Stan Greenberg came in and did the latest polling which was mixed, yet he felt the trends showed there was a chance of getting back with pretty much the same majority.

Thursday, December 2

Power was devolved [in Northern Ireland] at midnight last night. At the morning meeting, as well as trying to organise a fightback on rail, we agreed we should do a daily monitor of the *Daily Mail*'s anti-Labour stuff, which Philip and Douglas [Alexander] went away to organise from Millbank.

Cabinet was fairly brief, Northern Ireland the main thing. GB was in a foul mood, came in, head down, spoke to nobody, scribbling the whole time, or just raising his eyes to the ceiling. There had been a definite change in him, probably a combination of the baby [announcement] and Peter M doing well in Northern Ireland. JP took me aside at the end, said he was really worried he was going to get hammered for going to India [a six-day trip for the Indian Economic Summit] and they had learned the press were trying to get on the same plane.

Ireland was massive but I wrote the hand of history-type sound bite which Jonathan was against, but which made all of the headlines.[1] Gerry Adams called me and said he wanted to say thanks to TB and to all of us. He said it was a really emotional day which many thought they would never see. It was wall to wall on TB all day and Peter M was doing stacks of media well. There was one less pleasant fallout we had to deal with which was that with power devolved, John McFall and Alf Dubs were now surplus to requirement as ministers. They were both very grown-up about it and just pleased the thing was happening. JP called in a real state because the Tories had put down an Opposition Day debate for Wednesday on transport and he was thinking of cancelling the trip to India. I said that would be madness. He had to go because otherwise they would feel they had him on the

---

[1] Recalling Blair's words following the Good Friday Agreement that he felt 'the hand of history' on his shoulder, Campbell wrote for Blair of 'the hope that the hand of history is at last lifting the burden of terror and violence'.

run. He said he was tired, felt beleaguered and he wanted to get out of it. I talked him out of it. I learned the Treasury were going back on the pledge re [expansion of] the Metrolink [tram system] in Manchester, which we had been intending to be the story of TB's interview with the *Manchester Evening News* tomorrow.

Lance came in with the news, via Ann Keen, that Shaun Woodward[1] was about to be sacked for refusing to support their policy on [the retention of] Section 28, and he might defect. He was with Ann Keen and he wanted to talk to Cherie. I felt a bit uneasy at involving Cherie. I spoke to Ann and then to Shaun and said if he was going to defect, he must broaden out the issues and come over soon. Otherwise, no matter how strongly he felt on one issue, he would look opportunistic. He said he was also uneasy about Europe, their approach on the economy and tax, general illiberalism. He came over to see me at 8.15 and poured his heart out re what had happened and why it mattered so much. He said he couldn't support anything that in his view led to homophobic bullying, something that for family reasons he had cause to know about. He said several times it was about decency, what kind of society we want. I said that if he came over, though no promises could be made, he should look at the help we gave to Alan Howarth in trying to find a seat.[2] Cherie popped in and saw him for about twenty minutes and she basically just said he should do what he felt was right. He looked like he had been crying. He had put on some weight and was very emotional. I'd say he started out forty per cent in favour of defecting and ended closer to seventy. TB was amazed by it but agreed with me he had to be broadened out from Section 28.

Friday, December 3

TB agreed to speak to Shaun Woodward but Shaun wasn't returning my calls and Lance feared he was going cold. I suspected he was talking to lots of people who were talking him out of it. I spent most of the day working on the regions report with Paul Britton [Cabinet Office] and Bill Bush and working up a briefing plan based on the idea that it was an oversimplification to speak of a North–South

[1] Conservative MP for Witney and Opposition spokesman on London. Section 28 of the Conservatives' Local Government Act 1988 banned local authorities from promoting homosexuality and schools from teaching 'the acceptability of homosexuality as a pretended family relationship'.
[2] The Conservative MP for Stratford-on-Avon defected to Labour in 1995 and, after failing to win Labour selections in Wentworth and Wythenshaw and Sale East, was elected as Labour MP for Newport East in 1997.

divide. It led to the longest Sunday briefing I could recall and even they, not normally interested in this type of thing, were biting on it.

I then did a briefing for the ministers who were going to be doing visits and media in all the regions on Monday. Blunkett wasn't happy about it, he said there was a North–South divide and we had to do more to close it. I said this was about saying the argument wasn't as simple as that and that in all regions, we were pursuing policies that would improve people's life chances. Some of the worst poverty was in the South. Some of the best success stories were in the North, so let's stop feeding a caricature. We got quite heated and I ended up losing it a bit, saying why was it that ministers spent so much time moaning about the policies they were meant to be promoting. It was going to be very touch and go, because so many ministers were clearly against the basic idea, but we were already generating a lot of interest in TB's North-West tour.

TB finally saw Shaun later and Lance said he had pretty much promised him a job, whether in the Commons or the Lords. He said Shaun was clearly loving being the centre of attention, that he had been there for a couple of hours and was now hoping for another meeting tomorrow with me, Peter M, Lance, hopefully TB as well. I worked late with Mark B making a few changes to the regions report. Paul Britton had done a terrific job. I did a conference call with all the press officers likely to be involved, which went fine. We had a flurry of late calls from a story in *The Times* on Paddy Ashdown's diaries alleging that we tried to censor his comments, particularly on GB.

Saturday, December 4

Paddy called first thing and said sorry for all the fuss. He was now sure that the leaks came from within his own office and he knew that because of the format. We agreed to brief that he had said nothing untoward about GB. We chatted about [Charles] Kennedy. I said he needed to find an issue that he made his own. He was all a bit scattergun.

TB called and said he was pretty confident Woodward would come over. He was genuinely impressed by his intelligence and thought though there might be a bit of careerism here, his stand on Section 28 was definitely principled. But all of us felt there was something of the drama queen about him, and Shaun didn't like the comparisons with Alan Howarth because he saw himself as a much bigger fish, possibly even Tory leadership material. TB wanted me to go in for the meeting with him but Calum was in such a rage about me saying

December '99: Blunkett unhappy re North-South divide

I was going in on yet another Saturday, that I ended up joining them on the speakerphone. I tee'd up Peter M to be the one to emphasise the need to broaden it out from Section 28, and that was how the conversation was going when I checked in. Shaun clearly felt very strongly that he had managed to get over the argument about bullying. He said that in his heart he had moved over already, but he felt if he did it now, right now, his friends would know it was out of character. Chris Patten's reaction, he was sure, would be 'This is Alastair Campbell at work. I can't believe you didn't think about it more deeply.' The press would say it was a fit of pique.

My argument was that in a sense this should be seen as the straw that broke the camel's back, the last in a line of issues where he felt out of step with his own party, but actually he needed a bit of emotionalism in his explanation, and that the longer he waited, the more it might be seen as opportunism. TB and I then went into a bit of a soft cop/hard cop routine. TB kept saying Shaun should take as long as he wanted, and think about it deeply because it was such an important step. I was saying that if he was going to make a career in the Labour Party, the Labour Party was going to have to take to him and he wouldn't get much better circumstances than resigning over an issue of principle like this, and then broadening out. He said he thought he should disappear for a while and then come back and do it. If he did it now, people would say it was a stunt. On broadening out, Peter M said that as he had been a frontbencher, it would be difficult because there would be very little on the record to point to. I said Shaun needed to go through all areas of policy and decide which he genuinely opposed. The conversation went on for about ninety minutes, and I suspected there were going to be plenty more.

I took Calum to school for football and then went to pick up Mum at King's Cross. She commented that I seemed to be on the phone more than ever, which was bound to get the kids down. There was a good piece in the *Guardian* on the North–South report, but a bad piece in *The Times*, saying it would say there was no such thing as a North–South divide. It meant the Sundays would feel the briefing had been pre-empted, so after speaking to them we gave them pages on the deprivation section showing how much poverty there was in London.

Sunday, December 5

The Sundays focused largely on the idea of Blair saying there was no divide. I talked to him at Chequers and we agreed the argument we wanted running was that there was a greater divide within regions than between them. Blunkett wasn't keen to do the *Today* programme but after another fairly spiky exchange, we agreed provided he could say that there was a divide and we were dealing with it. I did two long conference calls to finalise the briefings scripts. I was conscious of the fact that I had spent several hours on the phone. Fiona was pissed off. Calum was refusing to do his homework.

Monday, December 6

The North–South report was going fine. Very big in the papers and a lot of supportive coverage for the main theme, and it was leading the news. DB did fine on the *Today* programme so all in all I was pleased with the way it was going. It was set up more or less perfectly. I was in early to brief TB re the Internet interview on *GMTV* which went fine. At the 8.30 meeting, I said we needed to be out there defending JP who was being hammered on [being in] India [while major transport policy issues were ongoing]. We also needed to be much more robust and confident about taking on the *Mail*. They did a big piece today saying I had lost my touch, so clearly we were getting to them again.

On the flight up north, TB read the report while Peter H and I worked on the speech for Chester. The speech was at the MBNA credit card company, which had an American feel to it. The sign 'Think of yourself as the customer' was everywhere. They were announcing 1,000 new jobs, so the backdrop was good. The speech went fine, as did the little press huddle afterwards. They were all buying into the main argument. It was good talking-point material which was generating a lot of debate about what the government was trying to do. We left for the [Manchester] Metrolink part of the visit. TB was having to deal with the withholding tax on the phone. It was clearly going to be a big problem at Helsinki but he was fired up about it and felt Schroeder was making a dreadful error in attacking us over it. After all the kerfuffle with the Treasury, the Metrolink launch [opening the new Salford Quays tram extension] went fine, then to the BBC for a phone-in. The lunchtimes were full of different packages about the report. Channel 4 were doing their programme from Manchester. TB was in great form at the press conference. [Tony] Bevins said to me we had thrown them a bone which had real meat on it.

TB did a [Manchester] city centre visit with Mo, then out to see the Commonwealth Games site, then to east Manchester to see the New Deal for Communities at work. We were also getting enormous coverage in all the regions, not all positive, but with the main messages out there. Mo was looking a bit fed up. Earlier in the car, she had intimated to TB that she would stand for mayor [of London] if we could get Frank to quit. I met up with Alex [Ferguson] at the reception at the Town Hall and we went off for dinner at a very nice restaurant outside Manchester. He reckoned he had another couple of years to go and then he just wanted to do a bit of work here and there, but basically travel round the world with Cathy. He thought we were doing fine. If the rest of the country was doing as well as Manchester, which was buzzing, we had no problem.

Tuesday, December 7

TB had stayed overnight in Liverpool with friends. I was out at 6 to go and meet him, and there was something slightly comic about the police presence around this very ordinary house, where TB had slept – not very well – in one of the kids' bedrooms. We did pictures of him wearing his glasses to go with his interview with Terri Tavner for *Woman's Own*. We worked a bit on the speeches for later, then set off for the business breakfast and the NHS Direct launch [having been launched as a telephone helpline, the health advice service was going online]. I was pleased overall with the coverage of yesterday. He was talking to Charlie [Falconer] and others about whether we could get Mo into the mayoral contest. Charlie felt legally there was no problem.

The press corps were still up with us from London and they seemed to be enjoying the whole trip. The NHS Direct launch in Bootle was fine, though in a bit of an odd place, right in the middle of a busy shopping precinct. Some of the hacks were quizzing me on the *Mail*'s attack yesterday when an old lady came up to me and said she was madly in love with me when I was at the *Mirror* and on telly and she loved me even more now because I hit the press and the Tories so hard. They ended up interviewing her, and then someone else came up and told me I should run for office. By now, the hacks seemed to be convinced I had planned the whole thing.

We left for a visit to a Catholic school where TB sat down with teachers in the staffroom who were pretty surly, but the kids in the sixth form were great. He was getting tired and started to whinge and whine. I said I was fed up with him complaining unless everything was easy and safe. And might he take the time today to thank some of the dozens of people who had worked flat out for the last few days to make it go as well as it had. NHS Direct was leading ITN. TB had to make a stack of calls on the withholding tax and then a lunch with the editors from the region who were pretty groany and whingey. We then went to Liverpool Royal [Royal Liverpool University

Hospital] where TB left dispirited by the private meeting with staff. They weren't hostile but nor were they remotely positive.

On the flight back, I was so fed up listening to him moaning that I went back and sat with Alison [Blackshaw, AC's PA]. And in the car I had a kip while he worked on his [ministerial] box. He called me after seeing the Queen to say he felt that both the trip and the report had gone well, but GB was continuing to say it had been a disaster.

Wednesday, December 8

At the morning meeting, several of those who had argued against the North–South report were big enough to eat their words and the general view was it had been a good success. On the withholding tax, the [European] Commission letter had come through suggesting we were going to win, but GB was not convinced and he and TB had a very heated conversation about how to handle it tactically. TB felt it was clear we were going to get our way, but GB said the detail was all wrong. Just before I did my Helsinki briefing, we heard from Gerry Adams that he was going to make public that they had found a bugging device in his car. It was going to be a huge story. I stuck to the usual line about not commenting on such issues and I strongly defended the security services. I did a long briefing which was mainly on tax. [Michael] Cockerell [documentary maker] was in filming, including TB and Bruce [Grocott] leaving for PMQs. He was a bit pushy but I still felt on balance it was right to get some kind of film [to be broadcast by the BBC in July 2000 as *News from Number 10*] which showed what we actually did as opposed to all the bollocks written about us.

PMQs was a bit flat. The four o'clock was all about Adams. Mike White seemed genuinely concerned that it was history repeating itself, security services fucking things up for a Labour government. I said I didn't share his concerns. I got back for a meeting with TB, Charlie F, Margaret [McDonagh], Anji, Sally and Pat McFadden re Mo/mayor. I felt we could do it, but TB was not so sure. It was such a fiasco, I felt, that it could hardly get worse. And in the end we had to decide who we thought could win. Nobody seemed to think Frank could.

At 10pm Jospin called TB with the news that the French would not lift the beef ban. We had a conference call to agree a fairly strong line but TB was still on the non-hysterical end of the market. The French decision was a real kick in the slats and he sounded very fed up. The problem was Jospin's government was divided and no matter how hard he tried to sort it, he couldn't. I wanted to make the point that the problem was Jospin's weakness but TB said there was no point. The French cabinet had apparently been discussing it for three and a half hours. He felt it was pretty pathetic that Jospin couldn't win the argument, and we knew it was going to be seen as a humiliation not for Jospin but for us.

Thursday, December 9

Beef was leading the news and a bit of a disaster area. I missed Cabinet for Calum's school concert but made it in to do the morning briefing where I calmly put the case and didn't go OTT. I sensed there was a lot of sympathy for our position and suggested TB did a clip ruling out a trade war but putting the case. He said he would do it but he had done his neck in and was in pain. We were still getting a bit of flak about the Adams business but TB seemed totally relaxed about it. On the way to the airport, he talked to Prodi about beef and the with-holding tax. GB was still very much against the Commission plan and was intending to hang tough in the evening when he flew in, separately from us as always. TB felt badly let down by the French but didn't want to up the ante with them. On the flight [to Helsinki], we went over with Robin the various tricky issues we had to deal with.

TB spoke to Adams about the bug, a call we had agreed to simply to let GA say that he had raised it and protested. But he seemed fairly relaxed. 'Sorry to bug you with this,' he said. Both of them laughed. On the way to PES dinner, I got TB to do a pool clip, sharper than the earlier one, and I got out the line that the French were doing this [continuing their ban on British beef] for their own internal reasons. TB felt that despite the humiliation headlines, we had to play resolutely by the rules. GB flew in and immediately caused mayhem on the with-holding tax. He went straight into battle and so annoyed everyone that the Finns came out and briefed that the Brits were being very difficult, finance ministers were unlikely to be able to resolve it and it would have to go to heads of government. Of course, I had to go along with the GB strategy in public, or risk a big-split story, and I got Julian to brief that TB would be raising the issue in very stark terms. TB just shook his head when I told him what had happened with the finance ministers. Where GB was right was that it was very complex and he had at least thought out his own alternative plan to deal with money laundering. Given that we were winning and could sort out the detail quietly, I agreed with TB it was an odd way to do business.

While TB was at the dinner John Sawers and I went over to the Irish hotel and had a good chat with Bertie [Ahern], half work, half play. He was regaling me with stories about [Cork-born Manchester

United footballer] Roy Keane's dad who was called Moss and now they call him Sterling Moss because Roy sends so much money home. When TB arrived, he was raging about the French and Bertie said 'You wouldn't have to read too many history books to know they were a bunch of untrustworthy bastards, Tony.' PG and PH called having been to a couple of focus groups which they said were the best for ages. There was real goodwill towards the government. TB got respect out of Northern Ireland, they felt warmer about him because of the baby, and they felt the report on the North–South divide took them seriously and didn't treat them like idiots.

Friday, December 10

I had another go at TB that we had to be a bit more in your face with the French than we had been up to now. But he said it was really important he didn't come over like [John] Major had, that if he was going to do all that fury and anger, there had to be a tangible result. You would never imagine from his demeanour with Jospin that he was angry at all. Our papers were taking it out on us when, had the Tories been in power, they would have been taking lumps out of the French. TB and I had a meeting with GB. GB had got to bed at 3 after the Ecofin [EU finance ministers] meeting on withholding tax. He had basically said we would not sign up to anything that covered the London Eurobond market at all and they would just have to live with that. [Hans] Eichel [Germany's finance minister] said the question was whether we accepted that tax evasion had to be dealt with and people had to pay tax on the savings. The obvious answer to that was yes but GB said if TB answered yes to that he would give them a green light to go ahead and push us over. TB actually agreed with him on the principle but felt that tactically he had screwed it up. Robin, needless to say, agreed.

TB said to GB we had to try to get it put off and basically kicked into touch. GB was motoring though, saying that only the Germans had a principled reason to go for this and the French were just causing trouble. TB said he was not much in the mood for letting the French cause us trouble. I had a separate chat with Robin about how we deal with the fallout from the French and what it said for our strategy of constructive engagement. Robin was happy to go up and do 'more in sorrow than anger' on the French.

The *Mail* monitor was clearly getting to them.[1] Dacre had said he was cancelling the planned meeting with TB. Though TB was edgy

[1] Campbell's team was publishing detailed daily rebuttals of *Daily Mail* stories.

about it, he said in the car they had to accept that if they were going to be nothing more than a propaganda sheet against, we could not let that lie. His more specific worry was that GB was partly manoeuvring on Europe as a way of winning the right-wing press over to him on that, by being more sceptical than TB, having already secured the left press by being Mr Social Justice.

TB felt that whilst it was perfectly acceptable for GB to try to build support, if he was deliberately shifting position on Europe to curry the right wing's favour, it was dangerous and divisive. He shared my view that a combination of the baby and renewed success in Northern Ireland had put him over the top again. He said GB was treating EU finance ministers in the same way he treated Cabinet colleagues during the CSR [Comprehensive Spending Review], but he had to understand these guys had less to lose by falling out with him.

TB was very keen that we maintain the basic pro-European posture whilst holding our own on beef and the withholding tax. GB meanwhile was killer drilling Eichel trying to get Eurobonds out, or into June [European Council in Cologne]. He was desperate to get the deal done, do a quick briefing and go. I got TB to agree to them doing the briefing together, after which, in the holding room, TB challenged GB over the continuing hints in the press that he was interested in the IMF [International Monetary Fund] job.[1] GB kept saying he was not interested 'for the moment' so regularly TB ended up laughing. TB felt it was all part of the same game, trying to unsettle him.

I bumped into Jospin, who was very apologetic, said he knew this had given us a big problem and he was still trying to resolve it. Schroeder seemed to spend less time in the meeting than out of it, was constantly wandering around smoking a cigar. I got TB out at one point to get them to agree bilaterally to a text on the tax directive. Schroeder joked to me that this was *'der siebente Weg'* ['the seventh way'] and then said, less jokey, 'Please do not put out false messages.'

The TB/GB press briefing went fine. We were in a better position on the withholding tax, but the main focus was still beef. Jonathan called to say that the story about Mo's book was out. We agreed a line. I had dinner with Jeremy H and some of the Number 10 staff

[1] The announcement by Frenchman Michel Camdessus that he would resign in the New Year left open the position of managing director of the IMF, a role overseeing the global financial system, stabilising international exchange rates and encouraging development in poorer countries through loans, restructuring and aid.

and bumped into David Hughes [*Mail*] and Trevor Kavanagh, who were both very hostile re the *Mail* monitor. I said that those who liked to give out are better learning what it's like to take it.

Saturday, December 11

There was a bit of a feeling of parallel universes, the media depicting everything as a disaster area, Britain isolated on beef, when in fact it was fourteen vs one, and on tax, we were winning the argument. I got Ricci Levi [Prodi's spokesman] to do a briefing for our Sundays saying this was only the third time they had put through the five-day legal ultimatum because as far as they were concerned, our case on beef was totally clear-cut. At the French press conference, Jospin went into a ten-minute tirade and Chirac just diddled on for a few seconds. So Julian and I went out and said this was a rare occasion of a totally isolated France having to defend the indefensible. TB and I had a fundamental disagreement about how to handle this. I felt he was coming over as soft and the French were just running rings round us the whole time. TB's press conference went OK but they [the media] had all decided on the script and that was pretty much that. We had a problem with the *Sunday Times*, who were saying JP was effectively demoting himself and getting Gus [Macdonald] to do the transport job. I worked on JP's transport speech on the plane.

Sunday, December 12

I spoke to JP and Gus to agree a big briefing to go out overnight on the transport speech. JP sounded quite chirpy and was happy for Gus to do the broadcasts. The Sundays weren't as bad as they might have been on Europe, and even though it was frustrating we were treated differently to how a Tory government would be, he said we just had to hold our nerve. It was hard to get the transport story back on track because JP's press office had effectively confirmed the *Sunday Times* story through an incompetent briefing.

JP was beginning to wonder whether there were people inside the department actively working against him. He said he should just have got on with it and never bothered with the media at all. I said 'Hold on John, this was totally self-inflicted.' I said there was no story about this till you gave it. And now we have to get back focused on policy. But he was seeing dark plots everywhere now, that somehow we were getting up the idea of breaking up the department. He sounded very depressed. His problem was that he loathed the media so much and couldn't work out how to deal with them.

The papers were still a bit grim for JP though some of the positive briefing got through. Gus did fine. At the office meeting, as well as lamenting transport, TB said he was worried about health, public services generally and the Dome. We worked on the Helsinki statement and I worked on his response to Hague, felt we really had to go for him as being unserious. TB was now very jumpy about the *Mail* monitor, felt we had made the point and should now stop it. I didn't agree, felt we were never going to get any mileage out of them so we should seek to portray them for what they are on a sustained basis. At the eleven o'clock, I was really on form with JP and the totally trivial press and was there any chance of getting some focus on policy?

I did a big number attacking the *Today* programme who seemed to be making their two-way [journalist to journalist] burbles the main focus and which were buying into the whole trivialisation agenda. And even though I agreed with them re Mo, I think I managed to keep that played down as well. The JP story was pretty much leading the news all day, but more focused on his role than the so-called downgrading. I went spare at the 6.30 headline which was 'Sacking denial'. We couldn't have defended him more, but it was a classic example of lack of planning and bad briefing getting us off on the wrong foot and leaving us unable to recover. It was also now being stated virtually as a fact that we were briefing against him and against Mo.

JP was still getting totally mauled and by now was very depressed about the whole thing. The *Mail* was hysterical today. After all their talk about a boycott of French goods, they were running a special offer for readers to go to France to do their Christmas shopping. We set off with Charlie F for the Dome. To my surprise, I liked it, both the mood and a lot of the content. I felt they had done a pretty amazing job to get it to this state. TB was definitely going through one of his down phases. He said he was having dinner with GB on Thursday and felt there had been a definite change there, that he [GB] was being difficult deliberately. Jospin did a briefing for the UK press which was supposed to be helpful but ended up saying they had offered to lift the ban in Scotland. Then and now, it was basically a divisive ploy.

At 1.30, I went with Lance to [broadcaster and writer on music, friend of Price] Paul Gambaccini's flat at County Hall and waited for Shaun W. He had written out a speech which we went through and we also had a draft handling plan. He made clear again, less subtly than before, that he felt he was seen by some in the Tory Party as a possible future leader. We agreed that he would do the speech on Friday, and defect on Saturday after seeing his constituency chairman. I think he had pretty much decided but he still needed a lot of assurance so we were in for another long meeting. He was worried that the speech would be seen by Hague as so over the top that they would withdraw the whip, which would make it look like the defection was in response to that, rather than the obvious natural consequence of the arguments he had made. I didn't feel they would do that but we agreed to go through the speech with that in mind and soften if necessary. After an hour or so, I felt confident enough that he was going to do it and started to map out a detailed handling plan. He seemed to be assuming he would be Europe minister. TB said I should make no promises but make him feel there would definitely be a role.

I got back for a meeting with TB etc. on the mayor situation. Frank was going absolutely nowhere. TB was also worried about Mo. Margaret McD said she had had dinner with Mo and Jon last night and he was saying that it was unbelievable that Mo wasn't at least Foreign Secretary by now. But TB was clearly moving to the view that Frank shouldn't stand.

Wednesday, December 15

We got very good coverage out of the rough-sleepers package [working with the voluntary sector to provide emergency hostels for rough sleepers]. Louise Casey [head of the Rough Sleepers Unit] was excellent on the broadcasts. The *Mail* splashed on a story, from GB at the [Treasury] select committee that the tax burden was rising and TB was pretty sure Hague would do tax at PMQs. TB saw Mo and told her to stop giving out so many vibes that she was fed up with the job. She claimed she had said nothing to anyone, which of course was nonsense. She had put it around variously that she should be Foreign Secretary, Defence Secretary, NATO Secretary General. She certainly had qualities, but she overestimated them and had over-inhaled the positive publicity she got for being a different sort of politician. Hague was reprimanded over his use of Archer's gym but TB didn't want to use the line I gave him about him having a black belt in bad judgement.[1] In the end Hague did well on broken

---

[1] Hague was told by the Commons Committee on Standards and Privileges that he should have declared judo lessons he attended in Jeffrey Archer's private gymnasium.

December '99: 'Why isn't Mo foreign secretary?'

promises, pledges, stats. It was one of his better days and at the four o'clock I got loads on the tax burden.

GB had another strategy meeting I couldn't go to. I was sorting out Friday's arrangements for the Northern Ireland meetings. I went out with TB visiting some of the down-and-outs near the Savoy, which was really grim, and then to [the homeless peoples' centre at] St Martin-in-the-Fields [Trafalgar Square] where he did a couple of interviews and then the press conference with Louise Casey and Hilary Armstrong [local government minister]. We walked back and he said he wanted me to have a drink with him and Shaun W tomorrow. There was a good poll in *The Times* tomorrow and I felt that despite all the problems, we were doing better on connection and also there was some sense of energy and direction again.

Thursday, December 16

Hague, deservedly, got a very good press for PMQs. I argued with TB that it showed he had to engage more with really sharp lines, but he disagreed. He also felt the Tories were making a mistake with setting up investment in public services as an issue as they wouldn't be able to match us on it. I was working on the [homeless charity] Centrepoint speech but we were unlikely to get strong coverage two days running on the same issue. Cabinet was about mainly the millennium bug[1] and the update on contingency plans, plus Northern Ireland and then a discussion on different systems of university funding.

I went to join Lance with Shaun at Paul Gambaccini's flat. Shaun had gone through the speech and also his letter to Hague and the articles he was planning. He had done a really good job and the letter was very powerful. It was quite a big thing he was doing and I was reaching the view he was doing it more for the right reasons than for the wrong ones. He had done an article for the *Express*, basically an extract from tomorrow's speech, and later [Tony] Bevins asked him if he was going to defect. Shaun, taken aback, said no, which had the potential to be a problem later. There was no doubt it was happening now. We had the chronology sorted and all the various statements. The doubts had gone, he was really up for it. I went back for a meeting with Phil Dilks [Labour press officer], who we were planning to assign to Shaun. Briefly I went to the Labour Party Christmas bash but had

[1] It was feared that there could be widespread failure of computer systems when the year 2000 was reached because of hardware and software which used only the last two digits of the year, e.g. 97, 98, 99, rather than all four. In the event, failures were very minor.

to get back for the next Shaun meeting. This time he was with his wife, Camilla, who was very pretty, and seemed genuinely supportive and composed. He led us to believe she had all sorts of concerns, but she actually seemed quite comfortable with the whole thing. He was full of it now, said he felt totally happy about it, totally at home. I sensed they hadn't really gone through the detail, e.g. what they would do with the children when it broke. I felt it was important she was with him, and posed with him, with or without the kids. I liked her. I thought she was very calm and would be helpful in the next few days. He asked me to tell TB he felt one hundred per cent happy about it and was sure it was the right thing. TB had read Shaun's speech [to be delivered to the Social Market Foundation] and told him how brilliant it was. I was beginning to get worried, because too many people knew by now and as with Howarth, it was important that this came out in the right way to get the right response, not least from the party.

Friday, December 17

The BIC/BIIGC [British–Irish Council and British–Irish Inter-governmental Conference] was running fine, though the arrangements were all a bit shambolic. Peter M was very funny quizzing me about what happened at the Good Friday Agreement that led to the Isle of Man being part of these discussions. TB was constantly fretting about what was happening re Shaun. Shaun's speech went quite big.[1] He did *The World at One* and Bevins was clearly convinced he was going to defect. I avoided all his calls. We went over to Lancaster House to greet all the different delegations like Guernsey, Jersey, Isle of Man. Bairbre de Brún [Sinn Fein Assembly Member and minister] was late and so came in on her own. TB realised straight away that if he greeted her, it would be the first ever public handshake with Sinn Fein, which was straight away the main story. TB and Bertie's opening statements were carried live. Then TB and Bertie left for Number 10 for the BIIGC. Trimble and Mallon were a bit late. The Irish were keen that Bertie did the press with TB, as a head of government, Trimble and Mallon to do it later.

I missed the lunch to go to a final meeting on everyone involved with Shaun. His researcher, Matthew Robinson, looked really nervous but was enjoying being part of a big event. The other amazing thing

[1] Woodward attacked Conservative support for Section 28 as 'wrong and bad', saying 'The consequence of the discrimination is to perpetuate a climate of fear and intolerance.'

today was that GB popped up on the nine o'clock news saying he was going to write off all Third World debt to the UK. Nobody, not even TB, was aware that he was going to do it today. TB tried to get hold of him but he wasn't returning calls. GB had gone right offside. The debt story led the news and some of the papers, especially of course the *Guardian*, relegating the Irish stuff which was being seen as a success for TB and Peter M.

Saturday, December 18

The rumour mill was starting. Bevins had taken a punt and Sky were running from 10am that a defection was likely. They said they had independent Labour sources. I had a chat with Shaun, wished him good luck. He said he was ready for a big onslaught from them, but he was happy he was doing the right thing. He saw his constituency chairman and it broke on PA around 12. It set the agenda for the day. There was a good response from the Tory Reform Group [attacking the 'personal abuse' aimed at Woodward] and others on the left of the party, and a very bitter response from Hague, who said Woodward had no honour.[1] Their basic line of attack was careerism. TB was worried the whole thing would be seen as a TB/AC operation and we should get Ann Keen up as the person he dealt with first. She was there to greet Shaun, Camilla and Phil Dilks when they came up from the country. Phil was doing really well and they clearly liked him. Shaun called later, said he was happy, felt great, felt that he was home. I got the Sundays. As well as careerism, the Tories were clearly trying to make it as much about me and Peter as possible, said we were more ruthless than the security services getting spies to defect. Shaun intended to use the line that their response showed how vile they were. I had a chat with JP, who was due on *Frost* tomorrow, and though he didn't really take to Shaun, he would be OK about it.

Sunday, December 19

Shaun was fine on *Frost*. [Conservative Party chairman Michael] Ancram looked dreadful. He didn't handle it well. The message that the Tories were getting more and more right wing was getting through. The *Mail on Sunday* went on a gay-slur line. The *Sun* were doing his sex-change sister Lesley ['Shaun Woodward's sister used to be a mister']. I kept in touch with Shaun through the day. He said he had

---

[1] Hague wrote angrily to Woodward saying 'If you were a man of honour, who valued his constituents as much as you say you do, you would resign your seat now, fight a by-election and give them the opportunity to judge who it is that represents their views and their instincts more accurately.'

spoken to friends who said it was the best thing he had ever done. I fixed for TB to phone him and tell him how well he was doing. He put Camilla on the phone and she said everyone was so nice and how well everything had been prepared. They were both clearly excited but also a bit nervous about some of the lines of attack.

Monday, December 20

The papers had even more background on Woodward than the Sundays. [Tony] Benn and [Jeremy] Corbyn [left-wing Labour MPs] were attacking him and Benn said New Labour was basically a Conservative party. The Dome preview press was very mixed. We needed big connecting endorsements and real news stories. The *Mail* did six different pieces by different writers, all negative. At the office meeting, TB was still livid that GB, without any consultation at all, wrote off Third World debt – £155 million over ten years – while telling us he could do nothing more for the NHS to pre-empt a winter crisis. I talked to TB afterwards and he said that when he's like this, the truth is he sees himself as being in opposition to us and he will only engage if it's to his personal advantage. I said take that to its logical conclusion, and he may one day see electoral victory as not being in his interest. TB said, I think for the first time, even to me, that he sometimes wondered if we might not be better off without him. The problem was there was nobody else who had his mix of ability, real strength, and reach into the party whilst being basically New Labour. But it was interesting he now felt GB was working against us.

The eleven o'clock was all about Shaun and Northern Ireland, where we were changing the law in relation to taking the oath. I had a long chat with Paul Howell [former Conservative MP, later to join the Liberal Democrats] re defecting. He was one of the breakaway pro-euro Tories. TB and I were both worried we would be seen as too pro-euro and it turned out he had already been expelled by the Tories. Piers and Yelland called to say someone was flogging a picture of Euan [Blair] with a girl at the Ministry of Sound [London nightclub] last night and Yelland offered to buy them out of the market, which was quite nice of him. Then we heard the *Star* was running the picture. I called them and they agreed not to. TB was seeing Adams and when I told him about the Euan snogging picture he said the one thing that would put him over the edge was that his kids were not allowed a normal life because of our wretched press. In fact the press were being pretty good about it. Bruce [Grocott] said MPs were very up about Shaun W and Hague was looking pretty lost and useless.

Tuesday, December 21

Woodward was still getting loads of coverage and he was due to come in to see TB. He told Lance that Camilla was now very shaky and would Cherie speak to her. The *Daily Sport* of all people ran the pictures of Euan. I had seen [Press Complaints Commission chairman Lord] Wakeham yesterday to discuss Lords reform and called him now re this in his PCC capacity and he said go for it, you have to. TB agreed, so we announced it at the 11. The *Mail* had a leak of the honours for [actor Sean] Connery, Richard Branson [businessman] and [outgoing BBC director general] John Birt. I spoke to Richard Wilson to say there had to be a leak inquiry. I had a meeting with Tessa [Jowell, education and employment minister], Ian McCartney, John Reid, Brian Wilson, Charles Clarke and Pat Hewitt [Labour ministers]. I wanted to build up the group that we could call on to do media at any time but also that we could put out words on their behalf. Charles, unsurprisingly, kept saying he didn't want to be seen as Millbank Man. John Reid wanted to hang back afterwards for one of his conspiratorial chats.

I had lunch with David Davis [Conservative MP and former minister, friend of Campbell] at Granby's. He thought Woodward would become trouble for us. He said Jane Clark [widow of Alan] was very lonely. I had another session with the dentist, and went home via buying Fiona's Christmas present. TB called. He said he had spoken to GB re [Third World] debt. Asked why he did it in the way that he did, GB said 'Because you asked me to.' 'When?' 'Six months ago.' We were able to laugh about it, because he had in the end done what we wanted him to but it was a very odd way to do it. TB and I were also laughing about 'Operation Myopia', the joke code name we had given to the plan to get publicity out of his *Woman's Own* interview and pictures wearing his specs.

Wednesday, December 22

I took a day off at home. Godric called with a problem, namely that Rex Features [picture agency] were charging £2,000 per picture for the *Woman's Own* interview. I got Terry Tavner [*Woman's Own* editor] to put one of them out on PA for free. JP called around 7pm. There had been a plane crash near Stansted. It was a Korean cargo plane. The crew were killed and amazingly nobody was hurt on the ground. We were chatting about whether JP should go [to Stansted] when TB came on the line and we agreed that he should. I was talking to Charlie F and Jez [Sagar, Dome press officer] about the Dome advance publicity. There wasn't sufficient sense of excitement about it. Jez had the idea of doing a new version of 'All You Need is Love' using our national anthem instead of the 'Marseillaise'.[1] Charlie felt it was naff and overruled it. In the interim, I checked it out with Geoff Crawford. The Palace certainly believed it was right to dump the French national anthem but felt even a few bars of 'God Save the Queen' would be a problem because people would think they should sing. They suggested something else very British like 'Rule, Britannia'. Charlie was really bright but he didn't always get creativity and it was creativity both in communications terms and in reality that they needed to generate excitement.

Thursday, December 23

The specs pictures were everywhere. The plane crash was a big story. I went to the dentist then in for a meeting on Honours. The right-wing press were already at it re New Year's Eve. The *Telegraph* ran a story saying that we were planning to upstage the Queen.

Friday, December 24

TB agreed with my analysis re the Dome, said we needed a real sense of excitement building, but it wasn't really happening. The *Telegraph* had a story that Prince Charles had a joke Dome at Highgrove [his country house in Gloucestershire] made of Cotswolds materials. TB said he was still playing around with us.

Monday, December 27

Jez Sagar came up with a list of ideas to build up to the Dome opening but it was all a bit *Tavistock Times*-ish.[2] I spoke to Nigel Dacre at ITN, Nick Pollard at Sky and some of the Beeb people and they agreed if we could persuade NMEC [New Millennium Experience Company] to be more accessible, they would do a lot more with it. Mark Damazer [assistant director, BBC news] came back from the Beeb and gave me the usual crap about how news values would decide, but there was some evidence the exercise was worth it. Sky said, at Nick Pollard's suggestion, that they would like to do an item from every zone hour by hour.

[1] The Beatles' 'All You Need is Love', voted the nation's favourite song in a recent poll, opens with bars from the French national anthem, 'La Marseillaise'.
[2] Known since 1986 as the *Tavistock Times Gazette*, the *Tavistock Times* was the local paper where Campbell cut his teeth as a reporter, covering the news of rural Devon.

Tuesday, December 28

I spent much of the day working on tomorrow's speech. We decided he should do an end of year, pre-millennium speech up in Sedgefield. The basic message was a lot done, a lot to do, pretty downspun, but it lacked any real millennium uplift so Peter Hyman and I worked on that. TB did a section on faith which we felt was very risky. The papers were full of rubbish in the main and we were just ticking over. Last year, we had said this would be the year of delivery, now we were saying so much done, so much to do, tied in with a message of confidence because of the British character. He was very wedded to the faith stuff. I said I was worried that the message that would come over was that he was saying to be a successful modern nation, you have to be religious, so we toned that down. There was a very funny piece in [the *Daily Telegraph* diary column] *Peterborough* about me and Peter M being godfather and godmother to the baby.

Wednesday, December 29

As ever, the speech was a bit last-minute, TB and I not finally signing it off until shortly before he left. In the end, it ran fine.

Thursday, December 30

We got great coverage out of the speech, with a lot of focus on the uplift stuff, and the downspin of the venue. The *Guardian* even published it in full. TB was back from Sedgefield. He came in for a chat. He was intending to do a note that would be 'positively compendious' over the next few days so we ran through the various problem areas we had to sort. He was clearly worried and unnerved by GB, 'Who only communicates to me by letter these days.' Cherie had been trying to find out if they could get access to part of the Number 10 flat once the baby was born, and GB had written to say he was willing to give them the whole flat, which of course was not what anybody had wanted. TB felt it was just a ploy both to make them feel bad about asking, but also to be used in future.

Anji paged me to say there were difficulties with the big new wheel that was going up on the river.[1] And JP called to say it was not going to be possible to fix passengers for it tomorrow. I fixed a conference call with him, Charlie F, Bob Ayling [chief executive, British Airways, co-owners of the wheel] and Anji. It was a bit of a disaster. Bob decided that the people who were coming would get a free flight to

[1] The landmark observation wheel on the Lambeth side of the Thames, known as the London Eye.

anywhere in the world, a party on the Thames, and be the first people to go on the wheel when it finally started. Added to the fact that thousands of tickets for the Dome event had still not gone out, we had the makings of a bit of a fiasco. Charlie was adamant the tickets would be sorted.

We went out for dinner with the Goulds and even before I mentioned the wheel, Philip said he thought the Dome was 'on a knife-edge'. Then Anji called after getting calls from both Trimble and Margaret Beckett that they didn't know what the arrangements were for getting back from the Dome. I did a conference call with Charlie and some of his people. They were far too trusting and assumed that when people said things were being done, it meant they were. Even though the wheel was not really our problem, we would cop it for it, as we would if the tickets weren't sorted. Charlie said let's save the witch-hunt for later. I said let's make sure we don't need one.

Friday, December 31

TB called at 9, a bit agitato, said he could not believe that on the eve of a new millennium we could not get the fucking wheel to move. 'I just can't believe this. We'll be a laughing stock.' While we were speaking, the message came through that Yeltsin had announced he was stepping down ahead of time, but after a brief discussion on that, he was back to the wheel and the Dome. He spoke to Charlie F and later called me back to say he thought Charlie was doing everything he could. We then broadened out for a conversation which, as I was on the mobile, we probably shouldn't have had. He said his two big problems for the year ahead were Ken [Livingstone] and Gordon. Ken was a problem in part because even people like John Burton [Blair's constituency agent] felt we were overstating his danger. Nobody thought Frank was going to win and we would probably have to do a deal with Ken. The upside, as Jon Cruddas [Blair's assistant political secretary] said, was that if TB needs a figure of dissent on the left, far better it's Ken than say JP or Margaret B.

The problem with Gordon was far worse, because he was part of the team, yet distant and offside. He was playing around over Europe. The reason he got such a good press from the *Mail* and the Murdoch press was not just because of the economy but because he was playing their sceptic game, which was dangerous. It was also another way of getting at Peter. But it meant TB was the only big figure taking on the sceptic argument, and doing it whilst still being attacked by the pro-European press, who GB courted on the social justice agenda, for not being pro enough. I said to bracket Gordon as a problem in the same bracket as Ken was quite a big step. 'The scales really have fallen then.' He said he was torn between the acknowledgement that GB was a phenomenal intellectual and political force, and a fear that GB was actively working to undermine his government. TB said if he plays around on Europe, it could actually destroy the government. 'It may sound melodramatic, but it is an indication of my concern. The danger is GB gets hooked on the drug of praise from the right-wing press on Europe, the left-wing press on the domestic agenda, and a real divide opens up.'

He went on like this for maybe twenty minutes before asking if the phones were safe and I said no, as I said at the outset, and reminded him of some of the things we had heard of through mobile phone conversations. It was pretty extraordinary that a relationship which not that long ago TB would have said was nigh on unbreakable was now just seen as GB a problem, on his list of issues to resolve in his compendious New Year note.

For the rest of the day, the phone never stopped re tonight's events, but it was basically a case of people talking themselves into a state. We had to accept the wheel wasn't going to move but he was still due to say something at its official opening. I went into Number 10 with Fiona and the kids and briefed TB on the night's events. TB said 'This is worse than the election. At least then we had a fair idea we were going to win. Here, we don't have a clue what is going to happen, but we feel it in our bones something is going to go wrong.' Rory and Calum and TB's boys picked up on our nerves and were making jokes the whole time about everything going wrong, e.g. let's take the lift. Oh what's the point, it won't work anyway.

There was a great atmosphere out on the streets for TB. There was a fair bit of hanging around, then over to the Lords, and down to the Underground, where Peter M was prancing around taking pictures of everyone. TB was in with the Archbishop [of Canterbury] and the Commonwealth Secretary General. There was something very Zil lane[1] about it all as we were whisked straight there. On arrival, we went up to the VIP room, where Marianna [Falconer] told me there was a problem at Stratford [station, East London], where lots of the media people were being forced to wait for hours to get their tickets. The problem seemed to be there was only one scanner. Philip was there and said it was a total disaster area. Greg

[1] In Soviet Moscow, high-ranking officials could take advantage of a separate lane for their Zil limousines.

Dyke [new BBC director general], Jon Snow [*Channel 4 News*], Peter Stothard [editor, *The Times*], lots of them, going absolutely mental. I was going into an absolute rage, especially as nobody seemed to be taking it that seriously. Nobody was taking responsibility to sort it out. Charlie kept asking for assurances, being given them, but then they weren't doing the things they said they were. I said to Charlie we could not allow these people to get away with such incompetence. TB said I shouldn't lose it with them but this had the feeling of a bit of a disaster. He said my rage was a bit too obvious, not least because my ears had gone red.

Fiona was showing the children around. Cherie had a dreadful cold but was soldiering on. Jennie Page [chief executive, NMEC] showed TB around and he felt it had the makings of a success. But not if tonight was a disaster. There was a good atmosphere but there were a lot of empty seats, presumably those of the people stranded at Stratford. The Queen arrived with [Prince] Philip, [Princess] Anne and her husband [Commodore Timothy Laurence]. Apart from the Queen, who at least managed the odd smile, the others looked very pissed off to be there. TB worked away at them, trying to charm them into the mood, but Anne was like granite. Cherie even curtsied to the Queen, a bit of a first I think, but it didn't seem to do much good. The pre-midnight show was not that great. It needed a compere to get everyone wound up and excited, but instead we just had a few acts, some good, some indifferent, but the climax of two young choristers was dull, and the moment itself was upon us too soon.

Fiona, the kids and I were sitting directly in front of Hague and [his wife] Ffion. At one point not long before midnight, I looked round at Hague, who was probably listening to my continuing phone calls about Stratford, as the list of angry hacks grew longer, when he said 'It's all going very well then.' TB and CB tried to get the Royals going a bit once 'Auld Lang Syne' came on but it was pretty clear they would rather be sitting under their travelling rugs in Balmoral. The Queen did kiss Philip and took his and TB's hands for 'Auld Lang Syne' but they did not look comfortable with the whole thing. TB claimed Philip said to him it was 'brilliant', but his body language did not radiate in that direction. Also, it would clearly have been better with the young princes there but Charles was never going to let that happen.

Afterwards the show was pretty spectacular and got people going a bit more than the build-up had but you would be hard-pressed to say it was the greatest show on earth. The fireworks outside sounded amazing and I sensed people feeling they would rather be out than in. At the party afterwards, again the mood was OK without being great. It just didn't feel that extra special that was needed to make it work really well, and create a mood that could give us a bit of momentum. The so-called river of fire, a flame down the Thames, had been a damp squib, barely visible. The TV news reports were seemingly fairly positive, but this was not a great buzz, and any of the papers whose editors had been stranded at Stratford were going to have their coverage dictated by their own diddums experience. There had just been too many things that didn't work. I enjoyed the boat ride back and the Dome itself actually looked quite impressive from that angle, all lit up. The boat must have taken half an hour or so, maybe more, then TB and JP were visiting some of the emergency services to thank them for working through the night. The mood around the place was OK, but there were a lot of people very pissed and it all felt just a bit debauched. The kids were beginning to wilt, and we finally got home about 3.30. Calum and Grace were asleep, but Rory and I watched a bit of the coverage on Sky, and it was clear Paris, Rio and Sydney were thought to have done best. In fact the picture of the night used as the TV headline caption picture was the bloody Eiffel Tower with fireworks coming out of it. Simple but brilliant, and better than anything that came out of the Dome in terms of single image.

Saturday, January 1, 2000

After a few hours' sleep, the phone went and it was TB, fretting about the way things had gone down. I said I felt it was about a seventy per cent success rate, but some of the other capitals did better. Also the Stratford strandings were going to hit us hard because they would all vent their own spleen. I also felt the show itself had been poor. I did a conference call with TB, Peter M and Charlie F. Peter and CF were both saying it had been a great success considering all the different pressures, but TB was worried the Sundays would revise the whole thing downwards and a fairly negative mood would settle. I said I thought we were a long way from persuading people it had been a success, given all the fuss over cost etc. Charlie F was down at the Dome doing interviews and of course the big thing there was going to be the first paying customers, and what they thought. It was a real baptism of fire for Charlie but he seemed up for it.

TB must have called me half a dozen times to find out how it was all playing out. Charlie was really keen to pile out the news so that we deflected attention from the fiasco at Stratford, but it was an uphill struggle. The tabloids were not that bad but the broadsheets were shaping up to be grim. We set off for Chequers and TB's New Year's do. Charlie arrived fairly late and seemed to think the Dome itself was going OK. We gave him a reasonably hard time, but he was coping pretty well I thought. The great thing about Charlie is he always managed to see a funny side of things. I suspected this was a quality he was going to need in large supply. TB felt in reality it had been an eighty-five per cent success. The problem was that the fuck-up at Stratford took us down to seventy rather than up to a hundred in the eyes of the media. He worried the papers would just go out to kill the Dome now.

Sunday, January 2

The press was definitely turning for the worse. TB felt that we must have it established within a couple of days that the Dome was a must-see, or we would be in trouble. It didn't feel that good, not least because the blame game was starting, between the police and NMEC, Jennie Page and Mike Lockett [Dome opening-night organiser]. I was angry with myself at not having done what I would normally do, namely work out what the picture was. The organisers believed TB and the Queen together, plus the Dome itself and the show, would be good enough, but the French had done what I would normally do, really go for a big symbol. It was Fiona's birthday, and we had loads of people round in the afternoon, but in between times I was doing a stack of conference calls. They [the Dome team] were already on defensive, damage limitation mode which was a real problem. There was definitely a delivery mechanism gap.

Monday, January 3

I left early for Notts County vs Burnley. TB called just before he left for Portugal, which would lead to the usual holiday bollocks. He was full of his usual 'you must get a rest', followed by half a dozen things he wanted done. GB was really worrying him now. He had written to TB saying he was moving out of the flat and it worried TB, who couldn't understand why he chose to write something like that, felt it was playing games, or part of some weird negotiation that nobody else understood. But he was a problem, and the IMF [managing director job] thing was still in the air. Robin was offside in a different direction, playing around on the euro. I did a conference call re Frank [Dobson]. Ken was still way ahead. But we had heard that he told the *New Statesman* he would stand as an independent if he lost among the members. We wrote to him asking him to withdraw. The plan was that if he didn't, we could do a rerun and get Mo in that way. He hadn't replied yet. Margaret McD went through the plans they had for Frank. We were coming up to a crucial phase and the relaunch had to be different, interesting, show a real step change. But none of us really felt that confident. We lost 2-0.

Tuesday, January 4

Calum and I had stayed up at Mum and Dad's, but the feeling in the office was that I should do the eleven o'clock by remote on to the squawk box. There was a bit of pressure building re the Dome, but I was pretty robust. They were trying to present the big-queue pictures as evidence of failure, whereas in fact we had to make clear it showed the level of interest there was. The truth was probably somewhere in between. On the drive back, the phone never stopped. I had a long chat with Piers [Morgan] trying to get him onside both re Dobbo and the Dome. I went into the office and worked through a stack of paper.

Wednesday, January 5

The first full day back. The holiday coverage wasn't too bad. The *Mail* tried the hardest to make it an issue, provoking JP who said it was an outrage he was criticised for having a few days off. There was more evidence of Robin's diddling in Alice Miles' [*Times*] piece on the lines that GB was pushing TB towards scepticism and RC was valiantly holding up the pro-Europe position. I had a Queen's Speech meeting with Jonathan, DM and Clare Sumner [private secretary, parliamentary affairs]. DM and I felt we had somehow to get Margaret B on board for a strategic approach. Jonathan was arguing that we had to find bills that were not briefed, kept secret till the end and which generated some excitement and momentum. My experience of the Queen's Speech, on both sides of the fence, was that nothing stays secret because the process was so long and drawn out, but we would try.

I had a meeting with RC's team re the euro, and lost it with David Clark [special adviser] for the way he was setting up GB/RC rows in the press, making it harder for TB to do what Robin wanted, namely a concerted push. He didn't deny having done it. He said the problem was the perception we were going back on the EMU policy. I stressed we had the right policy and we should all be promoting it. We had a carefully worked out strategy and one stupid briefing had put it at risk. They may have thought they were helping Robin's positioning, but in terms of what he was trying to achieve long term, they had damaged him. Shaun Woodward called, said he and Camilla were fine and both felt we did the right thing.

Tom Baldwin [*Times*] was somehow on to the letter that TB sent to GB about the flat. GB had written to Cherie saying he was willing to leave the flat totally until Euan went to university. TB wrote back saying there was no need for him to move out, they just needed one or two rooms. It was irritating that it was out there, and would just fuel the soap. I agreed a non-line with Hilary C.

Jonathan told me that TB and CB were going to stay with Cliff Richard [veteran pop singer] in the Algarve. I called him and said I thought it would become a real problem, parody material, if it became public. He said he just couldn't see why. Why couldn't they just chill out without always having to see famous people? His argument was that they couldn't have normal holidays partly because of security. Charlie F called, said that Jennie was really down, and the blame game was going into overdrive.

Thursday, January 6

The *Mail* was at it again, two pages on Dome disaster. *The Times* was still droning on negatively and there was no real fightback. TB called from Portugal in the middle of my meeting with Philip G and Dobbo. We were really trying to get Frank to go for Ken. I didn't get the sense Frank was improving. He was still all effing and blinding and bad jokes, and he said two things which made me think he was staying on in the wrong direction. First, he said he needed reasons to fall out with the government, which suggested he wanted to fight a kind of sub-Ken strategy. Second, he seemed to think more of the same would do. I said he needed a real gear change for Friday's press conference. Philip reckoned he needed thirty-eight per cent of members. Frank said he really needed GB to come out and fight for him. I spoke to TB again at the end of the meeting, which went on for an hour or so. He felt Frank had to go for Ken with a bit more oomph and imagination. He was determined to go and see Cliff Richard.

I spent most of the day dealing with the Dome. I spoke to the ghastly Simon Jenkins [journalist, member of the Millennium Commission], thought at the very least given his role in the whole thing, he should do something. Charlie F and co were keen on a Royal seal-of-approval story, so I called [Sir Robin] Janvrin [private secretary to the Queen] who was at Sandringham, apologised for asking, but he understood and said he would ask and get back to me. I acknowledged it was difficult. Charlie and I must have spoken close on half a dozen times during the day. He sounded fine, but I think shared my lack of confidence about the basic operation. We had to make it fashionable to like the Dome against all the chattering-class criticism. Ian Austin called in a state because GB was in an absolute fury about Baldwin and the *Mirror* enquiring about the flat. Both TB and Cherie were convinced, as was I, that GB or his people were responsible, though Austin's concern seemed genuine enough. I suppose it was possible GB would rage at him whilst letting somebody else put the stuff out, though what a waste of energy all that would be. We agreed we had to be totally dismissive of it.

Friday, January 7

Writing this at the end of a not untypical day at the end of which, when they called just before midnight, I told Switch, in answer to their friendly 'How are you?', that I was both homicidal and suicidal. The Dome press coverage, with the exception of the *Mirror* poll, was wall-to-wall dreadful. I did a conference call with Charlie F, Jennie P and Jez [Sagar] to go through the script for the Sundays. TB later said he thought me doing a briefing on it was a bad idea because it would lay it all on us, but if it failed, we were the ones who would cop it anyway. I also felt if we didn't show real support, it would look really wounded. My main pitch was to try to divide real people, who were overwhelmingly positive, from the chattering-class knockers. Jennie and Charlie were both getting more and more defensive. Also, I had been banging on for days about the need to get a few celebs down there, but it just hadn't happened. I wanted to say that the behaviour of the press was the longest tantrum in history, which Charlie felt was over-provocative, but we did need to make the point that coverage was overly influenced by a small number of editors having been inconvenienced at Stratford. I did an hour-long briefing, but the questioning was relentlessly hostile and there was no doubt we were losing the PR battle. I had started the day hoping to have a day off, but the Dome put paid to that. We just had to get up a dividing line between real people, and sneerers and cynics.

Hilary had discovered that in fact GB had effectively moved out of the flat already so our denials would be made to look ridiculous. She was convinced this was probably an operation to show GB doing his usual hair-shirt thing while TB needed two flats at the taxpayers' expense. It looked like GB's letter had been written to leak but it meant we were heading for another fucking episode of the soap opera. When TB called later, he said there was no question of taking over the flat. They just needed one or two rooms if people were staying, and they were the rooms currently used by staff. Dobbo's launch didn't really break through and by the end of the day Ken had turned it into a personal attack on him, which he believed Frank would regret. Robert Hill [TB's health policy adviser] was another regular caller as we were on the edge re an NHS winter crisis, though the health department seemed to be doing pretty well. We thought it would be a good idea to get up in the Sundays that nurses and doctors were set for a good rise, but needless to say GB was opposed.

TB called when I was watching Rory play football and said he had no idea things had been so bad in the last few days. I felt Charlie had been too trusting of the Dome people, that he had not wanted to bother us with problems, but they really needed more support. Ticket sales were not going as they should be. TB said he was having a good time but was preoccupied with this, Europe, GB. I said I was pretty close to the end of my tether, that today was meant to be a day off, and I had been doing too much work on too many fronts.

Saturday, January 8

The *Sun* ran my piece on Burnley over two pages. We were still getting badly hit on the Dome. The *Telegraph* reported me as 'interrupting my holiday' to help PR for the Dome. Baldwin [*Times*] had a line about GB advising TB to distance himself from the Dome, which again must have been briefed, because it was exactly what GB said to TB yesterday and lo and behold, there it was in black and white the next day. We set off for Coventry vs Burnley with Gavin and Oscar [Fiona's brother and nephew]. We arrived early and met Geoffrey Robinson [former minister, Coventry City honorary president] who was very solicitous of the boys. He was giving me advice about what we should be doing about the NHS, but I always found it hard to follow Geoffrey's logic. The Coventry chairman [Bryan Richardson] was showing the boys a model of the planned new stadium and was being quizzed by Oscar on the finances, which led to Geoffrey asking him if he needed a loan and wanted to go into business. We lost 2-0. We got the Sundays late on. The *Sunday Times* splashed on a story about GB's flat. When Ian Austin called, I was very hard on him. The flat story wasn't great, but I felt very little sympathy for GB, who rarely gave a toss when anyone else was in trouble.

Sunday, January 9

I got Peter M to put out words re the Dome critics. The NHS and winter problems was the main story of the day. TB/CB back from Portugal.

Monday, January 10

Robin C had given us one or two problems on *Frost* yesterday by suggesting that there would be a PR [proportional representation] referendum, that there would definitely be a euro referendum and every rational person wanted that. At the 8.30 meeting, Ian [Austin] was a bit woolly on the GB flat story. GB had responded to TB's note, which we discussed at TB's office meeting. On the political argument, there was a new non-argument between them, TB saying we had to emphasise reform, GB saying we had to be more focused on dividing lines with the Tories. They were not inconsistent. I felt we just had to get back to some of the earlier arguments and get radicalism tied to values. TB was confident we would win on health over time but that pushing reform was the key to achieving it. He seemed a bit subdued and asked Philip G and me to stay back at the end. He was very worried about Livingstone. We told him Frank was heading for a hammering. Also, the Dome was a problem and there was probably an overwhelming need for new management.

I agreed with Mo that she would do a speech about the Tories on Friday and their 'lurch to the right'. She was very pissed off at Steve Richards' [*New Statesman*] article ['Mo Mowlam's fall from grace'] saying Number 10 was exasperated with her. I assured her we did not brief against her, and that she was the one who emanated unease the whole time. She was pretty antsy but agreed to do the speech. At one point, it was clear we were talking at cross purposes because she thought I meant us at first when I talked about lurch to the right.

TB called a meeting on Frank. He felt there were three options – 1. MPs get members to vote for Frank by being told their lives depended on it (unlikely to be successful); 2. Frank pulls out willingly and Mo goes in; 3. we cut a deal with Ken to be a good boy with a Blairite deputy and staff. He felt we had to work on all three. I said this is fine, so long as we understand he is capable of doing deals and then undoing them once he gets his way. TB felt he might honour a deal if he felt all the guns would be trained on him if he didn't. But I had to understand if he won the nomination it would be a huge blow to New Labour, and also understand his ability to attract oppositionalist dissent around him. Philip G felt TB was OK on this because everyone knew he didn't want Ken. I said it was all dreadful and there was no point pretending otherwise. TB felt Mo was the best option, but that Frank wouldn't go along with it because it was so humiliating. None of the options were either easy or perfect.

The four o'clock was almost all about CB not buying a ticket on the train to Luton, where she was sitting as a judge. It was classic Cherie. She claimed the ticket office was closed but she was probably just absent-minded. I said it would be very odd for a 45-year-old pregnant woman to jump a fence and run away. They were fairly light-hearted about it but obsessing mildly because Hilary had said the ticket office was shut whereas I had said it was a kiosk. Flu was leading the news, which would create the mood for any bad NHS stories. Also, people were trying to make a problem out of something I said at the eleven o'clock, namely that there would be a gap between a general election and a euro referendum, which there would, but they were trying to say TB had never said that. TB was having dinner with GB to try to get him bound in to what we were doing again.

TB seemed pretty pleased with his dinner with GB, said that it had been better than other such events. GB had adamantly denied having a different position on Europe, and felt it was the Foreign Office that was trying to shift the policy in a different direction. Despite all that though today's *FT* had a story that he was pushing a different line on Third World education. The atmospherics between them had definitely changed and that was getting out there, and we had to get it back in a better place.

The Cherie train story was massive in the tabloids and the *Sun* wasn't very nice, talking about her being nabbed and nicked and what have you. She was pretty fed up. She had a cold, the pregnancy was tiring her and she found the whole thing embarrassing. Bruce G's take was that it was quality PR because it showed she travelled like a normal person, and she sometimes forgot things like everyone does. TB saw Frank D privately. He said afterwards that Frank was convinced he could do it so we would have to go for it. I think we all had the same sinking feeling, but TB said we would have to make the best of it. GB would have to go out and fight for him, so would Clare [Short] and anyone we thought might be tempted by Ken.

The other thing that was coming up fast on the radar was [boxer] Mike Tyson, who was due to fight in London, so there would be a big hoo-ha if he was let in, given his various misdemeanours.[1] I dropped a line to Jack Straw to say I thought he would be absolutely hammered if Tyson was banned. Coincidentally, the *Standard* splashed on it today in an editorial saying he should be banned. Jack's line was that rules are rules, and he had to play it by the book. I felt it was one of those where people who wanted him banned didn't feel it that strongly, and would be on to the next cause pretty quickly, whereas there would be a constituency that would really, really object if he was kept out of the country. I got a sense of the mixed views at the four o'clock. The sense they got from my briefing was that he definitely would be banned, because I was emphasising Jack's 'rules are rules' line. Frank Warren, who was promoting the fight, was out blaming me for breaking the rules re applications. Little did he know I was fighting his corner.

[1] 'Iron Mike' Tyson had been convicted in 1992 of the rape of eighteen-year-old Miss Black Rhode Island Desiree Washington and sentenced to ten years in prison, serving three. His 1988-89 marriage to actress Robin Givens ended in divorce, amid allegations of domestic violence by Tyson.

Wednesday, January 12

First PMQs of the New Year. [General Augusto] Pinochet was massive in the press, as was Tyson. I spoke to Jack a couple of times and said I feared the Tyson situation would be grim. TB briefed up mainly on health, Pinochet and the Neill committee report on special advisers.[1] He did fine and Hague was poor, but I worried that too many of our own MPs were a bit creepy. PMQs only really worked if TB looked like he was being tested. We had a strategy meeting post-PMQs, trying to put together a proper plan for Frank but also discussing how to get direction and momentum back. PG reckoned we were regularly five per cent behind the Tories in local elections.

Thursday, January 13

Jack was of course focused on Pinochet and I called him again to say I thought the Tyson situation was becoming a bit of a shambles. I was beginning to worry it would be the main focus of TB's *Frost* interview [on Sunday]. Peter Oborne had a piece about me controlling the press in the *Spectator*. Someone said it was the third *Spectator* front cover on me in less than a year. I went up to see TB and said I felt we were just drifting at the moment, there was no clear big message. Interest rates were going up today. Tyson and Pinochet were both tricky. I grabbed Jack before Cabinet and he gave me his usual line about playing by the book, but I really felt we were in danger of falling into the wrong place. Cabinet went over pay review bodies, flu, Northern Ireland. Peter M was very gloomy on decommissioning, said it was absolutely bleak. He said we were talking about very dark clouds. The decommissioning body would be unable to make a positive statement and that was very serious because decommissioning was to have started by the end of the month so that Trimble could report to his council in February. It meant the UUs would leave the executive.

The World at One led on Tyson and a union guy saying it was dreadful that an immigration worker would have to decide. That was indeed the logic of Jack's 'rules are rules' approach. I had finally got TB engaged and he agreed we had to get it sorted quickly. Otherwise, he said, it will be a fucking shambles by the morning. Jack was feeling a bit hurt, I think, and made a joke – though without much humour – about how he would happily give it up and let me do

[1] A report by the Committee on Standards in Public Life, chaired by Lord [Patrick] Neill, was expected to curtail the role of special advisers in government. However, it acknowledged their importance and concluded that it was right they should be paid out of public funds.

the job for him. I said we had to have it sorted by the four o'clock [briefing], because this felt like a shambles and we had enough of those at the moment.

Frank Warren made a submission and included the wider issues of businesses that would be badly affected if the fight didn't go ahead. After my briefing yesterday, he had finally realised that I was on his side and today invited 'you and your lady wife' to the fight! By the 4, Jack had discovered that he did after all have discretion and he was going to use it and review the situation. I knew the Tyson issue was moving towards resolution, but couldn't quite say so at the four o'clock.

We had a truly dreadful meeting of the TB/GB etc. strategy group. It was meant to be just the six of us (TB, GB, Peter M, PG, Douglas Alexander and I) but GB turned up with Ed [Balls], walked through the door saying 'This is an economics meeting, isn't it?' Ed marched in behind him. Embarrassment all round. At one point when TB asked what he thought was going to happen with long-term interest rates, GB said 'Ed's here, he can answer that.' At another point, discussing Europe, TB said the pro-Europeans were attacking him and making life difficult, Peter said we had to be more positive and Gordon literally turned away to look at the wall. He only opened up in any shape or form when TB and Peter left the room for a call with Gerry Adams. God knows what Douglas thought of all this.

TB had said after his dinner that GB was back onside. If this is onside, God knows what it would be like with him offside. The two of them didn't really communicate at all. GB referred questions to Ed B. We skirted round the Europe issue. Robin had been livid it had not been discussed at Cabinet. GB felt the FCO and others were deliberately putting out the line that we had gone negative. Philip G and I tried occasionally to get a proper discussion going but this was a totally dysfunctional group at the moment and I felt we were in bad shape.

Friday, January 14

We had been a bit slow yesterday to pick up on [scientist, doctor and Labour peer Robert] Winston's attack [on Labour's handling of the NHS] in the *New Statesman*.[1] It was now leading the news. The *Mirror*

---

[1] Winston had been quoted as saying 'Our reorganisation of the health service was . . . very bad. We have made medical care deeply unsatisfactory for a lot of people. We've always had this right but monolithic view that there should be equality throughout the nation at the point of delivery. All very good stuff, but it isn't working.'

January '00: Professor Winston's NHS broadside ...

had done three pages on it, no doubt in part because of Oborne's article in the *Spectator* to say they were all in my pocket. As if the general attack wasn't bad enough, even worse in a way was he talked about how Cherie was having a caesarean when he had no way of knowing if she was or if she wasn't. I thought he was meant to be a serious person. First, she wasn't. Second, who was he to know whether she was or she wasn't? And third, even if he did know, what the fuck was he doing talking about it in an interview? I got Fiona to call him and ask whether he said what he was quoted as saying. He denied it, not convincingly. I spoke to him, said we tried very hard to protect CB and he had given us a very bad situation. I must have been losing it a little, because he asked me not to shout at him. I said he had to make it clear he hadn't said it, or that if he had, he had no business doing so.

Tyson was also a bit of a mess as they were all on to the idea that Jack was made to do it by us. That resulted from them asking if TB spoke to Jack and I said I had spoken to him simply because it was a big media issue. TB was very exercised about Winston whilst CB was as livid as I have seen her for ages about him talking about her at all. TB felt we should encourage Winston to do interviews recalibrating what he said, but I felt little confidence in him. I drafted a statement which Robert Hill and I got him to agree to, which said that he supported the general direction of our policy, attacked the Tories, and denied the remarks about Cherie. I just about managed to get it out for the 11, where I said CB was upset and also that he had said he had been misrepresented. The briefing seemed to go on forever – Winston, Tyson, Europe – and in all of it they were really only interested in the spin/process etc. Cherie was even talking at one stage of a complaint to the General Medical Council. TB was against, and was more worried about what he was saying about the NHS.

Channel 4 News did a big number on Winston being gagged, presumably because he was complaining he couldn't do interviews. TB had wanted him to do interviews but I was worried he would just open up new flanks. It also emerged that there was indeed a tape, albeit muffled, of him talking about Cherie and *The World at One* played it. Cherie wanted to demand an apology but TB said to leave it. [Alan] Milburn did well doing the rounds, but it was all pretty difficult. The problem was that these kinds of stories always took a greater hold if we were drifting without direction or momentum. We went out for dinner with the Goulds. Philip said both he and Douglas were genuinely shocked at GB yesterday.

Saturday, January 15

TB spoke to Winston, who said he had been unbelievably naive and was very sorry and amazed that he had caused all this trouble. He had not meant to say a lot of the things he had said. TB was very nice to him, saying we may need him again. But the press was a bit of a disaster area, and I was pissed off that as ever I was the one getting it in the neck for allegedly trying to nobble him. I was also getting blamed for the Tyson decision which was now running as helping Warren and Sky [TV] to get even richer.

Meanwhile a bloke drove a car into the gates of Number 10, breaking a woman's leg. When I first heard, I guessed it would be a nurse or junior doctor, knowing our current luck. It turned out to be a lover's tiff. TB was at Chequers most of the day, and we chatted a few times. Re the press, he said they just moved from one frenzy to the next, without stopping for real thought. They are a mix of dishonesty, superficiality and rank hypocrisy. But he was till holding back from really taking them on. He said if he was asked about me tomorrow [on *Frost*], as he might be given all the stuff in the press, he would say they went for me because I was effective and because I went for them.

Sunday, January 16

I had briefed a bit on health pre TB's *Frost* interview, and it was leading the news. We had planned a number of stories – extra spending – more intensive care beds, NHS Direct extended, nurses' pay deal good, more specialist schools, stop and search. I went in to meet TB and we went over some of the tricky questions in the car. After he got made up, we had twenty minutes or so in the dressing room and we agreed to try and get up the idea of the narrative for the parliament with a real push on health now after education. It was OK as an interview and with a concerted ring-round afterwards, we got them on the right track. He had pledged to raise health spending to the EU average, which the experts were immediately trying to pick apart, and which had not got down very well with GB, even though it was the logic of what we had been saying. It certainly got us into a better position on health.

Mo did Boulton [Sky News] and admitted she had taken drugs so she got her way in the end. I had spent the last few days trying to persuade GB to do an article for the *Standard* pro Frank and anti Ken and the draft finally arrived, but they were still arguing against doing it. The *Observer* had run an interview with one of Pinochet's doctors who seemed to suggest Jack S had misled Parliament by claiming they had said Pinochet was not fit to stand trial. Jack now felt that he *could* issue the medical reports.

Monday, January 17

TB's interview only partially arrested problems re the NHS. The *Mirror* was dreadful again and I had another up-and-downer with Piers who as ever was being wound up by the anecdotage of someone he knew, in this case a doctor relative. GB was in a complete rage about it, ranting and raving at TB during our meeting later on, saying it hadn't been agreed, it wasn't sensible, and how his reaction to problems was always more money. TB was sure it was the right thing to do and we would have had to bind GB into doing it anyway. My worry was that we were making how much we spent vis-à-vis other countries the main thing by which we were judged, because these comparisons were rarely like for like. It also meant less room for modernisation within the argument and the judgements made.

Nurses' pay was running OK but that too looked like a money message, rather than modernisation. We were feeling and looking ragged and we had to get back on track sharpish. I told Ian Austin that also meant GB had to end his near invisibility on political issues and difficulties. At the office meeting TB was angry that someone had told John Kampfner [BBC] about a 'living with Ken' strategy based on an assumption he was going to win. The eleven o'clock was all about health and it was tough going. They just didn't buy the idea of progress. TB was confident by next year there would be real change, but we so lacked a big driving strategic narrative.

We planned out the next few days. I had a session to plan the Michael Cockerell interview up in the flat. It went fine, but by the end TB was fed up with being quizzed too closely on personal stuff. I left for the Jill Craigie [late wife of Michael Foot] memorial. It was nice to see Paul Foot, Geoffrey Goodman, Bill Hagerty, John Penrose and Annie Robinson [all former *Mirror* colleagues]. Tony Benn was effusive, thanking me for letting him film one of my briefings [for a television documentary]. 'I do hope you are a fellow diarist,' he said. I got back for TB's meeting with GB, which was a grim scene. Then we heard of a *Mirror* poll showing TB's ratings had fallen dramatically. Alex F called. We ended up having our usual moan about the press. He said all they could do with success is knock it.

Tuesday, January 18

The Home Office had done an OK job of explaining in advance the context re crime figures but the reality was it was going to be bad once the figures were published. The *Telegraph* splashed big that Hague was pushing private health care tax breaks and looking for an all-party approach on it. TB felt it was another Hague misjudgement, that it allowed us to get up the idea of a right-wing philosophy undermining the NHS. Also, the last time it was tried [by Conservative ministers] in the 90s, the effect was poor. I prepared a strong script for the eleven o'clock, and launched into it.[1]

Ken had done an interview in *The Face* [fashionable culture magazine] saying he supported the rioters in Seattle.[2] I called Frank to say he needed to go for him on crime. Needless to say, it never quite happened.

The eleven o'clock was mainly health and Livingstone, with no mention of crime figures, which was extraordinary, but may just mean they decided they didn't need much explanation at all. I looked up the big strategy document we had done for last September and although there was some progress in most areas, we had not followed it through with sufficient rigour.

Sue Nye [GB aide] had told Anji that GB was livid at *Frost*, felt that TB had totally undermined his strategy and said that he didn't trust any of us, that he was convinced I had been responsible for the 'psychological flaws' briefing [unattributed comment reported by the *Observer*'s Andrew Rawnsley], that Ian Austin had reported back me saying GB had been invisible and he had been trying to avoid the [*Evening Standard* pro Frank] Dobson article. So with GB offside, JP bruised, RC diddling, Peter on Northern Ireland, Blunkett low-key and Jack on anything but crime, it was not good.

I then learned that the CB/TUC parental leave story was going to hit us tomorrow.[3] I told her I thought it was self-indulgent, that she was being used by the TUC in hiring her for the case. She said she did what she thought was right. It should have been avoided and played right into our opponents' hands. Then came the news unemployment was going up too. So in no time at all we'd have waiting lists up, crime up, unemployment up and a sense of drift all over the place.

[1] Campbell, speaking as the prime minister's official spokesman, told journalists that the Conservative proposal was evidence of a 'clear right-wing agenda to promote arguments that the NHS cannot be sustained'.
[2] Anti-globalisation protests in Seattle, Washington, USA in November 1999. An estimated 40,000 protesters marched, destroyed property and clashed with police in advance of a World Trade Organisation conference.
[3] The TUC engaged Cherie Blair, as Cherie Booth QC, to challenge a government ruling on parental leave in the High Court.

I woke up and had that feeling of total grindology, too many problems, too much stuff coming from different directions. The press sensed we weren't on top of our game and were being even more ridiculous than usual. Something I said, in exactly the same words as TB had used, was now being described as a retreat and a U-turn. TB had seen [Paul] Dacre yesterday, whose general view was that we still got an easy time, that we were woeful on health – too Old Labour – and that we lacked strength and ministerial depth. TB was so charmed by his intelligence that he said he would stop me from going over the top in my attacks on the *Mail*. I did words on Livingstone from TB to give out at the eleven o'clock. The briefings were generally going on for at least half an hour these days, covering lots of subjects, which basically meant we weren't controlling the agenda.

I went up to see TB in the flat, where he was working on PMQs. He was mildly pissed off with Cherie re the TUC case but in the end felt it didn't matter that much. At the Grid meeting, we were discussing the rural [economy] report and ideas for what TB could do on the thousandth day [in office]. We had a Britain in Europe meeting with poor Simon Buckby, who showed us their latest crap poster on the day the *Guardian* poll said sixty-three per cent were against the euro.

Philip did a couple of groups last night and they weren't good. Traditional voters were OK, but the switchers were dreadful. The sense of failure on the NHS was particularly bad because it was a core connecting issue and trust issue because of its centrality to how we won. Philip was really concerned we were losing the plot on health and education. The public had very little idea of what we were trying to do. That was in part because TB and GB were not really pushing the same lines.

GB's body language at PMQs was dreadful, clearly livid still at the *Frost* interview. It was the same story when he arrived – late – for the Institute of Education Q&A [Labour Party members meeting]. TB said in the car that he was confident we could get things right but Philip and I felt we were too complacent, that we didn't have a clear message and we lacked direction and the policy agenda wasn't driving through properly. Added to which, ministerial capacity was worse than it had ever been with all of the main people variously offside or disabled so it wasn't hanging together. The Q&A was OK, though there was a fair amount of heckling [Blair and Brown were slow-handclapped on arrival fifteen minutes late]. The best bit was when TB really went for a woman who said we had done nothing at all. GB was pretty good too. On the way back, TB admitted that in part

Frost had been about trying to box GB into this NHS extra spending. He was not remotely convinced that the extra child benefit had been a good use of money. We got next to no political credit and it was simply part of GB's positioning around the equality agenda. The three lead stories on *News at Ten* all had TB figuring strongly in them – up against Hague on health, tackling Livingstone, then Cherie and the TUC. I suppose it was connecting after a fashion.

Thursday, January 20

The press were pretty much universal in saying we were currently a disaster area. [Trevor] Kavanagh said it was the worst week ever. Philip felt this was our worst period yet. But TB was strangely becalmed. He knew we weren't on top or motoring, but he believed this was just one of those tough patches we went through. We just had to keep emphasising reform over the long term. I was feeling tired and depressed. Normally I like a fight but at the moment I just couldn't be bothered with it. I was having to do too much for too many people, and too many people were wanting a piece of me the whole time. It was a nightmare. I was working on the speech and briefing for tomorrow and the idea that TB was more radical than Thatcher. Despite me trying to talk him out of it, Piers splashed the *Mirror* on Mo for mayor. Dobbo was whacked in the phone poll. Piers was probably successfully winding Mo up. I saw Jack to discuss the Pinochet plans.

TB was on much better form at Cabinet, really fired up about the expected defeat on the Mode of Trial Bill in the Lords.[1] Said we had to make it a crime issue, and go for the forces of conservatism. We had to be clear we would get it back in the Commons very quickly. Margaret Jay said there was a cross-party alliance being led by [Labour Baroness and QC] Helena Kennedy and we were going to be defeated. Jack said there was an unholy alliance between some of our people, Lib Dems and Tories. TB immediately saw it as an opportunity to show the Tories were no longer tough on crime, and to show the need for a more representative House of Lords. He said it was being defeated by a combination of vested interests [e.g. lawyers] and opportunists. He was very fired up, pointed out Scotland had been doing

[1] The Criminal Justice (Mode of Trial) Bill sought to take the choice of court away from defendants in 'either way' offences like theft, burglary and handling, where traditionally defendants could choose between magistrates' courts or Crown Court. The choice of court would be made by magistrates, with the safeguard of a right of appeal to a Crown Court judge. Opponents of the bill said that it took away the right to trial by jury.

this for ages without any problem, and he was more than happy to take on the lawyers over it.

On health, TB gave his assessment and there was a discussion. Echoes of GB's view had already been in the *Mail*. He said higher public spending could lead to higher inflation and he wouldn't be surprised if the Bank [of England] felt the need to put up interest rates on the basis of what we had been saying. It was a clear message delivered straight to TB. He was really smouldering at the moment. The eleven o'clock seemed to go on for ages. I was very robust re Mode of Trial and on reform generally.

At one o'clock, we had a strategy meeting of the group of six, which had become the group of seven, and which Douglas A had christened 'the group of death' after the last meeting. It was another classic. They were often saying the same thing but in a slightly different way, and it would be in the slight differences that GB would find huge arguments. TB looked tired and worried, which was exactly how I felt. I was sitting on the sofa next to GB and you could feel the smouldering, particularly when Peter M spoke. Every time two or more of us tried to agree a line, let alone a plan or a course of action, GB would say we had to go out and test it. Nobody was sure what we were supposed to be saying now. I said the emphasis had to be on reform for the purposes of delivering. TB wanted the focus on the sense of struggle. GB wanted big-picture delivery set on clear dividing lines. It should be perfectly straightforward to bring that together but we never seemed to agree on anything. We went round in circles for an hour. Peter M wondered if we shouldn't now distance ourselves from Britain in Europe because we were getting nowhere with them and we needed triangulation. It was pretty much what GB had been saying up to now, but today he was suddenly opposed to it. He felt the answer on Europe was a Britishness campaign.

I felt tired, angry, depressed and not at all on form. TB could tell I was down, kept trying to keep my spirits up but I told him he was wasting his time. He said we would get there, but I felt we were really lacking in firepower at the centre. I told Dobbo about the dreadful *Mirror* poll but he showed no sign of wanting to pull out. I spoke to Mo, who came up with, even for her, an unbelievably up-herself statement, namely that TB was now so unpopular that 'even I might not be able to pull it off'. I went to GB's press drinks do. He was doing the rounds big time. Gus O'Donnell [Treasury official responsible for EU monetary policy, press secretary to John Major 1990–94] asked me whether TB doing the EU average on health was deliberate or accidental. I said both.

Friday, January 21

The briefing on the speech [announcing hundreds of comprehensive schools would become specialist colleges] was leading the news with a mix of sticking to our guns and fightback, but the press was definitely in a totally ridiculous phase. Both yesterday and today I confided to Anji and Liz Lloyd [home affairs policy adviser] that I was seriously thinking about moving on. I felt no ownership of my life at all. I was in at half seven. Up to see TB who had been up since 5 working on the speech and had done a pretty good job. It was very much a 'stay the course' speech. We got it finished by 9, inserted some of the lines I had briefed overnight like politics being a struggle, then set off for West Ham. We were laughing with the cops as we drove past the Dome, head in hands, reminiscing about the effects of that dreadful December 31 fiasco.

The *Mirror* was massive again on Dobbo. [Front page headline] 'Dead as a Dobbo'. The *Sun* asked Mo to do a piece backing Dobbo as a way of stuffing the *Mirror*. I had to get Mo to pull it on the grounds she didn't want to be used in newspaper politics. Mo was clearly keen to run, but very unkeen to say so. Yelland called to ask whether I was pushing Piers towards this. The visit went really well, very good school, a newly knighted head who was clearly in charge. Both the speech and the Q&A went well, and the kids clearly liked him. Hague by contrast looked a bit pathetic when he tried to play into the media's whole 'week from hell' agenda. I then left for William Ellis [Campbell's sons' comprehensive school in Gospel Oak], where I was doing a Q&A with the politics class. They were pretty tough but my sense was the Tories had had it with their generation.

Saturday, January 22

TB's speech had settled things down a bit, though the comment pieces further revealed a new mood. TB called a couple of times, said things were basically fine and we just had to keep going. I was desperate for a quiet weekend so I transferred my pager on to Godric who only bothered me once, over a *Sunday Times* story about TB's dad having private health insurance. Margaret McDonagh was due to see Dobbo tomorrow with Tessa [Jowell], to underline the message that it wasn't going well. The Mo plan was only going to work if he went.

Sunday, January 23

The write-throughs of the week from hell weren't as bad as they might have been. There were also a few defence shortage stories which we put down to the usual pre-spending review skirmishes. TB's car was involved in a mild prang. Later Cherie told Fiona that he was very down at the moment.

Monday, January 24

The *Mail* was in full throttle, on mixed-sex wards and much else besides. Routledge [*Mirror*] had a piece on 1,000 days basically saying we were crap apart from GB. The *Sun* did a full-page leader on the euro suggesting GB was the man to save the pound. Throw in Simon Walters' [*Mail on Sunday*] piece of yesterday, which had GB's warning to TB, and the quotes from Cabinet, and I would say we had a bit of a serious GB problem at the moment. TB said he had a good one-on-one meeting with GB. At the morning meeting, I said I felt we needed to put together a proper strategy for the press, both taking them on, and getting them going at each other. I felt we had to define them and expose to the public the way they operate. When we did the *Mail* monitor, we had had an effect but now we were being hit day after day and not getting any gain for the pain. As Philip said, it was actually a successful government being defined as an unsuccessful government.

Bill Bush had done a very good note comparing our first 1,000 days with Thatcher's, and we had a long discussion about the extent to which we wanted to draw comparisons. GB or RC doing it would just be reported as part of the current soap so [David] Blunkett was the best one to do it. I said so deliberately at the 8.30 meeting, with both Ian [Austin] and Douglas A there, so that would get back to GB. Douglas was actually on good form at the moment, and had done a very good note on strategy. It was stronger on analysis than solutions but to be fair to him the reason was that it was so hard to be frank on paper about the central weaknesses. Strangely, Philip was very down, which was unusual for him. TB saw Dobbo again and there was still no sign at all that he felt like pulling out. Don Macintyre [*Independent*] was in for a chat with TB. He told me he felt GB was getting hooked on the drug of support from the right-wing anti-European press.

Tuesday, January 25

TB was in a real state about Livingstone. Frank had refused to come out. He was not remotely bothered, it seemed, about going back to Cabinet or a peerage, or anything else. His pride was at stake and that was that. Also Mo was not willing to push him too hard. TB said it was the worst of all worlds – we had a candidate in the ring who can't win and a candidate outside the ring who would probably walk it. I asked him if he could imagine himself campaigning for Ken. The thought filled him with horror. He said he wished he had never listened to the soft-left voices saying Ken must stand. He was going to be a total disaster from now on in.

Phil Bassett [special adviser] had drafted the Blunkett speech for tomorrow on the Thatcher/Blair comparison, which I rewrote then briefed and got a good row going at the 11 which meant at least, for the first time in days, we were on an agenda of our choosing. After the 11, we had a 'group of death' minus PG and Peter M who were away. It was more of the same. TB saying the reform message is key. GB wanting his Britishness campaign. A cursory discussion of Douglas' note. Me saying we needed a sense of struggle and conflict with vested interests. GB back on his dividing lines. Then another discussion on Europe, TB saying the worst thing was any sense we changed policy, GB saying it was all the fault of the FCO, TB saying they were just picking up the signals that he was cosying up the Eurosceptic agenda. I think TB had been seized with the point made by Don Macintyre, that GB could get hooked on the approval of the right-wing media.

I left for a visit to the new SIS building. They laid on a presentation about some of their information operations, and also some of the work they were doing on drugs in Afghanistan, Pakistan and Colombia. They were very good but clearly felt they were just picking at the tip of an iceberg. I had lunch with the new C [head of SIS], Richard Dearlove and John Scarlett his deputy. We discussed their profile. I suggested that the whole [Melita] Norwood episode could have been avoided if there had been proper work put into it earlier. They were still bedevilled by a combination of James Bond and the sense that they did things they weren't meant to, the downside of secrecy, whose upside was fairly obvious. If they felt it mattered to get a better press, I felt we should work up strategies to get profile for what they do in relation to drugs, organised crime, WMD [weapons of mass destruction], terrorism. Dearlove was urbane but also friendly, and with a real grasp of big-picture foreign policy. Scarlett was much more what we imagine a classical spook to be. He had very intense eyes, could hold your gaze but would then suddenly dart his eyes somewhere else. He was also immaculately dressed. He was once kicked out of Russia [in 1994, when he had been Moscow 'station chief'].

I told them that our people, including quite senior people, had little or no training at all on how to deal with this kind of thing. I also said that even if they had a good story to tell, they should be wary of becoming just like any other organisation that made itself too open and accessible. It was interesting that they felt we got a good press as a government, whereas I didn't. I felt they got a good press, but they didn't. I felt they were overly defensive about their role in the world. I assured them that TB was totally on their side. That we wouldn't support anything that they felt put the lives of agents at risk. I liked them both, thought they were impressive as characters and also dedicated and serious about what they did.

Wednesday, January 26

In general the 1,000-days stuff was fine and DB's speech was going OK. We guessed that Hague would do 1,000-days stuff [at PMQs] and a rap on non-delivery. TB was getting really panicked about the Ken situation. The ballot papers were due to go out today and we just couldn't get Frank out and Mo in. If only she had gone for it when she should have. We were getting a dreadful press in general but I wasn't sure it was damaging us that much, because the public knew a lot of it was ridiculous.

I was pretty short with them at the 11 and really wanted to go for the *Sun* on [repeal of] Section 28 after they had said that children of five were to be taught about gay sex. We were due to leave for PMQs but an all-night and all-day filibuster meant we lost the day's business, which was ridiculous.[1] So after all that preparation, no question time. A handwritten letter [complaining that Blair could have rearranged business to preserve PMQs] from Hague came in on the fax, then we got TB's reply out [responding that Hague should get a grip on discipline in his party] and away we went in a head-to-head PR battle. We got Boulton, Brunson and Oakley [Sky, ITN, BBC] in for interviews which went fine, the main focus 1,000 days, a bit of Ireland, and the Opposition being a joke [Hague had also challenged Blair to a half-hour television debate instead of PMQs].

Another meeting on London. Margaret McD said there was no way Frank would win and that Mo would, even though there would be a backlash. We all felt pretty desperate at the idea of Ken being a candidate. I said we had to do everything we could to get Mo in there. Margaret and Sally [Morgan] went to see her and eventually she said she would do it provided Frank wanted it, and we didn't pull him

[1] Conservative MPs filibustered for twenty-nine hours to oppose the Disqualifications Bill, which sought to remove the disqualification for membership of the House of Commons and the Northern Ireland Assembly of politicians who were members of the Irish parliament, while disqualifying Irish ministers from holding ministerial office in Northern Ireland. The move meant that parliamentary business was cancelled on Blair's thousandth day, though it deprived William Hague of an opportunity to confront Blair at Prime Minister's Questions.

out. I went home briefly before going back in to join TB to see Frank and Janet Dobson [his wife], to try to persuade him to pull out. TB was pretty blunt, said he felt that the very best prospect was that he would only just nick it and then lose the election itself, possibly with Ken as an independent. Frank said he was convinced it was moving his way, but I said there wasn't much evidence of that. Frank also said, and he admitted there were personal feelings here, he didn't believe Mo would do much better. If he really felt she would, he would have no problems pulling out. Janet said she thought party members in particular would be gobsmacked and appalled if we did this, that it was the worst kind of fixing. TB said what he cared about was the impact on the party and the government if Ken won. It would be a big disaster and he didn't want that. All the evidence suggested Frank wouldn't win, and Mo might. That says to us that we should get her in. Frank was adamant he could do it and that she would do no better.

He must have been hurting to hear what we were saying, and maybe it just made him more determined. I said Mo would totally change the dynamic because she had an anti-politics persona and it was clear that several of the papers, including the *Mirror* which a lot of members read, would just shift behind her. It may be unfair but the press had not let Frank put over a persona. Between us, TB and I must have tried eight or ten times, but he wouldn't move from the basic point, that he didn't think she was the answer. TB asked him, if he carried on and things didn't pick up, whether he would pull out later in the contest and he said no.

So that was that, we were stuck with it, we were going to have to try to get him a proper message and a proper campaign and try to get him to win but it was going to be very, very difficult. I gave Frank and Janet a lift home and we really just talked small talk. I felt sorry for him. He was almost certainly going to lose, and surely he must know that, and he'd be left with nothing. I had one last go, saying he could come out with dignity, but he didn't buy it. There was real pride involved there and nothing we could do. The truth was we were heading for Ken as mayor. TB called just after 11 and said 'I suppose you think I wasn't tough enough.' I said no, I thought you got it about right. And given Frank wasn't budging, it was important not to destroy his morale totally.

Thursday, January 27

By and large most people felt we got the better of yesterday's [post-filibuster] events. But the *Telegraph* and the *Mail* gave it to Hague. There was still no clear line on Section 28. JP came to see me and said he was worried TB was taking on too much and taking too many hits on too many fronts. At Cabinet, TB, at the two Margarets' [Jay and Beckett] behest, gave them a bit of a bollocking about the legislative programme process, warned bills may have to be truncated. On Section 28, he said it was a government measure and would go through as a government measure and we would just have to deal with the absurd misinformation campaign against it.

TB and I saw [Alan] Milburn to discuss Shipman and we agreed, despite the pressures from the department, that it was best not to have an inquiry.[1] I had another dreadful heads of information meeting, basically the same discussion as always. Philip G had decided to imbibe some real poison and had set up focus groups made up entirely of *Mail* readers. He said they were absolutely dreadful. The drip-drip propaganda against us was definitely having an effect.

Friday, January 28

I was up at the crack of dawn. Mike White [*Guardian*] came out on the plane with us to [the World Economic Forum meeting in] Davos to do an interview, mainly re London/Dobbo and 1,000 days. We had bilaterals with the Turks and then the Polish president [Aleksander Kwaśniewski] who was keen to know what we were going to do about [Austrian far-right leader Jörg] Haider.[2] I found the whole Davos thing pretty ridiculous, too many pompous people taking themselves far too seriously, but I guess it was a fairly good platform. We were late leaving because Mike White had got his times all muddled. TB was working on his boxes and showed me an extraordinary letter from George R about how he needed to keep his Special Branch protection in the UK.

Saturday, January 29

The papers had lots of stuff about Mo being 'whispered against' and losing her bodyguards, of which she was probably the cause.

[1] Dr Harold Shipman, a Cheshire GP, was on trial for multiple murders. After six days of deliberation the jury found him guilty of killing fifteen patients. He was sentenced to fifteen consecutive life sentences with the recommendation that he should never be released. An inquiry, headed by High Court judge Dame Janet Smith, followed and later reported that Shipman could have murdered as many as 260 people.

[2] In Austria, the Freedom Party (FPO), headed by right-wing extremist Haider, formed a coalition with the People's Party. Fourteen EU states were to announce that they would not accept contacts at the political level with an Austrian government integrating the FPO.

Sunday, January 30

I finished my *Times* article, and gave them the headline 'More spinned against than spinning'[1] We had various problems through the day re Mo, Robinson, Ireland, *Sun* rubbish about how we were doing soap-opera storylines. Both Philip G and Peter H sent through really good notes on the need for direction and focus, and how we might bring that about. We went out for dinner, and Martin Sheehan [press officer] called to say that Peter Kilfoyle had sent through a letter that said he was resigning [as junior defence minister] over 'heartland regional issues'. It was clear he was not going to pull back.

Tom Baldwin [*Times*] was doing the story, said it was perfectly clear Peter was setting himself up as an Old Labour voice. I told TB what was happening. His response was that it was all about ego and status. I drafted TB's reply to his letter, got it out and got TB to speak to him. I told Peter he should have spoken to TB first but he said he didn't know what the protocol was, he just wanted to do right by his constituents. I think Peter thought that by now he would be chief whip, it hadn't happened and maybe he thought it never would.

I got back to watch the Cockerell programme [BBC documentary, *What Makes Tony Tick?*] which was strong. TB was excellent. Mum said he should get more passionate more often. [Professor Peter] Hennessy [historian of government] was good, saying it was to TB's credit that he allowed me to operate as I did.

Monday, January 31

Peter Kilfoyle's resignation was going pretty big. Also, there was a very good example of the phenomenon I had pointed out in my *Times* piece. Carole Walker [BBC], who last night was saying there was no real reason for Kilfoyle going, was now leading the news with the idea that it was all about our traditional heartlands. All that had changed was that she had read the papers. TB and I agreed we should be nice about Peter, though TB felt nothing but contempt for what he had done. 'Two and a half years in, they all think they should be Cabinet ministers and they all want it to be easy.' The TB/Cockerell film seemed to go down pretty well, though the main focus media-wise was on [Sir Richard] Wilson saying he would be happy to say bollocks to TB. But with decommissioning about to go down the tube

[1] Responding to *Times* columnist Matthew Parris, Campbell complained that journalists were seeking to set the news agenda rather than report events, and broadcasters were unduly influenced by newspaper stories.

and the Kilfoyle story going big, the feeling was of another tough week ahead.

Mo came to see me just before the 11, in a real strop. She really did have the look of a wounded child. She wanted to know what I would say about the story that her protection was being scaled down, and about the so-called whispering campaign against her. I said there was no whispering campaign from here or anywhere else that I knew of and on protection, it was purely a matter for the security people and I would discourage people from writing about it.

TB was worried about health again, really felt delivery ought to be picking up faster than it was. Anji and I stayed at the end of the office meeting and had another go at trying to get an agreement on the strategy for the press. Do we make them an issue, and really go for some of them, or not? He said he felt the same about journalists as I did. The question is, is it sensible politics to be at war with them? I wanted to undermine them, divide and rule. He felt we could continue to woo them. I said the Dome was a good example of something being steadily killed by the press. He said yes, but we gave them a lot of the ammunition. It's the same with health. They distort and exaggerate but there is something there to complain about. That was why he was so livid with GB because if we had just raised child benefit by fifty per cent of the amount we did, and put the rest into health, it might have made a difference. TB did a series of calls about Jörg Haider. I put out a strong message on our opposition to him at the four o'clock and was amazed that they all seemed to think it was bad for EU member states to be expressing a view. I knew that politically it was tricky, but I felt totally comfortable with the argument.

Tuesday, February 1

Shipman was massive in the press, Milburn was doing a statement. The NFU [National Farmers' Union] speech was reasonably well trailed. TB rewrote it later and though he didn't get a warm response, as we knew he wouldn't, it wasn't that bad. Peter M called, said that the Irish were in a real state and living in denial about what was going on. They didn't want to publish de Chastelain's report [on decommissioning], and they were just hoping something would turn up. But nothing was emerging. Peter said he wasn't at all sure how we take it forward. The feeling was we would keep going through a day or two, make a statement on Thursday about legislation to suspend, unless we got more progress now, which was doubtful. We had to steer the line between realism, accepting this was bad, but not tipping it into disaster areas. It had to be clear we were fighting to save it and we had to do what we could to prevent violent reaction. If it was usually two steps forward, one step back, this time it was a very big step back.

Both the *Mail* and now [*Sun* columnist Richard] Littlejohn had run dreadful pieces about whispering campaigns against Mo. I complained to Yelland, said they had no evidence of it. We had a 'group of death', first of all without TB who was making calls on Ireland. GB was banging on about Britishness. It was his answer to the European problem. Partly he was right because we did have to win arguments on Europe and devolution. But part of it was also about ensuring that a Scot could still be PM of a UK with a Scottish Parliament. But when you pushed him on what it meant, there wasn't much there. Fair play, decency, pride in history, focus on the future, it was all about values not institutions.

TB felt there wasn't enough in that about people's self-interest, the motivation to do well for themselves and their families. It was an altruistic version of Britishness, not an invented one. The two had to be brought together. They had different takes on this, but pretended to agree, a mirror image of what normally happens, which is that they pretend to disagree on issues where there is only minor differences between them, which GB in particular then over-ventilates. I wasn't sure how this version of Britishness differed from what many would define as Englishness, which may seem odd given it was GB putting it forward. But it wasn't clear to me how the more overtly expressed Scots and Welsh identities fitted into this.

PG punctured the whole thing, and brought it down to earth, when he said if the people in the groups he did could hear this, they would wonder what on earth we were talking about. They just wanted delivery and they had no real sense of it. Nor did they feel any sense of enterprise in the economy. GB said that was in part because we had no real strategy at the moment, no coherence, we were just moving from one story to the next.

Peter M, Tom Kelly and I were all working on the Irish to try to get them to see we had to publish the report, but they were adamant we couldn't. Hague did a reshuffle and I agreed lines with the party about judgement and moving to the right.

Wednesday, February 2

We were trying to get the Irish over for tonight but it was difficult. Bertie [Ahern] was seeing Adams and McGuinness. Coverage of TB's NFU speech wasn't bad on content, but some of them said there was

February '00: Irish veto publication of de Chastelaine report

booing and heckling, when there was none. Hague was at the NFU and did a speech that had opportunism stamped on every page. He did asylum and the euro at PMQs, which wasn't bad. At the Grid meeting, we agreed there wasn't enough of the reform agenda for the medium term. We agreed to go ahead with the idea of TB's website broadcasts.

We had one of those classic little logistics fuck-ups that becomes a story. When I was speaking to Joe Lennon [Ahern's press secretary] about the idea of meeting tomorrow, and we fixed Northolt as a precaution, the office was talking to the BBC and somehow the conversation got mangled into them thinking we were about to meet at Northolt for a crisis summit. At the office strategy meeting, I was complaining as ever about ministerial capacity. Peter H wanted TB to focus, both with his time and his public statements, much more on education. Douglas felt we were really lacking politics in what we were doing, which is why [the resignation of] Kilfoyle was potentially so potent. Later TB said he was perplexed why we couldn't get up the basic message. I said partly because only he and GB really pumped out message in a disciplined way. Too many of our ministers just went down the track any event or an interview took them. I had a meeting with all the ministers who were doing interviews on the rural report tomorrow.

Thursday, February 3

We were doing OK on the rural report, despite the *Telegraph*'s 'Crisis? What crisis?' story. I went up to the flat to see TB. We agreed that the problem on the rural stuff was that 'farming is in crisis but the countryside is not' is OK as a message but lacks any sense of forward direction. Finally TB settled on a One Nation argument, against people like nationalists who want to break up the UK and separate Scotland from England, Labour MPs who want to split North from South, Tories who want to split town from country.

Cabinet was all about Ireland. TB and Peter M both spoke at length and didn't hide how bad things were. Peter was due to do a statement and we were looking like we would have to suspend the institutions which, as the Irish said, was going to lead to no decommissioning at all. Jonathan, John S and I were in constant touch with the Irish re meeting up later after TB's West Country visit [for the rural report]. On the way to the airport, we finished the speech and went straight to Exeter University on arrival. There were a few farmers protesting, but the speech and Q&A went fine. At the lunch, I was with Barrie Williams of the *Western Morning*

News and Ian Beales of the *Western Daily Press*, and both complained we didn't understand the countryside. The feeling was that Labour thought of the countryside as rich landowners, but most of the people living there were poor. Then the Irish came on saying the IRA had moved and were ready to say they would decommission in full by May 22.

We did a couple of good visits, then to Plymouth on the train. TB spoke to Bertie, who was saying there was progress. Peter warned us to be very sceptical. A load of Trots had turned out at the [Plymouth] Guildhall. We agreed the tone and tenor of the statement with Peter M, deciding to go for legislating to take the power to suspend, rather than just to suspend. TB wasn't convinced the IRA were really moving. It wouldn't be enough for Trimble just to get more words. I did a briefing for the UK and Irish press and I think got the balance about right, as did Peter on the broadcasts.

Bertie was flying into RAF St Mawgan [Cornwall] and we met at a nice hotel at Carlyon Bay. He arrived about 9.15 and we got straight down to it in a room set up with a mix of hard chairs and overly comfortable sofas. Paddy [Teahon, Ahern's adviser] showed me the second de Chastelain report which was further down the road and they believed showed they were ready to do the business. The problem was it was all just words. Only under pressure did Bertie admit that what we were talking about was that the IRA would disband in May, send in their weapons and say that war was over. I said would he be able to be that blunt with Trimble and he was honest enough to admit both that he probably wouldn't, and that it didn't go far enough. TB was sceptical. If Adams was asked 'Did it mean the IRA was definitely beginning to decommission?' he would just say it was a matter for de Chastelain. TB said without clear answers, Trimble was dead. We had to give Trimble some succour. We all understood though that suspension was incredibly difficult for Sinn Fein.

Paddy Teahon warned that if de Chastelain said he was content, there could be no suspension of the executive. Bertie said we had to get it. Brian Cowen [new Irish foreign minister], who always strikes me as a pretty tough cookie beneath the laid-back manner, said to TB we cannot proceed on the basis of irrationality. TB said why not, virtually every argument I hear from Trimble and Sinn Fein has large elements of irrationality. They did brief statements which were fairly strong, saying there had to be decommissioning and there had been progress, and then I did a longer briefing. John Sawers felt we had gone from zero per cent to fifteen per cent.

Friday, February 4

The Ceredigion by-election was a bit of a disaster.[1] TB was fairly relaxed and pleased he had got his argument about the politics of unity and division right in his head. We did a round of interviews. Peter M was very cautious about so-called progress. Gerry Adams had a real go at Peter today. We went to the Eden Project [gardens and conservation tourist attraction], amazing place, fantastic pictures and he did a really good speech. He was really fired up by the argument, about how it was easier to promote division than unity. He had found a way of putting the One Nation argument that he was comfortable with. Then off to a farm where I was accosted by a group of Countryside Alliance and Lib Dem activists with a vicar complaining he was losing his church because of lack of support for the countryside. I suddenly found we were surrounded by the media and it was hard to get out of it.

I had real sympathy for some of the farmers because you could tell they were in dire straits, the others I wasn't so sure about. I got some of them in to see TB. Some of them were pretty desperate, one or two close to tears most of the time. One farmer's wife said she felt like killing herself. I had a chat on the phone with the new Dome boss, PY [Pierre-Yves] Gerbeau [replacing Jennie Page], and wished him luck and said it had to become unpolitical. TB did another round table at another farm and seemed genuinely moved. I told TB that our next report, after North–South and now the countryside, should be 'the government is in crisis but the country is not'.

Saturday, February 5

I set off for Burnley and on the train worked on his speech for tomorrow on the politics of unity vs division, which he had trailed yesterday. Godric called to say some of the papers were clearly on to Jennie Page getting the boot. I set up a conference call with Charlie etc. and we agreed it was better to get out a more positive story, that it shouldn't just be about her, that PY Gerbeau was coming, pay tribute to her and say different skills were now required.

PY was a bit worried about our media. I said we would give him all the support we could, but it was really important it was all seen as their operation and not ours. Governments shouldn't run tourist attractions. Later Mo complained she hadn't been involved in the

[1] Plaid Cymru MP Cynog Dafis had resigned his Westminster seat after election to the Welsh Assembly. His party retained Ceredigion with 10,716 votes. Labour fell from second to fourth place, with a swing of 9.9 per cent against the party.

discussions. She said she had heard there were going to be more stories in the papers about her wanting to resign, presumably put there by her. It was one of the best matches so far this season. Frank Teasdale [Burnley chairman] took us to Blackpool where we had dinner. Calum and I stayed at the Imperial, waiting for TB tomorrow, and had the suite where TB had told the Shadow Cabinet about Clause 4.

Sunday, February 6

I was a bit worried that PY's achievements were being overspun and would come back to haunt us.[1] There was also bound to be a sense of backlash for Jennie. TB called on his way from Chequers, and we agreed he would do something on Ireland at the top, then the big One Nation message as I had drafted it on the train yesterday. He was very keen on the argument he developed up to last Friday. His car and the cops collected Calum and me and we went off to wait at Blackpool airport. We went through the speech [to Labour's local government conference in Blackpool] and he liked it. Ireland was tricky. We took out the line that he believed that the IRA had not broken their word. It was an attempt to recalibrate because the sense was Peter M was really hitting Sinn Fein and putting all the pressure on them. It was a good, rounded, measured statement but maybe there was too much in it because the press could only take one simple message. So when PA headlined it 'Blair issues decommissioning challenge' I was a bit pissed off. TB chucked away most of the prepared text and did a big-picture explanation of all that we were trying to do, and did it well. He took them through the whole argument in all the big policy areas and they liked it.[2]

Monday, February 7

The Stansted hijack was leading the news and taking up lots of space.[3] I joked that I wanted an all-female SAS snatch squad to get

---

[1] The Frenchman, a former professional ice hockey player, had been vice president of park operations and attractions at Disneyland Paris, and had been praised for his role in boosting the attraction after its shaky beginnings.

[2] Partly in response to the 'heartland' arguments surrounding Peter Kilfoyle's resignation, Blair told the conference 'The whole country is our core constituency.'

[3] Two Afghan brothers and six compatriots hijacked a plane from Afghanistan when it arrived in Moscow and forced the aircrew to fly to Britain. Claiming to be fleeing the Taliban, they surrendered after three days and were subsequently jailed.

them out in time for TB to announce the release at PMQs on Wednesday. PY was getting a bit of a mauling in the press [Gerbeau had already been nicknamed 'Gerbil'] but did well in his first interviews today. Charlie F said Jennie Page was totally devastated and was weeping when he saw her on Saturday. She did so again when she saw TB. At the morning meeting, TB went through some of the problems we had – Dome, NHS, delivery, Ireland, Scotland and Wales, Europe, transport, welfare. He felt we were in the right place on the big arguments, particularly the politics of unity. I said that lacked the other side of the argument, which was forces of conservatism. Philip felt TB and GB were not on the same message. Sally said GB was going round to MPs saying TB was preventing him from spending more money. He had also told someone he was not helping Alun Michael [First Secretary of the Welsh Assembly] because he was a Blairite. Alun was facing a motion of no confidence over the match-funding issue and our basic argument was there was no need to do the match funding now.[1] Pat [McFadden] did me a good note which I used for the 11 but GB should have been out on this ages ago. GB eventually did a Welsh media briefing. I did an interview with Bill Hagerty for the *British Journalism Review* and probably went on for too long and was too whingey about the press.

Tuesday, February 8

The Lords defeating the government on [repeal of] Section 28 was the splash in several places. TB was in worried and reflective mode in the flat first thing. He said we had a lot of problems. Cherie told me he was not sleeping well for the first time in ages. He was definitely worrying about GB, the latest thing being said was that GB was saying to MPs that TB was trying to block a rise in the minimum wage. TB asked me if I honestly thought GB could be prime minister. I said possibly but I would be worried how he would be in a real crisis or up against some of the big cheeses when they were on the rampage. TB was really fed up at the moment. A lot of it was about Ireland, but a lot of it was also about GB and the sense that there were a lot of problems mounting up.

Tom Kelly and I did a briefing for the foreign media at the Foreign

[1] Treasury match funding of EU Objective One funds, intended to help poorer areas of Europe. Blair had secured Objective One status for Wales, but this was dependent on Gordon Brown releasing funds, which had not yet happened. The issue was seized on by Plaid Cymru, becoming a decisive factor in the Ceredigion by-election (see February 4) and led to the vote of no confidence in Alun Michael.

Press Association. I did my line about how they shouldn't use British political journalism as a primary source because they were the real spin doctors. I was conscious of becoming more and more anti press. I got back for the Sinn Fein meeting but it was clear we weren't moving anywhere. Even though we were on a new time frame [for decommissioning] of December 2000, it wouldn't be enough to move Trimble. I had the usual line to take discussion with Adams and McGuinness and Gerry gave me his notes, including his warning about the slippery road back to conflict.

Hague was up saying we had gone soft on drugs. Mo was all over the shop. ['Drugs Czar' Keith] Hellawell was complaining he was totally without clout. TB saw the President of Romania [Emil Constantinescu] while I met Tony Hall [BBC director of news] to take forward my complaint about the way the press still have the upper hand in setting their agenda and also how these interminable two-ways were taking over from proper reporting.

Then the Jill Dando [murdered TV presenter] police came in. The guy said there had been three calls saying that the photofit closely resembled me and someone had told them I had an affair with Jill Dando nine years ago. They were taking it further because the guy said he knew my family. I said I had never heard of him and never had a relationship with Jill Dando, other than working together. I said I suspected this guy was a mischief maker put up to it by the press. The DCI [detective chief inspector] was perfectly nice, and said it was very unlikely any further action would be taken. He admitted they didn't have a clue at the moment. But eventually they would get there, he felt. If it was a contract killer, eventually somebody would go for the reward, and if it was a stalker, he would crop up again. Fiona said Cherie told her GB was back on the rampage about the flat, saying it was the whole flat or three rooms. Fiona felt TB was finally coming to realise that GB was basically trying to topple him. Tony Banks [former sports minister] popped in for a chat about the World Cup [bid for 2006] and whether the national anthems should be played at the Argentina match [a friendly at Wembley on February 23].

Wednesday, February 9

GB was in the *Telegraph* and on the broadcasts with a big number on charitable giving, yet another piece of pre-Budget stuff through the press. TB was very destabilised about it all at the moment, though he didn't want to admit it. He said they were going to meet again on Sunday. On Wales, TB was saying Alun was a goner and we might have Rhodri [Morgan, member of the Welsh Assembly] by the end of the day. On the [Stansted] hijack, with the papers basically saying they were all here looking for asylum, TB said if he hears a line from the Home Office saying they will be treated like any other application, he will go out into Horse Guards [Parade] and scream. He wanted them back home 'within hours'. Alun Michael called TB to say he was going to resign before the no-confidence votes, and then seek re-election as leader.

At PMQs, Hague raised the Michael resignation. TB, despite three questions, did not acknowledge that he knew what was going on, which was a bit odd. I had to say that he knew but he was so vague on the detail it was bizarre. What was clear was that Alun was in trouble. TB spoke to him afterwards and he was going to go. He was very upset. Rhodri was going to be a shoo-in.[1] Then to a totally hopeless strategy meeting. GB's Britishness, I was becoming more convinced, was basically an argument that a Scot could run England. He was also still playing games on the flat. When GB got like this, TB was discombobulated. Things were hopeless at the moment. TB called in me and Anji. He said he had made a bad mistake. He had been over the top in his assessment of Rhodri. He should have let the Welsh party do the job, not Millbank. It was a bad mistake and he would learn from it. Maybe it would have been OK with Ken, he said. Rhodri looks like he's going to be fine.

After I had gone to bed, I got an extraordinary call from Mo. She had seen Tony. She wanted to be Foreign Secretary but she realised it wasn't going to happen. She was not very happy where she was and she was going to be looking for something new. She *did* want to be mayor, and she suggested to TB that maybe she could be an independent. Two businessmen had offered her forty thousand quid. She said people were coming up to her the whole time urging her to go for it. She was looking for a way in. TB had grimaced at the idea of her being an independent. Amazingly, it was the idea I had put forward weeks ago and I still felt surely it was possible. Mo said whatever she did she was going to be a problem area for him and she needed to be out of it. She said the Tony crony thing was a real problem.

[1] Michael dramatically handed his letter of resignation to the presiding officer during his last speech as First Secretary, and later also as Labour leader in Wales. He told the Welsh Assembly 'It cannot be right for Plaid Cymru to choose who leads Labour. Nor is it right for the Conservatives and the Liberal Democrats to connive with that purpose.'

TB got a dreadful press on Wales, wall to wall in several places, lots of talk about humiliation. He said people would forget and in the end what mattered was we would get a bit of a lift in Wales. He said he had been wrong about Rhodri, who had shown himself to have leadership skills. The Stansted hijack ended at 3am but a large number were now asking for asylum. TB wanted them turned around and sent on their way. Phil Bassett had been attending all the meetings and was doing well getting them focused but Jack [Straw] came in with his usual blather about rules and lawyers and his worry that we get JR'd [judicial reviewed] and how they had a right to apply and to have an appeal heard. TB said he would much rather get JR'd than have the pain of this going on for weeks. I put together a very tough line for the 11 and got it through the Home Office.

TB was worried that the right wing were really getting up a right-wing agenda through the press – anti gay, asylum, Europe. At the 11, it was all hijack and then Wales and I turned it on with both barrels. We believed in devolution, they didn't. I then did the [Prime Minister's Office] website launch briefing. Interestingly the lobby barely turned out for it but it was definitely worth doing. There was a bit of interest in the fact that our main briefings would be written up and put on the site. Then a so-called strategy meeting. TB saying what do we do? GB saying Britishness. Me saying we had to get ministers to perform better and buy into a bigger message than haphazard day-to-day departmental stuff. PG saying last night's groups were grim.

We got no news back from Mo re her independent bid. TB said it was crazy that she felt so badly she now wanted to do it but we just couldn't find a way. TB did the first broadcast [webcast], without notes, just spoke. It was very strong but it later emerged it had recorded badly and wasn't of sufficient quality for the BBC to use. TB spoke to Bertie, put together a very downbeat line for the four o'clock where I virtually said we were going to suspend and it was important not to lose Trimble. TB was voting on the age of consent.[1] He called later, pretty down, and said we looked ragged and only the uselessness of the Tories was really keeping us on the road.

[1] Sexual Offences (Amendment) Bill, to equalise the age of consent for homosexual and heterosexual sex at sixteen years old. Blair's government would face a long struggle with the House of Lords to pass the legislation, eventually invoking the Parliament Act to do so.

Friday, February 11

The *Telegraph* were gleeful about 'Labour hit in the polls' though when you looked at it we weren't that far down. It was more the raggedness that was worrying us. TB was on the phone re Ireland all day trying to get a situation where de Chastelain could produce a report showing progress. Peter M was being very hardline, for example not buying the line about new words from the IRA being enough. He had signed the order suspending the institutions so Adams, aware of what Peter was doing, put out a statement that there had been a major IRA development, so putting us in the position of looking like we were at fault. Peter was not at all happy with the game-playing. De Chastelain was due to produce a report that would show progress which we wanted out there to welcome but which the Irish wanted us to say was the basis of reinstatement of the institutions. We couldn't do that because in the end the progress was just words.

TB spoke to Bertie and after the Adams statement to Bill Clinton and told him they were 'dicking us around'. But Bill was taking Sinn Fein's side, saying Trimble had to get out and sell this. Our view was it was best just to get Trimble through tomorrow and leave it at that. Adams took the high ground for a bit. Peter was slow getting out that he'd suspended. Trimble struck an OK note. I got Denis Murray [BBC's Ireland correspondent] to say there could be a second de Chastelain report and tried to persuade the Irish we would put it out by nine o'clock. Joe Lennon was up for it but Paddy Teahon was insisting it was accompanied by a statement from the governments that we could use it to reinstate the institutions. TB and Bertie discussed it right up to 9pm, when I cut off from the call and gave Denis the go-ahead to brief on the de Chastelain report and say there would be a statement from the governments welcoming this as a development of real significance.

As ever we were walking a tightrope between the two sides and trying to get the media not to be too downbeat so that we could avoid overreaction, not least on the streets. And as ever, I was grateful for the honest discussions you could have with Denis Murray. TB was pretty fed up with it. Bertie was realistic and pretty clear we had to suspend but desperate for us to indicate we wanted the institutions back up again. Paddy got more and more emotional. I came on at 8.45 to say it was important to get the dynamics changed and get this reported in a more positive light. Literally, seconds before nine o'clock, with the titles running and Denis Murray holding on for me, I said right, decision time. TB said go and get Denis to do it, as agreed. Paddy started up all over again about the need to say that Peter would now be going to Parliament to rescind. Denis did an absolutely brilliant job, got the balance right, and put it in the place we needed it.

Saturday, February 12

TB thought last night's conversation with the Irish had veered from hilarious to surreal. Paddy had been unbelievable. Most of the time, it had been Paddy not Bertie doing the talking, and so emotional. The papers weren't bad, many following the same line as Denis. We got Joe Lockhart [White House press secretary] to be reasonably positive. Calum was grounded so we couldn't go to Bournemouth vs Burnley and I got Rory on at me to go to Newcastle vs Man U. Bertie was going to be there too. TB gave me a brief for when I got there. It was pretty rollercoaster stuff and even though we were nowhere near where we needed to be, it did feel a bit better. Bertie was in great form. I said our biggest problem was that we never seemed to get clarity from Adams. The IRA had to be clear or we would lose Trimble off the other end. He [Ahern] was a lovely bloke. Alex popped up for a drink before the match. He looked really tired. Man U played badly and got hammered. On the train back, Mo called, emphasised she wanted to do it, said she was destined for it. The journey was spoiled by a dreadful hoity-toity public school women's hockey team making a racket in the carriage.

Sunday, February 13

Very quiet with Afghanistan the main focus. Thanks in large part to [private secretary for foreign affairs] Philip Barton's excellent work more than seventy [Stansted hijack] Afghans went home on Cambodian Airlines. TB said we were not in charge of the domestic agenda and the media were dictating the terms of the debate. We had to get back on top. Treasury were not engaged though, which made it difficult. I also thought in public presentation terms there had been too much of the liberal values stuff. We had had gays in the military, age of consent, Section 28 and now gay day at the Dome. Enough was enough. If only the Tories could land a blow, we would be in trouble.

Monday, February 14

We were doing OK on crime with *The Times* splashing on the new inspections though the broadcasts went with the new targets. TB was on *GMTV*, supposedly for a crime interview, but it turned out mainly to be about the new website. He said on the way back he should do a tough interview soon. GB was definitely up to no good at the moment and his people were out basically undermining TB. He said he was confident he could manage it. I felt it was reaching a bad enough state for us to have to do something through the press. Anji felt it would be the end of the government if we got into a full-scale briefing war with him, but I felt TB was just pandering.

Northern Ireland was tricky with the Irish briefing they were on a different tack to us, and that was the main focus of the 11. I had an internal meeting where I read the riot act a bit about the lack of creative input. I said I wanted Phil Bassett focusing long term, Lance [Price] medium term, and Godric doing the day-to-day, with Peter H working on message and Bill [Bush] and Lance ensuring ministers were properly briefed before interviews. But I found most of the team a bit too prone to telling me what the problems were.

Mo came to see me after calling me at the weekend about going for the mayor's job as an independent. She was up for it, knew it would be a disaster for the party and that she would have to leave but she said it would be better than the life she had at the moment. TB had told me it must not happen but she had the bit between the teeth. I got her in to see him. She said she was very keen and it was him who had put the idea in her head, at which point he grimaced. She was eating a huge pear very loudly, with juice all over her top by the time she had finished. TB's view was that it was impossible for her to stand as an independent. JP would denounce her and the party would be in turmoil. He felt it was possible to get her in 1. if Dobbo won by a slim majority, we told him he would lose to Norris and he agreed to pull out, or 2. Ken refused to abide by the manifesto. We ran round in circles and eventually agreed she should place a story that she wished she had gone for it, then build a clamour about it, particularly through the *Mirror*.

It was an odd meeting. It ended with her thinking she was going to go for it but she later came back to me and said she would wait for Frank to win and then get TB to do the dirty work. She definitely bought the argument that Frank's and Alun Michael's problem was that they were seen as TB's people against colourful independent-minded people, whereas the problem was that they didn't have clear personalities and message. I had a dreadful cold and got very bad-tempered later in the day. TB did his first group of ministers meeting with [John] Reid, [Alan] Milburn, [Geoff] Hoon, [Charles] Clarke and Estelle [Morris, education minister] where we tried to sign them up to the idea of doing more cross-cutting communication and some of the intellectual underpinning of New Labour. John Reid got it instantly, though it was very hard to stop him talking. Charles seemed a bit bogged down departmentally. I said we needed them to take a few risks, generate controversial talking points and break free of the stultifying hand of departments. I was called halfway through by GB who wanted to do the minimum-wage uprating [by 10p to £3.70 per hour] tomorrow. The best news of the day was Ian Wright [former England and Arsenal footballer] signing for Burnley.

Tuesday, February 15

GB did a good number on the minimum wage. It was perfectly clear he had briefed the *Guardian* before he came on to me last night to say he wanted to do it, and equally clear that [Trade and Industry Secretary Stephen] Byers knew even later than that. The *Guardian* treated us to their best breathless prose about his skill and brilliance, while the rest of the papers were focused on a series of NHS failings. I said to TB, at what seemed to be becoming a ritual morning meeting up in the flat, that I was reaching the view, dangerous I knew, that GB was trying to set up a kind of two-government system – the GB government was economic success plus dealing with poverty; the TB government was public service delivery going wrong. TB, and later Anji, said I had to be very careful about not emanating too powerfully hostile views and feelings about GB around the office. I called Ian Austin, said it was perfectly obvious they had briefed the 10p uprate before getting TB's agreement, and I was worried they were going back to a [Charlie] Whelan-style modus operandi. I would not put up with it for as long as I had put up with Whelan.

We were reasonably friendly but he said I had been sending out negative signals about GB at meetings and I argued they were building GB's profile at the expense of relations with colleagues. TB was adamant I do nothing through the media. He reckoned we just had to weather the storm, see real improvement in public services and, he added implausibly, turn the Dome into a success story. But he was looking tired and fed up. I knew how he felt.

Hague had announced his tour on a lorry to save the pound. He would get a certain lift out of it but not enough to sustain progress and there was a danger it would become a bit of a joke. But the *Mail*, which did four pages on stealth taxes today, and to a lesser extent the *Sun*, were definitely shifting and looking at him more favourably. I noticed the *Telegraph* had been becoming a little bit more reasonable and might be trying to detach itself from being seen in the same bracket as the *Mail*, which was becoming more shrill and ridiculous.

TB was doing a number of interviews, including with *The Economist* on Europe, which I used as the basis for my presentation to the

Europe ministerial group at 4.30. We had a big meeting on drugs planned for tomorrow and I was trying to get stories up on that, but both Mo and [Keith] Hellawell were a bit of a nightmare to deal with. Then at 4.45 Jon Smith [of PA] called to say that P. O'Neill [IRA spokesman pseudonym] was putting out a statement about the IRA pulling out of co-operation with de Chastelain and what was our response? We discussed calling off tomorrow's meetings on Northern Ireland but TB said no. I had a meeting with Hellawell, who constantly needed reassurance that we rated him and wanted him out there on the media, but he was finding the system very difficult. He was basically fed up because he felt he lacked any real clout or power, felt that [former Minister for the Cabinet Office Jack] Cunningham had a problem with him because of his ego whereas Mo was useless and unfocused.

Wednesday, February 16

The Ireland meetings were leading the news all day. I was pretty clear we would get nothing out of today beyond SF and UUP grand-standing. The drugs coverage went pretty well all day, despite Mo charging around saying it was all a waste of time. TB had had dinner with GB last night and if how he looked was anything to go by, it was a bit of a disaster. Cherie told me later that GB had arrived late and they were arguing for so long that the dinner just lay there on the table for two hours. GB was back to the basic notion that TB had betrayed him in becoming leader and that if he was going to carry on it must be on GB's agenda. TB didn't want to talk about it beyond saying there would be a hell of a fight over the Budget and also telling me that GB had taken offence at my berating Ian Austin. I said he had to understand we were not going to put up with a constant running sore in the press. In the end, I said, I had to leave it to him to sort but power and force was the only language GB understood and if he felt others were weak, he would exploit it.

At the moment, he was treating TB as though he were weak. There was an example yesterday at a Treasury presentation in front of civil servants. TB asked a factual question and GB spat out with a mix of venom and contempt that if he had read his brief, he wouldn't need to ask. I don't think I had ever seen TB go white with fury before, but that's exactly what he did. At the end, he took GB to one side and said 'Don't ever speak to me like that again.' But the overall effect was freaking him out. He was also livid with Mo and Jack Straw after the drugs meeting. He said there were excellent ideas from police and customs, real practical stuff, and he backed them, whereas Jack and Mo just wittered on endlessly about the ECHR [European Court of Human Rights]. He said he didn't have a clue what Mo was talking about.

Ian Austin wanted me to write a letter to deny Andy Grice's [*Independent*] story that TB made GB do the minimum wage early. I said what do you want me to write, that TB didn't actually know until after GB had briefed the *Guardian*? I really felt for TB at the moment. There were some very tricky issues around and he wasn't getting much by way of support from the key people. The Irish meetings were OK, first Bertie, then SF, UUs and SDLP. Peter M was getting very Mo-ish, claiming to be isolated, Number 10 taking up too much of the reins, etc. Joe Lennon and I worked on joint statements, but we really were in verbiage territory. Adams and McGuinness were pretty surly, lecturing TB. People were just going through the motions and going to their default positions. There was a natural cut-off point because TB had to leave for a banquet at Windsor for [Margrethe II] the Queen of Denmark, which was a white-tie job, prompting me to feel even more sorry for him.

GB called to say he had 'had to' brief the *Guardian* that child poverty would be the focus of the Budget. He had also caused mayhem with his Internet speech which was seen as a change of policy and wiped a fortune off BT's share price.[1] It also emerged he had refused to see [BT chairman Sir Iain] Vallance and [BT chief executive Sir Peter] Bonfield. He was off his head at the moment and clearly set on doing what he wanted up to and through the Budget. TB said if people knew the truth about the way the government was at the moment, it would be dreadful, because this just was not serious. Philip did some groups which were dreadful on public service delivery.

Thursday, February 17

We were running into problems on the [Sir Ronald] Waterhouse Report [into child abuse in residential care homes in Wales from the 1970s]. It turns out it was delayed for months because it had to be translated into Welsh and there were people named in it still working with children after its publication.

We got a very bad press for PMQs, with TB felt to be avoiding straight answers, and Jack Straw came to see me, said he thought it had been dreadful and TB had to answer questions because his evasiveness was harming us on trust. Although the *Mail* splashed on

[1] The value of BT shares fell by more than £2 billion after Brown was reported to be announcing plans to cut the cost of Internet access.

it, GB's BT balls-up wasn't as bad as it might have been though both BT and the Stock Exchange were in a state of fury about the Treasury spin. GB also had the lead story in the *Guardian* with his Budget for child poverty so I called Ian again and he just parroted GB's blather about how he had had to do it because otherwise they would have done a big number on tax. I said to Ian, knowing it would get straight to GB, that I was sick of their game-playing.

TB had mentioned a review of the adoption rules earlier [to allow an increase by forty per cent of the number of children adopted from care by 2004–05] and as he raised it in Cabinet, I briefed it out after squaring the relevant ministers. It ran pretty big, though the departments were pretty useless dealing with it. Cabinet was mainly Ireland, Peter M just taking them through where we were, good news and bad. He felt Adams and McGuinness had indeed stuck their necks out, perhaps too complacently. He said Trimble was saved but in a difficult situation. TB said later that Mo going through the Grid had been 'unbelievably excruciating'.

I had another discussion with TB re GB, but he didn't buy my basic argument that GB was currently doing him in. He said they would get there and I would have to leave it to him. In some things, his judgement had to be paramount, and he was in no doubt that if he and GB fell out publicly it would destroy the government. I said that meant GB had a total hold on the levers of policy and strategy. TB said I had to trust his judgement. On this, at this time, I didn't. We found a reason to cancel the 'group of death' meeting, and instead Peter M, Anji and I had a somewhat dangerous discussion in the White Room. Anji was basically pushing the TB line that we needed to play down these problems but I felt he was deluding himself if he felt they were working together in any shape or form.

Peter M felt GB had made his operation more subtle but he was still steadily building up support and subtly undermining TB, and the aim was to build a sense that TB was shallow, without values, that New Labour was just a brilliant piece of spin, that GB was the real driver on substance so why not let him take over and be the real PM? Peter M said he felt a bit out of it in Northern Ireland but his sense was GB was motoring, that the whole 'psychological flaws' episode slowed him for about a year, but he was back in gear. Jack Straw had also said to me he felt TB was quite vulnerable at the moment. He said he had been talking to Gwyneth Dunwoody [senior Labour backbencher] who said that the problem was the party felt TB hated it [the feuding], whereas GB didn't.

Peter M said GB was able simultaneously to court the *Guardian* by being left wing on their issues whilst courting the *Sun* and the *Mail* by being with them on theirs, at a time the gilt was coming off TB. At the four o'clock, they really tried to get me to jump on GB over the Internet fiasco, but I didn't. TB was doing a webcast on drugs and I was furious to discover they had written in a line – 'I can announce' – on something that had already been done. Towards the end of the day we got the news that 1,500 jobs were to go at Ford in Dagenham tomorrow. BNFL [British Nuclear Fuels, accused of faking safety records] was another problem.[1]

Friday, February 18

I think GB thought I was going to do him in through the Sundays, because he was on being very co-operative about his speech next week. He had just about got away with BT. The BNFL report and job losses at Ford took care of the news. I briefed the Sundays in a fairly half-hearted way on TB's Europe speech on Wednesday, and told them there was nothing new in it. Adoption had gone well media-wise and underlined the need for talking points as opposed simply to new policies. TB was at Chequers and had decided he should see Livingstone and Dobson tomorrow, which would mean them going there. I felt Livingstone would brief it but agreed with TB it was better if he saw them before we knew the result. I had a long chat with David Davis who was in charge of an adoption commission for the Tories, which we were going to be reasonably supportive about. He had clearly thought it through. Irwin Stelzer [Rupert Murdoch adviser] called Anji to say Murdoch had ordered the *Sun* to curb the hostility to TB which had been pretty clear in the last few days. TB was having dinner with Roy Jenkins [former Labour Cabinet Minister and co-founder of the Social Democratic Party in 1981].

Saturday, February 19

We were in the final build-up to Sunday's mayoral announcement. TB was at Chequers and as I left with the boys for Burnley vs Wigan [0–0] on the 9.20 train, Livingstone and Dobson were heading for two separate 45-minute interviews at Chequers with TB. I loathed the idea of TB having to see Ken at all, but according to Sally, the only witness, TB had not only welcomed him but said he clearly had ability and appeal. Sally felt Ken was slippery. TB said he did at one point feel

---

[1] A report by the Nuclear Installations Inspectorate (NII), the UK atomic watchdog, was to reveal a 'lack of a safety culture' at the BNFL Sellafield site. It also found that safety checks on fuel supplied to Japan had been falsified.

physically ill as it became clear just how highly Livingstone rated his own abilities and intellectual prowess. TB said he felt queasy in his presence. He was also preparing the ground for running the line that the ballot was bent. We got to Burnley and it was great to see the place full. Ian Wright did one or two good things and we hit the bar in the last minute of injury time. We should have won. Margaret McD seemed to think Frank might win. TB said Frank wouldn't be even near it if we hadn't pulled out all the stops for him. Mo was on again, desperate to do it.

Sunday, February 20

TB was very agitato, must have called about ten times. The first was to say that Frank had won [Labour's mayoral candidate nomination] and that I needed to speak to him and talk him through the day. He had to rise above the process and get on to policy. Frank came round after Margaret spoke to him and he was looking a lot more relaxed than before. We went over the script and I said he had to be policy, policy, policy and leave process to Ken. None of us really knew how Ken would play it. Frank felt he would go as an independent. I was suggesting to Frank that he didn't wear a tie, tried to be more relaxed and look a bit happier than of late, and also that Janet should be with him. She hated the idea because she didn't want to be the lady mayoress. I also felt Frank had to become more aggressive with the Tories and [Conservative candidate Steve] Norris, but the most important thing was getting above process. He also had to become his own man, not Millbank's, so he should do his interviews away from Millbank, out by the river or over at the Eye. The plan was that Margaret speak to the other two at 1.30 and as she was doing so, Phil Murphy [head of communications, Labour Party] told PA.

Livingstone did a thing in the street which came over as pretty self-indulgent. He didn't rule out standing as an independent but said people should stay in the party. He attacked the process and said Frank should stand down. We finally persuaded Frank to dress casually with clothes Margaret had bought, and to take Janet with him. Frank came over a lot better, nice bloke if a bit frumpy. He said he knew he could do a lot better at campaigning, and he would. The focus was all really on whether or not Ken would go as an independent. I was pretty sure he would. TB asked me why I sounded depressed. I said I wasn't aware that I did, but he was back urging me to rest whilst at the same time calling me every few minutes either for the same conversation as before or with a new set of instructions. Philip called twice, said he was now of the view GB and people were openly contemptuous of us and basically undermining TB the whole time, very open about their belief that we didn't really have a message. TB said that the mayoral situation was bloody but a lot better than if we had been landed with Ken. Norris said that if there was a God, clearly he was a Conservative, and I managed to crank up a bit of a storm.

Monday, February 21

I tried to have a day off, leaving Godric and Lance to do the briefings. TB was at Chequers. I sent him a note suggesting we get somebody out saying that if Livingstone stood [as an independent], the contradiction to his stated intentions of earlier, he would expose himself as a charlatan totally without honour. TB felt it was over the top. JP was up for being pretty heavy. Dobbo was doing pretty well in interviews but the only story was whether Ken would stand or not as an independent, with most of the papers encouraging him.

Tuesday, February 22

Livingstone was still the dominant political story and now we had the *Guardian* saying TB had a secret plan to dump Dobbo and put in Mo. The story could only have come from Mo or, TB and others feared, possibly Peter M, which I didn't buy. Mo insisted she was not responsible but it was odd that it was out there just as Frank was looking better. Frank felt we were being equivocal and we had to kill it but it was almost 6pm before Mo put out words that helped us do that. We also agreed with TB that we should put out the Vernon Hince [trade unionist, chair of the NEC] correspondence [with Livingstone] which was put together while the ballot was going on when it was rumoured he [Livingstone] was going to stand as an independent. Pat McFadden spoke to Vernon to get his go-ahead along with strong words that if Livingstone ran he would be exposed as a liar.

We were also having to deal with a story being whipped up about the idea of the army handing over guns in an act of NI reconciliation. Godric did the 11 and it all got a bit tricky because he couldn't rule it out. I didn't really get focused on it but later Trevor Kavanagh called and I sensed it was going to be big. I spoke to Tom Kelly in the States [Washington DC, on a trip with Mandelson] and we agreed a pretty robust line to get the thing in perspective. But we had too many of these ragged situations. JP's statement on rail safety was for some reason coming over as a U-turn and was a bit of a disaster.

Stephen Lander [director general of the Security Service] had asked me to go for lunch at MI5. We went over a brief history of the service, in particular what they did during the war. He said there were three main parts to what they did – first, following people, at which they were reckoned to be the best in the world. Second, interception of communications and third, counter-terrorism and increasingly, working on organised crime and drugs.

As with MI6, they had in my view an overly negative view of their own profile and image. Most of our discussion was about Ireland, drugs and the media. They had someone who responded to media enquiries but they were resisting the idea of having an official press office and I said I would continue to resist it if I were them, but they did need to have lines out that allowed them to explain properly when they needed to, or when they needed political support. I said they should always feel free to use us.

Lander was clearly more strategic than hands-on. He said the organisation had changed beyond recognition since he joined it twenty-five years ago when women were only allowed to be secretaries. Northern Ireland was clearly his focus and he said it was important that even decades after the event, sources should be protected. I understood better after talking to them why they needed a bit of distance from government but felt there was a good story they should be telling about an old organisation responding to new challenges. He said the CIA's press operation cost more than their entire budget. It was gone 3 by the time I left.

TB saw Mo and I got her to put out words backing Frank. The *Standard* splashed on 'liar Ken' out of the Vernon Hince stuff. Stan Greenberg brought in the latest polling which showed that while we were still way ahead on the state of the parties, beneath it we were falling away on delivery, Europe, trust, TB's rating. Stan said it was a dangerous moment and we had to address the fundamentals. I didn't much like TB's response, which was basically that if we had a good Budget we would get back on track. Health was doing us a lot of damage. Stan said the public just had a sense that we were running out of gas. He looked at TB and me, exhausted and slumped in our chairs, and we both laughed. Can't imagine where they get that idea from, I said.

TB had to leave early but when he called later, I said I thought his instinctive response to the poll, which was basically more of the same, was weak. He had subcontracted economic policy and now also strategy to GB, who was not, in my view, on the same track or even wanting as much as we did a massive second-term majority. There was part of him that wanted the majority cut. So as we had different approaches, there was drift. The Budget would come upon us soon and it would be his Budget, not necessarily related to TB's overall strategic direction. It might be, but we didn't know and we had to get a grip of it. At the moment, GB sensed weakness.

We were being hit on delivery, trust, now competence – the mayor situation – and we had no real agreed answer to the onslaught of the press. TB said all governments go through this kind of thing. I said I thought we were going to be different. We cannot keep coasting like this. The Tories were dead, but Stan's poll had shown again that even if they were struggling as a party, there was a foothold for the right-wing agenda and if they got their act together, they could revive quite quickly. Lack of delivery plus the press against us plus division plus the Tories get their act together and we would be in bother.

Wednesday, February 23

I was absolutely knackered and decided to stay rather than go with TB to [deliver a speech to European business leaders in] Ghent. Godric and Julian went with him and it was fine. It was a perfectly good speech though it led to quite a lot of attacks, e.g. from the *Sun*, saying they would withdraw support for us if we stuck to the line on Europe.[1] I had a kind of physical and mental crash during the day, couldn't get going at all, added to which I was slowly getting more and more tired and depressed. Partly it was the workload but also it was the extent to which I kept having to dig deep to raise the performance of the place. And yet I sensed we were drifting. On London, Livingstone was totally calling the shots. He was clearly going to go for it but would take his time doing it, which was all adding to the sense that we didn't really have control of the agenda.

Thursday, February 24

Dobbo called first thing to say he felt very strongly he had to say something slightly different to us on the Underground, namely that he would appoint a panel of experts to approve any deal on financing. TB wasn't sure about it, but I agreed with Frank. He went ahead with it and I think it came out fine. The main news was [a fall in] house prices and another dreadful report on health from the National Audit Office. We were really getting hit on delivery and that was taking us straight into trust. Throw in control-freakery and now, with Ken, we were getting hit on competence too. I also felt we were weak at getting

[1] Blair contrasted his pro-Europeanism with the warnings of an EU superstate that Margaret Thatcher had raised in her 1988 speech in Bruges. He said the United Kingdom 'should be leading the way in Europe, shaping the direction of Europe, participating in debates and working in partnership with the others for a more prosperous economy for our people'.

arguments out there properly. We were woefully short of people who could actually make a case publicly without sounding like they were reading a script.

Friday February 25

TB called and said he felt we were at quite a dangerous moment. He was not sure how to get out of it but he saw two different routes for Sunday's speech on the party's centenary.[1] First, almost apologise for the mess re Ken and for the fact we were not delivering fast enough, and second, say that he was doing what he was doing out of conviction and was going to stick to it. He felt the way to deal with [accusations of being] out of touch and arrogant was to show that he was leading out of principle and driving through change out of conviction after years of Tory decline and in the teeth of fierce opposition from the forces of conservatism. I said that was a speech to get us through a day or two but we had four weeks to the Budget and we were bereft of an agreed strategy and therefore there was a sense of drift. They were still arguing about money and GB was making clear that though there would be more for public services, he was holding out for some pretty big sums for his pet schemes. TB felt he had convinced GB that a big [parliamentary] majority was also in his own long-term interests because it would indicate a long-term change of mood and a new dispensation in the country.

Also, though the press was a nightmare over Europe at the moment, he felt long term we would develop strength for sticking to a pro-European strategy. He, I, Peter M and Philip G had a conference call to talk about Sunday's speech. PG wanted a sense of drawing a line and moving on. Peter and I both felt there had to be a very tough message about the job to be done and the difficulties in doing it. Philip worried it would simply retrench the electorate's currently basically hostile feeling. I was unsure how much of that was real and how much basically media-driven. TB was also tempted to say Ken should stand, but even though he would, I felt that was wrong too. The public clearly felt there had been a fix to stop him. TB wanted to explain why he felt so strongly about it. His worry was that history was repeating itself, that the party was fed up with the discipline of government already and was going to make all the mistakes of the past. The big difference between this and previous Labour

[1] Commemorating a century since a conference of left-wing organisations was held in London in February 1900, founding the Labour Representation Committee as a vehicle for supporting union-sponsored MPs to represent the working classes in Parliament.

governments was our basic competence alongside the Tories being useless and widely despised. But we were clearly going to get mauled in the local elections [mayor and London Assembly in London and councils in some parts of England on May 4] and that might change.

Saturday, February 26

TB was working on the centenary speech at Number 10 while I was working at home with Peter H. Ken was continuing to lead us a merry dance and we were still being forced to dance to his tune. TB said he was willing to see Ken but I felt Ken would just use it for a few more days' limelight-hogging and to remind people how badly we had handled the whole thing. The problem was that neither TB nor I were seeing this as the public were. TB said he would really like to go out there and say Ken was only allowed to get away with all this nonsense because the media were desperate to build him up. But at the moment that just wasn't sensible.

Ken was due to see JP on Monday and that was already being talked up as a big policy meeting. JP and I discussed it and agreed he would say it was just a deputy leader meeting to find out what he was planning, and that policy was settled. TB said GB had 'almost finished' the strategy paper he had promised. It had taken weeks. And I was still unconvinced we would see it. In the afternoon, we went to Wimbledon vs Man United, the first time the whole family had been to a football match. Sam Hamman [Wimbledon chairman] took Fiona and the boys down to the tunnel and Grace came back very excited because David Beckham touched her head. The kids were all filmed with Sam Hamman coming out of the tunnel in the opening shots on [BBC One's] *Match of the Day*. Peter H came round later to work on tomorrow's speech. TB had done some good passages about the betrayal thesis and why we are Labour.

Sunday, February 27

To my annoyance, the news was leading with TB's article in the *Independent on Sunday* on GM food. The BBC ran with it all day. It totally overshadowed the speech and of course in a way was our fault. We signed off the speech in a series of conference calls and got up the lines about Labour as a transforming force and the five goals for a new century. I also got the *Mirror* to agree to splash on nurse recruitment and briefed the morning broadcasters on it. TB as ever wanted a very New Labour message but we also needed something for the party to hang on to that was more traditional. The Old Vic [theatre] was a great venue for the centenary event. TB was in the

Lilian Baylis dressing room, JP in Laurence Olivier's. It was a tough speech, but strong, and it went down really well. We took the kids skating at the Sobell [Leisure] Centre and afterwards to Pizza Express where I had a huge row with a woman called Angelica, a friend of Jon Snow's, who said the government was less liberal than the Tories. I went to the car and got a copy of TB's speech and asked her to read the bit about how historically well-meaning people on the left helped the right to stay in power by peddling the thesis of betrayal. Rory was very supportive, said they were total losers.

Monday, February 28

The best papers for ages. The *Mirror* splashed on more nurses, the *Mail* on GB's plan to get more jobs for people through employment hit squads etc. and we got pretty good coverage on the speech except in the *Guardian* which had not a word on the front. I regretted taking out TB's line of yesterday that the right-wing press was ruthless and hostile and the progressive press useless and weak. But the nurses story was running fine on the broadcasts and we had a fairly chunky week ahead so I felt better. TB was in better form at the office meeting but we were still very weak in terms of our capacity for delivery.

I read GB's strategy note, which was comprehensive and good, but I was worried how many of the delivery points would fall to me. The GM [food] piece was still running as a big U-turn, which it wasn't. It led to a whole load of journalist as spin doctor crap, e.g. Nick Watt [*Guardian*] saying it was all about reconnection with the heartlands, as if they were all sitting there obsessing about GM. I had a meeting with the government chief nurse, Sarah Mullally, and we were getting up different stories for tomorrow in advance of the speech [on modernisation of accident and emergency facilities].

I saw Polly Toynbee [*Guardian* columnist] about the *Mail*. She thought we should be going harder at them. I gave her my thesis that Dacre justified himself because the Tories were so useless and he felt the media had to be the opposition. GB was angry that health was getting so much on the news when we had agreed to try to get the focus on his enterprise and employment speech. Peter M called, said that he had had a very thuggish meeting with Adams and McGuinness. He also said his security advisers had admitted that decommissioning would make little practical difference to security and that it was a non-issue so far as the real security situation was concerned. The problem was the Tories had got on that hook and we were on it too. I had a very good chat with [BBC *Newsnight* presenter Jeremy] Paxman about tomorrow's interview.

I wrote a private letter to GB after his complaints about TB's stuff on health downgrading his speech on enterprise and employment, pointing out that TB on health had been in the Grid for weeks and I could not easily promote his events if I didn't know what they were till the last minute. TB was not happy when he heard I had sent it, because he was still trying to be conciliatory. The general reaction to the [GB] strategy paper was that it was very GB-focused, very much seen down his end of the telescope. The media was going through another mad phase. [BBC] *Panorama*'s stuff on Livingstone was real poisonous propaganda stuff and I complained to [Tony] Hall. Then the *Standard* splashed on 'Crisis? What crisis?' out of TB attacking 'alarmist nonsense' in the press.

The main media focus was Paxman's interview at St Thomas' [Hospital, London], and we had a session to go through the really tough questions. Paxman was less in your face than usual, and let the audience do more of the talking, basically critical but not in an over the top way, and I think it was definitely worth doing. As one of the doctors said afterwards, at least he is on top of the issues and engaging on them. For my taste, he had pushed out the boat on greater use of the private sector a bit too far, but it was OK. Back at the office JP said re his meeting with Ken last night, that he still thought it wasn't certain he would run. We agreed to brief nothing out of it. There was a London poll today that had Ken on fifty-three and Dobbo on eleven. Even when Ken was taken out of the running, fourteen per cent said they would vote for him! JP said he had been perfectly 'comradely' but he knew he couldn't trust him. TB took a meeting on London to agree a plan of action should Ken go for it.

I had to work hard to keep my temper in check at the four o'clock. I was in a bad mood anyway and I knew the slightest thing from one of the wankers would set me off. I was also conscious of the fact I was firing off too many complaints at the moment. Trouble in Mozambique[1] was running big on the TV news and there were suggestions of MoD and DFID [Department for International Development] rowing over money. I was also dealing with the fallout from a silly Charles Clarke interview on BBC Online yesterday when he seemed to suggest we – i.e. Number 10 – were deliberately stoking divisions with Old Labour.

---

[1] Catastrophic flooding in Mozambique caused by constant heavy rainfall resulted in the deaths of around 800 people and 20,000 cattle.

Max Hastings [*Evening Standard* editor] took my letter complaining about their health coverage very badly. He did a leader and in later editions a two-page spread basically justifying the initial coverage. Also the *Sun*, no doubt because we had fed a couple of stories to the *Mirror*, did not just one but two leaders on me, including one saying GB had done well because I didn't taint his words! Polly Toynbee had a pretty vicious piece on the press which most of them would assume was my handiwork because it contained a lot of the arguments I was constantly putting to them. TB was worried I was going over the top, though Bruce [Grocott] thought it was a good idea to keep whacking them and complaining when they got things wrong.

We put together a string of ideas for PMQs – on a demand for clarity on bank charges for LINK [cash machine] services, volunteering (with TB and Number 10 staff included), extra help for Mozambique. The TV was taken up with Mozambique and amazing pictures of a baby being born in a tree. Tony Bevins came in for lunch and said I should do a book on how difficult government is made by the ridiculous media we have. PMQs was fine. I didn't sense the Tories had much of a plan at the moment and TB was a lot calmer than in recent days. We did *News at Ten* which [outgoing ITN political editor Michael] Brunson was really pleased with, said it was the perfect retirement present.

I got back for a meeting with [Sir Richard] Wilson, Jeremy [Heywood], Julian [Braithwaite], [Brian] Bender [Cabinet office permanent secretary] and [David] Bostock [European Secretariat, Cabinet Office] re the EU presentation unit. I argued against the idea, said that the problem was not the lack of a new unit at the centre, but one of ministerial will and capacity. We did not need a new strategy. We needed more drive in putting it through. I was unconvinced that a new group of civil servants organising visits and leaflets etc. was the answer.

I also discussed with Wilson whether to let [Michael] Cockerell make a film on the press operation. We both had doubts, mainly the obvious ones, but he also felt there may be a case for being more open and dispelling some of the myths. The only question was whether Cockerell was the vehicle. I was fairly confident he was the one most likely to be fair. TB was heckled by protesters at the road safety [strategy] launch event but he felt that was no bad thing, to be seen being reasonable in the face of emotion. He was obviously having an emotionless day – during the strategy meeting, his only reaction when someone raised the case of someone who died after being given the wrong kidney was that the public understand these things happen.

I was working first thing on his speech on volunteering for [the Active Community Convention and Awards] Wembley, which for some reason was getting close to zero coverage, though the volunteering initiative yesterday had gone well. I got CB to agree to record tapes for the blind as part of that. The main thing today was Jack S on Pinochet, release at 8 and a statement in the House later. Jack had handled it well throughout, as TB said at Cabinet. The other big issue was Mozambique, where we were getting hit for not doing enough. MoD and DFID were arguing about the use of helicopters, and who was going to pay for them, and it all flared up badly at Cabinet, where Clare [Short] accused MoD of briefing against DFID and said they were stupid.

Geoff Hoon hit back in a fairly half-hearted way, then Mo stepped in to try to calm it down, saying we had to sort out what we were going to do, going on about Clare's deserved reputation blah blah, before TB stepped in and said he just wanted it sorted. Margaret [Beckett] said to me on the way out that the problem was Clare thought it was all about her, and her so-called image, rather than sorting the problem. We had a quick meeting, TB, GB, Hoon and Short. TB said he didn't want to hear any more of the stuff about briefing against each other. He wanted to know what needed to be done, and whether we could do it. And he wanted me and GB kept across it all. We later agreed the RFA [Royal Fleet Auxiliary] ship *Fort George* should head there from the Gulf, and agreed to hold back the announcement for TB's webcast.

I briefed John Reid for *Question Time* but then we agreed it was better to put on Frank as they had Ken, Steve Norris and Susan Kramer [Conservative and Liberal Democrat mayoral candidates] on the programme. I had been very reluctant at first because I didn't like the BBC setting the agenda and dictating what programmes Frank should do, but there was now a danger Ken would run away with it. TB and GB both agreed he had to do it. Frank came in to see TB and me and we talked him through the best way to get the focus on him as policy and Ken as process and trouble. Frank looked nervous again, nodded and made lots of jokes, but didn't really have the edge he was going to need. As he left, TB said 'He's not going to come out of it well.' We had to set it up with a statement from Frank which we put together and got out to PA and it was good attacking stuff

250   *March '00: Row over aid for Mozambique flood victims*

which he would now have to see through. I gave him the line to use in the programme 'Ken, make my day and stand.' Ken of course was enjoying the limelight and we had to burst the bubble quickly. TB felt Ken was no longer the problem. Frank was the problem and we had to improve his capacity and the team around him.

Earlier, TB, GB, Peter M, PG, Douglas, Ed Balls and I met to discuss Gordon's strategy paper. We more or less agreed with the basic approach but also agreed we didn't have the capacity to deliver it, not least because of a lack of politicians who stayed engaged in politics rather than government. TB said the people in the room were the ones who knew best how to do it and we had to make it happen. GB wanted more resources and a series of new units working to him. I was worried we were over-complicating things. It was actually the basics we needed to focus on, not the ribbons and baubles.

I got home and after dinner watched Dobbo on *Question Time*. He did OK at the start, delivered the 'make my day' line perfectly well but then got very bumbly, didn't really go for Ken on crime, sometimes looked as though he was surprised to be there, made statements then looked around as though he was expecting someone to ask him to leave. Philip felt it had been a mistake for him to go on. 'Make my day' would win him the headlines, but he didn't really win the arguments. Stan Greenberg, watching in the US, felt that the process had hit TB hard.

Friday, March 3

Dobbo stole the headlines with 'make my day' but Mozambique was still the main event. Thanks to Godric, and TB's webcast, we were leading the news with TB sending *Fort George* [to help with disaster relief work]. The *Telegraph* had used a piece I had written on the media well and dead straight. Then on came Clare on the radio. Dreadful. I was in the car listening to her self-indulgent bilge, and was livid. She was making clear she and the MoD had been falling out and claiming she was being asked to pay too much. Like it was her money. Dreadful. Awful. Her back to her worst. TB was keen to get Dobbo up on crime. I called Frank and we agreed he should call for additional powers for the police on [criminal] assets seizure.

JP called as I arrived in the office in a total rage about Clare. He was planning to write to her to say she was selfish and stupid and had ruined the launch of the Countryside Bill. [Michael] Meacher [environment minister] had been bounced off the 8.10 slot on the *Today* programme so that [Shadow Defence Secretary Iain] Duncan Smith could respond to her verbal diarrhoea. JP said the problem was she had set herself up in such a way as to be virtually fireproof and she exploited it. She was a total disaster area. He said he intended to copy his letter to members of the Defence Committee. He hit the roof even harder when he discovered the letter she had sent to Hoon yesterday in which she said the government must speak as one voice.

I went to see TB who was working on the speech for tonight. I said I couldn't go on doing the day job, micromanaging Frank and dealing with idiots in his Cabinet like Clare who had turned a very good move today both for the government and for Britain into a presentational disaster area which would totally undermine the aid effort. I spoke to Clare and asked what was the point of generating a row that had virtually gone away and she put on her best sickly whiney voice and said sometimes in politics you have to tell the truth. I said it would hurt her and the government. She might get a good press short term but what she did was crazy. She said they were at it at the MoD. I said it didn't matter, all that mattered was getting done what needed to be done. She ended up agreeing but on the way saying she didn't like Hoon.

I called Geoff and said it was vital he didn't retaliate, that instead he should organise a phone call to the captain of the *Fort George*. TB felt it would blow over, which of course it would, but it meant time and energy wasted dealing with problems created entirely by her ego. Philip Barton was doing a brilliant job keeping on their [MoD and DFID] backs at getting things sorted, but by the four o'clock we heard that the four Puma helicopters we had said were on their way in fact were not on their way at all, but stuck because they didn't fit. It was a total fiasco and the Tories were piling into TB for not caring enough.

I met Cockerell and Anne Tyerman and decided to go for a film [*News from Number Ten*] on the press, despite the risks. I knew he was greasing to get us to agree to do the film, but I felt Cockerell did share the view that we had a real problem with the way the press covered politics. I did a lunch for the American press corps, and was introduced by them saying I had got a bigger turnout than anyone apart from Diana. They were quite a good bunch, desperate for more access. I did my usual spiel about the lobby. They were so much more serious than the Brits. Ireland and Kosovo were the main policy areas. One or two of them seemed to know that we were going to see [Vladimir] Putin [President of Russia], which surprised me.

TB had decreed that Clare should go out and do clips and say it was all a storm over nothing but she made it worse, as I knew she would, saying there would be a DFID [Commons] select committee inquiry into it all. Why on earth TB thought she would have improved the situation was beyond me. I did the Sundays which was mainly knockabout on Clare and Dobbo. TB called later and I filled him in on how dreadfully the Clare stuff had gone. He said he sometimes wondered if we were the most dysfunctional government in history. Quite a week.

Saturday, March 4

The exchange of correspondence between [Richard] Wilson and Andrew Tyrie [Conservative MP] ensured there was more stuff on me in the press, plus a *Times* cartoon. Wilson's line that I could do political work in my spare time was greeted with incredulity, not surprisingly. TB called to ask if I thought he should go to Newcastle vs Chelsea. I set off with the boys for Burnley and we had a fairly quiet journey until a call from [former Blair nanny] Ros Mark's mother Mig, who told me the *Mail on Sunday* were doing a story about a book Ros had written about her life with the Blairs. I sensed real trouble. I was shocked, as Ros had struck me as being very down to earth and not the sort to do this. She said she had written an account of her time with the Blairs to be a historical document. She had got in touch with an agent who said he wanted kiss and tell and that was the end of the matter. She said she had been contacted by a newspaper, intimidated and talked.

I said to Ros I couldn't believe she had written a book, how did she imagine our newspapers would use it for anything but harm? She said she would never hurt them, she loved the family and would never do anything without their consent. She admitted she had signed a confidentiality agreement. I advised her to write to the paper setting out the situation and complaining she had been bullied into talking to the reporter. That was about it until after the match, which was pretty dreadful [Burnley 0, Preston 3]. I suspected I would have to spend a lot of time on the phone and didn't much fancy being on the train so we arranged to drive back with Stewart and Lucy Binns [friends]. Simon Walters [*Mail on Sunday*] called as we were driving and told me they were running a story about the nanny's book. I said there was no book because she wasn't publishing one. He basically wanted, in the absence of a book, a 'Blair gags nanny' story, so other than being very nice about Ros, I said very little.

I dictated a note to the press office making clear we should stay very unfazed. I spoke to Charlie Falconer and Val Davies the solicitor. TB was really shocked at Ros. Cherie was upset both at the fact she was thinking of doing it, and also what she might write. I reminded

Walters of the confidentiality agreement. At no point did he say he had extracts or put any of the content to me. When the papers arrived, it was obvious the *Mail on Sunday* had a lot more than either they or she had let on. There was real detail and real words which came either from her speaking or writing. I called Ros who said she was amazed. I started to put together a statement with her to deny it all, which I got to PA around 11. I then did a conference call with TB, CB, Charlie and Fiona and after a fairly long discussion we decided to go for an injunction because of the principle of the confidentiality agreement being broken. TB was the most reluctant. Charlie and Cherie were pretty clear we had to do it to establish the principle.

Val Davies was instructed to go for an injunction, which we got by 2. I called Jonathan Harris [literary agent] and asked if he had had anything to do with the *Mail on Sunday*. He said he had peddled stuff to publishers but it had gone nowhere and they had amicably ended their relationship. I asked him three times if there was any way he may have helped get the material to the *Mail on Sunday* and he denied having anything to do with it. Val and I agreed we needed to be careful about him but Ros said he was the only other person she had shown it to apart from her family. TB and Cherie were both genuinely shocked and upset by it all.

The *Mail on Sunday* argued that I had been told by Walters that they were going to publish extracts, which I hadn't. I was up dealing with it till half two. TB was more worried about the content than the principle. Charlie had been impressive throughout. Cherie kept saying she couldn't understand how she could do it. The calls took a lot longer than they should have done because she was in Number 10 and TB was up in Durham. There was nothing much else in the papers apart from Dobbo coming out for not prosecuting people having gay sex in toilets.[1]

Sunday, March 5

The news was leading with the injunction. As I said to TB, it would now be a battle of spin. I called Ros at home. Her mother answered and was clearly angry about what we had done. She shouted to Ros 'It's Alastair – if you want to talk to him.' I said everyone was upset about this but we just had to get through it. We agreed another statement to put out which made clear she didn't get any money or try

[1] The *Independent on Sunday* reported that Dobson had told a mayoral hustings in South London that police should ignore victimless crimes. He said 'If they are wasting their time roaming around public lavatories or raiding clubs they ought to have something better to do.'

to sell it to the *Mail on Sunday*. She was pretty close to tears and said she would like to speak to TB. I listened in to the call. She said she wished she was dead, that she couldn't believe how stupid she had been, would do nothing to hurt them, and she was so, so sorry. TB was very nice to her, said he understood how it happened but she had to understand the media were not nice people and she should have nothing to do with them unless she stayed in touch with us about how and what she did. She cried her eyes out, went through the same story she had done with me yesterday. TB said they all still loved her. She said she didn't deserve their support.

TB wondered if he shouldn't go up on it and explain why we felt the need to get an injunction. Hilary [Coffman] talked us out of it and instead we went for a written statement. Ros called a couple of times to say she was being harassed. TB said Cherie was really on the floor with this one, had sat down with the kids to talk it through and was blaming the press but in truth felt pretty badly betrayed. The press were being broadly sympathetic but then Charlie explained there was a problem with some of the Scottish papers who were going to do a bit of attention-seeking boldness. I did a squawk-box briefing with Charlie at 4 to do the chronology and detail, said we didn't sit in judgement on anyone but there was surely a point at which any family was entitled to real privacy. We lined up lawyers in Scotland. The Scottish *Mail* were intending to do it so we had to get Val involved again to nail that down. CB called me later, said she felt violated and betrayed.

Monday, March 6

There was pretty massive coverage of the nanny situation. We did OK out of the briefing but Ros was marmalised and her mum called at 7.15 to say she really felt she had to set out her side of the story. I felt she would get nothing other than grief out of this. TB said he was minded to believe Ros' story that she had started off with good intentions but the press had done her in. It was interesting that even the *Mail* wasn't really defending the *Mail on Sunday*. During the morning meeting, the *Standard* called to say Ken was going for it. He had set it up very well, very quietly, and was going to dominate the news all day. I agreed a line for TB to do as a clip on his cancer visit. Frank's launch was all but wiped out but he had to go out anyway and did well. The eleven o'clock was mainly Ken and the nanny. I also announced the Russian visit. Ros' mum was desperate to put out a statement. I sent Jo Parkinson from the party in the North-West to help them deal with the press, but they weren't handling it well. The press found out the school Ros was at so they sent her home. She sent through a statement she wanted to do which was a bit OTT but just about OK. Frank was very pumped up and going for it. I gave PA a line re Ken, 'the ego has landed', which they put out as 'the eagle has landed'. I went to Brunson's farewell and Maurice Saatchi gave me 100-1 on Dobbo to beat Ken. I gave him a fiver which I suspect was lost.

Tuesday, March 7

Livingstone choosing to stand as an independent was wall to wall and he got a very good press without necessarily being endorsed. There was a sense running through it that we had really fucked it up. He was running rings round us. There was a poll in the *Guardian* which had him at fifty-five per cent, but still somehow he was the underdog. TB felt that too much putting the boot in would play into his hands. The strategy had to be to build up the policy arguments against him. His credentials on crime in particular were vulnerable. We also needed business people in particular to come out for Frank. Our big problem was the press and TV were doing his job for him. It was a conclusion of their desire to use him to kick us.

I had a long meeting with GB and Douglas, then with Frank and Trevor Phillips [Dobson's running mate, former mayoral hopeful now running for the London Assembly] to go through what they needed by way of people and arguments. I suggested they try to organise three head-to-head debates, on crime, jobs and transport. GB felt Frank had to be remade, that the policy positions had to be worked through first before we really started to go for Livingstone. TB was still very pro Ros but Val [Davies] felt that someone wasn't telling us the whole truth about the background.

We had a meeting with [Antonio] Guterres [Prime Minister of Portugal] on Lisbon and they did a doorstep.[1] I got a story in *La Repubblica* about [Italian finance minister Giuliano] Amato for the IMF [managing director job]. Schroeder was adamant that it should be a German and putting forward Horst Köhler [president, European Bank for Reconstruction and Development], who we were not keen on, and we had to try to get Amato in the ether without fingerprints. We pushed pretty hard with Guterres but he was basically keen to help Schroeder.

[1] A special meeting of the European Council in Lisbon was called to agree a new strategic goal for the EU in order to strengthen employment, economic reform and social cohesion.

There was a little flurry later on when Lord [Bill] Rodgers [Liberal Democrat peer, joint founder of the Social Democratic Party] had offered [to create] more [Lib Dem] peers in exchange for co-operation and they [the Lib Dems] had leaked it. Pat [McFadden] said it was basically true and he had had meetings with [Lord] Dick Newby [Lib Dem peer, Charles Kennedy's chief of staff] about it. Kennedy had said he couldn't control his peers anyway.

Wednesday, March 8

TB caved in to Schroeder on Köhler. I spent much of the morning doing my statement re the injunction. TB was angry at the way Ros' mum's interview had come out, making it look like we were trying to harm them financially, but they were now pretty much getting their own advice and no longer returning calls. Philip had done some groups on London and had concluded it was a lost cause trying to build up Frank. He was too much of a plodder and just didn't inspire. Yet Ken was beatable with a good candidate. At the four o'clock, John Sergeant [BBC chief political correspondent and lobby chairman] announced the plan for Cockerell's film and there was an immediate outcry led by Kavanagh, Jon Smith and Jo Andrews [ITN]. I suspected they knew what my motivation was, and also knew that put under the microscope, they were unlikely to come out well.

Thursday, March 9

The Times did a good piece on Cockerell, saying it was likely the press would object more to exposure than us. There was a fair amount of interest in TB's speech tomorrow [to the Scottish Labour Party conference]. TB and I were both fed up at having to do so much speech drafting. We had thought about doing a pretty full-frontal attack on the way the Scottish media operated and Bill Bush had done a very good piece of research but in the end TB, persuaded by GB, pulled out all the detail. Even that, nonetheless, would be taken by them as full-frontal, because they were such self-obsessed wankers. GB said the problem was there was a real sense that Donald [Dewar, First Minister for Scotland] was just drifting, there was no real drive so it was no wonder they were attacked the whole time. JP was in seeing TB and was totally on my side about going for them but in the end we went really for half measures. The argument for the visit had to be that devolution was working and that the media who had been virtually uniformly calling for it were tossers in now turning against it.

Cabinet in reality was mainly a discussion about how to handle

Ken, which I played down in briefing and emphasised the Northern Ireland element. In the car to the airport, I emphasised to him the problem of drift. GB was at least engaged at the moment but I was sure he was setting up parallel structures. Bob Shrum [American pollster and strategist close to Brown] was apparently coming in for ten days, which was fine provided we were all on the same strategy. We got to the Parliament, up to [Presiding Officer David] Steel's office for a bit of small talk and then into the Chamber. The speech was perfectly worded but a bit flat and there was no real atmosphere, though the applause from our side and from the gallery seemed genuinely warm. The SNP sat on their hands. It seemed a very nice building, which made me wonder why they really needed another one.[1]

We drove through to the Phoenix drugs project in Glasgow, TB meeting up with Hellawell and the head of the Scots Drugs Enforcement Agency, then to the Hilton where Pat and I rewrote Douglas' draft for tomorrow while TB did interviews. TB told me the kids had got quite troubled by the whole Ros episode, which was due to be settled tomorrow. He went off to do a Q&A in Kilsyth. He only got one question on Section 28 but the [Scottish businessman] Brian Souter posters [campaigning to retain Clause 2A, as Section 28 was known in Scotland] were absolutely everywhere and it was clear that Donald D and his press team were not challenging them at all. Donald seemed pretty cheery but TB felt he was very down in the dumps and all at sea without a paddle and with a great hole growing in the boat. We worked late on the speech for tomorrow. Fiona Ross [Scottish Television political correspondent] said on the news that today's speech was dull, and she was right.

Friday, March 10
A very good example of how ludicrous the *Record* had become. Their page 2 lead was on 'crisis talks' between TB, JR [John Reid] and DD, when in fact they had met to film for a PPB [party political broadcast]. The *Scotsman* led on a story that we were risking a split with the Lib Dems, the *Herald* on our attack on the press.

The speech was in better shape and TB did a passage himself on the Clause 2A [Section 28] issue. The posters, including one saying children would have to do homosexual role-playing, were absolutely

---

[1] It was in fact the General Assembly Hall of the Church of Scotland. The Scottish Parliament would have several other temporary homes before the purpose-built Holyrood building opened in 2004.

everywhere. It was actually profoundly anti-democratic.[1] Through the day we talked about how hard to go on it. TB wanted to say it was a vicious smear campaign. Donald persuaded us to tone it down to irresponsible scaremongering. TB's morning interview with BBC Scotland was classic, all about cost of the Parliament, special advisers, very little on policy and TB became a little bit peevish.

I spoke to Val Davies and Fiona to agree statements either for winning or losing the court hearing. It was a cause of a lot of tension through the day as Val reported the twists and turns in court. TB did a phone-in, then we got to the Glasgow office of the Scottish Office where he did a press conference with the American boss of [global employment website] Monster.com [Jeff Taylor], who was really positive about Scotland. The press sat there in their usual negative, numpty way, and by the end of it TB was laughing away and taking the piss. The American said he could not believe those people. GB called in the car, and was advising a bit of caution on Section 28. But I felt the campaign was so all-pervasive we really had to go for it and in the end we did. They also discussed the IMF with GB still pushing for Amato and saying that Köhler's dad was a German concentration camp commander [in fact, Köhler and his parents spent many years in various refugee camps]. As TB said afterwards, I bet the intelligence agencies have a field day with that one.

We got to the EICC [Edinburgh International Conference Centre] to finish the speech. It was one of those where you knew from the start that it was going to work and he got a good standing ovation. It was a very tough message to the party and the country. I sent through a very aggressive letter to Martin Clarke [editor] about the *Record* coverage and also put out strong words from Blunkett in response to the attacks on TB's earlier interviews on Section 28 by Souter's people. The truth was they could have exploded this argument a lot earlier. Donald insisted he had been trying but he didn't really get the stuff. He's a lovely bloke but sometimes not of this world.

Val Davies called from the court and we had a conference call with TB, CB, FM. The judge seemed to be supporting us on the injunction but was saying they could reprint the original article. The idea was that we should have gone for an injunction earlier in the day, but I had made clear I was not at all clear they had a book, the point on which the judge later called me naive and trusting, which was a first.

[1] Leader of the Keep the Clause campaign Brian Souter had also funded a private postal referendum, sending out four million ballot papers across Scotland.

The call I had from Walters had been recorded and released in court. The problem was if he allowed them to reprint the original, that would allow the other papers to lift the content. CB was very down because it also meant she was possibly facing costs. TB was more relaxed and I felt it was totally wrong that he allow them to benefit from this at all. We told Val she just had to keep going.

We were due to leave for Russia. We did a bit of schmoozing with the hacks on the plane. It was only when we got into reading the briefing and Tony Bishop the interpreter was talking to us that TB really got a proper fix on just how bad some of the stuff in Chechnya had been. It was odd that TB was only waking up to this now as Putin had been KGB all his life and was widely thought to be bombing Chechnya for votes. But on the big picture, though we knew it was difficult, we were defending the trip as being good for UK–Russia relations. As we landed, Tanya Joseph [press officer] called to say we had won on all counts in the case with the *Mail* and costs were to be awarded next week. Though pleased, TB said that probably meant the *Mail* would get even worse.

Saturday, March 11

I got very little sleep and was up to see TB who was muttering about the very difficult message we had to carry. He had only really been awoken to the full horror of Chechnya by Tony Bishop who had given us some pretty gruesome stories about what was going on there. We were definitely going to be getting flak from the human-rights people. Rod Lyne [UK ambassador to Russia] warned us we were likely to be bugged wherever we were so it was quite tricky to discuss how we intended to handle it. It meant whatever we said in private would be part of our message to them. TB agreed he would be reasonably tough but balanced. The press were moaning about lack of access and also the stories we were putting out and I couldn't basically give a fuck.

Putin came to meet TB and I talked to his press people to sort the doorstep we were doing later. They set off for Peter's Palace which meant a forty-minute drive in a green minibus. TB found the small talk quite difficult but Putin was clearly bright and very focused. He was clearly physically very fit, sharp-eyed but had a nice smile. He was definitely not going to be a pushover. Rod's basic advice was to be friendly without being overly chummy in case he turned out either to be bad or, in six months' time, in real trouble. He was a very good communicator, but worried about turnout at the elections. He took us on a long tour through the palace and then into a nice if rather dark room for talks. Rod broke his chair in front of the world's media.

Once they were out, and we got on to Chechnya, it was clear he was definitely a believer in attack is the best form of defence. TB set out our line in reasonably moderate tone and Putin said at least we were more balanced in our views than France. His basic line was the Islamic conspiracy theory, and also that criminal religious elements were at work and if they weren't dealt with it would cause the break-up of the CIS [Commonwealth of Independent States]. TB didn't really push him but the fact that it was the largest part of the conversation by far meant at least we could honestly say it had been the real focus, even if it was Putin who did most of the talking.

He said extremism was based on a very narrow trend of Islamic thought but they were up against weapons from Pakistan, Afghanistan, the Taliban, Arabs and Muslims. He said their approach was balanced and pragmatic. They were facing criminals who pretended their motivation was religious. It was aggressive extremism posing a real threat to Russia. TB urged him to do more to get out to the West the reality of what was going on down there. But people also needed to know any response was proportionate and that any allegations of human-rights violations are addressed. Putin pretty much point-blank denied there were any. He said Russia was prepared to accept some form of independence for Chechnya but they cannot be unlimited in the territory they choose.

He was pretty fired up about it and it was a relief when they got on to the domestic front, economic reform, developing a market economy. He said he intended to be tough on crime and tough on the causes of crime. Sound-bitesky. It was interesting he had a dig at the French because Rod had told us they were really worried that we were stealing a march with Putin. TB was sure that though we would get stick, it was the right thing. At the press conference, Putin's answers were way too long, which led to an overrun. The longer it went on, the more old-style he seemed and by the end he was very much on the offensive. TB found it a bit more hard going than he thought he would. There were times when Putin looked thoroughly modern, but then suddenly he would revert and be very much the old KGB man.

We left for the Hermitage, had a nice tour there with some very good pictures and then the second round of talks, which we left to TB and Putin alone and which seemed to go better, according to Tony Bishop. He said he opened up a lot more without all the officials around him. His assessment was that for the first meeting with a Russian leader – and Tony had seen them all right back to Stalin – it was a very good first encounter. We organised some very good pictures on the staircase and drove back to the hotel in the Zil but TB had taken the warning about bugging seriously, and was saying next to nothing other than how much he had liked him.

Later, he said Putin had told him he would be happy to see Milosevic go but didn't want that stated publicly. He had been very positive about Clinton and less so Chirac. On his own programme, he was determined to be modern and reformist. His view was that their version of socialism had poisoned the mentality of the people and it would not be easy. I did an interview with Catherine MacLeod [*Herald*] on why we had gone for the Scottish press. I probably went on too long, but as I told TB after he had been out at the Mariinsky [theatre] to see the premiere of [a new production of Sergei Prokofiev's opera] *War and Peace*, he had gone for the peace strategy and I was keen on war.

We had agreed with Putin that Malcolm Wicks [minister for lifelong learning] and David Miliband would visit them to discuss reform and I would work with [Alexey] Gromov [Putin's press secretary] and his people on how to improve their communications. On the plane back, TB did a couple of interviews for TV and he talked to the press about Putin and they clearly picked up that he liked him. He worked through his boxes and was in one of his rages at the Civil Service, said that when it came to e-commerce, asylum, Civil Service reform, they just weren't at the races. When I said to John Sawers the Civil Service wasn't delivering and he said people weren't paid enough, I said so why do they keep calling themselves Rolls-Royce? Maybe we should call it Vauxhall service. He reckoned it was more Volvo.

Monday, March 13

[Foreign Office minister] Peter Hain's interview in the *Observer* and [former Labour minister Baroness] Barbara Castle on *Today* meant that 'heartlands' was the new buzzword on whether we were going to do more for them. Michael Cockerell came to his first eleven o'clock without cameras, and Trevor K and George Jones [*Telegraph*] went off on a big thing about how it meant they ought to be able to name me. I said TB was the important part of the equation, but frankly I had given up losing sleep about what they did, but I wouldn't welcome being named the whole time. If Cockerell needed anything to show their self-obsession and self-indulgence, here it was. It took up the first ten minutes of the briefing.

I had a meeting on London with GB and Margaret McD. PG's latest note was very gloomy, said that Ken was going to walk it and they didn't much like Dobbo. We had to make a judgement about how much capital we tied up in this. It was John Sergeant's first day as ITN political editor and his first question was about Dobbo's beard. I said 'Is that the debut story?' to which he replied 'Is that the debut insult?' TB felt we should still be thinking about a way to get Mo in but it may be too late. GB felt we had to wait for Ken to give us an opening.

Tuesday, March 14

The *Herald* did a big number on my interview with Catherine [MacLeod]. It was leading the news in Scotland and would provoke another round of media attacks. It was interesting that the *Record* ended up with just Dennis Canavan and John McAllion [left-wing Labour MPs and MSPs] going for me. Both the *Telegraph* and the *Guardian* reported that I had agreed to be named in briefings, when I hadn't. There was far too much focus on me and on spin, with another dreadful *Panorama* last night [*Spin Doctors*, on positive 'spin' of NHS statistics]. Alex F had called after it and said they were dreadful and we should be doing something about it.

Hague's speech on tax was going pretty big so I got Bill Bush working on the tax burden and the notion of there being good spending and bad spending. George Jones asked at the 11 for the tax burden year by year. Stupidly I said I would give him the figures later. Philip had some new polling on the NHS which was dreadful, and he said TB's ratings were diving, in virtual freefall. At the four o'clock, I gave the tax-burden figures and when asked by George Jones whether the figures were higher at the end of the parliament than the beginning, I said yes and they went into an orgy of delight claiming it was a shift of strategy to connect with the heartlands – buzzword, buzzword. The problem was, even though the figures were there in black and white, it was the first time anyone had given a straight yes to that question. But they, as ever, made the assumption there was some big deliberate strategy at play and if anything it was a mistake, me just lacking the will to dance around the question. Some of the papers said they intended to publish the full transcript. TB was nonplussed. He felt at the moment there wasn't much we could do about the press. They were being absolutely poisonous.

Where the economic reports were good, for example the latest showing we were now the fourth biggest economy in the world, some of them wanted to give the credit to the Tories. We got into a bad situation on health with the report saying there was a fall in the number of cancer operations. It turned out the figures were wrong and there had been a rise rather than a fall, but yet again the *Mail/*

BBC axis was working. Later we were having to deal with the breaking story that BMW was about to sell Rover. Calum came in and we set off for Gillingham, 2-2, Ian Wright's first goal, and a good time. I got home by 11, watched *Newsnight* and several of the front pages were splashing on my 'admission' that the tax burden was going up. GB wasn't best pleased. On the one hand, we had danced around this for ages and it might be no bad thing we didn't have to dance around on it any longer. On the other hand, I hated being responsible for fuck-ups like this.

Wednesday, March 15

I didn't sleep at all well. The papers did the tax burden big and I feared it would be grim at PMQs. I called GB to apologise for the mess in the papers. He said his worry was whether he would have to reshape the Budget because we couldn't go into the next election with people thinking we were putting up taxes. That was why he had always tried to stay out of this. He was perfectly nice and friendly, on which Peter M's take was that it was probably to make me feel worse, which it did. GB said these things happened, it was very rare I put a word out of place and we just had to work a way out of this. The problem was I was doing too much, getting too tired, and making mistakes.

TB was also supportive, said it wasn't that bad, but I suspected he wouldn't be saying that at the end of six 'yes or no' questions from Hague. As it happened Hague wasn't that great and TB won on the argument but lost on the clips, e.g. Hague saying TB was less honest than me and being less honest than me was not something anyone wanted on their tombstone, ho ho. TB held up fine and felt we may have stumbled into the right position, because it was impossible to keep avoiding a question like tax burden forever. But it was irritating on two fronts – 1. it wasn't planned and it was my mistake, and 2. they were writing it all into this heartlands nonsense, their current prism.

Rover/BMW was a massive story and a problem for us. We didn't really know what was going on but we knew it was going to be pretty gloomy. We were momentarily cheered up by the Standards Committee report into Livingstone's earnings, a gift for Frank on his birthday.[1] I had a chat with Sergeant to try to get things calmed down re Cockerell. The truth was I was becoming too exposed at the moment

[1] A complaint from an ex-aide to the Commons Standards and Privileges Committee led to Livingstone being censured for not properly registering his earnings from journalism and public speaking.

Scenes of Kosovans using whatever means possible to flee Milosevic made it easier for Blair to make the case for action…

…and visits like this, to Stenkovec refugee camp in Macedonia, further fired his moral fervour.

In a speech he made to the Royal United Services Institute after the conflict, Campbell was highly critical of the media's sense of 'moral equivalence' between the democracies of NATO and the dictatorship in Belgrade.

Though General Sir Mike Jackson was sometimes suspicious of 'bloody spin doctors', he was a useful ally in Campbell's efforts to revamp NATO communications.

Charlie Falconer was heroic in the face of the abuse heaped upon his head as a result of the Dome he had taken over from Peter Mandelson.

At the Dome for the millennium celebrations, the Campbell family tries to keep smiling, but constant calls about stranded editors put a strain on the evening. Out of shot, sitting behind them, William Hague was enjoying the spectacle.

Cherie did her best to make up for the palpable lack of enthusiasm emanating from the Royals. By now, TB just wanted the whole thing to be over.

Even before the underwhelming show, TB had had to deal with the news that the London Eye was not turning.

Gordon Brown and his wife Sarah in happy times and sad times: at their wedding in August 2000, and a few months later at the funeral of Scotland's First Minister, Donald Dewar.

Northern Ireland was never far from the top of the agenda, and decommissioning a problem that bedevilled the peace process. Here Tony Blair and Bertie Ahern (right) take delivery of a report by the chairman of the Decommissioning Commission, Canadian General John de Chastelain.

Decommissioning provoked some strong feelings: this Republican graffiti in East Belfast speaks for itself; while David Trimble tells the media of his intention to resign as First Minister if the IRA fails to decommission its weapons.

Gerry Adams, flanked as ever by senior Sinn Fein colleagues, responds to an IRA statement saying it will cease all activity and decommission weapons.

The London mayoral campaign was an unhappy episode for Tony Blair, and for Frank Dobson (left), here with his fellow candidates Steve Norris (Tory), Susan Kramer (Lib Dem) and Ken Livingstone, who won as an independent after all other efforts to stop him failed. Holding the ring here is veteran broadcaster Jimmy Young (centre).

By the time TB and CB voted – for Dobson – they knew the Labour candidate was not going to win…

…and so did Livingstone. His victory, and a similar defeat for the leadership in Wales, would force TB to rethink his approach to devolution.

As the parliament dragged on, Campbell was determined to give up the daily briefings of the media – some of the spinning depicted here by Martin Rowson. Civil servants Godric Smith (below, left) and Tom Kelly (below, right) were to split the role of Prime Minister's Official Spokesman. But the press, having complained about Campbell, now complained that replacing the King of Spin with straight bats was like 'replacing Ian Botham with Chris Tavare'.

Student Laura Spence became the focus of heated debate about access to Oxbridge when Gordon Brown made an issue of her failure to win a place at Oxford; but the debate worried Blair, who felt it had touches of class war about it.

There were few people more trusted by the Blair family than nanny Ros Mark, which was why the news she planned to publish a book led to one of the few injunctions of this period, to stop the *Mail on Sunday* publishing her account.

The arrival of Leo brought shock but ultimately enormous joy to the Blairs and to Downing Street. But getting the balance right between privacy and life in the public eye was never straightforward.

Football, and particularly Burnley FC, was one of the few non-work outlets Campbell allowed himself. Here at Scunthorpe with son Calum (left) and his friend, Charlie Enstone-Watts, on the day Burnley secured promotion to the Championship. Campbell had left talks in Northern Ireland early to avoid missing the match.

Alex Ferguson was a regular source of support and advice to Campbell, and their friendship even survived the Manchester United manager's conversion of Campbell's son Rory (right) from Burnley to United. Calum (left) remained a Burnley fan.

As Campbell's profile rose, so the cartoonists appeared to see him as more attractive a target than most of the politicians. He was a regular on the front covers of *The Spectator*, *The New Statesman* and, here, *Punch*, trailing a piece about a forthcoming documentary, *News from Number 10*.

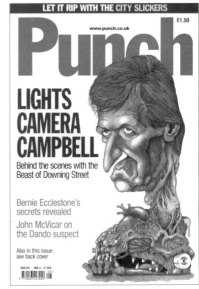

LET IT RIP WITH THE CITY SLICKERS

£1.50

www.punch.co.uk

Punch

LIGHTS CAMERA CAMPBELL

Behind the scenes with the Beast of Downing Street

Bernie Ecclestone's secrets revealed

John McVicar on the Dando suspect

Also in this issue: see back cover

and of course the risk with the film was it added to it all rather than exposed what I thought were the reasons. Peter M said they found me more interesting than most of the politicians and they also knew how important my strength was to TB and to the government as a whole. So they saw it now as a trial of strength between me and them. Sergeant said something similar, that I was too good a story to miss when I was sitting there in front of them the whole time.

Thursday, March 16

The Livingstone story was already rebounding in his favour with claims of dirty tricks, which no doubt he would get up whenever anything went wrong for him. I went up to see TB in the flat, who was livid we hadn't done more for Longbridge [Rover plant]. We feared that BMW had been putting out feelers for signals and we had sent out the wrong signals. Jonathan [Powell] had been warned about this six weeks ago. He had tried to get [Stephen] Byers engaged but nothing much happened. TB, annoyingly, was only really focusing on it now when it might be too late. GB, over for a strategy meeting, was also really steamed up, said there had been nothing in the way of proper intelligence. Geoffrey Norris [industrial policy adviser] said we now had clear information that they were going to sell. It was not clear what or to whom though apparently venture capitalists were now moving for it. We were looking like we were wrong-footed and without a strategy.

At the strategy meeting, GB made clear he didn't much like TB's *FT* interview and the focus on more health spending. He said every time TB did an interview he got up a spending rather than an economic message. TB told me I had to cool it with the press and start turning on the charm a bit more. He was pretty aghast at the violence of a letter I had sent to the *Mail on Sunday*. He was looking tired and his voice was a bit weak, which is what happens to mine when I get depressed. Cherie had told Fiona he was very down about Ken, about GB and about the media.

Cabinet was about Rover, with TB and GB saying more calmly what they had been saying in the earlier meetings, and they also had a discussion on Lisbon. But the truth was we were pretty much in the dark. At the 11.30 briefing, we were about to look even dafter because I said we didn't believe there would be a signed deal today. There was.[1] I had a meeting with Ed Balls on messaging for the

[1] A deal had been struck between BMW and venture capital group Alchemy Partners for the latter to buy Rover Group.

Budget. We somehow had to marry GB's desire for the focus on enterprise with the fact that we needed to be promoting investment in the NHS. Rover took up the first ten minutes of the news.

Friday, March 17

Godric did the 11 and we agreed it was time to stoke up anger on the BMW front, saying it was no way to do business. TB spoke to their boss later to voice 'anger and disappointment'. Peter H and I were working on health/Budget. He didn't think TB should do the health statement on the Wednesday unless he could announce the new CSR [Comprehensive Spending Review] figures. We were both worried GB would be big-picture economic success and TB tootling on behind with a bit of public service investment. I had a meeting with Balls and others from the Treasury who were being fairly cagey but it was clear the NHS was going to be the big story, and that although we would not reach the EU average of eight per cent, we were getting close. So it would be a good story to tell but particularly in light of past Budgets, it had to be downspun.

GB didn't think we were yet in a position to talk up delivery. We would only get the sense of it. He was still happier on dividing lines, the sense that the Tories were not the people to turn it round. Ed Balls and I agreed we needed a process story that set what we did in the Budget in the longer term. I later came up with the idea of a constitution for the NHS. It was a better meeting than usual, though TB and GB, meeting in parallel, was seemingly less productive. TB was still pretty down. He told me again I had to cool it with the press, that it wasn't possible to sustain a whole series of running fights.

Saturday, March 18

TB thought the anti-BMW stuff risked getting out of control and wanted it calmed. I got Godric to do a ring-round. TB was working on the NHS statement. The Sundays were full of stuff about GB really being in charge of the government, sufficient for Ian Austin to call and say he didn't know where any of it was coming from.

Sunday, March 19

TB was at Chequers, and called for several circular conversations on the Budget and the health statement, which Peter H and I had been working on. I took the boys to Hampstead Police Station. Last Sunday they had been mugged and had a whole load of mobile phone covers nicked and the police seemed to be taking it a lot more seriously than I thought they would. The Special Branch had been told because they were my kids and now we were sitting looking at pictures of mugshots, presumably of all the likely contenders in the area. They picked out the same kid independently. There was a very funny moment when Calum pointed at one of them and said 'That's so-and-so's dad.' The policewoman stepped in to say just because they were in the album didn't mean they were criminals, but Calum said he already knew that he was, but it wasn't him.

I got a call from GB to say could I go in and see him. He was with Douglas A, Ed Balls and Ian Austin when I arrived. He was worried about our positioning on health, said that though there was more money for health, the first question – because of TB's *Frost* interview – he is never one to let go – would be are we up to the EU average, and the answer is no. I asked whether he was saying 'This is your lot' and he said he was. He was stalking up and down, running his hands through his hair and grimacing. I said it would be odd to set spending according to the non-meeting of a target set by TB. He said that wasn't the point, but we had to be realistic and we had to be careful we did not set ourselves up for a process that would simply lead to more cynicism. People did not want to believe us. We had to set out what we were going to do with resources.

That was why, I said, it was important to tie extra money to a process of change, getting the system to deliver better. That was the answer to the question 'Why now?' We had failed because the system failed. Money alone would not make it work. We weren't actually that far apart, and a lot of it was going to depend on whether we could deliver a co-ordinated communications plan. GB wanted a range of regional press conferences which he wanted me to deliver, and I set that in train. Later Douglas said that their feeling was apart from me and TB there seemed to be nobody in Downing Street who could actually make things happen, whereas the Treasury was far more efficient. He also felt he was not personally empowered to make things happen in Millbank.

GB was in smouldering mood, partly probably nerves about the week ahead, but he was also railing at colleagues, saying they all just wanted more resources, and underneath it all was a resentment at TB having forced the pace in health spending. I was in there for a couple of hours and wasn't sure what the purpose was beyond getting me to organise a big regional hit for him.

Monday, March 20

There was a lot of pre-Budget stuff around, and the *Sun* had £3 billion boost for health and education, so generally we weren't in the right place. TB's concern was the sense we were being panicked into extra health spending, that it looked like a mix of weakness, Old Labour and more spin. Most of the day was taken up with meetings with GB, who was being more open and friendlier than in previous years, and now offering to help TB with the health statement. Peter H was convinced GB was setting TB up for a kind of second-best situation, whereas I was more comfortable with the idea of GB doing the big hit and TB taking it forward specifically on health. Where there was disagreement was that GB did not agree that we needed to do the CSR announcement. He felt a review-type process would be enough. My concern was that it set up too many expectations of the end product.

Milburn came in effectively to be told what the plan was and though pissed off at the process, seemed happy enough with the outcome. We went through the same thing with Blunkett and later with Jack S, but they were basically OK. The eleven o'clock was all about Rover – did we agree with calls for a BMW boycott, did we believe that an industrial policy based upon picking up the pieces was really an industrial policy at all, how do we reconcile this with the Lisbon agenda, which was a very good question. It was one of the trickier briefings I had had to do.

I did a note for TB for the Budget Cabinet and then worked on his NHS statement. TB was curiously nervous about it all, perhaps because of the second-fiddle bit, but also possibly because he knew the next couple of days were important for the way the whole parliament panned out. GB was doing a cut on tax on tampons, and I tried to persuade him to announce it himself in the speech, but he was very reluctant. He looked pretty embarrassed about the whole thing. I lobbied Ed B as well but it was clear he wasn't going to do it. TB said I had to get my mind in a different place re Ken. He was going to win whether we liked it or not and we had to start thinking of the plus sides because in the end we were going to have to do business with him.

Tuesday, March 21

Budget Day. I was worried we weren't really in the right place because there was no real sense in the build-up either of the enterprise agenda, or big investment in public services. TB and GB had several meetings through the morning but we were really just fine-tuning now. I saw Ed and Ian to agree the process for the day and review where we were on the follow-through. They were much more open this time but you still had the feeling they saw this very much as their thing and nobody had much of a right to interfere.

To the disgruntlement of the lobby, I didn't do the eleven o'clock, because by the end of the day it would all be overtaken. At Cabinet, TB went through the overall message script, then GB did the detail and did it well. He gave every impression that all the relevant ministers had been bound into the relevant bits for ages whereas e.g. Milburn wasn't really aware until yesterday. He said his big message was prudence for a purpose, the purpose being a stronger and fairer Britain. He wanted to link the economic and the social. It was because of what we had done on the economy that we were now able to build for the future. We could cut some taxes but not at the expense of stability. He took them through the extra spending but emphasised money and modernisation had to go together. Apart from a bit of a kerfuffle on pensions, it all went fine.

We then finalised his statement for today, just fiddling at the margins really, and TB's for tomorrow. We had the usual excitement in the street, including this time [photographer] Chris Harris of *The Times* hanging out of an upstairs window to get a picture from above of GB leaving Number 11. I had a last-minute go at trying to persuade him that it would do wonders for his image with women to do tampons in the speech but he was worried it would just be seen as a sop to women's groups. The statement seemed to go fine, though I thought our side would react better on health than they did. The thing they really went for was the extra help for pensioners but overall it was pretty subdued, partly because GB had deliberately gone for downspin. He was changing the way of calculating and presenting figures.

Hague had a lot of fun at my expense when he used the transcribed briefing on the tax burden which the *Guardian* had published. I just had to grin and bear it, even as the ghastly sketch writers were all looking over. Ed and I did the briefing afterwards which was fine, though again I think their expectations had been of something more dramatic. I went back to Number 10 to work with TB on his statement and plan the overnight briefing. I briefed Niall Dickson [BBC social affairs editor], who was really up for it. TB met a group of NHS professionals who were really positive. We had a real opportunity here to shift gear on health, and then keep going.

We had Blunkett coming round for dinner to meet Delia Smith [TV cook and food writer] who was really keen to push cookery in schools and wanted to help. David was very fed up with life at the moment. But he perked up. He was very funny recounting incidents either where he had been talking away and then suddenly realised the person he was talking to had gone, or where he was talking about somebody in detrimental terms, not realising they were there. He and Delia seemed to get on and we had a nice evening. The office were paging me with a readout of the bulletins, which seemed to go fine, and the Tories were clearly unsure about how to attack. By the time everyone left I felt really tired though.

Wednesday, March 22
GB got a pretty good press, though not the *Mail* and *Sun*, which splashed on [rising] petrol prices. We were leading the news on NHS reform, though the report on NHS cronyism was going to cast a shadow. I went up to the flat to see TB, who still felt the statement lacked grit. We put in more on challenges to the NHS, incentives, performance-related pay, targets and better inspections. The idea was, having focused on resources yesterday, to focus today on reform.

GB did the *Today* programme and though they tried to get the focus all on tax, he did fine. He was clearly relieved and on good form today, in and out helping with the statement. He agreed it needed more edge. He had a reception for women's magazines and women's editors. Cherie popped in for a while. It was all very jolly.

PMQs went fine, as did the health statement, though again the response was a bit flat in the House. But at the briefing afterwards, they clearly sensed there was real grit and edge in there and we could now get up reform better than before. TB was down to do [John] Humphrys as a pre-record for tomorrow's *Today* programme. Humphrys was very laid-back, almost chummy, even ending with something on paternity leave. But TB was a bit waffly and it wasn't terribly good. Peter M called, angry that Bertie [Ahern] had said there would be a new initiative from the two governments when there was no such thing. TB's statement was coming over really well on the news.

On the flight to Lisbon [for the European Council meeting], TB said it was becoming a problem that I was seen as such a figure in my own right, because it made the straightforward job of briefing harder. They basically saw it as their job now either to trip me up, or present things as news because I was saying them rather than because they were his views. I had been getting more and more concerned at the latter point. TB said he read the lobby notes and he could see the pitfalls and the traps they were trying to lay. I said I would be very happy to give up the briefings, but they were a means by which I kept on top of pretty much everything. We also discussed whether it might not be sensible for me to find a way of being more directly involved in Millbank, without it becoming just another great big hoo-ha.

We got to Lisbon and I did a very long but rather dull briefing at the conference centre. There was a lot of interest in whether TB would take paternity leave. Rover announced 3,000 redundancies. I had a long swim in the dark, which cleared my head, and after TB went to bed early, stayed up late talking to John [Holmes, UK ambassador to Portugal, former principal private secretary to Blair]. I had pretty much reached the view that I wouldn't mind getting out of it all, but he said TB wouldn't let me and I'd be there till the end.

Thursday, March 23

I did a couple of briefings through the day and felt that we were winning on all the main economic arguments but we were getting precious little coverage on that. The whole thing was overshadowed by the Haider issue in Austria and then later by the fact that TB, GB and RC all came out on different planes. The *Standard* splashed on it, which got them all thinking they had to do it. We were down to do an interview with [Robin] Oakley, who said he wanted to do it mainly on paternity leave and now planes. At least he looked embarrassed, but it was ridiculous that this was their agenda. It was a big problem that we had a political press that wasn't really interested in politics and was obsessed with the trivia. I was more convinced than ever we had to take them on. But TB said it wasn't really possible before an election.

At the second briefing, I said I would alternate between serious and trivial questions. George Jones eventually asked about the planes issue and I blasted him out of the water. It was ridiculous that we were sitting there having to explain different departure times etc. Robin was out and about on the media and said it was virtually impossible to get anything out on economic reform. I was reaching the point where I was losing interest in what they wrote. Even *The Times* said they intended to do the plane story on page 1. GB was developing the line, and I think was right, that the Tories were deliberately trying to foster cynicism in everything they did and the media was there to help them undermine the political process. I had done an interview for *Vanity Fair*'s profile of TB and said that if all journalists basically decided their job was to attack the government, the consequence was nihilism.

We were also dealing with the [Sir] Paul Lever [UK ambassador to Germany] situation. He had done an interview in *Die Welt* in which he attacked Rupert Murdoch and Conrad Black. I was pretty relaxed about it, felt it was handle-able. But he issued an apology under pressure from RC and the FCO. Then the *Sun* reported we were livid and TB had ordered him to apologise. I wrote to Lever to say it wasn't true and he shouldn't worry.

At the summit itself, there were real problems with the French, who were trying to water everything down, especially on aviation and transport. Then [Lionel] Jospin suddenly tried to link the withholding tax to energy and transport liberalisation. TB did bilaterals first with Bertie and then Jospin which we had to break up for the family photo [of leaders]. It was comic to watch because TB was placed next to [Austrian Chancellor Wolfgang] Schüssel and it really looked like he was trying to avoid him. Schüssel was desperately trying to talk to him and TB just carried on talking to Bertie. TB insisted afterwards he wasn't being rude and hadn't deliberately ignored him but the press were convinced it was a deliberate snub.

TB got bored in the afternoon session, came out to do interviews. He couldn't believe that the three planes story was their main focus. We went for a little wander in the press room and he got a taste of what I dealt with all the time – foreign media asking serious questions about serious things, our lot obsessed with trivia. We left for the residence before he set out for the dinner where he said Chirac and Schroeder were pretty tricky re Kosovo because Chirac was protecting [UN special representative Bernard] Kouchner and Schroeder was protecting [EU Stability Pact co-ordinator Bodo] Hombach. It was not the way to do business because most people actually wanted the best people there.

I sent a letter to Tony Hall saying that the Beeb's coverage today was further evidence of press-driven dumbing down. Julian [Braithwaite] had dinner with some of the hacks and said they were in very reflective mood, that they knew I had a point but they didn't know how to change. Both TB and Robin said they found it quite depressing you could have Europe's leaders meeting up to discuss issues that affect millions of people's jobs and prosperity, and all our media could care about was how they had travelled there and whether TB would take paternity leave.

Friday, March 24

In the car to the conference centre, we had a chat about Hague. TB felt we had defined his basic weakness, which was lack of judgement, but now we had to expose his strategy, which was to join with the press in creating as much cynicism as possible and so undermine all faith in politics. It was all about eating into the majority. TB told the summit that reform was working to France's benefit, because electricity to Downing Street was now supplied by a French company. I briefed it out as a way of making the argument that the French were standing out against change that was already happening. Jospin was not being terribly brave at the moment and in the bilateral, neither of them had really gone above polite level. TB had a real regard for [Spanish Prime Minister José María] Aznar, who adopted very tough positions and stuck to them and who said he was emboldened because he knew he couldn't stand at the next election.

Schroeder came over to chat and agreed to ask to eat British beef when he was over. He said he hated all the small talk and the hanging round at these summits. Schüssel was having a very hard time. TB's so-called snub got pretty big play in the papers but TB said he was about the only one who would speak to him and that when Schüssel spoke in the meeting, the others looked skywards. I worked on TB's press conference script and trailed it at the briefing where I was deliberately and tediously serious. I stressed it was an important summit and it would really change Europe's economy. I was trying to get them to be embarrassed to raise their usual trivia. I left and was on the way back to rejoin TB when I realised I had left my briefcase behind. Thankfully, and amazingly, it was still there when we got back.

I finalised TB's script which was long and detailed. He was a bit too warm on the euro in the Q&A, but all in all it was a good performance and he managed to get out some sense of the substance and we managed to get some pretty meaty coverage on the news. TB saw the guy from *Vanity Fair*, David Margolick, whose thesis seemed to be that the press hate TB and that something in him gets under their skin, but the public like him. I sensed that like Cockerell he was broadly sympathetic to our thesis about the media.

I got home to find Rory really playing up and Fiona and I ended up rowing about how to deal with it. It didn't help that I felt so tired but I was also having to deal with Val Davies because the *Mail on Sunday* did not want to acknowledge publicly that costs had been awarded to Cherie. I did not trust them not to spin it as a victory for them because the injunction was being discharged. I was adamant we had to make it clear it was a total vindication for Cherie, but it all added to the strain.

Saturday, March 25

I was all day out at Bracknell [Berkshire], where Rory was running, and sent Martin [Sheehan, press officer] to Oxford to meet up with

TB and Schroeder for the Königswinter Conference.[1] Both of them did a number on how Rover mustn't get in the way of Anglo-German relations. There was a story going around that I was leaving after the election to work for Man United. Total balls, but the *Sunday Express* and *Sunday Times* ran it. Michael Wills [learning and technology minister] had a good bit in the *Telegraph* splashing on Labour as the party of the Union [of the United Kingdom].

Sunday, March 26

The NHS reform stuff wasn't really flying and so when GB was on *Frost*, he was pushed more on the tax burden, added to which ITV later put something out claiming we were re-announcing new nurses. Both should have been avoided but both meant the press could go after us on spin. It was all part of an effort to poison the well of debate and make it look like we couldn't be trusted. The *Sunday Express* did a whole page on me going to Man U, and later admitted not only that it was balls but that they knew it was balls.

Monday, March 27

The papers weren't dire but nonetheless we were not getting a big post-Budget bounce. Added to which, focus on spin was undermining the good things GB had done. BNFL/Sellafield was a big story and post-Rover, we were looking a bit shaky on the industrial front generally. Health didn't really go anywhere despite GB on *Frost*. TB and GB were both wanting NHS stories day by day. Anji had been in TB's office earlier when GB had been complaining about our failure to get stuff up. Anji felt TB had been agreeing, and she had a real go at him, saying he never stood up for his staff. I walked in as they were arguing. She said Tony's complaining his operation is useless.

He was asking why he was doing a Britishness speech on Tuesday. I said because he had said he wanted to do it, but apparently GB had now persuaded him it was the wrong thing at the wrong time. On the NHS, I felt if we just did one story after another, day by day it would become another spin issue, when what we needed in communications terms was a sense of the long term and third parties doing the talking for us. He was back to worrying about stories and headlines and the need to persuade journalists, not real delivery which

[1] Annual Anglo-German conference of politicians, diplomats, business leaders, academics and journalists, established in 1950 to improve the relationship between Britain and Germany through a frank exchange of ideas.

eventually they would have to report. We were also diverging hugely on how to deal with the press. Anji and I were both pretty down on him at the moment. He kept asking for things to go in the diary, then complaining about them when the time came. A classic was his dinner with David Frost. We had warned it would come at the end of a packed day and he would wonder why he was doing it when he saw it in the diary. That was exactly what was now happening.

The eleven o'clock was mainly Sellafield and Northern Ireland, but I had a real go at their obsession with presentational issues. I said the Budget was serious and deserved serious coverage on health not the pathetic drivel we had about nurses. What had worked well post-Budget was the regional roll-out and I wrote to [Mike] Granatt [head of GICS] asking him to keep the regional operation on a permanent footing. We were working on the Commons statement on Lisbon and it was interesting that the Tories were not as strident as usual and TB felt they might be planning to soften their position. I got Julian B to get together European media coverage from Lisbon which again showed large and widely positive coverage for TB on the issues, on which there was a virtual news blackout in our own media.

Tuesday, March 28

Peter Kilfoyle's blast in the Budget debate yesterday, saying we were neglecting our heartlands, got more coverage than virtually every other speech. The bitterness was too obvious but the words were too strong for them not to carry through the media. Michael Wills' [Britishness speech] draft was OK but GB had discombobulated TB again and by the time I was in late, after taking Calum to school, TB had virtually torn up the draft and was starting again. I felt sorry for Wills who had worked very hard on it. TB felt we were walking into a great trap by talking about devolution but I couldn't see how he could make the argument without addressing it. TB recast the argument so there was more focus on Europe as well as the basic message of us being stronger together within the UK. I said it was a joke that he could rewrite a speech that had been in the diary for ages as late as this, and engage in what was essentially a different argument. But GB had totally wound him up.

Earlier he had spent the whole NHS meeting asking Milburn why the news wasn't leading on health, a question which, to be fair, Alan wasn't totally qualified to answer. The speech went OK, and the audience, basically regional media [newspaper executives], seemed to like the speech. In the car on the way back, he said he felt exhausted. So was I. I saw Andrew Rawnsley about his book[1] and then Kamal Ahmed [newly appointed *Observer* political editor] who gave me a big spiel about how he wanted to be a different kind of political editor. He was very nice but I suspected the cynics would be quick to get at him.

David Davies [Football Association] called about a possible joint bid with England and Germany for the 2006 World Cup, which presumably meant they had given up on the England bid. There was a very nice farewell do for Philip Barton and Rob Read [private secretaries], Philip was heading to Cyprus and Rob was going to be a student again. TB would miss them both.

Michael Levy [businessman, Labour peer and party fund-raiser] said he had had lunch with [Sir Richard] Wilson and I should 'watch out'. He reckoned Wilson was looking for me to fall flat on my face so that they could reassert after I went. Then we heard Mig Mark [mother of Ros] had done an interview for the *Today* programme. I agreed with Cherie and Fiona that we should take a pretty hostile line. TB called and said he thought I was really tired and I was getting too ratty with people. The *Telegraph* ran a story that I was getting more hits on the [Downing Street] website than TB, which was all part of their strategy for me and him.

Wednesday, March 29

The Audit Commission report on [the NHS providing substandard equipment for] the disabled was going big and was pretty grim. We had pre-empted it last night by tying to it the need for more reform, but it wasn't good. The other new concern was the *FT* splash saying the CBI [Confederation of British Industry] and the BCC [British Chamber of Commerce] were turning against the government. So today we had the *Mirror* doing us in over pensions, the *Guardian* and *Independent* on Sellafield [British Nuclear Fuels], the *FT* on business and every single paper was against us on drugs. I argued again with TB for a jihad against them. We had to make them more clearly part of the public argument. He said it wasn't possible this side of an election. He had a meeting [re equipment for disabled people] with the people in the NHS inspectorates which went fine and which we briefed extensively.

At PMQs, Hague went on BMW. They sensed that Byers was vulnerable and it didn't help that TB didn't directly say yes when

---

[1] Rawnsley's book *Servants of the People: The Inside Story of New Labour* would be published in September 2000.

asked if he had confidence in him. Also [Margaret] Beckett was determined to build up the story that she had a business communications unit leading the dialogue with business. Steve Byers was worried about it but she was doing an interview with Rosie Bennett [Rosemary Bennett, *Financial Times*] today and I suggested she make clear Byers had wanted her to do it. Margaret was a bit too status-conscious about it. TB really went for Hague on Section 28 at PMQs, and that's what dominated the afternoon briefing. I then had to deal with an Alex F problem. He had agreed to do an RUC [Royal Ulster Constabulary] dinner in Belfast tomorrow and the press there were whipping it up and the club was getting lots of calls. He was in Portugal for a match. I called him and he said his instincts were to get out of it, so I did a statement for him to the effect that he was not prepared to be used as a political football.

Thursday, March 30

GB was in real killer driller mode on health. He was very down on Milburn. He always thought it was possible to drive a message day after day after day, but in reality it wasn't. Added to which, I felt we were not nearly tough enough in challenging the media agenda, and I didn't note GB rushing to the front on that one. Cabinet was given over to a discussion on e-commerce, with Pat Hewitt [e-commerce minister, DTI] and Ian McCartney [e-government minister, Cabinet Office]. Ian did the presentation as though he was speaking to party conference. Otherwise it was fairly quiet. TB was seeing farmers' leaders. I was doing the four o'clock with Margaret [Beckett] and persuaded her not to do the business unit press release. I had a chat with Cockerell to agree when he would travel with us.

Friday, March 31

I was up late-ish and then a car came to take us to Chequers. There was first a three-hour discussion where GB made an OK presentation on strategy, followed by the usual mix of different statements that didn't really stack up with the odd insight. Peter M and Milburn were OK. Jack S all detail, Mo all over the shop. TB did a very good summary on the importance of New Labour in getting us here, stressing this was the first Labour Cabinet for a long time with no ideological divide and we had to ensure we didn't lose that. Equally GB was absolutely clear there was no inconsistency between a strategy for the heartlands and a strategy for Middle England. JP said we were not motivating our core people like the other parties were their core people.

Philip kicked the thing off with polling that listed as strengths the economy, TB, education, and a will to succeed. Weaknesses were in the areas of lack of delivery and trust/spin. But there was a hollowing-out of our support. TB said we had to keep the focus on reform and keep the coalition that built New Labour together. He said we had to stay absolutely focused on the possibility of a Tory recovery. Nobody thought we would win during the Thatcher era but they had still successfully made us the issue. The Tories may be weak but we still had to generate fear about them. JP did a number on turnout and argued for more politics and better organisation.

GB said that what was missing was a big central message and that in its absence other things fell in – spin, Middle England vs heartlands, individual policy areas. Between now and an election we had to be clear of the challenges, achievement in meeting them, and then the next steps. We have three enemies, he said. The Tories, the Libs and the smaller parties, and apathy. The Tories' weapon is not fear of Labour, it's cynicism. Read the *Mail* and see their strategy. It is an anti-politics agenda designed to damage us. As ever, he was strong on analysis of what was wrong but his solutions were pretty familiar. Empathy, message, story development. He was also keen that we do not fall into the heartlands vs Middle England trap. That is what the many not the few means. We are working for both and our appeal must be to both.

Once the key players had said their bit, the others tended just to make random points rather than actually discuss what was said with TB trying to bring it all together. He said our opponents want to make New Labour, New Britain a devalued concept. Why? Because it is successful. We have taken political territory we mustn't yield up. He said he didn't just want to win next time but win well again and that meant we kept driving modernisation. We have the right values but we have to be the party of reform.

Later TB, Peter M, Anji, Jonathan and I had a meeting to go through continuing problems. He was very open about the GB situation. He was a formidable strength but he was also fiddling and diddling around the whole time. He felt we just had to put up with it because there was nobody who could do his job as well as he did it. On himself, he felt the problem was the force with which opponents put the view that he lacked conviction and real beliefs. He felt the answer to that was delivery, to show you could do what you set out to do. He felt we had a weakness and apart from him and Peter, we lacked people who really put the New Labour case with conviction, e.g. to a business audience.

He said his next party conference speech had to be thunderingly New Labour, that the heartlands issue was a trap not to fall into, that New Labour was actually the route to a better life for people living in Labour's heartland territory. Forces of conservatism was the right concept but the wrong language. So he saw his big internal challenges as managing GB to get the best of him as close to his agenda as possible, and putting himself together again with the public. He felt New Labour was the solution to it all. We had another run round the block on the press, but he was now totally of the view that a full-frontal attack would backfire.

I worked on tomorrow's speech. I sent Peter M a draft of a note for TB. He felt that this kind of strategy work was what I needed to do more of. Like TB, and like me, he thought I should pull back from the briefings. But he felt as the note stood, it was too strong to send to TB, and might seriously undermine his confidence. Added to which, it might leak.

Saturday, April 1

GB did a fair amount of briefing out of Chequers, based on *Tribune* doing something on his presentation to the NEC. It came out fine but TB was clearly troubled at the moment. He had done a very good and rousing speech at the end of yesterday's meeting but he was still struggling to find his voice publicly. As Fiona and I drove up to Manchester for Alex F's testimonial dinner I had two big worries. How do we reconnect TB? And how do we deal with the media? On both, I knew that I should do something different but I wasn't sure what. I was also having second thoughts, too late, re the Cockerell film. The thought had been to get a proper focus on my profile and the profile of our operation. But it was clearly just going to be another load of profile. We got to the hotel and down to the G-Mex [conference centre, venue of the dinner]. Alex was very happy after winning 7-1 against West Ham. We won at Cardiff. There was some good people-watching to be done, particularly of the players and their wives and girlfriends. Teddy Sheringham's girlfriend had a dress slit so far up she might as well not have put it on.

I won a prize in the raffle of a trip to Chicago to see Bon Jovi. Bizarrely, [Everton manager] Walter Smith's wife had been going on over dinner about how much she liked Bon Jovi, so I gave it to her. Walter was very sound. He thought we had to do something about the press. He couldn't believe people like Peter Kilfoyle and how quickly some people seemed willing to go back to losing ways. He felt the longer we were in, the less people gave us the benefit of the doubt. It was a very British thing to bring people down if they flew too high. He, Alex, Cathy [Ferguson], Mick Hucknall [singer and Labour supporter] all also made a similar point in different ways, that TB was becoming a bit more remote, not speaking to people's concerns.

The problem was how do you communicate properly when you are so constantly mediated through a hostile prism? The spin thing was now virtually part of the language. Mick said that when TB came on the video clip, you could sense that some of them wanted to boo. Two years ago he would have been applauded, one year ago he would have been welcomed. What's changed is people doubting what drives him. I didn't sense anyone wanting to shift to the Tories, but I did think there had been a change of mood.

Sunday, April 2

We were up late-ish and watched *Frost* in the hotel. Hague was getting a free run for his Harrogate [Conservative spring conference] speech and we had no real operation to hit back at it.[1] We were also being badly hit on Rover with the sense that Byers was more interested in his own position than sorting it out. Yesterday's march [of tens of thousands of car workers and their families] in the Midlands was not a good sign. And yet I still felt as a government we weren't really pulling out all the stops.

Monday, April 3

I had enjoyed the weekend but in dipping into a different world, I'd felt too keenly that there was a real change in mood that had to be arrested. It was funny how these things happened. And others in the office sensed it too. TB had done a note which, whilst recognising the malaise, was woefully complacent about the solution. He was back to whether I could duck out of the briefings, as indeed I did today without too much of a problem. At one meeting, he was even wondering aloud whether I could go and run Millbank and be an upfront public figure. He thought it was bizarre that I was written about more than most politicians and yet most members of the public would never hear or see me.

At our various office meetings, it was the usual stuff on lack of direction, lack of delivery, TB reconnection. Charlie [Falconer] said to

[1] Hague told Conservative activists 'We are going to punish Labour for abandoning Middle Britain.'

me he thought TB was becoming a bit remote and we needed to address it. Godric did fine in the briefing but the problem of not being able to be political was exposed when he couldn't say when TB would be campaigning for Dobson, and that was taken as a signal of luke-warm support. I spent a lot of the day working on a six-page note on TB/reconnection. TB was desperate for me to take on the Peter M strategy role, which I was happy to do in theory, but Charlie in particular felt it would be impossible to pull me out of the day-to-day, and he also felt TB would lose something if I wasn't doing the brief-ings. I was alarmed at how Hague's [Harrogate] speech, which was poor, got pretty positive coverage and there's no doubt they were trying to give them another lift.

In the afternoon I spoke to our EU ambassadors at the FCO. Some of them – Michael Jay [France], Stephen Wall [EU], John Holmes [Portugal] – were phenomenally bright. Others you really wouldn't want representing you abroad. But I felt it was a useful meeting and I think they thought it was good to get the big-picture message, not least that we were trying to prepare the ground for the referendum, and also that we would welcome them taking risks and pushing the boat out in communications terms. It's why I was keen to correct the idea that TB or I had been angry at [Sir Paul] Lever, however daft it might have been [see March 23].

I had another long session with TB and told him that not just enemies but people like Philip, Gail [Rebuck, PG's wife], Fiona, some of the people I saw in Manchester, were expressing concern at lack of conviction, it was all about tactics and support. I went over the top to provoke a reaction and make him realise what people were saying. I said people were beginning to say GB had great range and depth. He had to reveal at all times not just that he was a clever politician but that he was motivated by the right things. He seemed pretty down by the end of it. But I think it was the right thing to do. And his self-defence and the way he framed it was helpful in putting together the plan I was trying to knock into shape.

Tuesday, April 4

I got TB to speak to Byers who was still very much on the back foot re Rover, dealing with situations we should have dealt with ages ago. He told him to get the focus back on help for Longbridge. Steve said he was trying to do just that but my sense was he was just hitting at the edges. Hague had now done two interviews on successive days on tax and spend. TB and I weren't sure whether to go for him hard now, or let him build the argument. The pensions rebellion was getting a fair bit of coverage and clearly harming us.[1]

I had a meeting with Trevor Beattie [creative director] and some of his colleagues at TBWA [advertising agency]. They were clever and I liked them and felt they were much more on our wavelength. I said welcome to the worst client in the world. The stuff they had prepared was lively and above all it had the right tone, for example 'a lot done, a lot to do'. They had a nice thing on the theme 'to be continued' and they did a terrific anti-Tory PPB to the song 'Memories'. Beattie was long-haired and scruffy, but I took to him because he was clever and his politics seemed in the right place. Trevor said we were doing quite a good job and even people who slagged us off expressed no desire to go back to the Tories, so what more do we want? I walked to the dentist and redrafted the TB note.

Wednesday, April 5

I felt very buoyed up by the agency people yesterday. They were more upbeat than we had been. I was reflecting that TB was basically a good thing and we shouldn't let occasional moments of disillusion make us overlook that. Independently, Bruce [Grocott] had done a note and clearly felt similarly to the way that I did. And though his solutions were more Old Labour, we shared the basic analysis. I missed another briefing today and Godric did fine though he said they were beginning to notice. Hague went for TB over Byers at PMQs and TB did fine so there was no real heat at the four o'clock. I was slightly concerned that Steve got me called out of PMQs because he was worried about something Hague had said. I said you really have to get out of who, what, where, when and just get on with helping the people at Longbridge.

Fiona and I went for dinner at Derry's [Lord Irvine] official residence [as Lord Chancellor] – very good fun. Charlie F and I had a little chat re what TB had meant when he talked about an upfront role. Charlie thought he meant me going to the Lords, becoming a minister and speaking for the government. I thought he meant Millbank but in the end neither would be right. We had a very nice, jolly evening and I couldn't help thinking all this official-residence stuff was bound to make people more distant. I felt the same when we travelled to stay with ambassadors in their big fancy residences with pictures of

[1] Forty-one Labour MPs had voted against the government's Child Support, Pensions and Social Security Bill in protest at a refusal to increase pensions in line with earnings instead of prices.

April '00: Upbeat ad agency impresses Campbell

the Queen all over the place. If you're not careful, you start to think it's normal to have people serving on you the whole time. I had a very nice chat with one of Derry's staff, who was straight out of Dickens, who said Derry was a very nice man and also that we were going to get back next time with a majority of 149.

Thursday, April 6

TB came round and we talked through the argument re Middle England. He wanted the speech targeted very clearly at the country, not the party, where it would be seen simply as a response to Kilfoyle. He said we just had to accept we were going through a bad phase and we would come through it. But we had to woo the press a bit harder. I had to stop whacking them so hard. He said he understood how it was impossible not to feel contempt for them most of the time but it wasn't sensible to let them all know that's what I thought. I had to try to quell the anger.

We had a meeting on local elections in London which was pretty dreadful. GB was still clearly not wanting to get involved. He was constantly analysing problems without saying how he thought we should resolve them. He was full of analysis of what was wrong with Frank and had no alternative. So we were heading for the local elections without a proper campaign and without a proper strategy for Ken. TB was fed up with the whole thing, livid that Mo hadn't got in and livid that Frank had not raised his game. The general feeling was also that Trevor Phillips talked a good game. So all in all things were looking pretty useless.

At Cabinet, Jack went through what was being done re asylum. It was beginning to pick up as a political issue and Jack was setting out how many of our current problems were a direct result of how the Tories ran it. The sums of money involved were becoming ridiculous, but of course there was a sense in which the Tories were using this to play the race card. Robin gave a very funny account of Mugabe at the Europe–Africa summit in Cairo. He said [Libya's Muammar al-] Gaddafi spoke for forty-five minutes. Did he mention the Third Way? asked TB. Apparently Gaddafi's very big on the Third Way, he said. No, said Robin, but he did wear painted nails. He said that on day two, Antonio Guterres rang a bell after five minutes of a speech. He said Mugabe had decided to cool the rhetoric against us for forty-eight hours but then went back to his potty ways and announced that Peter Hain was the gay lover of Peter Tatchell [gay rights activist]. 'Hain is taking it calmly,' said Robin. 'Tatchell is furious.' The place fell about, but Robin added that Mugabe had a neuralgia about us that was beyond any reason.

Steve Byers went through BMW/Rover both in terms of the sale and the fallout in the area. The news was totally dominated by the two Leeds [United] fans killed in Turkey [in violence ahead of a UEFA Cup match against Galatasaray]. We decided to keep TB out of it. We left for Paddington and worked on the train on the speech. Interest rates stayed unchanged. TB said 'That's a favour from my friend Eddie' [George, Governor of the Bank of England]. We agreed not to go into the heartlands issue at all in the speech but to do it in the Q&A down in Wales. We did a couple of Welsh interviews on the train, then to a jobs announcement, then to Merthyr Tydfil, then a Q&A on the New Deal [for the over-fifties] then heading for Wrexham. Cockerell was there with a crew and Tanya [Joseph] said some of them were really beginning to get edgy about being filmed. I briefed on tomorrow's speech. TB did a pretty dreadful phone-in. TB had a quick chat with Cockerell who looked hurt that he hadn't seen his earlier film [*What Makes Tony Tick?*]. While TB did the party dinner I went out with some of the hacks to the amazing new hotel in Cardiff Bay, St David's. Particularly once the cameras stopped, we had a good discussion about how we try to get the debate into a better place. I felt [Tom] Baldwin and [Don] Macintyre in particular shared a lot of my analysis even if they thought I sometimes went over the top.

Friday, April 7

We got low-key coverage for yesterday nationally, though good in the Welsh *Mirror* and the *Western Mail*. There was a sense too that TB and Rhodri [Morgan, First Secretary of the Welsh Assembly] made a very good odd couple. Rhodri had been very funny last night telling jokes about what it was like driving around in a bombproof Daimler. TB did a BBC Wales phone-in which was OK if a bit whingey. He gave a very strong hint on [EU] Objective One status and match funding. TB and I agreed that an all-out war on the press was off and that we had to do a lot to get more of them onside. They were fed up with both of us. Anji's view on my latest note was that most of it was right but that we shouldn't return to forces of conservatism, we needed to reconstruct the big tent, not pull it down.

At his NHS [pre-summit] meeting,[1] Alan Langlands [NHS chief executive] slipped me a note saying I must press TB not to micromanage from Whitehall because it was a disaster waiting to happen. He did a meeting with *South Wales Echo* readers which was pretty grim. One of

[1] Blair had called a summit with ministers from the devolved governments – the first of its kind – to discuss NHS investment and reform.

April '00: Leeds United fans killed in Turkey

them was in tears because his wife couldn't get treatment, another one said he had been betrayed over miners' compensation. We got them back a bit in the end, but it was tough. Then to two hospitals and I did briefings with Robert Hill [Blair's health policy adviser] at both, barely a line of which appeared anywhere. All day the hacks were asking what the story was and struggling to get anything out of it. It was quite good Cockerell material because we were clearly trying to get the focus on serious issues but they weren't really interested.

TB was enjoying it, really getting stuck into the detail though he did say it was going to be tough to persuade them to do all that needs to be done. We had the ministerial summit meeting at City Hall. Peter M clearly thought the whole thing was a nonsense and arrived totally unprepared and talked about the Northern Ireland Health Service much as he might talk about life on Mars. Rhodri on the other hand had a map to show where everything was. Jane Hutt [Welsh health minister] and Susan Deacon [Scottish health minister] did their own presentations. TB got well stuck into it and it all overran. They had also decided there should be a communiqué out of it all, which Rhodri was taking very seriously. Peter just sat there shaking his head. We did a very short briefing for the press, who were totally underwhelmed despite TB's enthusiasm. TB was quite keen for them to do absolutely nothing on it because it would show the conflict between their narrow definition of news and the honest endeavour that represents a lot of what governments do.

Saturday, April 8
Bernie Grant [Labour MP] died. I put together a tribute from TB which we released. I left the Sundays to Godric and felt absolutely knackered. I was very down and fed up with life, feeling I did nothing but work and when I didn't work I was either bad-tempered or exhausted.

Sunday, April 9
Asylum was really picking up and the Tories had briefed on the back of the local elections launch that they were going to make asylum the issue. This was going to be really difficult for us.

Monday, April 10
Asylum suddenly took off as the main political story. Some idiot in Millbank, stupidly briefing before we needed to our 'lots done, lots to do' campaign was also stupid enough to say the Tories were playing the race card, which of course is exactly what they wanted. Also, on

the policy, Simon Hughes [Liberal Democrat home affairs spokesman] was suggesting that we were as bad as the Tories. TB felt at least it allowed us to explain what we were actually doing as opposed to the various caricatures. He wasn't remotely worried about the Liberal attack. The more people knew we were trying to take a tough approach to this, the better. He also wanted it out that we were spending a lot sorting out the Tory mess. He felt, having read my note, that out problem was that we were not New Labour enough on policy, though how subcontracting the economy and strategy to GB would help this I don't know.

Cockerell was in to film the morning meeting, where neither I nor anyone else behaved like we normally do. It is odd how the presence of a camera can change people's behaviour, but there was no doubt it did. At TB's office meeting, he said again we had to be more New Labour not less. It was probably done to send a message to GB via Douglas. The eleven o'clock, with the cameras in, was pretty feisty, with them coming at us over race. At the four o'clock I announced Putin's visit. I got back to discover that TB and GB, in a rather bad-tempered call, had agreed GB would chair a meeting every morning before mine, which would be more political and allow more party people to attend. I was beginning to agree with Peter H that he was trying to set up rival systems and structures. It was also more pandering. What was definite was we lacked message discipline, strength and depth and capacity at the centre. Whether GB would help, I wasn't yet sure.

Tuesday, April 11
I was up in the flat, where TB was still fretting about asylum though he sensed the Tories would be worried about their own position. He wanted them hit hard on opportunism and hypocrisy. We had to show that while they were stirring it, we were sorting it out. But it was difficult. We also had to decide what to do about Govan [shipyard, threatened with closure if not awarded a £300 million MoD contract], which was the next one coming down the track. TB asked why I was so down. I said because my whole morning was now taken up with meetings, giving me less time to do the things that the meetings would decide I needed to do. Also, I wasn't yet convinced GB was really up for this.

To be fair, at the first meeting, GB was pretty engaged. He emphasised the need for us to be on the top of the news agenda the whole time. It was clear when we discussed asylum for example that he just wanted to play it down, which wasn't realistic, and suggested wishful thinking would take the place of really hard strategy when it was needed. Blunkett was there and on the way out said 'I hope we are not going to be doing this every morning. We'll all go mad.' I guess GB was just trying to bind people in. I left straight for my meeting, commissioned all the lines needed for the 11.

Anji was worried that the Cockerell thing was becoming *AC: The Movie*, that they would try to show TB couldn't cope without me. I reminded Cockerell we had agreed this would be a film as much about the press as about us. If it went wrong, I'd be pretty isolated. Fiona was totally against it, so was Anji. So was Pat [McFadden]. Peter M had his doubts too. I left with David M and Robert Hill for the *Express*, where we were trying to do a big push on NHS reform. I got back to see Phil Stephens [*Financial Times*] who felt we were looking very ragged. He felt we had to be more relaxed, more confident, less aerated.

Wednesday, April 12

GB's meeting was OK but his style was to make unrealistic demands as if somehow we could will a different news agenda into being. The best coverage was coming out of something we hadn't even discussed, namely the class-size pledge being met. There were a few revealing moments, for example we should get it out that twenty per cent of pensioners retire on £500 a week so why should we put up more money for them rather than the poorest? Jonathan came to this one but said nothing. Philip, Douglas and I made contributions but otherwise it was pretty quiet.

I was involved in a ridiculous row with Richard Wilson who had said I could not go to Milton Keynes for the local [elections] campaign launch because it was clearly political. I sent him a note saying it was legitimate both to liaise with the party and to brief TB on any issues that may be relevant but which may not be political. I was steaming about it, told anyone who would listen how crazy it was, and Richard agreed it meant that Godric or any other 'proper' civil servant could go, but I couldn't because there would be the perception that I was political. Bonkers.

TB was out campaigning with Dobbo and was very pleased with the line that when people turn to policy, they turn to Frank. On the way back, he bumped into people handing in three million signatures on a petition for sub-post offices. I had a chat with Hilary and Anji about how we could get the Cockerell film into a different place, away from just being about me, for example by focusing through [visits press officer] Magi Cleaver's eyes on the Putin visit. PMQs was pretty light, the Post Office was Hague's latest opportunism. Govan with a strong hint in the direction of help. On Putin, we announced that he would see the Queen but also learned that his wife wasn't coming.

Jeremy H had taken up my argument with Wilson re Milton Keynes. Richard's basic argument was that I shouldn't do any of this stuff. Jeremy made the point that if people like Godric could go to events like that, that really would give a perception of politicisation. Jeremy said he was really digging his heels in. They talked about precedent, but actually made it up as they went along, and now we had the utterly ludicrous situation where according to the head of the Civil Service it was fine for Godric to go to a party event, but not me.

Thursday, April 13

I wasn't sleeping well and I had a nagging feeling that Cockerell was a mistake and that I was heading for a fall. I was arguing all day on and off about Milton Keynes. Anji felt there was probably something personal there, but I felt there was a hardening on the position of what I could and couldn't do, and I was going to have to win. Cabinet was all about the local elections. TB said the basic frame was a lot done, a lot to do, a lot to lose under the Tories. He also said he wanted more of them involved in the campaign to help Frank. On the Tories, he said we had to link Hague's weakness to Tory extremism. It is because he is weak that he adopts extreme positions, e.g. on asylum, as a way of holding his people. I had a chat with Milburn who shared my worry at our inability to get up health on a sustained basis.

I went over to the Northern Ireland Office for a meeting with Peter M, Philip, Stan Greenberg, Bob Shrum and Ed Miliband. Stan took us through the poll and there were real problems beneath the top-line figures. I felt the real weakness was the sense that there was no well of conviction, that we needed to recapture the forces of conservatism concept if not the language. Peter M was totally opposed, said it was then that the big tent had started to fray and we should keep repairing. I said that only happened because we bottled out, we didn't stick to our guns, went back to being all things to all men, which has given us a different kind of definition problem. He said maybe he was still Blair '94–95 whereas we felt the world had moved on, but he was worried we were losing business. He felt a message focused on hard-working families was too class-based. I argued it meant working and middle class, but he felt many middle-class families didn't think it meant them, not because they weren't hard-working but because they thought it related to our traditional support. He was full of stories

April 'oo: More help needed in Dobson campaign

about Bobby, his dog. We weaved in and out of strategy, and him telling moderately funny stories about Northern Ireland.

Bob Shrum was very likeable, red-faced, avuncular, chewing Nicorette [gum] very aggressively. He said our weakness was lack of clarity about who we were for. TB and GB were more or less in the same place, but he felt TB's language was too abstract. I stressed conviction, and then direction and delivery as the key to TB reconnecting. Peter was fine on that but not at the expense of New Labour or new supporters. We must not risk alienating our first-time voters. I argued that they were the very people who wanted to see conviction, direction and delivery. PG was pretty down today, and so was Stan. I felt Peter's real point was valid, namely don't lose the big tent, but a lot of what he said by way of argument wasn't pragmatic.

TB got back from the [local elections] launch. He felt it had gone OK but there was always a risk of negative campaigning. I was doing a foreign press briefing at 5, got Tom Kelly along and it was mainly Ireland and Putin, who was coming on Monday. Philip and I took Bob out for dinner. He was a very positive force, clearly close to GB but wanted to help hold everything together. He said he thought my note was one of the best pieces of strategic writing he had ever seen, and he wished he could write like that. He felt that unless there was a total economic collapse, there was no way we could lose the election, and if we got our act together again, we could win big. A lot of the chat was small talk but I felt when we got on to substance that whatever problems we had, they were fixable, provided we all wanted genuinely to fix them.

Friday, April 14

Bill Morris [general secretary, Transport and General Workers' Union] attacked us over race in an article in the *Independent*. TB spoke to Jack to say we had to use it to get up a message on what we were doing to deal with asylum, but Jack had a bit of a wood-for-trees problem. Morris, Longbridge and more bad health stuff made it another bad day newswise. Milburn was due to do a big political attack on the Tories over health but was pissed off because no TV people turned up in the North–East. Godric did the 11 while I prepared for a meeting with student media. Their list of who they wanted to meet was interesting. Top was TB, then me, then a few others and GB was down at seventh, which was odd.

I had a meeting with special advisers, took them through key messages, and emphasised they had to get their ministers to be more political. They were definitely becoming too governmentalised. I had a meeting with the Russian ambassador [Grigory Karasin] to go over Putin's visit. He said Mrs Putin wasn't coming because she had a cold which she didn't want to pass to CB. It was clearly bullshit but he said I could say that to the Sundays, but then he changed his mind after the [Cockerell] cameras left. He brought me two videos on the Chechnya situation from the Russian information centre so they clearly weren't going to be defensive about that. We had a chat about how to get decent pictures out of it for both of us.

I had a chat with Jeremy about RW. I felt we had to fight against what he was saying because it wasn't based on principle or an intellectual argument. Jeremy thought he was getting grief from others and that we had to move some way towards him.

Saturday, April 15

I was briefing up the Sundays for the Russian visit which was in the wrong place with criticism about Putin stronger than before. The only problem Godric picked up on the ring-round was that [Charlie] Whelan said he was doing a rival film on me. The media were now trying to position the Cockerell film as being 'approved' so Whelan's, should it ever happen, could be the unofficial one. Burnley won in the last minute at Oxford, the third time in four weeks we won in the last minute.

Monday, April 17

Putin day. I went up to the flat to see TB, who was worrying re pensioners, re Putin and, after his dinner with Peter M last night, re the Millbank operation. He had decided, however, that I couldn't go over – first because he was worried things would fall apart here and second, because it would send a signal re the election. He was annoyed at the way it was becoming a given that the election would be next May. Even though it was his favoured date, he wanted to be able to keep options open. He was even thinking about sending Sally [Morgan] over full-time.

On Putin, the babble industry was going into overdrive re human rights, which was getting more play than when we went out there. That, pensioners, and a story in the *Guardian* about a 'bung' to the coal industry were the main things out of my morning meeting. TB's meeting was hopeless – just the usual complaints re Millbank and government departments, but no real direction about what needed to be done. Nor could we agree with Philip G about whether we should be saying the Tories could win, or whether they couldn't. I felt we had to talk them up. TB thought we should just be saying they could sneak in. The *Mirror* had splashed on an internal [Conservative] Central Office memo saying they couldn't win, so it was a strategic point we had to address and agree on.

I had a chat with Jeremy H and RW re the local elections and SpAds [special advisers]. Richard seemed a bit closer to our position and insisted his big worry was that I had become a target. We – TB, Rod Lyne, John Sawers, Jeremy and I – had a long discussion pre Putin's arrival. We were not going to get any change on Chechnya. They had announced some commission or other to look at the whole scene but Rod didn't think it stacked up to much.

TB was clearly getting irritated about Cockerell being around, and I think John S was stirring it a bit, with Jonathan away in Belfast again. There was another example of the presence of the cameras changing the nature of the event. As we waited in the hall for Vlad to arrive, TB would normally want to chat with me just by the door, but I could tell he was sensitive to the possible thesis that he couldn't do anything without being directed. So he wandered off. Putin arrived, good pictures outside, then came in and made somewhat of a beeline for me, which I could see Cockerell lighting up at. I was having second second thoughts.

We went upstairs for the first round of talks, which was very much Putin in lecture mode, first on the world economy, then Kosovo and then, briefly, on Chechnya. TB let him do most of the talking and said he would reserve his main points for the tête-à-tête, after which he reported that Putin was a lot more open on National Missile Defense, and less steamed up re Chechnya. TB said it was a very exciting time for Russia and we wanted Russia seen as an equal partner in the international community. Putin went through his economic plan, but when he went through the scale of some of the problems, and the restructuring he envisaged, it was clear he had his work cut out. Banking reform, pensions, housing, poverty and corruption, changing from Communist systems, it was a huge challenge and he made no effort to minimise it. The lunch was fairly relaxed. They went through India–Pakistan, Iraq, nuclear clean-up, then chatted about what they thought Okinawa [G8 summit in July] might throw up.

I was surprised at the way Putin made the odd joke at [Russian foreign minister Igor] Ivanov's expense, who in turn looked a bit hurt. He had quite hangdog eyes anyway, whereas Vlad's eyes were real killers', piercing blue and able to move from sensitive soul to hard nut with one blink. He was not as aggressive on Chechnya as he was at the press conference later when he really got steamed up. We had a little joint pre-brief before walking over to the FCO for the press conference. He was now in slight jaw-jutting mode and he was also, a bit like Neil [Kinnock], someone who clenched his jaw muscles if he didn't like what he was hearing, as when I said they would try to get him going on Chechnya and paint TB as being a bit soft with him on human rights.

TB went through the script Julian and I had drafted, but then Vlad totally stole the show, first with a really strong and passionate defence on Chechnya and then by commenting on the markets, and saying TB had said it was a bad blip – though his [Putin's] interpreter was dreadful. I did a little huddle instead of the four o'clock, and they were all basically in the same territory – human rights, Chechnya, were we too soft? The 'bridge of understanding' line was probably too weak and woolly to get through all that, and the 'blip' comment was a bit of a problem.

Once Putin had gone, we were back on to Northern Ireland. Jonathan's meeting with the UUs was leaked, so it was out TB was going tomorrow, which gave us another set of problems. I agreed a line with Tom Kelly and Joe Lennon to keep expectations right down. I did another interview with Cockerell and TB popped round, feigning surprise that he was there, and we had a not terribly natural chat about things before Cockerell drew him into a kind of interview, first re Putin, then re me, TB saying I was the best in the business but then, bizarrely, saying we never discussed policy. He was trying to downplay the media side of things and I stupidly undercut him as he left when I pointed out he had just wasted his time talking to Michael C. We then had the media reception upstairs, where the atmosphere was fairly relaxed, and they didn't seem overly to mind the cameras. Cockerell was interviewing and some were laying into me a bit. Cherie and Fiona popped in for a bit. It was actually quite a nice evening and the mood was generally OK.

Tuesday, April 18

Hague got a big hit with his asylum speech, particularly his line on them being kept in secure detention centres. He led the *Mail* and the *Telegraph*, so needless to say led the BBC first thing. Last night media monitoring had tried to get the Home Office to rebut properly but they failed miserably – no urgency, no drive. They were using the excuse of the fact it was a speech by Hague to say they couldn't really get involved. But it was a case of defending a policy under real attack.

I called Jack S who, with Alice [his wife] chatting away to him in the background, was keen to say that the Tories were inhumane, habeas corpus etc. I persuaded him that was exactly what the Tories wanted us to do, and it would be better to avoid falling into the trap. TB was worried at Jack's lack of subtlety on this, but it wasn't an easy line to tread – on the one hand we had to defend the policy, but on the other, we knew there were actual problems of implementation and on the politics, it was clear what Hague was trying to do – get us on the wrong side of a cultural divide. Jack said the problem was TB was 'suspect' on the issue, very right wing and didn't really get it.

At the morning meeting we agreed it was better if Blunkett dealt with it at the local elections press conference. But there was no doubt the Tories had successfully got up 'their' issue on their terms. TB was on the case all day. Peter M felt Hague had gone over the top, that he was looking a bit desperate. Plenty of others thought the same, but I was worried the papers were doing the job for him, and now he was legitimised in raising it the way he did. Asylum was playing out really badly for us.

We set off for the airport and out to NI, with Cockerell and crew in tow. We got helicoptered over to Hillsborough where TB did a brief doorstep before beginning his meetings, first with the chief constable and the General Officer Commanding, then Trimble, then the other parties. TB was trying to get a new IRA statement out of Adams and McGuinness, who Tom Kelly and I met going round the gardens at one point, Gerry pointing at the plants and telling us which ones he had in his own garden, being very much the nice middle-aged woolly-jumpered gardener. Tom and I did a fairly full briefing, but made clear to them all there was very little going on, and that they might as well leave for all the hanging around they were going to have to do for not very much to report.

TB remained optimistic though and when we went back in said he felt we might end up making progress. [Ian] Paisley [leader of the DUP] absolutely tore into him, and he more or less just let him. We then left for Dublin by helicopter. He and Bertie did another brief doorstep. They had a private session one-on-one and came out to say they had decided to meet on Thursday. Over dinner I was getting calls from Burnley where we lost 3-0 to Gillingham to pretty much fuck our promotion chances. Bertie was on good form, and interested in how the asylum argument was playing out. I think he felt NI was in danger of going backwards again but he was determined to keep going.

On the flight home, while TB talked to Jonathan re NI, Peter M and I talked about what to do re Millbank. He felt there were several big downsides to me going there – Fiona's opposition to a bigger workload, Number 10's capability, and whether I could manage Margaret [McDonagh]. I was worried more generally about my management skills. I was fine at the inspirational leadership stuff but less confident at all the more classically managerial stuff. Peter was curiously disengaged from it all, as if he were talking about something that was not really anything to do with him, giving advice from afar. He said it was impossible for him to do anything but, because in NI he was pretty much running the show and it was full on the whole time. TB was still very antsy re Cockerell, wouldn't let them film on the plane for example. Peter said it was a great big ego trip for me, and I would regret it.

Wednesday, April 19

Hague was getting huge licks out of asylum, though it was going to be interesting to see if he did it at PMQs, or would just leave the papers to do the dirty work for him and avoid being pinned in the House. I felt TB had to be more in the conviction zone than positioning vis-à-vis Hague, but it was difficult. Mugabe was the main story with RC pressing Kofi Annan [UN Secretary General] to get involved.[1]

I went straight to the GB meeting. Mo was there. GB was venting his spleen at the fact we had the best jobless figures for ages and we couldn't get coverage for them. There was more interest in [chairman of the Commons Education and Employment Select Committee] Derek Foster's report on the North–South divide. GB agreed with me that if we couldn't get the asylum dividing line on competence, we had to get it on big-picture conviction. There was definitely a feeling in parts that Hague was exploiting this rather than coming up with genuinely workable ideas, but getting the tone right was a tough call.

Faz Hakim [political adviser] came to see me re TB's stance on asylum, said that for example at [Guyana-born black Labour MP] Bernie Grant's funeral [the previous day] there was a feeling TB shied away from taking on racism up front, slightly ran away from the issue, scared.[2] I took her to see him to make the case, and she said there was a feeling among some in the ethnic minorities that we didn't really take on the politics here because we were worried the Tories were playing the race card and there would be white working-class

[1] In Zimbabwe, white-owned farms were being raided and taken over. The raids, and resulting racial tensions, were calculated to appeal to millions of black rural voters in the run-up to parliamentary elections.
[2] Blair had sent a videotaped tribute to the funeral, saying 'We had a shared belief that Britain is and should be a multicultural society.'

votes in it. TB said he would always challenge racism but the problem here was that there were problems in the system and the Tories were trying to portray us as friends not just of asylum seekers but of a system that wasn't working properly, and he wasn't prepared to let them. We had to accept there was a problem with the system being abused.

In the end PMQs went well. He got a couple of good hits on Hague re costs of government, which included money spent on the Opposition.[1] He was good against the Libs and got the tone right on asylum which was raised by three on our side, and it was interesting Hague didn't go on it. We had a bit of a JP pickle over the use of his flat.[2] Archie Norman [Conservative MP] had raised it and TB was worried he [JP] might have broken the ministerial code. JP was keen for a line to go out that TB accepted it was fine, but TB wasn't so sure. We put out a line that stopped short of saying he had not broken the code. There was no way the Tories would let up on it I suspected.

Ken Bates [chairman, Chelsea Football Club] called and said we were going to have to help out financially re Wembley. It was hard to tell how much was bluster and how much was genuine but it would certainly be grim if we lost the World Cup bid for the sake of a few million quid. He was in full flow, slagging off pretty much everyone in sport, and in government, and then saying he'd like to be invited to Chequers.

Thursday, April 20

There was a bad Queen story in *The Times* re the message of congratulations she sent to Mugabe on his twentieth anniversary. One of those routine but avoidable things. Geoff Crawford [press secretary to the Queen] was livid it had happened and I wanted to be able to say it was a mistake by the Foreign Office but it wasn't raised by the lobby so I let it go. There wasn't much appetite for an eleven o'clock so I delayed and we waited for Bertie's arrival. TB had to do his Dobbo press conference. Pat [McFadden] and I had worked up a script that

[1] Called Short money, not because of its amount, but after Ted Short, former Labour deputy leader, who introduced it in the 1970s. Total annual funding for opposition parties had been increased from almost £4 million in 1997 to over £10 million.
[2] Prescott had not registered the tenancy of a flat in Clapham he was renting at £220 per month, owned by the Rail, Maritime and Transport union. It was claimed by Shadow Transport Secretary Archie Norman that the tenancy presented a potential conflict of interest since Prescott's brief included transport policy.

promoted Frank and attacked Ken on policy whilst bearing in mind we may end up working together so it was slightly pulled-punches time.

The other problem story was Trevor Kavanagh's page 1 of the *Sun* saying TB was thinking of pulling in Peter M to the centre and sacking Mo and Ann Taylor [chief whip]. Peter M was convinced Mo was behind it. My own view was that it was George Pascoe-Watson [deputy political editor, *Sun*] picking up on my vague answer to a question at the briefing on Tuesday. The *Sun*'s judgement was that Hague 'lost by a whisper' at PMQs.

Grace was in when Bertie came in and he made a real fuss of her sitting in the chair in the corner of the hall. The meeting went well and there were clearly the makings of a plan on the table. We needed a joint statement by the two governments, an IRA statement, confidence-building measures to help both sides. Bertie as ever was more optimistic about the IRA going further than we thought they would. Peter wasn't there and pissed off not to be, but it would have meant [Irish foreign minister] Brian Cowen being there too and sometimes these worked better just with the leaders. They were at it for ninety minutes or so, then did the joint webcast.

I persuaded Joe Lennon not to go overboard about progress today, as this was not the time to overclaim. We were discussing third parties who could verify arms dumps. When someone suggested an American, I ventured Oliver North, just to lower the tone.[1] I did a briefing, also told them about TB being called up for jury service [as an MP and barrister Blair was disqualified], then home to collect the boys and head north to see Mum and Dad.

Both Phil Webster [*Times*] and Andy Grice [*Independent*] called me re an MI5 warning about civil disorder if race was stirred as a political issue. I spoke to Stephen Lander who said it was rubbish. I wondered if this was being stirred by the Tories to try to get us to bite again. I took the opportunity to brief Phil on the Mugabe–Queen situation. Geoff and I agreed a low-level story that saved face by making it clear it was a low-level FCO cock-up, whilst avoiding it being a big row, was the best way out of it. TB set off for Chequers. Re Frank, he felt he did as well as he could today. He said he didn't have much sympathy for him. If he had come out when we advised, we could have won London, but he was proud and stubborn.

[1] US Marine Lieutenant Colonel Oliver North, involved in the clandestine sale in the 1980s of arms to Iran, the proceeds of which were used to fund Contra rebels in Nicaragua.

We went to France for the week, staying at John [record industry mogul] and Roz [part-time adviser to Cherie] Preston's house near Cannes, via Burnley vs Millwall, where I presented some prizes to young volunteers and was booed by Millwall fans. We had a nice time, and for the first holiday I could remember decided not to get any papers and just kept in touch with the odd phone call. It was probably a mistake because day by day things were building up and the Tories were getting a bit more traction. Hague, having scored big time on asylum, was now laying into the Tony Martin case and we were unsure how to respond.[1] It was all basically about getting the right-wing papers back on board for them. We got back from France late on Saturday evening. The Sunday papers arrived and it felt like diving straight back into a vat of total shit.

Sunday, April 30

Alison [Blackshaw, AC's PA] sent over a box and I sort of eased back into work. TB had done reams of notes in the last week, some of them repetitive, all of them focused on the need for strategy to improve and for capacity at the centre to strengthen. He was now of the view I should stop the briefings if possible, move as full-time as possible into strategy, with Charlie [Falconer] taking over the Grid, and get going soon. It was the right decision but would be difficult to execute given his propensity to involve me the whole time in the day-to-day stuff. TB wanted me to go down to Chequers tomorrow with Charlie.

Monday, May 1

The *Sun* did a big page 1 editorial, 'Mayday, Mayday, Crisis for Blair'. As I travelled down, TB drafted a reply. It was basically just a rebuttal setting out what we had done, not brilliant but OK. Then stupidly, having said TB wrote it, I sent them through a handwritten extract and then learned they intended to present it on the front under the headline 'Rattled'. Rebekah Wade [*Sun* deputy editor] and [George] Pascoe-Watson claimed [editor David] Yelland was behind it because he was desperate to be talked about and was curiously fond of Hague. Using TB's reply in this way would look like pandering, which was silly and would piss off everyone else. Of those concerns, the more serious was that serious people would think it not very prime

[1] Farmer Tony Martin had, in 1999, shot two burglars at his home, killing one and wounding the other. Convicted of murder, Martin was sentenced to life imprisonment, a cause of widespread public debate. A later appeal reduced the charge to manslaughter and Martin's sentence was reduced to five years.

ministerial for TB to sit down and rush off a response to a *Sun* editorial.

We went through various problems, sitting outside in the garden. It was really hot, fine for TB with his tennis gear but a pain for the rest of us in suits. Re GB, TB was clear that if we could work with him on board, all the better, but if not, in a sense we had to work round him, drawing him in whenever possible, but we must not allow the 'paralysing mist' that descended whenever he felt like it to paralyse us and prevent us doing the right things any more. Peter M felt that I had to lead a core team inside Number 10 with him, Charlie, Philip and Anji. TB wanted Charlie effectively to take over the running of the Grid. I feared this would give him ministerial problems which bizarrely, as a non-minister, but someone known to have TB's support, I was less prone to.

We went round the old arguments about whether or not I vacate the briefings and try to get more focused on strategy and agreed it was time to go for it, however difficult to execute. TB let slip that GB had said to him we had to decide whether we wanted my briefings to dominate the agenda. Clearly he didn't. We were also thinking that maybe Phil Bassett and Pat [McFadden] should go to Millbank. Peter M really seemed to be gunning for Jonathan at the moment. TB was very defensive about him, emphasising he was very good at trouble-shooting, but wasn't there for politics.

After lunch we had a quick game of football, me, TB and Calum vs Rory, Euan and Nicky, 9-9. We drove back with Charlie. Neither of us were totally clear how things would work in practice but I could just about see a way through. Charlie was convinced Mo would be OK with all of this but as she had at points wanted control of the Grid, I wasn't so sure. Godric was going to have to take on more of my work and would need more support. The most important thing was that we got up a sense of mission and strategic purpose again. TB had GB down later and said he was on for being much more co-operative. The news was totally dominated by the so-called 'anti-capitalist' riots in SW1. Both Churchill's statue and the Cenotaph were defaced. I put out strong words from TB, but was alarmed later watching the softly-softly policing in the streets where people were tearing up the lawns and wrecking anything they could find. It was unbelievably depressing and wiped out everything else on the news.

Tuesday, May 2

I hadn't slept well, worrying about how to put these changes into practice. Rover was leading the news. There was an interesting spat between Kennedy and Hague as the Libs were going flat out in the Romsey by-election.[1] GB wanted us really to go for Hague, who got a very easy ride on the *Today* programme. GB wanted research-based evidence on extremism. He then suggested we get Jim Callaghan [former Labour Prime Minister] involved. I called Jim who was for him very grumpy, to the point of being deeply pissed off. 'So someone is bothered with me after three years,' he said. He said he would never say anything because he knew how difficult it was to be in a position of leadership, but he didn't like some of the things we were doing, and he didn't like the constant repetition of New Labour as a deliberate foil to Old Labour, as though nothing they had ever done had been good.

We chatted for a while, and it ended perfectly amicably, but I did a note to TB saying he really needed to keep relations with some of our big figures from the past in better repair. I think what pissed off Jim more than anything is the sense he would get through the media that TB would be more worried about Thatcher and [Roy] Jenkins.

Whitehall was a sight after the riots, boards up, graffiti everywhere. We agreed TB should go out to the Cenotaph and do a clip. He went further than Jack S by saying we would try to stop marches like this in the future. TB's hair was absolutely wild, all over the place. Jack was very Jackish about it, said that would be very difficult. He was with John Stevens [commissioner, Metropolitan Police] who also said we mustn't go over the top.

My routine was now see or speak to TB first thing, GB meeting, my own government meeting, see TB again, then do what was needed to get everything ready for the 11. I did both briefings today, mainly focused on Ireland, Rover and the riots, all quite difficult. We had to organise TB a postal vote for Dobson, having decided on the next trip to Ireland. Peter M was working out of my office most of the day because he was not at the Northern Ireland meetings and very pissed off not to be so. He felt Number 10 and Jonathan in particular were not setting meetings up well, and also that TB was too prone to buying the line from Adams. There was a rather nasty little scene at the end of the day when, in front of officials, he rather mocked TB when he referred to 'demilitarisation'. Peter M said 'We call it normalisation. Don't use your Sinn Fein methods just because you've been absorbing

[1] Conservative MP Michael Colvin and his wife had died in a fire at their house in February. The Conservatives delayed the by-election to coincide with the local elections on May 4, allowing the Liberal Democrats time to gain traction in the Hampshire constituency and win with a 3,300 majority. The Labour vote collapsed to 1,451 – down from 9,623 in 1997.

them all day.' Peter was clearly feeling a bit isolated and undermined. He was also getting more and more grand in the scale and nature of his anecdotes.

Today was a good example of how hard it was to separate day-to-day and strategic. The politics of Northern Ireland was such that TB wanted me briefing on it, to get the sensitivities right, which Godric would be able to do in time, but you only got them if you were immersed alongside TB. I was trying to work up a new strategy paper but was constantly interrupted. I announced at the four o'clock we would be going to NI on Thursday, but Sinn Fein threw a wobbly, said it was all pointless and then Bertie threw his own spanner in the works. Jonathan and Bill Jeffrey [political director, NIO] went to see Adams and McGuinness at the Irish Embassy. It was all very touch and go and only TB seemed at all hopeful. I bumped into JP and we agreed that at the count for the mayor, he should shake Ken by the hand and be reasonably friendly. He sounded very fed up. Everyone seemed a bit fed up at the moment. I got home and worked till 1 after the kids had gone to bed.

Wednesday, May 3

The GB meetings were getting better. He and I seemed to be pretty much on the same page about how to respond on the day-to-day and we were engaging in real dialogue that was leading us somewhere. But there was still a tension between him and TB over the extent to which we said reform was the key message. GB was much keener on the setting of long-term goals. He felt we had to get deeper into arguments, not just slogans, get beneath the discontent that existed.

Cockerell was coming in for a bit of flak himself, with the papers obviously trying to set him up as a patsy in the hope he would be pressured into being a lot more negative than he otherwise might be. If anything he and Alison Kahn, his producer, seemed emboldened. I had lots of chats with Godric about him and how we take the situation forward and, for once, a good 'group of death' meeting. GB couldn't help pointing out later that these meetings were better without Peter there, exactly as Peter always said if GB wasn't there.

Thursday, May 4

I woke up to the feeling that we had a bad day ahead, on the mayor and electoral front and also re Northern Ireland. TB, having worried for so long about Ken, seemed alarmingly indifferent, said Ken was going to be a problem but there we are. But we all felt it was going to require a real empathetic response. I really felt the GB meetings were getting better, and GB was even beginning to get back some of his old humour. Cabinet did Northern Ireland, Zimbabwe, Rover and then the local elections. JP had a terrific crack when Robin was reporting on Zimbabwe and said Mugabe's slogan was 'Down with British imperialism'. JP said it sounded like a variation of traditional values in a modern setting [a favourite Prescott slogan].

On the elections, TB said we had to use them to focus the country on long-term decisions that would be seen through. He felt there wasn't great hostility out there, but indifference making it difficult to get people to vote. Robin described it as a 'pretty modest midterm crisis' but that we would need to steady nerves and get people to keep a sense of perspective. Ann Taylor made the same point, that there was a lot of goodwill but some of our own people would be taken aback at bad results and would need hand-holding. JR felt our problem was that nobody took seriously the Tory threat. GB said what was important was a clear and agreed message going out in the next few days. If we use it to stay focused on our long-term strategy, long-term goals, a lot done, a lot to do, it would be fine. We have to fight their slogans with deeper arguments around change and modernisation. He felt Hague was going for momentum at the expense of credibility, which was a good line. TB, for reasons best known to himself, was having lunch with [right-wing journalist and historian] Paul Johnson.

We collected him from there and headed off to the airport to head for Belfast. Bertie arrived. Adams and McGuinness came privately for a couple of meetings before going off to get the IRA to agree a statement. Things felt a little bit more hopeful. Over dinner, which was pretty relaxed, Bertie said there were three options. They come back with a good statement and we go snap. A bad one, and we go home, or one somewhere in between that means a long negotiation. I felt a little bit unworthy that my principal selfish thought in all of this was how to make sure I managed to get home to collect Calum and get to Scunthorpe on Saturday for what was, after our recent run, Burnley's biggest game in years. The big bad diversionary story – there always seemed to be one – was a leak of an Ivor Roberts [UK ambassador in Dublin] telegram saying Brian Cowen was basically a Sinn Fein supporter. TB spoke to Clinton and said at one point the big difficulty was losing the word Royal in the new Northern Ireland police service. Bill said why can't you call it 'former Royal' or 'Royal pain in the ass'?

I stayed up fairly late to watch the election coverage. It was all pretty grim for a while but then Romsey looked like going to the

Liberals, which changed it. Blunkett and Beckett were excellent on TV. Romsey was a massive blow to the Tories, though they did better than we feared in the local elections and London was even worse than we thought it would be.[1] Ken was sending out conflicting signals, one moment conciliatory, the next clearly indicating he would go for GB on the economy. Philip was calling regularly, said the party press office was really fighting to get the focus on Romsey but we really lacked heavyweights who could move a story. It was the kind of thing I used to do. As TB kept saying, we've stopped doing the things we used to do as a matter of course. We really needed to find new people. Philip felt we were pretty lucky in that, but as for Romsey, it would be seen as a bit of a disaster for TB [14.9 per cent swing against Labour].

Friday, May 5

I woke up to pretty nightmarish headlines. I went to see TB in the Queen's bedroom [at Hillsborough Castle]. He was pretty unfazed. Said he wasn't complacent and he didn't think this was so significant, though he didn't like us being neck and neck in the GLA [Greater London Assembly, Labour nine, Conservatives nine]. He was furious at a *Times* piece by Linda McDougall [documentary maker] on her programme with Mo, which was all about us doing her in. TB said he was fed up of this stuff and wanted to speak to her. He did, during a lull in the talks, and though he wasn't terribly stern, she probably got the message. He said we had never briefed against her and it didn't do her or us any good to have this take hold as some kind of truth. He said he was fed up of reading we had done her in because it simply wasn't true.

TB and Bertie did a series of meetings and the parties were all coming and going, but it wasn't clear where we were heading. Adams and McGuinness came through with their IRA statement, which was fine though slightly watered down, Brian Keenan [IRA representative] having insisted on putting in a line about 'the causes of conflict' next to the line about decommissioning. But it was pretty good. However, it was becoming clear through the day that Trimble, whilst reasonably happy on the decommissioning front, was desperate for something new on [the recommendations on policing in Northern Ireland by Chris] Patten to avoid problems being generated by David Burnside

[1] Livingstone had won the mayoral election with 57.9 per cent of the vote. Dobson came third. Labour had won only nine of the twenty-five Assembly seats. Elsewhere in the country, Labour lost seventeen councils and 574 councillors, while the Conservatives gained seventeen councils and 594 councillors.

[Ulster Unionist candidate in the forthcoming South Antrim by-election]. We had a whole series of arguments about the title of the new police service, with Trimble desperate to get some kind of reference to RUC in the title. John Taylor [UUP] suggested we say it incorporated the RUC but Trimble rejected that. It was all a bit roller-coasterish. We all had our own reasons to want to get away. TB for his birthday, Bertie was intending to go to Old Trafford tomorrow, I was desperate to get to Scunthorpe.

We seemed to be on for progress again after a Sinn Fein/UUP meeting upstairs went better than we thought it would. Ronnie Flanagan [chief constable of the RUC] was around and was keen to get on with it. Stephen Lander let us know he didn't much like the IRA statement but even Peter was satisfied it was progress. We had to go out and do the media both on this and London. I did a script for TB after he spoke to Frank. The backdrop was good, out at the stables, he got the tone right. There was an embarrassing moment, me having lined up Mark Simpson [BBC] to do something on Ireland and TB slapped him down, saying he was really focusing on London. His best answer was when he said he wasn't going to pretend he had changed his views about Livingstone but he was going to do his best to make it work.

I did a phone briefing with the political editors, who had realised Romsey was significant. It was pretty vile watching Ken on the news. The Northern Ireland stuff was really up and down and TB was getting a bit frantic. He spoke to [former President of Finland Martti] Ahtisaari to get him lined up on arms dump verification. We were also going for [South African lawyer and politician Cyril] Ramaphosa. So there was lots to move on but it was hard. I asked TB if I could leave early and he said yes. I had a long walk with Peter who felt that the Irish were being unreasonable, that if everything could be left to Bertie, it was fine, but his people kept getting to him. He visibly cheered up when I told him that Ken had said of GB that a Chancellor who wanted to be prime minister would have to look after London as well as he currently looked after Scotland. Earlier, TB and GB had had a bit of an argument on the phone about the nature of reform and the extent to which we made that our key argument.

I did the Sunday lobby down the phone with Cockerell filming in Number 10 and Alison Kahn with me. Godric said Cockerell then interviewed Jon Craig [*Sunday Express*] and Mike Prescott [*Sunday Times*] who were quite hostile. TB was really getting down at the idea that this thing could come crashing down over what we called the police force. As the thing dragged on, eventually I left in an armoured police car that whisked me through to get the 9.40 flight. I felt personal pleasure at leaving and knowing that I would make the match tomorrow, but professional guilt because I could sense both TB and Jonathan felt I should stay.

On the flight, I watched a couple of women reading the [Linda] McDougall piece in *The Times* [re Mo Mowlam], which they read from beginning to end, and I could see them thinking it was true. By the time we landed, I called through and it was all moving. They had pretty much got the deal. There would be a joint statement, a brief doorstep with TB and Bertie, the expectation of an IRA statement within twenty-four hours, Trimble not too bad about it. Jonathan and Tom Kelly both sounded genuinely excited about it. TB sounded tired but the atmosphere had been transformed. The key was the SF/UUP meeting. It also allowed us to say that Peter M had done a real job in talks, getting the UUs to move. There were all manner of questions but it was pretty good. I followed it late watching Sky News. We could be pretty pleased with the last few days' work.

Saturday, May 6

The NI breakthrough came too late to prevent the papers from being a real Livingstone orgy. Peter M did some excellent interviews as we waited for the IRA statement. TB was getting very down on GB again. He said they had had endless crazy conversations, but they basically agreed that GB constantly pretended that they didn't. His latest big thing was a 'goals' argument, that goals was a better communications vehicle than reform. TB said GB considered himself to be a great strategist but actually was better on the day-to-day. TB also found it irritating that GB didn't want to admit that anywhere apart from the Treasury was radical. TB was in better mood re Ireland but still felt we should try to persuade the Irish to move on the question of the RUC.

He spoke to Livingstone at 10.30. Because I was on the way to the train, I didn't listen in. TB said if I had, I would have vomited. 'He was basically just giving me lots of advice about the way forward.' He made clear he would like to be back in the party and also that he would challenge the London Tube plans in court. As PG said, we had buried him and now we had resurrected him as an act of policy. I got on the train with Calum and Charlie [Enstone-Watts, friend of Calum] and set off for Scunthorpe. I did the Sundays in a conference call from the train. I was setting out the difficult questions on the NI process, making clear that we were almost there. As I was speaking, Adams called Jonathan to say that the IRA statement, exactly as agreed, would

May '00: Atmosphere transformed in Belfast

be out in half an hour at 1. So at Doncaster Station, I did a conference call with Tom [Kelly] and Julian [Braithwaite] to agree what we should do and how we should announce it.

There was a fantastic feeling among the Burnley fans but Scunthorpe scored, and we went through a pretty dreadful phase and it looked grim. But we equalised, setting us up for half-time. We scored again and somehow we hung on. Everyone piled on to the pitch to wait for the other results, then it came through that we were promoted [from Second to First Division]. Fantastic celebrations. Somehow Calum and Charlie managed to get on the team bus and got their shirts signed before they got kicked off. On the train back, Peter M called to say the Channel 4 documentary on Mo was an outrage, and totally libellous of me. Then, at [Fiona's brother] Gavin's party Philip called re a *Sunday Telegraph* story that he and I had been behind a covert campaign to get the *Mirror* and the *Express* to back Steve Norris. It was a total fiction and I exploded at Chris Boffey [journalist and friend], who was acting editor. I got a lawyer to call them and ask for the cutting to be sent through. They agreed to change the headline, take out the picture of me. It was a good job Boffey was in charge. He said he had never heard me so angry and accepted what I said. Both TB and Fiona thought I should sue. The Sundays just made up what they wanted now and it was like swimming through a sea of shit every weekend.

Sunday, May 7

Ireland was dominating, with the IRA the lead in most papers, Clinton up on it and Peter M on *Frost*. I was working on the *Times* interview, saying to TB that we had to get back into a sense of conviction, that he was doing what he was doing out of belief. Alex called re our promotion, said that Darren (his son) had been man of the match for Wrexham beating Gillingham, and that there had been hundreds of Burnley fans there cheering them on. His take on the local elections was that it was a bit of a wake-up call. TB was pretty close to the end of his tether re Mo, who was clearly pushing all this stuff about being done in by us. Julia Langdon had a big piece in the *Mail on Sunday* saying Jonathan was 'the Downing Street poisoner'. TB felt Mo had made up her mind to get out and had decided to go as a victim rather than have anyone think she'd been a failure. He felt that she was trying to damage others as a way of protecting herself.

The [*Times*] interview was in the flat with Phil Webster and Peter Riddell and we went for it as a kind of New Labour relaunch. TB was good on Ireland, excellent on the big picture, London, the baby, and volunteered a few lines on the Mo stuff being a tissue of lies. He said afterwards he was tempted to write a piece himself setting out the truth – that he did ask her to go for mayor but she didn't want to, the opposite of what she was saying now. Both he and JP, who was mega-supportive at the moment, agreed that she was behind all this stuff. TB reckoned JP's current support was because we had stood by him so strongly when he was being kicked about. We had lunch at the Goulds', and Philip still felt there was a danger of erosion because we were weak on crime and patriotism. I got home to work on a strategy note for tomorrow.

Monday, May 8

The *Times* interview went well. They used it big and with a good editorial. And as Cockerell said, it was interesting to see the difference between TB's own words coming through and the constant mediation that was the norm. GB was on the *Today* programme re his [London School of Economics] speech [announcing tax credits for pensioners], but it was obvious to me that he was deliberately trying to hit a slightly different message to TB, so it was a lost opportunity. He came back saying we should have better research than the *Today* programme. His office was being done up so we had to move, making the meeting more chaotic than usual, and he didn't really want to engage when I tried to get him to focus on creating more events to get up long-term message. His speech included stuff on pensions and there was a feeling we had been punished in the local elections because of the [much criticised] 75p rise and we had failed to get up other help. We needed a strategy to put that right quickly.

Jonathan was in Dublin and although Ireland was in a better place, there were still problems to sort. TB was supposed to see Pat [McFadden] to get him to go to Millbank but he did it so badly that Pat just felt he was being shunted aside and he thought fuck it. Quite a few people had seen Rory Bremner [Channel 4 satirical impressionist], who had done loads of stuff on me, which all added to the sense of profile getting a bit out of control. At the 11, *The Times* had helped settle things down. I was pushed on Sierra Leone and avoided saying that our troops would not go into other duties.[1] Afterwards I had a meeting with TB, Anji, Cockerell and Alison Kahn to go over some of TB's concerns. He said he had to be honest in saying that he didn't always behave normally when a camera

---

[1] The escalation of the civil war prompted the deployment of British troops to evacuate foreign nationals and establish order.

May 'oo: Brown announces pensioners' tax credits

was there, because it did change the nature of an event. I still felt Cockerell basically accepted our argument about the media, but obviously there had to be some TB input. We agreed on a couple of meetings he could attend.

We had a little flurry later over Bharti Vyas [holistic therapist and beautician]. The BBC did a package on her and said she was involved in the preparation for the Blair baby. First Fiona, and then after speaking to Cherie, I spoke to her [Vyas] and said we wanted absolute guarantees that she did no interviews re Cherie and the baby, said that nobody was interested in her other than because of her inflated claims about her connection with CB and I would go for her publicly if she carried on trying to use it. I did a letter to the BBC attacking them for using such an item and got it out to PA. I just didn't know how we were going to deal with all this soap-opera stuff. A bit like [London Oratory school headteacher John] McIntosh, she burbled on about how the media were interested in her in her own right. TB felt more settled after the *Times* interview because there was a big argument he was confident in.

Tuesday, May 9

I felt that we were just about getting up the long-term message, but GB was still on about the need to get 'goals' up in lights. It was, as TB said, a non-argument being presented as a big strategic choice. I felt this week we were only going to get up one stabilising message. He felt all it said was that we were standing firm, that we didn't have much new to say. I felt it was right to make a virtue of saying nothing new. What was new was the emphasis on seeing through the difficult choices for the long term. Where I agreed with him was that the NHS consultation was coming over like we were asking people what to do, rather than engaging with them as consumers of a service. If we weren't careful, it was just a vehicle for horror stories in places determined to do down the NHS. GB's view was that it would simply crank up the demands for more money.

During the meeting news came through that the Rover/Phoenix deal was done so that changed the mood pretty quickly.[1] That, Ireland, and sticking to our guns on NATS [National Air Traffic Control Services was to be privatised] was the agenda for the day. We had the usual last-minute rush with TB's speech. On Rover, TB's instincts were far too political, wanting us to take credit and use it to bolster

[1] Rover was bought from BMW for £10 by Phoenix, a consortium formed by four businessmen and former MG Rover chief executive Kevin Howe.

Byers. I spoke to Byers and said it was important we weren't boastful, that we should let others take the credit, but he didn't really heed it. The Bharti Vyas report had got a fair bit of coverage, as did my row with the BBC, and when they tried to defend it, I really went for them, ended up storming out condemning them as 'wankers' to Cockerell before going to see TB to finish the speech. When I was working on it in the Garden Room [offices of the Downing Street secretarial support], they were all going on about how hilarious the sketches of me and TB were in the Bremner show, but I had heard enough, plus we had the *Sun* leader today, to realise that this was all potentially damaging. His speech [to an audience of magazine publishers] went well, good on the big picture and the long-term sense of mission and project, and TB injected a good line on cynicism as a way of explaining the Tory strategy.

I spoke to Martin Cruddace [*Mirror* lawyer] who reckoned I had an open-and-shut case for libel against the *Sunday Telegraph* because it basically said I was prepared to sell the Labour Party's soul. Jack Straw was over for a meeting with TB and came to see me to say he was worried that TB's strength was being turned into arrogance, and also that I was being turned into a problem for him and had to retreat. In a way, he said, I was too good at my job, and too interesting, and it inevitably drew attention to me because they saw me all the time. He felt the Bremner programme was genuinely damaging. It had taken them years to satirise Thatcher successfully, but this really captured something about Tony and it would weaken him. Also, he was worried that though TB was clearly the main focus of the government, there was little sense of him being the main focus for the party and we had to change that. He said *en passant* that the Treasury was a total pain to deal with. I think he had been genuinely well-intentioned in saying what he was saying and I agreed with the basic thesis. The question was what we did about it. I certainly think if I had known pre-Cockerell that the focus on me would grow as it was, I'm not sure I would have done it, but I still felt we needed to get out some sense of how the media operated politically and how they were twisting the whole debate.

I had a meeting with [UK ambassador to Washington Sir Christopher] Meyer and of course Cockerell was keen to film the two of us together. Meyer was really just talking trivia but it was OK for them. Godric did the four o'clock, which he described as desultory, when I met Charlie F to discuss his role. He seemed to think it was more about policy co-ordination whereas I thought what we had agreed with TB was that it was more about presentation. I could tell that Jeremy,

Jonathan and DM weren't that happy with the new set-up. What we needed was clear strategic direction from the TB, GB, Peter M, AC, DA etc. group and that events flowed from that direction.

There was a pretty big rebellion on NATS [Labour MPs voting against the Transport Bill] despite TB and JP saying that the pilots were not in the public sector. Pensioners were going to be a real problem though. Everywhere I went at the moment, people said there was real anger at the [pension rise of] 75p. The free TV licences, etc., were all fine but were seen as gimmicky alongside that. It was a classic case where one part of a successful strategy – keeping inflation low – led you to make mistakes in another – help for pensioners. I said to GB we could spend all we want but 75p is what's sticking.

Wednesday, May 10

I was hoping to get Cockerell out of our hair by giving him some TB access today but at the first meeting, TB was so obviously not himself, and by lunchtime he just wasn't in the mood for it, and we called it off. By then the Northern Ireland situation was going backwards again. Sinn Fein was saying the CBM [confidence-building measure, e.g. verifiable evidence of IRA decommissioning] was off if we changed Patten, which was a real problem because we had already done a deal on changing Patten with the UUs. TB had a stack of calls on it through the day.

Because it was good news, Rover was downplayed on the media, who were anyway just moving on to problems at Ford [the company had decided to end car production at its Dagenham plant]. The FT had a leak of the report on mobile phone safety which was likely to be the big news of the day. Asylum was the main focus of the 11, and we were working up some good lines on Hague and opportunism for PMQs, but TB was reluctant really to go for Hague yet. He wasn't in a great mood all day, probably because of Ireland.

As part of the attempt to get more strategic, I was now working on notes for TB for Cabinet to set the following week in strategic context. It was quite useful as a way of speaking to ministers who had big events on the Grid and trying to drive some kind of narrative through them. At PMQs, it was OK but I felt he could have gone for Hague a lot harder and the overall judgement was pretty negative. I sometimes worried about his touch. For example, Richard Burden [Labour MP whose constituency included Longbridge] asked a question which surely TB should have used to praise the work he did on Rover, as we had done in TB's article for the [Birmingham] *Evening Mail*. The cameras were in for the post-PMQs briefing. I felt I was behaving pretty normally, but they weren't and the thing lasted twice as long as it normally did. Mobile phone safety and Sierra Leone were running big. Hague was hit on opportunism a bit but I felt we let him off the hook.

Thursday, May 11

At the GB meeting, we decided against a statement on mobile phones. GB was worried about Ford and the impact on manufacturing but when Byers briefed Cabinet later, it was all much better news than we had feared. There was meant to be a TB/GB pre-Cabinet strategy meeting but Northern Ireland was going wrong. It was another of those issues that you couldn't believe might scupper the whole thing, namely flags. [John] Taylor said there could be no question of any Union flags being removed from public buildings. Sinn Fein was saying that any retreat on Patten would lead to the IRA statement being withdrawn.

GB took the meeting instead, with TB tied up on the phone, and we talked about how to get the health plan better placed. His problem on health was that there was very little sense of hard choices. We had the idea of TB doing a sustained two-day conference just on the health plan. TB hadn't done his [ministerial] box overnight. I tried to get him to focus on the Cabinet speaking note but he didn't, just burbled a bit, upset Mo by asking her to go through the Grid when I had already squared her not to bother, and then just kind of ran through my note without any real focus, so they left with no sense of message at all. I know he was preoccupied with Northern Ireland, but it was a wasted opportunity when we had slowly been reasserting the sense of strategy.

Jack Straw came for another little chat, he felt we were doing pretty badly in the North-West. They discussed Sierra Leone and Ford, which were also the main focus of the briefings. I went with TB for lunch at the *Observer*. He was on much better form, terrific on Ireland, relaxed about Ken and good on Europe. Back at the office, Mark [Bennett, AC's researcher] and I worked up the note for Cabinet into something that could be sent to all ministers.

I had a meeting with Chris Boffey to sort out the *Sunday Telegraph* situation. He said Joe Murphy [political editor] accepted he had got it wrong, had been bollocked rotten and they wanted it settled quickly. I agreed to a donation to the kids' schools, a page 2 apology including the line that the allegations weren't put to us. TB was on the phone re Ireland all day, and at 11pm Trimble was virtually in tears, saying it was over, he was finished, and TB trying to assure him he would stand by him but eventually saying 'I can't believe we are going to lose this because of the bloody flags issue.'

Friday, May 12

TB was really struggling to get Northern Ireland back on track with flags and the RUC still the main problem. Peter M was losing patience with the Irish. GB came in for part of a strategy meeting, but wasn't really contributing because Peter M was there. TB was trying to get structures sorted. The Sierra Leone situation seemed to be getting worse. I was due to speak at St Martin's Hotel to the British Society of Magazine Editors, who were a much nicer bunch than the political hacks. There were a load of people from my *Mirror* days. Again, the Q&A revealed far too much interest in me as me rather than as TB's voice. It was pretty lively, and I think worth doing to go over the long-term message. I got back to do a foreign press briefing and then an internal press office meeting to go through all the changes to try to free me up from the day-to-day. Peter H gave me an excellent note re our current problems, but I sensed their general feeling was that both TB and I would find it hard if my hands slipped at all from the day-to-day levers.

Saturday May 13

Philip G was back from the States, said he had learned a lot from the Americans about how to campaign while in government. Doug Sosnik [strategist, Clinton's political director] said the key was big leadership events, a clear strategy, constantly reaching out to the public rather than the press. Andrew Marr [*Observer* columnist and former editor of the *Independent*] was replacing [Robin] Oakley as BBC political editor. I called Marr, who was clearly very pleased. On balance, it was probably good news though it was slightly alarming the extent to which he talked about himself, rather than politics or the politicians. He said he wanted to give a leadership voice to the BBC. I said it would be inevitable that our opponents would try to present him as a Blair stooge and I was worried that might lead to over-compensation. We could also say in all honesty we knew nothing about it until today.

Sunday, May 14

Oakley called me, to say he was really angry that he was being described as a Tory in some of the papers and he wanted me to know how angry he was. His anger went way beyond that though. He said he had simply been summoned to a hotel at 10pm on Thursday and told he was going before his time. He sounded devastated, said he was devastated and felt betrayed and very bitter. I said I had always found him fair and reasonable and I was sorry he had been treated so badly. I asked him if he wanted me to generate people to say he was someone of independence and integrity, which he did. The *Sunday Telegraph* carried the apology.

[Andrew] Rawnsley had a piece saying we had only ourselves to blame for spin and cynicism. Robin was on *Frost* and I was pleased that he used the top line from the note on strategic objectives. Both TB and GB felt my note on Hague, which we were going to get Margaret [Beckett] to turn into a speech, had to be more forensic. If it was just attack, it would make us look rattled. Hague was now moving into changing the law on double jeopardy.[1] I spoke to Jack who said yes, it was opportunistic, but hard to attack. Jack had spoken to TB, and told him that he felt he was becoming a bit distant, a bit southern and that our language on manufacturing was wrong.

Monday, May 15

Northern Ireland and Sierra Leone were the main issues for the day but Hague was getting the usual uncritical ride on double jeopardy. Roy Greenslade [*Guardian* media commentator] had a big piece on the background to my *Sunday Telegraph* apology. There was a lot of anti-BBC stuff re the Queen Mum[2] and the Andy Marr job. We were getting the blame for pretty much anything at the moment. Charlie F came to his first GB meeting. GB had a speech today, again with the focus on the long term, which allowed him to do his 'goals', e.g. on child poverty. We agreed that Margaret B should do the Hague speech on Wednesday.

TB really irritated me at the office meeting. He had done another note basically saying that nothing ever happened, that he kept asking for things, particularly from departments, and then they just collapsed into nothingness. But a lot of this was about the lack of drive and focus at the centre. I also said that unless big messages were totally rooted in conviction, we would get hit. He said he felt he needed to see more journalists himself. I said the more they thought we worried about what they thought, the less they thought this was all being driven by conviction and belief. I said his note was all short term when his focus needed to be long term. We had to get into a mindset

[1] The legal principle that a defendant could not be tried again on the same or similar charges following an acquittal or conviction.
[2] The BBC had dropped plans to broadcast Queen Elizabeth the Queen Mother's hundredth-birthday celebrations. The Corporation was criticised for being out of touch with the British people. The celebrations would be broadcast by ITV.

of governing and not campaigning. I was also irritated by his refusal to see that our problems might have anything to do with him and his operation.

Interestingly, he had read Peter H's excellent note on the contamination of the New Labour, New Britain project and yet I felt had taken the wrong lessons from it. He used it to argue for a few short-term fixes when I read it as an argument for exactly the kind of long-term strategy I thought we were trying to pursue. The eleven o'clock was all Northern Ireland, after Ahtisaari and Ramaphosa meeting on CBMs, Sierra Leone, GB, and the Queen Mum, the MoD having sold sponsorship tickets for the hundredth-birthday pageant. Peter H basically wanted to be my sidekick on strategy which was fine. Lance [Price] had agreed to move to Millbank [as Labour's director of communications].

Anji called, said it was obvious Tony and I were really getting on each other's nerves at the moment. He felt that I was not really committed to pulling out of the day-to-day and also that I brought a lot of the media's anger that I experienced on to him. I accepted some of that, though it was hard to pull out of the day-to-day when he expected me to be on top of everything. I also felt he needed to stand back more and analyse what if any of the problems he railed against stemmed from him and his ways. Also, I pointed out, this was all pretty cyclical in any professional and personal relationship where you spent so much time with the same person. We had had our ups and downs but basically I thought he was a good thing, he thought I was a good thing and once we got the show back on track properly, it would be fine.

Tuesday, May 16

The *FT* had a ridiculous story on page 1 about TB's CBI speech, saying he was going to lecture business about its influence – all because I said our purpose as a government was to help the many not the few. This led to all manner of business people calling to complain. Jack was leading the news today on [flexible] sentencing, which was at least in the tough-on-crime department.[1] Byers was awesomely on-message on the long term. Jack was due to do the latest of the big-picture speeches tomorrow. But GB was lobbying TB to get him to block Jack doing a big thing on police numbers, which he worried would just become a spending story. The minister

[1] Straw proposed a more flexible sentencing framework for petty offenders, combining custodial and community-based punishments.

really hitting the right notes consistently and regularly at the moment was DB.

We still weren't in the right place on the NHS Plan. Pensioners were a massive problem and we didn't seem to be clear about how we dealt with it. The *Guardian* poll showed TB's ratings now very low, comparatively. Mo's were very high. She came to see me at 11.30 and we agreed she should go on *The World at One*. But she was all over the shop. Wanted to say we had changed course, kept scribbling things I was saying then playing them back at me, usually with a totally different meaning. I thought she should be on social exclusion, she just wanted to 'do drugs'. She said she ought to explain how many Cabinet committees there were, as if that added up to a row of beans. She said she wanted to say TB had 'gone through his strong leadership phase'. We also agreed she would say we didn't comment on polls, but she ended up thanking people for their support for her. Mike White [*Guardian*] called me after the interview and asked, genuinely, if she was ill. I think her basic problem, and she said as much to me, was that she hated the job and was desperate for a real role.

I was also dealing with Margaret Beckett re her speech on Hague, which was coming on fine, and I tried to generate overnight interest whilst avoiding it being a story about us being rattled. At the CBI, [Sir] Clive Thompson [CBI president] was giving us a whack on regulation so TB was a bit on the back foot about that. GB came for a meeting with TB and had a copy of Peter M's speech in Belfast, which he felt was a real problem because he was pushing the boat out on the euro, suggesting we could not get stability for our businesses until we were in it. GB was in a total rage, said it was an outrage and why didn't he just stick to Northern Ireland? He felt it was crazy to get the euro up in lights at a time we didn't need to. I spoke to Peter in Belfast and he did his usual feigning ignorance as to why there should be a problem. Of course, as he knew I would, I gave the line to the press that it was not a problem, that it was in keeping with our policy but of course they knew different from the Treasury who were now on the rampage. GB wanted me to say that only he spoke on EMU, which of course wasn't possible. It indicated how wound up he was. The press was on to the idea of a big split.

It was all Peter's fault, self-inflicted, and there was a danger it would totally block out TB's [CBI] speech in the press, if not TV where he was leading the bulletins. TB said it was above all a mistake because it gave GB ammunition. It had not been cleared at a time we were trying to get greater discipline. As if to add to the soap, CB was doing a case saying the government had broken the law on parental leave.

May '00: CBI gives government a whack

GB was not going to let go. He was in a real strop, arrived, threw down the papers, shook his head. Peter M paged me as the meeting was going on to say this was only a problem because the Treasury was stirring it up. I decided not to show it to GB, who was close to explosion already. It had cut across our overall strategy, though I guess you could argue it was a long-term issue. It also meant we were struggling to get Jack up on crime and now we also had TB watering down the attacks on Hague in Margaret's speech. He said he thought it was OTT. I said I gave up, that he just gave out conflicting signals the whole time. One day, stoke up the attacks on Hague. Then we do it, and he changes his mind. It was less the fact he didn't want to do the dirty work himself than the fact we kept chopping and changing that annoyed me.

The eleven o'clock was all Peter M, which I did my best to shut down, and Sierra Leone after a big firefight. People were at least starting to notice though the improved message discipline. Milburn called to say the weekly note must be maintained as it gave them the big picture in language they could communicate easily. JP noticed too, saying they were all beginning to sound like parrots. TB was a lot better at PMQs, partly because we had some really good killer facts to throw back at them.

The four o'clock went on endlessly about the euro. I had a meeting with Alan Milburn, along with Charlie, Philip, Peter H, Lance P and Robert Hill, to try to work up the major communications plan for the NHS Plan, including a big event with TB and all the professionals. Alan seemed pretty much on top of it, knew what he wanted out of it, but was very wary of any kind of real battle with the doctors. I said to him we had to get away from being the defenders of everything NHS to becoming the champions of the patient. I had a meeting with JP to go over all the new structures. He was willing to get back into front-line campaigning, providing there were proper structures and Rosie [Winterton, Labour MP and adviser to Prescott] was properly involved. He was worried about Mo, felt she was a problem and he found her whole way of doing business difficult to handle.

Fiona and I left to go for dinner at Delia Smith's with Mike and Sandy Molloy [AC's former editor at the *Mirror*, and wife], which was nice. TB called halfway through to say they were leaving for the hospital because Cherie was having contractions every twenty minutes. As soon as they left, we got a massive rush of calls, photographers landed like locusts, but it seemed to be a false alarm.

Fiona went down there and felt the hospital wasn't totally geared up for it. Cherie was really pissed off at being swarmed by photographers through the car window. TB said it was grim down at the hospital, that they were literally swarming all over the place. Earlier, I told Don Macintyre [*Independent*] I didn't believe this stuff about there being political bounce out of the baby though there may be a bit of empathy towards TB that cooled at the edges the hostility against him.

Thursday, May 18

Phil Bassett did a very good analysis of the commentators which showed very clearly that most now saw it as their job to do in the government. At GB's 8am meeting, we discussed how to deal with Hague's speech [to the Police Federation, calling for prosecution appeals against lenient sentences]. He was definitely getting momentum at the moment and people would feel he was speaking up for them. There was a 'group of death' meeting, Peter only there for a bit and he didn't say much, which given GB's continued simmering over the euro was no bad thing. Charlie had been to a few of GB's morning meetings by now, and felt that GB perpetually wanted to put himself just to the left of TB. The strategy meeting was perfectly good after a bad start and at least we were all clear that we needed to keep going on the long term, laying down bigger arguments. At Cabinet, TB explained the changes at the centre and emphasised the need for them all to engage in bigger arguments. Robin and Geoff [Hoon] took them through Sierra Leone, and Peter set out where we were on NI.

TB used the note I had done to go through the political stuff, emphasising the long term and trying to get them to root what they did in bigger messages of economic stability, civic society, the responsibility agenda. The record of our campaigning, and our time in government, showed that we were best when we had these big-picture messages out there the whole time. I did the weekly note for ministers then had a meeting with Alistair Darling [Social Security Secretary] and Peter H to go over all of the problems in his area, 75p, how to get people to see there was such a thing as good welfare spending as well as bad, fraud, housing benefit. AD felt the best we were likely to get in his area was a draw, and he certainly had a lot of difficult stuff on his plate, but I felt we had a lot of good stories to be told, and some big arguments we could win.

I then left for the ad agency [TBWA] and was there from 2 till 8, going through the process, kicking around ideas. GB came down from 3 till 6 and we split into little groups to put together fifty-word mission statements. I was with Ed Miliband and we concluded on something like 'We exist to put power, wealth and opportunity in the hands of the many not the few so that lower- and middle-income families enjoy rising living standards and public services they can trust. And by confronting the forces that hold people back we liberate talent to build a fairer, more prosperous Britain.' It was quite a good exercise and what emerged was that people felt we were better at defining what we weren't than what we were. GB was back on his goals. Peter H was arguing we needed more enemies. But it was a good session and I wished we had more time to do this kind of thing.

GB and I were engaging well but he clearly felt that we played up New vs Old Labour too much and nobody really knew what the Old vs New Britain divide was. I wish we had been able to stick with forces of conservatism. We needed to be breaking more eggs for better omelettes. I also felt TB's fall in ratings was in part a consequence of a sense that 'all things to all men' meant no conviction.

Friday, May 19

I went straight to TBWA for the second part of what was becoming a brainstorm/bonding exercise. Charlie F and I worked together on a speech which we then delivered. We were moving towards the idea that the focus had to be on middle- and lower-income families, that tough decisions were being taken to improve their livelihoods and public services. What was clear was that GB and what TB sometimes called his disciples were convinced we needed an enemy, and that we had to be against the top people in our society to be in favour of 'the many'. TB was worried not just that they were wrong, but it meant they misunderstood what New Labour was, and its potency as a political force.

It was clear though that when the ones basically there with GB talked, they always positioned just to the left. They didn't really get the idea that business was a key to helping deal with social exclusion, that somehow one could sit in a separate silo to another. I said that yes, we were for lower- and middle-income families, but we should not be against people who were better off because we wanted them to support our position as being a benefit to the country as a whole. We all had to write little speeches. Philip's was very Philip but too solemn and too much like an opposition speech. Bob Shrum's was very good, all about connecting with people's lives, and I certainly felt we didn't have the strength Thatcher had at giving people a feeling she was fighting for them. We were really back to the forces of conservatism argument and the disagreement was about what they were and how to identify them.

After lunch, we split into pairs again and had to get the mission statements down even shorter. I was now with Charlie F and Johnny Hornby [TBWA joint managing director] and we wrote that 'We exist to give middle- and lower-income families life chances taken for granted by the privileged and so build a prosperous, confident Britain.' Douglas and Ed were in a different place to Philip and Peter, who were on the responsibility agenda, but Bob [Shrum] and Sally were still hitting the top ten per cent. The moderator had a voting system and Charlie and I won by seven with Bob/Sally second, PG/PH third.

TB, when I reported back, said it sounded like GB's people were basically in the wrong place, that we had to get back to a more New Labour message because it was the middle classes that we were losing and we would get them back through crime, welfare reform and the economy. And if we got them back we'd do better with our heartlands. He felt GB was buying into the idea of an either/or situation when it had to be both. We were doing lots with the poor, but we were losing support in the middle ground because there was a sense of stealth taxes and not getting crime. I was quite taken by the TBWA guy who did the focus groups, who said that if we were to say to the groups that Hague was extreme or for the privileged few, they just wouldn't get it. They saw us as privileged because we were in government. We really had to understand how some of these distinctions were blurring. I had found the two days useful, and the TBWA people were lively and clever, but TB was worried we had reached the wrong conclusions.

Fiona had gone off with Cherie to the hospital and they were pretty sure the baby was going to be born fairly soon. TB stayed in the office till about 8 and Anji said later he had been really nervous, nervous about the politics of where we were, nervous about the baby and what it would do for him, Cherie and the way we work. TB called as he was going to the hospital. I called Anji to get Cockerell down there to film the media outside. Fiona kept me in touch through the night. It finally came at 12.25 and we decided not to put anything out until they got home. I was in bed when Fiona texted that it was a boy. I called through, spoke to TB who sounded very happy about it. I heard the baby and TB said 'Here you are Leo, talk to your spin doctor.'

Saturday, May 20

Fiona got back about 4 and was still out to swim at 7. The media was going into meltdown on it, leading every bulletin, every spit and fart.

May '00: Leo introduced to his spin doctor

TB sounded elated and was pleased that he had been able to get home. But he was still talking about our political problems. He genuinely felt that our problems were as much of perception as of reality. I agreed with him that he would have to go out and say something in the street. Jonathan and his little daughter Jessica were all over the news coverage as the only people in the office to go through the front door. I thought it best to stay away, rather than have the whole thing seen as a spin operation. Fiona went in with Grace and said that before TB went out he was incredibly nervous but did fine, though they would no doubt have a field day with his mug, which had a picture of the kids. He still underestimated how much they gorged on this kind of stuff.

TB and I must have spoken four or five times during the day but usually about the political scene, which he was really running around his mind the whole time. He said we had to stay bang in the centre ground. 'I know I am right. I am where the country is. Hague is more right wing than the country and GB is more left wing than the country. We have to stay where we are.' I did a conference call with the press office to agree a few lines that we could put out. We were just about avoiding the accusation of spin but the press were desperate to push us there, while simultaneously wanting to fill pages and pages. Simon Walters [*Mail on Sunday*] was desperately trying to find out whether TB was going to have a vasectomy and asking as if he had a right to know. I watched the FA Cup Final [Chelsea 1, Aston Villa 0] which was about as boring a game as I could remember. There were loads of messages coming in from the Queen, Hague, Major, lots of foreign leaders. TB was genuinely baffled by how big it was around the world. He said sometimes he found it really hard to take in that everything he did was potential news. After a while I couldn't take any more of the endless babbling bulletin two-ways.

Sunday, May 21

TB was boasting about how he had been changing nappies. Nicky and Euan both got followed by cameramen so we had to work out how to handle that. And we had a little drama at the start of the day because Cherie had put a picture of the baby on the [Downing Street] intranet which Fiona got taken off pretty sharpish. We weren't going to be putting pictures out until tomorrow. As the *Observer* said, I was in a bit of a no-win situation: do too little and we alienate the press, too much and they would say we were exploiting it. Mary McCartney [photographer] was going in to do the pictures today and we were going to put them out tomorrow. We agreed with CB that she would put out a few words in a statement. Fiona went in when Mary was doing the pictures and said it was very normal (!) family life. Euan punched Nicky. Gale [Cherie's mother] was in tears. TB had wanted to wear one of his silly Nicole Farhi creations but Fiona managed to get him into a denim shirt. The Sundays were full of TB/GB/Peter. TB was worrying that they would never work together properly.

Monday, May 22

I got in and went up to see TB. The baby was upstairs asleep. There was a lot of focus on what sort of paternity leave he might have and we agreed that he wouldn't be doing PMQs and Cabinet, but he would do the Queen. I put together a script on the photos, and Robbie Montgomery [Mary McCartney's agent] came in with an assistant and assured me they were able to cope with the demand. We quickly chose the one free photo we would send all round and then picked fourteen others that could be used at £500 a time for two cancer charities, which was Fiona's idea.

TB had decided that we were doing the right things and in the right place but we were not communicating properly. I felt that that was arrogant and wrong. He didn't buy the idea that we should emphasise we were for middle- and lower-income families, or working families, because these were exclusive messages. People basically think it means working class and we had to be careful. He felt all our problems came from where we were not New Labour – on crime not being tough enough, on asylum sending out the wrong signals, pushing on the anti-poverty agenda without regard to the impact on taxation with the result that we got little political credit for doing the right thing. At least we were having proper strategic discussion again. He also wanted me to have one-on-one meetings with all the key ministers and get them all properly fitted into a strategy. The eleven o'clock was mainly about the baby though the first question was about the Dome, and the story that more money from the Lottery was to be used to help it. The Dome was becoming a total disaster area. But again, even on that, TB didn't want to admit he was wrong. My worries about the pictures were founded when Robbie's website system didn't work and we had to get staff down there to sort it. Jonathan and I went up to see TB a couple of times and he was just sitting there holding the baby, all gooey-eyed.

I had a big meeting with the SCU and the press office to try to get them more fixed on the broader agenda. I was trying to get a grip on strategy but it was bloody difficult when stuff just kept coming at me. Cockerell made an interesting observation, said that since some of the papers had decided to set him up as a patsy, they now talked to him when he was out and about and he ended up being quoted as a Downing Street insider. He felt he had been on the receiving end of a mild version of what we got the whole time. I got home with Fiona, and Frank and Janet Dobson were round for dinner. He looked a lot better and said he wasn't bitter but he felt the whole operation had been poor. Millbank lacked leadership and the campaign operationally had been weak. He felt that we had been up against someone in Ken that we didn't really understand.

The pictures were running fine but the Dome fiasco meant we were into scapegoat territory on that with Chris Smith [Culture Secretary] and Hezza [Michael Heseltine] calling for Bob Ayling's head as NMEC chair. TB called late after he had seen GB and said he had been pretty hard with him, said that people were going to start blaming him for what was going wrong because he was pursuing an agenda not always consistent with one on which we were elected. He felt that GB's people felt that we were the style and they were the substance and it wasn't a sensible way to think.

Tuesday, May 23

Apart from the odd columnist, the coverage on Leo was fine and I felt we handled it OK. GB at his meeting was angry and frustrated that we couldn't get up the NHS Plan, but the stories just weren't big enough. He said [health minister John] Denham sounded like a bank manager with no passion or conviction. He was beginning to see that it wasn't always easy to stay on top of the agenda. A quick look at the editorials showed Europe, welfare, Dome, [TB's] paternity leave, Sierra Leone, it was a bit all over the shop. I went to see TB in the flat and he said I had to make an effort to look less fed up because my moods had a powerful impact around the place. I said it was partly workload but it was also because I felt he was wrong in some of his analysis. He basically believed all the substance was right but we needed better systems to deliver a message. I felt that whatever systems we had they ended up with me doing more and more, and he kept saying he wanted me to do less and less.

I went to see Blunkett with Phil Bassett to try and get him properly plugged in to longer-term planning and also to get his agreement to do more with the [media] commentariat for the government as a whole. I signed up John Reid to do the same. Jack Straw came in later and I went through some of the polling on crime. It wasn't good for us, the Tories were moving and we had to get back focus and drive. We had to get the dividing lines back in the right place. We then saw

TB who set out his washing-line theory, the need for individual stories and items of policy to hang from a bigger message. Jack was up for it and realised we needed to do better to get it back and although there was a reality problem with police numbers we had to get proper focus on how things were under the Tories.

Later I had a meeting with Jack, Charles Clarke and their [Home Office] press people and special advisers to work out a system of communicating on crime. Although Charles could be very bumptious, they did seem up for the idea of doing this together. We had to be in a better place by the time of the party conference and we had to start hitting the Tories harder on opportunism. Liz Lloyd [home affairs policy adviser] said afterwards she had never seen them more motivated and focused. She said even TB had not been able to get them going.

We picked up that the Tories were briefing on pensions and their plans to give a bigger rise in the basic state pension. They were really motoring at the moment and getting out big policy hits at a time we were vulnerable. I was working with Bill Bush, Ed Miliband and Ian Austin on rebuttal. They had managed to re-create themselves as a blank page which meant the media were giving them a very easy ride and hitting us hard. I got home and told Fiona I was really fed up with it and felt that whatever changes we made, I would have too much to do. Anji was offering to progress chase and organise for me but I felt the problems were deeper than that.

Wednesday, May 24

I went up to see TB in the flat, who felt we had to turn the pensions issue against them and have it unravel by the end of the day. Darling was terrific in the head-to-head with [David] Willetts [Shadow Social Security Secretary]. It just showed how important these ministerial interviews were, not just through what the public heard but also because of the confidence they could inject into the system. TB felt we had to be more robust on the Dome. I said that was a good example of where whatever the reality, he wouldn't admit he made the wrong decision. Or what about putting Frank Field in the government. Even on that, he said he was basically right. On his chat with GB, he said he told him he wasn't right to think that if we did badly only TB would get the blame. It wasn't so. GB would get the blame too.

He called me up again in the afternoon, he was sitting with the baby again. Anji had mentioned that I felt despondent and he wanted to know why. I said it was partly because I felt there was too much pressure falling on me. He said that was why he wanted me doing

May '00: Frank Field for government job?

less of the day-to-day and he agreed it was hard. We had the usual round of meetings with JP pre-PMQs and I went over to the House with him. I had to work hard at persuading him not to tear into Frank Field.[1] He did fine. [Veteran Labour MP Dennis] Skinner came in and was helpful. Darling had done a terrific job all day and I felt by the four o'clock we were in a stronger position.

Mo was on, wanting to move the line on drugs again tomorrow. She really did need a role. There had to be a way of using the talents that had made her popular to help the government and the party and TB but none of us seemed to be able to work out what it was. JP agreed to go to Dunkirk for the veterans parade. At the Grid meeting, we agreed to try to reopen the whole issue of compensation for Far East PoWs, and the idea of a veterans minister. *The Times* did a poll showing what they called a mild 'Leo effect'. PG did some groups tonight and one of them was absolutely dreadful. Three out of the eight people felt the baby was conceived for electoral purposes. Philip said spin was really hitting us, though opportunism was getting through and hurting Hague a lot.

Thursday, May 25

The *Mirror* were doing a big number on Dunkirk boats being rejected for lottery money so we were trying to sort that out. At GB's meeting, we reckoned we had done OK on pensioners but now needed a bigger message on reform. GB said he might say something about the girl rejected by Oxford who went to Harvard when he spoke at the TUC equality conference.[2] It was a bit of a risk not knowing all the detail, but he was very up for it. I stayed behind to talk with him about TB's note of last night which said that our problems were Middle England issues. GB said he feared that TB wanted to get us to a different position and that we would cede too much ground. TB's argument was that we ceded the ground in the centre if we shifted to the left. GB believed we had an alliance which meant we could focus on jobs and the social justice agenda whilst maintaining support for it in the centre ground. He felt that the way TB was crafting the argument for his speech to the Women's Institute risked it becoming the equivalent of Back to Basics [moralising policy disaster for John Major]. Philip

[1] Prescott did in fact criticise former social security minister Field, the man Blair had asked in 1997 to 'think the unthinkable'. Prescott said if Field supported Conservative calls to scrap free television licences for the over-75s and the Winter Fuel Allowance, 'That is the kind of unthinkable thought that I don't accept.'
[2] Laura Spence, a pupil from a state school in North Tyneside, was rejected by Magdalen College despite her predicted five A level 'A' grades.

felt TB's note was very in your face and a direct challenge to GB's analysis. TB didn't believe we had a substance problem. He believed we had a communications problem, which was counter-intuitive because we were meant to be so good at it, particularly him.

GB had done his own note which he gave to me for comments. They weren't that far apart on the arguments but I put in a few more sections and changed a few words to make it more TB-ish and GB incorporated most of them. He was very much 'many not the few' but in a far more aggressive way than TB. I had another chat with TB later, on what I called the 'Is he ever wrong?' issue. I said his instincts were good but e.g. on the Dome, he had been wrong. He said actually his instincts had been against it but he was persuaded to do it, and though he wished he hadn't been, he still believed it was possible we would have endured damage of a different kind had we not done it. Likewise with Frank Field, he felt he had to be given his chance and had he not been, serious people would have felt that was the wrong thing to do.

Cherie popped in with the baby and I said I was telling TB how he got it wrong from time to time. She said where he was most wrong was letting GB have so much control. He said we must not make our problems more complex than they are. I had a pre-meeting with JP before Cabinet. I had done a speaking note for him and he pretty much went through it. GB and AD did an excellent presentation on pensions. I had been really impressed with Darling this week. Chris Smith went into far too much detail on the Dome. Mo was in a visible sulk. TB had seen her earlier and hadn't really hidden how down he was on her but I felt she was dangerous like this, a real loose cannon.

I went for lunch with Trevor Beattie. I liked him a lot. He was an enthusiast and an optimist and clever. He felt we were actually in good nick, better than it felt at the centre, and people were easily seeing through the Tories. I got back to a TB/GB meeting at Number 11 with a cast of thousands. TB spoke to his note, saying our problems were not of substance but of communication. GB was on the line that we needed greater definition and we would only get it through controversy, e.g. the Oxbridge row. TB was clearly exasperated, felt that they were trying to move to a class-based politics that was counter to the basic New Labour message, and also, he felt, politically stupid. He had seen now the alternative messages we had done at the agency away days and he felt the GB-people versions were workerist. We had to be inclusive. Don't forget that in attacking the top ten per cent, you had fifty per cent either thinking they were in the ten per cent or who certainly thought they should be. I said the enemy had to be the Tories. They were the ultimate forces of conservatism. We needed to work out where we wanted to be at the election in issues terms, on dividing lines, and work back from that. GB felt we weren't doing enough to set out next steps and big goals.

It was an OK meeting, and ended up with an agreement that I would oversee a long-term Grid. There wasn't that much disagreement between TB and GB. Ed Miliband and Douglas were putting a more leftist case and saying we needed to be even more focused on poverty. I had a two-hour Grid meeting to try to draft an outline Grid for twelve months. It was hard work but we had something vaguely in shape by the end of it. GB had pretty much slipped the Oxbridge row past TB. Godric did the four o'clock at which Oxbridge was raging as a big story. We went out for dinner with the Goulds and Tessa [Jowell] and David [Mills, her husband] for my birthday. Ian Hutchison [Baroness Helena Kennedy's husband] came in while we were there. I tore into him because of Helena's latest blast at us. She was more and more oppositionalist and it had definitely been a mistake to give her a [House of Lords] platform. There are too many people who owe their platform to the Labour Party and just use it to undermine us the whole time. GB was leading the news on Laura Spence.

Friday, May 26

I drove in with Philip and we listened to DB on the radio re Laura Spence. It was tricky. On the one hand, it was a classic opportunity message where there seemed to be a British elitist bias against a girl from an ordinary background. On the other it was always risky when politicians alighted upon individual stories without knowing all the facts. And of course it played into the current argument TB and GB and their people were having. My instincts said we had to fight for the argument and that meant supporting GB whatever the fallout. The fact that the BBC were moving on to Oxbridge domination of the senior Civil Service was, in my view, a good thing for the purposes of winning the argument. I arranged to get Robin motoring on what he was doing in the FCO to try to widen access [to senior posts]. At least we were dominating the agenda with a big argument again, though there were risks. TB was reasonably OK about it, provided, as he said to GB on the phone when I was up in the flat, we stay on it as an opportunity message, not some kind of class war against one of the best universities in the world.

The press were basically against what we were doing, so we had to hold firm. TB's worry was exactly as he had said re the ten per cent argument. Oxbridge may be an elite but an awful lot of people want to get into it. TB said he had reflected on yesterday's meeting and he was worried GB was being badly advised. He and I had a meeting with Charlie F on the Dome. I said we had to get the line running that the papers hated it but the people loved it. TB was getting more and more worried about it. Charlie said PY [Gerbeau] was determined not to let the politicians influence it, but he had to understand the politics of this. I left to work on JP's speech for Tuesday on heartlands/Middle England, which I felt could be an important message for the party. Unfortunately JP pulled out of Dunkirk. I had to deal with [Labour MP, former arts minister] Mark Fisher's nasty letter to his constituency members about me and the 'nauseating' campaign against Mo, so I put together a reply on that.[1]

Saturday, May 27

RC said he was 'apprehensive' about the elitism/opportunity debate, but he did fine on *Today*. Richard Wilson didn't like the Oxbridge briefing to *The Times* re the Civil Service, and called to complain. I said Robin had acknowledged the progress he was trying to make, so he should relax. GB wanted to do a bit of reshaping of the CSR to take the message forward, e.g. more money to help top universities find students from poorer backgrounds and schools in tough areas. I put together lines from JP's speech as the basis for a big-picture briefing for the Sundays, which I did just after the narrow but successful UUP vote on the IRA statement, leading to restoration of the institutions. I felt at the briefing that we were in the right place re opportunity for all vs privilege for a few, but we really had to watch them taking it into a big class-war splurge in the Sundays. Needless to say some of them twisted what I said and claimed it was a 'cool it' message from TB to GB. Either that or they were being led there, in Simon Walters' case possibly by Mo, others maybe by Peter M. Peter was totally opposed to what we were doing, and was winding up TB over the weekend.

I watched Brazil vs England [1-1], interrupted only by the *Sunday Times* who had got a leak of some of PG's memos on recent focus groups. So a big bad story was looming. Philip was worried. On Thursday he had taken a call from London Transport lost property re some of his memos, which he feared was a hoax, because we had already heard by then the [*Sunday Times*] Insight team were looking into them.

[1] Fisher's letter had found its way into the *Daily Mail* and elsewhere, saying 'The nauseating spin campaign against Mo Mowlam suggests that Downing Street is still in the grip of the southern, modernising spin doctors.'

May '00: Gould worried re memos leak

Sunday, May 28

The papers were not brilliant on GB/Laura Spence. The Tories were managing to lead the news with some new crapola written on the back of a fag packet on pensioners/war widows. PG was in a bit of a funk re his leaked memo. He was always leaving stuff lying around. Also GB had lost his gym bag and there had been papers in that too. TB said he had to get used to the fact we were in a tougher environment, and get more disciplined re paper. It was true there were far too many florid notes flying around and they were circulated far too widely. David Davies [FA] called saying they really needed our help in legislating to stop known troublemakers going to Euro 2000. Jack was setting out the difficulties but TB was adamant we had to make it happen. Jack was banging on re the ECHR and NCIS [National Criminal Intelligence Service] fears about compromising intelligence sources etc., which were classic Home Office arguments designed for inaction.

I had an interesting call from Rosie Winterton, who asked me whether I thought JP should give up his department to take on a more traditional deputy-type job, and to get more involved in campaigning, possibly based in the Cabinet Office. I doubted very much that she phoned without John knowing, and that he was testing the waters. I said it all depended on what he wanted to do long term, but I could certainly see a big role at the centre, motivating the party, doing loads of the committees and trying to help us keep GB and Peter M in order.

Monday, May 29

We got away with murder on Philip's memos, which barely featured in the press. It showed that there were times where provided we all exuded insouciance, they would just fade away as a story. I actually felt it could have been a lot more damaging. The Treasury had briefed [Phil] Webster on the CSR opportunity message which was the splash in *The Times*, focused on the extra education spending so we were still motoring fine on that. John Kingman [Treasury] called to say GB wanted me to find a way of taking it all forward, and with JP's speech coming up, we could do that, saying the CSR would get us right back on the people's priorities, meeting the demands of the heartlands and Middle England alike. JP hitting a basically New Labour message was exactly what we needed at the moment.

GB called later and was clearly still worrying about all the fallout, said all he had ever said was that they needed to look at how the [Oxbridge] interview system was working, and it was a scandal someone like this felt she had to go abroad. JP was totally up for the message we wanted and I put together an overnight briefing note based on my draft and some of GB's words from earlier. Peter M called, said it was a dreadful error to have got into this and the sooner I got us out of it the better. I said we had to keep going, to show confidence and to maintain a real 'many not the few' divide. I talked to JP re the lines for the *Today* programme in the morning. He was going down to Leeds Castle for a Tony Bennett concert and didn't want a radio car in case they realised that's where he was!

Tuesday, May 30

JP was the splash in several papers, the lead on the broadcasts and stayed there for much of the day, showing again that if you get up a theme, you can drive good coverage. He called to go through the difficult stuff and felt he wasn't fully up to speed on some of the education detail. He did fine. GB was a bit panicky, not just about our electoral position, but also his own position with quite a lot of fire aimed at him, *The Times* in particular. He and I both worked on the columnists and leader writers and agreed I should do the eleven o'clock. Philip and I listened to JP as we drove in and he was superb. There was a real sense of message and an agenda being driven. For all the criticism, I think GB did the right thing, and we did the right thing defending and promoting it. By the evening news, JP's speech was the focus of six minutes' coverage, including a big package comparing British and American universities, and I felt it was where we needed to be – opportunity for all while the Tories defend the status quo. We had done very well media-wise with the extra money for talent spotters. TB was still a bit nervous but happy enough provided we kept it on the right side of the tracks.

He was getting more and more frustrated about the system though and railing at me to the point where I said 'Don't rail at the one person doing his damnedest to get you the system you want.' PG and Peter M had separately seen TB yesterday and Philip felt strongly Peter wasn't really in the same place as us and was not responding to TB. Peter paged me later to say 'It's come to a pretty pass when JP has to rescue GB from himself.' I sent a message back that the commentators may be against us but I felt the public in the main were with us. The most important thing was that we had ministers now promoting what they were doing on policy in a more coherent way.

I had a long chat with Blunkett and then Milburn about their role in the next period. Alan still felt to me a bit cautious, very much wanting consensus in the NHS before really going for it. I felt our

May 'oo: Brown panicky on two fronts

problem in health was that delivery wasn't really happening and the reform message wasn't really flying. Both needed to happen. Seeing that we could still get good coverage for a speech, as with JP, should give the others more confidence. I had a call from headhunters asking if I was interested in going to Manchester United. TB was at Chequers and visited by Kevin Keegan, Alan Shearer, David Beckham and David Davies as part of the launch of the Football Foundation [sports charity]. During dinner, Ian Hutchison called round, on a clear pretext, but obviously wanted to discuss the row we had had about Helena. I said as far as we were concerned she had put herself beyond the pale by being so clearly oppositionalist. She abused the patronage and made our life a lot more difficult. Fiona said we had persuaded TB and others that she would be more than just a figure of opposition. After I went to bed, I got calls on *The Times* splash and universities charging more for tuition fees.

Wednesday, May 31

A combination of an end to the postcode lottery [for good NHS treatment], the waiting-list plan and bringing back matron gave us a real message on health. Milburn did fine and the combination of the NHS consultation exercise plus waiting lists led the news all day. TB and I had both been against the consultation, which was costing half a million quid, and by the end of the day the story was fiasco because it wasn't clear when replies were meant to be back. JP got great coverage but the commentators were really whacking us all over the place. The *Mail* had no fewer than three columnists on basically the same line – that the whole Laura Spence row was Old Labour instincts reasserting themselves. Anji said she felt the whole Middle England part of our coalition didn't like it. TB was unsure we should have had JP out on it. I said there was nothing in John's speech or interviews that could not have been said by TB before the last election. It was his language that had changed, it was him that was moving to the right and it was very depressing. His response was that he hadn't changed, but he had always known there was a danger if we tried to pursue one part of our coalition – the heartlands – in a way that might alienate the others.

I left with Robert Hill for a meeting at the *Telegraph*. Charles Moore [editor] clearly thought we had taken leave of our senses re Oxford. They were genuinely interested in the health plan and although politically we were miles apart, I felt at least they would give it a hearing. GB admitted to me later we should have done more to check out all the facts on Laura Spence, but he still felt justified that the focus was all on opportunity.[1] I got back for the Grid meeting, which was a bit bad-tempered and at one point I had a bit of a go at Anji, Charlie F and Phil Bassett re using private education [for their children]. Anji came round and said I really had to cool down on the class-war stuff. Stan Greenberg and Philip came round with the latest polling. The Tories were up three, we were down six and our loyalist core was smaller than at any time. Stan said there was real erosion. Our problem, compared to the Tories in power, was that we would never get that sense of pre-election boom that the Tory media always created. It was a pretty depressing meeting.

Charlie and I went to see Gus Macdonald and his team on the transport plan. Gus was very switched on, had got his team working well and I felt a lot more comfortable when I left. I went round to see GB, who was beating himself up a bit at not having thought through Laura Spence, but I assured him I felt we were still in the right place and he now needed to use the CSR to keep going with an opportunity message. We agreed to meet again tomorrow to agree some of these in practice. I got back for a meeting on the NHS, and there was definitely a bit more energy round the place. It was odd, though I guess inevitable, that if people felt we were driving an agenda publicly, it became easier to do it internally.

Thursday, June 1

Oxford dons were out attacking GB, and Boris Johnson [*Telegraph*] had a big piece saying the big split was the one between TB and me, suggesting this had all been my work as a militant state-education activist. I met GB and we worked up a pre-CSR Grid to get us in the right place, with the dividing lines where we wanted them. He was still worried that TB, in trying to shift from opportunity to responsibility as a main message, would make us look like we were retreating. Charlie F and I went to see Robin to bind him in and get a couple of dates in his diary for domestic political speeches. Robin was clearly made up to be asked. Every time I saw him, his office seemed bigger and bigger and he seemed happier and happier to have it. I spent much of the day doing interviews for new press officers. What was interesting was how many of them basically said Number 10's reputation round departments was dreadful. We really had to improve the two-way communication.

[1] Brown was being accused of 'ignorant prejudice' by the Conservatives and media commentators after it had emerged that Spence had not performed well at her admission interview and that other candidates for the five-place medicine course had equally good qualifications and had interviewed better.

I missed the strategy meeting, but Philip said TB was only really hearing from the polls what he wanted to hear, and that was the stuff about the middle classes. Then he plucked out the idea of hinting at tax cuts, which sent GB off the radar and which I said would just pump up the Tories to think their tax guarantee plan was working. Stan Greenberg said he had enjoyed listening to them but he did feel they were in different places, TB on Middle England, tax cuts, families, crime, GB on the poverty agenda which was too limited. TB felt we needed Peter M back more closely involved but because of Ireland that was difficult, and also when he did come back, it just gave him another set of problems with GB.

The Laura Spence issue had rumbled on and on and the internal opposition on the elitism row was pretty strong. Peter M, Anji and Charlie F were all winding TB up to varying degrees, but I was still very much with GB on it, that we keep driving it through. Philip felt that TB was sometimes put off by the sheer weight of propaganda against us, and the power of basically conservative assumptions. TB said something interesting later though, when I was going on again about the need to isolate the *Mail* and go for them. 'I do understand that Dacre and his lot positively hate me. They think this is a conservative country full stop. And they know that we are changing it.' GB, probably for the first time, had had his eyes opened about just how conservative the press can be. He was facing criticism of an intensity that we had to deal with pretty much all the time. This was actually a rerun, with a bit of the same backlash, of the forces of conservatism argument which I was convinced we could win, and had to win.

Friday, June 2

JP's speech in Gateshead was reported in the *FT* as an attack on Durham [University], and we got him on to *The World at One*, who were whipping it up, to calm it down a bit.[1] I was working up with Milburn a Sunday briefing on reform. GB sent though a draft article for *The Times*, trailing the [Peter] Lampl [independent adviser on education] Report on access to universities, so I worked for a while on that. It was going to be tough to weather this but we had to keep going. TB had lined up [former BBC director general] John Birt to do a review of the criminal justice system, which would obviously

[1] Prescott's speech had sought to praise the efforts of northern universities for their efforts in widening access, but Sir Kenneth Calman, Durham's vice chancellor, commented 'It is clear from some of the things being said by ministers that they have not been well briefed about the efforts that universities such as Durham have been making.'

attract a fair bit of attention, so I had a long chat with him about his role. It turned out that not only was he unpaid, but he wasn't even getting expenses, which suggested an over-defensiveness on everyone's part to me. We had a very nice chat. He said there were about fifty jobs in the country that were totally all-consuming. He used to have one of them, I currently had one of them and he thought basically we were doing OK. And in a very difficult environment, we got our message through to the public much better than most governments or big organisations.

TB called while I was working on a strategy note, said he had had a good meeting with GB, felt they were broadly in the same place but that his analysis of the latest poll was that it was on the Middle England issues that we were being hit hard, which was why in the end the Oxbridge row was of limited value. He felt GB had to draw the line on Laura Spence and move on.

TB was working on his speech to the Women's Institute next week which I felt at the moment was too conservative. He wanted to balance new and old, put the responsibility agenda up alongside opportunity. His worry was that in what was basically a conservative country, we were being portrayed as anti family, anti tax cuts, anti strong defence, all rights and no responsibilities.

Saturday, June 3

TB and I must have spoken a dozen times over the weekend about the WI speech. Independently, Peter H, Philip G and I reached the same conclusion, that this was not really him, that it was over-pandering to what he thought a certain constituency wanted to hear. He was adamant that he had to marry the old and the new and the key to that was opportunity and responsibility as the twin pillars of community. It was perfectly fine as an idea but the first draft was very defensive, almost apologetic about New Labour and about wanting to change Britain. Both Philip and I sent through notes which were pretty harsh. Mine said that the speech lacked focus and leadership, it didn't properly explain or defend modernisation and so risked being Majoresque nostalgia. He was clearly of a view that the Oxbridge row had done us substantial damage. Anji and Peter M were both telling him that 'their people' were really up in arms.

GB's article in *The Times* was the splash, keeping the Oxbridge row going. JP's speech yesterday was taken, whether we liked it or not, as a hit at Durham, so this was rumbling on big time. I was reading and rereading his WI speech and finding it very hard to get a proper handle on it. TB was adamant that this was his genuine voice and he had to have it heard. I said I thought it was what he thought they would want to hear, several thousand fairly conservative middle-aged women, at a time the political debate was dominated by an issue some of them would support us on but most of them wouldn't. But if he pandered, it could go wrong. What they probably wanted was a bit of humour, a lot of leadership, a bit of celebrity and a solid explanation. Peter H, Philip and Sally all said as it stood it was far too right wing and would not go down well. When the Sundays arrived, we had done OK in the health briefing and opportunity for all was in there in spades. But the downsides were the wave of criticism, the attempt to hit GB on credibility and a sense of some of our people losing confidence. The *Sunday Times* News Review did a very bad focus group in Worcester, whilst Hague was still chugging along pretty nicely.

Sunday, June 4

I had dreadful hay fever and sinusitis and had made the mistake of going for a swim in the [Hampstead Heath] lido. By lunchtime I could barely breathe. I briefed Margaret Beckett and Steve Byers for the lunchtime programmes, but then [former Labour Party general secretary Lord] Tom Sawyer came on *The World at One* to deliver a real 'out of touch' broadside.

TB called a few times and was still saying he didn't want to change the basic message in the [WI] speech, bringing the old and the new together. He believed that the country was where the party was when we first reviewed Clause 4 – in need of change but change rooted in our basic values and beliefs. The key to those were opportunity for all, responsibility from all, building a strong community. It was OK but it was proving a real struggle to turn it into a strong speech. He said he felt this conflict when he went to the local church near Chequers, and he could sense there were people there who wondered why he was a churchgoer when he was constantly being defined as standing for all things modern. He did believe in a lot of traditional things and traditional values, but the country had to modernise. GB of course felt this just showed up how hard it was to get people to believe there was a Third Way and he felt we needed to be more direct in forcing change. But we could only do it if we held the [New Labour] coalition together and he felt the Laura Spence issue had risked fracturing it for some people. But the draft was proving to be a nightmare.

With the exception of Peter M and Anji, everyone thought it was ghastly. Peter H was so violently against it, I thought he was going to have a seizure. Philip thought it was dreadful. I thought it would be sensible to get others outside the usual inner circle to read it. Part of the problem of course was that we were giving TB conflicting advice. I got Godric, Hilary and Mark Bennett to have a read and none of them liked it at all. Mark said it was 'all wool, no thread'. On that note I went to bed.

Monday, June 5

Health was running fine and at least we were getting up the existence of the plan. The Lampl Report was out, and going OK, though not big on the broadcasts. GB called and said we really had to pump it up. When it came up at the 11, I briefed according to what TB had written in his weekend note and it was taken as a bit of a rowing back. GB was livid and PG livid on his behalf but that was where GB had wanted it relocated, so I felt that was what I had to do. We had several meetings on the WI speech. Peter M and Anji argued that it really was TB's voice and would do the trick of connecting him back in the way we wanted. I felt it was too whimsical and there was a real danger it would be seen as whimsy and nostalgia and was open to parody. But TB felt strongly all our problems were Middle England problems and also that we had a problem with older people because they felt excluded from the 'new' the whole time. I don't recall a speech taking up as much time as any outside of party conference, and I don't recall a speech provoking as much division. I, Philip, Peter H and Bruce were totally against it. So, perhaps more unusually, was Jonathan, who told TB that it made him cringe. Anji and Peter M were arguing strongly in favour.

TB and I went for lunch at the *Express*. As ever, most of their points were presentational. Once you got on to policy, they weren't really interested. I sat in on TB's meeting with junior ministers which was an attempt by him to get them to be more political. He was a bit vague but it was probably worth doing. Blunkett had written to TB complaining about GB. I spoke to him and sensed he had been somewhere behind the stuff criticising GB in the *Mail*. Philip felt it was dreadful that TB didn't just want to stand by GB. TB felt the whole thing had been damaging because it wasn't really his voice. Jon Cruddas [Blair's assistant political secretary] believed that GB had done it very deliberately for his own internal reasons in the party. I didn't buy that, and felt it was the right message for the government as a whole.

June '00: Blunkett complains about GB

A potentially seminal two days. Ever since Saturday we had been doing virtually nothing but work on TB's speech for the WI tomorrow. We had a fundamental disagreement that was simply not resolving itself. TB was convinced we had to set out the old/new balance. The rest of us kept reading the changing drafts, where he wasn't taking any of the stuff we did to recalibrate the message. Paul Johnson of all people was sending over his advice and it was drivel, including a paragraph, which at one point TB included, about the new being a glittering sword and the old a sturdy shield. We went round and round in circles all day and I was there till gone 10 trying to get it sorted.

We weren't helped by the fact that TB was getting diametrically opposed advice. He was definitely, post-Laura Spence, of a mood to tack to the right. I felt if we lost our nerve on opportunity for all, we would get hit. TB wanted his key message to be responsibility plus a mix of the old and the new. Philip, who was at Buckingham Palace for [his wife] Gail's CBE ceremony, felt that TB had done some kind of deal with the *Mail* and also that Peter and Anji were up to something. I put together a briefing note based on the draft. Normally, TB would assume my briefing notes were fine or, if I did show them to him, would sign them off pretty quickly. But this one he rewrote for ages. As I waited for him, John Sawers said he spent too much time worrying about politics and the media and not enough governing the country.

JP came to see me and asked the same question Rosie [Winterton] had asked. Should he dump his department and become much more a deputy at the centre? He felt things were a bit grim at the moment and that TB would never resolve the GB/Peter M situation. My bad vibes about the speech got even worse after the four o'clock, when I went through the briefing note on the speech. Even Don Macintyre, who was more friendly and more serious than most, was basically taking the piss. He said it was just an orgy of abstract nouns. When would we get something that would really connect again? When I said opportunity plus responsibility equals community, they asked if that could be said in any order. My problem was I shared the cynicism even if I had had to hide it.

Afterwards, I met with Godric, David M and Peter H and said the only way to rescue this was to get some hard-edged policy stories. I then briefed on adult literacy and on some of the stuff on sport. At first flush, the papers weren't too bad, the *Telegraph* splashing on recapturing Middle England and the *Guardian* on TB exposing a new

elite front. Hague was meanwhile getting a total free hit on school
sin bins. I had a pretty dreadful scene with TB when I said people
would not understand why he was making this kind of speech at this
time to this audience. It was almost year zero. Poor old Julian
[Braithwaite], who was meant to be the speech co-ordinator, was
trying to work out what he had let himself in for and he was there
till the early hours with TB doing most of the writing while I was
now at home trying to get more policy that might take away from a
message that, if the four o'clock was anything to go by, was just not
going to work.

Wednesday, June 7

We just about got away with things in the press, and Blunkett was
excellent on the radio. TB was upstairs in a dressing gown, writing
away. He said he was sure it was the right argument. Amid it all, we
did not heed a call from Lucie [McNeil], who was advancing the visit,
who said it must not be too political. We didn't think our way through
that. The thing had now been built up over days into an enormous
political event. We had been so worried about getting the message
right that we had overlooked the fact they probably didn't want
anything overtly political at all. I missed GB's meeting as we tinkered
around with the final version. Monica [Jelley] from the Garden Room
said she had never done so much typing on a speech in all the time
she had been there. TB set off with Tessa [Jowell]. I had decided not
to go because I had a series of meetings, including one with JP.

He turned up after TB's speech had started and which I was
watching on Sky, having postponed the lobby. It seemed to start OK,
and I turned the sound down a bit as JP and I talked over things.
Over JP's shoulder, I could see there was a bit of reaction around the
place and then the clear sound of slow-handclapping and heckling.
It was pretty obvious the speech was a goner. I turned up the sound
and both of us watched as TB did what JP called his Bambi look,
really startled but with the smile still there as he ploughed on and
eventually scythed through the speech. This had the potential to be
a disaster area. I paged Anji, who called back and said it was a very
odd atmosphere. It was clearly the wrong speech for the wrong audience and we had a PR disaster on our hands in media terms. I said
to JP it's a good job we've got lines in there about being more relaxed
and chilled out. But it was clear to TB that he was no longer loved
or even understood. The TV news people were loving it of course.

He called me as soon as he got in the car and said it had been
really bad. It wasn't just the slow-handclapping. Every element had

been wrong. He was really down and I said he was going to have to get himself lifted for PMQs and get up and at them. The eleven o'clock was pretty difficult for obvious reasons and they wanted to run the line that basically Middle England had given up on us. I was pushing the message that he was a politician of conviction who believed what he was saying and would not be fazed by a few hecklers. We would keep on keeping on. We also had a process story problem in that we had said they had invited us and they were saying we had invited ourselves. Their main complaint was that it was a political speech, to which I said what did they think politicians were for? Of course there was no way we would win a war of words with the Women's Institute, so all we could do was use the huge coverage there would be to get ministers up live talking about what the government was about. I briefed Reid, Beckett and [now social security minister Jeff] Rooker and they were excellent. PMQs was actually not that bad and TB had some good hits on Hague, but in truth there was only one story anybody was remotely interested in. My office became the focus for all the coming and going as we tried to handle it as best we could.

I went round to see TB later and he was just sitting in his chair, with his chin in his hand, looking hurt and worried. He was really angry that we had spent so much time on a speech that was now defined as a disaster area. He asked if I really thought that people of this country were so stupid that they could kick us out and go back to the Tories. Is it such a conservative country that they will do anything to get us out? He was very down. I said it wasn't that bad, and that our real bonus was that people didn't like the Tories and wanted to keep them out, we really needed to come out now and show some fight. He still felt we had the right arguments. [Former Labour deputy leader Roy] Hattersley was out and about saying it was the PR department's fault and we had to understand Tony could not please everyone all of the time. He felt TB would get more support if he made more enemies and people believed what he was doing.

Thursday, June 8

The papers were a bit of a car crash though in scale it could have been a lot worse. Jack did the *Today* programme and despite me saying he should be robust he did far too much on the need to reflect and learn lessons. Hattersley was out again attacking the spin machine, which would run for a while, and I had camera crews following me a bit later. In the car on the way in, Philip reckoned they were the worst papers he had ever seen, which was an exaggeration, but it was being seen as a seminal moment at a time the Tories were felt to be on the up. GB was keen for us to get the shift back to the opportunity-for-all agenda. We also needed to get more pressure on the Tories and the NHS was the obvious area. Also GB was planning to write to every local paper in the country on the Tories and the New Deal. GB and I went over to Number 10 for a meeting with TB, Peter M, DM, Douglas A and Ed Miliband and maybe because things were so grim, for once GB and Peter M were at least engaging.

TB and Peter M wanted TB to go and do an interview but I was against. For a start, they were not going to let him get out a message and the whole point at the moment was that people were saying he was all words and no delivery so why just do more words? I thought we had to take the hit and come out fighting at the right time. Concepts had been far too airy-fairy. We also needed to get real with a strategy for Hague, who was being totally driven by focus groups. TB was OK but a bit flibbertigibbety and so he gave out rather panicky vibes and what we needed was to be as hard as nails at the moment.

At Cabinet, he didn't get off to a great start when he ran through the absences and said Robin was in Florence, when everyone knew he was in Sierra Leone. They opened with a tribute to the murdered military attaché in Athens and the discussion of the fallout.[1] On the political scene, whatever the noise, TB said we had to keep going on opportunity and responsibility. GB was supportive. Both Clare and Mo said the problem was spin and we had to address it. Reid was excellent, said we had to be really careful because what our opponents were trying to do was stop us being professional and coherent with our message and go back to being ill-disciplined.

I did the 11.30 and felt it went pretty well. I felt we shouldn't concede at all, that we had to use this to promote the basic message. As the day wore on, I felt more confident that if it was damaging, it was of a passing nature. The WI later put out a statement trying to draw a line. The *Mirror* tracked down the WI ringleader. Of course, if Thatcher or Major had been on the receiving end, the story would have been their rudeness. I said to TB I felt we were paying the price for not being hard enough with papers like the *Mail*. He felt there was nothing to gain. I disagreed, felt that as they were now as much players as spectators in the way the debate was framed, we had to treat them differently. They were the cancerous elite. There was a bit of a post-mortem.

[1] Brigadier Stephen Saunders had been shot by motorcycle gunmen on his way to work at the British Embassy. The killers were members of the Marxist revolutionary group 17 November, which claimed Saunders had been involved in the bombing of Kosovo. In fact, Saunders had no connection with Kosovo.

June '00: Paying the price of being too soft

Anji and Phil Bassett had been the ones pushing for the WI event, and if we made a mistake, it was not to pin down early enough the dangers of doing anything too political. Byers gave an interview on the euro which was pretty stupid. As Jeremy H said, he seemed to have a death wish with GB. Blunkett was brilliant on *Newsnight* and even Clare called before *Question Time* to get the line and apparently did OK. TB called and said we just had to hold our nerve. I agreed, but he had been the one recently being more short term than long term.

Friday, June 9

TB was back on the kick that we were making the right decisions and doing the right things, but we lacked the ability to get the message out. I felt that the longer we had, the more people would work out the reality, but it did mean defining change in the way the debate was conducted. I also felt he had to change his style and stop talking in such ethereal language. We had to bring on more people. We had to improve our operation in the office. And he had to be more political. But he wasn't having it, said it was just a question of keeping our nerve. He said I was too angry at the moment, and being nasty to him. He said if we could get better people fine, but where are they? I also said there were too many people around who told him what he wanted to hear and he said 'For God's sake, who? Nobody does – you, Gordon, Peter, Jonathan, nobody does. That is ridiculous.' He said we simply had to hold our nerve and have balls of steel. I said fine but we should not pretend that because we defend ourselves the whole time, there are not things that we defend that don't actually need changing. He said on the big-tent approach, he was insisting he was right and we had to back his judgement on that. There came a point when we couldn't keep having the same arguments, and in the end he had to make the final calls.

TB asked me to go and see him and asked whether it was getting to me that there was so much shit about me personally in the press. I said I didn't think so, and actually you could argue that it could be worse. The things that annoyed me were having to deal with a media I didn't much like or respect, and from time to time the politicians expected too much of me, and sometimes that included him. I always felt I could justify to myself and the family working flat out if it was in a way and on an agenda that I supported. But when there was drift and disagreement, and I felt too much of the pressure fall on me to sort it, I did get angry. He said that in most organisations, lots of people would do things, but very few people could assume real leadership, and I was one of the people who knew how to step up to the mark. He agreed there were problems and said it was possible we were in trouble. His own feeling was that we could lose narrowly, though it was doubtful, or we could win again with a big majority, which he felt was more likely, but it did mean the key people sticking together. He also said if the biggest criticism they could mount was that he tried to be all things to all men, he could live with that.

Cockerell was in for the Sunday briefing and I really went into the whole real world vs medialand agenda, how much of what they wrote was actually spin, and they complained they were just extras in a film I wanted making. What was clear was that they were lining up for more 'Blair's worst week yet' bollocks. There was a very funny moment when I said 'I've seen some guff in my time,' and was interrupted 'You haven't seen the background pieces we've done yet.' They were all men, and I wondered how many groups and organisations today were still all male.

Saturday, June 10

The papers weren't too grim though the Byers [euro speech] situation was a problem because of a story in the *Mirror* that Number 10 had let him act as an outrider. Max Clifford [publicist] had a piece in the *Independent* saying I should go on TV [for briefings] because people would then see the arguments. On [proposals to ban fox] hunting, the Tories were being quite clever, going on 'What's the point?' rather than running up to defend the status quo. On systems, TB and I were both moving to me giving up the briefings altogether, while he was thinking of putting Anji in charge of Millbank/Number 10 liaison, which might be a problem with Sally M.

PG called in a flap from Alton Towers [Midlands theme park], saying the *Sunday Times* Insight team had a copy of the memo that he sent to me last weekend on the WI speech which was full of very colourful language, e.g. saying TB was not being left by Middle Britain because of lack of balance between old and new, but because he wasn't believed, all things to all men, spin, failure on delivery. He was in a terrible state, convinced that someone must be tapping the fax. TB was reasonably relaxed, though he had mentioned before that he sometimes worried how frank we were in these strategic notes. The Sundays were full of WI post-mortems, including one or two calls on me to quit.

Sunday, June 11

I did a long note to the Garden Room on the *Sunday Times* leak. It was clear they [*Sunday Times*] had three memos. One from Philip to me, one to TB, and one from the Garden Room sent to six of us with the speech. Richard Wilson called in Stephen Lander. They were taking the leaks pretty seriously. We had good ministers out, Reid, Milburn and Darling, who were excellent. I briefed Margaret Beckett for the *Today* programme on Europe. The Byers interview fallout plus his speech meant he was being whacked by GB a bit. GB felt that because it was first Peter, then Byers, someone was authorising them to go out and do this.

Monday, June 12

Hunting was big, there was a lot of PG [memo] fallout. Bill Hagerty ran my interview with him for the *British Journalism Review* in *The Times*. Peter M sent through a note on systems. His main point was that up to now, we just got on with the governing and if there were any problems, I would sort them out, but the mood had changed. The press were bored with us and we didn't really have a driving narrative to get them onside. We had been too complacent and meanwhile the Tories had made themselves interesting again. TB had sent a note through on Saturday saying that he has absolutely decided on the big-tent approach and he wanted it implemented, no questions asked. Peter M said, in a very Peterish way, 'It's very good that you have finally decided to agree with yourself.'

I was also trying to work on a message note that would take us from the CSR to conference to the Queen's Speech to the next Budget. Philip was around and said he was surprised I didn't tell them all to fuck off because I seemed to be the one person working his balls off because every change they made to the systems seemed to require more work of me. It was a point I made to TB in the car on the way to lunch with the *Telegraph*. TB asked what I thought of Douglas. I said I thought he was bright but I was sometimes worried GB didn't really give him his head. A good thing at the moment was that in different ways GB and Peter M were getting more involved. He said we all had to raise our game. That includes you, I said. He said he wished he could have more rest. I didn't particularly enjoy the lunch. He wasn't on great form and they were a pretty nasty right-wing bunch. There was no way in the world we would ever win them over.

On hunting, alarmingly, he dropped a hint that he would go against his past position. I couldn't much care about the issue either way, but he would get hit hard on conviction if he just about-turned without a very good reason. The Tories were doing very well on the line it was all a waste of parliamentary time. I got back for a meeting with GB on the CSR. He had done a good paper on how to set it up.

He was also trying to draw me in against Peter, Byers and Cook re the way they were trying to play the euro. TB in fact felt GB was too rigid and not wanting to set out the benefits. I felt the real danger on EMU was of TB looking Majoresque between two different positions.

I went to see Richard Wilson and Philip. We agreed the security people should have a look at our faxes and phones and speak to all the people copied into any of the notes. He and I then discussed my profile and whether it was possible to get it down again, even if I stopped the briefings. I got home to watch the football, England 2 up against Portugal only to lose 3-2. TB called on the final whistle, said how depressing is that. Godric suggested we say it was a metaphor for the government. I said we had the best strikers in the business but they wouldn't play together. TB said there's no need to panic. I said I'm not panicking but I'm depressed at how crap we are at the moment.

Tuesday, June 13

Today was the second day I didn't do the briefings and Godric came back to say nearly all the questions were about me and my absence. By the four o'clock they were all at it. The BBC were doing packages from the lobby room. These people are obsessed. The euro row was rumbling which pissed off GB. TB was getting worried about hunting. He called an office meeting – Jonathan, SM, DM, Pat and me – and said he wasn't happy about going for a new law and wanted to get out of it. He didn't much like fox hunting or the people who did it but is that a good enough reason to ban it when it is a way of life for a lot of these people? He and I went for lunch at the *FT*. I thought Richard Lambert [editor] was genuinely nice and intelligent. TB was pushing the boat out on the euro and sticking up for GB. GB's worry that TB was pushing too far on the euro was exacerbated by the joint article he did with [José María] Aznar in the *FT*.

I left early for Rory's parents' evening. He was doing brilliantly. Then back in for a meeting with PLP researchers. I did the big picture, the hit on the media, a bit of motivation and it seemed to go fine. There was too much in the papers about me bowing out or cutting down and I was worried Godric was going to get a bit of a hit once they realised what we were doing. But the press had gone totally mad and it was better for me and better for the government that I pull out. The latest thing was *Punch* [satirical magazine] and the front cover of me with a vile cartoon and yet another piece which undermined Cockerell, who told Anji he realised he was being set up. He told her he had never done a more fascinating film and that he really did feel the press was now ridiculous.

Wednesday, June 14

There was lots in the papers about me not briefing. [Peter] Oborne was on *GMTV* saying Godric was boring and it was like replacing Botham with Tavaré.[1] God I hate these people. First they say we spin them too much and then when we take it away they say they need more spin. At PMQs, we were trying to work out how best to deal with the Philip G memos. TB thought it best just to be dismissive. PMQs was fine really. Hague wasn't brilliant. There was one question on me, but TB was fine. We then went to the four o'clock, and as [Martin] Sheehan [press officer] said, they were like a jilted lover. It was packed out, far more people than usual, very hot and sweaty. I was perfectly calm but made clear this wasn't for discussion, I had decided to pull back and do very few briefings myself. They were straight away on to the idea of it not being good for them but I gave no ground whatever. Godric and David Bradshaw [special adviser] had both warned they were not going to be very nice about this but I really didn't care what they thought. First they complained about being spun, now they complained about being snubbed. It was pathetic.

I was followed down the road by ITN and said the fact they did me rather than the job figures as their lunchtime political story said more about the media than it did about us. I then literally, by an extraordinary coincidence, bumped into Gus O'Donnell and swapped notes about the time he did my job for Major.

TB told me he was seriously thinking about moving Jack because he seemed to be getting captured by the Home Office and the change agenda wasn't happening quickly enough. He had seen Jack yesterday and given him a warning shot. Jack came to see me and said he didn't really know what TB was saying. Sally said there was a bit of a 'Sell Blair' feeling around, and people were going around getting support for GB 'in case anything happened'. I was doubtful of that.

Thursday, June 15

The press from my briefing wasn't as bad as it might have been. There were some very funny cartoons and Boris Johnson had me laughing out loud. I sensed it was a bit of a one-day wonder, that we had got

[1] Ex-England cricketers. Ian Botham had a reputation as a swashbuckling match winner; Chris Tavaré as an obdurate blocker.

through the pain barrier and who in the real world cares anyway? The big story was Milburn saying we would co-operate more with the private sector. I drove in with Philip. Both of us, whilst in our different ways we had caused some of our recent problems, felt that the main problem at the moment was TB not really offering clear direction and leadership. The euro row was a case in point. We didn't really have a problem on the policy, but we had allowed a sense of division to grow because Peter M, Byers and Robin C thought they were satisfying TB's pro-euro bit, while GB thought we had agreed at a strategic level it wasn't right to push the boat out. TB felt GB was in the right in saying we didn't want it to be the dominant issue but wrong to be saying we should be setting out the benefits. Philip and I went to see GB at 8. He threw down a file of cuttings, said there was no real disagreement but this was all about profile and personality. Byers wanted it as a diversion from other problems. Peter was Peter, just causing trouble, Robin wanted it to be a Foreign Office issue not an economic issue. But, he said, it will haunt us all the way if we don't grip it. TB tried to write something as a line to close it down but GB wasn't happy with the formulation.

Then Milburn came in to discuss private health. GB was worried, post-Laura Spence, that we really had to get the facts all right, and not let them off the hook. I was pretty impressed with Milburn, who didn't get pushed around, was in fact pretty tough with him, said we had enough to go on and at one point forced GB to back off. The strategy meeting at Number 10 was without GB, who had gone in early to complain to TB about the briefing against him and then just went back to the Treasury. Peter M was feeling confident enough to make jokes about the euro row and TB's reaction made me think he was overstating it when he claimed he had bollocked him privately. I thought it was crazy, to have this row running, and we had to find a way of shutting it down.

I saw Stephen Lander who felt that on Philip's memo, they had wanted to do a real inquiry but TB felt that was over the top. They said they were checking all the phones but they felt this was a human source. I suggested he used it to force the tightening of security more generally, because I felt we were a bit loose. At Cabinet, TB did slap down the pro-euros when he said GB would set out the policy and that was it and there was no need for further argument about it. We later got into a mess when Robin's Commons speech had to be changed but the text went out without the changes, and we were left with a story about TB taking out the pro-euro bits. All silly and avoidable.

Byers came to see me, said the problem was the Treasury would now brief this as a slap down. Peter M was stirring, even had a line in *The Times* about GB's 'territorial fetish'. I think TB underestimated the damage all this was doing. GB came round to my office to talk about a statement that would settle it. I had a meeting with Charlie F on the Grid process. Paul Brown [Grid co-ordinator] was proving to be an inspired choice. Milburn told me he was liaising with the Lib Dems on the NHS Plan, they would come on board for it and make it a big alliance against the Tories. I had been impressed by him today, thought he was tough and clever. Craig Reedie [chairman, British Olympic Association] came in to see us about the Olympic bid. I got a lift home from a very nice taxi driver who said he thought we were doing fine and should just ignore the papers.

Friday, June 16

Europe had now reached such a ridiculous situation that when [Michael] Portillo [now Shadow Chancellor] was on *Today*, the interviewer said that the government was no more divided than the last one. This was absolutely crazy. The last government was fundamentally split over massive questions of principle and sovereignty. We had an agreed policy, but squabbles between ministers on tactics. But it was showing up TB as weak. GB did *Today* and tried to hold it together but he was also doing some heavy briefing against Robin, Peter, Steve Byers and they seemed to be responding. The bottom line was that there was going to be zero coverage for TB's event in Carlisle. He was really down when I spoke to him in Scotland. They were all denying briefing against each other. He felt GB had a point in that Peter M started this up without thinking or talking it through. But they have a point in that he gives the impression nobody can talk about the policy. When I was briefing Godric before he did the 11, he said there was so much of this poison around and it would be the death of us. I said ego and division had been the death of every Labour government.

We also had other ingredients for a bad cocktail – non-delivery, spin, out of touch, and now division and weak leadership. TB looked and sounded absolutely worn out. We had to get him back on education and schools. I did a briefing on the Feira summit [European Council meeting in Portugal] and bizarrely didn't get a single question on the euro. The yobs were really starting to flare up and 400 were arrested by the end of the day.[1] I had a very good meeting with Jeremy on the CSR. We were looking at a six per cent per year real

[1] English football hooligans were rioting in Belgium during the Euro 2000 tournament.

terms increase for education and there was good stuff right through that. Crime was five or six per cent, a lot more police. A lot more for asylum. The more we went into the detail, the more it was clear we could get up both investment and reform. Philip was very down on Peter M, felt he was really going for GB at the moment. TB was looking terrible. I said to Anji we had to grip it. He was wasting too much time seeing journalists and wasn't fixing the fundamentals.

Sunday, June 18

The Sundays were reasonably full of rubbish and spin, *Sunday Times* Focus, Rawnsley, Whelan saying I should quit, Jon Craig saying I was about to quit. The big news though was the football and in particular the violence which was about to whack us very hard indeed. GB had decided to come with us [to Feira] which was written up needless to say as TB banging heads together. In fact the flight out was OK, lots of false bonhomie between GB and RC. I said we just had to get through this period on the euro and then move on. But the truth was we were in one of those periods of a total media spin fest. Most of the discussion on the flight was about tactics on the withholding tax. We were in a better position than before but it was still tricky. I felt we had to watch out with the way comparisons between TB and Major were developing. I did a briefing on arrival after which Martin Fletcher [*Times* Brussels correspondent] said he felt our relations with the media were like a war zone.

Then just after I left to go back came the news that UEFA had launched a bitter attack on us and were threatening to kick England out of the tournament. Bye bye World Cup bid. We put out a warning to the supporters to that effect whilst doubting it would make a blind bit of difference. TB was playing tennis with John Holmes when I spoke to him. 'This is a disaster.' He asked me to speak to Jack and wanted a whole package of measures that would make a difference. I called Jack who was as fed up with TB as TB was with him at the moment, and he said there was very little that could be done. He told TB the same and when he said one of TB's suggestions wasn't lawful, TB said that's because I'm asking you to change the law. At the very least, we had to establish that people sent back would not be able to return, as many would try. He was very wound up. I said to Jack there was a two-ton train coming down the track and we were staring in the headlights. TB was even worse. Recalling all the times he had asked if the Home Office were on top of this. 'I warned this would happen and we didn't do enough. We have fallen down on the job.' However, as he said on the way to the PES, Jack was one of his biggest supporters in Cabinet and he didn't want any sense of division but he was totally exasperated by the Home Office.

Helpfully, David Davies attacked the Tories for point scoring. We got Wilson, Jonathan and David North [private secretary] working on proposals. Then came the news of the discovery of a lorry load of dead Chinese asylum seekers [found in the back of a lorry in Dover]. I said to TB that football violence was Thatcher's children at play. He said it was more a vile and violent nationalist press. Columnists like [Richard] Littlejohn [*Sun*] pandering to low common denominators, a culture of drink and a belief we should be allowed to beat up foreigners.

Monday, June 19

David Davies called at 6.30 to find out what we had decided overnight. TB did an interview with [*Today* presenter James] Naughtie on violence, the euro, WI fallout, where he got the tone right. Then Adam Boulton [Sky]. Then to a fairly difficult breakfast with Jospin, starting with football and asylum seekers and then going to the more difficult summit issues. He said he was in the same place as us on the united states of Europe. Jospin said Ecofin ministers weren't happy because their meeting had been delayed because [Jean-Claude] Juncker [Prime Minister and finance minister of Luxembourg] was out enjoying himself. On the future of Europe, he said he was not in the same place as Chirac. He felt he was more *européen* than *européiste*. GB was pretty steamed up because he clearly believed that he had talked up the idea of TB laying down the law, simply because the press were saying TB ordered them to come on the plane with us. He would not communicate at all and it was clear they all thought I was behind it. I confronted him to ask if that's what he thought and said he must be crazy. And TB said to him later 'You really think I would ask him to go and tell the press I ordered you on the plane?' He said the papers felt licence to make these things up because they knew there were difficulties.

During the course of the day, he told both Gordon and Peter M they were in danger of bringing down the whole project. And he said to GB 'History will be very unkind if we fail. It will say that the two of you were deeply flawed and I should have done more to deal with you, but nobody will remotely understand why we let this happen.' He said the whole thing was about their personalities and their personal agendas and it was pathetic. GB said none of it would happen if we had proper discipline. TB said how can we have discipline if you are at it as well?

The news was dominated by football violence and the fifty-eight dead Chinese, and Jack doing statements on both. I got David Davies to agree that we could say that the clubs would impose a life ban on anyone convicted or known to be involved [in violence]. GB was motoring on the withholding tax which was now moving our way but there was no real sense of this being an important summit. Schroeder was enjoying our embarrassment on the football front, joking to me about how we were a national disgrace. On the drive back to Feira, TB said he had reached the view that the French really didn't want us inside the euro and that they were terrified of us building a different sort of relationship with the Germans. There was a lot of hanging around today and the more time I spent at these summits, the less I enjoyed them.

I watched Turkey vs Belgium and went out to dinner with Jeremy, John Holmes and David Bostock [European Secretariat, Cabinet office] and talked mostly about our inability to get a grip. In his new, slightly more detached position, John H had reached the view – which he pretty much held before – that the GB/Peter problem was insurmountable.

Tuesday, June 20

GB rumblings were still going on. The *Express* had a story that was a bit near the knuckle on the flight out, which again had Gordon in a bad light, so he started the day very grumpy, and the rest of it trying to get away. TB had a meeting with GB early on to take stock of the withholding tax. TB had to do a lot of one-to-one schmoozing but in the end we pretty much got what we wanted. There was also a sense of a different mood towards us. TB was no longer the shiny new thing. He was an established part of the furniture. As we went to the press conference Schroeder shouted out to me 'Stop your hooligans.' I said we were trying. He shouted 'Try harder.' TB was thinking about making a big Europe speech because he wanted to get to the French before we got to their [six-month] presidency [of the EU starting in July] and we started to commission some blue-skies thinking specifically for ideas on political direction. He had a good chat with Patten and RC on the flight back. He said that Chirac was the only leader who never said that they wanted Britain in the euro. [Wim] Duisenberg [president, European Central Bank] did a speech to the European Parliament and said we were converging but 'psycho-political' problems were holding us back, so that was the story for the day. Duisenberg, another of TB's great appointment successes.[1]

---

[1] Duisenberg was appointed president of the European Central Bank after a bad-tempered summit chaired by Tony Blair.

The press conference was OK though GB was very brusque. We left for the airport after a few one-on-ones. TB's mind was whirring on the European front. He obviously sensed big opportunities. He felt the French were vulnerable. He also felt we had to develop ideas to deal with the rotating presidency because it would be ridiculous with an enlarged EU. England were dreadful and deserved to go out [beaten 3-2 by Romania]. As Godric said, feel-bad factor descends. TB was also pretty down on the Civil Service. He said of David Omand [Home Office permanent secretary] 'He sits there thinking why don't these guys get off my back and go away and let me get on with my job which is running the Home Office without politicians?'

Wednesday, June 21

GB was in a bit of a sulk and cancelled the morning meeting. TB was at the PLP which went OK. PMQs was fine. TB was in very confident form in the statement on Europe. I think he felt he had handled the discussions well and shown that it was possible to win arguments without upsetting too many people. I did the four o'clock which was OK, though there was no doubt they were not at all keen on me at the moment re having pulled back. There was a funny moment when I said to Jon Smith that I would put a line out on PA later and he said he might not put it out because he had decided to be more strategic. Godric was feeling it a bit because of the sense they didn't really want him but me, I felt he was doing fine and would grow into it. My asthma was dreadful at the moment.

Thursday, June 22

The press was like swimming through treacle at the moment but I was at last beginning to feel I had more time to think. Godric was effectively lowering the temperature of the briefings. There was an extraordinary piece in the *Daily Express* by Sarah Helm [Jonathan Powell's partner] attacking TB over Europe and bizarrely Jonathan seemed unaware she had done it. We had a 'group of death' which was joined by Ed Richards [media business policy adviser] because the idea was to discuss David M's paper on the manifesto. GB immediately said he had not been able to look at it properly and therefore there was no point discussing it because all the ideas in it would have to be costed and he wasn't prepared to make snap judgements. Ed, who having worked for him knew Gordon more than most, looked genuinely shocked. This was his sulky worst. Whenever anyone else spoke, he just sat there reading his papers.

TB tried to get a discussion going on my message note on the CSR, but GB just was not up for discussion at all. TB was trying to tease out how explicit we should be about the choice between tax cuts and public service investment, but he just wasn't up for it. TB was getting more and more exasperated, GB was glowering. We then discussed the attack we were planning on the Tories on health, but GB had gone off that idea too. The whole thing was ridiculous. When GB did engage, it was to say that the CSR had to follow the polling and he said that showed we had to invest for the many and not the few and that 'One Nation politics does not work'. It was a very direct attack on TB. I felt somebody had to respond and said you could also argue there was no sense of an economic narrative leading to the CSR so the danger was it would all be seen as spin. After they all left, TB said that if GB carried on like that, he would have to go for the nuclear button. It was absolutely intolerable. Apparently JP had a real go at Gordon yesterday, telling him to get over his obsession with Mandelson.

I chatted to Ed Miliband and said we had to get GB's meetings going again. But they were so sensitive and went over the same old things again and again. They genuinely believed we had deliberately talked up the [Feira] flight story as a way of undermining him. But what we had seen in the last couple of weeks was that when we worked with GB, things went OK and when we didn't, things went badly. It wasn't a capacity point. It was just that we needed the best minds working together. Peter of course was milking Gordon's behaviour, telling anyone who would listen how extraordinary it was. Cabinet was ghastly, a total joke. It wasn't much more than a discussion of what was on the Grid. Godric was there as part of the new arrangement for him doing the briefings. He looked genuinely shocked. I told him not to be, said it wasn't usually as bad as this. Then Clare Short attacked the various lines to take that we send round as 'inane' and JP defended them. Blunkett talked about performance-related pay but nobody seemed terribly interested. GB just glowered. I had a meeting with Peter M and the party team on conference. Pat had done an excellent note on how the Tories had used their conference in 1986 [the last before the 1987 election].

I went over the road to the health department for a meeting on the NHS Plan launch. Alan Milburn told me Nick Harvey [Liberal Democrat health spokesman] was up for a joint approach and what about them doing a press conference on Tory health policy together. I liked the boldness but worried it would be seen more as a Lib-Lab story than about health, and that it would build up Hague. Alan and I went over for a meeting with TB. The substance seemed fine but it was going to be difficult from now on in and we were clear the Tories

June '00: Cabinet a total joke

were going for health next week. We had to pin them on their health insurance policy. Alison took me through next week's diary which was a total nightmare. It did not look like the diary of someone being freed up to be more strategic. I went briefly to GB's latest party for political and economic editors and then home for a row with Fiona saying I was hardly ever there and the minute I walked through the door the phone rang.

Friday, June 23

My asthma was dreadful and the papers were grim. TB was up in Sedgefield. The *Express* and the *Indy*, wound up somewhere, did silly stories on me as the real Cabinet enforcer because I was going round departments with Charlie. I went to a hotel near Gatwick where I was doing a speech and Q&A for a conference of left-of-centre parties, which was fine, though I did feel some of them didn't quite get it. It was clear in the Q&A that their media was very different and so they couldn't really understand, particularly the French and Germans, why we operated like we did. I went back to do my main interview for the Cockerell programme, which I rehearsed with Godric, Martin [Sheehan] and Tanya. I think I got the tone about right.

As we finished, Jonathan came in and said that Insight had got hold of Michael Levy's tax returns. I was rushing out to meet Fiona to go to the Wingfield House do with Jamie Rubin [chief spokesman for the US State Department] and Christiane Amanpour [CNN chief international correspondent, married to Rubin] and I wasn't really concentrating. Later I saw the letter from the *Sunday Times* and the draft reply from Levy's lawyer, Tony Russell. Stupidly, Jonathan – already in my bad books because of Sarah's piece in the *Express* – urged him to get more expensive lawyers who advised him to go for an injunction. Sadly, they never got on to me because I would have advised along the lines of Tony Russell's letter setting out the facts and saying they would sue if they intimated wrongdoing. Instead we went for an injunction and lost.

DFID faxed over a draft Clare Short article for the *Observer* which was partly an attack on the lobby but would be taken as an attack on me because of her stuff on spin and her 'delight that the spin doctor's arts were discredited'. After swimming through the usual guff about how she had to tell the truth and her complaints of multiple announcements she agreed to make some changes that would make it less provocative. The US Embassy do was very jolly with the usual crowd, [David] Frost, Warren Hoge [*New York Times*], Naughtie, Michael Pakenham [Cabinet office]. Conrad Black said the Tories were trying to go for me because I was a genius doing a great job. 'I'll get Charles [Moore] to do a piece on it,' he said and wandered off.

Saturday, June 24

Jonathan called with news of the Levy injunction. It was mad and I was livid because no doubt I would have to sort it out. I did a conference call with Levy, Tony Russell and Tony Grabiner QC and we agreed to pre-empt with a statement that focused on the *Sunday Times* breaking the law. I changed it to take out any reference to breaches of privacy and concluded it was more a story about the *Sunday Times* and its techniques than about Michael Levy's tax returns. Needless to say TB didn't want to make a deal of it. Grabiner admitted he had made a mistake in going for an injunction because it gave them a story when a letter dismissing it all would have been fine. I wanted to get an MP out backing Michael. Ben Bradshaw [Labour MP] said no.

By 3 we got the statement agreed, with lots about the *Sunday Times* and their dubious methods and a reference about the PCC. There was no way the *Sunday Times* got these tax returns without someone breaking the law somewhere. Michael was keen to say in the press release that he had paid millions in tax in the past, but Tony Grabiner and I advised against, which in retrospect was a mistake. A lot of the day was taken up with it. We were out at Philip Barton's in the evening. Jeremy said he thought TB demeaned himself by spending so much time with the press, who didn't really respect him for it. I had to agree.

Sunday, June 25

After discussing with Peter M, I then spoke to Michael and agreed he should do *The World this Weekend*. It was a risk, but he sounded on top of it. We went through the various lines and difficult questions. He did extremely well, as most of the press acknowledged. Lots of people called him to offer support. I spoke to him three or four times and then tried to get people out criticising the judge because his ruling was a green light to go for people's private tax returns and this kind of thing would put anyone off going into public life. It was hard getting Michael off privacy and on to press conduct but he did fine and on the back of it we arranged another interview. Mo didn't want to help and told me she had told Tony ages ago that 'Levy was trouble'. Margaret said she didn't feel she should attack a judge. Gareth Williams [Attorney General] advised us to hold back and we did.

After another crap weekend ruined by work, I was in no mood for TB. GB cancelled his meeting again but asked me to go over for a one-on-one. Levy did well yesterday but the papers were bad, and the *Mail* vile. We should never have stopped Mailwatch. Also, the [Mr Justice] Toulson judgement on Michael was being seen by the press as an excuse to break the law to get any piece of information on people in public life. I wanted us to have a real go over that but TB didn't. We had Ahtisaari and Ramaphosa coming in and I got them lined up for a very positive statement on the progress being made, which was a good start for the week. At the office meeting, I felt TB was like a glorified Grid manager. At one point, I suggested we get Paul Brown in who was the only man who knew more about the Grid than TB. Peter M said he had a 'make your vote count' speech on Wednesday, no doubt written by [Roger] Liddle [policy adviser], which would get coverage. I complained about it and said what's the point of calling for a system and not sticking to it ourselves? It was a dreadful meeting, people just raising random issues.

I went over to see Gordon at 11. He said we had to get a grip on Europe. He said because we hadn't slapped down Peter when he started this off, he was now taking advantage. He believed TB was limbering up for a change, possibly tied to the inward investment figures, and it would be a dreadful mistake. Unless we got back to the kind of discipline we had in opposition, we were in trouble. It was becoming accepted we were divided. The press are going for us because we lack a big message and sense of direction. They sense weakness and when they sense weakness, they are merciless. He put the blame firmly at Peter's door and then at Tony's for allowing it, and then those who followed because they felt they should. He said 'I could go out tomorrow and say the Treasury won't foot the bill for the Patten reforms or that I want to rename the RUC – what would he say to that?' He said he had no doubt TB was moving on the euro and it was stupid. I said what are you saying, that all those – Peter, Robin, Steve Byers – should be sacked? He said there had to be discipline and nobody should say anything unless it went through Number 10 and the Treasury.

We then went over general message and he said again he thought the One Nation message didn't work. He felt the many not the few gave us more edge and took us to our issues – education, crime, health, poverty. I said we needed to get back to his daily meetings for the politics, and mine to drive decisions through the machine. He said he would, but wanted me to know how fed up he was with recent events. Everyone seemed fed up at the moment. TB, no doubt wound up by Peter M, was fed up. Godric was a bit fed up, feeling the pressure a bit. I was working on TB's human genome speech. Clinton's was so much better. He looked better, sounded better, the words were better. This is what happened when TB and I weren't working properly together. I had a meeting with Alan Milburn and the Treasury people to agree how we get up the political dividing line on health which had to be about taking their policies seriously and going for them about private medical insurance, and their inability to answer questions. Alan eventually agreed to a press conference tomorrow. Genome and IRA decommissioning were massive on the news but Godric got fifteen minutes of Michael Levy at the four o'clock.

Tuesday, June 27

I woke up to Zimbabwe and more intimidation of the Opposition, followed by a story that Mo was calling for the Queen to move out of Buckingham Palace. Lucie called to ask if I thought Mo should go on. I said no. She went on anyway but with TB as the ardent monarchist, anything we said would take us to 'slap down' territory and so it duly proved. The full transcript was even worse. It was now becoming a given that we saw her standing ovation at conference as a problem, and also a given that there was a Number 10 briefing operation against her. Both were nonsense. We had pretty much organised the reaction during the speech, with Peter M deliberately sitting with her, and I was now pretty convinced the so-called briefing operation consisted of her and her friends just going around saying it. It just wasn't serious.

I was also pissed off with Peter M who was going to be speaking tomorrow on AV [alternative vote, proportional representation system]. What is the earthly point? TB said just make it un-newsworthy and I said you can't with Peter. I called him and he said he wasn't saying much, he wouldn't go for PR, but not rule out AV. I said that wasn't the point. We were trying to get more discipline in the system and he was springing this on us. He said he didn't believe it would go big and he did not really see why he should be in contact with Paul Brown about his contributions to public debate. It was a deeply unsatisfactory conversation. If we couldn't even grip Peter in terms of basic discipline systems, why should the others bother? I told TB I felt there was a lack of respect for him which was damaging.

Of course he knew I had a real downer on him at the moment because I felt he wasn't motoring. Milburn was up on health, then Darling came in and agreed to do a vaccine damage statement based

June '00: Mandelson's pro-AV speech

on GB agreeing to more money. Godric did the 11, lots on Mo, and Chirac's speech to the Reichstag which was a problem for us. He seemed to be going for a two-speed Europe. TB and I went for lunch at the *Sun*, during which I wrote the script on NAFTA [North American Free Trade Agreement, a favourite – if unrealistic – alternative to the EU for Eurosceptic Conservatives]. In the car on the way there, TB said the problem on EMU was that in Gordon being so determined to shut it down, we were giving ourselves a problem with inward investors. He was still basically defending Peter over his Belfast speech.

At the lunch, Trevor K was doing his usual paranoid Europe stuff. TB was OK but very defensive. They were very big on the crime/yobs agenda and I got very close to saying a lot of it was down to the fact we had yobbish newspapers with yobs like Littlejohn the loudest voices. Trevor used the meeting to lobby TB re me not doing the briefings and TB, instead of saying it was their own fault for constantly going on about me, said he would think about it. I said I worked for him and not for the press, and it would be wrong to change. I was not terribly friendly, could just about deal with these people individually but as a group, I didn't like them or their politics.

I met my security liaison guy from the Central Unit, who said re the Philip leaks it was very easy to get stuff from rubbish bins and that was a possibility. He said they were taking the nuisance stuff seriously. Michael Levy came in and we went through his tax returns with Jonathan. Not surprisingly, Michael was very fed up that he was having to do this. He was very emotional and we had to calm him down . The press were getting into this and we just had to know all the facts. I got home late, told Fiona I was really getting fed up with the workload and constantly having to sort other people out. Philip called, said he had just done his worst focus groups ever. They felt TB was weak and for the first time were saying they felt Hague could be PM. He said all the warnings we had been given were coming through – drift, division, lack of conviction. For One Nation, they just read all things to all men.

Wednesday, June 28

The *Guardian* had got hold of my summer planning memo, along with an internal Cabinet Office memo about it. We put it round the system at 11am and they had it by 3pm. At the GB meeting, Ian McCartney had a go at him saying he was holding things up that needed to be sorted for the Policy Forum. I was really worried now that TB's Tübingen speech would be seen as eccentric. The audience at the event were expecting something big and international. He was thinking of something very domestic. I told him about last night's groups in London and Rochdale and said he really had to get a grip. We were not driving an agenda and he looked weak. At the moment his modus operandi was partly the problem. We may be doing the right things but we lacked drive and direction. Peter M doing the AV speech with TB's blessing, and possibly at his behest, was hardly designed to get us back on the core issues.

A Mirror poll showed his ratings down again. PMQs was OK but Hague had the best lines. Also TB failed to back me when Teresa Gorman [Conservative MP] had a go. The Standard splashed on a CBS report about violence in Britain which was totally over the top and I really wanted to go for the report by attacking the BBC's coverage of it. I got Charles Clarke to agree to it but then Jack S vetoed him from doing it. I told Pam Teare [Home Office press officer] they were losing the plot. Jack came on and we had a big row, with him saying I was not always right and no doubt I would tell TB again that the Home Office was full of wankers. I said no, but it was one of the worst departments to deal with. There was right on both sides but I was infuriated at the lack of a real crime message from the Home Office.

Mo apologised for the Royal gaffe, ensuring it ran for another day. TB called to say I was right about Peter's speech. I couldn't understand why he had let it happen. Crazy. Losing the plot time. I had a nice meeting with Joe Haines [former press secretary to Harold Wilson] who agreed with me we should go for the Mail and paint Hague as their poodle. I was probably too frank about how disillusioned I currently was. He felt basic ill discipline and too obviously trying to win the press were giving us problems. I got home by half seven to see the guys who were going over the phones and the fax, but they felt the leak was probably from Philip's end, possibly his bins, but they were going to recommend all manner of tightening up.

Thursday, June 29

Trevor Kavanagh had a piece having a go at me and there were a few pieces running out of TB failing to back me yesterday. I said to him he never instinctively stuck up for people. He apologised and said he hadn't meant it to come out like that. He asked why I was so down on him at the moment. I said I thought he was being weak in sorting some of our problems. Later, at the hotel in Berlin, he said he had been discombobulated by the baby and was also at a loss to know what to do about GB/Peter. He was worried now about positioning re the meeting with Schroeder, which was being seen as a reaction to Chirac.

After the GB meeting, he and I went over to Number 10 for what was meant to be a manifesto meeting but turned into another discussion of tax cuts vs public spending. I persuaded him that we should bring back Mailwatch. I felt it had been a real mistake to drop it because they sensed weakness. I had done a CSR note and GB agreed it without changes so we put it around to all ministers. Cabinet was a bit scratchy. JP was as angry with TB as I was at the moment and told him yesterday he had to start showing more leadership and get a grip. He had a little go at Cabinet, saying perhaps we should review and report back whether we had managed to stick to our agenda. It was a not very subtle dig at Mo over the Palace and Peter re PR. JP and I saw him together afterwards and told him the drifting has to stop. For Tübingen, TB wanted to get up opportunity for all, responsibility from all as a message. I met GB to discuss it and said I wanted to get up on-the-spot fines. TB did a Cockerell interview and was a bit too Prince Charles-ish, but OK.

We left for the trip to Germany and on the way to the airport, he said he was thinking of splitting the Home Office to have a separate department dealing with crime, he would put Blunkett in charge, put Jack S to Education, which we would rename Education and Sport. He was also thinking that we should have a department focused on work rather than unemployment, and a separate department dealing with the non-working age side of DSS – kids' benefits, pensioners, veterans etc. The non-crime Home Office stuff would go to a beefed-up Lord Chancellor's Department. Gaming to DCMS [Department of Culture, Media and Sport]. He was thinking maybe Byers for NIO, maybe Darling to DTI, maybe Mo to a new Pensions department. He was also thinking of coming out firmly for the euro, while on fox hunting saying it was not a priority and he was not prepared to let it get in the way of legislation on things that were. All pretty bold and he wanted to do it just before the CSR to get back to a position of strength. He felt we would go down further before we came up again.

On the plane, we worked on the speech and I was trying to get the religion out and more politics in. We were working up on-the-spot fines as the top policy line. He had recovered some of his confidence, and I some of my confidence in him, by the fact he had at least come up with a few bold plans. We met Schroeder on the bridge where they used to exchange spies, which made for good pictures. They did their doorstep. As he walked over, Schroeder, who always liked to have a laugh and a joke with me, asked if I was always there when the spies were swapped. I like him but didn't get on with [Michael] Steiner [Schroeder's foreign policy adviser] at all. We left them to have dinner and I went back to the hotel to work on the speech. TB came back full of beans, said they got on very well and on the big European stuff he felt we could do a lot of business. TB was being exceptionally nice because he knew I was at the end of my tether.

Friday, June 30

We worked on the speech till 2am and were back at it at 6. The press were almost all leading their political coverage with crap. I put together a note and we got it on the website by 11, making the point that the press did not want a grown-up debate and their coverage of Europe was a joke. ITN used it and the *Guardian* said they were printing it in full. TB seemed up for stepping up the battle with them. TB apologised again for not sticking up for me in the House, said he had felt discombobulated, but he felt better now he had a proper plan. The Chief Rabbi had sent some very good lines through which we used in the sections on community. He agreed we should try to get up on-the-spot fines and I had written in a line about police having the powers to take people to cashpoints. We argued on the plane about whether to keep it in and in the end agreed to. We got to Tübingen. There were a few protestors who stood up and whistled during the speech but he handled them fine. I did a squawk-box briefing back to London.

They all bit on on-the-spot fines, which had been pretty last-moment because the Home Office had been so useless. They had got nobody lined up to support it. It was going big and TB was leading most of the bulletins on something domestic rather than Europe. Charles Clarke was livid because nobody had told him we were doing it. And he told me he thought it was half-baked. I said we needed to take it through the weekend and into Monday as a way of showing we were serious about tackling low-level nuisance crime. Needless to say it was being slammed all over the place by the obvious pressure groups. So what? It was bang on the agenda we should be on. It was getting huge coverage and it wasn't on Europe.

On the flight back, we were briefed that Special Branch were planning to investigate claims of a plot to kill Gaddafi.[1] TB said it

---

[1] Former MI5 officer David Shayler claimed there had been an MI6 plot to assassinate Gaddafi. Despite Robin Cook dismissing the allegation as fantasy, the FCO later admitted 'We have never denied we knew of plots against Gaddafi.'

was totally wrong and scribbled on the report that we should do everything we legitimately could to stop it going ahead. He was on better form, and we both felt better for having had it out over the past few days. When the cashpoint idea started to unravel, in part because the Home Office weren't firm enough, he stood firm, said he was totally up for it and agreed we should keep going. I had a long chat with Jack Straw's son William. He was being pursued by the *Sunday Times* over a false claim that I stopped him sending a letter to *The Times* complaining about GB/Laura Spence. John Patten [former Conservative minister] had kindly tipped me off about it so I wrote a letter to [John] Witherow [*Sunday Times* editor] saying it was rubbish. William called, said he had been planning to write something critical of GB in his capacity as president of New College [Oxford] junior common room. Jack said it was a mistake because he would be asked to back either GB or his son.

Saturday, July 1

On-the-spot fines were being savaged all over the shop. The *Independent* and *Guardian* both had typically wanky leaders. Petrol was becoming a huge issue. I sold the idea of a TB article on it to the *News of the World*. We had to show there could be no pandering, that we were capable of tough decisions, real choices etc. TB felt we had to put the choice in very stark terms – cheaper petrol or hospitals. I had a row with the *Northern Echo* over a picture of Cherie and Leo and was criticised for being heavy-handed when I put out an advisory that it was done without consent. The downside of workload vs family was badly apparent in the afternoon.

I promised the boys to take them to the shops and told them to go ahead without me while I was on the phone sorting something with Rebekah Wade. They got mugged on the way and came back pretty shaken up. They knew the kids involved so Omar [Pallas, father of the friend the boys were with] went out to find them. God knows what we were planning to do, but I really felt the gorge rising. We found them, about eight of them, rampaging around and were about to confront them when one of them said 'There's that bloke who works for Tony Blair.' I let Omar do all the talking. They were classic out-of-control estate kids, pinch-faced, skinny, contemptuous of any authority. I called the cops who said they had twenty incidents waiting to be attended to and no support officers. And the Home Office wondered why we kept banging on at them.

Through the evening, I got a stack of calls about a vicious attack from Ken Follett [author and husband of Barbara Follett, Labour MP] in the *Observer*. Really lurid over-the-top stuff and very personal. I got the *Observer* to change two lines, first to deal with the bollocks that TB tried to blacken Mo's name, and second that I poured poison into their ears. I gave PA a statement that it was sad that there were always people on the left willing to peddle the propaganda of the right.

Sunday, July 2

TB's *News of the World* article was leading the news, followed by Follett. I called Eddie Mair [BBC] to challenge Follett if he had any evidence. OK interview. *The World at One* wanted a minister and Margaret B agreed to do it. She and I had a good bitch about Mo. Mo called, bright as a bee, and said 'Hi Ali, just to say if you want me to go up and say whoever's doing all this to me, it's not Tony, I will,' and I really lost it. I said the best thing she should do is what she should have done months ago and tell the truth, namely that it's total balls that anyone was doing her in from Number 10. She could say that she was too busy dealing with serious issues like drugs and social exclusion to worry about gossip, but no, we had to deal with this fucking rubbish every weekend because people were too self-indulgent and because wankers like Ken Follett wanted a few more minutes of fame. She was clearly taken aback and for a while there was total silence. She said was I aware of her discussions with TB about leaving government to try to get an international job and we needed to talk about how to make it a good story for Tony. I said I wasn't in the mood.

I spoke to TB, who also said to her she had to make it clear that the stuff about her being briefed against was rubbish. He was pretty forceful and she sounded close to tears. She later called Anji and said I had blamed her for the whole thing, which indeed I did. I knew TB hadn't said anything untoward about her, I knew I hadn't. Most of the journalists Jonathan spoke to complained he never said anything to them. I was convinced she and her pals were the ones putting it about. I was also dealing with Byers who was doing *On the Record*, then a leaked memo saying we risked manufacturing meltdown if we didn't join the euro, then Piers Morgan came on offering me space to respond to Follett, which I did, then Levy on pissed off and depressed at the *Sunday Times* getting into his tax affairs, then a stack of ministers doing interviews. Follett was doing the rounds. Beckett was excellent in response and even Alan Simpson [left-wing Labour MP] was pretty supportive on the radio. The boys were running at Hammersmith, so I took them down there and got Alex F to speak to Rory who was still a bit shaken up, then we got back to watch France win Euro 2000 [2-1 vs Italy], which was very annoying.

Monday, July 3

Pretty much wall-to-wall Follett, and the leaked memo on the euro, though the crime summit was leading the news. Needless to say, by the end of the day it was a disaster area with the sense of a U-turn on on-the-spot fines. At GB's meeting, he was raging about the leak. Then later we had the leak of a telegram from our ambassador in Japan saying much the same thing. Milburn cancelled at the last minute the Lib-Lab health plan for tomorrow.

At TB's office meeting, we went through Europe/EMU. Peter M continued to argue for a more forward position and for being more relaxed. We were still pondering the tax vs public services line. TB basically wanted to be pro investment but without ruling out tax cuts. Media cynicism at the moment was totally corrosive and really eroding faith not just in us, but in politics. On fox hunting, I said that if he moved from his *Question Time* position he would be dead with some of our people. He got very sharp with me.

Later, he took the rest of the office through the changes we talked about last week and they were pretty underwhelmed. He also said we needed a big strategy to 'cuddle' people and get more of them back on board. I said I felt our problem was pandering, and cuddling sounded a bit like that. I could see he was beginning to worry that I was losing it. Maybe I was. Maybe I was just off the reservation at the moment, and my strengths were becoming my weaknesses. It was certainly an odd position to be in where his main conduit to the press couldn't much stand the press and the feeling was often mutual.

I had a CSR meeting with Ed Balls and co to work out the follow-through programme, though Margaret B wasn't keen on having too many statements in the Commons. I felt we had to get the CSR dominating the news agenda for two weeks if possible. As I ranted and raved about the crime summit coverage, JP popped his head round the door. He had just seen TB. Like me, he was worried we were losing the plot. He wanted to get back into a deputy role with less time on the DETR and more time making sure our top people did their jobs properly and behaved. He also felt he had to engage more, taking on the nay-sayers. The nine o'clock news was dreadful – crime climbdown, spin, euro disaster area. As I said to Blunkett, it's like swimming through shit, you have to hold your breath and keep your nerve.

Philip called from Putney and said the *Mail* agenda was pouring out of them. He too was totally persuaded we had to isolate the *Mail* and hammer it. I spoke to TB later who said once we decide war on the media, that's it, there's no coming back from it. I said I was advocating war on the *Mail*. I talked things over with Fiona and we were both beginning to think maybe I should move to Millbank.

Tuesday, July 4

The press was full of spin stuff, several pieces vile about me. The GB meeting was more angst than anger. I was working on Thursday's speech on race and exploring whether we could take the fixed penalty idea further, e.g. for parents of unruly kids. TB called me in and asked if I was all right. He said there was so much anger in me at the moment and it's not sensible. He said there weren't many people he was dependent on but I was one of them and angry advice was not always the right advice. He relied on me for the right advice. He said he relied on me more now than ever because GB was always in a rage and always calculating, which meant he gave warped advice, whereas Peter M was incapable of not being devious. But they were both brilliant and we still needed them.

He said my problem was that most Cabinet ministers, certainly the important ones, trusted and respected my judgement, so I was unique. It wasn't like [Margaret Thatcher's press secretary Bernard] Ingham because in the end I was on a par with the senior Cabinet guys. He had thought about whether I should go upfront as a government spokesman but felt that would just lead to more noise about propriety, but he just wanted me to get in a better frame of mind so that I wasn't always fighting. He said it wasn't sensible to be at war with the press the whole time. It's what they want. He said in the end he had to take most of the strain because he was the top man. But when it came to taking the strain and the pressure, I was second in line and he knew that I was talking more than most people were capable of. But somehow I had to get more time off and I had to delegate more, and I had to try to rebuild some of the relationships with the media.

We had an office meeting on the reshuffle and the restructuring of government and every proposal seemed to bring its own problems. I felt the most pressing question was whether to put Peter M in Millbank. Byers to Northern Ireland might be seen as a bit of a slap down. We rejected the idea of Reid, Darling or [John] Denham for Millbank because we knew Peter would still be diddling. I got home and JP called in a rage, having heard about Milburn's Lib-Lab stuff. He said what's the point of saying we were going to be a team and he doesn't even tell me about this? He knows I'm going to be totally

July '00: Blair relies on Campbell advice

neuralgic about it and what does he say? That it doesn't matter, when the NHS is what our people really love and we are sullying that by cosying up to the fucking Liberals. I said only TB, Alan and I knew about it, possibly GB, and that it had been postponed. It ended fine after he had let off steam. I was also getting it from Cook and Byers who said they were constantly being briefed against by the Treasury.

TB said to me later GB was playing games again because he sensed he [TB] was weak. He also said it was important I understood the press were going for me because they knew I was important to him. But we had to watch out for the 'real deputy PM' gibe, because if people believed it, it wasn't good for him or me.

Wednesday, July 5

PMQs was grim beyond belief. TB mixed up Australia and America, said that we were spin not substance. We had planned all day on Hague coming on all the crap. We had the *Mail* leader of yesterday covering all the difficult issues of recent days and we had had Steve Richards' column saying they worked out the strategy for PMQs by seeing what was in the *Mail* the day before. We worked up really strong lines but TB didn't really want to get stuck in.

The new inward investment figures, partly because of the leaks, were leading the news as a problem and briefing against ministers was still going on. The *Guardian* for example had said I was responsible for on-the-spot fines, TB/GB loathed each other. Jack was livid that we were still pushing on-the-spot fines. I got back for a meeting on tomorrow's speech [to the black churches conference in Brighton] and told TB it would be one of those that would be a total disaster or a total triumph, and he didn't much like that.

Thursday, July 6

At 2am, Godric called to say Euan had been picked up by the cops, drunk and incapable [in Leicester Square], and the *Sun* and *The Times* had been tipped off. I told him to emphasise he was still sixteen and try to get them to hold off. I got in, went up to the flat and saw TB. He said he hadn't slept at all, he was cross with Euan, and had been up all night dealing with it. We then had an extraordinary meeting with Peter M, PG, Douglas A, DM in the flat, where Peter said we had to get off Europe and division and on to core priorities. If Douglas had not been there, I would really have gone for him, but I was so angry now I could barely bring myself to look at him, he having started off the last wave on Europe.

We were having to put together a plan re Euan. The cops said he had been found alone, lying on the ground. Some of TB's Special Branch guys had identified him. He was released with a reprimand and a caution. Cherie was in Portugal with the baby, so I spoke to her on the kind of line we were using, fairly light. She sounded very calm about it. Jack came in and briefed Tony more fully, having been briefed by the deputy commissioner. The guy from the Met came through for a meeting with me and Jack and we put together a more detailed statement. I had written to Jack to apologise for the cashpoint business, whilst defending the overall thrust on fixed penalties, and in the meeting he and Ian Johnston [assistant commissioner] were making lots of jokes about on-the-spot fines and why they hadn't marched Euan off to the nearest cashpoint.

Cabinet itself was mainly the legislation to deal with hooligans. JP had a bit of a go at Jack for not being tough enough. The briefing was fine. Mike White was terrific, as when I said they wanted him [Euan] to have a normal upbringing and Mike said 'He's doing very well on that front then.' There was actually going to be a lot of sympathy both for TB and Euan. Fiona came down to see me after the briefing and said that Euan had seen the news and was distraught. He was lying in bed, looking pretty grim, and said he had gone out with his friend James and two kids from Bristol. He had only had three pints, and there was no way he would have been drunk and incapable on that. He said he had drunk a lot more than that before and not been drunk on it. He was sure his drink was spiked because the others had not felt bad at all while he was totally all over the place and didn't have a clue how he got to the Square. He said he was worried his mum would never forgive him. I said it would be grim for a few days but then fine. I felt sorry for him because the press would now see him as a fair target on the socialising front. I called [PCC chairman Lord] Wakeham and agreed he would put out a friendly line, as we had accepted it was fair to report this.

On the train down to Brighton, we heard that Germany had won the World Cup bid. TB asked if things could get any worse. But the black churches conference cheered him up. There was real sympathy about Euan. They loved the speech. They loved the line about Britain one day having a black prime minister. There couldn't have been a better audience on a day like this. Then came news of a massive pro-hunt demo and we were kept waiting before we could go. We got driven through a pretty unpleasant bunch of people. We arrived at the school where he was doing *Question Time*. TB was pretty nervous but got into his stride, dealt with Euan, went for it on EMU, was good on leadership. He missed one or two tricks but it was pretty good. I went in to meet him at the end and one of the audience came over and said make sure those Tories never come back.

He spoke to Cherie in the car and it was clear he wasn't buying Euan's theory that the drink was spiked. TB said he wanted to stop for a pint, very rare, off the beaten track. The cops found a very nice little pub and the locals were gobsmacked, including a barman who was only working there for that day. It was interesting how people reacted. There was a couple in the corner clearly having an illicit meeting who scarpered the minute we arrived. Some of them just wanted to be left alone and ignore us. Lots of them wanted their photos taken, one or two wanted a serious chat. Cherie was really steamed up about how the press had got to hear about Euan before either she or Tony did, and going on about needing an inquiry. We were going to have to work out how to get Euan to go to the cops for his caution. By the time we got back to Number 10, and up to see Cherie and Euan, I was so knackered I was even nice to Carole [Caplin, friend and adviser to CB], who was looking tanned and pretty fit after their little break in Portugal.

Friday, July 7

The press wasn't bad, felt we handled Euan OK. We had a strategy meeting in the Cabinet Room, TB, GB, Peter M, AC, PG, AH, SM, Ed B, DM. We went through the war-book draft and it was interesting that TB was really focused on the Tory attack, more than us getting up a positive message. GB and I both said we had a real problem with discipline and unity on Europe, Robin having last night said it was inevitable we would join EMU. TB said we would have to slap him down on it. Peter argued against that. PG's polling showed all the main indicators down for us. Unity, delivery, competence, we were even in a minus on the economy, which was probably just a general slump in mood. We had given the agenda away. GB had to leave early as he was going to Japan, and after he left Peter was being ridiculous, constantly complaining about lack of economic message and then going to pick up the sword on the table opposite TB and waving it around like a samurai.

I did a long interview with Cockerell, where he had another go at me over psychological flaws and talked through Euan, Follett and Mo. Hilary was advancing Charing Cross police station and Jack called to say it was perfectly proper to get cautioned at a different station to the one he had been taken to. I spoke to TB and Cherie and agreed he should go to Kennington. I went up to the flat and TB was sitting there with Euan, who looked pretty sheepish, and Cherie was telling him not to give the police any of that nonsense about spiked drinks. Euan said he was really nervous. There was a load of press at Charing Cross and none at Kennington. They went out through the tunnel to the MoD and got in and out without being seen. I had a statement ready to go. I saw Euan when he got back, clearly relieved. We put out the statement once he was back in the flat.

Saturday, July 8
I'd done a briefing on JP's new role which went fine. I briefed on [John] Birt's role and then did a note to all relevant ministers. Joe Murphy got hold of last week's strategic context note on the economic narrative. The *Mail on Sunday* were doing a big number, stating as a fact that I called GB psychologically flawed. We went out to Kew to see Stewart and Lucy Binns [friends] and Frank Teasdale [Burnley chairman]. I took the boys to a little cafe where a couple of blokes started trying to wind me up. Rory was all for me steaming in but I ignored them. The kids gave me strength as ever.

Monday, July 10
At the office meeting, we discussed Cockerell, and after all the mauling I had been getting in the press, there was quite a lot of distancing going on. I hadn't exactly helped myself. It was almost certainly a mistake, both the fact of the film, and also pulling back from the press during the filming. TB felt the best line to run was that I was more spinned against than spinning, but long term I needed to get back on an even keel with them. Fiona was convinced that Peter M was using it all to stir against me. Philip felt Peter would be worried that I was back working closely with GB. TB had gone back on the idea of major restructuring for the moment because he felt it would look like panic and just before a long recess wasn't the right time. JP called, very friendly, just asking how I was bearing up with all the media shit. So did Kilfoyle, and Dobbo. As ever, though, quite a lot of people ran a mile once the going got tough. Apparently the bookies were giving odds on my successor. I had a CSR meeting with Ed Balls. Ed was obsessing about something Peter had said about the need to move to a different kind of battlefield to take the political world by surprise. He assumed he must mean either Lib-Labbery or Europe.

Milburn came in to discuss his paper on alternative funding systems which he was keen to brief to the *Telegraph*. But when he heard about it, GB was storming around because it rejected social insurance out of hand and he felt it wrong to rule out options. We had a meeting

July '00: GB storms out over health funding

– TB, GB, AM, AC – where GB was in killer driller mode and eventually, as he wanted, Alan said well let's not bother then. GB then went off, worked on it himself in Miliband's room and called me out of the NHS Plan meeting to discuss.

I was aware through the day that people were looking at me and talking to me in a different way, asking me how I felt as though something terrible had happened. What had happened was that the level of media focus and criticism had moved up a few notches. When I got home, Fiona said Cherie had said to her that Peter M had done a private note to TB on the media operation. Fiona said she feared I was being set up for a fall, to be redefined as a bad thing and go with my reputation shattered. She was very down about TB, who I spoke up for, and even more down on Peter, who I spoke up for less convincingly. I said it was natural for TB to want other advice, not least because I had been making mistakes, e.g. cashpoints, e.g. Cockerell. I hadn't been enjoying it and therefore I hadn't been adding much value. Also, because of the way I treated them, the press were determined to see me off. It was just one of those things.

Tuesday, July 11

I took the day off to take the children to my mum's. The main political event was Hague and Portillo doing a double act effectively dumping the tax guarantee, or at least turning it into a cuts guarantee. I worked on a draft statement for Thursday. TB on the economic narrative and the jobs scene looking good had to be right. GB was trying to talk him out of it. The *Sun* had a leader, not very nice, is the end nigh for Campbell?

Wednesday, July 12

The press was bad for the Tories. I put together, at Philip's suggestion, a proper handling strategy for the Cockerell film when it came out. TB was doing our press conference and with the Tories in trouble it was fairly straightforward and we led the news for most of the day. If we could put together a good PMQs we would be in a strong position. It went well. He was recovering his confidence and also so were we. I had a meeting with Margaret B and Murdo Maclean [private secretary to the chief whip] who wanted to explain why there were real problems with the legislative load. Mo was due to do the *Today* programme and had decided she wanted her top line to be that it was a year where we didn't exactly cover ourselves in glory. At the four o'clock, TB having stormed it at PMQs, the first question was what was he on, and I said he was on substance. Betty [Boothroyd] announced her retirement [as Speaker], which would obviously get a lot of play.

The Cockerell people had started their hype and were sending round postcards trailing it – a picture of me at my desk, TB looking down a bit anxiously. It looked like I was the boss and he was explaining himself, which got me worried. Today showed again the importance of getting it right in the House. He had easily won it and it led to the best press we have had in ages, though we had another GB surprise, an overnight briefing that there was more money available in the CSR than we first thought.

Thursday, July 13

Cockerell did an interview in the *Telegraph*, which was pretty straight, and made me think his programme might not be so bad. Peter Hain had done an article for *Progress*, placed in today's *Independent*, which said ministers were like automatons. JP called him to blast him out of the water. Hain said it was cleared by Number 10. Balls was it. He had told Sally he was doing it, Sally suggested changes and he just did it. I went up to the flat to work with TB on the Annual Report statement and the debate Hague had called on the relations between the executive and Parliament. Jack Straw came in to talk about the hooliganism legislation and was very friendly, said he had been worried about me, thought I had been down. The Tories had reneged on a deal on the bill.

Cabinet was reasonably good-humoured. There was a funny moment when JP's phone went off and he was tut-tutting loudly at the idea someone had their phone in there, before realising it was his. The other big laugh came when Jack said he had been dealing with Simon Hughes who was pretty straight. GB was in Scotland so TB set out the picture pre-CSR. He said it was because we had tackled debt and got social security spending falling in real terms that we were now able to make further investments. He said he couldn't exaggerate the importance of the Tories falling apart on the tax guarantee. Blunkett made the point there must be no funny money and double counting. Several of them told me Mo had been dreadful on the *Today* programme. I got a transcript, which confirmed they were right.

The press went in droves to a screening of the Cockerell film, which I watched in the office. It seemed fine, worthy, neither great nor disastrous. The only moment I cringed was when I seemed to be taking the piss out of TB. There was a real sense of access but some, e.g. Peter H, felt it made TB look weak and me look strong. Jamie

Rubin did me proud on *Westminster Live*. It certainly wasn't a hatchet job, though the press were bound to go for the bits they wanted. We went over to the House for TB's statement on the Annual Report, which led the news, and the debate. Hague was very funny. TB was having dinner with Dacre, Rothermere and wives and I felt that was a bad move, that we shouldn't be going near the place. TB insisted if we were not going to have a jihad then we had to try to get them on board as best we could. I said I believed 'Operation Pander' had done us a lot of damage. TB seemed fine about Cockerell. He didn't watch it but had relied on Jonathan, Anji and Sally for their views. Fiona felt it did me no harm but it still hadn't been worth the hassle.

Friday, July 14

TB's worry, that the Cockerell film stood up the Rory Bremner analysis, was slightly borne out by the press. The *Mirror* leader said I could take over, several said TB looked weak but at least it wasn't meltdown and most people thought we came out better than the press. Peter M felt we had to sue for peace now. TB ditto. Jonathan felt we should go all out for on-the-record televised briefings. TB felt I had to go on a major schmooze. He did admit his dinner with the *Mail* lot had been ghastly and they were just basically right-wing shits.

Saturday, July 15

Blunkett lost his performance-related pay case to the NUT which was the main news of the day.[1] We went to Tessa's [Jowell] in Warwickshire and I managed to avoid doing much work.

Sunday, July 16

Phil Webster called to say he and Trevor Kavanagh had been given a copy of a note done by TB on April 29 re the need for us to engage on 'touchstone issues'. He started to read it to me and I knew instantly which one it was. It was clearly very worrying if notes done by TB for a fairly small number of people were going missing. When I called him, he said it was ridiculous if he could not write this kind of thing. It was also very destabilising. Yesterday's *Guardian* ran a story about emails from Anji about last night's Cockerell programme. Fiona pointed out that everything that had been leaked so far had been sent to me, so maybe it was something to do with the fax. Wilson talked

[1] A High Court judge ruled that David Blunkett's Education (School Teachers' Pay and Conditions) Order, effectively rewriting the contracts of 400,000 teachers, was a 'hybrid and flawed document'. The judicial review was brought by the National Union of Teachers.

to Lander again. News management-wise, it was probably best to get the focus as much as possible on the leak rather than the content, which wasn't terribly edifying.

Monday, July 17

The leak ran very big, splashed in the *Sun* and *Times*, picked up by the others and straight off as a broadcast lead. It was a very grim start to the week, just as it had looked like things were getting better. It also played into the idea that TB was more interested in presentation than substance. And we were wondering how many other notes like this were stored away somewhere waiting to be leaked. After the black humour, we agreed at TB's office meeting it was pointless talking about it and instead focused on CSR, Europe, and our continuing hunt for a full-time speech-writer. TB felt there was no problem with the note itself and we had to emphasise it showed how focused he was on people's priorities.

Post-Cockerell, he said we now had to draw a line with the media. I felt they had to be challenged more. He said we weren't in a position of sufficient strength. I felt that was cowardice. I had a long meeting with Julia Eastman [security adviser, Number 10] who said she had never met TB properly. I asked why they couldn't put phone taps on the entire staff to see who was shipping stuff out, and she said, very nicely, that that probably wasn't allowed. She felt that our systems were quite loose. I said I didn't believe anyone in our inner circle would do this but she was very keen on getting a heavy inquiry going. She was right to do so because if this kind of thing was being leaked it meant potentially whoever was doing it had access to really sensitive stuff. TB and I went for a stroll in the garden. He said we just about got away with Cockerell, but that's enough. He asked if I had a problem with Peter and I said I felt him wheedling away whenever he thought I was working too closely with GB.

Tuesday, July 18

They were now into line-by-line analysis of Philip's memo. I believed strongly they were as bad as they currently were because of pandering. There wasn't much point trying to work out who did it. One theory was Peter M to take the gloss off the build-up to the CSR. Another was GB because it would show TB as all spin at a time he was all substance. GB did an excellent presentation to the CSR Cabinet and was well received. The figures on debt as a share of national income were impressive, thirty-seven per cent to thirty-six to thirty-three. The costs of unemployment were down £3.5 billion. Good growth delivered up an extra £6 billion. Eighty per cent of the new money was for public services. He went through it all then department by department, and most of them ought to be able to do something pretty meaningful with what they were getting. He was on the right track on the big picture and he had some good individual moves to do with children. Bruce said the PLP feedback on Cockerell was totally positive, that they basically felt reassured there was someone in here who was really Labour.

I went to Richard Wilson's office for a meeting with him, Jonathan, Stephen Lander and others on the leaks and general security. The general belief was that it was a mole of some sort. I said there was a case for a police inquiry. They agreed that even if it was unlikely we would find the culprit, we might deter them by the nature of the inquiry. I pointed out that all the leaks were political/strategic and combined to make one central point about TB personally being about spin not substance. I went over to the House with TB. GB was excellent and Portillo hopeless. Earlier I had spoken to Phil Webster and said to him 'I wonder what the next thing will be.' He called me later in the afternoon and said 'Are you ready for this?' He then read to me another leaked PG memo about TB getting the right place in history. It was a very colourful piece of writing with several dreadful lines for us. Phil read it to me. He believed it was clearly a political operation, possibly involving the Tories, he didn't know. I felt we should start to go with allegations of dirty tricks. GB was worried it would just blow out the CSR if we went very heavy and we were better being dismissive. That was probably right. But the truth was we were probably going to get knocked off course once *The Times* was out which was a real pain. We had to assume someone had a stack of these things. They were being used in quite a sophisticated way.

Wednesday, July 19

Though the BBC led in the headlines on the CSR follow-up, the bulk of their stuff was on the Gould memo. The best thing was a panel of three who said they liked the CSR and couldn't care less about leaks. But it was another blow. PG came round first thing, obviously worried he might be becoming a liability and would have to go. But to be fair to TB, there was no way he would allow that. He said we shouldn't worry too much. We should start to prepare people for the idea there would be one of these a day for weeks. He did not buy the idea this would be GB. But he was worried about the PLP. Bruce said the feeling among MPs was we had to get a grip of all this nonsense that gets written, all the soap-opera stuff.

Godric did the 11 while I did a planning meeting for September and had a real row with Anji about the sheer volume of speeches going into the diary. They were not being linked strategically. TB saw Eduard Shevardnadze [President of Georgia] then prepared for PMQs where we were really up for going for Hague if he went on the leak because we could show again he never bothered with serious policy. It went OK and TB rallied the troops well. Clare Short was speaking to the press gallery lunch. She had a real go at the lobby but also at the 'New' in New Labour, which was seen as a whack on Philip. Blunkett also had a mild pop and made the mistake of saying there was a 'mole' at Number 10, which put the story back where we didn't want it.

We set out for the airport, neither of us feeling terribly well prepared for Japan. We agreed TB should do an off-camera on-the-record briefing on the plane to blow away all the leak stuff and set up G8 properly. He did well and went back to the front and I had a long session with them. They felt I came out of Cockerell fine but they knew it was a bit of a stitch-up idea. I said I was minded to go back to more sensible arrangements if things settled down and they stopped the relentless focus on spin and me. I agreed to have lunch with them in Japan. I had dinner with TB and said he had to flap less, be stronger in the signals he sends out to ministers and staff. He had to be more like GB, focusing more on long-term action than short-term 'what do we say?' The irony is GB is probably more short-termist in reality but he hides short-term questions in long-term language. We arrived to be met by the ambassador and went straight to the new Otani hotel. We had a meeting with [missing British bar hostess] Lucie Blackman's dad and sister. It must be terrible being caught up in something like they were, a daughter in trouble and possibly dead.[1] JP's Transport Plan was going well, so I was quite keen to play down coverage here, much to the broadcasters' annoyance.

We left for the G8, at a palace up the road from the hotel. Clinton was late because of MEPP [Middle East peace process] talks, Schroeder didn't bother, Chirac came last and in the end TB was in hysterics, said it was possibly the most pointless meeting he had ever attended, enlivened only by Chirac's extraordinary rudeness to Larry Summers, [US Treasury Secretary]. 'Intelligent and determined to make sure everyone knows it,' said TB. He said Chirac went on for twenty minutes of cliché-ridden waffle and then when Summers started,

[1] Blackman had in fact been abducted and dismembered. Her remains would not be found until February 2001.

Chirac leant back in his chair, threw his head back, snored loudly, came to a couple of minutes later with what TB called a loud snort and then shouted 'Too long, too long,' in English as Summers went on and on. TB said it was as impressive an exhibition of rudeness and anti-Americanism as he had ever seen.

We had a bilateral with [Japanese Prime Minister Yoshiro] Mori who was more enormous in the flesh than in pictures. We had just been watching the sumo wrestling on TV and I was mouthing 'sumo' to TB to try and get him going. Mori told us he was at fourteen per cent approval ratings which put our problems in perspective. They did BNFL, Blackman, EMU, Korea, G8. We set off for the flight to Okinawa. Alex F called, said he had seen the Cockerell film, that I did well because I kept my temper but 'What's important is your relationship with TB – nothing else really matters. Provided you two see the big picture clearly and work together, you'll be fine.'

John Sawers had a chat with us on the plane [to Okinawa] and said he felt TB spent far too much time worrying about the media. He didn't think they were as influential as they thought they were. TB said he might yet come to my view that we go for them publicly and consistently but he certainly wasn't there yet. John felt we were operating too much like in opposition. As we were in Japan, and Mori had welcomed our commitment on EMU, there was the mood for another Europe story and Godric called to say he feared Peter M's speech on Europe, cleared by TB, would be a problem, so we got changes put in. Jonathan called to say we understood *The Times* and *Sunday Times* were working in concert on leaked memos and had another one ready to coincide with the health plan.

I slept through OK and seemed to have avoided jet lag and went out for a swim in the Pacific which was nice while it lasted but my eyes were stinging like hell when I got out. TB had been up since 4 and was clearly knackered and was wondering why we bothered with these summits anyway. We had a bilateral with [Romano] Prodi who was rambling even more than usual. And the more he rambled, the more whispery he got so that by the end he was inaudible. TB was nagging me the whole time to be more friendly to the press. We drove out to a school where he did a little speech and a Q&A and enough for clips to tide us through the day. It was incredibly hot and I went for another swim in the pool later. I had a chat with GB who was feeling the CSR had been pretty much wiped out because of all the leaks. I read the latest draft of the NHS Plan which was coming on really well. TB set off for the summit with Jeremy while the rest of us were put into a cottage which had a tiny office. It was a very odd place indeed, and of course being Japan the protocol was even heavier than ever.

Our hacks weren't much interested in the stuff they were discussing on debt and instead were making a big hoo-ha about the $500,000 cost of the event. I had a brief chat with Clinton who said he was hanging in there on the Middle East, that he felt something could happen and he was going back early to finish the talks. On the elections, I sensed he was feeling they weren't necessarily going to adopt the same strategy as he did, perhaps be less mainstream as a way of differentiating. He said if the economy's the issue, Gore wins. TB had a Putin bilateral. He was less aggressive on Chechnya, but really wound up with the Yanks over National Missile Defense, and he was clearly irritated at Chirac for not totally buying his line on Chechnya. In the car, TB said he felt we needed an identified Hague-basher because he shouldn't do it all, maybe Peter because he was ruthless and sharp enough. He said he was getting a lot of sympathy from the other leaders over Euan and the leaks.

Saturday, July 22

TB said over breakfast that in eight presidential suites in eight five-star hotels there are eight leaders asking eight sherpas and eight press secretaries 'What the hell are we all doing here?' We were staying in a beautiful part of the world, in spectacular and luxurious surroundings. But it was all a bit unreal. There didn't seem to be any 'real people' around the place, other than those brought in for a swim. The agenda was fairly big stuff, but it was doubtful much of it actually needed the leaders to resolve. A lot of it was ceremony and small talk and a few half-decent bilaterals. I had lunch with [Phil] Webster, [Charles] Reiss, [David] Hughes and [Trevor] Kavanagh. I gave them a bit of strategy and dividing lines leading up to the election.

On relations with them, I said I felt latterly it was all counter-productive, the briefings were a waste of time, because they danced on pinheads and spent the whole time just trying to wind me up and catch me out and though they wound me up they hardly ever caught me out. But it was a waste of time and energy. Phil agreed. Trevor and Charles felt I underestimated the mutual benefit of a constant dialogue with someone inside TB's mind in a way that Godric or any other civil servant was never going to be. I said they had to understand it was a two-way thing. If they were going to make spin such an issue, then why should I play into that? They knew I didn't brief against Mo so why had they never written that? Reiss said the reason spin was such a story was because there were no big divisions of an ideological nature, no big crises or scandals. I said if there are no real scandals, it's not their job to invent phoney ones. I said I might come back to do more briefings but I was more inclined to open them up to more people. It was probably useful but Phil was really the only one who seemed to see things from my perspective as well as his own.

I went back to see TB at the cottage. He was wearing one of the silly shirts they were all being made to wear. He said he was bored and we needed to get some muscle back into the deliberations. We were not getting very far on the new trade round. Apart from Putin's idea of an email network between them, and TB and Chirac arguing hard on debt relief, there wasn't much to brief out. TB came down with me to where the media were to do a very sweaty doorstep, after which he needed a towel to wipe himself down. Then we left for the Okinawa reception where the leaders were clapped in one by one, with Putin easily getting the loudest applause. On the way, TB was lamenting GB's failure properly to get stuck into the Tories and also said he sometimes felt I had bought into the propaganda that he was weak. He said if he really felt we had to take on the press, he would. He was unconvinced it was the right thing to do.

Philip called. It was now going from the sublime to the ridiculous. The *Sunday Times* had got hold of the note he had faxed to me that Grace [his daughter] had had a dream in which we lost the election and Tony and Cherie moved in with them. Where the fuck did that come from? It was sent from him to me and I put it straight into the shredder.

Sunday, July 23

The Sundays were full of the usual crap though there was more than expected coverage of the summit. TB was due to do [Adam] Boulton and we agreed he push on the froth vs fundamentals line. The *Sunday Times* leak story was a joke and treated as such. Boulton ran off at the end with the draft communiqué complete with Jeremy's markings and comments, which we had to get back from him. We went to Clinton's hotel for a brief bilateral breakfast. Their hotel was even smarter than ours and the Yanks had done the usual fine job with the room for the meeting. They did a brief doorstep largely on GM food. They travelled down together to the summit. Bill seemed about as bored as we were. I went into a bar with Alison [Blackshaw] and bumped into Schroeder who had nipped out, so he was bored too. He was on a roll though. The *Herald Tribune* had done a piece contrasting soaring Schroeder with stalling Blair.

It had been a nice enough place, and technically well organised, but everyone was glad to get back to the airport and head for home. TB and I were working on the NHS Plan. Then Tanya came down with a look of panic on her face and said there had been a near riot at the back of the plane. Alison had gone up the plane to say TB was coming back and Kavanagh and [John] Sergeant were watching a movie and said there was no real appetite for a briefing. When the others heard, they went berserk. I went up and was greeted by a round of applause, as was TB when he came back. I took a sleeping pill and slept through what I later learnt were 140 mile an hour winds.

Monday, July 24

We had an ongoing row all day with Jack over transsexuals and sex offences. Why on earth Jack was so keen to do all this was beyond me. I had a meeting with TB and Bruce. We were worried [Chris] Woodhead [chief inspector of schools] was going to resign and switch openly to the Tories. TB, unbelievably, was still keen to defend him. We had an office meeting to plan August and September but it was pretty meandering. Eventually I snapped and said none of this will happen unless you get a grip of GB and Peter M, and unless we properly empower Millbank. GB has done the CSR, since when nothing. Peter is barely visible at Millbank. I felt myself close to losing it and I could see that some of the others were shocked, but I really had had enough. He was asking us for miracles. Added to which I wasn't convinced people wanted all this stuff during August and I knew we had the usual scrabbling around for people who were even willing to stay in the country in August. I said he may have a point but as ever it was going to fall to me to put it all together, and I wasn't having it.

The meeting ended OK but then after a few minutes he called me back, and was a bit steelier than usual. He said you cannot talk to me like that. It's wrong and it unsettles all the others. He said this is not about vanity or *amour propre* because I am the least status-conscious politician I know, but that was bad. And the reason we have things like Rory Bremner is because that kind of thing gets out. I kind of apologised and said I felt completely stymied by the lack of follow-through from ministers and the lack of basic discipline and professionalism, and the extent to which he expected me and one or two others to pick up all the pieces. But I accepted I was too easily slipping into a mode of being critical of him. He said it was OK for me to go at him in front of Sally, Anji and Jonathan but that was it. I got round to my desk and a call from Fiona to say the kids were fighting and could I go home.

Tuesday, July 25

The launch of the Football Foundation with Keegan went pretty well. At the GB meeting, he was worried about health dividing lines and how we squared our concordat with the private sector with the attack on the Tories over private medical insurance. Anji told me TB had been really taken aback yesterday when I lost it with him, especially as we had got on really well in Japan. He said he felt we had gone ten steps forward, twenty steps back. I noticed for the first time that he looked a bit irritated when I stole a piece of his fruit. I did my note on August/September, then news came of Concorde crashing in Paris.[1] We took the kids to Walthamstow Dogs, which Calum wanted to do for his birthday. We were stuck in traffic on the North Circular when a man in a convertible sports car said he really enjoyed Cockerell, didn't envy me my job at all but 'keep sticking it up them'. Fiona got a call from a friend saying there was a big profile of me in the *New York Times*.

Wednesday, July 26

Obviously the Concorde crash wiped out everything. Philip [leaked memos] was on page 1 of the *Guardian* which said Max Clifford was at the centre of it, plus Benji the Binman.[2] PG was keen to push the boat out but I felt it best that it just went away.

Alice Miles suggested in her [*Times*] column that GB wasn't keen on some of the private sector stuff in the health plan. Sally was convinced GB was organising against TB, not really defending him, and not really doing much for the TB agenda. He had done the CSR and was now barely visible. Concorde took some heat off Jack's sex offences review, which I had taken to calling the Shagging in Public Bill. Charlie and I went to see Blunkett to go over a twelve-month Grid. He had been getting a great press recently. Too great, he said,

[1] The Air France plane, en route from Paris to New York, crashed in Gonesse near Paris, killing one hundred passengers, nine crew and four people on the ground.
[2] The paper claimed that Clifford had acted as a go-between in the leaking of five Downing Street memos after they had been recovered from discarded rubbish by Benjamin Pell. When 'Benji the Binman' had previously been convicted of stealing documentary waste from a law firm, the court was told he suffered from an obsessive compulsive personality disorder in the form of 'collection mania'.

adding it won't be long before GB sets upon him. Hague did Section 28 as expected at PMQs and TB was excellent, really stood up for it again. Milburn, Darren Murphy [special adviser] and I worked up a pre-briefing plan on the NHS Plan and we had to be particularly careful not to overbrief because Betty was doing her valedictory statement. PH was drafting TB's health statement with Robert Hill speaking to the key professionals.

Then we heard the *Sun* and *The Times* had another leak. Britain in Europe polling by Philip and Stan and a short note from TB on the euro. We gave them a very dismissive line, that the public had lost interest in these yellowing memos. I had another meeting with TB on health but there was very little real warmth between us at the moment. I told CB I didn't particularly want to go to the christening [of Leo] on Saturday, me not being a christening-type person. The *Sun* splashed on the memo, needless to say claiming it showed TB had made up his mind on the euro because he said the politics were overwhelmingly in favour. PG said he was now convinced it was the binman.

Thursday, July 27

The health plan was going fine but *Today* couldn't resist leading on the leak. Clive Soley [PLP chairman] went on to say obviously there is a conspiracy between News International and Central Office. Les Hinton [News International executive] called me later to complain. I said he shouldn't be too surprised if the odd MP slags him off from time to time. The surprise was it doesn't happen more often. We were preparing for the health statement in the usual last-minute panicky kind of way. Milburn seemed a bit taken aback when he came over. TB had told us yesterday it was too long. He got up at 5am and by the time he had finished, it was fifteen minutes longer and he said it was now exactly the right length.

TB was a bit hurt I think that we didn't want to go to the christening, but I explained that my children would be entitled to feel we gave too much by way of time to TB and CB already, and going away on Calum's birthday to do something with their kids might make them think that even more, added to which we didn't do the God thing. I was just tired and knew we all needed a break from each other. At Cabinet, I had done a note for him and he and GB went through the economic narrative and the dividing lines. GB said that £16 billion cuts had to become as embedded in the debate as twenty-two tax rises. He said he couldn't even remember what the twenty-two rises were, but we made them stick and we had to make £16 billion stick. TB cut it fairly short to carry on working on the statement, which went well. Hague was hopeless, with no real policy at all, and TB dished him. Milburn and I did the four o'clock together and again I felt when we were on substance, we were hard to stop. I got back for a conference meeting with TB, GB, Peter M and all the usual suspects. GB felt it had to be very downspin, that we couldn't really motor on delivery yet. Peter wanted a confident sense of progress. I was tired with TB because I felt he was trimming too much, with GB because he was still so secretive and difficult, Peter because he wasn't getting stuck into Millbank.

Friday, July 28

I did a strategy note and a couple of speeches for Beckett and [Ian] McCartney. I had a very jolly lunch with David Frost. Northern Ireland was the big story because of prisoners leaving the Maze [prison]. TB was up in Bishop Auckland to lay the stone for a new hospital. We spoke a couple of times but knew we both needed a break.

Saturday, July 29

Hilary was up [in Sedgefield] for the christening, managing the photographers and the crews. I stuck to the line that we should not encourage publication of photos and that given we had asked the press not to attend we would be asking the PCC for their guidance. It was a difficult area and I called Wakeham to say we would be winging his way.

Sunday, July 30

The second story on the news was us referring the press to the PCC about the christening photos, which sounded a bit harsh, so I drew up a statement that sought to reflect a better balance – on the one hand accepting people want to share in their happiness etc. but on the other we don't want open season on the kids or charges of exploitation. TB said he really didn't want to be seen as churlish on this, or heavy-handed. But I felt that if we encouraged them in any way, they would quickly turn it against us and say we were exploiting it.

Monday, July 31

The silly season [journalists' phrase for slow summer months] was starting, with JP's carpet for his residence the big story with several papers. GB saw the Grid notes for the first time and was really seized of them. It showed him some of the problems we had been dealing with. How could we get next to no coverage out of a major campaign to clean up hospital wards? Why was there yet another calculation for crime figures? TB decided re the pictures that it was better if I could just reach an agreement with the editors myself rather than use the PCC. On [his forthcoming speech to Labour Party] conference, TB wanted a washing line to hang everything from, I wanted something prosaic about more jobs, better schools and hospitals. Trevor Beattie agreed with that approach but TB and GB wanted something more thematic like opportunity, or building a better Britain. I had lunch with Adam Boulton to go over the lobby issue. He felt we should go for my three to four briefings a week, using ministers whenever we could, scrap the four o'clock but do a ring-round. He said the Tories were doing better but still didn't understand the broadcasters. TB said we really had to think how to get the *Sun* back on board. They needed a reason to come back other than the fact that they might be on the losing side. He said I had to put my personal antipathy for some of the people to one side. I had a good meeting with Bruce and Graham Allen [Labour MP] about how to get more of our stuff to MPs and how to get them better tied in for ministerial visits. Graham wanted me to see the MPs region by region. I spoke to Cockerell who said that he had more coverage for this film than all the others put together over the last five years, including on several prime ministers, and felt that we came out of it OK.

Tuesday, August 1

We got fairly badly hit on saying there would be no holiday photo. I wrote a long letter to Wakeham yesterday, and a shorter one to editors today making clear we would do a photocall at some point with TB, CB and Leo. I was sure we were right to be on the side of the argument protecting the children, where there was a danger we looked a bit petulant. I spoke to Wakeham in Wales who drafted a statement with Guy Black [director, PCC] that leant too much towards the suggestion he was asking us to do one. I made some changes to make it more neutral. TB had said it would definitely only be Leo, but then CB told Hilary she thought if one of the kids was doing it, all of them should. It felt to me like Wakeham was looking for a bit of kudos with the press. We were never going to win this one because they basically wanted their cake and wanted to eat it.

GB was still going on about the health stuff that he felt we should have made fly. Milburn was doing a poster launch which went OK, but not massive. We were also trying to agree the conference slogan with all the roundabout discussions that involved. I wanted something very prosaic like 'jobs, schools and hospitals' but TB and GB wanted something more values-based, like a future for all. TB headed off for Chequers, still telling me that I had to be nicer to the press and get back on decent terms with them. Lance got Ivan Massow[1] lined up for defection with an article in the *Independent* tonight.

Wednesday, August 2

CB was adamant that for reasons to do with her hair, she now wanted to do the picture on Saturday, which would piss off the dailies. Lance brought Ivan Massow in and we went off to see Mo, who was as unstructured as ever, before they went off to do a photocall together. I emphasised to Lance he had to make sure this was not just seen in terms of gay issues. It seemed to go fine and he came for a cup of tea. I couldn't really work him out, half suspected one day he would move on again. It ran second on the news, not great for Hague. It wasn't setting the world on fire but it wasn't a bad way to kick off August. Late in the day, just before 9, I got a call from Ian Austin to say they were about to put a line out that GB was getting married tomorrow. TB had only got to hear around 5 when GB was talking to him about something else. Although TB thought it was a bit odd that they had kept it so quiet, he nonetheless thought it was about time he got married. Fiona's view was that he was just making sure nothing stopped him.

Thursday, August 3

We stopped at a hotel halfway down at Beaune [Burgundy, France], and caught some of the TV coverage of GB's wedding. It was interesting to see [Baroness] Mary Goudie there as well as, more obviously, the Eds [Balls and Miliband], Murray Elder [special adviser], but it was all a bit odd, and GB didn't look at all comfortable with all the attention.

August holiday

We had a house in Puyméras, a little village on the other side of Ventoux. We had an OK time, though there were too many party people around in one go – Neil and Glenys at the bottom of the road, the Goulds in the village, Jonathan and family about a mile away, and the Kennedys [Ian and Andrea, with their sons]. Some days, I

[1] Entrepreneur and prominent supporter of the Conservative Party but at odds with its illiberal stance on gay rights issues.

was chronically depressed. Philip's view was that I had moved from characteristic glumness to anger. We were all pretty much agreed by the end of the holiday that I felt I had to give my all and was asked to do too much and pick up too much of the slack left by TB and his colleagues. Neil could tell I wasn't terribly happy and after ten days or so we sat down at the bar in the village and talked it over. He asked what was wrong and I said I felt I had to work round the clock to hold the show together. I asked if he thought there were any circumstances in which I could quit. He said no, because he worried it would fall apart. I said that was the pressure I felt.

His view was that TB had to reassert a grip but it maybe meant understanding that GB and Peter M could not work together, and one of them had to go. He was pretty down on both of them but felt on balance Peter should go, or at least be told to concentrate on Ireland and nothing else. Neil recalled [former Labour leader] John Smith's death, when his line to them had been that they had to decide it amongst themselves. He was always clear it should be TB but that was an agreement the two of them had to reach. Six years on, it was extraordinary that the feelings aroused by that period were still felt to be so relevant. He worried GB was in danger of cutting a pathetic figure if he allowed the narrative to be perpetuated that he felt cheated of his rightful inheritance, and that he was angry and bitter. He was still a strength but there were areas of policy and personality where he had let himself down, particularly pensioners. It was a nice chat but the bottom line was that he felt I just had to keep going. He also felt there wasn't that much I could do to change the way the press operated. I was conscious of my bad moods getting everybody down, though Philip and I had the usual good laughs. But he felt I had changed, become more introverted, less outgoing, angrier. He said he felt I was disappointed with TB.

The office didn't bother me much, maybe a couple of calls a day and I only really got involved when the press were chasing Euan in Rome.[1] TB felt the papers really just saw him as fair game now in relation to anything to do with drink. I got involved too when the Blairs went to France and TB undercut our strategy on photos, when he seemed to go along with the paparazzi who were down there. He had done a speech outline for conference about the need for a big-mission statement around which the nation could unite. I

[1] It had been reported that sixteen-year-old Euan Blair and two friends had been ordered to bed by staff of an Italian hotel after complaints about noise from other guests.

felt we needed to come down from the high-falutin' stuff and do something much simpler like Clinton's speech to the Democratic Convention, which was strong. I felt his arguments were sounding a bit stale. I was also conscious I was allowing my own moods to affect what I thought of him. I had Fiona on the phone to CB at one point saying how fed up I was, and that it came from a feeling that I did too many bits of other people's jobs. Northern Ireland took up a bit of time. Peter M called when he put Johnny Adair [notorious Loyalist paramilitary Leader] back inside. Another high spot was when Hague did an interview saying he drank fourteen pints [in a day as a teenager]. But as Audrey [Millar, Fiona's mother] said when we got back, most of the news was one-day wonder stuff. The kids seemed to have a good time, but I was beginning to worry whether I needed some sort of help on the depression front. I felt almost as tired when we got back as when we left, and it had been a strain on Fiona too.

Her basic take was that all our problems stemmed from me going to work for TB against her advice, because in the end I always did what I wanted regardless of the consequences. She felt she had had to toughen herself to avoid being hurt by it. Philip's view was that even Fiona didn't fully understand the cumulative effect of months and months of sustained pounding against me, but part of her felt I had brought it all on myself. We agreed it would probably be best if I quit after the election and then looked to do something maybe in sport. I also went on a few runs with Rory, who was having a go at me for lounging around by the pool, getting fat and lazy. I got into it fairly quickly and by the end of the holiday was thinking about doing a marathon.

Tuesday, August 29

I really didn't want to go back. I had an anxious night, woke up several times in a sweat, and had a really disturbing dream about the kids leaving home. We had had three weeks off and I didn't feel at all recharged. I wanted nothing to do with the press, I didn't want much to do with the politicians so it was all a bit of a disaster area. It felt worse than the usual first-day-back routine. TB was due back lunchtime. I went in with Philip, and sensed too that Bruce, Sally, Peter H and DM were all struggling to get motivated. We were actually in a better position because of the CSR, health, transport, Tory mistakes, but we were still lacking a bit of confidence through the system. I went to JP's final morning meeting in the chair, which he clearly didn't want to end. He was fairly happy at the way things had gone but equally felt several departments had not pulled their weight or even left in place adequate systems. He was particularly down on Straw, Milburn and Blunkett. He saw TB later then popped in for a cup of tea, and reopened the discussion about TB briefings. He felt I should go the whole hog and do televised briefings because he felt it was the only way to do in the lobby and break their monopoly on interpretation. He knew that TB had doubts after the Cockerell programme because it made him look weak but a lot of the people he had spoken to thought it made the point about the media well, but we now had to take it to the next level.

TB called me up to the flat when he got back. We did a bit of small talk about holidays. He defended the Strozzis [Vladimir and Irina] vehemently and said they had a great time, though that wasn't the sense I got from the cops. He said he was set on his idea that the conference speech was about unifying the nation behind a vision of change for the many not the few. He felt that Gore's 'with the people not the powerful' beat 'prosperity for a purpose' every time because [Republican presidential candidate George W.] Bush was not clear what the purpose was. I said I had spent some of the holiday thinking about leaving, that I had been pretty badly depressed and that if the modus operandi, particularly between the politicians, didn't improve, I wouldn't want to stay around for long. He said I could not possibly leave and we just had to go through it. His take was that I had become, in the literal sense of the word, un-nerved, not lost courage but realised we would lose it all because of the way people behaved, and got very angry. I said I also got angry at his inability to use the power he had to resolve it. He was adamant that in some senses it wasn't soluble. We had to take the bad with the good with some of the key personalities. GB, he said, was brilliant but flawed and always with part of his mind on his own future. Peter could be infuriating and exasperating but his perspective was always worth hearing.

On positioning, he said the speech would be important to keep us bang in the centre and push the Tories out towards the extreme. We had an office meeting at 5 where Peter M gave his assessment of where we were, with the public ready to give us a fresh hearing and with TB needing to raise his game personally. Nobody was very keen on TB's speech outline. He also said he wanted to say at some point why it had been right to keep the best of Thatcherism. Even Peter M said that one jarred a bit. I said I couldn't work out why he had to define himself against Thatcher rather than as his own man. He said we had to make people feel that just because they had voted Tory during the 80s, it didn't make them bad people. He was clearly rested, certain this new drive for the centre ground was what we needed. He was emphasising crime and the importance of respect. He was also a bit more abrupt with everyone, which was no bad thing.

Wednesday, August 30

TB's note on yesterday's meeting had got everyone talking. Peter H, Philip, DM and I all felt he was in a different position His feeling was that we had all gone a bit lefty, possibly under the influence of GB. He was even thinking about making tomorrow's crime speech another big Women's Institute-type event but we just hadn't put the work in and we persuaded him to go for low-key. Today, as the argument went on, he was emphasising the political positioning, how establishing the centre ground would push the Tories to the right leaving us reaching out, more inclusive than ever. He said it was important I understood why this needed the argument that parts of Thatcherism were right. Later in the day he came up with another belter when Peter H, trying to get him to be more progressive and radical, asked what gave him real edge as a politician and TB said 'What gives me real edge is that I'm not as Labour as you lot.' I pointed out that was a rather discomfiting observation. He said it was true. He felt he was in the same position he had always been and we were the people who had changed to adapt. Re me, he said I had to learn to be less het up and emotional about this because in the end it was my political judgement he wanted me for. I said I felt he was becoming a bit aloof and out of touch. In another conversation later, he said the problem with schools was uniformity of teaching. I said the problem was the background of poorer kids and he just rolled his eyes at me.

Philip couldn't understand why, having established the investment message, he now wanted to move off it into unity behind change. But I could tell TB had basically decided and we were going to have to trust and accept his judgement. He always wanted a bigger intellectual argument that we could then distil and make simple. We had a long meeting re the UN speech, then conference. Peter H really got quite intense with TB and told me later he was very disillusioned. Then TB called me in and said one of his strengths was that he had never had differing camps within his own outfit but there was a bit of a gap opening up with him, Peter M and Anji in one place and me, DM, SM and some of the others in another. He said we had to be very careful not to undermine his self-confidence.

Overnight the French ferry blockade was going big. Also some of the Sierra Leone hostages were freed after TB had had to authorise movement of special forces.[1] Whilst he was in Kent, doing a police Q&A, he said he felt we should really go for the French. Philip and I went in together and agreed we now had to make his speech work on his terms rather than just argue about it. On the train back, Jack Straw and I argued with Tony that we weren't doing enough to get ethnic minorities into the police. We were on a low-key re-entry but at least the Q&A allowed him to work his way back in on the public stuff and he wasn't too bad. JP was on top of the blockades which were called off eventually. We got back and I was trying to work out how to avoid TB's Scotland visit tomorrow being overwhelmed by the exams fiasco. Martin Clarke was sacked at the *Record* which was good news. Paul Keating [former Australian Prime Minister] came in to see TB and was full of the usual gruff but usually clever advice. He wasn't personally sure about the euro but said the most important thing was that we took decisions and staked out clear positions the whole time. He believed if TB really came out for EMU, it would break Hague. I was surprised how anti-American he was compared with the last time, in tone at least.

Friday, September 1

By the end of the day the only story was going to be TB backing Sam Galbraith [Labour MP and education minister in the Scottish Executive] over the exams crisis. It was a perfectly good leadership issue and TB was up for a full-throated defence. In the car to Northolt I listened to quite a lively debate between Keith Vaz [Europe minister] and Charles Moore on xenophobia in the press coverage on Europe. TB arrived. Both of us were surprised that we got as much as we did out of the DNA speech yesterday and that we were back on crime successfully. We visited the Drugs Enforcement Agency and then Strathclyde police HQ where he did a good little speech to the new recruits. We then set off for Edinburgh for the JMC [Joint Ministerial Committee]. The Scots press were as mad as ever and as difficult as ever but the mood up there was much better for us than in general. Anji told him that she thought several of us, certainly me and her, would leave after the election. TB said he didn't believe I

---

[1] Eleven members of the Royal Irish Regiment had been captured and held hostage by the rebel group known as the West Side Boys. Five were later released but when the rebels threatened to kill the remainder Blair authorised the SAS to attack and extract the remainder.

would leave. He headed off to Balmoral, while I got the 5.15 flight back to London.

Saturday, September 2
TB called a couple of times. He said [at Balmoral] the Queen Mum had taken a bit of a shine to Leo and they had been taking pictures of him. He said the Queen was much more relaxed with them than a year ago. It was a fairly quiet day, though we had to deal with the papers about a story of a Euan Uglow painting of CB.[1]

Sunday, September 3
The Tories did quite a good job getting up Europe out of their 'Believing in Britain' stuff. TB called, anxious that we push back on it.

Monday, September 4
GB's first meeting since his return from honeymoon, and it hadn't done much for his mood. He looked tired, his left eye was badly bloodshot and he was full of the usual gloom and complaint. We agreed AD would do a briefing to try to get the £16 billion cuts idea implanted in people's minds. I wanted to do ten questions for Hague, all of which were answered by £16 billion, but GB thought it gimmicky. I went back to see TB to try to resolve the Mo situation. Yesterday the *News of the World* said she was thinking of going at the election and today's *Express* had a quote from her agent saying she wanted to go. TB said we should deny it but that wasn't possible. He spoke to her by phone and though he believed she said she was staying, that was not the impression either Jonathan or John Sawers got listening in. She came to see him. She decided she was not standing at the next election and wanted to make sure she didn't damage the party or the government. She wanted a different job and didn't want to be a running sore between now and conference and beyond. She wanted to announce it today. TB wanted to stop her but I felt the sooner we got it out of the way the better. She had drafted a statement, full of sentimentality, which included the line she was resigning today. I said 'I thought you were announcing you were standing down at the election, not that you are resigning today.' She said simply 'Is that a bad idea?' And I said 'I think it probably is.'

[1] Whilst a 22-year-old pupil in Lord Irvine's legal chambers, Cherie had posed nude for Irvine's friend, the painter Euan Uglow, for a work entitled *Striding Nude, Blue Dress*.

TB then got a little bit heavy with her, said that if he was to have any chance of getting her a big international job she needed to understand it was hopeless if this line kept running that he was trying to get rid of her. He wasn't and never had been, and yet all this victim stuff meant that people would think twice. He said she was the only one who could kill the idea that we had done her in or forced her out. After she left, he said we underestimated the extent to which good media could turn people's heads. I said she had inhaled the propaganda in full. What had been extraordinary about the conversation was that basically she had just talked about herself. She had said she was worried that she might dominate conference so maybe she should 'get ill' during her visit to Colombia. Maybe she should 'disappear' for three weeks. TB had been pretty frank with her, but was trying to be helpful. He said she would be wiser to make sure something was lined up before she went because 'politics is a very rough trade and people can be quickly forgotten'.

She and I met in my office and agreed a plan. We would announce it at the 11, she would put out a statement then do interviews today and tomorrow. Mo was fine but of course the press had their line – she had been forced out and we couldn't cope with characters and there was very little we could do to stem that tide. What was awful was that they knew we hadn't briefed against her, but they couldn't resist running with it. TB didn't like how big and bad it was running but I felt we just had to be confident and relaxed. If we briefed the truth, e.g. that TB had offered her Health and later asked her to be mayor, it would just be seen as more briefing against her, so we were as well just to stay schtum. TB called after the Jospin dinner and said re Mo that he didn't believe she had thought this through at all. He felt her husband had bought into this whole notion that she was briefed against after the standing ovation at conference.

Tuesday, September 5

Hague was leading the news with his 'Believing in Britain' manifesto. He did a dreadful interview on the *Today* programme, for once Naughtie put him through it and he was hopeless. I met the Millbank people to go over some ideas on how to respond, for example giving out calculators to the press as they arrive. We agreed to do a big rebuttal document and I got JP up for doing the press conference. GB then decided he didn't think JP should do it. Stan Greenberg came in to see TB, partly to brief him on Gore but also said re our own position that he had to reconnect pretty quickly, because we had been in a bad way for a while. The *Standard* came in for lunch in the Small

Dining Room. It struck me, listening to Max Hastings, who was basically felt to be on the reasonable end of the media spectrum, just how right wing our media now is. We left for the airport. Concorde had been grounded so we shared a scheduled flight [to New York] with, amongst others, [President of Kenya Daniel] arap Moi. TB spoke to him briefly. Ghislaine Maxwell [daughter of late tycoon Robert Maxwell], who had come in to see me yesterday and told me I was the only person at the *Mirror* that she had really liked, suddenly pitched up on the plane and was coming down to see me the whole time and suggesting we meet up in New York. She talked as though we were far closer than we were back in the days at the *Mirror*.

Cherie had Leo with her, and his presence seemed to improve TB's mood. I was a bit more relaxed than usual, to the point where TB said he trusted that Zen would not be replacing my old karma. We chatted a bit re the euro and he said he would definitely want me around for a referendum. I asked him if he would quit if we held a referendum and lost. He said he probably would but for God's sake don't breathe a word of that because it would give GB ideas, would it not? Meyer called as we landed. Clinton wanted to speak to TB re pressure he was getting over trade tariffs on Scottish cashmere. Senator Trent Lott was pressing the White House to put cashmere on the carousel retaliation list. I feared this could go big if we were not careful when we saw Bill for a bilateral tomorrow. We were due to do *Good Morning America* but I pulled it when they said it would be with Diane Sawyer [TV news anchor] because she had done us before and was dreadful. More money for the Dome was leading the news and the papers were killing us on it.

Wednesday, September 6

I got woken at 4am New York time to call Calum before he left for school. As the day wore on, TB got more and more exercised about the Dome. Godric said Charlie F was touring the UK studios 'manfully' but it wasn't easy. TB was fretting more than usually about the speech which wasn't going to fly very high. He did a brief doorstep on the way out on peacekeeping. We crawled through the traffic to the UN. Finally gave up and walked in. TB did a few bilaterals through the day with [President Ricardo] Lagos of Chile, [President Rexhep] Meidani of Albania, in exchange for swapping slots in the speech times to the General Assembly. We saw Bertie briefly and later [Palestinian leader Yasser] Arafat. TB came up with a great line at the end of the Arafat meeting. 'If I had a bit more time, we could definitely sort out this Middle East peace process.' Arafat had told him the Jerusalem problem might be insoluble. TB was also doing his usual thing abroad, asking why it was that foreign politicians and media took the Third Way seriously, but it was derided at home. I was more concerned about the cashmere problem which the press were getting on to. We finished the speech. He delivered it perfectly well, better than most, but interest was limited. There was something very phoney about these big international gatherings where everyone came, trotted out their few minutes of cliché, tried to do a bit of business bilaterally and basically everyone was thinking it was a bit of a waste of time.

TB recalled how he and GB used to go to New York most years and that it was here that they had dreamed up 'Tough on crime, tough on the causes of crime.' We went for a walk, had a nice chat and then got back to see the cuttings on the Dome, which were grimsville. They were all moving towards calling for Charlie's head. TB did a really dull TV interview on peacekeeping, the American elections and the baby. Magi [Cleaver, press officer] was losing it with Cherie for letting Andre [Suard, her hairstylist] and Leo become very visible. TB saw Kofi Annan and raised the idea of Mo getting a job. Kofi didn't rule it out but the body language wasn't great. They were much keener on Paddy Ashdown. Mo was still getting lots of attention in the papers as being a great thing. That, plus the Dome, plus interest rates if they go up, plus the bad health figures that were coming, plus 7,000 jobs lost at Coats Viyella [textiles group], and we could be heading for disasterville by the end of the week.

TB went out to his Third Way dinner. When he came back, he said he was worried they would try to make the Dome a metaphor for the government. The papers had killed it and now they were dancing on its grave. He had spoken to Peter M and GB. Peter was running a mile from it while GB had always been against it. And he would be enjoying the current phase. TB wanted his meeting with Bill as one-on-one but Sidney Blumenthal [former journalist, adviser to Clinton] gatecrashed with David M. David was in heaven with all this policy-wonking going on. But it meant TB wouldn't be able to raise cashmere properly, except in the margins at the end. I drove back with TB to the Carlyle Hotel. I called Charlie to suggest a slight change of tone to the line that it wasn't the runaway success we hoped for but it wasn't the disaster the press were portraying.

Thursday, September 7

Peter M and I both thought TB should do something on the Dome but he felt he should stay out of it for now. We had breakfast with [Israeli Prime Minister Ehud] Barak, TB giving him his tuppenceworth of advice. I sensed Barak was more on top of things than before but he clearly despised Arafat, felt he was a liar and that he just used the other Arab leaders. They went over the Jerusalem problem, TB saying he could see how hard it would be for any Israeli PM to hand it over, that it would be like giving Westminster to Germany. We left for the UN and, as yesterday, there was no real story so the Dome was continuing to get far too much attention. He went to a round table on Africa, which was actually a really good exchange and then to a Security Council meeting on peacekeeping. At the meeting, TB was I think the only one who really spoke off the cuff, not from a script, and so made an impact. Meeting with Bono on debt and then bilateral with Putin re various bits of business. I spoke to Charlie F who was worried that by us not engaging re the Dome, it would be said that we were distancing ourselves. There was enough to do to keep busy but by the end of the day I was not at all sure what if anything we had achieved.

Friday, September 8

We had a meeting of the P5[1] at the Waldorf Astoria. Clinton was trying to tease out the idea of a specific proposal which in the end was just that the five of them would appoint an official to work with Kofi on the implementation of the Brahimi report.[2] When we got to the P5 Sandy Berger [National Security Adviser] sent me a note: 'For seven and a half years I have been trying to get Clinton to do what Blair just did at the UNSC. Fuck you!' I looked over and he was smiling and doing a thumbs up. Jiang Zemin [Chinese President] talked about it being historic and that the P5 should try where possible to support the UN together. Even Chirac was quite supportive of what TB had been saying about conflict in Africa. He said if there were no diamonds in Sierra Leone, there would be no war. He said it was only if we worked together that we would be able to deal with issues like drugs and money laundering. But he was also very tough about the benefits we gave to countries that had no democratic rules. He said he had been saying this for years 'But it will not prevent me from repeating myself again.'

Clinton had a particular problem because of the hostility of a lot of American politicians to the UN. He felt people were with him more than the politicians, but we had constantly to explain if we could

[1] UN Security Council permanent five: US, UK, China, Russia, France.
[2] Report of the panel on United Nations Peace Operations, chaired by UN envoy Lakhdar Brahimi.

prevent conflict and reduce conflict overseas, there was a relevance to our people at home. He cited what we had done in Sierra Leone, but also thought re e.g. Ethiopia and Eritrea that if we could resolve that conflict for good, and the two leaders be seen as models for the future, it would have a big impact elsewhere. The discussion went wider and wider, TB's next intervention being on the rise of extremism and its links to terrorism. Jiang Zemin said he felt it was possible we were entering a phase of peace, prosperity and stability and that if the five countries in the room stayed together, that was more likely. Putin said it was better to talk among five than fifteen. He said all our countries have a certain capacity so if we set our minds to do something, we can do it, we can make things happen. But it must not turn into a new bureaucracy. He said the world has more than enough big public organisations. Bill chaired it very well as ever. He loved meetings like this, wanted it to go on forever. God knows how he was going to cope when he had to leave the job.

David M got back from Washington and said he sensed really big tensions between the Clinton people and the Gore people. He sensed the Hillary campaign for the Senate wasn't going too well and that she might have to rely on him pulling in a landslide. We had a brief bilateral with Clinton but then Leo arrived and that was that. He was wearing a very cute Stars and Stripes jumper and Bill loved it so much he took him down to see Chirac, who was cooing over him as well with the usual Chirac guff, saying to TB and CB he was the most beautiful baby he had ever seen. There was a very odd incident at the airport when we learned that Andy Marr had told the airline staff that he would be sitting next to TB on the plane to do an interview with him. British Airways put the Secret Service on to it because they thought he was behaving oddly. TB did a bit of general schmoozing on the plane re the value of these high-level discussions with other leaders. He didn't get drawn on the Dome. I took one of Magi's sleeping pills and woke up just before we landed, feeling very groggy. TB went off to Chequers to work on his education speech, which was OK, good attack on the Tories, strong on the need to modernise the comprehensive principle, which, to our amusement, later led the news. I went in to meet JP and Charlie, who was feeling very battered.

Saturday, September 9

The media were getting very excited in anticipation of the [Andrew] Rawnsley book. Some of the papers were suggesting Rawnsley was going to name me as the author of 'psychological flaws' [comment re GB] so I put together a defensive line. I agreed with TB we should just have a general line dismissing these books as having no real merit and all being about serialisation money and the need to have something sensationalist to say to justify it. TB was much more worried about petrol. GB was in Paris for the OPEC [Organisation of the Petroleum Exporting Countries] meeting trying to get the OPEC countries to increase production to get prices down. There was a lot of talk of more blockades coming to Britain.

We went to [Crystal] Palace vs Burnley, where we met Ralph Coates [Burnley player, 1964–71]. It's very odd to see boyhood heroes looking a bit old and overweight and normal in their Cotton Trader casuals. Then we left for Chequers. I had a swim with the kids. I had a chat with Charlie on the Dome, then with TB re the SAS and Paras operation about to be launched in Sierra Leone to get the UK hostages out, which was going to be incredibly risky. TB did a nice little speech at dinner re Bill [his brother], said he was a great friend and support and that he was blessed to have him as a brother. Lydia Dunn [Baroness Dunn, former Hong Kong politician] was there, said she had seen the Cockerell programme and was going to show it to CH Tung [chief executive of Hong Kong] to tell him that was how to deal with the press. I felt distinctly aware of an irony she may not have meant when I got home by 11 to be greeted by a seriously crap set of papers.

Sunday, September 10

The Sierra Leone operation had gone ahead. CDS [Charles Guthrie] was on *Frost* and told a little bit of the story. Then we did a conference call, TB, John S, CDS, Jonathan and me. Charles briefed TB on the operation. He said there had been an extended firefight, that it had been very difficult, that there were certainly casualties and there may be fatalities. TB said these people really were the bravest and the best. It later emerged there was one dead and eleven walking wounded. Charles had been very keen for us to do this and said to TB it was helpful to have a prime minister who was decisive about this kind of thing. Later he and Geoff Hoon did a press conference which was fine, and there was huge interest in the detail of how these guys actually did it. What was bubbling big time up the agenda though was fuel prices which was becoming a bit of a disaster area. There were clearly well-organised demos being put together, and blockade-style action that was going to cause us a lot of grief. Anji called me later and said she had spoken to TB at Cranfield [postgraduate university] where he had done his education speech. He said that Anji and I could never leave him.

In for a GB meeting. He had AD in to tell us about a pensions speech – the first we knew about it. We then went round in a few circles on various stories that were running, but he was just skirting around the petrol blockades, which were clearly going to be trouble. I asked whether he was happy that we just keep putting up random ministers with no specific brief for the problem like John Reid, who was doing a fine job but was hardly the right minister for it. He said he was. I tried again to engage him, said that this was going to be a real problem taking over the entire agenda, but he wasn't on for it. It was not the best tempered of meetings. His only advice on fuel was that we tough it out but clearly not with the help of the Treasury.

I left to meet up with TB and head off to the station. Both of us were a bit worried to be leaving London. He said he regretted not having gripped this earlier. There followed a day of us, and particularly him, applying endless pressure on Straw, Jonathan and Byers, trying to get it gripped. We seemed unable to get the police to focus in the way they needed to. The oil companies were pusillanimous. Every time we spoke to Jack, he gave us all the problems, which we knew well enough, but little sense of solutions. TB said at one point that if this was Thatcher and the miners, the police would waste no time wading in. We were just pussyfooting with small groups of people threatening to bring the whole of the country to ransom. He felt the whole thing was political, that as they couldn't get Hague off the ground, as the 'dump the pump' [petrol boycott] campaign had flopped, now they were going for direct action and those forces that would normally abhor it if it came from the left, would ventilate it.

On the train north, TB spoke to Jack and said we had to get the oil moving out of the blockaded refineries. We got Jonathan to attend Cobra[1] and the Home Office meetings and he called back in a state close to despair, said they just didn't have a grip. We drove from Leicester to Loughborough and wrote in a tough message on fuel at the top, about the importance of not caving in. I travelled to Derby with the press corps, and was perhaps lulled a bit by the fact they didn't seem to be as obsessive about fuel as we were. On the long drive to Hull, TB was trying to sort out Jack and Byers but said it was like fighting blancmange. GB kept telling him and me it would be wrong to put up a Treasury minister, that it should be transport or law and order. Both of us felt this was GB diving for cover. We

[1] The committee intended to lead responses to national crises; named after Cabinet Office Briefing Room A.

stopped at a nice three-star hotel for a briefing of the press and sat and drank tea with them out in the garden. TB was on form but both of us were getting really worried that the fuel situation was basically getting out of control. Jack had gone to bed at 11, saying he wasn't to be disturbed. GB was still going on about it not being a Treasury issue.

We were due in Hull for a dinner for JP to celebrate his thirty years as an MP and we arrived to the usual chaos. But JP's instincts were usually pretty sound and he was exactly where we were in terms of where the fuel situation was heading. Then, as if we didn't have enough to deal with, news came through that [Japanese bank] Nomura were pulling out of the Dome purchase because of the financial mess they had uncovered. Charlie F called around 11pm and felt that if they did pull out, he would have to resign. JP got into one of his absolute rages as we left because the gates weren't opening properly and we had a stack of police cars all doing three-point turns all over the place. Some constituent was passing by, asked a perfectly polite question and got an earful. We got to City Hall where about 250 anti-hunt protesters, needless to say described as fuel protesters by the media, made a real racket. Security was pretty heavy. TB did an excellent little number on John for party members, after which the police took us into a side room and told us that all the streets on the way in to the restaurant we were due to be holding the dinner in were closed. I could tell JP was very disappointed, but the police were pretty clear that it was all getting a bit nasty and we should call it off. We were taken out by a side door, but even there TB and I only just made it into the car before a group of protesters found us and were chasing us down. This is getting ugly, he said. In the car, we had another long round of calls but he wasn't happy about the way it was handled.

We were staying at the Sheffield Hilton but as we arrived agreed it was probably best to go back and take charge tomorrow. There was a really nasty feeling in the air now. The hauliers were threatening to bring Leeds to a standstill. TB could not understand why the police were not stopping it. The go-slow of tractors earlier even had a police lead car leading them along. He kept banging on about the difference in their handling of the miners.

Tuesday, September 12

He wished we had gone back yesterday. We had a security briefing first thing and they advised that we cancel the visit to the school in DB's constituency. David was very, very pissed off, but the cops were pretty adamant. The hauliers seemed to know our movements and it wasn't a risk worth taking. There was very little change overnight and all the promises of tankers coming out came to nothing. There was a real sense of drift. The press was grim and getting very personal re TB. We didn't tell the press what was going on, because the police assumed the info would get straight to the protesters. We just left for the station, bought a cup of tea, and came back via a change at Leicester. We decided TB should go up on it when we got back and focus on the impossibility of a government changing policy in the wake of protests like this.

As ever, TB wanted fact rather than all the blather that departments pumped out. He was convinced that while there was not a conspiracy as such, a lot of the forces at work were political. When we got back to Number 10, he was appalled at the lack of grip. Jack was not inspiring confidence and TB felt the police were getting mixed signals. TB took a meeting at which we were given the same promises as yesterday that things were about to move. TB was looking nervous and was getting irritated. He decided personally to call all of the main oil company chairmen and urge them to raise their game on it. The police insisted that whatever problems there were re intimidation or access, they could deal with them. TB felt they had been getting very mixed signals but as the day wore on, it was clear we were not getting the movement we needed. It was obvious TB was going to have to front this until we had seen it through. We fiddled around with the press statement we had drafted on the train. He said it would be twenty-four hours before we saw progress. We should have foreseen that the press in their current mood would misrepresent it, which they did, into saying it would all be solved in twenty-four hours.

We had another meeting with ministers and officials and ACPO [Association of Chief Police Officers]. I could sense TB's irritation every time David Omand [Home Office permanent secretary] tried to convey the idea that everything that could be done was being done. At the end of it, I said TB's voice had to be heard, we had to say that the oil companies could move, the police could police it. The protesters were still strong and they were playing quite a clever game in letting the odd one through and saying it was for emergency services. But it was clear the drivers were being intimidated. TB spoke to Bill Morris [general secretary, Transport and General Workers' Union] and John Monks [general secretary, TUC] and the unions were being terrific. It was business that was sitting on its hands while the Tories were just exploiting it as ever, and the media, claiming to represent public opinion, were supportive of the cause. But it was getting more and more serious by the hour and there was a real sense we were losing control. Milburn called me, and said we should play the NHS card soon because real problems were developing. He was probably right, but I said we should just wait a bit. TB did a press conference in the State Dining Room at 5.30 and I knew as soon as he said it the 24-hours line would be a problem. But his tone overall was good and his manner prime ministerial.

GB finally began to address the issue at the TUC and when he came back sent through a fax with his thoughts but said he didn't want to be disturbed. TB was now fully seized of the seriousness of it all, said it could be the end of him. 'This is a real crisis, make no mistake. I can't back down now and if we don't get things moving pretty quickly, I'll have to let someone else take it on.' I went out for a couple of hours to meet Calum and go to Fulham vs Burnley, missing the first goal. By the time I got back to the office, the full horror of the situation was mounting. We weren't far off a crisis in the basic infrastructure of the nation. Fuel shortages leading to food shortages, and an inability to run public services. There was some movement of tankers but not enough to change things. TB was with JP and Gus [Macdonald], when I got back and we were now looking to step up the military options as well as putting pressure on the oil companies. I left just after midnight, TB's last words that it would get a lot worse before it got better.

Wednesday, September 13

I was longing to wake up and hear of massive movement of lorries and tankers, but it wasn't happening. For an hour or so it had looked OK, but then nothing. It was grim and getting grimmer. I did a conference call with JP before his interviews but he was very wound up. We were starting to get some focus on to the protesters, putting them under pressure for the first time. I went up to the flat to see TB, who said we are in deep shit if we don't get things moving soon. GB came on, said that the oil had to move but had no real idea how to bring that about. We called a meeting with the oil company executives who came in at 10.30. They were not a very pleasant, compelling or impressive group of people. The only really strong voice there was Jeffrey Sterling [Lord Sterling, executive chairman of P&O], who said the companies had to get the message to the drivers that if they didn't get out, they would get other drivers to do it for them. There was a lot of comic interplay between him and JP, but the BP and Shell people were not impressive. I guess part of them was happy for this all to be seen as a government problem. I said why didn't they operate in this together?

TB said they had to get things moving. He left them in no doubt of his frustration. They all had stories of intimidation, and said the protesters were becoming more violent. They wanted police escorts, but they understood the police were stretched. TB said we could get out 200 military drivers. I did a little gaggle with them at the end and suggested they had a single spokesman out there. The guy from BP said he was worried they would be left holding the baby. I said don't worry, when the shit flies, most of it ends up here. They agreed at least to get a senior representative from every company into a room with government and police so we could finally get some proper co-ordination. I did a statement, no questions, leading to Jon Snow chasing them all the way down the street.

ACPO rather pooh-poohed the idea of intimidation. We finally got GB up on the media. Through the day there were endless rumours of big breakouts which never really happened. The media was a big part of the problem here. TB said he accepted this was all about trying to break us undemocratically but he would need a second term to do anything about it. The entire pitch of the media coverage was to create rather than report problems. The protesters were treated like heroes, the government like villains. Jeremy Heywood was doing a brilliant job but Cobra, defended to the hilt by Richard Wilson, had been useless. I did a round of some of the editors, asking if they felt comfortable urging mob rule. They were turning a bit, but slowly.

Milburn and I discussed a strategy to put the NHS at the centre of this. We got some excellent NHS people to visit some of the picket lines and directly accuse the protesters of doing real damage to essential services. Milburn put the NHS on emergencies-only red alert and went up for a round of interviews, and there was a real sense now of it turning a bit. Hague then called for a recall of Parliament. TB did a press conference, more assured and measured this time, and the new top line was running hard that they were putting lives and jobs at risk. There was also a hint in there at using the army. We were also having more success getting the media to focus on some of the intimidation stories. Milburn was doing well.

We were having trouble getting GB to engage on the [fuel] tax issue. We got Sainsbury's and BP out talking about intimidation. We felt better at the end of today than yesterday. TB said he felt strong because he was sure we were doing the right thing. Gus Macdonald had been impressive. The oil companies had got their act together a bit following the meeting. JP was fine though he lost his temper a bit too much. Byers was too Zen-like. The polls on it were bad but I felt the Milburn interviews, and the NHS people out on the picket line, were a turning point.

Thursday, September 14

I woke up to news that the protesters at Stanlow refinery [Merseyside] were calling it off. Milburn was doing the morning media. I called and said we should of course welcome it but emphasised we would not be intimidated. He got pushed hard on the difference between illegal and unlawful [blockades] but held up well. Both the *Mirror* and the *Mail* had urged the protesters to call it off. They sensed opinion moving away from them. But it meant if they got the timing right, the protesters could keep the moral high ground and we would take a big hit. I loathed the press and the way they had handled this. Work had been going on in government on a list of essential services, and the newspaper industry had been added belatedly. Whilst it would be hard to exclude TV and radio, I felt the press had been largely irresponsible and in part to blame and we should not be helping them.

TB called, said GB had been on and wanted me to brief the news that there would be uninterrupted tanker movements from Grangemouth. I advised him to wait because we had had so many false dawns. His worry was that the protesters had the moral high ground. Maybe, but all that mattered was we got things moving properly. GB was no doubt keen to have it said that he had sorted out Grangemouth, and started a domino effect. The day became a swirl of meetings. Jack came in after Cobra and he and TB had a row about the difference between illegal and unlawful. Then he was pressing for a statutory rationing plan. He really was a nice guy but not great at putting his case to TB. TB said afterwards the problem was at one point he had stopped listening and just nodded so God knows what Jack thought he had agreed to. TB's bottom line was that we couldn't cave in. Although everyone had been caught up in it, we were actually dealing with small numbers of people who were vested interests, so the media labels of 'people's protest' and 'taxpayers' revolt' were misleading. He felt the media coverage had been an outrage but he didn't want to say so publicly.

The oil crisis dominated a long discussion at Cabinet. TB was critical of the oil companies, and of the media and of the way the Tories had exploited it. Jack went through the facts, reckoned we were operating on fifteen per cent of normal deliveries and prioritising essential services. Byers said we needed 900 deliveries even for that and we were facing real difficulties. As GB spoke, and spoke well, I couldn't help thinking how different it might have been if he had engaged earlier. But he was still not keen to make the arguments that we make it a tax issue. He said the press had become the Opposition on this and the Tory Party were just echoing them. On the question of tax and spend, we had to broaden it out, make it about schools and hospitals, and the cuts they would threaten. He said it was limited the extent to which we could put pressure on OPEC. Nick Brown [agriculture minister] had met leaders of the food industry, who had basically said there was a danger the country would run out of food. Animals would have to be slaughtered. He said the oil companies were favouring their own in the distribution and intimidation was getting worse.

TB said we had to get the focus on the impact on health, schools, the military, agriculture and business. He felt yesterday was the first time he got the public more on our side. JP did a very effective rant, said our resolve was being tested, the oil companies hadn't faced up to their responsibilities but we have to. TB said we shouldn't rule out the recall of Parliament. He said he intended to have a very frank discussion with the oil companies. He felt if we caved in then this kind of thing would happen in a different way again. It was a good discussion and TB summed it up well. We worked on TB's press conference statement and again he was calm, measured, had a good tone, took all the questions. Esso put their prices up 2p a litre, which TB said was incomprehensible, and we started to press them to put it down again. But we were kidding ourselves, though the press felt he was on form, if we thought we were doing anything other than minimising the impact of a big hit.

We then had a meeting with the oil companies. TB said he wanted to read the riot act because he wasn't happy with their systems, and didn't really feel they had pulled out all the stops. Mark Moody-Stuart [Shell chairman] was dreadful. He had earlier asked if TB minded if he sent his deputy. Yes he would was the answer. It was pretty tense at times, not least when JP had a go at their contracts system. TB said we didn't want to brief against them but the press were making up their own minds. There was a feeling they were only seeing it from their own perspective. Jack said the price rise was a PR disaster for them. The guy from Esso explained how it came about. TB said they should reflect on how this thing had developed and concluded it was not an industrial dispute but a dispute with the government which had exposed weaknesses in their operation as well as ours. We needed to work out better systems in the future. TV as ever was being led by the press and they were focusing almost exclusively on members of the public supporting the protest. I felt that if we saw it through, people would step back and think deeply about whether they wanted this kind of thing to happen again.

Friday, September 15

Though some of the papers were willing to acknowledge TB had stood firm, the sense was nonetheless of a victory of sorts for the protesters and a defeat for TB. Philip did some groups last night which were not as bad as they might have been. It had felt absolutely terrible at the centre, an almost palpable feeling of a gulf opening between government and country. But Philip's view was that whilst there was real anger about fuel prices they had not seen this as a seismic event. The *Sun* printed the unpublished Number 10 switchboard number so we were inundated with calls and I got TB to write to Murdoch explaining the number was used by a limited number of people and it was a seriously irresponsible thing to do. Up in the flat, he said he felt as if he had been the one trying to shut down the nation, the way we were being treated. I was doing my usual rant about the press and he said I had to understand this was a power battle and it was only worth going for if we knew what the outcome would be. Under Thatcher, they got drunk on the power she let them wield and then they tore Major to shreds, in part with our complicity. Also, for pragmatic reasons, we entered into a whole series of basically dishonest relationships with them and now they realised that. They realised that they actually have less power than they did and they see us as all-powerful and they want their power back. So there was no point in all-out war, because at the moment we have the upper hand. But I promise you, nobody despises them more than I do, and if you want to take them on we have to be sure that it's worth it.

We had a conference speech meeting. Obviously the context might change but he was on the same basic 'many not the few' message. GB was worried that ministers were overemphasising the 'listening mode', giving the signal too strongly that we might cut fuel prices. TB was worried he was going to use this to make a stand. TB said he had had an extraordinary conversation with him this morning in which he claimed he was being briefed against yet again, in which GB again raised 'psychological flaws'. TB said to him the fact that he keeps going on about it is what leads people to conclude it might be true. Yet even after the last few days, TB was still arguing that GB's brilliance meant he was worth persevering with.

Saturday, September 16

TB called as I was listening to GB on the *Today* programme. He said all we can get out of this now is strength. I spent much of the weekend briefing ministers for various interviews. The Sundays were grasping for any piece of colour for the big background features they were doing, which would be a disaster zone. The *News of the World* called with a poll that had the Tories two points ahead of us, I think for the first time. Though in a sense inevitable, given the pounding we had taken, TB's worry was if it became a self-fulfilling prophecy. My worry was that we couldn't really work out exactly what had happened here. Though it was to a large extent media-driven, there must have been something deeper for it to take off as it had and when you looked at the jobs and economic figures, that can't just be tax. There was also maybe a sense that large numbers really didn't like us. Yet whenever I was out and about with TB, he still seemed popular.

I worked a bit on the conference speech. The main point TB wanted was that we had the strength to take the tough decisions needed to build the Britain we had promised. The Sundays were pretty bad and the commentators were all coalescing around the same negativism. We had so few media people on our side. There was a lot of briefing going on against GB and the latest instalment of Rawnsley's book was all about Peter, was vile about GB and showed me in a bad light too. At least the [Sydney] Olympics had started. The other good thing was that the party had been terrific. During the day, Blunkett, Straw and Byers all called me and said GB had to listen.

Sunday, September 17

I was really tired and TB must have called half a dozen times. I was having to brief a stack of ministers who were doing all the different programmes, and TB, having wanted Margaret Beckett to float the idea of a right-wing conspiracy, then wanted that pulled down quickly after GB had been on to him. Paula Yates [TV presenter] killed herself, and the media caravan seemed to move off us and on to that.[1] But the press was now putting up so much cynicism about us and about politics in general that it was almost impossible to get up a positive message. I talked to Stan Greenberg who felt that at the moment a big 'on your side' speech would fall on deaf ears. It had to be about pushing through change, tough choices, strength for the long term. When Hague praised the protesters as 'fine, upstanding citizens', I felt it was a mistake, though we had to be careful. The press were giving them legitimacy.

---

[1] At the inquest the coroner ruled out suicide and it was found that Yates died of an accidental overdose.

Monday, September 18

Philip called to say GB was in a real strop because I didn't go to the morning meeting and he assumed I was retaliating for the fact that he failed to go up on petrol last Monday. In fact, I just wanted a day to work exclusively on the conference speech, me and Peter H at home, TB at Chequers. Fuel was still the main political story but the heat was going out of it. GB was still digging in on fuel and on pensioners, despite the enormous grief we were taking on both. TB did an interview with [Phil] Webster and [Peter] Riddell [*The Times*] which was meant to be on the 'listening but firm' line but it came out very much on the tough end of the market.

I went with TB and CB to GB's [post-wedding] party at an art gallery near Blackfriars. It was not exactly my kind of event and TB was pretty uncomfortable too. It was unbelievably crowded and the first people I saw were the Folletts, followed by Richard Littlejohn and David Yelland [*Sun*], John Edmonds [general secretary, GMB union], John Humphrys [BBC], Harriet Harman [former Social Security Secretary] and Clare Short. I fought my way through them and then ran into Will Hutton [*Observer*], Jonathan Freedland [*Guardian*] and Diane Abbott [Labour MP]. I could not wait to get out. Freedland told me the ICM poll had the Tories four points ahead and politics was interesting again. As he struggled his way through the grim crowd, TB said he was less worried by the polls than by the effect they would have on these ridiculous media people. I was one of the first to leave.

Tuesday, September 19

Rawnsley had sold second rights [of his book *Servants of the People*] to the *Mail* who led on 'Blair lied' over Ecclestone.[1] A big bad story back to bother us. We could deal with the allegations pretty well, not least because they misquoted the *On the Record* interview on which the lie claim was based. It wasn't running massively but had a bad feel to it. I called GB to apologise for not being at the morning meeting. He said it was pointless him doing these meetings if the person in Downing Street who knew what was going on wasn't there. I said I did have another boss, namely TB, and if he wanted me working on the speech, I should do that. He said we all have speeches to do. He then said if I didn't get a grip of Number 10 we were in real trouble. And so we went on. He was worried about the stuff running that

[1] A donation to the Labour Party from Formula One boss Bernie Ecclestone led to an enormous controversy in November 1997.

he had been aware of the Ecclestone donation, which sent the lobby into a total tizz, and him into an even deeper funk. With the news agenda now dominated by the Dome, polls, petrol and Ecclestone, we were going through a real *Pravda*-in-reverse phase.

I went to watch a couple of focus groups in Weymouth Street which were much better than I feared. TB was doing fine, there was a greater sense of delivery and Hague was nowhere. If there was one big criticism, it was that we weren't really listening to people. One woman said we didn't get their concerns or 'honour our lives'. Stan Greenberg reckoned they felt we were doing the right things but they didn't feel warmth towards us. But it was interesting that when we played them TB's petrol statements in full, they all responded better. If they could see things in detail, rather than through the wretched prism of a clip here and a clip there, eroding his full voice, we would be in a better place. The men were more hostile but even they, when they heard the whole argument about investment and tax, came round. Later the buzz went round that the Tories were going to announce a petrol tax cut tomorrow.

Wednesday, September 20

There was a lot of anger that Rawnsley had flogged his book to the *Mail*, though there was no sense of it really going anywhere. We were putting together a big attack on opportunism with the Tories now promising lower fuel prices. The Tories were getting away with murder. TB and I were arguing again about how to deal with the press. Rawnsley had trotted out the old stuff on the People's Princess [Diana] and TB said there was a deliberate strategy to say he was incapable of doing anything without a spin doctor telling him what to say. JP called, anxious about the talks with protesters. The last couple of weeks, maybe when we had needed them most, I had not found the time to do the weekly strategic notes. We needed to get back to it pretty quickly. On Ecclestone, I warned Ian Austin of the note I had done at Canary Wharf on the Friday morning, which would confirm GB had been involved in our discussions. He was in a panic about it. ITN did a special report on 'Labour's awful autumn'.

Thursday, September 21

Ecclestone still bubbling away. To appease GB after his grumbling yesterday, I went to the 8.30 meeting, which was mainly about pensions and the economic commission that afternoon. Little did we know that by the end of the day, unbeknown to anyone, he would do big interviews with the BBC and Channel 4 on fuel, Ecclestone, and try to buy off the problems on pensions. At the meeting, he said we would not get through conference week with the announcements we had. I said we had to talk to the public through a wall of cynicism, and that meant big arguments as well as big announcements. I still wanted to do a big sports announcement even though the papers would say it was Olympics-created opportunism and that we were trying to avoid real political questions. Despite the groups, Philip was now worried the recent shift was real, TB's that it was a referendum on a disastrous week. I agreed that if we could get the Tories up in lights for a while, we would be back in a better position.

On Ecclestone, TB was worried that GB's line was untenable. It got worse when GB said he was not aware of the true story and that he never got involved in donations. It was as if he had been bothered with it by TB and then told TB he should not discuss it, whereas in fact it was GB who had the idea of referring it to [Lord] Neill [chair of the Committee on Standards in Public Life] and who also attended meetings on it with Derry Irvine, [Sir] Robin Butler [Cabinet Secretary at the time of the Ecclestone row] and others. When I showed TB the transcript of his Channel 4 interview, he could scarcely believe it. To get himself out of a hole, he had made it look like TB was some kind of money grabber. 'Who pays for his operation? Who pays for all those parties?' TB said when the going got tough, GB saw everything from his own perspective. I said so to Austin, that GB ran his own operation without regard to other people and he had taken a hit recently because of that. JP called me after GB's interviews and said much the same, that he had done it to protect himself and his position in the party in the run-up to conference and couldn't give a damn about anyone else, especially TB. And it was out there a bit. Don Macintyre was doing a profile of GB and asked me 'Do you think he would prefer TB to succeed or fail?' In the speech, TB was OK with the main argument but we were desperate for lines that connected. There was a mortar-bomb attack on the new MI6 building, which would dominate the news for a while.[1]

Friday, September 22

Clare had been on *Question Time* last night saying the Dome was a flop and a disaster. GB's interviews had done OK for him, but he had planted another potential time bomb, by saying he didn't know what

---

[1] A missile believed to have been fired from a rocket launcher, from a range of between 200 and 500 metres, shattered an eighth-floor window. Dissident Irish Republicans were believed to be responsible.

was happening. He put us all in the position, including TB, where the only way to protect him would be to go along with his version, which was a dreadful thing to do. GB was absolutely of the view that he had been right to do so but when TB and I were preparing for the *Independent on Sunday* interview, it was clear that if he was pressed hard, it would be very, very difficult. I could see this coming back and really hitting GB. Meanwhile, we had agreed to spend £50 million propping up the euro.

The *Sun* was vile again, with Trevor K clearly in control. I thought TB looked a lot greyer and older today and whilst he said he felt fine, I think he was finding it hard to come to terms with some of the hatred for him that was out there. He was genuinely worried about GB, felt he could only operate if he was getting his own way at every turn. We were getting into the pre-speech black humour. James Purnell [policy adviser] suggested TB should say to the country 'I put my trust in you and you have betrayed me.' I spoke to Rawnsley to tell him he may have burned his boats with some people, that it wasn't a serious book and we were astonished he had given it to the *Mail*. He felt that overall the book was clear this had been a pretty good government. The *Independent on Sunday* interview was OK. He emphasised that we would listen on pensions and the 75p rise came from us strictly applying the rules.

Saturday, September 23

We were working up the sports element for my briefing of the Sundays at 11. I was up early doing a kind of public opinion assessment. It was humble, almost apologetic re the Dome, fuel etc., and making clear that we accepted the fuel protest was also about something deeper. I was trying to persuade TB to give a bit more than he had planned to in terms of tone and substance. The idea that he was arrogant and out of touch was becoming a bit of a buzzword. I went into Number 10 to do the briefing and then sat out on the terrace with TB and went through the speech. Philip, Peter H and I were determined to try to get it into plainer English and with a simpler structure.

Just before we left, news came through of an eight-point lead I assume for the Tories in a Channel 4 poll. TB said there was a danger the party would go into panic. In fact the party had been absolutely brilliant in recent days. We went down to Brighton by train and TB was a bit wired and distracted. He did a dreadful doorstep on arrival with his hair wild. We went up to Room 104/5 to work on the speech. I showed it to one or two people who thought it was pretty good for where we were. We now had to hone and polish, and manage the politics. Certainly the process felt better than in previous years and that was because we had agreed the structure early on, and the fuel protests had prevented us from over-obsessing, though no doubt we would make up for it in the next day or two. GB's people seemed to be setting up Peter M re the Ecclestone affair. The real downside of the Rawnsley book was that it set off lots more division. Whenever one of them did something, the other retaliated, and neither felt they could ever be sacked. TB was worried that they both had self-destruction buttons, but they cared more about their own places in things than about the bigger project. Burnley won at Huddersfield.

Sunday, September 24

Brighton: *Frost* was OK though TB got bogged down a bit on Ecclestone and some of the other shit stories we were up against. But he was OK tone-wise and was beginning to roll out some of the arguments that he would meet on Tuesday. GB protested about what he said on the euro and intervention. Now we were just plugging away on the speech. Peter H and I both felt a bit flat and were struggling to get going. We kept promising TB that the purple patches would flow but inside I was worried that it wasn't happening. Policy content was working better than usual and I got Bill Bush to work up a report on what £16 billion worth of cuts would mean for people. I pretty much locked myself away while TB was doing the rounds [conference receptions] and though the media was still in a frenzy, provided we got the speech right, we could get ourselves into a better place fairly easily.

Monday, September 25

GB's conference speech was the main event, which I watched in the hotel. I didn't think it was that great but it played brilliantly in the hall. Neil felt it was another little dig at TB, but he'd hit all the right buttons. He just did enough on pensions and fuel. He then had to leave for Prague [IMF meeting]. I was beginning to wonder if I was losing my feel for these things because so many people were saying it was brilliant, and I just didn't feel it. The Treasury were briefing heavily against pension rises and causing difficulty with the unions. TB was getting more and more angry with GB and Peter M, and it was interesting how little he was really consulting them on the speech, particularly GB.

Tuesday, September 26

We had been working till late but TB was up at 5, and me at 6. I did the final uplifting 'spirit of Britain' stuff and worked on a couple of jokes about Hague. Both Neil and Bruce were very against the section I had done as an apology. They worried if we went too far, it was all anyone would take and actually there wasn't that much to apologise for. I redid it, and then TB redrafted the section that tried to do a tone of apology without straying into weakness. TB had written a very powerful section on his 'irreducible core', which we thought would work best as an almost unscripted ad lib towards the end. He worked on that while I worked on the 75p line, admitting we'd been wrong to limit the inflation linked pensions rise to 75p, and I think we just about got the balance right. We had the usual rush of last-minute changes, fact checking, points from departments. Neither GB nor AD was happy with the 75p pensions passage because it would be used to throw back millions of words used against us. But it was clearly the right thing to do. We actually got things finished in reasonably good time and TB was panicking less than in previous years.

We left for the conference centre by foot. We got JP to introduce him. TB was very quickly into it and as in previous years, I knew early on it was going to go well. I was standing next to Jeremy Paxman [BBC *Newsnight* presenter] as we watched it and he seemed impressed, as did others when I did the rounds afterwards. The big trivia point was the amount he sweated.[1] There was also a bit of forces of conservatism RIP but nonetheless you could feel things settling down. I went back to the hotel to watch the news and he had really done the business for us. However, the BBC reaction packages were bad, no doubt long planned. We had to start thinking through how to prepare for the fuel protesters' sixty-day deadline on their demand for a fuel price reduction. At the ITN party, Phil Stephens [*Financial Times*] asked me, almost casually, how we were going to stop the 'GB stroke Peter cancer' destroying the government. The speech had caused less angst than in previous years, but seemed to work pretty well. Partly because we hadn't put so much into it over such a sustained period, I didn't have the usual plunge afterwards, and actually had quite a nice evening for once.

Wednesday, September 27

Press for the speech was pretty good, despite all the sweat headlines. But I had a sense the story was moving quickly to GB/Peter M and TB's inability to get a grip of them. After his school visit, he, Jonathan, Sally, Anji and I had a chat about it. He said the truth was GB was

[1] Blair wore a blue shirt which grew darker with perspiration as he gave the speech. *Guardian* cartoonist Steve Bell depicted Blair as a puddle on the conference platform, with the caption 'Boiling down to our irreducible core'.

effectively indispensable because he was brilliant and outside capable of doing real damage. He could threaten him with all manner of things but GB was unlikely to believe it. Threatening Peter was more realistic. But Peter always denied doing anything to do GB in. TB's big worry was whether he could maintain a properly reasoned dialogue with GB. I said the party was fed up with it all and we had to sort it out. TB was still having to sort out pensions with Rodney Bickerstaffe [UNISON general secretary], asylum with Bill Morris and get Milburn to drop his commitment to the freezing of prescriptions in the health speech. TB felt it was far better for Milburn to be seen as a reformer.

I went in for Blunkett's speech then up with TB to the *Mirror* lunch which we had to cut short for the NEC meeting on pensions. TB thought we had persuaded Bickerstaffe last night to remit the motion restoring the link with earnings, but not so. Bickerstaffe had been wound up by [John] Edmonds. John Monks, realising it was all leading to a big hoo-ha about a bust-up with the unions, was keen to play it all down. I went over to the conference centre and was being asked the whole time if GB was coming back from Prague to sort it out. It was nonsense, but that was the story they wanted. The unions were putting it around that TB was ready to compromise but GB was being more firm. It was all perfectly ridiculous. GB was working on Bickerstaffe in one room, TB on Edmonds in another. GB turned round some of the constituency delegates [Labour members], which Ian Austin immediately briefed. I told GB I thought that was the wrong judgement. He said we can talk about judgement later. He was hardening it all up and making it look as confrontational as possible. TB was of the view we should not turn it into a massive great thing and simply say the NEC statement would take priority over this vote.

Eventually he asked JP to come down with GB for a meeting in our office. When they arrived TB was holding the baby. 'What a lovely baby,' said GB. Cherie said do you want to hold him? 'Don't be ridiculous,' said TB, handing the baby to her. I said we should surely get the message out quickly that we were not going to abide by the vote and what was important was what money we got to pensioners. GB kept going on about how we would get a bad press. JP finally snapped 'Gordon, we know we're going to get a bad press, it's no good going on about it, being obsessed with it, what are we going to do about it?' During the debate I called Austin and said that their operation would end in tears. He said he wouldn't be threatened. I said I blamed GB for this because he couldn't get his act together with Peter. I said that on fuel, the handling of Rawnsley, and now this, we should have had an agreed plan based on openness, not constantly briefing splits. Yet from their perspective, they behaved as though GB was the victim of a never-ending briefing operation. I said TB was the prime minister and leader of the party and all this reflects on him and the government as a whole.

Ed Miliband came to see me later and said we had to sort it out. They felt GB, PG and I could work together pretty well but they just didn't trust Peter. Fiona felt there had been a turning point at the time of his wedding, that it was really weird they so obviously didn't want us to know about it. The vote was all a bit of a mess and I put the best possible gloss on it. I went back to the hotel, went out for dinner with Fiona before coming back to work on JP's speech.

Thursday, September 28

I was up very early for a swim then to see TB before his interviews. He said he could cheerfully kill Edmonds and Bickerstaffe, felt they had given us a bloody nose for no reason other than to damage us in the process. The interviews went fine though he was still very much on the defensive with the focus on the things we were apologising for. He wasn't on great form though, for example on pensions saying 'What we have to say is' rather than 'What we are doing'. But he was at least beginning to get over a message about investment. We bumped into Peter M as we came out of the *Today* programme interview and even though there was a risk of being earwigged, TB was pretty sharp, said the briefing war had to stop, he was going to have to shape up or be in trouble. Peter of course denied everything, said he was the victim not the perpetrator, but TB held pretty firm. I did a line for JP that we had to stop feeding the press agenda and the message that it applied to the party 'from top to bottom' was rightly seen as a warning shot. TB had asked JP to get directly involved in trying to get a grip of them.

TB later saw GB and told him he was more than happy to see him take over at some point but that if he carried on the way that he was, or if he thought he could do it by constantly undermining him, he would do everything to make sure it didn't happen. He also said that if he had to get rid of Peter to keep him on board, he could do that but he would resent having to do it and that would not bode well. 'You know you are largely indispensable because you have power and you have ability but I will not allow the current situation to carry on.' GB was still going on about the Rawnsley book, about psychological flaws, but agreed to tell his people to be more grown up and work with us more closely. TB said afterwards we had to take it at

September 'oo: Blair 'happy to see GB take over'

face value and that undermining vibes coming out of Number 10 about GB had to stop.

[Former South African President] Nelson Mandela came in and brought with him the usual mix of charisma, grace and wisdom, all laced with the deep warmth and humour. He took hold of Leo, said hello Leo, and Leo looked at him a bit puzzled and Mandela said 'Clearly you have never before seen an old-age pensioner from the colonies.' Peter Hain was in for part of the meeting with TB largely on AIDS and Congo and worryingly, Mandela was being more supportive than we thought he would be of some of the more worrying African leaders. The office staff were all hanging around hoping to see him and he agreed we could bring them all in for a photo.

We went over to the conference hall where JP's speech, a few good jokes and a good rant at the Tories went down well. There was an eight-minute ovation for Mandela as he came up the ramp with TB. There was a fantastic atmosphere and really moving film with 'He Ain't Heavy, He's My Brother' as the backing track. Mandela had them in his hand the whole way through and made a solid, serious speech, including a bid for cash for AIDS, a warning about the downsides of globalisation, but great on our values and then back via another ovation as he left. He was a phenomenal personality and everyone was buzzing. As he left the hall, Dennis Skinner came up and said he felt the recent shift in mood was real and it would be impossible to get it back.

Friday, September 29

The Danes voted *Nej* [No] in their euro referendum. The Olympics were going well and the press was pretty low-key on conference, with Mandela stealing the show. There was an extraordinary picture in *The Times* of TB with Paxman and me in the corner like something out of the shroud of Turin. TB was now worrying about reconnection. He felt we had done OK at conference but not much better, and the unions had been a setback. Also, divisions at the top were now doing real damage. I felt a lot of it was about his style and language, and the way he lived. Some of it was unavoidable, but some of it we could change. I spent much of the day taking weekend TV and radio interviewers through the argument about £16 billion cuts.

Saturday, September 30

I planned the weekend around football, Burnley vs Portsmouth today, Arsenal vs Man U tomorrow. Godric picked up in his ring-round that the Tories were briefing on pensions that they would give more than whatever we promised, alongside a more modern approach for young people. We did a quick conference call with the Treasury and the party people and put together a strong briefing line to get round the Sundays. The match was pretty dire, 1-1, but at least work-wise it was a quiet day.

Sunday, October 1

David Frost did me proud with Hague, effectively taking our briefing note and turning it on him. After the programme, we regrouped with Margaret B who was doing *On the Record*. But she didn't quite pin the Tories and they were getting away with far too much at the moment. Though the polls were back marginally in our favour, we weren't popular at the moment and the Tories could get a dangerous lift with a good week. I got Spencer Livermore [GB adviser] in to do a rebuttal document on their tax and spending but we weren't really getting lift-off. We needed a lot more imagination. I took Rory to Arsenal and met Alex F for a brief chat.

Monday, October 2

I felt we could quickly lapse into drift again. At GB's meeting, he wanted to get us back on boom and bust. TB was looking really tired and we were lacking a big forward agenda. He said the most important strategic objective for the short term was to get him back with GB. We had a Dome meeting with Charlie F. He wasn't sure about legacy. David North made a joke about arson. We were beginning to get focused on the Europe speech, though TB had done his own draft, and the carers' package for tomorrow. I had a meeting with Cherie on Wakeham's [Press Complaints Commission] reply to us. She wasn't happy that he took seriously enough her concerns about the kids and I wrote Wakeham a very downbeat reply.

Tuesday, October 3

The Tories were getting good straight coverage of their conference and we lacked the politicians or the imagination to break into it. TB and GB felt we just had to hit back with rational argument but while that may be OK for the opinion formers, we lacked the people to drive that message through. GB wasn't motoring and Peter was disengaged. Also Margaret McD was running into problems in Millbank. Her view was our big problem was lack of politicians really up for a fight with the Tories.

TB took a meeting on his Poland speech [for the Polish Stock Exchange] with Stephen Wall, Roger Liddle etc. and what was

October '00: Cherie unhappy with Lord Wakeham

extraordinary was that they actually wanted to argue about whether we could say that the nation state was more important than the European Commission. I said that if real people heard this discussion, they would not believe it and they would certainly never vote for us again. We weren't helped by [Commission President Romano] Prodi's speech today saying intergovernmentalism was not the way forward.

I had a meeting with Balls on the PBR. He was worried that both TB and GB felt the PBR would solve all our problems on fuel and pensions when it won't. He felt we had to get up an early message about all the threats on spending. The media was wall-to-wall Tories. [Michael] Portillo did an ad-libbed tour de force [speech] and Hague a pretty good Q&A.

Wednesday, October 4

I took Paul Brown [Grid co-ordinator] to the GB meeting for the first time and it was a real boon. Not only did he know everything that was going on, but he talked very straightforwardly, without the slightest hint of fear to GB, whatever the mood or the question. The Tories were definitely getting a lift and I was making the point that to break through we had to be edgy and even consider [media] stunts, like taking a bandwagon down there [to Conservative conference]. We might also need advertising to get up £16 billion cuts.

During the day, a gift presented itself when Ann Widdecombe [Shadow Home Secretary] came up with the idea of £100 fines for the first offence of cannabis possession. Police, drug groups and Shadow Cabinet colleagues came out against her hard and by the end of the day it had unravelled. It totally cut across their overall strategy, which was to be One Nation/centrist, a move we had to deny them. TB, Stephen Wall and I were up in the flat trying to agree a central argument for the Europe speech. We settled on the idea that the main question was what do Europe's people want and expect, as a vehicle for emphasising a stronger [European] Council, which set an annual agenda, a work programme, with a charter of competence which made clear which organisations and institutions were meant to do what. Stephen suggested a call on Europe to wake up to a new reality, Europe widening and deepening simultaneously. I then worked up a briefing script, having a while ago agreed I would go to Brussels to do a briefing of the correspondents there.

TB did not want to be sceptic, but he did want to stress the nation state as the key to legitimacy. We had so far in recent days had big speeches with Chirac, Schroeder, [Italian Prime Minister Giuliano] Amato, [German Vice Chancellor Joschka] Fischer and others and this would be seen as part of that debate. TB gave me and Stephen one of his little sweeping statements. He said the thing about Europe is that France and Germany always count. We and Italy and Spain sometimes count and we count at the moment and Spain counts because of Aznar. The others count less, so they rely on the Commission more. I left to go to parents' evening at the boys' school and then back to Number 10 before leaving for Waterloo [for Eurostar]. On the train I worked on the speech. It was quite nice to get away without TB, even if just for a night. I went to [Nigel] Sheinwald's residence [as the UK permanent representative to the EU] and went over the main lines for the briefing. The cuttings came through and although Widdecombe had spoiled their day, the Tories were still doing too well and the *Sun* was totally up their arse.

Thursday, October 5

The fall of Milosevic, which was brilliant. I had breakfast with Jonathan Faull [European Commission chief spokesman]. He said Prodi felt out of favour and was pissed off with the Brits. He felt we snubbed him in New York and didn't give him enough support. He was clearly a very prickly character. I went through TB's speech. It was clear that we were still seen as a bit of a back marker. He said there was a lot of talk around the place that we weren't that much different to the Tories, that we weren't really pushing the boat out on the euro, and they couldn't understand why a leader with such personal skills and a huge majority was not going for it.

The briefing went well and they clearly felt it was a substantial speech with a lot in it. I was explaining that the purpose was reconnection and that the governments and parliaments were the key to that. That was not a sceptical view. On the train back, I spoke to TB who was wondering whether he could use the line about Europe becoming a 'superpower, not a superstate'. Stephen Wall and I worked on a new ending to the speech.

I got back in time to see Hague's speech which I thought was really poor, lacking in substance and even the jokes were not his usual standard. Only the *Sun* were likely to give it big licks though even Trevor Kavanagh said it was dull. The uprising on the streets of Belgrade was growing and growing and we were witnessing a revolution that was fantastic to watch. I was hoping he was as scared as he deserved to be. Clinton went out to do a clip, then we got TB out to say Milosevic must go before there was more death and that we would offer the hand of friendship to the Serbs if they embraced democracy. It felt great that Milosevic was so clearly on the way out and hiding in a hole somewhere, really panicking. It also meant that Hague's speech was going nowhere.

We left for Warsaw. TB talked to Prodi to calm him down a bit, then we worked on the speech, which he wanted to be less forward on the euro, but strong on vision. We were meeting in a building that used to be KGB offices and then did a joint interview with Polish telly but TB was tired and relieved when we got back to the Sheraton. He was a bit taken aback by how the Polish interviewer clearly believed we were very much in the slow lane. He had seen GB and Peter when I was in Brussels and it had not gone brilliantly. He was wondering again whether I should go to Millbank, though of course it would be quite a signal re the election. I got to bed late and watched events in Belgrade for ages. Needless to say, despite the significance of what had happened in Kosovo, we were getting zero credit, and indeed Robin's attempts to link us to events was being whacked by the commentariat.

Friday, October 6

Hague's speech was totally overshadowed by Belgrade and although the *Sun*, *Mail* and *Telegraph* were desperate to give him a lift, the sense I got talking to most people there was that it hadn't really happened for them. As well as the Europe dividing line internally, there was now social tolerance vs social authoritarianism that was damaging them. This was likely to take off as a Widdecombe fault line over her approach on drugs. TB was worried as ever about whether the central argument of his speech was strong enough. After a long discussion we decided to go with 'superpower not a superstate' which played well through the day. We wrote a new section at the top on Milosevic to underline the depth of his barbarism. The speech felt strong, superpower not superstate, key to reconnection national governments and parliaments, second chamber to police it all, proper charter of competences. First we had a meeting with the president [Aleksander Kwasniewski] who was a big Arsenal fan. I was a bit alarmed when TB indicated he wouldn't mind if Milosevic wasn't tried for war crimes so long as he went.

The big question for the Poles was EU membership and TB was pushing a strong line of support without giving a date. We had a long meeting with the prime minister [Jerzy Buzek], again mainly about Europe, NATO and one or two bilateral issues. At the press conference, TB basically just repeated the message on Milosevic. While he visited the tomb of the unknown soldier, I briefed the broadcasters on the speech. The venue was good, it went down well with the audience and the media thought it was pretty meaty. TB was having lunch at the [Koniecpolski] palace while I sat out in the park briefing a few columnists by phone.

Saturday, October 7

TB called, happy enough with the speech. Trimble did well in his no-confidence conference.[1] TB said that every time he has forced a fight he does well, but he always takes too long to get fighting and he is too slow to see the problems emerging. The *Mail on Sunday* got seven members of the Shadow Cabinet to say they had taken drugs – clearly because they hate Ann Widdecombe. England played Germany [England 0, Germany 1] and then Kevin Keegan quit [as manager]. Philip came back from the US feeling that Al Gore could lose because they liked Bush's plain speaking.

Sunday, October 8

Major was on *Frost* and attacked us over Kosovo, as well as saying we had squandered our majority. I called Robin who did a very good attack over Major's Bosnian record and his failure to stand up to Milosevic.[2] I went up to the running track while Rory was training and did twenty-four laps, and started to think I could really get into running.

Monday, October 9

The Tory drugs shambles was pretty big and Hague did interviews to try to calm it down. But it was also moving to us with the press saying that as Shadow Cabinet members had been 'open and honest' about whether they took drugs, so should the Cabinet. GB did pretty well getting up childcare today, the third story after the Middle East and the Tories on drugs. Our usual line on not taking part in surveys was broken first by Chris Smith and then by GB, worrying about his own position. I drove in with Philip, who was full of his trip to the States, but feeling a lot less confident about Gore than a while back. He said the biggest difference between here and there was that they had a big serious press.

At TB's office meeting, he had done a note on the processes he

[1] Trimble had survived a vote of no confidence in his leadership orchestrated by disaffected Ulster Unionist Party members who felt he had been too conciliatory towards Sinn Fein.
[2] Major had been prime minister during the Bosnian War 1992–95, when 200,000 people were killed, some 50,000 women raped, and 2.2 million people fled their homes.

now wanted. It was back to a basic structure of him, me, GB and Peter M and everything driving out from that. Yet when he spoke of both of them, it was in pretty negative terms. He felt Peter had become too grand and too prone to dump on colleagues. Andrew Adonis [education policy adviser] had confronted [Chris] Woodhead over the claim, slightly different to what we first heard, that he was going to resign, attack us in the *Mail* or the *Telegraph* and eventually take a job in a Hague Cabinet. TB said he felt betrayed but the problem was the right-wing press would seize on it for the obvious politics and the left-wing press as a way of questioning his judgement about people, rightly in my view. TB felt it would be difficult to win a war of words. It would just inflate Woodhead's standing in the area he wanted to be strong. The other focus of our discussion and a subsequent meeting with Charlie was the continuing effort to make the Grid more strategic. Paul Brown was doing a fantastic job, though in showing GB the shape of the Grid as it developed, he was beginning to nick the best of it.

TB felt we needed to see Murdoch fairly soon, but the *Sun* was pushing the boat out so hard for the Tories they wouldn't be able to come back in line. He said it would be fantastic to win without any press support but it wouldn't be easy and it was better if we had some of them with us. We had a big health meeting to discuss ways of avoiding a winter crisis. We had a meeting on the Dome with Charlie setting out plans on legacy and TB asking rather hopefully whether a last-minute rush would lead to a more balanced balance sheet. I was feeling a bit out of sorts, no longer driven and obsessive, which some would say was a good thing, but it meant when I was like this I wasn't really motoring. Peter Hyman did me an excellent note on how I could make myself more strategic. The end of the day presented a very good example of just how hard that was. GB and Smith having broken the line on surveys by saying they had never taken drugs, it proved virtually impossible to find a minister who would go up tomorrow. JP was livid at GB for dropping them in it. GB said he hadn't wanted to answer but it was very hard when asked direct. I said anyone who now didn't answer would be assumed to be saying yes. DB called, said he was thrilled Woodhead was leaving.

Tuesday, October 10

We were drifting back to governmentalitis, lacking a big political message, not really focusing, departments dribbling stuff out without impact or regard to the big picture. Also, since I'd been taking Paul Brown to GB meetings, GB was now working the Grid to his own advantage. Three stories from it had been shipped straight into the *Mirror*. The *Mail* were now chasing every member of the Cabinet and we had to send a message that no matter how irritating it was, and no matter what stick we took, we had to reimpose the line on not taking part in these silly newspaper surveys.

The Middle East was bad and getting worse. Ditto Northern Ireland, and TB was having to get more involved again. He also had a meeting on hunting but believed if we went ahead as planned there would be massive civil disobedience which would disrupt the election campaign. He was back to asking whether we could just dump it. Even the idea of local referenda, which is where it felt like we were heading, was unlikely to do much good and was very fraught.

I got a call from Brian Fitzpatrick [the First Minister's head of policy] that Donald Dewar was ill, that he had fallen and was now in hospital again. He said he would be kept in overnight and it was fine, but it was clear things were a lot worse and as the day wore on, it became clear things were a lot, lot worse. I could tell from the tone of the calls from Fitzpatrick and David Whitton [Dewar's spokesman] that he was on the way out. They kept us in touch through the day and virtually every call sounded a bit more desperate. I promised to take Grace and her friends to see Britney Spears [pop singer] at Wembley, and I was in and out the whole time taking calls about Donald. I was also hoping to avoid being seen but just as we settled down for the second half, Matthew Engel from the *Guardian* popped up behind me and said he was doing a piece on the crowd.

Wednesday, October 11

Donald was on life support and they were basically just waiting for Ian and Marion [his children] to turn off the machine. I called Ian and suggested they entrust someone like Jimmy Gordon [Lord Gordon of Strathblane, Labour peer] to take over the management of the funeral, and I offered Hilary C and Anne Shevas [Downing Street chief press officer] to help. He died officially at 12.18, while TB was seeing the Czechs. He did his own tribute.

GB cancelled meetings with TB and Peter M because he was working on an obituary of Donald and he also did extended interviews. Everyone was really sad about Donald. He could be maddening at times with his old-fashioned ways, but he was a truly solid citizen and he had been a great help to me so many times. The *Record* called for an article and I said TB would also do one that we would offer to everyone and back came the answer 'Fine, but it would be nice to get a couple of gimmicks just for us.' And they wonder why I loathe them.

TB did his tribute to Donald for the broadcast media which was fine and then I went to an extraordinary meeting chaired by Peter M to go over Peter H's paper. Peter H, largely at my prodding, had done a paper on strategy which TB had sent to GB yesterday and he had gone into a total funk about it. It was an attempt to force the pace on those who were meant to be doing strategy for the election to do so, but GB's only point was that we hadn't consulted him properly. Douglas was good on stuff like one-to-one campaigning but lacked the drive or power to get things done. I made the point that we had dysfunctional systems and we had to have a new approach based on openness.

I was called out to do a conference call with DB, Conor Ryan [special adviser on education], [Michael] Bichard [permanent secretary, Department for Education] and AA. Blunkett had just seen Woodhead who was 'shambolic and unpleasant' and clearly wanting to be sacked. He later claimed to Andrew [Adonis] that he was being hounded out. I said to David and later to TB that I felt it was a mistake to run the two-trap approach. Woodhead was Frank Field with knobs on and would use it all against us later. I felt David should write to him and ensure that if the letter leaked later, it would not harm us. I still felt this was all likely to end in a full-frontal battle but TB in particular still didn't want Woodhead to be able to claim convincingly he was pushed out.

Back in Peter's meeting, Anji had mentioned the GB irritation at this meeting, Ed Miliband reacted, Peter went mad first with Ed and then tore a strip off Anji with what she called his 'histrionic Hitler' bit. I said I felt they were all mad, that TB had no idea how weak his operations were, that he had put in position a fundamentally unstable structure founded on two people capable of destroying each other and I was not going to spend the next period of my life going through with this nonsense day after day. I said there's no point, it's no fun and life is too short. Peter did his aggrieved bit, said he didn't need to do this, he had plenty to do in Northern Ireland, as for GB, it was clear he felt if his job was strategy, Peter should not be doing meetings like this. Earlier in the meeting, when I had said we had no real strategy, Anji said that was reported back as an attack on Gordon and Douglas.

When we went back to see TB later, we ended up laughing about it because it was all so ridiculous. TB was taking the mick out of PH as 'the man who caused all the problems'. And he came round to see us later and said we couldn't go on like this. We had to get a grip and find alternatives. He said he thought of every possible alternative but GB was head and shoulders above the rest on politics and strategy, and Peter M had organisational skills we needed in Millbank. GB was anti big tent, Peter was centre ground and TB could hold it all together. He said it was really bad that I gave out vibes of being unhappy and blaming him. If there was a workable different idea he would have gone for it by now. But there was none. He, GB, Peter and I were the four people he needed to drive all this and unless I had alternatives, you just had to get on and make it work. He said GB had to be totally bound in to our success or failure. JP was totally signed up for that approach. They were due to have dinner soon and JP would make clear to GB that if he did not deliver the whole party would be down on him, TB and JP included.

The report on race and ethnic issues was going big; we were trying to get it focused on Britishness. During the briefing on the Biarritz [European Council] summit, I slipped a note to Hilary asking her to leave the room and plant a question with Jon Smith of PA on Britishness. Five minutes later, Jon Smith said he had just been paged to ask me if I had any comment on the story about a British nurse!

Blunkett came home for dinner. He admitted he was mildly paranoid about Gordon because he feared he was just plotting away the whole time to put his people into the big jobs where he could control policy. He said TB operated like a human being whereas GB ran a military campaign. He would now be fixing the Scottish [First Minister] succession. TB was less obsessive because he was more human. He said he dreaded the idea of him handing over to GB. He thought GB was an amazing bloke, capable of doing any job in government apart from the top one.

Thursday, October 12

I was livid about the *Sun* whose story and editorial totally misrepresented my briefing yesterday and presented it as an attack on Britain. I sent [David] Yelland a demand for a correction and apology. I told Trevor Kavanagh that if they were in my office I would splatter them against the wall and I wasn't going to put up with it. Yelland called after Cabinet, said he accepted it was a mistake, was not going to haggle and agreed to make a donation to the kids' school. I said I had left him alone because it was clear they wanted to go down a different track. Fine, but we weren't going to put up with total misrepresentation.

The papers were otherwise full of huge tributes to Donald, some of them warm and genuine, the bulk utterly hypocritical. It wasn't

October '00: Blunkett mildly paranoid about GB

that long ago that Donald came to see me, almost begging for help with how to deal with what he called Rottweiler journalism. The same people who had made his life hell were now writing about him as though he were a great personal friend. GB was motoring on getting [Henry] McLeish in as a shoo-in [as First Minister], much to the irritation of Jack McConnell [Scottish finance minister and leadership candidate]. The Scottish press were seeing GB as a kind of kingmaker. It was at times like this we realised he had in some ways a much deeper political and media operation.

On the flight out to Biarritz later, TB showed me a piece of intelligence which showed that the Germans assessed our problems on Europe not as one of public opinion, or the Tories, but a sense that TB and GB were on a different track to each other. So it was out there, probably picked up when some Foreign Office people were in Berlin. At least my morning meeting with GB was a bit more political and a bit more strategic. Later TB saw him and Peter and said it was fifty-five minutes of pure hell followed by five minutes of pure gold when GB properly turned his mind to strategy. His big point at the moment was that the [US] Democrats had allowed the economy and economic strength to become a given without a dividing line and we mustn't let that happen. The general feeling was that Gore lost the [presidential] TV debate earlier this morning.

Donald was still a big political story, and if anything the sadness around the place was even greater today. But the Middle East peace process was going up in flames. TB spoke to Robin in the region and also spoke to Bill C and sent messages to Arafat and Barak. The Israelis really were kicking shit out of the Palestinians including Arafat's HQ. Then came the bombing, probably [Osama] Bin Laden's lot, of a US ship.[1] Grim.

Gus [Macdonald] came to see me to plan a strategy for the [fuel protesters'] sixty-day deadline based on 1. the dangers of what happened last time, 2. better preparations and, 3. building an alliance of reasonable people. Cabinet began with a minute's silence and TB said that because of Donald's death and because JP was away, it wasn't appropriate to have the planned political discussion. GB did a pre-PBR presentation on the overall economic strategy. He defined the background as cynicism, disillusion about delivery and an attempt to portray us as anti-patriotic. The Tory problems meanwhile were

[1] The USS *Cole*, a destroyer, had been targeted by al-Qaeda bombers while refuelling in the Yemeni port of Aden. Seventeen sailors were killed and thirty-nine injured.

£16 billion cuts and opportunism. He got very passionate about how the Democrats had surrendered and allowed the economy debate to neutralise and become a debate about who would best spend an illusory surplus. The press want to push us to that same position. On fuel and pensions, for example, we can only argue about how to spend money because we did the things needed to create stability. It didn't happen by accident but by difficult decisions.

Both GB and TB emphasised we had to pin the Tories on boom and bust versus prudence and stability, and present every step of progress on health, education and crime as a choice that we were making, which they could not because they would not invest to build a strong economy. Investment in the talent of the many or tax cuts for the few. TB said that if the economy becomes a given, we lose our strength on the fundamentals. They did bits on Serbia, Middle East, Europe and fuel, but the mood throughout was pretty subdued. I got GB to do more DD tributes. John Reid called me a couple of times to say TB underestimated how much GB was 'at it' in terms of policy and personnel. I also learned from Anne Shevas that GB would do the main address at the funeral, with TB not really in the script. TB was worrying re the Middle East [peace process] that oil could be up to $900 a barrel and Iraq exploiting the situation.

I did the strategic note for the weekend, then worked on a letter to [Lord] Wakeham re Leo. Fiona and I sided with CB but TB said he really didn't mind Leo being pictured. I had quite a good meeting with Philip and some of GB's people to agree a series of speeches tying the two of them together. On arrival in Biarritz, we were warned to be very careful about all calls, pager messages, conversations in open places and paper security. The Charter[1] became the story for my briefing. We were staying in the Hôtel du Palais, a beautiful, very French five-star hotel. I got Tim Livesey [press officer] briefing on Robin's Middle East visit. We bumped into Schroeder who asked me how the polls were. I said fine, in part because we didn't really have an opposition other than the press.

Friday, October 13

The Scottish press was full of TB/GB out to square it for [Henry] McLeish. I asked Lance for a line to settle it down and before I knew it GB was on the phone to me saying it was important for TB not to

[1] The new EU Charter of Fundamental Rights, setting out the economic, political and social rights of EU citizens. Initially briefed as a 'showcase' for existing rights, the Charter would be seized upon by journalists as an opportunity for European courts to overturn British laws.

be involved. He had no vote or locus. I said I just wanted a defensive line. He blamed the press for cranking it up but it was obvious he was angling and manoeuvring. I got my apology in the *Sun* plus a cheque for the school. The papers were filled with the Middle East and the row over the Charter, Keith Vaz having said that the court [European Court of Justice] could take it into account having sent them into a bit of a frenzy.

We had breakfast with the Norwegian PM [Jens Stoltenberg], largely talking about oil. We had to square Chirac that Stephen Wall could sit with TB. Chirac was clearly pissed off that Robin was in the Middle East as well as [Javier] Solana [now Secretary General of the European Council]. TB felt the French were constantly trying to undermine us in a way the Germans were not. I did a briefing partly on the Charter and the IGC issues but mainly on Robin seeing Arafat and later Barak. I called Blunkett re Woodhead who claimed he was being hounded out. He had asked for more time and David reluctantly gave it to him. Woodhead was really pushing his luck with DB who felt [Richard] Wilson had been too soft with him and he was feeling he could push us around.

Vaz having got us into a bit of a mess on the Charter was now saying it was no more than the *Beano*, a line he had picked up from me at breakfast.[1] That became a different sort of problem. At the morning session, Chirac was trying to push QMV [qualified majority voting] on tax and social security. TB was pretty firm on both. He said tax was a fundamental point for national parliaments and governments.

TB got back from the dinner and spoke to Clinton and Robin. RC had done well, but was modest enough beneath the pompous tones to say that TB's relationship with Barak had helped and also that [Michael] Levy had done well for him and that he was right to keep him involved. TB said Chirac was reluctant to speak to Arafat who was under pressure from other Arab leaders and we had to push and push to get him engaged in the summit. Clinton wasn't too confident. But the oil price was soaring again and a summit might bring it down. TB was worried at the way the French were gunning for him the whole time. He felt they were jealous of our growing position both in Europe and with some of the Middle East countries.

---

[1] Referring to a children's comic in an attempt to downplay the significance of the Charter, Vaz had told journalists it was 'no more binding [on British courts] than the *Beano*'.

Saturday, October 14

I was up early and went for a swim in the seawater pool in the dark, which was really nice. Then breakfast with TB, RC, Stephen Wall and John S. TB did an interview with Humphrys [BBC *Today* programme] but it was a crap interview by both, very scrappy. Humphrys went on about Yvette Cooper [Labour MP, wife of Ed Balls] 'confessing' on *Question Time* that she had taken cannabis. I sent a message afterwards to Humphrys and Rod Liddle [editor of *Today*] – serious journalism RIP. TB was angry with himself that he had not really driven through a message on how positive engagement benefited Britain. He was very nice about Robin, who was listening with me, and was almost visibly purring. TB said to me later he was a very good Foreign Secretary, who gave us more support than problems. Later TB was walking through a crowd with Robin, everyone recognised TB then someone went up to Robin, slapped him on the back and said '*Vive l'Autriche*' obviously thinking he was [Austrian Chancellor Wolfgang] Schüssel.

I did a briefing for the Sundays in a restaurant and went through the usual shit and charade of them pretending to be interested in the serious stuff before we got down into all the crap. On Donald, the *Mail on Sunday* totally misrepresented what I said by suggesting we were at odds over the funeral. Scum. I tried to calm down the Scottish situation by saying TB had not expressed a view on the succession, but that was misrepresented too. I did TB's press conference speaking notes. I had a nice chat with Chris Patten who said we were the victims of our own success, the press having been so much our slaves for a while that they were now turning against us. He said we had to build up pockets of sanity within the media. He said one problem was that the average intelligence of editors had fallen markedly.

I was getting into my usual summit malaise. I had a chat with TB, Schroeder and Aznar on football transfers. Schroeder said he reckoned I was the only person who hated summits more than he did. TB's press conference was fine though he was strangely hesitant, full of 'erms' and 'aahs'. He was full of praise for Robin again. He announced the summit with Arafat and Barak which was good, and did some strong pro-Europe, strong Britain, picking apart the lunacy of the Tory position on Europe. Robin was singing Levy's praises to me. Afterwards I did a huddle, then talked to Phil Webster [*Times*] and George Jones [*Telegraph*] on the next stage, and the need for big choices. TB and I both had a kip in the back of the car on the way to Paris airport. [Former Paymaster General] Geoffrey Robinson's interview in the *Mail* signalled the next frenzy coming our way. On the flight home, we read Blunkett's detailed notes on the Woodhead meetings. He had given him till Tuesday for a final answer. The big news when we got home was a plane hijack with forty Brits on it.[1] I was glad to get home, see Fiona and the kids and was hoping for a quiet day tomorrow.

Sunday, October 15

David B was on *Frost* and had a whack at [Geoffrey] Robinson being self-indulgent over his book [*The Unconventional Minister*] that was being serialised tomorrow in the *Mail*. I talked to Peter M about how to deal with Robinson's book. Peter was worried, said the problem was God knows what it would say. I said it would cause a frenzy which would pass until the next one came along. I got Blunkett to put out a line later challenging Geoffrey to say how much he was getting from the *Mail* and give it to the party or charity. Apart from a couple of calls from TB, and from Robin who was dealing with all the foreign policy stuff going on, I managed to have a quiet day, swam with Grace and played tennis with Calum. I did thirty laps at the track and really felt I could get into distance running.

Monday, October 16

Middle East was the main story but GR in the *Mail*, and the allegation that Peter M lied [about the £373,000 loan from Robinson], was going big. Peter called, anxious, and I said he should just put out a short but non-inflammatory statement. At the GB meeting, we had a very good discussion on longer-term strategy, PG and I arguing for a big campaign on cuts and Tory economic illiteracy. I felt we had a chance to hurt them on the economy, if we could link cuts to boom and bust. GB said it was difficult to campaign in government against an opposition that people didn't think could win. It never stopped them when we were in opposition. There had to be a mix of hope and fear and the fear had to link cuts to boom and bust and we had to make an economic case for investment. GB was in a far better mood and had thought about things, and between us we could see the shape of a series of interlinking campaigns.

GB was really firing and there was a bit of contrast when we went over for TB's office meeting. He was a bit fazed about fox hunting again, also not confident we had sorted a proper plan for the fuel

[1] A Saudi Arabian Airlines plane en route from Jeddah to London had been hijacked by five armed men – four Saudis and an Ethiopian – and forced to land in Iraq. The hijack ended peacefully the same day with the hijackers detained by the Iraqi authorities.

protests. He wanted to be dismissive of Geoffrey's book but knew it was bad and may well be TB/GB-related, with [Charlie] Whelan almost certainly operating for GR. He spoke to GB and we suggested he make clear he hadn't wanted the book written and that he thought Peter M was doing a good job. I wanted GB to go further and distance himself publicly from Whelan. GB said that would only make a martyr of someone who is bitter because he feels we got rid of him. I had a meeting with Dickie Attenborough [Labour peer, film director] who said he had been asked by TB to help on relations with GB. He had called a friend of GB who said what TB needed to do was say privately, and preferably publicly, that two years into the next parliament, he would make way for GB. Ridiculous. Dickie had some good insights, for example that apart from JP, ministers almost always talked about 'I' and their department, rather than the government, and they rarely talked up TB. He felt TB should do more in Parliament and that if he did, it would be easier to rule out a TV debate. GR was running big and DB getting next to nothing out of his schools stuff. I took a meeting on Peter H's paper on strategy and the war book, which we needed to develop. I saw TB who wanted me to go for the media for the way they were ignoring health and education for GR. I talked him out of it and he said it was good that I was moderating him for once.

Tuesday, October 17

I was in early for a breakfast with the Trinity Mirror top brass plus editors. They did their usual whinge about us not giving them enough stories. I said they had to start treating the Tories like they could win, as the Tory papers used to do to us. It was OK but not much better. Margaret McD came to see TB and said the party was getting more and more fed up with all the talk of division. He said to her, like he said to me, find me an alternative. TBWA [advertising agency] had done some good work and I felt on that front we were in good shape. Bandwagoning and opportunism was really hurting the Tories. They had put together a very good 'Thank you' campaign, the idea being to link delivery to the people who voted for change. They also had some very good knocking ideas re Hague. But the latest big internal poll suggested the Tory message was getting through better than ours and TB's ratings were poor. I said he had to come out fighting, show more spirit and determination.

News came through at lunchtime of a bad train crash [at Hatfield, Hertfordshire]. It blew out any hope of coverage for health without blowing out Robinson, who was today beating the drum on Europe and saying TB should deal with Peter M. Geoffrey was looking ridiculous but making the government look ridiculous too. Even though Hague was bandwagoning, he was hitting the right notes on it. Peter M spoke to [Piers] Morgan yesterday, who ran a positive line for Peter but he was livid that he was quoted. He put out a statement to PA saying these were not his views and Piers hit back saying the words came direct from him. Then Andy Grice [*Independent*] wrote a big story that Peter was saying to friends that GB allies were out to destroy him. Ridiculous. I felt we were moving towards one of them saying that they absolutely wouldn't work with the other. But both could be a real problem on the outside. TB accepted the current situation wasn't working but he kept saying he just didn't have an alternative.

I spoke several times to JP in Beijing about whether he should come back to deal with the rail crash. We both felt that probably he should. Earlier, about half one, I popped round to see TB. He said some of the Cabinet were in a state of revolt over GB/Peter M. On their way to the health speech, Alan Milburn said ministers felt they were working hard and doing the business for him but 'these two clowns' were pissing everyone off and doing real damage. He got Sally and Anji to join us and we were back to the old stuck record – that he had no alternative. I said I was no longer sure about that, that yes GB was good but the negatives were pretty powerful. As for Peter, none of us were actually sure what kind of planning was going on. At least we should be building other people up, and he had to do more of the strategy himself and not subcontract the whole time to GB, Peter and me. He also had to find a way of making them more fearful of his authority.

TB said this time he felt they did realise how bad it was, and that the mood in the party was turning against them. He said it wasn't realistic for GB to turn on Whelan because Charlie knows so much about him. 'How do you think I would feel if you were out there as my enemy not my friend?' He said GB had in some ways treated him dreadfully for years and logic says put someone else in there, but he remained unpersuaded that anyone else would do it as well. He said Peter is not indispensable, but he is talented and it would be wrong to push him out just because someone else wants it. I think it was the first time he had said overtly that if there was a replacement for GB, he would welcome it, but he also said he still felt personally very fond of him though 'at times like this the reasons tend to elude me'. He said he believed they would both learn from recent events. I said I didn't believe they would. They were like a couple of old stars in a long-running soap and they couldn't rewrite the basic script.

Normal politics was suspended for the day for Donald's funeral. The [Hatfield] rail crash was leading to calls for [Gerald] Corbett [Railtrack chief executive] to resign from Railtrack. He told Gus Macdonald he would resign if it turned out to be a broken rail. I spoke to Gus and told him it was best for him to stay in London. After a pretty desultory morning meeting, we left for Twickenham where TB was doing one of [film director and Police Federation supporter] Michael Winner's police memorial events. In the car, TB was looking really tired, his face a bit grey and his hair clearly thinning and greying. I was reading Paddy Ashdown's diaries and was angry that Jonathan had held them back from me because there were all manner of dreadful stories in there. But TB was always keen to keep Paddy fairly happy.

On the plane up [to Edinburgh], TB settled Blunkett, who was filling him in on Woodhead, and they agreed he would step down on Tuesday. We were going to take a big hit but TB was convinced we mustn't give him any excuse to say he was hounded out. The Robinson stuff was dying out but TB believed there had to be a GB/Peter M rapprochement story soon, and it had to be real, to get things back on an even keel. The mood on the plane north was a bit school outing. I chatted to Cherie, who was in good form, Andrew Smith [chief secretary to the Treasury], Sally and Peter H. Jack Straw was angry at the note I'd sent on the handling of the drugs announcement and my suggestion that the Home Office wasn't working well with us. Margaret and Leo [Beckett], Mo, Hoon, Paul Murphy, Milburn, Ian McCartney, Margaret Jay were all on the plane. Further back on the plane, there were a host more ministers. Sally pointed out that if the plane had crashed, only GB and Peter M would have been left. What a smooth handover. I said GB wouldn't know which queen to call first.

As we arrived I attached myself to David Blunkett and looked after him for most of the day. We were taken by bus to the Scottish Executive building and met by Henry McLeish who shook hands with everyone and said 'Thanks for coming' as though it was his event. John Reid was busy stirring. Wendy Alexander [Scottish minister for communities, sister of Douglas] was clearly wanting to have a serious discussion, but I wasn't really up for it. I talked to Derry and Alison [Irvine], and it must have been a particularly difficult day for them. Alison looked very nervy.

It was a nice atmosphere on the bus to the cathedral. Because of the security, we were in for a good hour or more before the service started. I noticed that Hague was seated in front of a pillar after being separated from [his chief of staff Sebastian, Lord] Coe. Bertie was across the way. Ruth Wishart [journalist] made a reasonably funny speech. Douglas [Alexander]'s dad [a Church of Scotland minister] was conducting the service and I felt his welcome to TB was a bit patronising, and maybe I was too sensitive, but it was like he was welcoming him to a foreign country.

GB's tribute was very powerful, very socialist, more of the Old Labour than the New. I loved the Gaelic singing, which reminded me of our holidays in Tiree [birthplace of AC's father], but I wasn't as emotional as I normally get at funerals. We filed out to the Internationale [socialist anthem] and were back on the bus and then to the Kelvingrove Art Gallery. I had a nice chat with Elizabeth Smith [widow of the late Labour leader John] and the girls. TB did a bit of business with Trimble. Robin and Gaynor [his wife] joined us for the flight back. They were fussing over the baby.

We had a discussion about the trip to [the Asia–Europe summit in Seoul] Korea. It was odd how quickly everyone just moved on to the next thing. What I had picked up very strongly through the day was how virtually everyone in the Cabinet was really fed up with the GB/ Peter M situation and that they saw the Robinson book as part of that. I worked on a script on tough choices for TB to use when he saw the press on the flight out to Korea, but he didn't really go for it. Stupidly, he said that if there was a referendum tomorrow, we would vote no, which though blindingly obvious as the conditions were not met, set the press off into a total frenzy. My last words, as he had taken off for Korea, and I headed home, was that if he saw the press he should do it all on the record, as virtually every off-the-record briefing he had done on the plane had gone wrong. His last words to me were that we had to get GB and Peter working together.

Thursday, October 19

The GB meeting was very much focused on rail and we felt we needed JP up and about on it quickly. GB was anxious that we weren't going to be able to get up the big themes properly in time for the PBR. I stayed on at the end and asked him if he thought he could do something publicly with Peter, e.g. a press conference. He said of course he would, but I suspect the theory would be easier than the practice. I said if they joined together at an event attacking the Tories, it would be powerful. He said it would just look stage-managed, but I felt we had to do something that people noticed and created a new dynamic between them. TB's speech came through, a watered-down version of what we had done on the plane. His euro comments were going big. Godric filled me in on what happened, which had unleashed a total media wank. TB came on and said it was totally his fault for not planning what he intended to say, and agreeing to do it off the record. He said it was impossible just to have a sensible chat with journalists any more.

Peter M and I had a meeting with the [advertising] agency. GB's lot came and we agreed that the balance between positive and negative in the campaign should veer to the positive. Peter M felt that some of the Hague ideas, him as a schoolboy, him looking like Thatcher, were too personal. But they were funny, and they would work. But we needed the positive first base, and the 'thank you' campaign was probably the best for that. JP came to see me to go over plans for rail with the HSE [Health and Safety Executive report] due tomorrow. JP was very onside at the moment, said it sometimes dawned on him just how dreadful TB's job was. He wanted to do his bit to get Peter and Gordon working together and to bind in the Cabinet. I was pressing for the idea of TB doing regular Commons debates. I felt our problem at the moment was that we weren't really acting as agents of change according to a big message but drifting. Even education was feeling flaky again.

GB called me over and we discussed where we needed to be by March, stability vs boom and bust, investment vs cuts, jobs vs unemployment, productivity vs stop-go. TB called halfway through. He had done a clip to try to calm down the euro, but looked like a ghost when I saw it on TV. He was also very worried about fuel, as was GB. GB and I also had a long discussion on Scotland. He said McLeish was not perfect but with Wendy Alexander as Number 2 he would be fine. He was worried about McConnell and said Reid would wind him up. I warned him Peter Cox [*Daily Record* editor] was going to support McConnell. GB said I must try and persuade him not to. With a pretty heavy heart, I did just that. Peter said they thought they had been misled by McLeish about Jack's intentions. Also, when he asked him what his plans for Scotland were, he said he was sure we could get the Ryder Cup. Peter said he would back him but reluctantly. GB said Jack would flirt with neo-nationalism. Instinctively, I had always related much more to Jack, but TB was keen we work with GB.

Friday, October 20

EMU was pretty big, e.g. the *Sun* splash and loads of confusion. [Keith] Vaz did OK in interviews and people quickly realised it was a bit of a non-story. TB did his little speech to the ASEM [Asia–Europe meeting] and then they started the thirteen-hour flight back. Despite the fuck-up, I was glad I had given it a miss. I spent most of the day working on his environment speech. Pat McFadden came to see me, the latest to say he thought I should go full-time to Millbank, where he said things weren't good. The *Sunday Telegraph* were on to some story about Jonathan and Geoffrey Robinson, presumably given to them by Whelan or GR. TB landed around 6, and we went over the same old ground.

Saturday, October 21

A quiet day work-wise, mainly briefing on the environment. Burnley were at QPR. Gavin [Millar, Fiona's brother] and Mark [Bennett] came with us. It was Grace's first game, but she didn't exactly follow it closely. We won 1-0. Later JP called pre-*Frost*. We agreed he would suggest Geoffrey pay the money from the *Mail* to the campaign and we would put 'sponsored by the *Daily Mail*' on JP's [election] battlebus. We were also getting geared up for Ashdown's diaries which were going to be very detailed on TB meetings. JP said he would be dismissive, but I emphasised it was very important not to create a division story between him and TB.

Sunday, October 22

TB called while I was at the running track. He said we had to get out better overall explanation of what we were trying to do. GB had promised a strategy paper again, but again, it hadn't materialised. The *Observer* led on BSE [bovine spongiform encephalopathy, 'mad cow disease'] compensation and I was worried because it would raise expectations so high. TB was unconvinced we should go for compensation on the scale being considered but it had gone beyond that at the meeting chaired by Margaret B on Friday. TB was sounding pretty down.

Liz [Naish, AC's sister] called and asked me whether the pressure of all this hatred of me in the press was getting to me. Bizarrely, maybe because I was getting too used to it, I had felt things hadn't been that bad of late. PG spoke to TB and said he was back on the idea I should go to Millbank but Philip felt he was worried about my outlook at the moment. My fear was that it was him who didn't get where people were with us. He felt that provided we gave a rational explanation for everything, it would all be fine. But we weren't just dealing with rational and reasonable emotions. That went for our own operation, it went for the media and to a lesser extent an irrational and unreasonable world outside. Even Philip was feeling down at the GB/Peter M situation. Douglas and Peter

H were both getting dispirited. Philip felt that TB gave too much and didn't take enough from GB.

TB called, said we had to rebuild patiently, that it may be after Christmas before the mood starts to turn and we just had to accept we were going to be treated like any other government. 'Why should we be different?' he asked. Because, I said, the Tories were useless, we were better than them, and the vast bulk of our problems were self-inflicted. He said 'That's politics. There's not much you can do about it. If it wasn't me and GB, or him and Peter, it would be something else. What matters is that we know what we want to do and we get it done despite the difficulties.' Also, he said GB acted as a unifying force and that the Cabinet's loyalty to TB strengthened at the thought of GB as the alternative. So we just have to explain and converse. I said we lacked good explainers and conversers. He was both buoyant and down. Down about some of the realities, and the basic unfairness of the way we were depicted, but buoyant because he felt we were doing the right things and making progress and also because he had resigned himself to the idea that if we lost, we lost, and it wasn't the end of the world. He had clearly been chatting to his maker again. I said if Britain was ready to elect the Tories again, then I was out of here. Deep down, I think we were both confident the mood would turn.

Monday, October 23

Another week of drudge and struggle ahead. I drove in with Philip. Neither of us were on very good form. GB seemed a bit lost too. Philip felt we should get straight on to the [Conservative £16 billion] cuts message. GB thought we had to get positive stuff up first because the public would be more receptive to it. After my morning meeting, I saw TB and Peter M who was looking exhausted. The meeting became a dialogue between TB and me, him just saying we had to rebuild slowly, that it would be wrong to do anything suggesting a major change of course, we were going through a bad patch and just had to work through it with constant explanation as the pace of delivery quickened. He asked if we had a proper system linking us, GB and Millbank. I said no, only in theory. He was basically right, but we had to watch we didn't become becalmed and start to lose fight. Bad patches could end, but they could also last an awful long time.

There was a lot of interest in the election of the new Speaker. GB and JP both voted for Michael Martin [Labour MP], who was also getting all the Catholic [MP] votes. TB said history suggested governments sometimes do better with Speakers from the Opposition, but Michael looked like he was going to win in it and [Sir] George Young [Conservative MP] had little chance. The eleven o'clock was fairly quiet, mainly Ashdown [diaries] about which I was dismissive. I had a meeting with Henry McLeish and Wendy Alexander. Henry talked a good game but I think was going to need a lot of help. I talked through my usual spiel on strategic communications. They were going to go for Peter MacMahon [former political editor, *Sunday Mirror*], which was probably OK. They also wanted Moira Wallace [former private secretary to Blair]. I dropped into the meeting at the Foreign Office of all our EU ambassadors. The guy from Belgium [David Colvin] was very anti euro. Helsinki [Gavin Hewitt] suggested I do a tour of all the capitals. I thought Michael Jay [France] was very clever, as was Nigel Sheinwald [EU]. Fiona picked me up to go out for Rory's birthday dinner. Philip called from St Albans, said the groups were disastrous, just replayed the *Daily Mail* at us without an alternative agenda. Wes Clark called for a chat about his future. He said Gore wasn't looking good. The Speaker's election was also a bit of a mess.[1] There was a very depressing *Newsnight* piece on how people in an all-white area of Norfolk just absorbed the media line on asylum, as though the place was being overwhelmed.

Tuesday, October 24

TB had done a note on the plane back from Korea which I was trying to turn into a plan of action. David M used exactly the same word as I had about TB, felt he had become becalmed, lost some of the old fight. I wanted us out there with direction and message but he wasn't really up for it at the moment. The GB meeting was pretty hopeless, thrashing around on various subjects. Douglas could look extraordinarily peevish when he wanted. He and Lance [Price] weren't getting on [at Millbank]. The environment speech went OK but the overwhelming noise was the great whinge from the green whingers.[2] We had a fuel meeting – TB, GB, Gus [Macdonald], Steve Byers,

[1] After a tortuous debate in which the various merits of a dozen candidates had to be debated one by one in the House of Commons, Michael Martin beat nearest rival Sir George Young by 317 votes to 241. MPs protested that they would rather have had a straight ballot.

[2] Blair's speech to a joint conference of the CBI and Green Alliance had called for 'a new coalition for the environment, a coalition that works with the grain of consumers, business and science, not against them'. The speech was being dismissed by green activists as 'chicanery' and 'ecobabble'.

Jack S, and we seemed to be in better shape. But it still wasn't clear what was going to happen. TB didn't really chair it so GB took over, said we had to address the question of extremists, make clear that their expectations were not going to be met, get the PBR in the right place, work on editors to be more responsible than before. The guy from ACPO said we shouldn't overdo the intimidation claims. The tactical question was whether we cranked it all up or not. Blunkett and Woodhead did another round of letters and he was probably now going to go on Friday. JP was now fully on the case re GB and Peter M and wanted me to do a note analysing our campaign strengths and weaknesses in advance of a meeting next Monday.

Wednesday, October 25

I finished a long note to TB which was measured, but fairly tough, eleven pages in all. I broke down his problems into three areas – leadership, disconnection and the press. In each, I tried to set out an honest analysis and then put forward ideas for improving things. At the heart had to be serious speeches setting out the choices as we began to lay the dividing lines, an interview programme that really allowed people to see him examined at length, and above all grip and authority at the centre. I had another good meeting with the agency and I felt we were getting the balance right between positive and negative. TB did fine at PMQs. Earlier, despite the Foreign Office opposition, Keith Vaz went up against Trevor Kavanagh on the radio and did well. I left after the four o'clock to go to Notts Forest with the boys. I had a stack of calls on the way, mainly from JP and DB. We got there a bit late, were 1-0 down when we arrived, then 3-0, finally 5-0. For the first time, I had a bit of aggro from some of the Burnley fans who were involved in the petrol protests, and they warned it was going to get even nastier. On the way back, I was dealing with the response to the IRA statement [on arms inspections, accusing the British government of 'bad faith']. I also dictated a speaking note for TB at Cabinet tomorrow.

Thursday, October 26

In early for a meeting with JP. Rail was becoming a real problem because they were overreacting now and shutting down lines all over the place. JP really wanted to have a go at [Gerald] Corbett. I showed him the note he asked for on our campaign and communications problems but said I didn't want to send it out of the building. It brutally went through all the problems, the relationship fault lines, the structural fault lines, the personnel and personality problems, the

October '00: Aggro from some Burnley fans

loosening of discipline, the lack of cohesion and strategy, the departments refusing to buy into the Grid process. It was a deliberately bleak picture but he was clear he wanted to be properly armed when he saw GB and Peter M. Gus came to see me again, and was worried the Home Office wasn't gripping preparations on fuel. I had been slightly taken aback by the hint of menace at the match last night and the very brittle mood.

We had the Cabinet photograph done. Cabinet itself was mainly rail and BSE. TB was pretty distracted, yawning, stretching his arms, looking around, once or twice ignoring questions. His tie was undone because his shirt was too tight. He did an OK political pitch on the choices though. JP said there had to be unity, Clare said we should stop the books and the briefings. TB said it was impossible to stop all the little people around the place, she said it's not the little beasts that do it, but the big beasts, and we all know it. Mo murmured in agreement. It wasn't a very happy discussion and we were nowhere near cohesive enough for an election campaign. JP went through the rail crash in some detail, and made sure they had the figures on underinvestment down the years. There was a general feeling that there had been an overreaction. Nick Brown set out where we were on BSE. Clare threw in her view that MAFF was dreadful. Milburn made the point that it was unacceptable if all the compensation went to farmers not victims. TB led a fairly long discussion on political strategy, delayed from last week. He echoed what GB had been saying about countering the strategy of cynicism. He felt on delivery that people accepted progress in schools but that health was not motoring like it should. He said they needed to be far more engaged, all of them, in the bigger political arguments. He said we had to avoid what had happened in America where the Republicans had successfully neutralised some of the key issues, and the Democrats had let them, to the extent that Clinton had told him it was either choice on big issues or [of the two candidates] 'who would you prefer to go for a drink with?'. He felt confident we could get them on cuts and make them nervous about going for their traditional tax-cutting agenda.

I went over to the Home Office for a meeting with Jack, people from the Treasury, DETR and DTI on the fuel protest. We agreed Jack would do a statement on Thursday and that we would work up third-party pleas against going back to the blockades. The preparations weren't quite as bad as Gus had indicated. There was some intelligence of animal rights extremists and other groups infiltrating the protests. I felt we had to publish reports on just how bad things had been during the earlier protests and also do a better job of mobilising business. I had a meeting with Douglas and Philip to try to get to the bottom of what was happening inside Millbank. It was difficult for me because I couldn't really go in there without the risk of a hoo-ha. But I feared creativity was being stifled and that the divisions at the top were a real problem for them. Douglas clearly felt disempowered, lacking clout and that he was the lightning rod for the grievances of others.

I said we had to start taking more risks, and stop allowing initiative to be stifled by the feeling that everybody has to agree everything before anything is done. Douglas needed to be more open and flexible. We had an internal meeting on fuel. Jeremy H was excellent. A lot of this was about the tone we struck and the kind of stories that appeared between now and the deadline, which needed to be about the nature of some of the protesters and the damage they were prepared to do. We had to use the regional media better too. The Home Office officials were a bit resistant to being directed from the centre, but I felt we had to grip this one tightly. TB had been in Northern Ireland and we had got another statement from the IRA. When he came back, he was really wound up by the railways. The kids came in and went up on the wheel with TB's boys and Putin's daughters. The boys were convinced they would be huge Russian monstrosities and were very pleasantly surprised.

Friday, October 27

I had been working late last night, woke up tired again, not keen at all on going to Spain. BSE coverage was huge, but there was next to no sense of how it was the last government that was responsible. [James] Bulger was the other big story.[1] TB returned my note and had written 'Yes' alongside all of the recommendations, including the speech series and the interview programme. The only thing he didn't tick was the idea that we look for ways of symbolising a changed style. I got in and straight into his meeting with Corbett who struck me as a first-class bullshitter, and one who was trying to put a wedge between TB and JP, and between JP and Gus. JP couldn't much stomach him, and hadn't wanted TB to see him. TB claimed later to him that Corbett had just turned up, which was pretty fanciful. I had to speak to JP to calm him down and make sure he wasn't going to go off the deep end. JP felt TB was allowing Corbett to play games with us all.

[1] Two ten-year-old boys had murdered two-year-old Bulger in 1993. Now, reviewing the minimum ten years to which the killers had been sentenced, Lord Chief Justice Lord Woolf reduced the term to eight years, adding that the young offenders' institutions were a 'corrosive atmosphere' for them.

October '00: BSE crisis blamed on government

I was also struck, as was Jeremy, by how flippant he seemed. He didn't seem to take it all as seriously as we had expected. But he pretty much rolled over TB, who just wanted his assurances the job was being done. When Godric did the 11, they gave him a hard time about why we were putting out such a soft message.

Gus stayed back for a discussion on the PBR. We had a few billion to spend and the lion's share was going to go on £5/£8 pension increases. On fuel, there was a choice: just do hauliers, with a cut in diesel – they use a litre a mile – or £50 cut in car tax. Gus was in favour of the straight cut. The problem was the reason the public supported the protests was as an expression of their anger about the prices they paid. So we might buy off the hauliers, and I wasn't even convinced 5p would do that, but we lose the public again. TB said that was why it was so important to get out a sense of difficult economic choices. We decided to use the press conference in Madrid to begin that, say you could have tax cuts but then you have to understand what happens when you get interest rate rises. On the plane [to Spain], I sensed TB was moving to a general cut for the hauliers, feeling the public would see the £50 road tax cut as a gimmick. We discussed the last protest and TB said it had been totally ridiculous that GB had refused to do interviews because it 'wasn't a tax issue'.

I was also trying to resolve the Wakeham/Leo situation. TB had told me Cherie agreed with him we should be more relaxed but when I spoke to her, that was clearly not so. But TB didn't want to discuss it. As for the Spanish, we had been hoping to push the economic reform statement, but the Spanish press was full of HMS *Tireless*, a nuclear sub being repaired in Gibraltar which, according to the Spanish ambassador in London, was as neuralgic an issue as Pinochet. They had asked to put Spanish technicians on board to check safety but we had refused. [José María] Aznar was being very good to us but it was a difficult issue and TB was keen to help if we could. We arrived, did a school visit with a video link to [a school in] Lambeth, then a business lunch while I went to brief the Brits at the embassy. The bilateral at the Moncloa, Aznar's new, purpose-built and very swanky offices, was largely about the *Tireless* and how we deal with it. TB emphasised there was no risk whatever. It's a nuclear reactor, not nuclear weapons we are talking about. We worked out a form of words, but at least eighty per cent of the questions were about it. And they weren't really biting on anything else. We tried football, pre-PBR warning on interest rates going up and I got a question planted on fuel. Aznar seemed pretty straight, went out of his way to help us.

He and TB left by helicopter for Toledo. I flew back with the Number 10 team and got a lift home with Terry [Rayner, Government Car Service]. It was the first time in ages he had driven me without TB there and we agreed TB was a bit disconnected.

Saturday, October 28

The only story from Spain was the submarine, with the Tories saying TB was spineless like a jelly, Hague's line from PMQs which was clearly going to be their next line of attack. I didn't see [impressionist] Rory Bremner on *Parkinson* [chat show], but PG thought it was dreadful because it got TB as a startled rabbit, the look of yesterday when he was asked a planted question about fuel, and he looked like he had been told something dreadful. He called about the note he was doing on choices and options. I got some of the Sundays to do stories on how both the TUC and the CBI were urging us not to go on a massive spending spree. The only other story to deal with was the *Sunday Mirror* saying CB was trying to gag [documentary maker] Linda McDougall's book [*Cherie: The Perfect Life of Mrs Blair*]. It was total crap but the *Sunday Mirror* still ran it. Rail mayhem was dominating the news. Rail plus weather plus fuel shortage plus NHS winter crisis could build up to be very difficult for us. But there was no sign of the Tories coming back, which meant the ground was shifting, possibly for good.

Sunday, October 29

Darling was on *GMTV* and made clear there was going to be more for pensioners and less on fuel. The tornado in Bognor Regis[1] was leading the news and I suggested to TB he went but he said it would be seen as a gimmick. I thought people would read empathy and connection into it but he wasn't up for it at all. We got [environment minister Michael] Meacher to do it instead. I went running and bumped into Jeremy Corbyn [left-wing Labour MP] who was out for a run. He was always very pleasant, and I could never quite work out why his politics were so off the wall.

JP called, still pissed off with TB over the Corbett meeting. He said he understood that sometimes leaders had to dissemble, but this was so unnecessary. The truth would not have been hard to deal with. He said if he treats me like that again, he can fuck the job. I'm loyal but not a lickspittle, and I have to know what's going on. TB was unpicking

---

[1] Several people were hurt, houses, caravans and cars were damaged and trees uprooted when a tornado struck the West Sussex seaside resort.

the fuel strategy I had agreed with Jack S and was worried about him doing a Commons statement. I played tennis with Calum, then got Jack up for the *Today* programme. In his [ministerial] box Jack found a British Chamber of Commerce report on the fuel protests [estimating the cost to the UK economy of the protests at £1 billion]. We briefed on it, emphasising nobody really wanted to go back to this kind of thing.

Monday, October 30

Violent gales again. Jack S did a good job on the radio, very measured, got over the message about the cost to the economy and the link between big tax cuts and an interest rates rise. [Michael] Portillo was in *The Times* saying they could have £8 billion of tax cuts. GB was leading a fight to head it off, and we were saying Portillo had confirmed the cuts plan that would lead to boom and bust. We had a meeting – TB, AC, HC, AH, SM, PG – on TB's position. PG went through some verbatims from the groups and some quantitative figures on disconnection. TB was still of the view it was simply a response to a hostile press strategy and we shouldn't overreact. Philip and I tried to persuade him that he was a bit disconnected, that he didn't speak the real-people language as well as he used to, that he wasn't motivated by real people in the way say Clinton was, that he sometimes seemed more interested in talking to right-wing journalists than the people we were trying to help. I was deliberately a bit over the top because I felt we had not been getting through. But it seemed to just push him deeper into his own position. He said the only time we have made mistakes is when we hadn't followed through his instincts. Afterwards he apologised for being so sharp which was ridiculous as I had basically attacked virtually everything he said.

He said he didn't mind doing some of these things we suggested for reconnection, so long as we understood they were stunts and we would get nothing out of it. I said he would always get things out of meeting people outside the bubble. To be fair, he agreed for us to fill the diary with a stack of the things I had put in the note. After the 11, I had another fuel preparations meeting and was angry that the one thing I had asked Mike Granatt [head of GICS] to do, namely find me a co-ordinator, hadn't happened. We needed to work up more third-party endorsements and warnings of economic damage. Yet again I was having to lift up this hopeless bloody machine and shake it into doing something useful.

TB saw Murdoch and Irwin Stelzer [Murdoch adviser]. He had asked them outright whether they were going to back us. Murdoch said the Tories were unelectable and that was that. TB seemed to take it at face value. I still felt we were using too much of his own time on journalists, time we could be devoting to him doing things that would make a difference and get a different sort of coverage. He did at least agree to do some phone calls to people in the emergency services dealing with the floods.[1] But this created its own problems with JP thinking it was much more than it was, and raging at me that first he took over transport – the Corbett meeting – and now he was taking over the environment. 'If he doesn't think I'm up to it, I'll go.' I said he was being ridiculous. 'Let me make that judgement, not you. You're trying to present him like Superman.' I said I had been trying to get him to do things that will connect and help us to deal with this out-of-touch tag, and it's crazy that it has this effect on him. We had a five-minute shouting match with the door open in front of lots of people in the office. As ever, we more or less calmed down by the end and I think he got the point. I had a meeting on honours, where I was pushing for more gongs for Olympians, then saw [Richard] Wilson re his [Public Administration] select committee appearance on special advisers.[2] I felt I was beginning to motor again and was more on top of things.

Tuesday, October 31

JP decided to do a Commons statement on floods and gales. When he spoke to me, he didn't even mention yesterday's row. I liked that about him, that you could have an explosion like that and just get on with things the next day. I think he knew he had gone over the top. Jack's [House of Commons fuel] statement and my briefing were helping to turn the media. We had another leader in the *Mirror* attacking the fuel protesters and both the TUC and the CBI on the radio. David Handley [Monmouthshire farmer, chairman of the People's Fuel Lobby] was putting himself around a lot and though he was quite a good polemicist, I don't think he was doing their cause much good. GB wanted us to go for them on extremism, intimidation, and a threat to food and medication. He was becoming almost as obsessed as I was about the way the *Mail* influenced the agenda of the BBC, but whenever I put the idea of taking them on, he backed off.

TB had a whole series of foreign visitors, plus an interview with

[1] Intense autumn rainfall had led to severe flooding in England and Wales.
[2] The committee's report would be published in February 2001, entitled *Special Advisers: Boon or Bane?*

October '00: Floods, gales and Prescott rage

Never had so much effort been put into a speech that went so badly wrong. Blair's attempt to woo the Women's Institute led to one of the most famous slow-handclaps in living memory, leading Blair to resort to what a watching John Prescott called his 'Bambi look'.

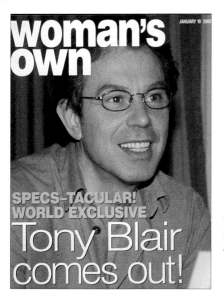

When you're PM, even the news that you need glasses can make for a good front page somewhere.

Fuel protests, floods and foot-and-mouth disease: it is hard to imagine a worse lead-up to a general election campaign.

Fuel and foot-and-mouth were probably the biggest domestic crises of Blair's entire premiership, the latter still raging when Blair's favoured election date neared. Campbell is photographed on the day the PM announced the election would be postponed.

American presidents are big players in the politics of every country in the world. Clinton (top left; right), here with Campbell on his farewell visit to the UK as outgoing president, was a political soulmate of Blair's. But the PM stayed well out of the election to choose Clinton's successor: either George Bush (above, right) or Al Gore, here at one of their televised debates.

Once Bush had won, Blair was determined to get close to him, and they got on well from their first meeting. Here they are at Camp David where Bush bemused the media, and Blair, by saying (accurately) that they used the same toothpaste.

Another summit, another signing: Nice in December 2000. Here Blair and his European counterparts applaud, as the European Charter of Fundamental Rights is signed.

Blair at his desk in Downing Street, working on a draft Campbell has prepared for him.

Campbell's profile rose considerably during this period, even prompting Rory Bremner (as Tony Blair, left) to hire his own Campbell impersonator (Andrew Dunn, right). The Blair-Campbell double act became a regular feature of Bremner's satirical show.

There were certainly ups and downs in the relationship between Campbell and Peter Mandelson, as between Blair and Brown. Here cartoonist Martin Rowson shows Brown suggesting to Blair that Campbell and Mandelson created him, control him, and can also kill him.

Mandelson's second resignation from the Cabinet: both Blair and Campbell have since said if it had been anyone else, they might have toughed out the furore over a passport application. Mandelson has tended to blame Campbell rather than Blair, but on the Saturday after his resignation he nonetheless attended a family party at Campbell's home. Rory took this photo of his father and Mandelson looking at newspaper headlines declaring them to be at war.

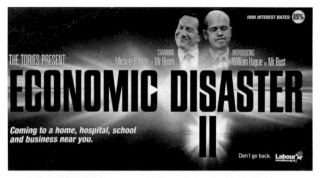

Campbell took an active part in the campaign preparation and loved working with the advertising agency TBWA. The movie-style *Economic Disaster II* poster and that of William Hague with Margaret Thatcher's hair used wit to make heavy political points which struck home during the campaign.

Having successfully launched the manifesto with a 'schools and hospitals' slogan, Blair visited a hospital only to be confronted by Sharron Storer (left), who leapt to the top of the news with an impassioned attack.

The 'Prescott punch' also enlivened what was otherwise a rather dull election campaign.

Another happy family snap on another sunny election morning, at the end of which Labour would win another landslide.

Campbell's son Rory, being hugged by Neil Kinnock, and Philip Gould's daughter Georgia waited for Campbell to get back to Millbank from Sedgefield in the early hours. After a couple of hours' sleep, Campbell was back in Number 10, but uneasy about the future.

All smiles from Gordon Brown as Tony Blair arrives at the victory party, but there had been tensions throughout the campaign, and soon Brown would be asking for Blair's departure date.

September 11th, a date that would immediately write itself into the history books, changing the course of both Bush's presidency and Blair's premiership, and making Osama bin Laden the world's most wanted man.

Blair returned from Brighton by train to London to deal with the crisis. As he and Campbell are driven from the south coast conference centre, the PM is already thinking through the big decisions that would inevitably flow from the terrorist attack.

the *Mirror*. It was meant to be [new political editor] James Hardy's big moment but Piers [Morgan] did most of the talking, and was obsessed with the singing fish that JP had given TB [Big Mouth Billy Bass, an animatronic in Blair's office that sang 'Don't worry, be happy']. It was a good interview generally but the impact would be limited. I had lunch with [Trevor] Kavanagh at the RAC [Pall Mall club]. There was the usual tension between us, but he made clear they were going to support us and that the pro-Hague line was going to be softened. The big disagreement would still be Europe. TB took another fuel preparations meeting and seemed more confident. But he told GB we could only mount the extremism attack if we had the economic arguments out there too. There was no guarantee we were going to be able to sort this out on our terms. We were trying to take it to a situation where bit by bit, public opinion was clear in its opposition to protests as before. GB wanted to be far more aggressive but TB felt we had to be more subtle. The floods were getting worse. I was then staggered to discover Morgan was intending to splash on Billy the Fish and the line 'Don't worry, be happy' which would inflame people re the floods. JP had his dinner with Peter and GB, but by the sound of his call afterwards, it didn't go well.

Wednesday, November 1

The *Today* programme led on their own survey of [NHS] Trusts' winter preparations which they said showed real worries. It was totally bent journalism. Both the Department of Health and Number 10 complained but they continued to peddle it inaccurately and designed to mislead. Bill Bush drafted an excellent letter of complaint for Tony Hall [BBC director of news]. GB was still keen that we go for the fuel protesters as extremists but I felt we were better relying on third parties. And that we don't waste too many bullets too soon. We also agreed to do a paper on what a 26p petrol cut – as they were demanding – would do to the economy. I was getting more and more frustrated at the time I was having to spend kicking the basic infrastructure on communications into gear.

We got Bill Connor [general secretary] of Usdaw [Union of Shop, Distributive and Allied Workers] to do an open letter to [David] Handley who was becoming more and more rattled. We got Tesco up on it via David Hill [PR consultant, former Labour communications director]. Shaun Woodward found a fuel protest website that was racist, homophobic and very unpleasant. We got up 26p as being irresponsible and we successfully linked it to pensions and meals on wheels. Things were getting better for us. TB easily won PMQs. I was working up a report on the North-East, one of the ideas for the note I did. TB was worried about going there by RAF plane but it was fine as we were going via various flooded areas. I was by now having regular meetings with Douglas, Philip, Peter H and the Milibands and I felt we were starting to make progress on strategy and planning. The *TES* [*Times Educational Supplement*] called about Woodhead, so that was clearly about to break. We had a reception for the ethnic minority media and quite a few ministers came.

Thursday, November 2

The floods were massive and fuel was also building up. The *Mirror* did me proud with a front-page whack at David Handley. But the *Mail* did 'Here we go again' on a picture of an empty pump, clearly trying to get panic buying going again. I so wish we could go for the *Mail* big time. They are absolute scum. I saw GB at 8. We were both worried that Jack's statement lacked clarity, that he needed to go on a single line and hammer it. Handley was poor on the *Today* programme. The more he was on, the better, because he appeared so extreme. I had a whole stack of meetings but was in and out working with Jack S on his statement. We were also putting together TB's floods visits.

At Cabinet, TB went through the arguments on fuel, focused on the irresponsible economics of a huge tax cut, and how we could use this to mount a bigger argument. Everyone is talking about a surplus but it only exists because of the way we have managed the economy. He warned that our opponents would try to say we were picking a fight, which is why we were releasing an account of all the meetings we had had to try to listen to their concerns. It must be clear we are trying to avoid confrontation but we cannot yield up the right to govern. If we do, time has run out for democracy. John Reid said that first time round we had bad intelligence, bad organisation and we lost the political argument. There was no need for any of those to happen this time. There was a general feeling that Handley and some of the others were playing into our hands by being so over the top.

JP briefed on floods and GB brought them up to date on the PBR. At the 11.30, I think I just about got the balance right between a tough message on preparations, and listening. Jack's statement went OK and Ann Widdecombe went over the top. TB and I set off for Battersea [helipad] where we got an RAF Puma that flew over the floods at Bewdley [Worcestershire]. He got an OK reception apart from a few local hospital protesters and a handful of lippy kids. We left for

Shrewsbury to tour the emergency centre. Really nice people doing a fantastic job. TB's dad [Leo Blair] and Olwen [TB's stepmother] came down to see him and they had a little chat together before we set off for York. It was dark and pouring buckets when we arrived, just as Woodhead finally resigned. I spoke to DB to activate the briefing plan we had agreed.

Some of the flood stories were pretty terrifying but again the people at the flood centre were doing a great job. I was impressed by Elliot Morley [fisheries minister] who could look a bit hamsterish, but was a patently nice man and his manner with people was terrific. We drove up to Sedgefield, working on the speech and talking through the PBR. Jeremy was worried we were doing too much on fuel now but I didn't agree. We had dinner at the Dun Cow [Inn] with John Burton [Blair's constituency agent] who clearly felt the protesters still had a lot of support. The flooding was worse up there than we thought and we had to do a big detour to get to Myrobella [the Blair's constituency home]. Bill Bush had done a good job on the North-East report. I worked late on the speech for tomorrow. Anji called to say the visits had looked terrific on the news.

Friday, November 3

I was out before 7 for a run. Jeremy H had sent up overnight the OECD [the international Organisation for Economic Co-operation and Development] report on tax which showed that we [the UK] were relatively lightly taxed, the eleventh highest in the EU. TB wanted it up big, even the centrepiece of the speech and the press conference. He spoke to GB who was totally against, reminding us that last year we rubbished it. Also soon the tax burden would be going up again so it wasn't a sensible thing to do. TB spoke to him for about half an hour, exasperated, and later said that the part of him that wants to appeal to the *Guardian* doesn't want to say we have relatively low taxes. He said 'Shall I follow my instincts?' I said yes, so we started to brief up the figures though of course the broadcasters were more interested in fuel and panic buying, being generated by the usual *Mail* and BBC route. The speech was actually pretty good, and TB was really keen on this tax argument, felt we could win it.

The report we had done on the North-East with the Government Office up here was a decent piece of work and exactly the kind of model I wanted to use for other visits to get up what was happening in the regions. Then we were off to Newcastle airport to open the new terminal. Then to the University of Northumbria. His speech went well[1] and it was a good idea to have Milburn and Byers there for the press conference. It was a fabulous day weather-wise and it was unbelievable to think the floods were so bad elsewhere. The Times ran a story, I assume out of one of our meetings, that I was masterminding a plan to do in David Handley. He was doing himself a lot of damage. I felt the press were currently more supportive of us on fuel than the public, many of whom still had sympathy for the basic point of the protesters.

Saturday, November 4

The general feeling was that TB's speech, and the sense of more big speeches to come, had gone well. Ditto the press conference. I started planning a repeat exercise next week in Brighton. TB called while I was out running and we agreed he should do a broadcast interview to keep pushing forward. I tried to get [Michael] Parkinson for his radio show but ended up with Eddie Mair [BBC] who came into Number 10 at 2. I went in with Grace. JP was also in with a new package of help on floods including £51 million extra for flood defences. TB did Mair but it was crap because he thought he could just sail through it. He was still smarting a bit from our 'out of touch' conversation. JP asked me to rewrite the script for his press conference in Number 12 before he went to York. There was a bit of a sense with rail, floods and fuel that the country was kind of grinding to a halt. Gus Macdonald called to plan his meeting on Monday with Brynle Williams [Welsh farmer and fuel protest leader], who was more sensible than Handley and Gus wanted to bind him in a bit. But we had to be clear we couldn't appease these people. Burnley drew [1-1] at West Brom.

Sunday, November 5

TB saw GB for an hour and a half to go over the PBR and was clearly still a bit worried that he didn't have the full picture and he was worried that GB was over-complicating some of the tax credit schemes. JP did *Frost* from York. TB kept saying to me 'They can't blame us for the floods as well, can they?' because quite a few of them were. GB called to say they were briefing the *Mirror* and *The Times* on the idea we could freeze fuel prices for two years. He said he wanted to use that to get up the interest rate argument. Ed Balls was doing the

[1] Blair told an audience of politics students 'People forget that in coming to office we introduced, literally, a revolution in economic management. Our aim was to defeat the age-old British millstone of boom and bust, high growth followed by recession.'

briefing but I felt it was a mistake – first, it was wrong to leak tax measures, second, it was misleading in part of [Phil] Webster and [James] Hardy, third, it pissed off all the others, and fourth, having got into the right place with the focus on their 26p [fuel levy reduction] demand and the behaviour of the protesters, it was now back in the wrong place. I guessed from the tone of his voice that he also felt it was probably the wrong thing to have done and was looking to bind me in post facto.

Monday, November 6

I said to GB at the morning meeting that I didn't get the strategy. There was a danger that leaks would be the issue. I understood the need for interest rates as part of the message but I wasn't clear how this helped get us there. It was all too clever by half. TB agreed with me that we had got to the wrong place having been in the right place. I also said to GB I didn't agree with putting out other stuff from the PBR in advance but he insisted it was all old. The fact they got so much out of it was evidence of a very effective spin operation. At my morning meeting, I spotted a quote from a group of hauliers threatening the M25 and airports so we got BAA [British airports operator] to get up strong lines on it. I also spoke to Tony Burden at ACPO [chief constable of South Wales police Sir Anthony Burden, ACPO president] who said they had been making it clear there would be very vigorous policing of the so-called 'Jarrow crusade'. There was a growing feeling of a political agenda here and he said the forces were up for pretty tough policing.

TB told me that he thought some of us – he basically meant me and Jonathan – sometimes surprised ministers by our lack of deference to him. I said OK, the key to dealing with arrogance and out-of-touchness is to have staff bowing down and scraping before him the whole time. I also pointed out he had given a dreadful example at Cabinet recently, when he so clearly wasn't listening and concentrating. He said the problem was he was too readable. If he was tired, it showed. If he lacked confidence, it showed. He currently felt in control and that showed too. He thought GB's overnight operation on tax was stupid but not of lasting damage. The Palace phoned to tell us the Queen Mum had broken her collarbone. We were clearly getting to Handley, who did an interview with the *Telegraph* saying I was to blame for the press turning against him.

TB was back worrying about fox hunting. He thought we could go for local referenda and he also wanted a big number on the rural White Paper. There were a whole load of meetings on Far East prisoners of war which we were doing tomorrow, finally giving them compensation after years of being told it couldn't be done. GB's speech went OK, Gus Macdonald did an OK doorstep with Brynle Williams, the BAA threatened an injunction. I was just falling asleep when Anne Shevas texted me to say the *Sun* was splashing on the £100 VED [vehicle excise duty] rebate for truckers. There was virtually nothing left in the locker now, added to which we had a problem with spin and the Speaker [over the briefing of tax measures before announcement in the House of Commons]. God knows what GB thought he was playing at.

Tuesday, November 7

Philip was more and more worried about the US elections. The TV was saying neck and neck but though Gore had closed strongly, it was not looking brilliant. They had been daft not to use Clinton properly. We had been right to stay out of it but now it was going to be important to be on the right side of the result, and there would be a real desire to present a Bush win as a disaster for us. I tried to engage GB at the morning meeting but he was only really interested in the PBR. I said I didn't understand the strategy. I felt we were putting the focus of pressure away from the protesters and on to the government. He said he felt we had pummelled them so hard there was a danger of sympathy, but also we had to get expectations down from 26p. Also, contrary to what he intended yesterday, we did not really get up an interest rates message as planned. We had a mix of headlines, some saying we were defiant, others caving in, and when I pointed that out he went all sarcastic, saying 'Oh it's all terrible and a total disaster,' and I said 'I am simply trying to test the strategy because I don't understand it, and if we have a disagreement we should resolve it.'

He said he was trying to get to a situation where 1. there is no traction for protest, 2. we can get up Tory cuts and boom and bust, 3. we make the argument for long-term stability, and 4. we are dealing with problems like pensions and fuel. He was defensive at first but eventually allowed it to open up into a proper strategic discussion. What was clear was that instinctively he, Douglas A and one or two others would prefer not to be having to go for tax cuts and instead put everything we had into anti-poverty initiatives. I was worried we were conceding too much on lack of delivery. We ended up agreeing a way forward that understood the need to take out the sting on fuel whilst pressing ahead with the other priorities. He asked me to stay back at the end and we went over it all again. I said I was not prepared just to accept a strategy that I would be expected to explain and to some extent implement and he should not see fair questions as unfair criticisms. He said he knew it wasn't perfect but he was worried where expectations on fuel were, following the protesters' 26p campaign.

TB said later he didn't care how irritating and maddening GB was with us, provided he did the right things. Certainly extra help for fuel and for pensioners was the right thing to do. TB was constantly asking for the latest draft statement for the PBR, which we eventually got at 6pm. It was unacceptable the way they kept things from TB like this. I suspected also it was an early draft. It was lacking clarity. GB was angry as well that TB had pushed him into accepting Far East PoWs compensation. I could tell TB was pissed off though he was also saying GB was brilliant and we just had to put up with some of the nonsense and the madness. TB had an OK meeting re pensioners with Jack Jones [retired trade union leader turned pensions campaigner], Rodney Bickerstaffe and Sally Greengross [director general of Age Concern], which went fine. Jack was a wily old bugger, and pressing all the right buttons.

The big story of the day was the cops foiling a massive diamond theft at the Dome, which was the best publicity the Dome had had in ages.[1] We did the Far East PoWs event at the National Army Museum and it was a terrific event, and a sign of how government could do something useful and important without it always being about huge sums of money. Bruce and I had been nagging away about it for ages and I was glad Bruce came along to see it happen. The Royal British Legion had organised it well and I found the whole thing moving, and the background stories of some of these characters really inspiring. Needless to say very few of the Westminster hacks could be bothered to shift their arses out of the Commons, but it went well on TV and the atmosphere was great. Stan Greenberg called, sounding very worried about the state of things in America.

Wednesday, November 8

The US elections scene was unbelievable. I went to bed thinking Bush had won, then woke up to 'too close to call', then on the way in Gore seemed to be conceding defeat, only to retract as the day wore on amid suggestions of real jiggery-pokery going on. There was nothing

[1] Metropolitan Police officers had sealed off the Dome to prevent what they said would have been the world's biggest diamond robbery. The robbers had smashed their way into the Dome using a mechanical digger, to steal twelve diamonds on display in the Money Zone – including the priceless Millennium Star.

we could do but wait before we could begin to put in place a strategy for either outcome, but it was going to be the only show in town for a while. Meanwhile we were trying to get the PBR in the right place. They had even leaked the move on low-sulphur petrol to the *FT*. Our daily fuel meetings were going fine and we were getting some good regional coverage and overall winning the arguments I think. GB presented the PBR to Cabinet, good on the big picture, lots in it on inner cities, youth unemployment. Obviously the moves on fuel prices would be important and the general feeling was that he got the balance right, that there was enough of a shift on prices to have an impact, without it looking like we were conceding too much. We had the usual bombardment of facts and figures on tax credits, but overall he did well. Prosperity for all, moving to full employment, rising living standards, the messages were in the right place.

We went over for PMQs and then stayed for the PBR, which was fine. Ed Balls and I did the briefing afterwards. They were all very cynical and wanting to make the story the tax burden again so we had to push hard on fuel and pensions and the overall strength of the economy. Ed was good on detail but not good on message and he had a habit of just repeating what GB had said, when what they needed was a bit of nuance and the main strategic message hammered through. I had a meeting with Gus Macdonald re Handley who was now very much on the back foot and we had to keep him there. I got back to track the US situation, which was surely one of the most amazing election stories ever. Hillary Clinton did brilliantly in New York and we sent through a [congratulatory] message on the q.t.

Fiona and I had dinner with TB and CB in the flat. TB knew I had not been very happy of late, and also that Fiona was pressing for a decision on how long I went on. I said I would probably want to go after the election, and he needed to understand others would want to do the same and so he should be looking around for new people. He said there was no way I would go because I would not be able to resist the challenge of a euro campaign, and if we went for it, he would want me around. I said I was not that bothered about the euro. It didn't move me like a Labour vs Tory battle did. He said it would be tailor-made for me because we would have to win the argument with huge swathes of the media against us, and it would be the time to make them part of the argument. I said we needed a get-out date, and he said he couldn't give one at this stage. He said if he could get new people, that would be great, but he didn't know where they were. He said New Labour was largely built by him, GB, Peter M and me. We were all better than anyone else at what we did. He accepted that GB and Peter could not really work together but even with that, they were still brilliant.

Reluctantly, he said he had had to accept that part of GB's strategy was that he put himself in a slightly different position to TB. But even that was worth bearing to keep his input. I said that was all well and good but it was incredibly draining because I had to deal with so much of the fallout. It was different for him, because he was prime minister and when all was said and done would get the kudos, the place in history, and the knowledge that in the end he had made so much difference. I sometimes felt like I was just picking up the shit left by everyone else. He said he couldn't have done it if I had not been with him every step of the way. Fiona said that I ended up doing other people's jobs as well. TB said that was because of my personality and it would be the same whoever was there. Cherie said TB had never been good at bringing people on, that he settled quickly on what he wanted and then relied on the people he felt he could trust.

He said he would love to rely on more people, but he came back to his basic point – GB was special, Peter M was special, I was special, there were plenty of very good people but very few who could just take you to a different level, and I had to understand he would not let go easily. In between the heavy stuff, we had a lot of laughs and Cherie was back to her old self. Between us we gave TB a bit of a hard time, said he *was* becoming a bit out of touch, that he was no longer seen as having North-East connections, that he spent too much time at Chequers, that he didn't get the empathy stuff. But as he said himself, he was about as normal as any politician could be given the weird circumstances of his existence. 'There aren't many prime ministers who could sit and listen to their missus, their spin doctor and their spin doctor's missus all telling him how useless and out of touch he is, and still keep smiling.' He then pretended to call through for executioners to come and take us out and hang us on Horse Guards [Parade] for rank insubordination. The upshot was he was determined I should stay but accepted we might have to do things differently.

As we left, he said that in politics today you need intellectual ability, nous, judgement, a thick skin and a very strong personality. He came back to his point – though we were all flawed in some way or another, he, GB, Peter M and I were the ones that had that and he wasn't going to let go of that talent lightly. We also had another go at resolving our approach to the PCC. TB wanted to be relaxed. He said we just had to accept he couldn't go out and be a normal dad taking his kid for a walk in the pram, without the press and public being interested when it happened.

GB got a good press for the PBR. His interviews were a bit scrappy but the Tories didn't have much to say, the fuel protesters were divided and we got an OK reaction from OAPs groups. The daily fuel meetings were going well, showing again that if we had an agreed message, and systems for communicating it, we could usually win arguments. ACPO put out a very tough warning to anyone thinking of fucking up the motorways. York police said they were up to their ears in floods. Handley was clearly looking for a way out from the kind of protest they had been planning. The police told Gus that if Handley met TB or GB, they reckoned he would call it off. GB was reluctant to see him, which was right, and TB certainly shouldn't see him. We arranged for Gus to see him tomorrow.

At the TB/GB strategy meeting, TB was much more in control, and said we had to decide whether we made a direct offer to people on tax. He felt we had to be more subtle on the questions of tax, cuts, boom and bust. They mainly did rail, floods. Mo was pushing to get herself in charge of a committee looking at some of the longer-term problems we were likely to face around the election, but neither TB nor JP wanted her doing it. Re the PBR, TB said GB had done an excellent job, the question was how do we build from here. He said we need to emphasise tough decisions paying off, that we are only able to get more help for pensioners and a better deal for drivers because we took the tough decisions early on. Second, we needed more of them setting out a bigger narrative. Stability leading to lower mortgages, higher growth, more jobs; investment in public services; help for families. None of it happening without tough decisions, which the Tories would shirk. Blunkett praised the work we had done centralising operations in response to the fuel situation, and *en passant* described Handley as an obnoxious little individual. I worked on the weekend strategy note, then the nursing speech and got the *Mirror* to splash on it. Gus was still pressing for GB or JP to see Handley. I felt both were too big for it. Maybe Jack. The US situation was becoming farcical, making them a laughing stock. TB did nine regional TV interviews, and said afterwards he felt totally confident in our basic message.

The US elections were still confused. I felt the Democrats should really go for it and not give in. There were more and more stories of how

November '00: Fuel protesters divided

people thought they voted Gore and in fact voted Buchanan.[1] The whole thing was a mess and whoever finally won was going to be weakened at the start, at a point they should have maximum strength. The best news was that the lorry convoys were basically fizzling out. Handley had virtually gone into hiding and Brynle Williams was asking them to call it off. I went up to the flat where TB was signing off the nursing speech and hardening the line on investment/cuts. He was still mulling over GB. The press today had loads of stories on NICs [National Insurance contributions] going up which, although not new, was a bad story for us, and TB said that GB lacked the feel that he had for people in the middle, the vast bulk. GB felt there were poor people and there were rich people.

We were getting hammered over the Dome again. He felt that though Charlie F had the ability to do the job, because of the crony tag it had always been hard for him. We got a helicopter down to Shoreham [West Sussex], then to Hove School to record something for Channel 4. Bill Bush had done a good report on investment and the Department of Health had put together an excellent paper on nursing. The speech [announcing a new recruitment agency to tackle the shortage of nurses] went fine, the questions at the Q&A were pretty tough, but he did an excellent peroration and it went fine.[2] We did a press conference with a nursing backdrop which was fine. As we left, a woman in the audience came up, said she had never voted for us before but she would now, having seen him speak like that. It underlined the need to get him out and about more, and to find ways of getting his own voice heard, not mediated the whole time. We flew down to Chichester, then to Gloucester where the flooding was even worse. Elliot Morley was doing well, really knew his stuff. There appeared to be no side to him at all, a nice man, good manner. We visited the police HQ, where TB was really well received, before flying back to London.

[1] Pat Buchanan, the Reform Party candidate, received an unexpectedly high number of votes in Palm Beach County, Florida. It is possible that this was caused by a 'butterfly ballot'. The list of candidates was laid out in two columns, divided by a single row of holes. Punching the second hole did not register a vote for Al Gore, the second name in the left-hand list, but for Buchanan, the first name in the right-hand list.

[2] Blair said 'The majority we won in 1997 was never a reason to rush it and fail; but to do the job properly. Stage by stage. Economic stability. Then putting people back to work. Then investment in our public services. Then help to those like pensioners who need it most. At each stage, a choice. A vital decision about the future. I believe we have made the right choices. And I believe that if we can explain those choices, the British people will make the right choice too.'

Saturday, November 11

The [fuel protest] convoy from Jarrow to London was turning into a flop. Philip had done some groups last night. The PBR had gone down pretty well and he felt people were getting warmer to TB again. TB called, still worrying about GB, said the problem was GB would happily live on supplementary benefit so he couldn't understand why many people actually wanted to be wealthy, or at least well off. GB believed that people on twenty grand were doing pretty well. The only stories I got bothered about were the *Sunday Times* chasing me over Jill Dando and the *Mail on Sunday* claiming to have the minutes of the Cabinet meeting on the Dome. We went to [screenwriter] Shawn Slovo's fiftieth birthday party and I think I upset [actor] Richard E. Grant by saying I thought he was very good in the Spice Girls film.

Philip called from the States. I said I thought the Democrats were being useless in not generating any real anger about what was going on. What was happening was that because the media had called it early for Bush, they now had a vested interest in that being the outcome. The Democrats were being far too proper about the whole thing.

Sunday, November 12

TB called, wondering whether he shouldn't see the protesters. GB was a bit meandering and messageless on *Frost*. Gore/Bush was still massive, and ridiculous. I was working on the Mansion House speech tomorrow. Alex [Ferguson] called, he was on the 9.20 to Cape Town and had lost his passport. I sorted him with the chief immigration officer at Heathrow. I picked up from one or two of the hacks that Hague was planning a big speech on the West Lothian Question,[1] and was planning to say Scottish MPs at Westminster should not vote on devolved issues. Both TB and I felt that while there was an obvious superficial appeal in it, it was a mistake because it created second-class Westminster MPs, and it was an argument they had never mounted in relation to Northern Ireland.

Monday, November 13

I woke up, and was surprised to hear leading the news that TB and RC were to lead a concerted fightback against Euroscepticism. This

[1] First posed in 1977 by Tam Dalyell, Labour MP for West Lothian, this questioned the ability of MPs in Scotland and Wales to vote on matters affecting only people living in England. Conservative grandee Sir Malcolm Rifkind later proposed the 'East Lothian Answer': an English 'Grand Committee' of English MPs to debate and vote on relevant bills.

had come from John Williams [now FCO director of public and press affairs] and briefing Robin's speech, with a few lines on TB's Mansion House speech thrown in. It would be hard to shift off it. I was less worried than GB, who felt it pushed us right off course, just as we were regaining traction on the economy. TB said Robin's problem was that he sometimes had very poor political judgement. He said we had got Europe into a better place and this would take us back out of it. GB felt we had regained momentum on investment and this would take us back. Gus came to the morning fuel meeting and with the numbers of protesters dwindling, and their ringleaders attacking the press for not supporting them as before, we were definitely winning. TB asked me to do a similar operation in relation to health and winter preparations, which was getting up in a very negative and dangerous light.

On the *Mail on Sunday*'s account of Cabinet discussions on the Dome, I agreed with TB and RW that we should say there would be no leak inquiry because there had been no leak of any document, contrary to the impression. In truth, the account in the paper was more complete than the written record. It was clear someone who had been there had taken notes and then briefed them. Richard Wilson's face was a picture when I said I was sure it was not a special adviser. The *Telegraph* had done a story on how the Tories were moving from guarantees to commitments on their main policy areas. I was pushing for a party press conference in response but it didn't really go anywhere. We lacked a political killing machine at the moment. I was also working on my press gallery speech for Thursday, trying to get the balance right between nice and nasty. GB wanted Michael Wills [learning and technology minister] to do an article responding to Hague on the Scottish issue.

Tuesday, November 14

Bush/Gore was still rumbling on. When I saw the *Newsweek* team for a chat, they were pretty contemptuous of both. Europe had definitely knocked us off the post-PBR roll-out. Godric described it as a fiasco. Robin and [John] Williams getting us into the wrong place, Tim Livesey over-briefing on TB's video conference with Chirac without telling us. With the lorry protest pretty much fizzled out, we held the final meeting of the daily fuel group, but I told them they may be called in again to deal with the NHS 'winter crisis'. I had a good meeting with Nigel Crisp, the new NHS chief exec, who seemed pretty sassy about what we needed in communications terms.

I saw GB to discuss how we get back on track on investment. He then came over for a TB meeting where we agreed we should do a series of 'next steps' speeches in the next couple of weeks. GB felt that as soon as we got to January, everything we did would be seen in the electoral context, so we should be getting the big arguments laid down before the Tories got going. We had an election planning meeting, and I was a bit alarmed that there were so few new people. It was good to have experience but I felt as a group we were a bit tired. I liked the agency, though, and the 'Thank you' campaign had grown on me.

Wednesday, November 15

GB had flu so cancelled the morning meeting. We thought Hague would do health at PMQs but in the end did Europe and the Dome. TB was much more confident in himself at the moment and the general feeling was Hague was not doing as well at PMQs as before. I was working on tonight's event in St Albans to launch the 'Thank you' posters. Pat [McFadden] was doing the words and sounded very fed up about things. I was also working on my speech for tomorrow. Philip was urging me to be very soft with them, try to charm them rather than hammer them. At PMQs, we were trying to do Hague as 'the weakest link' but it didn't quite work.[1] TB did get him on band-wagoning though. We got the train to St Albans and I briefed the press on the thinking behind 'Thank you'. There was such resistance to politicians citing improvements, or taking credit for them, so the idea was to give people the credit for having voted for change. The Q&A went fine but the audience was a bit too professional and TB needed to be a bit more sparky.

I had been agonising about whether I could really go to the Britney Spears party without Grace. Eventually I went with Kate [Garvey, diary secretary], Steve Pooley [Number 10 duty clerk], Laura [Hester] from Fiona's office and Douglas Alexander. We met up and snuck in, or so we thought. We were taken up to the VIP room. Britney arrived late and went into a corner with her mum and her minders. Kate was running around sorting out arrangements, like she was still at work, when a guy came over and said 'Britney will see you in ten minutes.' I then saw the girl from the *Sun*, and photographer from the *Telegraph* gathering with one or two other snappers I didn't recognise and I thought fuck this. The atmosphere was all a bit seedy and sleazy. The

[1] A reference to the popular television quiz show. Blair would return to the idea in the debate on the Queen's Speech in December, saying of Hague 'I know he's very keen on summing up policy in six words – well how about this: You are the weakest link – goodbye.'

best thing out of it was that Douglas and I had a really good laugh together. Kate was taking the piss that I'd bottled out, but it really did feel a bit sad. There was something ghastly about the people around her. I was glad I went, if only to know that it was the kind of event I really didn't enjoy.

Thursday, November 16

I woke up to another load of balls on Europe and the euro. Peter M had said to a dinner of business people that we had made a strategic error saying that we just had to win the political and constitutional argument, and the *FT* were on to it. JP was livid that Peter had reignited it. I advised Robin not to do the *Today* programme but he did and was run ragged. Everyone assumed Peter had put the story in the *FT* to crank it up which of course he denied. He admitted he felt GB's approach was wrong but denied he had flammed it up. TB took a meeting on our revised communications plan. He wanted more emphasis on business enterprise. He felt that we were not appealing enough to aspiration. He felt GB was on business' back. GB came in later, still suffering with flu and was raging about Robin and Peter. We had had a plan post-PBR, and been derailed. TB said if it happened again, he would reprimand Peter. GB said 'You said that last time. You cannot have this indiscipline.' I was with GB on this.

At Cabinet, TB was pretty tough, saying that he was fed up that we agreed an advance Grid, and then so much crowded in to make it completely different at the last minute. He wanted ministers to get a proper grip of their departments and he didn't want to have to keep coming back to the same message. Otherwise it was pretty quiet. He called in Peter at the end, said he was fed up with all the diddling and he had to understand he did not want Europe up as a big election issue, he wanted it shut down. Peter gave an unconvincing account of how it all happened, that he had been trying to prevent one story and inadvertently created another. He said we had to understand GB was helping the Eurosceptic line in the *Mail, Sun, Telegraph*. He felt TB was allowing himself to be bullied by GB, that he assumed, rightly, that Gordon had been in shouting at him before Cabinet and had wound him up. He said it was ludicrous that the Foreign Secretary was not supposed to make speeches about Europe.

TB was getting more and more agitated and finally said 'I am losing patience on this. I want it shut down, end of story. You had better understand that I am the prime minister, and the leader of the Labour Party, and you do what I say.' Peter looked a bit taken aback but eventually said 'I sometimes have to think of my own interests too.'

TB: 'In my experience, you are the worst judge of your own interests. If you are trying to get back in synch, you have failed. Worse, you are creating a situation where GB can build a base around the issue of Europe.' Peter: 'I do not believe the Labour Party will go for GB because the *Mail* and the *Sun* back him on Europe.' TB: 'You are going to have to listen to my judgement in this and I want an end to it. As for Robin, he is very clever in some ways but occasionally adept at putting his foot in it. And if what you are saying is that you will do whatever you feel like doing then understand that is not something I will put up with.'

This verbal tennis went on for a bit longer. Eventually I said 'It is fucking ludicrous in a week we had an agreed plan to get up investment that I'm now about to leave for forty minutes of questioning on the single currency.' Peter later called me, after a predictably tough and tiresome lobby briefing, to say he felt he should put out some words on it all. JP called and said Peter was impossible to work with, that at least GB was serious. With all the fuss going on, I had very little time to prepare for the press gallery lunch, but it went fine. My impersonator on Rory Bremner, [actor] Andrew Dunn, was there and I complained he was too fat. Unfortunately, the only story out of it was TV debates [between party leaders during general elections]. TB was worried it would become a self-fulfilling prophecy. I didn't actually say anything I hadn't said before but the tone was probably too positive.

Friday, November 17

Europe was still a problem and the US elections were still bubbling away. TB was up early finishing his biosciences speech. As I said to the broadcasters, if it had come at a time when the *Mail* was rampaging on GM foods, it would be leading the news. But we were struggling to get coverage. The audience [of bioscientists] liked it though, and he was sure that a very strong bioscience message was an important part of our economic approach.[1]

I drove down with TB to Chequers, to go over his spiel to the political Cabinet. There was real anger at GB and Peter, and TB could strengthen his position. He also had to read the riot act at their lack of politics, the inability of most of them to deliver a message. He said that after I had left his meeting with Peter to brief the lobby, he had told him if he did it again, he would be out, that there was no reason

---

[1] Blair said 'Biotechnology is the next wave of the knowledge economy and I want Britain to become its European hub.'

for him to be making speeches on Europe. He was clearly losing patience. 'Why the fuck was Northern Ireland and Millbank not enough for anyone?' We arrived, and I was the subject of considerable piss-taking over the photo in the *Sun* of me arriving at the Britney party, clearly trying not to be seen.

The meeting itself was good. TB was on superb form. He was clear, determined, didn't pull his punches in saying they had to raise their game. He laid out the strategy and the dividing lines, the need to take things to a choice and a personal offer of prosperity. GB was also more New Labour than usual. Philip did a polling presentation, 54–37 wrong direction-right direction, floods and fuel creating a bad mood, but we still had an eight-point lead. Hague was being hit on opportunism and poor judgement, but the Tories could make inroads in standing up for Britain. TB emphasised the need for people to be given a personal offer about their future, that we had to be less general and more specific. And he warned that patriotism was an area the Tories would try to take back. He said it was a stupid mistake that a week after the PBR we were arguing about Europe. We have to be far more focused. We also had to expose the Tories' back-door strategy which was to make people as cynical as possible, depress the vote, and get their own vote out. He felt the dividing lines were clear – stability vs boom and bust; investment vs cuts; prosperity for all vs social division; opportunity and responsibility together vs social disorder; leadership vs engagement. On all the big arguments, we were on the right side of them but we lacked the capacity for explaining them. Ministers were too departmentalised, lacking in politics. He went through the reform areas coming up and said again they had to raise their game politically.

GB went through some of the electoral arithmetic and said apathy was the big challenge. If one in five Labour voters stay at home, we lose sixty seats. We were fighting the Tories, the press and apathy. He felt the New Year had to be the time to launch bigger attacks upon the Tories, particularly on the economy and cuts. He was also worried that they had a better definition of Britishness. JP went through the campaigning structures, was very nice about the changes I had made, e.g. the Grid, on managing the fuel issue centrally. But he said divisions were causing problems. Peter M reported on election planning, and went on a bit too long, but at least they felt a proper plan was being put in place. Robin talked about how Thatcher, even at the height of her powers, managed to campaign against us whilst in government. He said he agreed we shouldn't campaign on the euro but said we couldn't ignore Europe. Margaret B said she felt the public were turning against us a little, and we shouldn't ignore the extent to which the Tories would seek to exploit asylum. DB emphasised unity. He said the recent Millbank press conferences and weekend speeches were a waste of time. Milburn said we weren't doing enough to inspire people. They all chipped in.

Then TB summed up, and pretty much repeated what he said earlier. He said we had to build the case that the glass was half full not half empty. On Europe, the referendum pledge makes clear it can be dealt with separately. He felt Milburn had been right to say we have to give real emotional power to the choices we put before people and that means they have to feel they would be better off with us. He said we had to go after Hague and Portillo and Widdecombe etc. Neil Kinnock was thirty times the person Hague is and they went after him big time. Hague is dangerous because he is weak and he has bad judgement, and people have to know that. He ended by saying we have to go into this fight as though our lives depended on it. Over lunch, I chatted to Milburn and also got TB to call Mo who had left early feeling snubbed because he hadn't called her to speak early on. I got back and we put together a briefing based upon the discussion, emphasising that the economy would be at the centre of the campaign.

Saturday, November 18

We got more out of the post-Cabinet briefing than I thought we would. I felt we had established stability vs boom and bust, and now had to pin down investment vs cuts. I sensed we had an opening in the next few weeks, though European defence was building up as the next problem area.[1] We went up to Birmingham vs Burnley, lost 3-2. By the time I got back in the car, European defence was running hard and the *Mail on Sunday* had another so-called leak of Cabinet discussions in the early months of government. The Sundays arrived and Fiona was pretty pissed off about all the pieces on me and Britney. The *Sunday Telegraph* splashed on Cook saying that GB would never be PM and that he had a psychological need to damage anyone who disagreed with him. Gore/ Bush was still unresolved.

[1] It had been agreed at the Helsinki European Council a year earlier to create a European rapid reaction force that would be able to deploy 60,000 men within sixty days for peacekeeping and other operations. Defence Secretary Geoff Hoon had recently raised doubts about the capability of some EU countries to service such a force.

Sunday, November 19

The right-wing press and the Tories were trying to build up the defence situation as us going for a European army. TB called to say we had to kill it. On the Cook/GB story, Robin agreed to put out a statement rubbishing it. He said he feared someone had spoken loosely to Joe Murphy [*Sunday Telegraph* political editor] who had put the usual topspin on it. I suggested he also put out a line on the EU army idea as a way of moving it to a different territory. Robin was trying to get back in the good books and was blaming Peter for having kept the euro row going last week.

I did forty-three laps at the track, my longest run yet, most of it in pouring rain. In the afternoon, I did a seven-page strategy note, partly based on TB's presentation to Cabinet, to set out how we could use the Queen's Speech, speeches and events and talking points to lay those dividing lines clearly in the New Year. The Britney picture was leading to piss-taking wherever I went. I watched Rory Bremner with the kids. I ended up being fired, kicking the Queen's corgis, ending up working for her and getting a knighthood. Although the bloke playing me was overweight, it was uncanny how he got some of my mannerisms, and the nature of some of the exchanges between me and TB.

Monday, November 20

The EU army stuff was going big and I didn't prepare properly for the eleven o'clock. I had thirty minutes of it and wasn't terribly convincing. Stan Greenberg was over with the latest big poll. We were six points ahead but we hadn't had much of a lift out of the PBR and the trust issue was beginning to hurt us. TB had signed up to the note I did yesterday but now we had to see it through which meant a lot of his and other ministers' diary space. He agreed to a press conference for Wednesday on the White Paper. I sent the note round to departments on the plan for big-picture speeches. I told TB that GB had said the speech plan was impossible because of Europe. TB just shook his head, said we would just have to work around him, which was very unlike him.

On the plane out [to Moscow], he was wading through the briefing on Russia while I was drafting his script for Wednesday's press conference. The message came through that TB should dress casual. We went straight from the airport to a kind of beer cellar. We had a drink, ate some goose, and they went over MEPP, Balkans and Iraq, plus a lot of small talk. TB then went off to Putin's place and came back a bit pissed. I had dinner with John Sawers and Rod Lyne [ambassador], who really knows his Russia. TB said Putin had been on great form, and was determined not to get pushed into an anti-American position.

Tuesday, November 21

Rod and I went for an early morning run along the banks of the Moskva. It was freezing cold and sleeting, the air was dirty and my asthma kicked in a bit, but I felt terrific afterwards. The right-wing press was dreadful on EU defence. I briefed TB on it and said that when [Andrew] Marr came for a clip on Putin, we should really go for the press on it because they were being fundamentally dishonest. I got Jonathan and Julian B on the rebuttal case. TB was pretty wound up. He was looking out of his bedroom at the residence towards the Kremlin, said that if we listened to the people who wrote this bilge, we would do enormous damage to Britain. He had enjoyed his session with Putin and was very much up for another round. As he met with some young business people, I wrote to Yelland and Dacre saying that their coverage was dishonest, and offering a piece from TB, suggesting they wouldn't take it because it might mean their readers being troubled with a few facts. Both came back saying they would take it.

We went to see Prime Minister [Mikhail] Kasyanov who according to Rod was very fond of himself. He gave TB a hard sell on various commercial issues. He had a very irritating laugh, took a long time to make simple points. They went over oil prices, bilateral relations, air services, climate change. We then drove to the Kremlin for the meeting with Putin. The vast bulk of it was TB and Vlad on their own, just with Tony Bishop [interpreter] and the Russian interpreter. Putin took TB up to show him round his apartment and also on a mini tour of the Kremlin. Tony Bishop said that for a Russian leader, he was really making the effort and that there was a warmth there that was quite rare. While we waited, I worked on his education speech for Thursday and the investment script for tomorrow's press conference. Eventually, we were called in for the plenary session. After their night out, Putin seemed tired and failed to stifle a yawn when [foreign minister Igor] Ivanov was speaking about the Middle East.

Eventually, as Ivanov blathered on, Putin said simply 'Lunch?' and TB said 'That is a very good presidential initiative.' Ivanov looked crestfallen. There were no real problems at the press conference. Putin was being fairly human, not going on as long as he normally does. TB repeated his whack at the press over Europe. It was pretty obvious the Kremlin still had a fairly tight grip on the media. At one point I suggested to Alexey Gromov, Putin's press guy, that it would be good to get a question on the Blair/Putin relationship. Gromov nodded at one of the journalists, called him next and he asked the very question. 'I'm psychic,' he said.

Lunch was very good-humoured, oodles of caviar, nice salmon, not nice meat. Putin was much more confident and humorous than before. When the waiters came round with vodka for a toast and I put my hand over the glass, one of the Russian diplomats was harrumphing, and Putin noticed. TB said 'It's OK, he's not allowed, he's a reformed drunk.' Putin said 'I hope you redeem yourself in other areas.' Later, I sat in the Zil trying to fix tomorrow's investment event and sent through a note making clear it was not about Thatcher ten years on but about the future, linking investment for the long term. TB made a few changes on the plane. On Europe, he felt the defence row was another consequence of Robin and Peter doing what they did. GB was determined to exploit it. Having first had the idea of the investment press conference, he was now going cold, saying that because of Europe, it wouldn't fly. Europe was bound to hurt us in the by-elections, West Brom in particular.[1] We were paying a heavy price for Peter's self-indulgence. On landing, there was a box waiting which had a revised version of tomorrow's script. I went up to the track to see the physio who diagnosed tennis elbow and weak foot muscles. She said I had the flattest feet it was possible to have and should get orthotics for my running shoes.

Wednesday, November 22

The *Mail* and the *Sun* both carried the TB articles, but overshadowed by [Margaret] Thatcher saying European defence was a 'monumental folly'. It would also cut right across TB's investment press conference, so Bruce, Peter H and I persuaded TB we should use our intervention to launch an attack on the 'four fundamental failings of Thatcherism' – boom and bust, mass unemployment, underinvestment in public services, and the wrong turn on Europe. I planted a question at the press conference and TB did a couple of very strong clips on it. Although there was a lot of coverage on Europe, the investment message got through and it was definitely worth doing. GB was still wallowing in it all as a way of reminding us that Peter M had fucked up.

[1] The West Bromwich West by-election of November 23, caused by the resignation of Betty Boothroyd as Speaker of the House of Commons. In addition, there were three other by-elections on the same day, Glasgow Anniesland (UK Parliament and Scottish Parliament seats), caused by the death of Donald Dewar, and Preston, caused by the death of Labour MP Audrey Wise.

I lost my rag later when Anji came in and said TB had decided he wasn't doing a speech Sunday or Monday as agreed. Both he and GB had now pulled out of events they had agreed to. I said it was pointless, there were maybe sixteen weeks to go before an election campaign and we weren't even at the races yet. PMQs was fine and at the briefing I did the dividing lines again. Richard Desmond of *OK!* [celebrity magazine] fame bought the *Express*. I was now working on the education speech for tomorrow. Philip told me Stan had been very hard with GB yesterday because he felt GB was in the wrong place politically.

Thursday, November 23

I had bad vibes about the by-elections. David M and I went to the *Observer* to do one of our strategy and policy double acts. At Cabinet, TB did a big defence of [General Sir Charles] Guthrie, said the attacks on him for being too close to us were an attempted form of intimidation. He said our opponents were mounting these dishonest debates because they couldn't damage us on the economy, on investment, on jobs, so this was all they had. On Guthrie, Hoon rightly said can you imagine the fuss if Labour MPs had ever attacked a Chief of Defence Staff under a Tory government. They had a discussion on BSE and the French. Nick Brown and Alan Milburn gave very alarming accounts of how bad things could get. Clare, to a number of shaking heads, said we should tell every parent not to be feeding beef to their children. The discussion rambled around and TB let it wander before GB said there should be a team working on this which reports back. TB said we should work on it but we had to understand that if it was a question of banning it, then he would do that. Milburn was really up for something quite dramatic.

We agreed to brief that we would ask the FSA [Food Standards Agency] to send people to France to assure themselves that procedures there were OK. That, plus my robust defence of Guthrie and attack on his attackers, meant two big stories out of the Cabinet briefing. [Tony] Bevins called to say he was thinking of quitting [the *Express*] over Desmond.[1] I had a meeting on Europe with Stephen Wall and some of the FCO people. We had to get up bigger arguments about the benefits of EU enlargement and how some changes on QMV could be good for us. I left for lunch at the *Mirror* hosted by [Trinity Mirror

---

[1] As well as owning *OK!* magazine, Desmond was more controversially the publisher of such titles as *Asian Babes*, *Horny Housewives* and *The Very Best of Mega Boobs*.

chairman Sir] Victor Blank. The German ambassador [Hans-Friedrich von Ploetz] was there, totally on-message for us. Thought Hague was useless. Milburn called halfway through saying we had to toughen up our line on French beef.

Friday, November 24

We won all four by-elections, but turnout was low [all under forty per cent]. I called Byers and said he should emphasise in interviews that we were worried about turnout and we should start to expose the Tory back-door strategy. Godric was with TB in Zagreb [Croatia] for the Balkans [stabilisation] summit, where he was making another big pro-EU speech. Chris Patten had a letter in the *Telegraph*, and Heseltine in *The Times*, so they were beginning to turn against Hague on Europe. TB later spoke to Chris who then did an interview with James Robbins [BBC diplomatic correspondent] making clear he was appalled at what Hague was doing on Europe. I did a good briefing for the dailies, then the Sundays, and felt that after a bad phase, TB and I had rediscovered both our confidence and our teamwork. Guthrie called and said he appreciated our support and the fact that TB called him yesterday. I did a long conference call with Peter M and Peter H. Peter M said that at their meeting last night, GB had been vile to TB, said he was giving no direction or leadership, no sense of vision. Peter said it was unbelievably rude, but it meant there was no real agreement about what we were going to do next.

Saturday, November 25

By-election coverage was low-key. Defence was rumbling on on the back of TB and the Balkans [summit]. I went with Calum, Gavin and Oscar to Watford vs Burnley. We arrived in a downpour followed by a pitch inspection, a fifteen-minute delay, after which, without anyone even going out there, it was called off. We were queuing to get out of the car park listening to Radio 5, who said I had been seen on my mobile but 'even he couldn't get the game back on', as if I had been trying to do that when in fact I had been talking to Godric. Things felt more stable. TB called me, said he had been trying to get hold of GB who had gone AWOL. It was quite extraordinary the way that GB treated him sometimes. I think a lot of other people would be shocked if they really knew.

Sunday, November 26

Robin was fine on *Frost*. Bevins told me he was definitely going to quit the *Express* because he hated the new people and everything they stood for. [Lord] Hollick really did have a lot to answer for re the people he got into newspapers – Monty [David Montgomery, former Mirror Group chief executive] at the *Mirror*, now Desmond buying the *Express* off him. I worked up a script on EU enlargement, and chatted to JP about the collapse of the Hague summit [the United Nations Climate Conference in The Hague had finished without agreement after eleven days of talks]. TB wanted a big thing up on red tape for tomorrow. JP was keen for TB not to get too involved in the rail situation, which was silly.[1]

Monday, November 27

Bush was declared US president but Gore was fighting on. We were planning a Clinton visit and I was hoping to get the ITV special on the 12th when Bill was here. We were in a better place with the public re TB. The media were also picking up more of our agenda. The *FT* led on red tape. The *Express* did fine on the EU enlargement briefing. But some of them were determined to build up an NHS winter crisis. JP had a real go at the French environment minister [Dominique Voynet] who he blamed for the collapse of the Hague environment talks.[2] We had plenty of decent stuff to roll out through the week, rural White Paper tomorrow, TB press conference Thursday, plus Chirac, speech Friday.

At TB's office meeting, he wanted to put more pressure on re rail and he felt we were not yet in shape on enlargement pre-Nice [EU summit]. The Queen's Speech debate needed to be a hit. The eleven o'clock briefing was almost all about JP and his attack [on Voynet] and I defended him very robustly. I had a meeting with John Reid who was being done in by [Elizabeth] Filkin [parliamentary commissioner for standards].[3] I felt it ought to be possible to make her the issue. Apparently Major was up for it. A lot of MPs were appalled the way it was leaked at the weekend to do him in. He also had legal advice saying she had been working

[1] Following the Hatfield crash, a report was commissioned on Railtrack's management of broken and defective rails. Subsequently the company was urged to put in place a more robust and thorough system for replacement.

[2] Prescott had told the BBC that French environment minister Dominique Voynet 'said she was exhausted and tired and could not understand the detail and then refused to accept it. That is how the deal fell.'

[3] Investigating claims that Reid's researcher son was paid from public funds when campaigning for Labour. The commissioner found some rules had been broken.

against the laws of natural justice and ECHR.[1] TB took a meeting on Europe, and told [Stephen] Wall etc. that he wanted them to go to the Germans to show that we would listen on tax but then rule out what they were suggesting. Wall said even that would drive GB crazy because he was adamant we couldn't move on this at all.

Tuesday, November 28

The papers were bad for the Tories again. I met Stephen Wall on the train to Brussels and went over the arguments we were going to deploy when briefing the Brussels media. I did a big number on enlargement benefits, gave out TB's note to ministers which I tried to push as the main issue and detach from the tax issue. Stephen was worried that TB's 'listen about tax' would be seen by others that we were in trouble and ready to move. The briefing we did played quite well as a political story, not least because I was whacking the Tories in a way that was bold and confident. I was warming to Stephen, who really knew his stuff, and was able to help me out on the detail once or twice. I felt the media bought the argument pretty well and they bought the political pitch because they had a sense of our confidence on it. PA did it straight – Blair orders Cabinet fight against sceptics. We then went to see Jonathan Faull, Prodi's right-hand man, with Steve Morris, another Brit who worked for them. They were very defensive. Faull felt we were not as strong on Europe as we thought. I then did a meeting of the Labour MEPs which was quite friendly and I hope gave them a sense of what we were trying to achieve.

Wednesday, November 29

Today were leading on some rubbish about a proto-EU constitution, an old document presented as new. It led to GB muttering again about how we had sabotaged ourselves by getting up Europe. Jack Straw had got up a ridiculous story about the idea of a UK football team. He apologised for it and I dealt with it by saying he was a Blackburn fan and giving out my all-time Burnley team. But both he, and later DB when he attacked *Who Wants to Be a Millionaire?*, were knocking out their own stories.[2] Portillo in the *Telegraph* was ruling himself out as leader which was being seen as a problem for the Tories. We thought

[1] Vaz's solicitor had warned Filkin that her enquiry could be in breach of the European Convention on Human Rights and conflicted with natural justice. She disagreed. One complaint out of eighteen was upheld against Vaz without disciplinary action; others complaints were not pursued.

[2] Blunkett said the TV quiz show undermined social responsibility by fostering a culture where material wealth was all that mattered.

Hague would do Europe or rail at PMQs, but he went on community health councils. We had successfully disabled him with the jokes and the bandwagoning attacks. The Damilola Taylor murder was dominating everything.[1]

GB wanted us to be out on crime Monday to Wednesday. I felt we could keep going after Nice as well. GB came over for a strategy meeting. I asked what his plan was for tomorrow and he went through all the next steps, including some of the things that when I had suggested them a few days ago he had ruled out. Then, when discussing Portillo, I said Portillo was using Parliament for therapy and Philip said 'He's got the right opponent then.' Which was not meant unpleasantly, but GB snapped 'What's that supposed to mean?' We were actually in much better shape at the moment but GB constantly made people feel less confident.

Thursday, November 30

I went in early with Philip who said he had noticed that TB and I were getting on much better. GB had effectively stolen from Blunkett and Darling the 'two strikes and you're out' New Deal initiative [to stop the benefits of anyone twice found guilty of benefit fraud]. TB said that when they saw the New Dealers, GB's body language had been really odd and he wondered if he wasn't a bit depressed that we had picked up recently, and also that we had launched a fight against the sceptic press last week and appeared to have won it.

At Cabinet, JP did rail. TB said they were in a position of risk paralysis. The reaction had been way over the top, and it was creating risk aversion elsewhere. Blunkett said the rail companies' handling of it had been woeful. London was in a state of gridlock because more and more people were shifting from rail to car. Jack said something on the Peckham murder and there was a brief discussion of Nice. TB and I left for Northolt, had another discussion about the Tories and about GB. TB remarked again how difficult GB seemed to find it to relate to people. We flew to Yorkshire, went to Salt Grammar School, which is not actually a grammar school, where he got a pop-star welcome, then to a clinic in Bradford, a New Deal visit in Leeds, then to Newcastle General [Hospital]. Tony Bevins was with us, having nagged me for ages to do visits which would allow him to show public service improvement and I was glad he was able to do it before

[1] On November 27 the ten-year-old Nigerian schoolboy had been killed on his way home from a library in Peckham, South London. Four youths were subsequently acquitted of murder charges but in 2006 fresh DNA evidence led to two brothers, Ricky and Danny Preddie, being convicted of manslaughter.

he left the *Express*. He was dead impressed. He said he was as depressed as I was about the state of the lobby and the state of the press. At all of the visits, we had seen real evidence of real progress, but how do you break through the cynicism?

TB and I had a few good laughs on the running gag about how Chirac would take to Sedgefield, and whether he would bring himself to do what he normally does, which was to describe every event as the best organised he's ever been at and every meal as the best he's ever eaten. We met him at Teesside airport. He had a gift of a really nice photo of TB, CB, Leo, Chirac and Clinton. They did a brief press conference which was fine, and then we headed for the County Hotel. There were a few egg-throwing farmers. We got inside, settling down to the meeting over dinner. Chirac entered into the spirit, saying how charming it all was, but I could tell one or two of his people thought the whole thing was a bit grim. Also, the door from the kitchen was unbelievably squeaky and the noise every time the waiters came through became increasingly irritating. The dinner confirmed that the problems between France and Germany were real, but that Nice was going to be difficult. It was a friendly enough discussion, including on climate change. TB and I went back to Myrobella to work on the speech.

Friday, December 1

I was up for a run at 6, a few miles, then back to work with TB on the speech. We put in a strong passage about responsibility and promising a Queen's Speech that would be tough on crime. It was another good, heavy speech that would get OK if limited coverage. But the effects of a more serious and sustained strategy were apparent in Phil Stephens' [*Financial Times*] column where he wrote of the more mature dialogue we were now having. There were good pictures out of the Chirac dinner, and the substance of the coverage was good. The Franco-German row was beginning to come through.

For once we got the speech finished early and I set off for the 9am flight south, on the way briefing Godric on how to push the speech. On the plane down, I was sitting next to a couple of working-class Geordie women on the way to New York for a holiday. One of them said she was a Tory but she was thinking of voting for Tony now because he took Chirac up north. Takes all sorts. As we landed, Godric called. TB's dad was ill and the press were on to the hospital. I organised Fiona Gordon [Labour Party official] to go down there and we put out a line about privacy. TB called after his speech, worried about Leo.

Saturday, December 2

The Tories were in real trouble now. We got limited but OK coverage for yesterday's speech. Leo was a bit better. But there was another family-related problem. Stewart Steven [*Mail on Sunday* columnist] was doing a piece saying TB knew all about bullying because his kids had a very rough time. There were three arrests over Damilola. The Britney thing was getting even more out of hand, with *Have I Got News for You* [satirical TV news quiz] doing something on it.

Sunday, December 3

Stewart Steven did the stuff on the boys so we had to work on others not to follow it up. We did a conference call to plan how to get up the NHS for tomorrow and respond to Hague's speech on Tuesday on how he was going to save £8 billion. TB called re the press conference on the NHS, which Milburn trailed well on *Dimbleby* [ITV political show presented by Jonathan Dimbleby]. I did fifty laps at the track.

Monday, December 4

The NHS briefing overnight went a bit awry, with *The Times* splashing on 'Blair says there will be a crisis' and the broadcast advance coverage was too negative as well. But at least it was out there and it was us identifying the problems, being honest about them. I went up to see TB who was exercised about getting the right message on health and working up to the Queen's Speech debate. He was also trying to think through the Clinton visit, and how we put together the right relationship with Bush. Jonathan and John Sawers were feeding him the usual diplo stuff, but this was going to require some pretty acute political skills.

I had a meeting with Richard Desmond. He looked and sounded a bit wide boy, but was pretty bright. I gave him an assessment of how I thought they should take on the *Mail*, be campaigning but from a spirit of optimism, promote what's good, don't just run everything down. He was not a fan of Hollick. He was clearly going to sack loads of people, would ideally like to run newspapers without journalists. His grasp on policy was pretty tenuous. It was all really about himself – he hated Hague because he hadn't returned a phone call. The German ambassador [Hans-Friedrich von Ploetz] came in, very bright and clearly wanting to help [in advance of the Nice summit]. He was doing the *Today* programme tomorrow and was up for putting a message that was helpful to us.

GB was the lead in the *Independent* with some rubbish about 'progressive universalism', which I took the piss out of at our morning meeting. He accepted it was unlikely to get them marching for us in Burnley. TB was working on the Queen's Speech while I was doing a seminar for ministers and press officers, pushing the same old stuff about co-ordination, need to be more political. I did a big number on the Nice summit, me doing the big message, Stephen Wall dealing with the tough questions. I had a real go at the sceptics, said they should have the guts to say they wanted to quit Europe. The main news was Hague's speech promising tax cuts. Darling did a very good job in response. We also sent round a poster van with Mr Boom and Mr Bust [a mocked-up movie poster with Hague and Portillo starring in *Economic Disaster II*] which got on TV. TB was doing his own draft of the Queen's Speech debate speech. We had a bit of a problem from Bill Cohen [US Defense Secretary] who was saying the EU rapid reaction force would be bad if it undermined NATO.

Wednesday, December 6

Queen's Speech. Yesterday's briefing came out not too bad, pretty aggressive in some quarters. The papers were full of pictures of CB and Leo from yesterday, when she had taken him out in the street. Fiona was livid with her, feeling it was ridiculous that she asked us to complain at the slightest intrusion but she took him out there when she knew the street was full of photographers. We had successfully got up crime as the main message pre-Queen's Speech. TB was working pretty much solo on his speech, just asking us for lines and facts. We felt Hague would come at us on policy but in the end he played it for laughs. It meant the broadcasters were bound to give the Commons exchanges to Hague. I felt that TB did fine and Hague was poor but that was not what the viewers were going to see on the news. TB called later. He felt we won on the arguments but Hague was very witty which would be enough to get a good press. Margaret McD called, said that Millbank was pretty hopeless at the moment and there was a real case for me going down there and taking over. She said Peter M was too remote.

Thursday, December 7

Queen's Speech coverage was OK, but dreadful in the *Sun* with a big attack from Trevor [Kavanagh] and a leader saying Hague was more prime ministerial. I complained to the *Mail* about a totally made-up story that I watched the Queen's Speech at TB's desk with my feet on the table. Europe was up there as a bit of a nightmare for us, even though for most European media, the real story was France vs Germany. On the way out to the airport we agreed to try and get up the issue of power, related both to reweighting of votes and also to the issue of competences in advance of the 2004 IGC [Brussels]. But it was going to be tough. As we arrived in Nice, we heard Chirac had done a press conference pushing the boat out on the EU having a different capability of planning. TB was up for a photocall with the enlargement countries, then a doorstep. He was strong and confident at the moment, had his voice, which was discombobulating GB.

The French and Germans, according to the spooks, were exploiting the fact that GB was seen as a rival to TB, to try to divide them further. I rounded up Stephen Wall, John Williams and Emyr Jones Parry [deputy political director at the Foreign Office] to do a briefing. It was all about Chirac and defence after what he had said. I did what I could to get it in the right place but it was difficult. The words 'independent' and 'co-ordination' were exciting them all. Wall and Emyr believed it was probably deliberate. Emyr went on for ages and then said that [William] Cohen's comments were 'valedictory' and that he was probably 'in his cups'.[1] I passed him a note asking what that meant. He said it meant 'gloomy' in Welsh, so I 'translated' for the media to try to avoid a story of a British official saying the US Defense Secretary was a pisshead. But the defence story, no matter how hard we pushed it back, was the only show in town. That much was clear when TB did a series of one-on-ones.

I called Catherine Colonna [Chirac's spokeswoman] and she agreed she would ring our key people to try to get them in the right place. In the end she did a conference call organised through Switch but it backfired when she said EU defence could not be subordinate to NATO. TB got back late from the official dinner and we went out for a little walk on the front. He said the whole thing felt like a therapy session for the French and the Germans. Chirac had said the Franco-German motor had to be the motor of Europe and it was terrible when Britain first joined. Schroeder said let the past be the past. Jospin said how dreadful it was that people always accused the French of being arrogant. TB said the whole thing had been very odd and people had ended up being pissed off by the French. It meant they would

[1] The American Secretary of Defense had warned that if the EU created a defence capability outside NATO's structure, NATO could become a 'relic of the past'. This was interpreted by some as a warning that the US would withdraw its military presence from Europe.

come at us very hard over tax but he was clear we would not give in. He was looking really tired.

Friday, December 8

Went for a run first thing and then back to go through the cuttings, which were a bit of a war zone on defence. Overnight the French had rewritten the text on defence to contain a few more weasel words when all we wanted was for the presidency report and the annexes to be accepted. Stephen Wall put forward the idea of simply taking all the language out and stating that they endorsed the report and annexes. With the help of the Dutch, we secured that. Unlike Stephen, TB did not believe Chirac had done this deliberately. TB was still full of last night's dinner, as were the others. The general feeling was that the French had been embarrassing. Schroeder said it was '*unglaublich*' [unbelievable]. Chirac had even said that over the next twenty-five years the French would catch up in population terms. [Michael] Steiner [Schroeder's foreign policy adviser] told me that Chirac had given them a huge problem, constantly talking about parity.[1] I briefed our broadcasters that the French were basically going for us as a diversion in their problems with Germany.

Schroeder had said they were acting for France, not as the presidency. TB was worried that it was all pointing towards them coming towards us big time over tax. Stephen felt it was more likely they would come at us over social security because we were more isolated there. Catherine C told me they would help us on tax if we didn't go for them on trade, and on defence asked me not to present them as backing down. They finally agreed the slimmed-down proposal on defence which the media took as us having won. At Godric's suggestion, I put together a script about some of the previous summits where in the build-up the media had been saying we would be defeated – on border controls, tax, the rebate, social agenda, economic reform, now defence – and we won the argument every time, so grow up.

We were getting huge turnout for the briefings and doing pretty well on the substance. Over lunch Chirac said they would now go into bilateral 'confessionals' so that the really heavy negotiations could start. For an hour or so TB sat down with me, John S, Wall, Sheinwald and Angus Lapsley [former private secretary to Blair, now EU Institutions Unit at FCO] to go through the various difficult situations.

[1] European Council votes were allocated according to the size of population, with weighting in favour of smaller countries. Proposed changes favoured larger states, but France wanted to retain parity with Germany, despite its smaller population.

TB was clear that the French real red line was not trade but parity. We agreed we would say we had no problem with Germany getting more votes – our problem was that the Germans won under whatever system was agreed whereas we did less well under double majority. His argument was that we had given lots on enhanced co-operation, 2004 IGC, size of Commission, some QMV. But he still didn't want to be standing out alone. We had to get reweighting of votes. I was called out to deal with another Peter M problem. He had hosted a party yesterday that was interpreted as him saying that Bush would be pro-Sinn Fein. Pretty idiotic. Sometimes he just couldn't keep his mouth shut.

TB went to see Prodi, who was pushing for more QMV. TB was arguing strongly against, arguing actually in a broader EU the bigger countries should not lose out. Then news came through that Gore had won one of his appeals, and the race was back on. TB and RC went to see Chirac and Jospin and came out feeling they had made progress. We couldn't really work out how Chirac would manage to break through all this tomorrow. He was going to have to bulldoze. But his problem was people were gunning for the French from all sorts of directions. Our only real isolation was social security because the Irish and Swedes were with us on tax. It was only when you were at these events that you realised just how different the politics were country to country. As TB said, to most Brits it's mind-blowing that the Italians will be judged by how much QMV is agreed to, while [Belgian Prime Minister Guy] Verhofstadt was under real pressure from the people of Belgium to get more QMV. TB said he didn't believe a single citizen was looking for QMV to be extended. It was a totally ridiculous statement. But Chirac had so fucked it up we were more confident than probably we deserved to be.

Saturday, December 9

I went out for a run along the seafront and up to see TB. The French presidency text had retained tax and social security QMV and TB was worried they would come at us in a pretty hard way. There was a long hard day ahead. We met with Robin and his team and went through it all line by line, and that was without doubt the big problem. We got to the conference centre where everyone seemed pissed off. Schroeder felt the latest text didn't remotely reflect yesterday's discussions. His interpreter told me she had never seen him so angry. The Chirac/Schroeder relationship was bad, and Chirac/Jospin was even worse. There was clearly very little trust between them. The Dutch were angry because they were given too few votes, Spain were happy

December '00: US presidential race back on

enough to be lagging just behind the big four but everyone else was pretty fed up and we decided to put together a storyline that the French were basically losing the plot. Our big worry had to be that the French cut a deal with the Germans and then come after us together on tax. But it was clear the French were finding it hard to see a way through. Lena [Schroeder's interpreter] suggested we speak to Schroeder and at lunch he, TB and I went out on the balcony and agreed we should try to work together with Italy to try to put together a proposal people could live with. Schroeder was sufficiently fed up with Chirac to go for it.

The French seemed clueless, for example offering the Belgians the idea of holding every second summit as compensation for more votes for Holland. TB started to do bilaterals, to keep people off our back on tax and social security and also start to put together a plan on reweighting proposals. I briefed the broadcasters on all the different points of anger being directed at the French, then went into news starvation mode. I went for a long walk with Godric and Michael Jay round some old haunts and got a nice present for Fiona from an art shop. We got back for a TB/Schroeder meeting before I went to brief. [Shadow Foreign Secretary] Francis Maude's press guy was there and I encouraged him to ask questions so I could have a bit of fun on the politics. Our problems were no longer top of the agenda even for the Brits.

TB and Schroeder were now working together on trying to get a plan. TB said the tragedy for Britain in Europe was that if we didn't have the crazy politics and the crazy media, we would be running the show with the Germans by now, but if we come back after the election and don't do the euro, things could slip away again. We took the plan we had worked out with the Germans on reweighting to Chirac and Jospin before dinner but it didn't really fly. Meanwhile [Swedish Prime Minister Göran] Persson came out saying TB had won on tax and Schroeder started to go for the French on article 133 on trade. The French refused to move. Schroeder then suggested TB send the French a note with the trade stuff taken out. Sawers and Wall took it to them. TB and Schroeder said Chirac's chairing had been lamentable but that Jospin had been even more difficult than Chirac. TB, Robin C and I went for a walk on the beach. TB said he had never seen anything quite as bad as the way the French had gone about things and could not work out why.

Schroeder agreed Chirac had made a mess of things by setting such store on the issue of parity and by making the point earlier that as they had been on the winning side in the war they had nuclear weapons. 'It's not easy for me to say to twenty-year-old Germans, dear German citizens, because your grandfather occupied France we got a very bad deal from President Chirac at Nice.' Top man, really, tough and by and large straight. TB's worry now was that Chirac would take our proposal to e.g. Spain, Belgium and Austria who wouldn't like it. In fact the French were so relieved to have a decent piece of work before them that they felt it was OK. We now had to bind in Aznar [Spain] and Amato [Italy]. It looked like not only were we winning on tax but we were getting our way on the overall package, and TB and our officials had pretty much turned it.

Sunday, December 10

Persson's quote that TB had won the day on tax went well in our press. As I came back from a run, TB was on the phone to Amato trying to work through the new deal we had done with the Germans. Then we went to see Aznar which was a bit of a problem because it was the first time he heard there was a proposal for Spain to have their votes reduced from twenty-eight to twenty-six within the system. TB assumed the French would put it around that this was our idea but it gave us a bit of an Aznar problem. Aznar's basic line when we met at the Negresco Hotel was why should he care about Poland? Harsh but understandable. We went to the conference centre where France tabled a slightly modified proposal that boosted Poland and Holland but was pretty grim for Lithuania. We had a basic position that if we, France and Germany voted against something, it didn't happen. Seems fine to me. Some of our team were getting more worried about being fair to Lithuania than fighting for the UK.

TB and I had another meeting with Schroeder on the balcony. Schroeder was pretty fed up but agreed they should carve up another round to push the case for our deal once more. The Portuguese and the Belgians were now threatening to veto it. Then the Austrians made clear they weren't happy so it was far from over. The crowds for the briefings were getting bigger and bigger. I had a very funny exchange with Mike White [Guardian] on my past in Nice and again with Maude's [press] bloke when I reminded everyone that Maude had signed the Maastricht Treaty. TB was working on the smaller countries. He came out from the lunch to go over the latest text. It was going to be difficult for the smaller countries and the mood was bad. About 5pm, it looked like we were OK on tax and social security so we got together the Brits in one room to brief them where we had won and pushing the idea that we were building alliances to sort the blockage on votes. TB was motoring. Chirac was basically saying this was the deal. Portugal, Greece, Belgium, Finland, all had real problems. Ditto Prodi. As Bertie [Ahern] said to me, as the pressures rise, you see all the difficult old tensions come out.

Dinner was a few tired cheese sandwiches then up to see TB when it all broke up in disarray. He said we had to find ways of helping Belgium and Portugal. It was feeling slightly like crisis time. We met Schroeder to go over a few ideas, then joined by Chirac and Jospin with interpreters kneeling around, everyone talking at once, slightly mad. We had to get more votes to the small countries but preserve reweighting. It was getting very fractious and faintly embarrassing that they couldn't work it out. Chirac looked lost. Jospin just shouted. Schroeder looked angry. TB said we should just get the big five in a room, crash it through then take it to the rest. Why they didn't do that earlier is beyond me. Belgium was the problem, proving hardest to break down. Chirac asked TB to work on Verhofstadt. Meanwhile Schroeder said to TB, as did Verhofstadt, that all it would take to break the logjam was for TB to say to Chirac that he could solve it all by giving one more vote to Schroeder. We were using Angus Lapsley's laptop to bang out all the various options.

Monday, December 11

We were now down to twenty-nine votes for the big four, which was cutting down on reweighting, and the whole thing was not brilliant at all. It was taking a fair amount of strong-arming to get the medium-sized and the smaller countries to go for it. At one point TB and Schroeder literally had Verhofstadt pinned into the corner of the room, his smile getting thinner and thinner as TB did the charm and GS did the exasperation bordering on anger. Chirac was even more aggressive, at one point telling the Belgian foreign minister he was a coward because they wouldn't take the deal. His handling of the whole thing had been bizarre, making such a totem of French parity with Germany without regard to some of the long-term friendships and alliances that were bound to be affected by the nastiness at the end. At one point, though he was meant to be chairing it, Chirac asked his staff to get some letters to sign and just sat there working at his desk on his own. Schroeder was sitting a bit further round the circle, just staring out, looking tired. Aznar and [Portuguese Prime Minister Antonio] Guterres walked out.

The last bits of haggling were done in the margins and largely by officials. Finally around 5am it was all done. I had worked on a script with Mark [Bennett] for TB and it was important we go for the big message on how well we had actually done for Britain, as a result of being more positive. TB was tired, as were the hacks, some of whom had been kipping out on the floor of the press centre. We also had a bit of repair work to do to persuade Aznar that we hadn't been responsible for a last-minute anti-Spanish bounce. Prodi was wandering around looking more depressed than ever. John Sawers was bollocking me and Robin, saying we didn't care enough about Lithuania and Malta! Bertie and I were chatting about the need to change the way the whole thing works. It's ludicrous that these negotiations were sorted in this atmosphere of frenzy, with everyone exhausted and losing their tempers. Bertie was really grateful to TB for sticking out as hard as he did on tax and was full of praise at his own press conference. We got back to the hotel for a couple of hours' sleep. Stephen felt the deal was OK but not brilliant but the media were pretty positive about what had been achieved for the UK. I agreed with TB he should do a doorstep as we left saying it was a good deal for the UK but we have to reform the way Europe works. We worked on the statement for the Commons on the flight back. TB said afterwards it was a tragedy that Britain was held back by so much scepticism. If we were really in there, we would be running the show.

Tuesday, December 12
David M and I did a breakfast at the *Express*. They clearly felt we were in a very strong position at the moment. I tried to set out how I thought they could go for the *Mail* but they seemed to lack confidence. There was definitely an opening for a paper that wanted to reflect the new spirit of the times, but I feared they lacked the imagination or the courage to swim against the tide. As part of the new communications plan, we had arranged for an ITV special, *Ask the Prime Minister* with Jonathan Dimbleby and an audience. TB wanted several sessions to prepare and was worrying about the audience just being made up of activists. ITV were giving it a huge build-up. In the car to Northolt, we had another chat about Peter, and TB's increasing concern that Millbank wasn't being run properly. We flew up to Leeds, going over some of the difficult questions that might come up. The TV people were in their usual state of overexcitement, but the programme started out rather dull, and Dimbleby was too fond of his own voice to make it really work as an audience event. TB could sense the audience getting pissed off that so few people were getting in to ask their questions, so he stayed on for forty minutes after the recording had finished. Even then, Dimbleby seemed to think it was about him not TB, and TB finally cut out the middle man.

On the flight back, TB said he preferred these events when there were genuinely difficult questions designed to elicit proper answers, rather than the game-playing of most interviewers. He said he had decided it was far better to try to be clear even if people thought you were wrong. He felt that Harold Wilson's problem was that the country reached a judgement over time that he was more interested in keeping the party together than in the overall purpose for the country. The pressures internally led him to that. We had to avoid allowing the pressures to build up so that the same thing happened to us.

We flew on to Belfast where the plan was that we try to get something done on the observation towers as a signal of commitment to the normalisation agenda being pushed by SF, and get them to do some kind of engagement in decommissioning, but it was going to be tricky. We met up with Peter M at the Hilton. He said we wouldn't be able to do the normalisation measures because all the towers were essential for the security operation vis-à-vis the Real IRA [paramilitary organisation split from the Provisional IRA]. The plan was that we try to get Clinton to put the deal forward. Bill and Hillary arrived and after the small talk, and a bit on Ireland, Clinton wanted a rundown on Nice. He had an extraordinary grasp of detail on the varying economic performances round Europe. Like TB, he found it hard not to like Chirac and his roguish qualities. TB put to Bill the specific plan on Ireland. He felt sure Clinton would be able to give it a real push.

Wednesday, December 13

I went for a run in the pitch black round the grounds of Hillsborough, falling over once or twice and landing really badly on my shoulder. After breakfast, TB had a session with Ronnie Flanagan [RUC chief constable] and the new head of the army in NI [General Officer Commanding (GOC), General Sir Alistair Irwin]. They were reasonably helpful in trying to get some moves on demilitarisation but the big symbolic things Sinn Fein wanted were not going to be possible. Peter was a bit odd at these meetings. He was obviously so used to being the main man here and lording it and found it hard to adapt when TB came in and was clearly the focus. He was very good in describing other people's positions, usually in exaggerated and sometimes disparaging terms. TB was getting more and more exasperated by his manner. We left for Stormont and were left hanging around for ages waiting for Bill, who was seeing Adams and [SDLP leader John] Hume at the hotel. He finally arrived forty-five minutes late and did the rounds of Assembly members and we then met some of the leaders. We did a photo call, TB, BC, Trimble and [SDLP deputy leader Seamus] Mallon, before a meeting of the four of them. Trimble was worried about Patten and the effect it would have on the unionist community.[1] Seamus was clearly worried that Sinn Fein would outflank the SDLP. TB was worried later re Seamus, felt he was a lot more difficult than before, that he was being driven by the SDLP not being clear about their purpose in all this. The politics were clearly in flux and all of them seemed a bit unsure how to deal with it.

It must have been odd for Clinton to be trying to help us deal with all this, in what was ultimately a fairly small part of the world, albeit one that had a resonance elsewhere, and back home there were pretty seismic events going on. I spoke to several of the Clinton people about the Gore situation. They obviously felt the campaign could have gone better if Bill had been more involved. The Supreme Court judgment had basically been that a recount was unconstitutional so that was basically that. Gore was planning to concede 2am our time, then Bush would speak an hour later. Clinton was reasonably discreet but he clearly felt his legacy was at risk, that they lost by allowing the Republicans to neutralise the issue of the economy, by allowing their basic message to move leftwards, and by not using him properly. He was right on all three counts. He also clearly felt some of the strategists had not done the business.

TB saw the UUP, SF and SDLP, and the meetings were more convivial than usual, which sometimes meant progress was not being made. Trimble was pushing hard on decommissioning. Ken Maginnis [UUP] was pressing for proper recognition of the RUC and said we were playing a very dangerous game if we were going for an amnesty for the 'OTRs' [on the run terrorists]. Then Sinn Fein. Martin McGuinness said he liked doing education and he felt most people felt he was doing his job. But we kept coming back to all the old impediments to progress and it pissed him off. He said he would welcome it if more of 'our people' joined the police but they are not convinced that a new police force genuinely represents a new beginning. He said he was the guy going out to Republicans saying Blair is a good guy, different to every other prime minister, but they laugh at me if I say that policing is a good deal for us. Patten did not go far enough for them. He said we don't come from where they come from and we have to understand the psychology. People hate the

---

[1] The Patten report included recommendations that the Royal Ulster Constabulary be abolished and that recruitment to a replacement force establish parity between Catholic and Protestant officers.

RUC even more than the British Army, but there is an appreciation that there must be a policing service. People are up for that but are badly disappointed. TB said what's your beef? We've done everything the SDLP asked for in the implementation plan. Bairbre de Brún [Sinn Fein public safety minister] said their people just weren't going to join as things stood. It was interesting that McGuinness did more of the talking this time than Adams. Gerry Kelly and [Martin] Ferris did the strong silent bit as usual. Policing, demilitarisation and decommissioning were coming together as real problems. TB wrote a passage for Bill that put pressure on all sides to move.

We set off for the Odyssey [Arena, Belfast]. Tom Kelly [NIO] and I did a briefing which went fine. It was an OK venue. TB didn't really get going. The audience wasn't as fired up as when BC was in [Courthouse Square in] Dundalk yesterday. He had some good lines but he must have been depressed by the Gore/Bush situation. We were getting something out of the tripartite attack – UK, US, Irish – on terrorism though Hague was about to wade in on a different front with a hit on the liberal elite re the impact of the MacPherson Report on police morale. The *Sun* was driving some of this and was hitting us pretty hard, as well as welcoming Bush like a best friend. Clinton seemed more tired than usual, at one point nodding off on a long black sofa in the holding room. Hillary was also clearly having to really fight within herself to put on a brave face about what was happening back home, and she was if anything even more discreet re Gore. But they were very anxious about the future.

Thursday, December 14

I went in with Philip and chaired a meeting on next steps but the only thing that mattered today really was Bush. It must have been so weird for Clinton, who was down at Chequers and giving TB a tip or two on how to make sure he got in with Bush. TB and I spoke a couple of times before he came out at 11.30 and did a big number on the US–UK relationship and how we would work with Bush. He also lacerated Hague for his MacPherson speech. He was up for really going for him for bandwagoning.

We got flown up by helicopter to Warwick University, where TB did a little walkabout and then he, Jonathan and I were taken up to the vice chancellor's office where a phone had been put in for his call to Bush. There was something almost weird about us sitting there waiting for the call while outside, everyone was getting very excited about Clinton. Bush came on, and made a point of saying it was the first call he was making. Neither of them mentioned the recent turmoil.

There was lots of laughter and joking, then the standard stuff about the special relationship and the importance of working together. They didn't really get into substance at all, it wasn't that kind of call. He sounded friendly enough. Bill arrived and we were put into a very poky little holding room before they went down to do the speeches. He was going out of his way to help. I had been trying to get their speeches to work together to show the Third Way as being something more than just an electoral device. As he came off the stage he said 'I hope that did something for you.' I said I wasn't the biggest Third Way fan in the world, but we may as well try to get something out of it. He said he always preferred the first way.

There was definitely an end-of-era feel to things. He said he wanted to thank us for all the help we had given him. I said he was the best political communicator I had ever seen or heard and he said thanks for everything. I reckoned he would find it quite hard to adapt out of power. Hillary looked sad as well. She said say hi to Fiona and keep in touch. Then they walked out, smiled and waved at the small crowd over the road, into the car, and off they went. There was something about a presidential motorcade that looks both impressive and sad at the same time. Impressive in that it sweeps all before it, but sad that they need that kind of support and protection, and for an outgoing president what was once a symbol of power becomes a symbol purely of status of what he once was. You could feel that the power was no longer there, but had moved.

Friday, December 15

TB was doing a policy unit awayday which I managed to get out of. I had to get a new mobile phone post-Nice because the spooks assumed the French were tapping the ones we used there.

Saturday, December 16

TB called. He wanted me to meet up with him and Peter M tomorrow, but I was going to be at Burnley. I had just done radio with Jack Straw on the Burnley–Blackburn rivalry. I managed to get in a bit of government message when Nick Robinson [BBC] asked at the end if I wanted to say anything in advance of their discussion on the Tories. I said if there were any Tories listening who felt their party was too right wing, they could always come to a party that had delivered economic stability, jobs, public service investment and a new role in the world. TB felt Peter M was panicking a bit and also that GB was like a deadweight holding him down. I was dealing with another silly Scotland-related TV row. As a result of the *Ask the PM* programme, the other four parties in Scotland were demanding an hour's TV pre the Falkirk by-election.[1] Ludicrous. TB was worrying that Hague scored a hit on MacPherson with the police themselves. Hague did another round of interviews and clearly thought he was getting something out of this.

Sunday, December 17

Hague was up attacking us on police numbers and linking to Damilola Taylor. I put together a strong line of attack, said that even by his standards this was low. We had to somehow get into £16 billion cuts. I spoke to Milburn because expectations on the nurses' pay award were being set too high, e.g. *The Times* yesterday saying eight per cent. I had the usual difficulty motivating the Home Office to engage with Hague so I got Dobbo out but he focused on race rather than Hague's judgement. We lost the Blackburn match [2-0] and took hours to get home.

Monday, December 18

Hague was still going strong and race/police numbers dominated the eleven o'clock. Little did I know, as I was laying into him once more, and saying politicians should choose their words with care, that Damilola Taylor's parents were putting out a statement accusing Hague of using their case as a political football. It should have been the cue for apology but the Tories ploughed on, no doubt thinking he was connecting at a certain level on police numbers and race. I got Margaret B up later to try to do what I had asked Frank D to do yesterday. Nurses' pay went better than it might.[2] We even had senior nurses out welcoming it. TB and I had an inconclusive discussion about January. Peter M was keen for a party document setting out choices. GB believed that if we did that now, everything would be seen in the context of the election and that the longer we were seen as the government rather than the party, the better. This was setting itself up as the next area for TB to fail to resolve GB/Peter M tension. TB was strangely unconfident again though the polls were good and Hague was getting a rough ride. TB felt the Home Office had been

[1] Caused by the resignation of Dennis Canavan as MP for Falkirk West. Having been rejected as a Labour candidate for the Scottish Parliament in 1999, Canavan stood as an Independent and was expelled from the Labour Party. He continued to sit as Independent MSP for Falkirk West.

[2] Senior nurses were to be awarded a five per cent increase but staff nurses would receive only 3.7 per cent. The salary of newly qualified nurses would rise from a minimum of £14,890 to £15,445.

pretty useless in dealing with the police and race issues over the weekend and Jack admitted as much when he came to see me, ostensibly to gloat about Blackburn. We had a long-term diary meeting and I was still pressing for more space for proper speeches and real engagement.

Tuesday, December 19

Hague was still not getting the kind of kicking he deserved re Damilola, though the Bishop of Southwark [The Rt Revd Dr Thomas Butler, whose diocese covered the scene of the killing] came out today, which was good. TB was visiting the Dome and got a good reception while Hezza whacked the press for trying to destroy it. It was worth doing, though there was a problem getting there because the Jubilee Line was down. I spent a lot of the day trying to plan out Christmas and the New Year. TB said we needed a clearer political line but getting him, GB and Peter M on the same page wasn't easy. I wrote round to ministers about the [parliamentary] recess plans and also the need for loads of them to be involved through the regions in the Neighbourhood Renewal launch.

Wednesday, December 20

PMQs was the only work thing to worry about apart from a Guthrie speech leading the news, saying that disabled people have no right to be in the military front line. The speech itself wasn't that bad but the media spin was heavy so I had to do a bit of a rescue job and ended up supporting him. Blunkett called me in a total rage about it, but I felt Charles was speaking common sense. I went up to the flat and TB still felt Hague was getting something on crime. TB was currently showing his least convincing side on the irreducible core front. We went over for PMQs. TB wasn't great with Hague but he did use a good line at the end – 'I'm not saying he is racist, I am saying he's an opportunist.' It had been a struggle to get into Parliament because of pro-hunting demos, which needless to say set him off wondering again whether we couldn't get out of it. In his heart, he would like to dump the whole thing. Later I went to the Palace for [the Queen's press secretary] Geoff Crawford's farewell. It was nice to see some of the old royal hacks and photographers, and Geoff was a pretty unstuffy character considering where he worked, but he was in the minority.

TB called me as I was on the way back and said he had been unsettled by the idea of me and maybe Anji leaving after the election. He said he had a very clear idea of what he wanted to do in the second term and he really needed me to be there. He said if I could find someone else he would be happier letting me go, but currently he couldn't see it. GB would be hovering, the press would be after us more than ever and he would need his key people around him. He was also worried that Peter M was having judgement problems. His Christmas card with himself and his dogs [Bobby and Jack] at Hillsborough Castle was the latest little thing to suggest detachment from political reality.

Thursday, December 21

TB was up on adoption, which he wanted to make easier for couples. Good visit, good pictures. Hunting was bubbling away, but things were reasonably quiet and I was winding down a bit. I had a meeting with the Swedish foreign minister to discuss the Swedish presidency [of the EU]. TB was up in Sedgefield. He had been pressing GB for his promised strategy paper but it turned out when delivered to be a series of random ideas and random diary dates.

Friday, December 22

The *Mail* splashed on Prince Charles 'privately' expressing opposition to our position on European defence. As TB said when I told him about it, 'I'd be amazed if he's even looked at what the real proposals are. Mark Bolland [deputy private secretary to the Prince of Wales] will just be trying to get him big licks in the *Mail*.' The Tories were straight on to it. I was talking to the BBC about them doing a feelgood film for our Olympics reception. We held Falkirk, just [by 705 votes, with a 15.9 per cent swing against Labour]. John Reid was cleared by the Standards Committee, who effectively ignored Filkin.

Saturday, December 23

TB called. He felt that the reason we were quite strong at the moment in public opinion terms was that we took the whole show over and got back in control over the last few weeks. GB and I had worked reasonably well together. We had had a proper plan in place and more or less seen it through. But the pace of the media was such that moods could shift very quickly. When we lost energy, we lost momentum and conceded the agenda. Burnley lost at home to Bolton [2-0], three crap results in a row.

Sunday, December 24

I did sixty laps, the most yet, in the pouring rain, and felt knackered afterwards.

Tuesday, December 26

We set off for Chequers, the usual mix of old friends and relatives. TB was on great form. Ditto Charlie F, whose character assessments of ministers could be very cutting but always funny. We played football and then watched Man U beat Villa [1-0]. TB and I went to his study to work through the next phase, he was genuinely worried at the moment that the GB/Peter M situation was irreparable. There was a bad poll of OAPs in *Saga* magazine.[1]

Wednesday, December 27

TB called re whether to go to the Dome or not, one year on, and we were also working through a draft of the New Year's message. I was in two minds as to whether these New Year messages were worth the work we put into them. I suppose at their best they are a free hit during the quiet season, but I could never remember them from one year to the next.

Thursday, December 28

I managed to draft TB's New Year message though it was a bit pedestrian. TB sent through his own ideas and I tried to work them together. We were still going over whether he should go to the Dome. He was also raising the idea of David M becoming an MP, which was probably right for David, but it meant looking for a new head of policy. We were still pushing for a document to set out choices as a vehicle for generating debate and laying down dividing lines.

Friday, December 29

The New Year message just wasn't right. Neither of us could really generate much enthusiasm so it felt a bit tired. GB was pressing to make investment the main message. It may be right. We certainly need something simpler than what we had drafted. TB was also in a bit of dither about whether or not to go to the Dome.

Saturday, December 30

The car was broken into overnight. The cops were terrific but they were all saying how badly stretched they were at the moment. I read the Social Exclusion Unit report on neighbourhood renewal, which

[1] Sixty-nine per cent of pensioners polled by Ipsos MORI said they would be certain to vote in the forthcoming general election, fifty-seven per cent saying they would vote Conservative. Sixty-two per cent said they were dissatisfied with Blair.

was good and had real communications potential. I put a note round the system on it.

Sunday, December 31

TB was getting a bit more geared up after a quiet few days. He said he wanted a meeting next week to go through all the difficult issues, policy, organisation and personnel. He said he intended to say to GB that he wanted him to work with Peter but if they were going to behave like children, it was going to be impossible. He was also getting more concerned on asylum, which was emerging as a big doorstep issue. Heseltine did a big attack on bogus asylum seekers and Mike O'Brien [Home Office minister] used a very tired line, which sounded pathetic, about Hezza being ill informed. In the end, we decided against him going to the Dome. It would make him the whole focus one year on, whereas Cherie could do it and be a bit more downscale. The coverage on the Dome was actually pretty good. PY Gerbeau was doing a good job on interviews. We took the kids to the Dome, and enjoyed it more than I thought I would. If it hadn't been for the dreadful press at the start, it could have gone a lot better. But I would reckon the vast bulk of people there enjoyed it. The atmosphere was good, and the show was pretty good if not totally my cup of tea.

We went to Charlie and Marianna [Falconer]'s to bring in the New Year. TB was on good form, very relaxed, and clearly enjoying showing off Leo who was busy eating lots of salmon. But I was tired and keen to get home. I found these times of year hard, when most people seemed to have loads of time off and loads of fun, yet even on days off I seemed to be dealing with stuff, and the phone was always going. Even tonight there was a steady flow of calls, mainly hacks with nothing to do but follow up rubbish.

Monday, January 1, 2001

The main political story running was the 'mystery £2m donor'. TB called, a bit worried about it. We had to decide whether to shut up shop, or go up front with the name. Michael [Levy] told me we had in fact two of them. The one I knew about was Paul Hamlyn [publisher and philanthropist]. ML was convinced this was MMcD loose talk re donors. I wasn't so sure about that. It wasn't exactly the best way to start the New Year though. We spoke to Paul H who was not at all well, had pneumonia, and said he would think about it overnight. As the pressure built on it, it was another example of the double standards operating against us on this stuff. The Tories could get away with far more on the funding front. TB was worrying it would still be running by the time we got to *Frost*. I took Calum and Grace swimming then went out shopping for Fiona's birthday.

Tuesday, January 2

The funding story having rumbled since Sunday, it now really took off. The *Today* programme was full of it, Clive Soley, Peter Kilfoyle, Glenda Jackson all up saying we had to come clean. Milburn was on and said he had no idea if it was true or not. JP called me to say the position was untenable. Bruce G felt exactly the same. We were still however in the same position, namely that if the person concerned didn't want to be named, there was not much we could do. It was a bit of a mess. JP was working himself up over it, said he wanted to speak to TB and also got on to the party finance director to demand a briefing. He was better once TB spoke to him but it wasn't an easy wicket. And if we ended up with this, the Dome and hunting as the main stuff out of *Frost*, it wouldn't be great. TB must have called six times making the same point, namely we had to make clear there may be others who did not want to be identified. Hamlyn finally called Jonathan to say he was fine being named so I drafted a statement then did a conference call with Hamlyn, Levy and Jonathan. Paul sounded very ill and we apologised on TB's behalf that it had come out like this. He was happy for us to point out that he had cancer, Parkinson's and pneumonia. He made one or two changes to the statement.

I told Andy Marr who was first out with it on News 24 [BBC news channel]. It was fine as limitation but basically a pain in the arse, a crap story about nothing to do with people's lives, Westminster bollocks that would get millions of words about process. There was also a danger we would piss off other donors, and deter new ones. Levy said fund-raising as practised up to now was finished. TB sought advice from GB who simply said he didn't want to be bothered with it. After what happened last time, I don't want to know, he said. It was another 'when the going gets tough' moment. TB said to me later you just have to accept Peter is becoming a bit semi-detached and GB will be fine provided our interests coincided with his. If they don't we'll have to do it ourselves. Once Hamlyn was named, a lot of the heat went out of the situation, but they were now turning it into a big process story. We took the kids to *The Lion, the Witch and the Wardrobe*, and I was in and out dealing with some of the hacks on the funding story.

Wednesday, January 3

The Hamlyn stuff came out fine and it was off the broadcast radar, with meningitis[1] leading the news and petrol prices picking up again. TB was now worrying about the other £2 million donation from [Sir Christopher] Ondaatje [philanthropist] and during the day we were putting pressure on Michael to get him to do what Hamlyn did, which later he agreed to. This was never going to be better than a score draw for us, but the more upfront we were about the donors, the more we could make it part of a narrative about business support. The phone was going, as it had yesterday, and Fiona was getting more and more pissed off and eventually said that the job was now such a massive pressure that it was very hard to live with. She said the problem was I used up so much emotional energy dealing with GB and Peter that by the time I came home, there was no time or energy for a normal life. It wasn't a good scene but I did point out she had

---

[1] Health officials issued a nationwide alert after the deaths of seven people from a strain of the disease.

always known I was driven and obsessive and she also knew if I was going to do the job, I had to do it full on.

She accepted I did as much as I could with the kids, but even with them, there was no escape from the phone, and being at the beck and call of people who always expected me to pick up the pieces. It was kind of reaching crunch point. She was basically saying I had to leave. TB was saying I couldn't and I was genuinely torn. I felt for the first time that I was doing something that both mattered and made a difference, and I knew there were bad knock-on effects. Yet I couldn't envisage how to do it in a way that made a difference without being pretty full on, and staying on top of everything as much as I could.

Thursday, January 4

TB was getting more and more hyper and putting me under more pressure. Fiona was putting on the pressure from another direction. She had talked to CB, who had mentioned it to him, and he was pressing all the buttons – about commitment, about his fear that he'd find it much harder if I wasn't there, above all the appeal of the scale of the challenge. I also knew that Anji was telling him she wanted to go. Fiona and I had dinner with Jamie Rubin and Christiane Amanpour. JR was clear I should get out before the end and have a plan. He said it was obvious to everyone that TB and I had a very special relationship, that there was trust and respect there. 'But in the end, at some point you have to be you. You can't always be an extension of someone else.' He felt TB would be fine about it as long as he knew that I wouldn't go against him and would always be there to help him get re-elected. He had made a very interesting observation about his own time with Madeleine Albright [US Secretary of State], said he was never a hundred per cent sure, even when he was speaking privately, that what he was saying was what he really thought, or what he thought he was meant to think.

Lance [Price] was doing a briefing for the party on our big funders and was clearly a bit nervous. I said that he had to be really bullish, and challenge the Tories to name past donors. It got more complicated because *The Economist*, wrongly, were claiming we were only going up front because they were about to break the story. There was a general worry that Peter M was not really motoring on the Millbank side of things, partly because he was worried about constantly being undermined from elsewhere. We were preparing for a meeting with GB on Sunday to bind him in. Just how much that was needed emerged pretty quickly when we discovered he was doing an interview with *The Times* effectively ruling out across-the-board tax cuts. TB felt we had the basic message and policy positions right but we were still lacking organisational capacity.

It was the familiar cry, and it was right, but I wasn't sure how we dealt with it. He was worried in particular about health. He also felt there was a bit of complacency on the education front. Hunting was still nagging away at him. As ever, we seemed to be clearer on message than on delivery. Pat, Sally and Anji all argued that now everyone knew it was an election year, I should go full-time to Millbank, particularly to focus on Tory attack. TB said no, because that would mean he [AC] couldn't come back. I said that was the attraction and though most of them laughed, he looked down and said again later he wanted me to stay the course. He had done a good note, and it was a good meeting, but the scale of what lay ahead was occasionally a bit petrifying.

Friday, January 5

Working at home, I did a conference call to generate story ideas for *Frost*. I had an eighty-minute chat with TB on the phone. He said to have me and Anji telling him we were thinking of leaving was really unsettling. I said he had to understand the pressure I was under, and also my fear that I wasn't really motoring like before. He said don't underestimate how much of the burden a very small number of us have had to carry. He said most people would kill for your ability, and for the place where you are, and you shouldn't give up halfway through. Fiona had never wanted me to do the job in the first place and yet found every day of her life effectively run by that decision. At the very least she wants a date that we can start to think about as a point of departure. He said he believed things would be easier in the second term because we would be more experienced, it would be much more our mandate, the press would have to see the country had changed. He was clear about the agenda for the second term – public service reform, the euro if the conditions are right, international leadership because there was a vacuum. He honestly didn't know if he would go for a third term. A lot would depend on whether he felt GB could do it. But he felt he would be very exposed if he lost his key people.

He felt both Anji and I gave him something nobody else could. He said the reason he was like a cat on a hot tin roof at the moment was because this was worrying him. He said in the end I can't stop anyone leaving but I would be disappointed if you don't feel a sense of the size of what we are trying to do, get to a situation where something we created, New Labour, could be in power for the next decade and more, and really change Britain. That's such a big thing, do you really want to miss out on that or have people say you were only there half the time? He said I just can't imagine anything sadder than you turning up on *Newsnight* in two years' time talking about what the government is doing, rather than being here doing it. It was a mix of flattery, threat, blackmail, an appeal to my better nature and also his insight that I was committed and wanted to be part of this for the long term. Just as he had made it impossible to refuse in the first place, so he was making it hard to leave.

Saturday, January 6

The BBC were leading on some shit about Robert Bourne [businessman] making a donation to Labour. I told Lance to get out a line that the Tories calling for an inquiry on party funding was like Milosevic calling an inquiry into war crimes in the Balkans. Blunkett called with a few ideas for *Frost*, and also to let off steam about GB doing another New Deal speech without discussing it with him. He said he had done an interview saying the country wasn't ready for a blind PM. What about half blind? TB OK'd my pre-*Frost* briefing on the economy and we phoned round on that.

Sunday, January 7

I went out just after 6 for a run. I got a message to Barney Jones [*Frost* editor] that TB would welcome a question about what he had learned most. TB was keen to get up the message that he preferred to do the right thing rather than be liked. He looked and sounded good and there were plenty of stories out of it – police numbers, teachers' pay, economy the key electoral battleground. I did a ring-round from the car and most were going on the lines we wanted but Kavanagh said he was going to do TB saying he would serve a full term as a snub to GB. TB said the *Sun*'s support was often in word only, that they did an awful lot to try to undermine us. He said there may come a point when he decides to go for them but not yet, and in the meantime I have to do more to woo them, he said. I said I felt it weakened us to be seen to be courting them. Before we were winning them through argument. Now they were behaving like players, wanting to do deals. They had to fear we could damage them more than they could damage us. TB said never forget Machiavelli's rule – don't wound, kill. If you can't kill, don't wound. I took Rory to Fulham vs Man U and met up with Alex beforehand. He was going off on one about the sort of money agents were demanding for players. Man U won 2-1.

TB saw GB who said he hadn't liked the message of the interview, felt it was too static, that economic competence was not a forward message. We then had a much bigger meeting in the study to go through the long-term note TB had done line by line. Though it wasn't perfect, it was superior to the rather brief note GB had done, which was more an annotated diary short on strategic direction. TB was in charge and directed the meeting OK, though as DM said to me, GB's people tended to show neither fear nor respect. The main areas of disagreement were the handling of next steps, the language we use for the Tories and how we attack Hague.

GB felt we had to portray the Tories as extreme. I felt that may be where we end up but for now they should be seen as a joke, hopeless, and we should be making it unfashionable to be associated with them. TB was getting a bit exasperated with Peter, who was explaining why he couldn't really spend much more time at Millbank. But the mood of the meeting was generally pretty good. GB was more engaged than usual, Peter less hoity-toity and TB just stuck to his note and went through it.

Monday, January 8

The *Frost* interview coverage was good and the economic message was out there, which was probably why GB didn't much like it. The *Sun* was good, the *Mail* hostile on virtually every page. In the car on the way in, Philip and I were chatting re our respective family situations. Gail [Rebuck, PG's wife] felt that Peter, Philip and I had all become much harder and as a result our personalities had changed. At the office meeting, Peter was still baulking at the idea of spending more time at Millbank. They all seemed to think I should be leading the attack work on the Tories, and I pointed out that it wasn't possible for me to go there and stay here. TB was questioning the quality of the people round GB. He felt he was hopelessly reliant on Ed Balls who was clever but sometimes lacked judgement. Andy Marr was doing a package on the economy. He had bid for GB and been pushed back, so I sorted out Milburn for him. Interestingly, as I was on the phone to him saying Alan would do it, the Treasury got back to him offering GB. There was a big turnout for the eleven o'clock and I felt strong and confident. I was determined to try to maintain a reasonable humour at these briefings, I met TB re his speech, which he had drafted, I redrafted and then the two of us were trying to work out the positioning. The Tories were out with some new posters and I felt the party was being too reactive, not creative enough with how it dealt with these kinds of things.

January '01: GB's people show no respect

Tuesday, January 9

I spoke to Clare Short, who we wanted to do a speech that would surprise people by being more New Labour. I had forgotten how stressful it was being out on the road with TB, his constant agitation. Got the train down to Bristol. We were warned by the cops that that there was a hundred-strong demo but they would be OK. We arrived, at a college, and were immediately showered with tomatoes. TB was hit by one on the back but he just kept walking. Inside he did a Q&A, toured about and then we left, the crowd having dispersed. He was all for making a joke about tomatoes, but I couldn't see the point. The speech was strong, and the Q&A was tough and he did well. All the main political editors were there, and had to acknowledge he was very good at these events. We got the train back and he was angry at security being so badly organised. He was pretty sure that if we pressed on with hunting, we would be dogged by protesters every-where we went. I still felt that if he tried to do a U-turn on this, the risk was enormous. His big problem with it was that he felt it was basically illiberal, and not him. Despite the tomato, he had enjoyed getting out and about and said he wanted to do more visits outside London. Chris Meyer came to see me re Bush. He said Bush was determined to make every effort with TB. Meyer thought [Donald] Rumsfeld [GWB's Defense Secretary] would be a problem for us and also he wasn't sure whether Condi Rice [GWB's National Security Advisor] would have real clout. He was assuring me that Bush had no interest whatever in helping Hague, that on the one occasion they had discussed it he referred to him as Jim Hague.

Wednesday, January 10

Millbank turned up a good one for PMQs, namely something from a website article by Nigel Hastilow [Tory parliamentary candidate] saying the Tories were basically crap. TB used it to very good and humorous effect and though Hague had one good clip for TV, TB pretty much killed him. Also they were increasingly coming on to our ground, namely investment. I was trying to get Fraser Kemp [Labour MP] in as a part of the Tory-attack unit. I felt there was a real gap that Fraser could fill provided he and I stayed in constant touch. PMQs was fine and the four o'clock was all about the pledges and what damage it would do if we failed to meet the youth justice pledge. I toughed it out but the reality is we must meet all the pledges. Burnley were playing at Man U training ground to give some of Alex's recovering players a run-out. Alex called to tell me we lost 7-1.

Thursday, January 11

I went up to the flat to see TB who was thinking through when best to launch a big economic attack on the Tories. He was not very confident again and said that he thought that I was a bit discombobulated, which I wasn't really, other than by the contrary pressures from him and at home. I was working on the Olympics speech which I wanted to go big. TB took a general-election meeting at which Peter M was very critical of the planning and organisation. TB looked frazzled. He felt our message on the economy wasn't rooted enough in living standards. It was a bizarre period where we seemed to be on the right side of all the arguments yet everyone seemed strangely unconfident. Maybe it was always like this for the party of government in election years. Cabinet was an RW collector's item in that the discussion was almost entirely political. JP even talked about the need to get more propaganda into departments' annual reports.

GB said the Tory plan was deliberately to spread cynicism, to focus on what we have not done rather than what we have. He said we had to fight with facts, show there was progress, show they did not have a key programme. A few of them chipped in but it wasn't a great discussion. It was another prolonged *Today* programme training session, people just trotting out fairly tired views. I took a big meeting on the neighbourhood renewal report, which was pretty strong. On hunting, TB was still trying to think of a way out. One idea now doing the rounds was that it would get blocked in the Lords and we could then put a middle way in the manifesto for the next parliament. Kavanagh said on *Question Time* that the *Sun* would back us again.

Friday, January 12

I went to the agency, where Trevor Beattie presented some really good stuff, including a terrific picture of Hague with Thatcher's hair. TB would be nervous about it but it was funny and he would buy it if we ran it alongside something positive. The recent groups were mixed but there was no doubt we were getting some traction with the Tory attacks. It was a good meeting, I felt if I worked more closely with them, we would make more progress. They had done a fair few focus groups and felt we were in OK shape. I went back to Number 10 where Stephen Lander was speaking to staff on our threats and vulnerabilities. I didn't think he put enough fear into people about e.g. paper security, though he did say we were all potentially targets and that we should all be careful with documents and in our discussions, that there were foreign powers constantly after us, that emails weren't very safe and mobiles were totally unsafe.

Saturday, January 13

It was fairly quiet work-wise. TB and I didn't speak much, though we were both worrying that though the neighbourhood renewal document was strong, there was no obvious thing for the media to bite on. I took Calum down to Gillingham vs Burnley. Crap game. 0-0. The Sundays came. Bugger all in any of them.

Sunday, January 14

The only story out of Hague on *Frost* was challenging TB to a TV debate, which was fairly easy to bat aside. Frost also pushed him on tax and spend and he was pretty hopeless. I did a conference call with Darling, Reid, Douglas [Alexander], Treasury and party people to agree a response we would get out on the airwaves. The best line was that he had nothing to say on policy issues so went for a process media issue. The press could sense we weren't really up for the TV debate. Both TB and I were far keener on the audience participation programmes. The TV debate route would just take us into media self-obsession and legal challenges from small parties. He wanted to turn the neighbourhood renewal speech tomorrow into an attack on governments left and right re inner-city policy.

Monday, January 15

TB said he had been trying to get hold of GB all weekend without success. Peter was still not spending much time at Millbank. Anji and I both told him again he should be looking for a new cadre of people. We finished the speech and set off for Stepney with JP and Oona King [Labour MP for Bethnal Green and Bow]. TB was worrying about the hunting vote on Wednesday and when Jonathan said there was a case for going to Northern Ireland, jumped at it. He was wondering about saying he would vote for the ban but support the middle way if the Lords blocked the bill. The Stepney visit went fine and we had loads of ministers out doing different media. Oona told me she had real problems in her constituency. 'The Islamics hate me because I am a Jew, the whites hate me because I am black. The Bengalis hate me because I am the wrong kind of black.' There were some fantastic people there, especially the woman from the local housing trust and some of the New Deal people. TB seemed to enjoy it. In the car back, he said on TV debates we should just say no and take a hit and move on. We are not America, we have Parliament. Also, we elect parties not just leaders.

Tuesday, January 16

More angst from TB and GB – TB because he thought we were about to take another wave of great hits on public service non-delivery, and GB because he thought we had set ourselves up for every day to be a referendum on us, not a choice on the future. How on earth he thought we could stop the media referring to the context of it being an election year was beyond me, but it was the current mantra. I spoke to Jack S, felt we just didn't have a strong enough big-picture message to blast through the bad individual stories that inevitably came around from time to time. We had a situation where car crime and burglary were being brought under control but all the media focus was on violent crime, and we could not allow the perception to develop in the way it was. We planned for TB to do a police recruitment visit later in the day. TB was still banging on about hunting. The Tories thought he was being very clever and cunning. In fact he was agonising because he did not feel comfortable about the position he was in. You could argue that we would never win the support of most of those who opposed our position, but that we would lose a stack of support if he tried to shift the position back. But he didn't like doing things he didn't instinctively feel were right. Anji was as ever whispering in his ear what all her right-wing friends were saying, and the whole thing was unsettling him. Peter M was pressing for us to go to NI tomorrow. Maybe he wanted to miss the hunting vote too.

Wednesday, January 17

Even though we had trailed it, there was inevitably cynicism at TB heading off for NI on the day of the hunting vote, though we made clear he would have maintained the same position as before – voting for a ban – had he been there. PG had the latest poll in, which was pretty good. GB felt we were lacking message about a forward agenda. TB was worried we had peaked, and also that we were about to take an onslaught on public services. Once we briefed we were going to NI, we decided it was also time to kill the TV debate idea. I was working on a letter to the broadcasters ruling it out. When I briefed on it, they were all pretty sceptical about the arguments, but I was sure it was right just to get it over and done with. I genuinely worried that if we went for it, process not policy would become even more dominant in the election coverage, but they basically felt we were ducking it because it was a risk it wasn't worth the favourite taking. In Belfast we had dinner with the SDLP, who were not at all happy, and clearly felt the UUP were driving our agenda, but it was definitely the UUs' precarious political position that was worrying TB. We then had a meeting with Sinn Fein, who were doing their usual of maintaining they were being reasonable given the difficulties whilst maintaining everyone else was not. TB spoke to Clinton by phone. He said he was happy to do anything we wanted, now and in the future, so long as it didn't cut across anything the Bush people wanted to do, 'Not that I guess they will want to do that much.'

Thursday, January 18

TB said he was really worried, that he had not quite realised how much ordinary Unionist opinon had moved away from us. He had been alarmed by the meeting with the DUP. Even without [Ian] Paisley there, they had been very chipper, cocky even, and he sensed that they sensed things were moving their way. They told him straight out that Trimble was going down the pan and he'd better get used to dealing with them. I didn't like the tone or feel of it one bit. TB now felt that unless there was decommissioning – and that meant product not words – then he feared Trimble was dead, and without him there was no peace process as things stood. He felt that was confirmed by the Alliance [Party] and the women's group, who though not big players were very good barometers. He really was worried, more worried than I had heard or seen him for ages. TB told the Irish it was not good enough for us to be expected to do something on normalisation in Armagh now, whilst all we got from SF–IRA was the vague promise of something down the track. He said we had to get a deal that would help DT. He said without Trimble there was no peace process and no Good Friday Agreement worth saving. He was getting irritated by the way the Irish officials overstated where we were with SF. They were saying what they wanted to be true, rather than what they knew to be true. He said he feared we were going round in circles.

He spent hours with SF, then said to us he wasn't actually sure what they were saying any more. They were pushing for more demilitarisation measures and up to twenty changes to the Patten proposals. The SDLP were nervous about SF getting the political credit for any change. They constantly felt squeezed, and maybe felt they were punished for being reasonable, wheras the UUs and SF got somewhere by shouting louder. TB was trying to persuade the Irish and SF that electoral disaster for Trimble would not be good for any of us. He called me through to a meeting with Adams, McGuinness and Gerry Kelly, who all seemed very relaxed and jolly given the circumstances. TB asked whether we could get away with a meeting at Chequers without the media knowing, and I said of course. We ended up talking about TB's neighbours, and chatted re Jackie Stewart [former Formula 1 world champion] and somehow we ended up discussing whether we liked Des O'Connor [TV entertainer], and Adams said maybe in the absence of anything else concrete to report, I could go out and brief that there was agreement that we all liked Des O'Connor. I said you just like his surname.

I had to fish TB out to meet Ronnie Flanagan and the new GOC [General Sir Alistair Irwin] who had been flown in by chopper to avoid being seen either by the media or SF. TB was very upfront with them about wanting to concede something on the demilitarisation front, provided we got something back, but he also wanted to assure them if they had genuine security concerns, he would not press. I sensed Flanagan was more up for doing something, but this was very tricky stuff. On the flight home, we chatted re Europe. TB was going off Jospin. I stopped by at Philip's on the way home to see the agency efforts on £16bn cuts posters. I spoke to Peter M in Paris and took the piss out of him being there for the Anglo-French colloque rather than doing his real job(s). He said it was important someone flew the flag for a positive European policy. Maybe, but it was also important we got our act together for an election campaign.

Friday, January 19

TB was down at Chequers seeing SF and the Irish, and we were putting together contingency lines. The SF lot were staying at a local pub and they were bound to be seen by someone. It wouldn't be the end of the world, but we were likely to get more done if we could keep it quiet. I was working on the 'next steps' document and also trying to sort Nissan–Corus. I wanted to do Nissan [plans for a new car plant in Sunderland] on Monday, but there was a real problem in that Corus were planning to announce 8,000 job losses on Thursday. Godric briefed me on his up-and-downer with Jack S yesterday, who had refused to go up on the crime bill. Godric said the problem was if I was not there, ministers were less likely to do what we asked them, because he lacked the political clout or the personal relationships. I said we had to work on that, but in any event Jack may have had a point with all that was going on yesterday.

Saturday, January 20

TB was very buoyed up by the talks yesterday which, amazingly, hadn't leaked, even though Gerry etc. were seen in Amersham. He felt they made real progress and felt that if we could pull them off some of their demands on policing, and above all get actual decommissioning, it would be the biggest thing since the GFA itself. Bush's inauguration provided a news sponge for the day, so work-wise things were quiet, though we were planning another possible NI trip on Monday to keep the thing moving. TB was saying if we went we may need to stay to Tuesday too, if we felt progress was being made. He clearly thought yesterday had turned things. Yet again, the lack of the 'crisis talks' spotlight had helped. There were one or two pieces in the press re a new play, *Feelgood*, which was meant to be based on me. TB called after his Chequers dinner which must have been a collectors' item – Bono and Bob Geldof, Jackie Stewart, Polly Toynbee and her dreary bloke [David Walker, also a journalist], John Denham [social security minister], Kate Garvey. He said it was totally surreal, but the real star was Dickie Bird [former cricket umpire], who was singing my praises all night, saying I was a good lad because I stuck with Burnley, and how he was so honoured to be there he would happily have walked all the way from Barnsley. TB said he arrived two hours early and was mesmerised by the place. Dickie asked Bono whether he had had many hits. TB said Bono and Geldof were a good double act, and deadly serious on the policy front.

Sunday, January 21

I went for a run and then was playing tennis at Market Road when I finally got hold of Peter to get a line on the story in the *Observer* that he tried to help the Hindujas get a British passport.[1] He denied it but I could tell he was in a real state. There was something bizarre about the sound of tennis balls getting whacked all around me as I tried to concentrate on what he was saying. He didn't want to talk about that story, but the page 2 story in the *Sunday Times* re him and GB criticising each other. There was something about it that really got to him, which was odd in that there had been a fair few stories like this before. He said 'these people' had destroyed 'half my life, half my career, half my future, and they would not rest until the whole job was done'. He said I had to understand that ultimately it was the prime minister they wanted to destroy and they would stop at nothing to do it. I said the problem was that the media was on autopilot on this. They knew they didn't get on, and so if ever they were short of a story, it was an easy one to do. Peter said what he

[1] It was claimed that Mandelson had helped Srichand Hinduja's application for a British passport. A subsequent inquiry found he had not made representations but by then he had lost his job.

hated was the sense among others – maybe me included – that there was an equivalence, that he and GB were 'both as bad as each other'.

He said he had no desire to destroy GB, but he had no doubt whatever GB was determined to destroy him. He said these stories only appear because GB and his people want them to. Routledge's book happened because of GB, so did Robinson's. I said here we are talking about a page 2 story unlikely to be followed, and nobody knew for sure they briefed it, and he just exploded. He said it was unacceptable to have a group of people determined to destroy him and all I could do was say that it was six of one and half a dozen of the other. He said he did not know when, but he intended to remove himself from the situation before too long. He was basically signalling he had had enough. I tried to pin him down a bit more re the Hindujas, but he just said the story was wrong.

Monday, January 22

Hinduja/Peter M was low-level but had a bad feel to it. The GB morning meeting was dire, him just complaining that everything was terrible and eventually I said there was no point just berating everyone, we had to have an agenda and then drive it through. Far better that we stopped moaning and started fighting and operating properly as a team. As we left, the mood was bad. GB did not lift people at times like this. On the polling, we were fine on state of the parties, and on TB vs Hague, forty-nine to twenty-one, but on issues like asylum, crime, Europe, we were not in great shape, minus twenty-six on asylum, minus twenty-one on Europe, falling back on standing up for Britain. Our numbers on non-delivery and out of touch were also rising. TB made the usual pitch for greater co-ordination, though when GB was in his current mood, I sometimes felt the morning meetings set us back. Peter H was pushing for the big policy plans to be at the heart of a next-steps comms plan, which was right, but were the plans compelling enough? GB didn't like the posters we were planning. It was not a good meeting. This did not feel like the core of an election planning team due to spring into action in a few months' time. TB said afterwards he was going to have to do more not less of the communication because it was clear GB and Peter M were still disengaged.

I didn't do well at the 11, because I think they sensed my worry about Peter M, and I was not sufficiently on top of the detail. Peter had been very dismissive yesterday and I did not follow my own instincts sufficiently to get to the bottom of it. It went on for ages and had a bad feel to it and they clearly sensed something here. Then it emerged that we having said it was all handled by a private secretary, Peter M seemingly did speak to Mike O'Brien about it. So we were heading for a process/handling drama that would have them obsessing. Peter M had been adamant yesterday re non-involvement. The Home Office finally told us of there had been a call with O'Brien at 3.45 and we went into a stack of conference calls, the most important of which was me, Tom Kelly, Godric, Peter M and Mike O'Brien, where I said we had to get all the facts. The position was defensible but not if we were saying different things or the story was changing and we had to get the facts quickly. It was another wretched weekend situation, where departments had not bothered to grip until the next day when things were often too late. I should have done so myself yesterday. TB was adamant we must not let the press create a false firestorm if Peter had done nothing wrong at all. Even if he had pressed for citizenship, there would be nothing wrong with that provided the normal rules and procedures were followed. The problem was the changing line, Peter having first said it was all handled by a private secretary, us sticking to that, but then the Home Office saying there was this phone call. It was not good. I called Peter M to say I was really worried about the Hinduja story and we had to get it sorted. I had a flurry of calls with GB, Austin re the Tories and then Trevor Kavanagh and Phil Webster who had another PG memo.

I got home and went running. As I was heading for home by the track, there was a hell of a noise up on the path and I could pick out four kids kicking shit out of a bloke on the ground. I phoned home to get Fiona to call the police, and as there was no reply tried Switch but they weren't answering either and meanwhile I was thinking about the security advice of not getting involved, and should I just walk by. I started shouting out 'police' in different voices and ran towards them, and they ran off. The guy was badly cut, bruised and shocked but didn't want to go to hospital. I walked with him down to the main road, said he should call the police and gave him a note with my name and number. He looked at it and burst out laughing. What's so funny? 'I really don't like you or your government.' He then launched into a big attack on our youth training policies and I thought this is surreal. I said, let's argue about our record on jobs. OK, he said, I accept you're better than Hague but I'm a Liberal Democrat and I really don't like you. And then he walked away, without so much as a word of thanks. What's more, he really meant it because when the cops called me to take a statement, they said he had even been going on with them about what bad people we were.

There was an odd feeling to the Hinduja story, which on one level was going away but I still feared the damage to be done if it came out later that Peter had spoken to O'Brien. Worse, we had known about it yesterday and indeed Jack Straw and Mike O'Brien both told us they had reminded Peter of the call last week. Jack felt we had to get it out because we were bound to be asked about it. I felt my own position was difficult because inadvertently I had already misled people. TB was worried an admission out of the blue would simply set the touchpaper alight. Peter agreed that we brief that he had asked for all the facts and had not recalled the conversation but Mike O'Brien had. It was a bad scenario and he sounded worried. He was also not consistent, for example trying to say that what he told me at the weekend was consistent with what he was saying now. TB wasn't helping much because he was going into his righteous indignation lather, saying what mattered was whether he had actually done anything wrong, not the press trying to present the handling as wrong. But the fact we had to change our story meant we were going to be lacerated. TB felt it was a classic firestorm and we should not concede. But he had to accept Peter had not given us the whole picture on Sunday, or at the least had been vague and unclear when we were asking for clarity.

The Home Office were useless at setting out the facts clearly. Only when TB was asking for the facts, and Clare Sumner [private secretary, parliamentary affairs] was pressing them, did they start to get going. Peter came over for the Northern Ireland talks and was nervous. The eleven o'clock was not as bad as it might have been, but we were still far from out of it. I did my best to appear calm and controlled but it was going to be grim, as was clear with the BBC now leading on it and by the four o'clock, they were in full cry and the facts were getting lost. Peter was in and out of my office. TB now felt the situation was bad but we had to get the facts out. Peter and I agreed he should do the rounds at Millbank and defend himself, but he opened new loose ends, for example saying he had not forgotten anything, alongside unravelling the Home Office version too. He was strangely detached through the day, almost as if he was talking about someone else, not himself. TB was by now irritated we were having to spend so much time on this, which he said had nothing to do with real people and real lives and yet would get millions of words devoted to it. He accepted it showed a loss of judgement by Peter, who had damaged his chances of a top job post-election. I meanwhile was fed up having to pick up the pieces and draw so much of the blame. This was going to do us real damage. The press could sense how bad it felt. I was up till past 12 briefing people for the morning programmes. I was also sensing that if Peter was moved on, I would be the next target, and I was going to take a hit on this stuff anyway.

Wednesday, January 24

I slept really badly and woke up with a strong sense that Peter was a goner. Though John Reid did a good job on the morning media, I felt there was no way out. I went up to the flat where TB was going through it all. He had spoken to Derry and asked him to look at all the facts and Derry later joined TB, me, Jonathan, Bruce [Grocott] and RW. It was clear that even if there was no problem with the application issue – and Derry was not convinced of that, feeling there was too much information about it in the July 2 memo – there was an insurmountable problem with the stuff about Jack reminding him last week that he had spoken to O'Brien. Jack also told Jonathan and me that Peter's office had called Jack's private office on January 11 to say Peter didn't see why the existence of the phone call had to be acknowledged. Peter had earlier called me and said we needed a chronology of the last few days squaring all the different statements. I said the problem was he did say to me that his sole involvement was via a private secretary and that I had passed that on to the media, as had Chris Smith in interviews based on what I told him. Also, his statement on TV last night, that he hadn't forgotten anything, did not sit easily with what Jack and O'Brien were saying. His friends, particularly Robert Harris [political journalist and novelist] and to a lesser extent Anji, felt I was going for him. I simply said that he had misled us. It was all so piddling in one way but he had made it a big problem because of the way he had allowed us to handle it on Sunday. Again, as on Sunday, he was strangely disengaged but now there was just a hint of panic. He asked if I was still hating my life and I said at times like this, yes.

I said to TB that the worst-case scenario was that he was asked direct in the House whether he had been aware of any evidence that Peter did know about the call. TB would have to say yes. TB spoke to Jack himself and I could tell from his tone of voice was satisfying himself that there were grounds for Peter going. He was asking whether he could stay for the duration of the next part of the process but we all agreed that wasn't possible. Also, whether he should say he was satisfied there was no wrongdoing in relation to the application but in any event we should have an inquiry. That's what we did in the end, and RW got hold of Anthony Hammond [QC, asked by the government to carry out the inquiry]. I was clear we had to get this sorted before PMQs, preferably by the 11. Derry was clear we either had to get rid of him or have an inquiry, or both. The mood was ghastly and it was pretty much curtains. TB said I cannot believe we are going through this again. The guy is finished. Is there nothing we can do for him at all? If not, it's his life over. He also said to me later that GB would feel more emboldened. Peter came to see TB at 10.45. I went in at 10.55 and said I needed a line for the eleven o'clock. Peter said things weren't resolved. He was resisting the idea of going. I said we had to be clear that if any new information came out, for example Jack's call last week, it was curtains, and I feared that was where it would end. TB said can't you just busk your way through it? I said no, I had to have something to say. He and I popped out and agreed I should say Peter was here because TB wanted to establish for himself the facts before being questioned in Parliament.

I did the 11, was as calm as I could be, maybe too calm, because they read from the body language a mix of feeling down and accepting inevitability re Peter going. I hadn't deliberately signalled it, but they sensed something was going on. After a while I said I was no use to them down here, I was better off upstairs, establishing what was happening. I went back up and TB looked absolutely wretched. Peter looked becalmed. TB said he had made clear to Peter he had to go and that though he wasn't sure, over time he would see why it had been necessary. TB seemed much more emotional about the whole thing than Peter. TB was writing what Peter might say. Peter went up to Anji's office to do the same. Up till now, I had pretty much dealt with it like any other difficult handling issue, but seeing him sitting there, looking pale, almost poleaxed, but trying to keep a very brave face on it, I was suddenly hit by how awful the whole thing was. Also there was a line emerging, e.g. via Andy Marr, that what this was all about was a blazing row between me and Peter, that I had said to TB it was him or me. It hadn't been like that, but here I was again, just me and Peter, drafting resignation letters, statements to the press, etc.

Peter was far less emotional than the first time, much more matter-of-fact. I said he was a good thing, and he didn't deserve this happening to him again. He said maybe I did. He was strangely quiet and unmoved, maybe even relieved. We agreed he should be allowed to do Northern Ireland Questions and we went round to my office with Tom Kelly to prepare for that. In between I was backwards and forwards to TB to agree lines and letters and help him prepare for PMQs. Peter finally went out to the street to face the media. It was windy and his hair was flapping about but he was pretty dignified and his fears that he would fall apart were unfounded. Fiona and Cherie came into my office to see him, and again he seemed strangely unmoved. In the House, Hague was too shrill and misjudged it. Because it had been Northern Ireland Questions, Peter was on the front bench alongside TB and only now I think started to realise this was probably the last time he would be there. The four o'clock was packed, standing room only, and I think I did OK. I tried to kill the stuff about Peter and I falling out. TB wanted to do interviews but I felt the stuff in the House was better than any interview, and he could always do more tomorrow.

We now had to work on the reshuffle, John Reid to NI, Helen Liddell to Scotland. Brian Wilson was really unhappy about it. In the end, TB got Hain to move to DTI and Brian into Hain's job. In all of the calls, TB said it was a tragedy for Peter M, that he had paid a terrible price for a small sin. Peter called me from the airport and was perfectly nice. There was a delayed reaction to come, I was appalled at Robert Harris going on TV effectively saying I had pushed him out. GB was advising TB to use the cover of the reshuffle to get me to go to Millbank, which was positive on one level, but TB was still worried it would make it impossible for me to go back after the election. There was a real sense of vengeance in the media, Peter getting his comeuppance. TB said Hague would regret being as lowlife as he had been today. TB said he was heartbroken for Peter but now we just had to pick up and move on. Peter H said I must get Tony to look a little less like his child had been run over by a bus. PG, as ever looking for the bright side, said maybe now GB would start working properly with us. I had my doubts. The only good thing out of today was people saying we had acted decisively, but by the time I got home, I felt drained and low, and Rory and Calum were both sad for Peter.

Thursday, January 25

Papers totally crucified Peter as expected. There were loads of predictable inaccurate pieces about me being the assassin. TB said all we could get out of this now was a sense of government as normal straight away. Peter, having slept on it, was now feeling a sense of injustice and was penning a self-defence that was wrong. At Cabinet, TB opened by saying there would a political Cabinet on Tuesday, and there then followed a totally political Cabinet anyway. He dealt with the Peter business fairly quickly, said it was a tragedy for Peter, serious for the government, but provided we moved on quickly, and got back on to the fundamentals, we would not sustain lasting damage. I was always struck at how quickly Cabinet business returned to normal, got over the shock of something like yesterday.

I decided to use the eleven o'clock to get up a business as normal kind of message. Rory was in and sat in at the back, started laughing when I went at Nick Robinson earlier, said the Hammond Inquiry was not being done for the convenience of him going out to blather breathless rubbish in the street. TB was heading off to Tyneside and did a few clips, on much the same message, if more politely. I was worried that my profile was going to be up again. Sky were running a piece again and again. I spent most of the day talking to various ministers doing interviews. I felt I had not done as well this week as I should have done, that I should have picked up on Sunday with the way Peter was deliberately distracted by the GB stuff and skating over the thin ice of the Hinduja story. I had too much on, and hadn't focused properly. If we had been thinking properly, we should have found a way to get out the facts re the Jack calls as soon as we knew. As I was running later, up on Kite Hill, Jack called to say *The Times* had asked whether he spoke to Peter re the PQ [parliamentary question] and he was minded to say yes. I agreed. It sent Godric into a real stew. He feared it would end in a dreadful situation for me, but I felt we just had to get all of this out there and done with. The Sundays would be in meltdown. I did a conference call with Jack and advisers to pin down all the lines we needed for the Sundays.

Friday, January 26

Another bad night on the sleep front. The press had now moved on to Keith Vaz, who was accused of all manner of things.[1] TB disagreed with me and Jack re our approach of getting out the stuff about Jack speaking to Peter. I said it would be a disaster if it came out as a new fact. Through the day, we had a series of conversations about whether to divulge or not. He and I were in favour of disclosing both that Jack spoke to Peter pre the PQ, and that Jack's revelation to us had been what tipped it towards being a resignation issue. But Derry, TB and Richard Wilson were all in favour of saying the inquiry would establish the facts and leave it at that. TB was more worried about Vaz, though again felt a lot of it was media nonsense. I chaired a handling meeting and made the mistake of mentioning the JS/Peter call, and became worried it would come out not on our terms.

Peter then called on the mobile and said his ex-assistant private

[1] The minister for Europe was also accused of assisting the Hinduja brothers.

secretary, Emma Scott, had called him and said she was absolutely sure that it was she who spoke to O'Brien's private office, she did not recollect Peter speaking to O'Brien and therefore she vindicated his account. He had recovered himself, and was now convinced he was the victim of an injustice, not the perpetrator of a resignation-worthy mistake. He said there had been funny business at the Home Office and he intended to speak to Richard Wilson. He had been treated unfairly, his career and his life had been destroyed and he had to get his side of the story out. He said it was possible that everyone was telling what they thought to be the truth. There were funny things going on at the Home Office, but I couldn't ignore what Emma Scott was saying. He said I had a responsibility to sort it out. I said I had thousands of things to do. He said this is my life, my reputation, my future and you have to grip it because nobody else can. I said this was why I hated my life, because everyone told me only I could grip these things, but how was I to make sense of the conflicting stories, the Home Office clear there had been these calls, him denying it, not recollecting fairly recent events. I said I will try, but he had to understand why it was difficult. I had taken the call at Alison's desk, and it was becoming embarrassing because there were people walking in and out, and he started to sob down the phone, please, please, please help. This is my whole life being destroyed and I don't know why. I have not been wicked. He said he got something wrong but was it really such a bad mistake? He said he was in there seeing Tony and he hadn't even marshalled all the facts, then you come in saying you have to have a line for the wretched eleven o'clock, a bunch of total bastards, and we didn't have all the facts, hadn't examined all the facts, and on that basis I am destroyed. You have to believe me, please believe me, I've been telling the truth. I said OK, I'll try but please understand the pressures I am under. He said he was desperate. We had pushed him out and he was a dead man. Jack Straw's version was wrong.

He then called Derry and RW, both of whom called me to say they were worried enough to want to shut Jack up. We had various calls on it ending at 8pm with TB, Jonathan, Jack and I agreeing we should just say the Home Office handled it properly and we would now leave things to the inquiry. We got Richard to ask Hammond to make clear he did not want potential witnesses to give interviews whilst he was conducting the inquiry. Peter agreed to that and also said he was thinking about his future. TB had said to me Peter might not stand again but when I put that to Peter, he said it was nonsense. I said he definitely needed a break from it all, but he was talking about fightback. TB felt I was being too brutal with him and that as a result

Peter had refused to take our advice. He had to feel we were on his side. The Sunday lobby was the usual crap, going over and over the same questions. Again though, I didn't handle it well and inadvertently gave them the idea that Peter had been a bit mad. Peter called late in the evening and was very different to earlier, calm, friendly, asking about the kids.

Saturday, January 27

TB called, having just spoken to Peter, who was now really angry, believed we had forced him out without allowing him to put a case. TB said he was genuinely worried about how far he might go, that he really felt deeply aggrieved. There were still a lot of difficult questions in this. TB felt that Peter had a case in saying we hadn't properly marshalled the facts, if it hadn't been Peter, and we lived in a different country without our mad, wretched media, Peter might still be in government. I still felt we couldn't square the different versions of events. TB called to say Peter had sent an article to the *Sunday Times* and we should be careful not to get into a slanging match. The Sundays were taking my briefing yesterday as me attacking Peter, and Godric and I were ringing round trying to calm it down. Andy Marr called and said he felt Peter's article damaged him more than us.

We were having a birthday party for Audrey [Fiona's mother], and I had asked Peter to come round. To our amazement, around half nine, he and Reinaldo arrived. Shortly afterwards, the papers arrived, full of stories about me and him being at war. Rory took a very funny picture of the two of us reading papers with big headlines about us being at war. Some of his oldest friends, like Chris and Illtyd,[1] were there, but partly because he had not been so close recently, they weren't as sympathetic as they might once have been. But he was on pretty good form considering the nightmare he had been through, and was very nice to Audrey. Given how bad the Sundays were, it was not unhelpful for us to be able to put out a line saying that far from being at war, he had been here for a family birthday party.

The problem was I had said he was curiously detached and had been unfocused and for the tossers of the Sunday lobby, that was enough for them to flam it up as me saying he was off his trolley. We didn't really discuss his *Sunday Times* article. Some of them were amazed at his nerve in being there at all. They arrived just as Grace and some of her cousins were doing a dance and so had to stand and

---

[1] Christopher Downes, theatre dresser, and Illtyd Harrington, former chairman of the Greater London Council.

watch, while loads of the other guests were muttering about them being there. But the boys were very nice to him and having a laugh, particularly once the papers arrived. He asked me why I said he was detached, I said because he was, but I shouldn't have said it to that lot. It was a surreal evening. TB was at a Holocaust memorial event and called on his way home. He too was surprised that Peter had turned up, but on balance he felt it was a good sign. We actually spoke very little about recent events and he seemed to want to talk about other things and be with other people. Reinaldo said they were just about coping but it was hard.

Sunday, January 28
The broadcast media were still talking about little else and there was endless stuff about my relationship with Peter. I felt I had to do something to correct the dreadful coverage of my Sunday lobby briefing, 'Number 10 knifes Mandelson' kind of thing. I put together a statement after an early morning run making clear I had been misrepresented. The truth was I should not have got involved in their amateur psychology games. I called Peter and he too felt they were worse in the cold light of day than when we had first seen the papers last night. He said he was determined to rebuild his reputation. He repeated that there had been funny stuff going on at the Home Office. TB, Jonathan and I had a conference call. TB felt it was all going to move to questions about me and Peter, and they would also be piling in on Vaz. He said Peter was in a dangerous mood and would be assuming we were advising him for our purposes not his. TB said he intended to have very sharp words with Richard Wilson on the quality of factual material that came back from departments. TB was clearly beginning to doubt whether he should have gone. He said it may have been he genuinely forgot, and it may be it was O'Brien who placed the call, and a private secretary who made the enquiry.

Monday, January 29
The broadcasters were desperate to keep the story going. There was reams of AC/Peter stuff. I had the cameras filming me leaving home. Philip felt Peter had just lost it in recent days, and would now move against us unless he felt we were genuinely advising him in his own interests. TB felt it remained a difficult situation, which we had to close down as best we could. We must not play the games the press wants us to play. Re Vaz, Jonathan felt we should simply, even on that, be saying leave it to the inquiry. TB's worry was that our opponents would just create a massive fog around this, and nothing else

the government is doing gets seen. Godric and Hilary came to see me before the 11, said I must try to keep my cool, not attack the press, shut it down, refuse to engage. I must have been OK because afterwards they were complaining they couldn't take the story on. Brilliantly boring, Godric said. TB took a meeting on next steps, which was obviously more important than ever. The agency did an excellent presentation to TB. He laughed out loud when he saw Hague with Thatcher's hair. He left for Germany feeling a lot happier about things.

Tuesday, January 30

The Peter/Hindujas stuff was dying down a bit though the *Mail* led on MI6 advice that we should have rejected their application, which was crap but impossible really to deny because of our usual line. Godric and I put together a jokey line to deal with it. Robert Harris was all over the place and several other commentators taking the same line against me. At GB's meeting, the issue wasn't even raised, GB still pressing to bring forward next steps and saying we had to respond to the Tories trying to change strategy from tax cuts to public service reform. Philip and I were getting more and more irritated by the indecision of these meetings, the constant moaning and the desire to plan strategy according to what we wanted to be the case rather than what was the case. Philip said the groups were not that bad. TB said he had had a terrific time with Schroeder.

The political Cabinet was good. TB was on form, went through his note, strong forward strategy and dividing lines, and the contributions round the table were much better than usual. TB said the Tories were fighting a back-door strategy, using the *Mail* in particular to spread as much cynicism as possible, trying to depress the vote while getting their own core vote out. We had to emphasise – 1. progress made through choice not chance, 2. substantial improvements, 3. we understand the major challenges ahead, 4. people will be personally better off under Labour, 5. unchanged Tories unfit to govern. He said as well as winning the intellectual arguments we have to win on vision and values. GB made much the same point, and said we have to avoid the daily debate becoming a referendum on us. Blunkett and Robin both said it wasn't enough to focus on achievement, but we had to show we better understood the future. Although there was nothing much to brief out of it, I felt the mood was better than usual, and also that their instinctive feel for arguments was better. The stuff about me in the papers must have been worse than I felt it to be, because everywhere I went people were commenting on it. I suppose if I thought about it, I was getting a lot of stick and because it was usually

January '01: Blair calls for victory on values

me that organised people to stand up for people getting stick, there was nobody really standing up for me.

Wednesday, January 31

For PMQs, we worked on Vaz, Peter M etc. I sent Richard Wilson a note saying TB didn't like his draft note to the select committee on me, which as drafted would be spun as a reprimand. TB was more of a mind to tell them [the committee] to get lost. GB's meeting had been the usual angst. I later sent him an angry letter because the crime plan, long in the Grid, was going to clash with his 'children's initiative'. His hair was wild. Late pm I had a meeting with Tessa [Jowell] and [Baroness] Margaret Jay who were both worried that the language dominating political discourse was alienating women voters.

Thursday, February 1

I wished I hadn't sent the letter to GB. It was perfectly sortable, and another sign I was just not on top of my game at the moment, and making bad decisions under pressure. I had a meeting with SpAds to try to steady the ship a bit and give them a sense of where we were going. TB was very tired at the GB strategy group meeting. I felt tired and unmotivated and sensed that GB really was motoring now. TB said we had to understand that GB was far and away the most talented politician of his generation and probably he would be a good prime minister. I said he was obsessive and lost focus because of it. TB said he believed his three key people, GB, Peter M and me, all had touches of genius and touches of madness about them. Of all of us, he said, he was the most normal. Anji had told Sue [Nye, GB aide] not to show my letter to GB, which was good news.

Friday, February 2

Richard W was in a complete tizz over an article saying that we were riding roughshod over him. Jonathan and I tried to explain to him that this is what our opponents do, present anyone who works for us in any capacity as being somehow politically corrupted, and he had to ignore it. TB was quizzing me about going, said that Anji was determined to go some time after the election but there was no way I could leave. I said he may not have finished his job but I felt I had done the bulk of mine. He said I was like an alter ego, that we had done it together and he couldn't believe I didn't want to see it through. I said I had to get a life back outside. We then got a message from Peter M about another *Sunday Times* article. TB felt sympathy would drain from him if he carried on like this. The press were using Peter's departure to talk up GB again. TB said he would happily hand over once he felt he had done the job he had set out to do.

When we got back, RW was still in a real tizz about the article saying he was becoming a poodle. I agreed he should do a letter making clear he had pointed out the limits of my role. I wasn't too bothered about a 'reprimand' story but TB was adamant we shouldn't have that. I felt we needed to give Richard something he could point to. He sent a revised draft down which Jonathan and I agreed even though we knew it would lead to a rash of 'Campbell rebuked' headlines and the Tories going for me again. So what. I felt for TB at the moment. Peter M gone, me under pressure to go and not performing at my best, Anji going, GB rampant. The twin pressures, one set at work, another at home, were doing my head in. Fiona felt the problem was my basic perfectionism, that if things weren't happening entirely on my terms, I wasn't happy. So at work, I kept taking on things I thought needed to be done, without regard for the knock-on effects. Kosovo was the worst example, she said. For four months, I might as well not have been here.

Saturday, February 3

We got OK coverage for TB's speech. He insisted I did nothing all weekend and today I managed to avoid too much work. I had a quick run before setting off for Crewe vs Burnley. There was evidence of a Peter M 'fightback' including a 'leaked memo' which purported to show Mike O'Brien could not recall the phone call. There were also lots more Vaz stories but as yet nothing that was lethal.

Sunday, February 4

I dreamt that I had my left leg blown off in a bombing, and at the hospital where I was being treated, they didn't allow family visits. They said they only made exceptions for people who could sing like Barry White![1] Work-wise it was quiet again, with Milburn up on organ transplants. Philip had spoken to Peter who was by all accounts still very much on edge and determined to prove he had been wronged. We went out for dinner with Tessa [Jowell] and David [Mills, her husband], which was perfectly nice but I was conscious of not being on form.

Monday, February 5

The papers were in full cry on Vaz and most of us had a sneaking feeling it would end in tears. But with Robin C having stood up for

[1] Gravel-voiced singer, nicknamed 'the walrus of love'.

February '01: Mandelson fights back

him yesterday we had to do the same today so I was very dismissive and curt at the 11. Any positive agenda was just being submerged at the moment. Peter Hyman, who had been working for weeks on next steps, was exasperated with TB, said he was showing no leadership, even hinting he would drop Thursday's speech if it wasn't big enough. He wanted to do meritocracy as the big idea, both Bruce and I felt he was tilting at windmills, for example re modernising comprehensives, he was saying schools have to stop treating all children the same, which they don't. It was all geared to a right-wing prism so a bit depressing. PH said that while GB was powering ahead with a real values-based agenda, TB looked like he was the pragmatic manager of different day-to-day problems. Forget what we knew, said Peter, GB was doing well on the economy, had a message on society and was delivering, had taken over debt and Africa. He looked like someone with vision and drive whereas TB was drifting, looked and sounded destabilised, felt isolated re Peter M and let down by the Civil Service.

It was an interesting take, and at TB's office meeting, it did strike me how much he was currently focusing on short term, day to day. He knew he wasn't on form but said he would get through it. He said the *Mail* was now beyond parody but I said it had been a huge strategic error to drop Mailwatch. What had we gained from trying to court or neutralise them since the election? Nothing. Page after page every day doing the Tories' dirty work for them. And because there was no concerted message out there about the *Mail*, they still had a disproportionate influence over the rest of the media. TB was really looking for big impact from the next-steps plan, and I took a couple of meetings on that, but I wasn't motoring.

Tuesday, February 6

I got woken at 3.30am by someone saying they were the IRA and there was a bomb in the house. I ignored it, but then couldn't get back to sleep. The Tories got a bigger hit than they should have done out of their savings press conference yesterday [Shadow Chancellor Michael Portillo announced the Conservatives would scrap income tax on savings for people on low and middle incomes, as part of £8 billion tax cuts]. I was worried the *FT* seemed to take it seriously, while the GB response was attacked as being too complex. I felt we hadn't really hit them hard enough on £16 billion cuts [to public spending]. I couldn't get properly involved in Millbank. The team was certainly not gelling. Pat McF and Lance lacked authority there. GB's lot spent far too much time moaning about what was wrong rather than coming up with ideas to put it right. I was working with Jeremy to push the Treasury for £18 million to announce free criminal record checks for charities and voluntary groups for Blunkett tomorrow.

TB took a meeting with JP, DB, JS and Alan M to go through how we needed to use the [Labour Party] spring conference as a big next-steps event. It was an instructive meeting because in different ways, all of them complained of constant second-guessing by GB and the Treasury. When they were talking about the problems of public sector recruitment and retention, Alan said it was the first proper discussion they had had on it. Blunkett complained how he would discover GB's plans for education spending the day before they were announced, when everyone knew it was too late to change anything. JP made a joke about how GB was becoming the new warrior for regional assemblies. 'Yep, the plates have shifted.'[1] The clear unspoken message was that TB had to get a grip of the Budget. I said to TB afterwards that I heard what he said about us being nice to GB and talking him up, but it would be nice if there was a bit of give back. At the moment, GB was courting the right, and TB said he didn't mind if that helped ensure a Middle England Budget. He said it wasn't in our interests for people to think we were fazed by GB.

I left for the Savoy where I was doing a lunch and Q&A. Tim Bell [Lord Bell, former public relations adviser to Margaret Thatcher, chairman of Chime Communications] was incredibly flattering in front of all the others, while the guy who said thanks at the end was equally fulsome, said I had elevated communications to a new level, was the best in the business. It was mainly New Media people and a few advertising executives. I quite enjoyed it because they were serious people, actually more interested in politics than the political press.

Wednesday, February 7

We were one day away from the next-steps launch and still unclear about some of the basics. I had worked till late last night on a script. TB called as I was leaving home to go through PMQs. He thought Hague would do something on married couple's allowance to screw us up tomorrow. He felt Hague was striking a chord recently, and he was slightly spooked. He was fretting we did the wrong thing re Peter. Philip and I went to see GB who was arguing there had to be

[1] Prescott would revisit the phrase in 2004 in relation to Blair and Brown, when he was quoted as saying 'The tectonic plates appear to be moving' in relation to Blair's leadership and Brown's succession hopes.

a big policy story tomorrow, that it couldn't just be process. The problem was getting agreement on what we put up in lights. He was keen for TB to do university access. I wanted GB to do that on Friday but he was pushing to do his own thing. Meanwhile, he had seen my angry letter on the crime plan and sent back a perfectly polite reply. TB was beginning to doubt whether we were ready for the next-steps agenda. He seemed a bit scared of his shadow again. In meetings, I noticed Douglas trying to be more assertive, but the way he looked was a real problem for him. He looked so young, almost boyish. We were all pretty sure Hague would do savings tax but in the end he did EMU, to pretty devastating effect. We had a group of seven to go through an outline plan for the election broadcasts. We still couldn't get agreement on what policy meat to put in tomorrow.

TB having said at PMQs that there would be an assessment on the euro within two years had really got everyone going. It meant that at the briefing after PMQs I struggled a bit to get them interested in the speech briefing. TB knew he had fucked up and as I was briefing, my pager was going endlessly with messages to call him and GB. The sceptics would use it to say basically we were going in and we would rig the referendum. We were never going to convince anyone it was a great strategy but it had happened and we had to be relaxed about it. The *Sun* were gearing up to say this was the clearest sign we intended to 'kill the pound'. Peter M called me and was asking me to go over old conversations we had had. He was clearly putting together a case.

Thursday, February 8

GB needless to say was in a mild rage re the euro, said it had not been sensible to expose ourselves to the next line of questioning and we had to close it down again. He looked at me and said I had to get more discipline into the operation or we would be in real trouble again. In truth, TB had been surprised by Hague going on the euro and so hadn't thought through fully the consequences of saying what he did. But at least we were back on him and difficult decisions for the future, not the rubbish and personality stuff. I bumped into CB and said we had to get more oomph in him, get him worrying less about the *Mail*, the *Sun*, what GB's up to, more confident, more himself.

At Cabinet, they came very close to having a real discussion about the euro but GB made very clear he wanted it shut down, and between them they managed to stop a big divisive debate opening up. In the end, though the assessment was key, we were talking about a political decision here. Robin did a bit on the US, and there was an OK discussion on next steps. I wanted GB to do a big follow-through interview tomorrow post TB's speech but he was convinced all he would get was Europe and the euro and so he wouldn't do it. We had pretty much had the final [next steps] speech for the 11.30 briefing so I briefed loads of it and then had to get Marr off the line that it was Old Labour. He later said the language was left wing and the politics were right wing.

In the car up to Enfield [Southgate, symbolic of the 1997 victory, where Stephen Twigg unseated Michael Portillo], TB was trying to persuade me of his idea for a revamped Prime Minister's Office with three big departments. Jonathan looking after policy and what you might call government issues, Anji doing politics and people, and me in charge of communications. I felt he was trying to revamp systems according to people and in the case of two of the three, it was not clear we would be staying. That was something he was not even acknowledging now. Also, though Anji had many skills, she was seen as being of a very particular strain of Labour, namely his. He would be lucky to hold on to Sally if she was meant to be a subordinate. On Hammond, TB was hoping that we would end up in a position where it was clear Peter didn't lie but he had been responsible for creating a real muddle. According to Charlie [Falconer], Richard W's basic line was that we panicked. The speech venue was good, a terrific new school, and he delivered it well.[1] The audience got a bit agitated when Laura Trevelyan [BBC journalist] did her two-way at the back whilst he was still speaking, which captured their self-importance. As a launch, it was fine, but the follow-up would dictate whether it was a success or not. Meanwhile, Peter M was putting his version of events all over the place.

Friday, February 9

We got good coverage last night for the speech but now Peter M blew us out of the water. He had been to the *Telegraph* and the *Mail* yesterday and they went big on it, including the idea that he could be a European commissioner. Added to which Peter was also setting up a bit of a circus in Hartlepool. Apart from the Special Branch guys, he seemed

---

[1] Blair said 'The first phase of New Labour was essentially one of reassurance – we weren't going to repeat the economic mistakes of the past; trade unions would be treated fairly but without favours; there would be no old-style tax and spend . . . [now] it is time for a second phase of New Labour, defined less by reference to the old Labour Party, than by an agenda for the country, radical but firmly in the centre ground, the ground we have made our own in the past few years, as our opponents have drifted sharply rightwards.'

February '01: Peter M for Europe, say papers

to have nobody looking out for him and at the moment the more he did, the worse he made it for himself, particularly in putting out partial and different versions of events. When we got to Cahors [France, Anglo-French summit], TB was adamant we should not engage, just be nice about Peter and refer all questions to the inquiry.

TB was more worried about the summit, with the politics between us and the Germans, and between the Germans and the French, in something of a state of flux. Neither Chirac nor Jospin were comfortable with what Schroeder was saying on integration. Chirac also made several rather eccentric tirades against various African leaders, then a real onslaught against our aid and development policy. For once, I found myself on the same side of an argument as the absent Clare Short. Congo was his big friend and he felt we were destabilising there. Then he turned on Michael Jay, saying that the embassy were constantly briefing against France re immigration and asylum and 'it's bad and it has to stop'. Jay was genuinely angry, later asked Catherine Colonna for chapter and verse and she apologised, said it was a bad thing to say and some days he was like that.

The really tricky stuff was defence, where they pretended they agreed, but TB pointed up the real ambiguities in their position. Chirac attacked the Americans on NMD [National Missile Defense] and then said the same at the press conference, about how the sword will always beat the shield. At the meeting, TB warned that there would be people within the American administration not as well disposed as others to European defence. He said he intended to persuade them that it was positive, but we must watch out for the strong voices in Washington who would try to cause trouble. Chirac, slightly damning with faint praise, said there were some areas where the UK had to be a leader in Europe and defence was one of them. There was also an unspoken tension over the different interpretations of NATO's role. He was very fiery all day. Jospin was also in an odd mood, wanted to talk politics but went very shy if any of Chirac's people were around.

They had a tricky discussion on immigration, and the need for us to have each other's officials properly working on each other's transport networks. TB felt Chirac was a man under pressure and beginning to look his age. He had another difficult phone call with GB on teachers' pay and the writing off of student debt. They were in pretty much pre-Budget skirmish the whole time. The food served at the lunch was exceptional even by their standards, particularly the sweet, and I left feeling overfed and tired. The plenary was over pretty quickly and we agreed to try to play down a big bust-up on defence, an agreement broken by Chirac straight away with his big attack on NMD. TB looked embarrassed to be having questions about Peter. On the flight back, TB said he felt there was a big opportunity with Schroeder at the moment and we needed to build up relations further. I got back to find the news leading on Peter with TB's visit third, even though there was nothing new on Peter. The Tories did a U-turn on pensions, saying they would give people 'choice' on what they wanted to do with their money.

Saturday, February 10

TB spoke to Peter again and said he feared he was on the edge. If we were speaking to any media, we should be nice about him. We agreed to try to get someone saying that we understood why he had to try to clear his name. Tim [Allan, former special adviser] called saying that Peter had asked him to do it and what did I think about him making clear to the *Observer* Peter didn't want to damage anyone, but he did want to clear his name. It was crazy that Peter couldn't phone me himself. My worry was that in the current circumstances, it was impossible for us to do or say anything on this without it becoming a big thing. Nor did I think it could be doing him any good with Hammond. I felt he should go back to his original statement and his desire not to be the focus of all these stories of division. TB for example had been clear in recent days we may have done the wrong thing, but said the longer we saw behaviour like this, the more he thought we probably did the right thing. Peter eventually called me when I was out for a run. He said he hadn't intended the *Mail* and the *Telegraph* to do big stories and he hadn't intended for yesterday to be a great circus. I said none of us could control these things at the moment but things would only calm down if we said nothing at all. I agreed he should say to the *Observer* he meant to harm nobody in the Labour Party but it was important he defended his reputation. It was like he couldn't stop being the focus of a one-man soap opera.

Monday, February 12

TB had a perfectly good speech planned for the education summit but it wasn't really flying. I gave it a bit of a lift by saying the day of the bog-standard comprehensive was over, little realising how high it would fly after that. Philip and I drove in together and he said we really had to get moving, that the entire operation was being run on largely dysfunctional bilateral relations. TB/GB, GB/AC, even at times TB/AC, while Peter was now effectively out of it. Also Douglas and Margaret McDonagh were not getting on. She and Waheed [Lord Alli,

February '01: Peter M trying to clear his name

Labour peer] were of the school that thought we had forced Peter out and that his departure meant we would lose sight of the election. TB was still confident that we could pull it all around for the election. TB was worried that I was offside and under strain again. I certainly felt we weren't motoring, was down on GB and several others. I had a series of meetings with departmental teams on various big things coming up. But I didn't feel I was anywhere near my best form.

TB was still pushing me re his new office plans. I said I still wasn't sure I wanted to stay. 'I can't believe you said that,' he said. He said he agreed I should keep pulling back from direct contact with the press, that I was too big a figure to be doing it every day because I was seen as doing it in my own right rather than as his spokesman. He felt we needed to get a civil servant doing it while I did strategy. I went with Margaret and Waheed and Lance to the *Express* where [Richard] Desmond did most of the talking on their side, including the occasional pop at his editors, deferring only really to [Desmond's editorial director] Paul Ashford, his rather quietly spoken sidekick. We did a fairly good pitch about how our political objectives – staying ahead of the Tories – could mesh with their commercial objectives – going after the *Mail*. Eventually Desmond clapped his hands and said right, it's war, Labour against Tories, us against the *Mail*, let's go for it. Hope vs cynicism, I said. They were a pretty uninspiring bunch but if they summon up the confidence to go for the *Mail*, they would do everyone a service. Philip said the [focus] groups were a bit grim at the moment, particularly women. The Tories had definitely been noticed recently.

Tuesday, February 13

My 'bog-standard comprehensive' comment got the schools story up rather larger than I intended. TB pointed out that he had used it before and nobody batted an eyelid. It was the headline in several papers and on TV it was a debate about where the phrase bog-standard came from. There was a terrible irony in me being the one who said it, as the one who was constantly defending comprehensives, and going at TB about it. I had also been the one always defending Blunkett. Andrew Adonis [education policy adviser] told me DB was going to denounce the comment if asked about it, which he would be. All I had been trying to do was make a point in favour of modernised comprehensives, with the emphasis on both parts of that. But it was too colourful a phrase for them not to turn into an attack. Blunkett was very pissed off, wrote me a pained letter saying his job was difficult enough and this didn't help. I apologised to him when he came over for a meeting with TB. It was going to be very tough to get it back on the terms we intended. Philip felt at least we had a message up about schools.

TB had another good meeting with relevant ministers on the spring conference and the various policy areas we could get up as next steps. He didn't do nearly enough of these meetings of small groups of ministers binding them together around politics and themes. I took Jack Straw aside at the end and said I was surprised Hammond hadn't asked to see me, and so was he. He felt it was vital I gave evidence.

Later Richard W came to see me. He was really upset at one piece by Hugo Young [*Guardian*] and another by [Edward] Heathcoat-Amory [*Daily Mail*]. He even said he wasn't sure he could take much more of this kind of criticism. I said 'Oh come on, it's only a couple of articles, it's nothing compared to what some of us are used to,' and he said he had 500,000 people in the Civil Service to worry about. He then said, astonishingly, that I had never suffered articles like these, and he held them up. I said I had had books' worth of it, but that's not the point, they are doing it to undermine your confidence in yourself and in us, and don't let them. We also discussed my future. He said he knew TB wanted me to stay and he knew I had reservations, so he would like to help find ways of making my life better and organising my time so I could be at home more. I said the problem was TB couldn't change the way he worked, and nor could I change the way I work.

The truth was I was totally split – a large part of me wanted to leave, a large part wanted to stay. The bit that wanted to stay was the bit that sometimes I felt stopped TB from being rolled over by GB. He felt too I should stop being the spokesman and be more strategic, stay lower profile if possible, though he said the press will never let go of you as a story. Even though Richard would never fully be one of us, I felt I could talk to him very openly about this stuff, and that when he said he wanted to help, he meant it. Nor did I mind when he pointed out where he felt I overstepped the mark, because truth be told, from time to time I did.

I had a meeting hosted by [assistant director of BBC news Mark] Damazer with some of the key programme editors. I switched the venue from Millbank Tower to 4 Millbank [Westminster broadcasting centre] because I didn't want a story running that I held meetings at Millbank. It was a perfectly friendly discussion though they wanted to know about access, notification times, logistics. And I was making my point about the excessive use of two-ways [broadcast conversations between two journalists], news and comment fusion, the need for them to watch not thinking they had to scrutinise us harder than the other lot because we are ahead in the polls.

Wednesday, February 14

The GB meeting was a bit jollier than usual, though with a lot of angst as ever. He said the knowledge economy White Paper was the most expensive White Paper per column inch in history. He was also worried about Prodi coming tomorrow and getting Europe up in lights again. We thought Hague would do asylum and the Dome. In the end he did asylum and Community Health Councils. I was worried [Charles] Kennedy would do 'bog-standard' which was one of those statements that had cut straight through and not to our advantage. We were getting loads of bad reaction and of course the explanation was too long and complicated compared with the simple idea that it was an attack by us on comprehensive schools. David B said the PLP was up in arms. Party members were resigning. The cartoonists were getting in on the act, which was always a sign we were in trouble.

TB was supportive, though said I had to be careful re language, and said as ever the real problem was the party overreacting to something that with a few moments' thought could be justified. Bruce [Grocott] was sympathetic, said that he knew what I meant, that it was saying all comprehensive schools should be good schools, and he felt I had enough cred in the party on the issue for it to blow over fairly quickly. He said it was amazing I didn't make more mistakes given the pressures I was under at those briefings, and the problem in his view was not the phrase but the policy. TB said the problem was not the policy but the phrase, because it sounded insulting. I had a stack of meetings to get through – GB, office, TB, Group of 6, Cabinet Office lot re regional communications. But 'bog-standard' was following me wherever I went. Some got it, most didn't, but the net effect was bad.

Thursday, February 15

There was an extraordinary splash in the *Telegraph* saying economic conditions were better than they had been for twenty-five years. But asylum was bad and TB's hectoring of the Home Office had not achieved much. Philip said it was coming through the groups as the number one issue, and though largely media-driven for a lot of people it was real. TB called re Hammond, who I was now due to see later today. TB was very keen for Peter M to have some way of rebuilding his reputation and the best possible outcome was for it to be clear he did not lie but he did cause an avoidable muddle. He was worried my account would basically be of a changing story. However, I felt that tonally I could do it in a way that did not need to 'kill' him. And as Richard Wilson said when I discussed it with him, 'Better you kill Peter M than kill the PM.'

RW came to see me again, said TB had asked him to establish whether I was going to stay on after an election. I said it was ridiculous he had to do this. For me to stay, I had to be committed to this heart, body and soul, and at the moment I felt demotivated because I felt things would never change, because he would never change his ways and nor would I. RW said what he really values is my opinion and my judgement and we have to find a way of him getting those without me then having to execute the outcome of our discussions. Maybe if Godric was PMOS [Prime Minister's official spokesman], I could do strategy and communications and general troubleshooting. I told him Fiona was also very unlikely to want to stay, so Tony and Cherie needed to start thinking about that too. I said we had to think about what kind of life we were going to lead long term. I was also beginning to wonder whether I was as good at the job as I used to be. I'd done it for a few years at a heavy pace, and it may have taken its toll more than others, even people close in, always saw.

I then went off down Whitehall to see Hammond, who had been given an office over the road to conduct his inquiry. He surprised me a little by going through a rough sketch of what other witnesses had said. The impression was that most did not buy Peter's story, but he was alarmed that there was no hard evidence of phone calls at the Home Office. We didn't spend that long on the weekend. He was pressing me on what happened on the Wednesday, and why TB had felt it was necessary for him to resign. I was determined not to dump too hard on Peter, but I did say I found it odd that he didn't tell me about Jack Straw's call to him the week before the PQ. He asked me if I thought he should see TB and Jonathan. I said maybe Jonathan but my own view would be against the PM having to do this. I wasn't convinced this was the place for inquiry into whether it was right or wrong he left the government. The issue was whether there had been wrongdoing re the application.

I was there for over an hour, and felt it went OK, but strongly sensed it was not going to come out as well as we would like. I didn't get the impression he was too impressed by the Home Office. He was clearly baffled, as was I, that Peter did not tell us everything at the outset, as it would probably have been defensible even if there had been a call. I said I could see why he said he didn't lie, but I didn't feel we got the whole story, which was a pity. He seemed to be casting around for my views on what happened and why. I stuck pretty much to what I had said at briefings, was perfectly nice about Peter, but had to convey the view that he had not been full and frank. Dickie Bird was in for a tour and a cup of tea when I got back. He was sure we were going to get another landslide.

Friday, February 16

I was trying to help TB get the Glasgow [Labour Party spring conference] speech in shape. Peter H had done an OK draft but Philip wrote a demolition of it, leaving Peter very dispirited by the end of it all. TB was holding a business seminar down at Chequers, to hear their complaints on red tape, interfering Treasury. I discussed leaving with Jonathan and he said TB would not want either me or Anji to go, but if he had to keep one, it would be me, and he would be very surprised if he let me go, and I would find it hard to leave if he was asking me not to. 'He needs his comfort blankets.' I suggested to TB he was wrong to put Richard W in charge of getting me to stay, because there must be a part of Richard who would love the idea of me leaving and them being able to reassert a 'proper' Civil Service operation. TB felt, and was probably right, that if he asked RW to get him structures to make things easier for me, he would do so. But on the new ideas for the centre, it was clear TB had told RW HE would be in charge, whilst Jonathan thought HE would. He was asking me to sign up to something that remained unclear. With Glasgow looming, I did a joint TB/George Robertson article for the *Sunday Mail*.

Later the balloon went up over US–UK attacks on Iraq outside the no-fly zone.[1] None of us in Number 10, including TB and John Sawers, had known the exact time it was going to happen. It would clearly overshadow the spring conference. I had to scramble together a useable line. JP called from Glasgow, said he was cancelling interviews because he was bound to be asked whether and when he knew – this was like the old days when 'Prescott excluded' was the first headline they thought of. It wasn't much comfort to tell him I had been excluded too. He didn't change on this kind of thing. I stopped short of telling him TB had been unaware it was happening tonight too. We just had to deal with this. Geoff Hoon was reluctant to go up on it but I persuaded him he had to. Robin C was equally reluctant but said he would do the morning media. He said he felt the MoD did not quiz

[1] In what US president George W. Bush described as 'A routine mission to enforce the no-fly zone', twenty-four American and British fighter jets struck five targets radar monitoring north and south of Baghdad. It was the first such operation for almost two years.

the US sufficiently on their military planning and added 'I'm not sure the US military planners really gave much thought as to whether their actions would wipe out your well-laid plans for the Labour Party's spring conference. You might wish to make them aware of your displeasure at this.' He can still make me laugh can Robin.

Saturday, February 17

The media was totally dominated by Iraq. What coverage there was for GB's speech was OK but his disciples seemed to think we had deliberately bombed Iraq as a way of minimising coverage. They really seemed to believe it too. JP was still in a rage at not knowing about the action in Iraq. The only minister who knew the truth about how we too had been in the dark was Jack S. He had been on the phone to TB and had seen the news of the air strikes on TV. 'How long is the bombing in Baghdad going on?' 'What bombing?' 'You are bombing Baghdad.' We did our best at explaining it, saying simply it had gone down the military chain of command and as there was no change of policy there had been no need for a TB/GWB call on it. But it was seat of the pants stuff and clearly someone inside the MoD had fucked up. Their political antennae were hopeless.

It was perfectly clear the Yanks were cranking this up. Jack S' stuff [announcing new rights for victims of crime] was running fine at Glasgow. Then, as often happens with party audiences, DB and JP indulged in twin self-indulgence. First, David had a pop at me re 'bog-standard', which would get it up in lights when it was dying down. Then JP waded in, said let's have less spin, more substance and hear no more bog-standard. Joe Irvin [Prescott's special adviser] admitted to me later it was all because JP felt he had not known about the Iraq action before it happened. Given how often I stuck up for JP and DB, I thought both of them could have held out against a bit of self-indulgence at my expense. Some of the Sundays intended to splash on it, and the TV were doing bits too. Mum was down staying with us for the weekend and said why do you work so hard for people who turn on you when the going gets a bit rough? Good question.

TB and I were sending speech drafts back and forth, him at Chequers, me on the fax at home, and it was getting there. There was a strong argument in there. We worked on the various policy bits that had to go in, which worked fine, though [plans for two weeks'] paid paternity leave was a bit vague and woolly, but adult literacy and the drug-dealers' register were strong. Devolution complicated things, as we would be up in Scotland announcing in some cases policy that would only apply to England. The overall message was strong, and I felt we were getting into a better stride on speeches.

Sunday, February 18

GB was not happy at how we were doing paid paternity leave. He was also still smarting re Iraq wiping out his speech. JP rowed back a bit on me on *On the Record* but it was still bloody annoying. On the flight, TB said JP's policy record was not great, because a fog descends on whatever issue he was dealing with – Dome, rail, Tube – and people ended up not sure what they were meant to be doing. Philip had dinner last night with Douglas Alexander, Ian Austin and Ed Miliband. He said it literally felt like being in a different camp. They saw everything through a very narrow GB lens. The speech process was a lot less frantic than usual, and TB seemed on top of things. He did a few good ad libs and though the venue was not the best for getting an audience going, it went OK. Neil [Kinnock] liked it. It was a New Labour speech but it was also warm about the party.

At the briefing afterwards, I pushed the policy stuff hard, and they felt it was a pretty meaty speech. It was seen by some, rightly, as the beginnings of the main election script and message.[1] TB said he felt confident in the speech message, and he was on good form on the way back. We were getting a fair bit of flak re Iraq as we built up to the Bush visit. Back home, I had a row with Fiona because when I said I was pissed off at DB and JP having a pop, and JP's was a reaction to being excluded, she said she knew how he felt. I said I spent all my life helping them out of fuck-ups and when I made the slightest mistake, their instinct had been to pile in to please a few teachers and activists, and stoke it up again just as it was dying down.

Monday, February 19

The speech got good coverage yesterday, and was the lead in all the broadsheets, pretty straight albeit focused on the election, yet at the 8am GB meeting, the mood appeared to be one of deep gloom. GB's basic outlook was that JP's ill discipline lost us Saturday, while the paid paternity leave policy story lost us any basic message out of TB's speech. This was bollocks. He was right re JP but actually TB's

[1] After praising Brown's handling of the economy, Blair told 3,000 Labour delegates 'This is a Labour Party that will enter an election ready and waiting to fight on the economy . . . today the government can be proud of a hat-trick of good economic news – the lowest unemployment for twenty-five years, the lowest inflation for thirty years, the lowest sustained interest rates for almost forty years.'

speech worked well, on TV and in print. Maybe that was what pissed him off, but the mood was ridiculous. Also Douglas was chipping in that he was taken aback how cynically the Sundays had taken to everything, and GB was growling as if everything was a total disaster and after a few minutes of this, I had had enough. I said 'For God's sake can we stop this depressive, inward stuff and start to get a bit of fight and confidence into these meetings?' He then said 'I thought the message for the speech was going to be crime.' I said no, Gordon, like we agreed last week, it was a big-picture message speech to set out how strong economic fundamentals had been won by choice not chance and now they allowed us to invest and modernise public services according to our values.

It was impossible not to be left with the conclusion that GB was pissed off that it went well. He had been the one arguing for new policy in theory as the drivers of these next-steps speeches but when it was done in practice, he suddenly objected. I told TB afterwards that the people from Millbank must go back feeling total failures and with no confidence at all. He made everything feel so difficult and wrong the whole time. The Millbank people put their hearts and souls into it but the message they got from GB when he was like this was that everything was hopeless, including them. GB was meant to be in charge of strategy but wasn't delivering, and wasn't leading, leaving us to do it.

I called Douglas afterwards and said he had to do more to motivate people in a positive way, not just inhale and then exhale all the GB angst and nonsense. The media and the Tories were still pushing on Derry being used for fund-raising, and later [Conservative Party chairman Michael] Ancram called on him to quit.[1] Derry was keen I stress the difference between his judiciary position and his politics, which are well known. It was just another example of the Tories picking on anything but policy, but in truth a lot of people would think it unacceptable that the Lord Chancellor raised funds from lawyers. We had to be far more careful on this kind of thing.

TB called a couple of times from Chequers, but didn't mention my situation, though CB told Fiona he talked to her about little else. Fiona had mentioned to Carole Caplin I needed some new suits and she fixed for me to go to [fashion designer] Paul Smith's, who quickly sorted me with three suits. Carole seemed very pleased that I had

[1] In what was being dubbed the 'cash for wigs' row, Lord Irvine, who as Lord Chancellor had the power to appoint judges and Queen's Counsels, had written to a list of solicitors and barristers inviting them to a Labour Party fund-raiser at a London nightclub.

February '01: GB not delivering on strategy

anything to do with her, but I said, smiling, that it did not mean I had mellowed towards her at all. I'm not a menace, she said, I promise you. The suits were OK.

We had an internal meeting plus GB. After our spat in the morning, GB was a bit more engaged and less down on everything. DM was defending the policy process and said they were expecting too much too soon, that we had to work towards the manifesto properly. PG and I were both arguing for far greater focus on an economic message. We felt that GB was not visible enough on the economy, and that we needed to find a simple message and just keep banging away at it. We had to decide whether we actually believed our own propaganda – I was constantly saying to the media that over time the big arguments got through and the public got the point. If so, we should focus far more sharply on our economic message, yet GB seemed strangely reluctant at the moment. We were weak on a narrative related to the economy. It was a better meeting but GB really needed to snap out of the negativism.

As I went home, I felt more and more drawn to the idea of the exit door, but Fiona said she didn't believe I would leave. She felt I was hooked on it, had to be central, had to be totally immersed and I would find it impossible to pull back. Part of me felt like that, but some days I woke up and just didn't want to be there.

Tuesday, February 20

I slept in for once, and missed GB's meeting, which was a relief. Derry was giving us problems, and it was getting bigger in the media. He agreed to do a [House of Lords oral] starred question on it tomorrow. I got in to work up a script for my briefing on the US visit, which was already getting a fair amount of attention and interest. It was an important visit and I was looking forward to it as being maybe more interesting that some of the stuff that had been getting me down recently. We had an internal meeting on the election, where I gave TB a fairly frank analysis of problems, then I did the US correspondents which was fine if a bit flat. Fiona was taking Calum to Suffolk and was late back. I had been hoping she would be there at the start of our latest session with TB and CB to try to settle what we were going to do.

I went up to the flat on my own, and once we had settled down in the sitting room I told TB I was feeling tired and demotivated. I felt I had given him my best for several years and I no longer felt on top form, and I wasn't convinced I would recover it. He said he went through phases like that too, and felt election years always produced this kind of mood, particularly at the start of the year. He said the problem was a quality-of-life issue, and we all felt our quality of life was poorer than it should be. He said I was key to the election and after that we had to make sure I had less pressure, less to do with the media, became more strategic. He was sure we could make that happen.

He said I was underselling myself. I may have had bad days but he felt my bad days were more use to him than a lot of people's best days. I was a politician not a pressman. I had a mind that gave him something extra and he was loath to lose it.

He felt I had become too big a figure to be seeing the press all the time because they were as interested in me as they were in most of the politicians. But he promised things would change. We would be strengthened by a second mandate. He was not at all sure he wanted to fight a third election and so he would go for it on his own terms. We would have new better ministers, a new chief whip, a new chairman, Charles Clarke, who would take a lot of the weight. I said that was all fine for him but I did not believe my job would change. He said it would if I let it. CB came in and he picked up his guitar and started strumming it, which clearly irritated her.

Fiona arrived, while Cherie was telling him he had to listen to people more, and listen to their concerns. Fiona pitched straight in, said our education policy was crap and the party was moving too far to the right, and she had a pop at Jonathan and Anji for good measure, saying that if they were given more responsibility, I would end up doing a load of their jobs for them. TB seemed taken aback. I tried to calm it down, said that he had to understand we had given an awful lot and Fiona's worry was that the changes he planned would just load more on to me, and that had a knock-on effect at home. I repeated my view that I didn't feel I was as effective as I used to be, and it meant he should be thinking of how to find someone who could do better. He wouldn't have it. He said I had a special talent and he needed it, and at the very least I should give it a go for a few months after the election. This went on for an hour and a half, fairly heavy at times and I did feel I would be letting him down badly if I left when he wanted me to stay as much as he did. I said I was unconvinced things would change. Fiona said TB would be making a big mistake if he promoted Anji or gave Jonathan even more clout, but he said in the end, he is prime minister and he has to be able to make judgements and they cannot be made on the basis of who likes whom. He needs a range of talents around him, and so far he has been well served, he said.

CB and FM said a lot of people feared he was taking the party further and further to the right. He said that is a different argument, and it is wrong. We have moved to the centre and we are staying there so long as I am leader, and none of us should forget the mistakes we made in the past that kept us out of power for so long. He was perfectly nice but by now getting irritated and feeling he was being overly attacked. Fiona and I had a row in the car home, because she said it was clear I was going to stay. TB called as I arrived home and said 'Be nice to her.' He was taken aback at how angry she was. He said she probably felt totally boxed in and subservient, and I had become such a big thing in politics that it was difficult for her, and I had to be more sympathetic to that. But the scene was bad all round.

Wednesday, February 21

The argument with Fiona continued once we got to bed and the cloud had not lifted by the time we got up, so our farewells were very muted, and I felt really low. She asked what I was going to say to TB, and I said I would tell him I wanted to leave still. 'Good.' She said she had found him patronising and insulting, that he thought he was always right and he basically thought she was an imbecile. When I saw him later, he said 'God, do I have a problem with your missus – I had no idea it was so bad.' He said he was willing to work at improving things but he could not have Fiona telling him whether he could or could not keep Anji or give Jonathan more responsibility. He had to be able to make judgements himself. I said the problem was Fiona was not happy with our existence at the moment, felt I was so immersed in the job I had no time for her, and he was copping it as well as me.

On the plane out [to Ottawa, Canada], he said we had to be dumb-bells if we couldn't make our lives a bit less stressful. On my position, he said he was the prime minister, not the chairman of a company, and if he took the judgement that in running the country he needed me to help him, surely I had to respond to that. The first year after the election was going to be hugely important. He had GB breathing down his neck. He was clear what he wanted to do but he needed his best people to help him do it. I said I just had to decide if I was up for it one hundred per cent, because anything less was a waste of time. He was very open re GB. Said he had told him that if he actively plotted and tried to force him out, he would make sure he never took over. If he played reasonably straight, he would help him all the way. He said he wanted Fiona to do a bigger job that took account of her abilities, but he couldn't be told who he should and shouldn't employ.

I sensed in his own mind he had no doubt I would stay. He said in the end, there are big people and little people. You are a big person and this is a big project, changing the course of a country and it's better and more important than anything you will ever do.

Derry did his statement in the Lords on his fund-raising dinner. I spoke to him before, said it was vital he wasn't arrogant and gave a sense of humility, and he said he would. But afterwards he called and said he was 'very, very good' and now thought he should do an interview with [*Telegraph* legal editor Joshua] Rozenberg. I said no. He later called to say that [Lord Justice] Auld [conducting a review of the operation of criminal courts], having agreed we should include some of the criminal justice reforms in the crime plan, was now saying we could not. TB, Derry and I had a conference call and agreed we would have to scrutinise it further.

We then got the news that Hammond was saying he wouldn't be able to publish his report till the day of the Budget, which was a total disaster so far as we were concerned. Over dinner on the plane, TB said he was genuinely shocked at how rude Ed Balls was to him during their discussions on the Budget. Anyone watching would have been hard pressed to imagine he was the prime minister and Balls an aide to one of his ministers. John Sawers did a note for TB on [Canadian Prime Minister Jean] Chrétien and what he should say on arrival, including pointing out that he had won three elections, over which I scribbled 'As I intend to – Gordon'. Godric did a script for TB to deliver a story on the plane [to travelling journalists] about the planned prison visit and the crime plan, and there was a lot of interest. We worked on the speech for tomorrow at the Canadian parliament. The media were in a fairly good mood, though the papers were bad for Derry. It was freezing when we arrived, TB as ever resisting wearing a coat.

Thursday, February 22

It was minus twenty-seven degrees in Ottawa, sunny but freezing cold. I went out for a run but my asthma kicked off so I used the gym. TB was up at the crack of dawn to work on the speech which was in good shape and had a good section on the false choice for Britain between Europe and America. He had had a good time with Chrétien, who told him the hilarious story of how opposition leader Stockwell Day [Conservative] made a pledge that if three per cent of the population wanted a referendum on any issue, they could have it, so the Liberals got a TV station to organise a three per cent write-in campaign for Stockwell to change his first name to Doris. It really took off, to the point the Liberals even adopted 'Que Sera Sera' as their campaign song. Chrétien was genuinely funny, constantly told stories against himself and was obviously a good guy to work for. He had screwed up yesterday on NMD, giving the impression that the US would allow others to veto it. So I told him at the bilateral that our press was very exercised by it. He got the point straight away and wanted it sorted quickly. He told me that the Canadian press were as into me as they were into TB 'because of your reputation for liking a fight'. TB did a business breakfast before going off to the parliament, which was a terrific venue for a serious speech. He got a fantastically warm reception and the speech itself went well. After a reception for some of the MPs, we set off for lunch with Chrétien at his residence. He was very relaxed, very self-deprecating, particularly about his language problem. He only learned English after he became a Cabinet minister. He had some interesting advice on election timing, said that twice now he had called it early to avoid six months dominated by rubbish and speculation. He was also in teasing mood with his foreign minister [John Manley] about how long he might stay. In between the pleasantries, we covered a lot of serious stuff, NMD, European defence, Iraq, the Balkans, China and Russia but more than anything it was a nice lunch in a nice atmosphere with a real political pro. He had spoken to Bush that morning. TB was arguing for Putin to be given a seat 'at the top table'. He said the key to understanding him was that he was a Russian patriot, and he would be OK provided we treated him with respect. They had a very frank discussion about Chirac and both felt the political situation in France made Chirac worse. Chrétien described Putin as highly intelligent, very serious, contrast to Yeltsin who was 'a lovely bear of a man. You never knew what was going to happen next.'

Godric was doing a brilliant job with the hacks on the crime plan, and gave me a sense that maybe it would be possible for him to take care of the press while I did strategy. We had another [Lord Justice] Auld problem and another conference call. He clearly had decided to go for us and I said surely it was time to take on the judges as real forces of conservatism. To my surprise, TB agreed, saying it was time they realised their job was to apply the law, not to make it. There was a case of foot and mouth back home and the Tories were blaming us for it. This could become a real problem if it becomes another farming crisis. Chrétien heard Godric and I briefing TB about it and came over all concerned, said be very, very careful. That is the kind of issue that can quickly get out of control. He was a real wily and interesting character. TB liked him a lot. He told us a very funny story about a trip to a World War Two commemorative event in Holland when he was first introduced to Prime Minister Kok, and next in line was a mayor named Prick. At the dinner, I was seated with a few Tories who had clearly bought the line that we had won on media manipulation. Chrétien made a little speech in which he said the last Quebec separatist leader [Lucien Bouchard] had a flesh-eating disease that took his leg but he survived and the separatists viewed it as miracle. 'It was quite hard to contest that even with my surname and the initials JC.' We set off for the airport and off for Washington, TB worrying about the tone to strike on NMD.

Friday, February 23

I was up before 6 to prepare TB for three US interviews, which helped us straighten the lines on NMD, European defence and Iraq. John Sawers had done a very good job in advance with Condi Rice and we had a good joint statement worked out even before we met which was very good on EU defence, and would help us push back some of the sceptic nonsense, and was OK for us on NMD. The first big meeting was with [Dick] Cheney [US Vice President] at Blair House [official guest house]. He was very dry, quite quietly spoken. If he was a Brit, you'd say total Tory. TB did OK but Cheney was clearly very sceptical about European defence. Oddly he managed to seem relaxed whilst at the same time emanating tension and a hint of menace. He was very well informed about pretty much all the issues they covered. And in a way a straight warm-up man for Bush, who would later seem warm and friendly and personable by comparison.

TB kicked off with a bit of US–UK, then on Iraq said he took the view that Saddam was a significant threat to the region. On the Middle East, Cheney was clear they would not rush in but get involved at the appropriate point. He was clearly sceptical about Arafat's commitment and ability. TB likewise felt we may have reached the limit with Arafat. Nor could he see a way round the Jerusalem problem. They had a long discussion on the sanctions before moving on to European defence. TB said 'I hear you have your doubts.' Cheney said if it enhanced capabilities and doesn't weaken NATO they could support it, but they do have concerns. TB said it was an article of faith that we would not do anything to undermine NATO's collective security. He acknowledged we and the French had a different approach but we had to be in these arguments and winning them. Bosnia showed up the failures of European defence. At a time the US didn't want to be involved, the French tried with us and we failed. Sierra Leone was a success. Kosovo was a situation where both the US and Europe were involved but there would be other situations where the Americans won't want to be. Europe has to improve its capability. On NMD, Cheney set out their concerns on Iran, Libya, Korea, Iraq. TB said that if the capability existed to improve defence, we understood the reason for wanting to develop such a capability and that nuclear and WMD were clearly concerns. He said the French were fiercely opposed, but he felt America could win more support if they handled it in the right way. He felt Putin could be brought to a different position. They danced around the timing issue, and Cheney would have had to be pretty astute to pick up all the nuances TB was trying to express.

We got driven out to the helipad for the fifty-minute helicopter ride to Camp David. Bush was out to greet TB and the rest of us, all smiles, very warm and with a nervous laugh at the end of his first few sentences. We were given little bungalow-style huts, pretty plush without being over the top, mainly named after trees it seemed, with 'Laurel' the big one in the centre where most of the work would get done. Jonathan and I were in Maple, TB in Birch, Bush in Aspen. Bush himself took care of the introductions to [Colin] Powell [Secretary of State], Condi, Andrew Card [chief of staff], Ari Fleischer [press secretary], Steve Hadley [Condoleezza Rice's deputy], etc. Bush's style was very informal and relaxed, and he was clearly one of those leaders who made a point of talking to officials on the other side almost as much as to the leader. He was very solicitous of TB and you had a strong sense of both of them making an effort. We went through lunch and kicked off on Iraq. Bush said the policy wasn't working. Sanctions weren't working. He let Powell do a fairly long presentation on sanctions, no-fly zones, WMD. He said they were losing support in the Arab world and in the P5 [UN Security Council permanent members]. Saddam had succeeded in creating the sense we were hurting his people, not him. TB felt there was a case for reforming sanctions around the things Saddam wanted to acquire. Bush said the no-fly zones 'scared the hell out of me' because we had pilots at risk the whole time. He said if we hit the guy he has to feel it and they have to understand why. He was very plain-speaking. He said we have to make Saddam less of a factor on the world stage. He's a pain in the ass. If he gets WMD, he's a very dangerous pain in the ass. He said the Saudis were nervous as hell.

On European defence, TB again set out the reasons why we were keen on this, the lessons of Bosnia, Sierra Leone and Kosovo. Again he stressed it would be NATO-friendly. Again, Bush was less subtle than Cheney in his response, said he appreciated the commitment to

NATO and said the US was sick of having to do so much peacekeeping in the world. TB repeated his basic line that if the US and Europe were together, there were few problems we couldn't sort. He was frank about the depth of opposition in Europe to NMD, said that all European countries had to live with their history, the Germans with their guilt, the French with their shame, the British with our victory. But he felt Schroeder was changing Germany, that he was not somebody that would spend his whole life apologising for his country's past sins. To understand France, he said, you have to understand de Gaulle. The French resent having been bailed out. They resent any sense of America telling them what to do. Throw in Russia and it becomes even more complicated.

Bush said he was pleased with some of the things Putin had been saying. He said that 'we owe it to humanity' to get a system that works and the ABM treaty[1] stops us doing it. He said one day Putin will wake up and see Iran gunning at him. He felt he could work with him. His big concern was China, and he said India and Pakistan worried the hell out of him and we all had to work to calm it. He let Powell again do a fairly long spiel on the Middle East. Bush said they were going to take their time. TB thought Arafat was a problem and did quite an interesting read-across to the Irish situation, said the Israelis were the Unionists, the PLO were the Republicans, for the Irish read Egypt, for the Americans read Britain. Bush wasn't as up to speed on the NI detail as Clinton, but he asked the right questions and said if we needed help, pick up a phone. TB pushed him hard on Africa and we tried to make the link between poverty there and potential problems here and again Bush showed a bit more sensitivity to the issues than we had expected. He was a curious mix of cocky and self-deprecating, relaxed and hyper. He liked to see everything in very simple terms, let others set out complicated arguments and then he would try to distil them in shorter phrases. He was very clear about his own positions on the big foreign policy questions. He clearly hadn't warmed to Putin and TB was urging him to give him a chance, also speaking up for Schroeder.

After lunch, they went out to do some pictures and there was a dreadful moment when Bush clicked his fingers for his dog to follow him and the media were trying to make it look like Tony turned and walked towards him. Once the cameras had gone, they went for a walk without officials and TB said afterwards they got on very well.

[1] The Anti-Ballistic Missile Treaty of 1972, agreed between the US and USSR as part of the Strategic Arms Limitations Talks.

February '01: China is Bush's big concern

We sat down and went through the tricky stuff for the press conference, and a bit like TB, he liked to be grilled a bit and go over tough questions so we did Iraq, TB/Clinton, Middle East, European defence. The press conference was in a fairly odd venue a short drive away but very homely, and our lot were clearly surprised at GWB's presence and the little bit of pizazz that he showed. He was fulsome re TB and totally played to our line on EU defence. I did a little huddle afterwards and it was obvious our lot were surprised at how relaxed they were with each other. We got back for drinks before dinner where Bush made a point of talking to me, Jonathan, John and Meyer while TB was talking to the American guys. He gave us a spiel about Mexico, his analysis of Gore's campaign and where it went wrong, his take on Clinton, where he was probably being diplomatic in that he was fairly positive about him. He was clearly worried about France and was picking our brains about how best to deal with them. He said we were absolutely right to avoid TV [election] debates because they were a menace. TB, Bush and the wives had dinner while we had one separately where Condi made a nice little speech. Ari and I agreed to do a joint phone briefing for the Sundays back in Washington which went fine. It also meant I got out of watching *Meet the Parents* [film comedy] with Bush, TB etc.

Saturday, February 24

TB clearly felt yesterday went well, that Bush pushed the boat out both in inviting him to Camp David, and also in the way we were treated. They had had a couple of fairly long conversations alone and he said he found him clear and straightforward. But also, for example on Putin, willing to listen and adapt. When they first discussed Putin yesterday, he was very down on him, felt that he was just your typical KGB guy. But TB had opened his mind to a different way of looking at him, and it was interesting that Bush probed him on that this morning. He was a bit fond of chucking out one-liners whenever anyone was mentioned – [President of South Korea] Kim Dae-jung 'naive', [Yasser] Arafat 'a busted flush'. On Europe, TB was also trying to show him a different way of thinking about it, that it was silly for us to keep having our views of each other negatively defined by wars. He just didn't want to let the French run European politics, which was why we had to engage e.g. on defence. TB said that on one of their little walks they talked about God and about their kids and Bush, clearly having read the potted biographies, asked TB why so many of his senior staff weren't married, and TB said he was constantly trying to persuade us.

Breakfast was a kind of help yourself set-up just down from where we had dinner, and Laura [Bush, First Lady] was more visible, very chatty about her kids and quite prim and poised. When he [GBW] came in, I was sitting in his rocking chair and he asked if I liked it. I said yes. 'It's yours.' He was clearly pumping out the personal charm but beneath it you got a real sense that if he didn't get his way he would be, to quote himself, a tough son of a bitch.

We had come out fine from yesterday, having effectively traded support on NMD for GWB backing on EU defence, and the general feeling was that his words of support for us were stronger and clearer than TB's for them. He wasn't a big fan of the press, but wasn't really buying my line that they had it easy compared with us. He said the reason he thought we were right to avoid TV debates was that the press made them all about themselves. He also thought there was a case for changing the Constitution so that you had one six-year term rather than two times four, which was an interesting idea I had never seen ventilated. He was critical of Gore, didn't pile into Clinton and said to TB he had been absolutely right to make clear he was still a good friend of Bill. Every now and then, he or one of the others would say something that exposed just how much further to the right they were, but he was obviously on his best behaviour. Cherie seemed to be getting on OK with Laura and they agreed to do a joint breast cancer event in October. We met George Tenet, the head of the CIA, and TB had a separate session with him. As a first meeting, it had gone well, and also the teams seemed to get on perfectly well. Condi was a sports nut and she and I talked a fair bit about that. We did the long walk up to the helipad, with TB and Bush locked in conversation, farewells then off to Andrews Air Force Base, where TB did five interviews and was pretty pumped up. We talked about Bush over dinner. Cherie and I had both felt a bit uneasy at times, but you couldn't deny he had a lot more charm and nous than the caricature. TB said he liked him, thought he was straight.

He had now enlisted Cherie in the persuasion game of staying, said he would get me more money and more support. Said he would rather have me 9 to 5 than someone else twenty-four hours a day. Cherie said we were all bound up together and it would be really sad if I didn't see the whole thing through with him. She added that TB needed strength vis-à-vis GB and I was part of that. She felt TB had to enthuse me to stay and she and I needed to persuade Fiona that there was a real job there for her. They both claimed after the election there would be a new wave of energy and direction.

As ever, there was disproportionate interest in TB's terrible sense of style, e.g. the awful pullover he wore on his walk with Bush and the dreadful creation he wore on the plane. He was hopeless at casual clothes. He had put on what was to all intents and purposes a vest and I said you can't wear that, and he said why not? I said because it's a fucking vest and you're the prime minister. Eventually he agreed to put a sweater on, which was some ghastly Nicole Farhi creation, on top of the vest, and it looked ridiculous. I said please, please take them off and wear something else when we see the press. Eventually, by persuading him that he would have to answer questions about foot and mouth, which was getting more serious, I persuaded him to wear a shirt and tie. The Bush stuff was fairly low-key in the papers which had stuff about Hammond either saying Peter M had not been cleared or that I acted peremptorily.

Sunday, February 25

Up to Manchester with Rory. It was a terrific match. United thrashed Arsenal. I had a good session with Alex afterwards and asked for his advice. He fully understood why I was pissed off but said there were two questions I had to ask. One, how many people could TB really trust? He guessed not many, and I was one of them. Two, how many jobs are there that really matter? Again, not that many, and I had one of them. If you took my main interests, it was probably the best job there was. He said you are working for the most important man in the country in one of the most important positions and if you left it, you would regret it. You do it well and your future is taken care of. The reason why people go at you all the time is because they want to stop you doing it well. He felt that Fiona could leave if she wanted to but shouldn't make me feel I had to. We chatted for half an hour or so and it helped clear my mind before we went for a drink with his boys.

Monday, February 26

Foot-and-mouth disease [FMD] was getting worse and we agreed both that TB should do media but also see Ben Gill of the NFU. TB did his prison visit and the crime plan was getting good coverage but FMD was clearly moving towards a sense of crisis. There was more hostile stuff from Kavanagh in the *Sun* and TB said he intended really to go for them on Thursday at lunch. I'll believe it when I see it. Fiona had seen Anji with CB and said she had heard nothing to suggest my life, and so ours, would be any easier.

After the eleven o'clock, I asked Adam Boulton [Sky News political editor] up to the office to sound him out as a possible replacement in the event I went. He was clear he would want to do it as a civil servant, he would want to wait till the New Year, partly for share options, partly to be distant from the election. I was clear with him that it wasn't certain I would go but that what we were talking about was a director of communications job rather than PMOS. He was basically up for it but not straight after the election. Fiona feared if I stayed even for a week after the election, I would never leave. She was also taken aback by how clear and forthright Alex had been.

We had a good election meeting with TB who was a bit more focused and political. He said he wanted to find an opportunity to say Thatcherism had its day and that the *Mail*, *Telegraph*, *Sun* agenda was the Tories' problem not solution. He was also clear that in terms of his own campaign on the road, there had to be a sense of struggle. He couldn't work out whether I was better with him on the road, or based in Millbank as a counter to GB, which is what most of the others thought. We were agreeing a list of key campaigners – as well as the obvious, Beckett, Hoon, Milburn, Byers, Estelle [Morris, education minister], Hain, maybe Reid.

I called Peter M later. He was obviously worrying about Hammond. My confidence in Hammond had been somewhat undermined by the incomplete account they sent over of my evidence, and I spent much of the day with Jonathan and Clare finishing my reply to it. We had a good Budget roll-out meeting, though Jeremy worried that the Budget was going to be a total bore. I doubted GB would let that happen. TB was anxious Hammond would overshadow the Budget and remained of the view we wanted Peter effectively cleared of wrongdoing, even if it meant we took a bit of a hit. He did his FMD interview and both of us were having alarm bells ringing louder and louder.

Tuesday, February 27

More cases of FMD, [horse] racing cancelled and a growing sense of crisis. I told TB I had no sense of it being gripped properly and no confidence in the machinery of government. Though Nick Brown was getting quite a good press, he was beginning to look strained and I wasn't convinced MAFF could handle it, despite all the assurances. We agreed he should do a ministerial meeting and a webcast. GB missed the morning meeting. I felt there was enough around for us to do a big number on Tory U-turns but Douglas didn't bite so I got Fraser [Kemp, Labour MP] up on it. Philip told me Douglas was having one or two problems with people at Millbank.

TB had another go at me about the job and said he had been shocked that Fiona was so hostile. He thought it was more about Anji than him. Fiona had got more hostile as a result of Alex's advice, which she could tell had been persuasive. FMD was not only bad in reality but also now damaging the government on the level of competence. David M said to me he felt I had to be at Millbank for the campaign. Bruce felt I must go on the road with TB.

Wednesday, February 28

FMD was massive throughout the media and if that wasn't bad enough, then came news of a train crash in Selby.[1] It would have the effect of further demoralising everyone. People were starting to talk about whether you could have an election with FMD. TB spoke to JP before he left for Yorkshire. The mood at the PMQs preparation meeting was pretty low although actually questions were much more straightforward when there were such obvious issues. We had a group of 6 meeting to go through the outline manifesto shape, what the pledges should be, and what economic disaster posters we should use. I had a very good meeting with David Hill [former Labour Party director of communications], agreed that he should be at Millbank for the campaign but that he and I should effectively be interchangeable, whether on the road, in the lobby or at HQ. I felt glad he was coming back [as a volunteer] because his relations with the lobby were good, much better than mine.

I went to TB's meeting on Hammond. He said he didn't mind ending up with a bit of egg on his face providing the thing went away quickly. The problem was if Hammond said clearly that the Peter M/O'Brien call took place, we were in the clear but Peter would be in the stratosphere. If Hammond was unclear, Peter was in the clear and TB was left having to explain why he resigned. He said he would prefer that to having Peter on the outside feeling vengeful. He also felt let down, that the Civil Service had been cavalier in saying there was a record of the call when in fact there was not. Peter H was worried about it, said I had to persuade TB he was not going to be helped by a report that vindicated Peter M. George Pascoe-Watson [deputy political editor, Sun] told me there had been a meeting at the Sun and their plan was to do a tough audit of what we had done but then come out for us at the end. But he warned me that Trevor K in particular was really going towards the Tories.

[1] An InterCity 225 had been derailed by a Land Rover on the East Coast main line at Selby, North Yorkshire. Ten people were killed and eighty-two seriously injured.

Thursday, March 1

A combination of FMD, the rail crash and the weather [questions raised about flood defences after heavy rainfall] meant we were in for a bad period. Cabinet was obviously dominated by FMD and rail. Nick Brown said that any hopes of FMD being confined to one or two regions were long gone. He said the tough conditions put in place were having some effect but what was emerging was that it was well incubated before the restrictions were put in. The chief vet [James Scudamore] thought we might be able to announce limited movements tomorrow but even if some trade were possible it would be nowhere near normal and the movement restrictions will stay. He had been to the council of ministers and there was enormous pressure to blame Britain for exporting another disease. TB said Nick and the chief vet had handled things well, but I think both of us thought they were close to being overwhelmed. TB was talking about cancelling his visit to Gloucester and Wales because he wanted to stay on top of this, and also on the Budget and Hammond.

The Hammond report came in. Jonathan basically said a call took place but Peter M wasn't happy with it. It was actually not that bad and probably got the balance about right. Peter had not been dishonest but had created a bit of a muddle and a call probably took place. We had lunch at the *Sun* with [Les] Hinton and [David] Yelland. TB said he felt the paper had been pretty hostile, said it's up to them to decide what to do but he found it hard to consider the *Sun* as a supportive newspaper. They denied there had been a change of policy but I said what they did was say they supported us, and constantly push a very right-wing agenda. The truth was they would love to go back to the Tories if they could. Yelland said the press is now the Opposition. I said why don't you stand for Parliament then? It was friendly but frank and TB did deliver the message he said he would. Sally went to Gloucester with TB while I stayed back and worked on the Wales speech. He did a Q&A [with Labour supporters and farmers] and launched the long-term review of agriculture.

Friday, March 2

TB's apparent attack on the supermarkets last night was going big.[1] It had not been planned and when the supermarkets came back at us through the day he got a bit discombobulated. He didn't like the draft

---

[1] Blair had told the audience at Hartpury Agricultural College 'We all want cheaper food in our shops, but on the other hand the supermarkets have pretty much got an armlock on you people at the moment.'

we had done, felt there was too much Tory-bashing in it, that it wasn't statesmanlike enough. We learned through the day that Peter M was seeing Hammond again and did so for three hours in the afternoon. If this went wrong, we could have Peter back on the rampage soon. I spoke to him later and he sounded relaxed but he had clearly convinced himself the call with O'Brien never took place, also that I had hardened up things at various crucial points and therefore that my role as the person responsible for his downfall was not crystal clear in the report. He said Hammond was reeling from it all. I said the next few days were not going to be very nice but we had to get through them as best we could. He said the Sundays – not briefed by him – were going to say he was cleared, which wasn't very good, or at least wouldn't be when he [Hammond] reported that a call took place. He said he had tried to get Hammond to be more inconclusive. The supermarket thing was really running and we had to put out a line making clear we were not saying that they caused the FMD epidemic.

Saturday, March 3

I had a long chat with TB re FMD, which still did not have the feeling of being under control. Peter M called re Hammond. He was working on a note about handling, but it would be totally from his own perspective. TB clearly didn't mind taking a bit of a hit, but we had to be careful it wasn't too big a hit. I went to Portsmouth vs Burnley [Portsmouth 2, Burnley 0]. TB called at half-time, felt we had to get deeper into the FMD situation. Gavin [Millar, Fiona's brother] was with me and I had a good chat with him. He felt, and so did Audrey, that I should definitely stay, that it would be disloyal to go and that the party wouldn't like it. But Fiona was adamant. And I was still having to deal with Peter M and Hammond, TB fretting re the same.

Sunday, March 4

It was working out to be something of a weekend from hell. Peter M was on the rampage, sending me long memos on how he thought I should handle Hammond. Fiona was upset. TB could sense I was under more pressure. I took one look at my diary for the week ahead and got an instant headache – election planning, Budget, loads of stuff on. I also had a meeting planned for today and Fiona not unreasonably couldn't understand why I couldn't have done it on Friday. Eventually, I cancelled the afternoon meeting. She said when it came to a choice between the office and home, I let them hold sway. I went for a run and bumped into Richard Desmond who was out walking with his wife, and we had a brief chat about the *Mail*. Peter M was clearly trying to press us to build our entire handling strategy around the notion of him being cleared. I couldn't quite see it but TB was clearly willing to take some heat. Talking to Peter M it became clear he basically believed I was responsible for pushing him out by: 1. hardening up the line we gave to the *Observer* beyond what he actually said, and 2. by demanding a line for the eleven o'clock on the day of his resignation when I could have got through with an existing holding line. He said he bore me no ill will but he did believe that to be the case. I watched Rory Bremner and there were far too many TB/AC sketches, including Burnley, Britney Spears, and me as the leader.

Monday, March 5

I slept really badly and was genuinely worried both about Hammond and FMD. Peter clearly wanted to push us into presenting Hammond as a vindication, which would mean saying we took the wrong decision on his departure. TB was clearly giving him the impression that was OK. I spoke to Margaret B who agreed she would do interviews on it and to Jack S, who said he was damned if he was going to apologise to Peter over his 'untruth' comment.[1] Margaret was clear she would not be happy about saying Peter did nothing wrong but that tonally she would lean towards him.

I drove in with Philip who felt Hague was connecting more than we imagined. TB's view was that he may be picking the right issues but the public didn't like Hague doing them. At TB's morning meeting, he said he thought the Budget was OK but that too much of it was already out there. GB was going for stability and prudence as the big message. FMD was still raging and TB had had about a six-page letter from Prince Charles full of *Daily Telegraph* speak suggesting it was all down to closed abbatoirs, lack of understanding of the countryside, etc. TB said this is likely to be down to one farmer who didn't boil pigswill and should be prosecuted but Charles can't resist jumping on the bandwagon as though I caused it. I saw GB re the Budget roll-out and he too was concerned it had been over-briefed in advance. Peter M sent over his suggested Q&A script on Hammond which started 'Q: Does this exonerate Peter M? A: Yes.' You had to hand it to him. He had thus far been pretty successful spinning the whole thing to his benefit and had pretty much persuaded TB that he was

---

[1] Straw had said in a January television interview that Mandelson 'by his own admission . . . told an untruth'.

victim not perpetrator. I did feel that if it had been anyone but Peter, we could have got through it. It was in many ways a perfectly sensible note but there were still a few circles we were finding it hard to square.

Bruce told me he was leaving [the House of Commons] at the election, Sally that she was leaving to go to the Lords. I said I was probably going to stay but Fiona was totally against and it would be difficult. She was a strong and wonderful woman, but when TB said it was hard not to see this through, and when Alex F said there weren't that many jobs really worth doing, they were right. The challenge for TB was delivering on saying he could make it easier for me, and the challenge for me was being more understanding about why Fiona hated it as much as she did, and doing something about it. Truth be told, I doubted his ability, and I doubted mine. I decided to try to give it a go, and to give up if it became clear we couldn't change. TB was growing more and more concerned about Northern Ireland again. I told the lobby we wanted to go there later in the week, but tried to play down expectations, so it didn't become a great media circus.

Tuesday, March 6

I started the day with a forty-minute call with Peter M. He said that not only should we say he was cleared but also that we took the wrong decision. I said we would bend over backwards to be helpful but we couldn't have a situation where TB was humiliated or his judgement called into question. He was very hoity-toity again, said he could prove the Home Office was behind all this, that the O'Brien phone call was an invention. He said that unless we were very generous, and the Home Office did not do him in, he intended to get his lawyers to tear their evidence apart. I spoke to him a couple of times through the day and said he was asking too much for us to say it was wrong he went. He said you are just going to have to swallow hard. He later sent through another Q&A script which hardened up the previous line. TB said he would not be intimidated, that he didn't want Peter further damaged by the report but that he did feel Peter had been less than frank with us at the time. However you looked at it, there was an inconsistency between what he told me on that Sunday, and what subsequently emerged.

We were working on TB's environment speech which was fine though surrounded by the usual cynicism about him not being terribly committed to green issues. I had a long meeting with GB at 12.30 to agree the Budget roll-out. It was perfectly clear there were some announcements planned which he had not yet agreed with the relevant ministers. He was extraordinary. For example, he was planning to announce a big nurse-recruitment campaign but Alan Milburn wanted more money for GPs and they had a very acrimonious meeting later on. He was very much up for a big macro message, plus investment in public services, help for mothers and families. TB, GB and I then had a meeting on Budget presentation, then over to see GB again later, then back for another meeting with TB on Hammond. Fiona told Cherie she was definitely leaving. She said she was not going to allow me ever to blame her for me leaving so I had to make my own judgement. It ended in another row, and her in tears again.

Wednesday, March 7

GB had yet again upset his colleagues on his big day. Yesterday Milburn, today Blunkett who said to me before Cabinet 'He's yet again trying to say there's lots of new money which in fact is going to have to come from within other internal budgets?' Milburn had protested to TB last night after GB called him on his mobile in the back of a car to say what the NHS was getting. It was a pretty disgraceful state of affairs and no way to run a government. As a result – and I rather admired him for it – Alan played hardball later, refusing to do refurbishment of maternity wards tomorrow, as GB and I had agreed on the roll-out plan. He said it wasn't ready to go, and he needed more time to line up opinion formers in the health service, plus he had real problems with the midwives, so no way. I tried four times but he wouldn't budge. GB was livid but refused to speak to him himself. I couldn't understand why he didn't square his colleagues in advance of things and why he then blamed them for things like this. The Budget Cabinet was subdued, didn't go down as well with them as in previous years. He kicked off with his usual rat-a-tat-tat on figures which on inflation and interest rates were impressive. The tax burden was up. Debt well down.

There were one or two coded attacks e.g. DB saying he represented a very poor seat [Sheffield Brightside] where people were getting lots of help but he would still be lucky to get a fifty per cent turnout. He also said a lot of people didn't understand the tax credits system. Others made slightly less subtle pleas that we should do more for Middle England. By the end of the day, the package was in fact getting a pretty good reception, but GB was still bad-tempered and grumpy. I also felt the Budget was just too complicated, too many tax credits, not enough politics, though stability was a good message.

On Hammond, Andy Marr last night did 'Mandelson cleared', probably briefed by Peter, who called me to say people would think that I did it because it helped the government to bury it on the day of the Budget. Come off it Peter, I said. I worked on a redraft of his handling paper and the Q&A but it wasn't easy. I had another bad scene with Fiona, her saying she was no longer prepared to take second place to TB and saying if I stayed it meant the job meant more to me than she did. I said the family meant more to me than anything but it was very hard to give this up when there remain so many challenges. Surely we could find a way of doing it differently.

Other people in the office were beginning to notice what was going on. DM came to see me, said Fiona and I were the strongest couple he knew and the best people there, and we had to sort it out. He was also thinking about his own future and whether to become an MP or not. I strongly felt he should. TB did fine at PMQs and the Budget went much better in the House than it had when presented at Cabinet, and despite Ed Balls' dull and at times repetitive briefing afterwards, the press seemed to think it was OK. I worked on his Inverness speech before we set off for Belfast. GB was still livid re Milburn and we were still scrabbling around trying to get something decent for tomorrow as we took off. TB said even by GB's standards, his treatment of his colleagues on this Budget was beyond belief.

Thursday, March 8

Despite all the worries, the Budget got a very good response. TB was focusing straight away on the Northern Ireland talks. The IRA statement took everyone by surprise, and by the end of the day the feeling was of progress, if not perfectly so. John Reid seemed to have settled in pretty well [as the new Secretary of State for Northern Ireland], though my God does he smoke. In between the various meetings I was working on the Inverness speech and preparing for Hammond. Peter M called first thing as I was looking out over the gardens at Hillsborough and he asked 'How exactly is my castle from which you evicted me so forcibly?' It was a joke, I think, but he was pretty focused when we got on to what we intended to say about Hammond's report tomorrow. I said we had to give a plausible reason for his resignation and that was that people came to be misled and he had taken responsibility for that.

The final report had come through and it was clear Hammond was trying to be fair to everyone. Peter had now redrafted all the lines, so many times that I didn't know if I was coming or going. I didn't want him to know that I had a copy because he was complaining Hammond wouldn't give it to him. There were bits in it that would cause problems for him, e.g. in relation to intelligence advice and also a suggestion that he had helped them before, and that he himself spoke to a private secretary at the Home Office. But he felt it was effectively a total vindication. Derry went through it with a legal mind and he thought we came out fine, Peter less so. A lot would be in the presentation. Peter was clearly only going to be happy if we accepted we had been wrong to get rid of him.

Later in the day TB spoke to Peter from the sitting room upstairs at Hillsborough and when he said he intended to say it cleared Peter but that he had inadvertently caused the public to be misled, Peter became quite menacing and rude. 'I see where you're coming from. It's all about saving your face. You say what you have to say. I'll say what I have to say.' He said the whole thing was a squalid exercise, that he had been pushed out for the sake of expedience, that I had hardened up the line and created the problem. TB listened for a while, then lost his rag, said 'Just listen to me for one second. I have bent over backwards to get this thing to help you and I have to tell you I don't think you come out of it as well as you seem to think. There are real difficulties there for you and we are still trying to help'. Peter said there was confusion, that's all, and he should never have been made to leave the Cabinet. TB said whether he liked it or not, people had been misled but Peter would not accept that.

TB eventually hung up but, showing Peter's intimidating manner can work, TB did take out some of the more critical parts of the draft statement. They spoke again later. Peter said the top line had to be that he had been cleared. He said you have given me no adequate explanation as to why I left the Cabinet. 'Liable to misrepresentation' is hardly a hanging offence. He said resigning was the biggest mistake of his life, that we should have waited for the inquiry but that we had pressed him. If a bit of confusion was the problem, why am I alone in being blamed? He said I [AC] contributed to the confusion and so did the Home Office. TB asked if he intended to shut it down tomorrow. He said it depended on our reaction, and if we were unfair, he would react. He said the whole thing had been squalid. TB: 'I resent that.' Peter read out his draft statement and TB shook his head at me as we listened and mouthed 'impossible to reason with'. TB was dreading tomorrow now. Philip called, said the groups had been really bad.

Friday, March 9

I was woken up by a message to call Peter urgently. He was livid at Norman Smith [BBC political correspondent] on the *Today* programme saying very negative things about him and blaming us. I said I had briefed nobody. He said I had a negative mindset about him and as a result had handled things badly. I said if we had a situation where he and I were saying different things we would be at war by the end of the day and what on earth is the point of that? In the end, we agreed the best thing was to say nothing about the resignation and simply not reopen it. It was the right decision. TB said later Peter saved us from a big mistake, that if we had gone for a big explanation of why he resigned, it would have been much harder to shut down. Even in this stuff, there was a GB element, with Derry, wound up by GB, believing Peter M had been briefing against him. TB, Godric and I did a conference call finally to agree the line we would deploy, and then we put up the shutters. The speech for Inverness was pretty much sorted, though we had the usual last-minute scrabble for jokes. But the basic message of no complacency and Labour the party of the economy was fine. Cherie had read Hammond overnight and her take on it was pretty undramatic, that Peter came over as a bit of a prima donna but it wasn't so bad for anyone.

We went by helicopter to Aldergrove for the flight to Inverness, signing off the [Scottish Labour Party conference] speech on the plane. I called Peter, after our terrible row earlier, and said he was right about not mentioning the resignation. On arrival in Inverness, I was conscious of being filmed everywhere I went because part of the Hammond story was Peter and me. We did a school visit, where TB did a doorstep, tone and body language good, Peter having done his thing already, then into the car and off. TB said he felt no real difficulty. We had Jack Price [film-maker making election broadcast] at the hotel filming TB working on the speech. I did a very people-friendly section while Tony did a mini rewrite. The speech went fine without really taking off.[1] Philip was worried that Hague's core script was beginning to strike a chord whereas ours was still a bit complicated.

Saturday, March 10

Papers were full of the Peter stuff but things could have been worse. And despite the media focus, I didn't feel this was going through to the public much. We now had to shut it down. Peter sent through a fax, almost comic, saying that he could not guarantee that 'friends of Peter Mandelson' may not be out causing us trouble and pointing the

[1] In a pre-election rallying cry to Scottish Labour activists, Blair said 'We were warriors against complacency in 1997. We must be warriors against complacency now. Polls don't deliver elections. People do and the people are the boss and they will decide and we have to re-earn their trust . . . we should be proud of what we've done and humble about what we've still to do.'

finger of blame at me but he would do all in his power to ensure that didn't happen. We spoke and I agreed it was better if I stayed out of things today and instead let Godric put out the line that nobody was more pleased than I that Peter was cleared and we remained friends.

In any event, the big worry remained foot and mouth, which was simply not clearing in the way that MAFF had told us it should. DB called to say that GB was trying to cut TB out of the plans on one million jobs by postponing Monday's policy event. Separately Alistair Darling told me GB and he may do a press conference tomorrow. DB said 'Call me paranoid, but I am worried TB is being cut out of things whilst GB is in the ascendancy.' He thought GB was trying to position himself as Mr Economy and Mr Jobs, and position TB as FMD, Peter M, plus any other passing disasters.

Sunday, March 11

There wasn't much in the Sundays, some crap about Nick Jones' silly book.[1] Philip was still worried, felt the Tories were breaking through more than we thought.

Monday, March 12

I had gone to bed early last night but been woken by JP in a rage, accusing me of trying to run his department because I had got Nick Raynsford [housing and planning minister] on the *Today* programme. I said to John it was hardly worth bothering him with, and there was no need to get wound up about it. Also, we had to develop a cadre of ministers who could do general thematic stuff, like challenging cynicism, not just departmental issues. Philip said on the way in he thought Peter had detached us from the public again. He also felt since GB became more involved in strategy, TB had slightly lost his voice and his power. There was definitely too much in the press at the moment about the inevitability of GB taking over and I didn't like this notion of GB being the big ideas powerhouse while TB took control of Ireland, foreign affairs and things that went wrong. At his morning meeting, Pat and I tried to persuade him he was ceding too much control of the levers at Millbank. Pat said he had to understand there were a lot of people there who were not for him, they were for GB.

Later I had a crazy runaround with Douglas Alexander and Ed Miliband over GB's refusal to get involved in the launch of an

---

[1] The BBC journalist had written *The Control Freaks: How New Labour Gets Its Own Way*, which was being serialised in the *Mail on Sunday*.

anti-Tory poster because he was the Chancellor and thought TB should do it. So Chancellor was now more important than prime minister was it? TB had spent part of the weekend reading up everything we had on foot and mouth, and was really fired up, worried, felt we weren't on top of it in the way that we should be. He met Nick Brown and Jim Scudamore. They told me and Godric afterwards we were in for a very long haul. Cherie and Fiona had a meeting with Jeremy and Jonathan and it was clear that RW was blocking some of TB's ideas, e.g. not allowing Anji to manage civil servants à la Jonathan and I. Jeremy and Jonathan were both a bit taken aback by how angry Cherie and Fiona were about some of the planned changes.

Peter Hyman, when he heard about the planned new tripartite structure, said 'Why are we giving a big managerial job to the worst manager in the building [Jonathan], the job of managing Labour to the least Labour person in the operation [Anji] whilst taking you [AC], our best communicator, out of front-line communication?' He felt I would be miscast as a communications director. I had lunch with Peter Hill and Hugh Whittow [editor and deputy editor, *Daily Star*] who both felt [Richard] Desmond was about as difficult a man to work for as had ever been born. But they said Desmond was totally up for us and dead keen on TB and me. I was trying to get more on top of FMD communications. Nobody for example seemed to be gripping the impact on tourism, different government departments were doing their own thing.

Tuesday, March 13

Before I left for the office, I said to Fiona, maybe the only way we can get a life back is for us both to get out of Number 10 but I would be very worried about leaving TB right now. The problem was she had grown pretty much to despise him, and therefore didn't share my sense of commitment and support. Jeremy told me his and Jonathan's meeting with Fiona and Cherie was the most difficult he had ever had to handle. Meanwhile Anji told me she was definitely going, because she felt she had CB, FM, SM and DM all ganging up on her and if that continued, she wouldn't last. Fiona was in tears again later, said this was about whether I had proper respect for her or whether I would just always do whatever I wanted.

I met GB to go over the week ahead. He was in quite mellow form. He had failed to stop Blunkett from doing his New Deal next steps and I did feel with Gordon at the moment that he had a forward agenda being mapped out. We were now getting into a rhythm of regular FMD meetings. We had the NFU in again. TB asked me where

I was on my own position. I said I was still minded to leave, that it was getting close to choosing between family and job. He said if it has really got to that, you have to choose the family but it leaves me with a real state. He said it was also a bit much if any member of the staff thought they could have a veto on whether other members stayed or went. He said he had Gordon and Peter fucking up his Cabinet relations and now all this to deal with in the office. Deep down, I didn't think that whatever changes were made to structure that it would make much difference to the way I worked so in the end I just had to make a straight decision, stay or go. After lunch I went to TBWA [advertising agency] for an election Grid planning meeting. I liked the people there, and the atmosphere, and we got a lot of work done. TB felt he was going to need to spend more and more time on FMD. He wanted to go for May 3 as election day but felt it would be impossible if this was still going on. Later, Calum called twice, first to say his watch had been stolen, then to say Burnley beat Watford [1-0].

Wednesday, March 14

A number of councils were now urging us to call off the local elections because of FMD. Part of me felt the whole thing was a political ploy by the Tories, but TB was anxious we did nothing that could be seen or thought to be insensitive. He called twice before I had even got out of the house and was also desperate to speak to GB, who later came over to Number 10 for a meeting about it. GB and I felt we shouldn't get drawn, should basically just shut it down. I felt that only if it was genuinely logistically impossible should we call them off. Later, we spent ages talking about how best to answer it if TB was asked at PMQs. But in the end he was never asked and instead I was asked at the four o'clock. I said there was no doubt we could manage the local elections and we had to be careful not to send out a signal that life as we knew it had come to an end. Also, the implications for tourism of the message that the countryside was effectively closed were pretty grim and had not been sufficiently understood at the start of the outbreak.

In Cabinet, JP complained the Green Paper on jobs had not been circulated or discussed properly. FMD was the main focus and TB said it was serious, the number of cases growing day by day, the future unsure. Most of it was traceable back to one farmer and two dealers and it was now affecting large parts of the country. He said the farming sector was in difficulty even before this and we were going to have to provide a lot of help. Tourism was also being badly hit. He felt some of the restrictions on movement may be over the top but we had to be at the tough end of the market. He said Nick Brown was doing a terrific job in desperately difficult circumstances. Nick did a more detailed factual briefing. Blunkett was the first who pointed out the sheer emotional power that this was unleashing. He said there were industrial, employment and political problems arising from this and the government had to keep its nerve. Nick was looking tired. He was doing a statement tomorrow announcing massive slaughter of sheep. PMQs was OK, TB fine on FMD. Hague went on [calling for the sacking of] Vaz and TB really went for him. TB was worried that I had been too hard in the line on local elections. Blunkett's intervention preyed on my mind. A lot of this was about emotion, the sense that we were urban and didn't get the rural community, the sheer power of animals being slaughtered, and the mood in the country the whole thing was engendering.

Later, I asked the boys what they thought about me packing in the job. Calum seemed to think it was a good idea. Rory was appalled, said it was the best job I'd ever get and added 'You have to understand that it's good for my image at school.' Fiona was really piling on the pressure though and said she just couldn't understand why I would not give it up when she was asking me to do so. Also, as I had ended up pretty much hating the press, being driven crazy by the politicians, she didn't understand why I didn't want to leave anyway, and she was totally unconvinced his planned changes would make any difference at all.

Thursday, March 15

TB was up north and must have called half a dozen times in the morning, like a phone-in caller making random points to a radio station – about FMD, Vaz, anything that came into his head. Prince Charles was leading the news with the Prince's Trust £500,000 donation to rural charities. It's amazing he can lead the news with small change given their wealth and we can get fuck all for spending billions. I had a very good meeting with GB, Douglas and Philip re the first five days of the campaign. We had pretty much decided to go on 'the choice' rather than ambition, and use the main events to get the dividing lines down quickly. GB felt we should be positive for as long as possible whilst hitting the Tories hard. Philip felt I had lost a lot of my drive recently, which was true, because of all the difficulties and distractions. He said GB and his people had all the levers, and I needed to get my hands back on them. But it had been a good meeting and I felt re-energised. Stan Greenberg's latest poll showed that we had made real strides since the Budget, particularly among women with kids. We were at forty-six to twenty-seven. TB was up as well. I was struggling with words at the moment and forced myself to work for two hours trying to improve the basic core script, and I got somewhere in the end. I worked a bit on Nick Brown's statement on FMD. Nick was handling the politics just about OK but this was such a big job for any minister or department.

Friday, March 16

FMD was big, bad, more and more difficult. Prince Charles was getting a very good press for his intervention which was actually deeply unhelpful. TB said he knew exactly what he was doing. He also asked whether Charles had ever considered help when 6,000 jobs were lost at Corus [steel manufacturer]. He said this was all about screwing us and trying to get up the message that we weren't generous enough to the farmers. He asked me about my situation again, I said things were bad. He said surely we can sort it, and asked me to go in and discuss it with him. I went up to the flat. He said whatever happened he would always call on me because he valued my judgement and friendship. He said part of my problem was that I like responsibility and I was good at big decisions but I hated hassle and the hassle of endlessly dealing with egos and phone calls and our ridiculous media was getting me down. He said we could get others to deal with the press but he still needed me for advice, politics, my feel for the party, my words and my ability to motivate.

He said he also believed that GB would at some stage strike against him and if he was going to repel him he needed me to be part of that operation along with a new party chairman, a new general secretary, and a much stronger political operation. He felt that GB was currently overreaching himself and in any event despite his phenomenal strengths, the quality he lacked which he [TB] had was natural humanity. He said when he really wanted to wind up Gordon, he reminded him of Clinton and Gore and told him to be careful not to be Gore to his Clinton. That applied to the politics, but also the personality. You can have a strategy for everything, but you can't have a strategy for being human, a real person. You either are or you're not. He said I was the only other person in our operation for whom GB had any fear or respect. He doesn't like you like he used to, but he does respect you and he does fear you. He said he felt deep down I wanted to stay and I was trying to find reasons for going so that I could please Fiona but he felt I would resent it if I went. He

March '01: Polls show real gains since Budget

also felt I was underselling myself if I thought I was more suited to press work than strategy. In the end, the one argument he would always support was the family coming first, but he hoped I could find a way to stay.

Saturday, March 17

Fiona was adamant, said stay if you want but I will never forgive you. She saw it all as black and white whereas for me it was grey. I had been the first one to talk about leaving but it became harder as it became nearer. Partly because of the responsibility, partly leaving the team I was building up, partly the insight that amid all the bad there was a lot of good, but also because it actually mattered. I also had a dread of becoming a has-been rentaquote wanker like all the other pundits. Tom Bower [investigative journalist and author] did a piece today saying Fiona was pressing me to ease up and saying I could name my price in PR, books or punditry. Exactly.

FMD was becoming more and more of a problem and despite all the promises, it was clear MAFF didn't have a grip. We were certainly going to have to take over the presentational strategy. TB called, said he wanted a strategy to put the scientific case for the cull, and also get up the message that the countryside was not shut. He was beginning to sound a bit panicked. This was our opponents' last shot at moving us off strategic course. I did a conference call with him, Nick, David North [private secretary] after Scudamore, the chief vet, had warned us it could go on for months and months. I felt we had to start to identify some of our opponents and their arguments as politically motivated, e.g. the Duke of Devonshire [former Conservative minister in the Macmillan government]. David Handley's mob were also now getting involved. TB felt MAFF were incapable of subtlety. The key now was to do whatever it took to knock out the disease. There were some suggestions of farmers moving livestock illegally, which was likely to spread the disease. But for us to get too heavy on that risked playing into the town vs country divide that our opponents were trying to grow. The pressure to suspend elections was growing. The 'countryside is open for business' message was sitting uneasily alongside the fact we had to kill hundreds of thousands of healthy animals.

I went to Sheffield Wednesday vs Burnley [Wednesday 2, Burnley 0] with Calum but was on the phone re FMD most of the time. There wasn't much in the Sundays. Mixed views on May 3 [as the date of the general election], but a general sense that FMD was not being handled as well as it should be.

TB was working on FMD all day and did a very good note setting out a forward strategy. Nick Brown had done well early on but it was getting more and more ragged and though the NFU was still trying to be reasonable with us, a lot of farmers were getting more and more critical, while the public imagery was bad. Tourism was really getting hit hard now. We were going to have to take over the whole of the presentational strategy and a good deal of the operational management as well. TB wanted us to go for a subtler differentiation approach – focus relentlessly on areas where it was really bad but try to get restrictions lifted on other areas. Philip was getting very nervous about the impact of FMD on public opinion more generally. GB asked me to get Alex F involved in the drugs campaign. He was keen, but felt to do it properly he needed more time than he had. I told him his name was currently mud with Fiona because of what he had said re me and the job. He said he could have never kept going without support at home. I watched Rory Bremner which had a hilarious *Big Brother* [TV programme] spoof of TB, me, Derry, Robin and Ken Livingstone.

Bad start to the week. FMD plus sleaze with the *Mail* still pushing on Vaz, [Geoffrey] Robinson up again. TB did a 75-minute meeting with Nick Brown and [environment minister Michael] Meacher on FMD. Everything depended on us doing everything possible to knock out the disease, to re-establish a sense of basic competence and develop a forward strategy for the countryside. He said we must have a sense by the end of the week that it's turning. We need to be promoting tourism alongside. I felt we had been far too sensitive early on to MAFF's concerns that a Number 10 takeover would spark the feeling of a crisis. If there was one thing we should have learned by now, it's that once you are in crisis mode, you need more not less centralisation. With TB clearly signalling we were taking it over, I now sensed relief rather than alarm across the table.

He was still keen on May 3, and felt it could be possible. What was clear was that the Tories wanted to put it off and wanted more and more of this rubbish from the *Mail* agenda. TB had to leave to do an NHS speech to GPs. The eleven o'clock was mainly FMD. When TB got back, we had a long meeting with GB, DA, the Eds [Balls and Miliband], DM, PG and PH re election strategy. GB was not sure about the concept of the pledges. We won him round on that but then there was an argument about whether we should include a pledge on a referendum as one of the key pledges. TB, GB and I felt there was no need. Philip felt we needed it for defensive reasons. It was a good meeting. TB was finally willing to let us really go for the *Mail*. We sanctioned Byers to go for them legally re the Tom Bower book [*The Paymaster*] on [Geoffrey] Robinson and the *Mail* accusing Byers of suppressing a report that was not his to suppress.[1] TB agreed we should never have dropped Mailwatch. GB was clear we had to be positive for as long as possible but really go for them on division and competence. We had a meeting on the leader's tour at which a few good ideas came out. Philip did some groups tonight, said the women were good, the men terrible.

Tuesday, March 20

TB was on the phone before 7 and a few more times before I left. He was worried we were looking very insensitive on election timing and was obviously being spooked by GB who, though denying it, was putting out signals that he doubted the wisdom of a May 3 poll. GB was also, according to Peter H, deliberately neutering the manifesto so that he could present the Budget and the CSR as the real political agenda and TB's little manifesto as the damp squib in between. I didn't mind GB having a strong agenda. I did mind Ed Balls being rude and cocky in meetings with TB and told GB so. TB felt we probably had to give some kind of palliative, for example postpone the locals for a month to June even if there was no clear intellectual case for it. But we did have to watch the signal it would send re tourism. He had another meeting with Nick Brown and Scudamore which was difficult because they were now more resistant suddenly to the extra support from the centre. Nick was tired and stumbling. Scudamore seemed to me to have an unrealistic view of things. Nick told me afterwards that the middle-ranking people at MAFF were all just interested in covering their own backs. Stan G and Philip both took the view now that the public would think there was no need for an election and ministers should all be concentrating on FMD. TB had a meeting with tourist chiefs, then farmers, then internal. FMD took up most of the day.

I had to do a pre-Stockholm [European Council] briefing to push economic reform. I was feeling real stress at the moment. A combination of the day job, election planning, the constant rowing with Fiona and trying to resolve my own future was resulting in a feeling almost of being overwhelmed. Hague broke ranks and started to move

---

[1] Byers' solicitors threatened shops selling the book.

towards calling for the elections to be off. I got Margaret Beckett lined up to go for him. We had a good meeting on TB's [election] tour which had to be about him strong and confident, taking the arguments out to people. I was still putting the case for a May 3 poll. I had run over the Heath in the dark last night and fallen over, twisted my ankle and hurt my knee. I tried to run again today but it hurt.

Wednesday, March 21

We were getting badly hit on competence re FMD and also the sense that we were more interested in the election than dealing with it. As GB said, we should shut up about elections and get on top of it. But TB said he was getting pissed off at the way, as ever, that when there was a real crisis on, GB ran for cover, didn't properly engage on the issues. Both TB and I were moving to the view that any talk of election would look like putting party before country. Hague had helped in a way because he was making the case that would allow us to postpone both local and national. We had pretty much lost confidence in MAFF now. David North and Jeremy Heywood were pretty much full-time on FMD. TB felt we could only go for May 3 if it was absolutely clear we were on top of the disease.

We put together a good script for PMQs which went well. He focused on the logistical operation required and on tourism. On PR, TB had seen [Charles] Kennedy yesterday to work out a deal and Don Macintyre [*Independent*] had got hold of it. I later discovered he had had lunch with Roger Liddle [special adviser] and I let rip at him. I went way over the top and when I apologised Roger said 'Of course this is what happened to poor Peter, you all jumped to conclusions.' PMQs having gone well, TB agreed to do a stack of TV and radio interviews. Actually he had done better in the House and maybe we should have stuck to that. The questioning was pretty aggressive and he said afterwards, some farmer in Northumberland starts all this, it costs us £100 million and destroys tourism and I cop the blame. He agreed to go to Stockholm via Carlisle on a foot-and-mouth visit.

There was a feeling GB was now exploiting our problems on FMD. It's what fuels the doubts about his leadership abilities because he is always calculating his own position. Why isn't he out there putting the case about the economy? Tony Bevins [former *Express* political editor] was very ill. Mishtu [his wife] died just after coming back from the US to see him. Dreadful. The four'clock was all FMD plus a new inquiry into Vaz. I tried to pick his brains on whether the Queen was a hundred per cent happy at the way Prince Charles was piling in. He was unbelievably discreet though, occasionally told the odd funny story about their meetings, but even with me, rarely let slip anything of substance from their discussions.

Thursday, March 22
At least Fiona and I were talking properly again, though the pressure was doing my head in. She accepted there were some upsides to me doing the job but she felt the downsides were far heavier, and she felt that if the roles were reversed, and she was doing something I wanted her not to do, she would listen more than I was. She felt I was not being honest with myself, that I was worried about losing status and power, and there might be something in that. Truth be told, there was a lot about the job I hated, particularly the press, dealing with ministerial egos the whole time, elements of TB, his modus operandi and his personality, and there was a long list of reasons I wanted to leave, but a very powerful pull to stay.

TB was at me again, stated explicitly that he needed me re GB, that I was the only person he feared and 'He needs to know I still have my exocet around.' He said Peter having gone again, he [GB] would love it if I went. I said the problem was Fiona and I used to have a partnership of equals and I was now seen as dominant and because of our positions, it was impossible to have views of our own or a life outside. He had had another meeting with Nick Brown and Jim Scudamore at the end of which he said he felt their grip was lessening and this thing was potentially out of control. He was beginning to fear a May election was impossible because of the insensitivity point. Most of us remained instinctively in favour of May 3, but I could tell he was moving against it. We couldn't just press on regardless of what anyone felt.

After a rather subdued Cabinet, I chaired a meeting of all the departments with a bearing on FMD. On the communications front, we were going to have to take it over completely. I got [Mike] Granatt [head of GICS] involved in beefing up the operation centrally and co-ordinating regionally. I was worried we were getting the usual talk a good game while not delivering. I decided that Godric, Anne [Shevas], Martin Sheehan and Bill Bush's outfit were going to have to be involved full-time on FMD. GB was being difficult still. At the morning meeting, I suggested he did something on tourism and its importance to the economy but he said no, the real economic problem will stem from all the money being wasted on this. He had later gone ballistic when TB agreed to a £100 million animal welfare fund. It was not a day that filled either TB or me with much confidence in the Civil Service.

Brian Bender [now MAFF permanent secretary] was clearly finding it really difficult to deal with Nick Brown. The 'top officials' sent into Carlisle to sort things out struck me as being out of their depth. TB was in Carlisle for about an hour and sat round the table listening to all the various organisations and quickly got the message they were having to cope with all manner of stupid bureaucratic problems. He came away a bit shocked. He later spoke to Hoon who said there was lots more the MOD could do if MAFF would let them. He then spoke to the boss of the Environment Agency [Sir John Harman] who said he had not really been asked before about the best place to find big burial sites. TB was really angry with Nick who had been telling us everything was being done that could be done. He was livid with GB for ducking out of the front line and with Nick for being truculent and difficult. He was getting clearer and clearer that May 3 was impossible. And later in the day I got Andy Marr to say that for the first time we were thinking about delaying. On the flight to Stockholm, TB was raging about incompetence, said we had made assumptions that basic things were being done, which weren't.

Friday, March 23

[John] Major had done a letter to TB on the election timing and was now embarked on his little media operation which included the *Today* programme 8.10 slot, going on about TB's disreputable spin machine. I really wanted to go for him but wiser counsel prevailed and we ignored it. But it all added to the sense that May 3 was impossible. TB felt it would be insensitive. We had breakfast with [Giuliano] Amato, which was a total waste of time. I spoke to Vaz about how to do his media. TB travelled to the summit centre with Amato, thereby totally screwing up the protocol order. His mind was never far from FMD with the epidemiological report due out, which contained some pretty gruesome material likely to cause a bit of panic. TB had to be in the main meeting most of the time but was calling us in and out wanting information, and wanting to feed in ideas. GB came out and asked for a call to Nick Brown which I fixed. It was obvious GB was telling Nick not to listen to all this stuff about presidential style, that he must not let the centre take over. I was picking up from elsewhere that Nick complained he had to spend all his time listening to rubbish from Number 10 about what they should be doing. Jonathan said it was as clear as daylight GB was using it to stir against TB.

TB said later GB's big weakness, which in the end made him less of a leader type, was that he found it hard to see beyond his own agenda. GB had now got into his head that Godric should go to MAFF to run the operation from there, said it was bad for Downing Street if it was an obvious takeover because it would fall to us and TB in particular to take the hit. Especially given what he was up to with Nick, it was just too transparent. I told him Nick had been offered help several times and refused it. GB particularly disliked these summits because they were so obviously a pecking order and TB was so obviously Number 1. But when there were no foreigners around, GB occasionally displayed a disrespect bordering on contempt. TB had given up trying to maintain even with us that there wasn't a malign side to GB.

I did a briefing on the epidemiological report and on the summit and was very downbeat. But then ITN ran pictures from a host camera picking up TB answering a question from Prodi about elections and that sent our lot into a total frenzy which we had to damp down as best we could. Of course it totally cut across our message that we were working flat out on FMD rather than worrying about the elections. We had a bilateral with Putin who was much more relaxed, told a few funny spy stories from his KGB days, said there were all kinds of diplomats kicked out of the US for spying who weren't really spies. TB filled him in on Bush, said his impression was that he would be open with Putin, and the best approach on NMD was to say frankly what the worries were. Blunkett called, said the news coverage on FMD was dreadful, that there was a real sense we had been over-whelmed and didn't know how to deal with it. News came through that Tony Bevins had died, just a few days after Mishtu. I put out words from TB and a tribute of my own. He was a huge loss, to political journalism as much as anything because he was one of the last who was really serious, amid all the mischief. He had also always been absolutely brilliant with me, supportive and full of good advice.

Saturday, March 24

I was hoping that yesterday was the real low point in media terms re FMD. Godric was doing a good job. GB was still pressing me to send him [Godric] to MAFF, but that missed the point. TB was up early making a series of phone calls on FMD before we had a meeting to go through the summit conclusions before breakfast with Bertie Ahern before we left for the summit. Schroeder stole the show when somebody lobbed in a football during the photocall and he did fifteen kick-ups. The summit stuff was reasonably straightforward though we just about lost the energy row with the French. I did the Sundays with a couple of strong lines Godric had worked up on pigswill and 21-day movement of sheep. For the first time in days, we were pushing our own story. I spoke to Nick to try to get him to push on the same lines.

I slept on the flight back to Devon while TB did a couple of boxes. We were driven to Exeter. Lucie [McNeil] had done a terrific job advancing [the visit]. Despite a small number of protesters, it went fine. TB met NFU leaders, businessmen and hoteliers, and said he wanted to hear for himself any changes they thought we needed to improve operational effectiveness. The NFU guys went through some of the hurdles they were facing. They had some pretty desperate stories to tell. As well as the emotional and economic trauma, the constant imagery of burning pyres was really hitting tourism now. There were constant complaints about communication, which meant rumour was too strong a currency. Again, TB was left feeling that things had not been done that should have been, there was too much red tape, that we were pulling levers but not always in a way that made things happen. Rural MPs were getting really jumpy. TB said that with the media as it was, demanding instant solutions to complex problems, we were always going to be behind the curve on an unexpected crisis as bad as this, and the Civil Service had not covered itself in glory.

Sunday, March 25

We had a series of conference calls on FMD. TB had a series of ideas on things that needed doing following the trip to Devon. He was amazingly resilient at the moment, had basically decided we just have to put everything now into sorting it. I went in for a Cobra meeting at 2pm and although things were still too slow and cumbersome, at least they had the message that TB was basically on their backs. Fiona and I had another long session trying to resolve what we do post-election. We were both now worried that if I left and felt forced out, I would always resent it. She now felt that because she had accepted a secondary position and a lesser job, I had ended up respecting her less. We had dinner with the Jowells [Tessa and her husband David Mills] and Gavin [Millar] and family. Jessie [Tessa's daughter] had an interesting take. Said I had made my mark, the mark would not get any bigger, I had carried too much for too long and I should quit while I am ahead.

Monday, March 26

I still had a sense we weren't really on top of things and that was confirmed at the 9am Cobra meeting. The MAFF people were tired and lacking in clarity. The things TB had asked for yesterday were still being promised for tomorrow. He pointed out for example that a decision on the Solway cull was taken ten days ago and we were still talking about it while the farmers were all saying get on with it. Scudamore was giving reasons why things couldn't happen rather than explaining how they could. TB later told Wilson the Civil Service had shown itself very good at setting up new committees but we kept announcing policy approaches which they could not implement. On election timing, Jack Straw was still urging May 3, TB was pretty convinced we had to go for June as a way of taking out some heat. At Cobra, we agreed to try to implement a policy of twenty-four hours from diagnosis to slaughter, forty-eight hours for contiguous farms.

I spoke to Nick Brown up in Cumbria before the 11, which was not as tough as I feared it would be, and at least they were accepting the argument about the scale of crisis we were having to deal with. I took another meeting to get more people into the central operation and into MAFF. TB had to do a statement on Stockholm which was dull as hell and in questions FMD was the main thing. Godric and co were making a difference but it was ridiculous that every time there was a crisis, departments fell down. There wasn't the cultural change through the system that we needed. I know MAFF had a reputation for being useless, but people would be genuinely shocked. The argument was now moving towards vaccination. We went over to the House, where TB went for Hague on opportunism, then back to do *Farming Today* [BBC radio programme]. TB was going to have to front much more of this, and we needed to see him out there dealing with it, as well as running it from the centre.

Tuesday, March 27
The Tube financing plan was finally going down the pan it seemed, with Bob Kiley [transport commissioner] walking away, and Ken [Livingstone] suing us.[1] I had a chat with Pat McFadden re my future and was alarmed at his alarm. Pat was never one to overreact, but he said if I went he was worried the operation would collapse and GB would move in for the kill. He said TB totally underestimated the extent to which GB had a rival operation at work. If TB slipped, Gordon was 'ready to roll', and we had very little by way of

[1] Kiley, along with London mayor Ken Livingstone, had expressed vehement opposition to public-private partnerships – PPP – in the running and renewal of the London Underground network.

resistance. Tessa had told us on Sunday that GB was embarked on a major charm offensive on the PLP and of course though he was busy, he had far more time to play with than TB, who was probably still too sympathetic re how GB spent that time.

At GB's morning meeting, he said absolutely nothing re the MAFF situation, except for 'We have to be seen to get on top of it, and I'll leave that to you, Alastair.' He saw everything through his own prism. This was so obviously the most important issue at the moment, but he didn't want to be over-drawn into it. Ian McCartney [Cabinet Office minister] gave me a look and a flick of the head that said 'He's running from this one.' I went to Cobra and then had a meeting with Mike Granatt and Robert Lowson [MAFF director of communications], which was pretty dispiriting. Mike talked a good game but the output was not great, while Robert seemed lost. We had a conference call later at which they both kept explaining why we couldn't do this or hadn't done that. Unbelievable. Cobra was poor as well, lots of things promised yesterday which were still not happening, and a total lack of focus from MAFF. We had been banging on about the need for a report on pigswill, and on sheep movements, but they were so slow. I know they had a lot on but I had the impression they went back and had more meetings about meetings and went into headless-chicken mode. There was a danger as we gripped the communications that we now started to get the media image ahead of the reality, which would bring its own dangers. Some of the papers were saying they had 'FMD fatigue', which probably meant they thought we were getting on top of things, but we weren't. TB was getting exasperated again. RW was just chipping in to finish other people's sentences. The MAFF people looked shot to pieces.

I had lunch with David Frost who was very strongly of the view May 3 was a no-no. TB went to the NEC then up to Worcester for an FMD visit while I worked with Nick B on his statement and tried to get some decent message into it. Mum called to say the *Mail* had been round when she was out and for some reason Dad had asked them in and was chatting away when she got back. She said he was talking away quite the thing, but she gripped it straight away, told them to leave there and then and they had absolutely nothing to say to them. I reminded Dad these were the people who had said he was dead, but he had fallen for the old trick of them wanting to do a piece about how proud he must be, blah di blah. TB got back from Worcester for his audience with the Queen. I filled him in on how dreadful MAFF had been.

A bad story in *The Times* re Anji, badly done in re job moves etc., and TB was getting more angered, saying he was being thwarted from doing what he thought was the right thing to do, and he had to be allowed to make the final judgements re personnel. FMD was still raging and we still lacked the basic factual information that allowed us properly to track and respond. I went up to see TB to work on his speech. I had trailed a few lines on tourism which was leading the morning news, again giving a sense we were more on top of things than we were. TB felt that better media management would actually lead to a better operation, because partly this was about calming people within the system, and also lowering the temperature among the public. If people knew how hard it was to crank our machinery into gear, they would be appalled. We saw Chris Smith [re tourism], then Nick Brown and Scudamore and the argument was all pushing towards vaccination, maybe Cumbria and Devon first. Scudamore had the eyes of a man who had been shot to bits. NB was tired and deflated. I sent him a note re my assessment of the MAFF operation which he clearly copied around because soon after Robert Lowson called and asked if he retained my confidence. I said yes, provided he accepted the need for more support. I was in fact losing patience with him and with Mike Granatt because I kept being told things were being done but by the next meeting I was being told the same thing. Godric did the 11 and did fine considering we were so badly armed on the figures front. I had a GB meeting on pledges, manifesto format and timing, where the argument was becoming more open and public. We went over to the House, where again despite a lack of proper facts and figures TB did fine. He was so much better at the tone than Nick or anyone else.

I got a call about a *Times* poll which still had us nineteen ahead, so that would get people thinking May was still a possibility but TB was pretty much settled against it. I was trying to be objective, and concluded it was probably my own situation that was pushing me to May, and he was right to delay. To go for May would mean calling it in days and it just wouldn't be right. It would also be the worst possible backdrop for the launch of a campaign. I used the poll to brief the line that all he cared about was getting on top of the disease, and that re local elections, what mattered was whether logistically they were impossible because of all the restrictions on movement. He had discussed the timing issue with the Queen and said she seemed relaxed either way. I also felt we maybe needed a bit more time to get ourselves in shape campaign-wise. We were not exactly at the peak of our form, so a bit more time, however frustrating, was not the end of the world. But TB's big point was the insensitivity it showed to people really suffering, and the sense it would give to the broader public about our priorities. You didn't have to think about it too long to know he was right about it, so that was pretty much that, though we continued to have people bending our ear re May 3.

Thursday, March 29

Philip had done some groups in Shropshire last night and said people were appalled at the idea we could be considering a general election with FMD as bad as it was. Then tonight he did some groups in South Norwood, who said go for it, so there was clearly a rural/urban divide on it. But TB had pretty much decided. He had a number of NFU meetings today re vaccination, and later with a group of scientists. We did a webcast later, as well as some US interviews to try to push the tourism message and explain that the countryside was not all on fire, which is the impression the media coverage there was giving. The NFU were clearly reluctant on vaccination. David North had been clear from the start we should be going that way, but they were leaning more to vaccination plus slaughter, which improved compensation. Ben Gill [NFU president] said he wanted to stay plugged in to all our discussions re vaccination.

Cabinet was all FMD, and a bit of Macedonia. GB gave a little lecture on the potential enormity of the public spending implications as the bill was running to the billions. He was not getting his hands dirty on this one at all, and tonally the sense was that this was money he was having to shell out because everyone else was fucking up. Nick Brown did a presentation and then TB went on even longer. He had become an 'expert' and went into so much detail some of them started to glaze over. There was no mention of election dates, apart from a couple of jokes at the end. After Cabinet, Jeremy H and I discussed with TB whether David King [chief scientific adviser], who TB had taken to, and was affectionately calling 'Dr Strangelove', should do a media briefing showing various possible projections. There was at least a sense we were getting a grip of the government machine, and media-wise Princess Margaret's illness was taking over as their main focus. GB was still being difficult, said to me after Cabinet 'At some point, Cabinet government will have to be reimposed and TB will have to extricate himself from being in charge of this.' I said what are you talking about? – this is one of the biggest crises we have faced, with enormous implications, MAFF have been hopeless, and the idea TB should not be taking this over is absurd. It would help if he had more support. He was a bit taken aback, but I knew he had been stirring with Nick. I said that there was no point pretending MAFF could handle this and rather than stirring re presidentialism, he should be weighing in with us. Milburn sent me a note during Cabinet, saying had I noticed how GB ran for cover every time the shit really hit the fan? It was hard not to.

I met David King and we agreed to go for a detailed, heavy briefing Sunday for Monday. I felt that despite the risks of it being misinterpreted, he would do it well, and it was important we give a sense of being on the front foot, and stop the whole thing being dominated by burning pyres and a politically driven agenda from elsewhere. Peter H and I were writing lines to take re election timing, which was now much more obviously a public issue that had to be addressed. TB and I walked round the garden, established final clarity in our own minds it was the right thing to delay, and then talked through the various basic management issues that would have to be addressed. I went over to the Treasury for a meeting. They were all there – GB, Bob Shrum [US pollster and strategist] was over for a few days, DA, the Eds, Sue [Nye] plus DM, PG, Pat. GB was still sitting on the fence re timing, said 'You could do May 3 if you think the machinery is in place,' then 'You could do June provided you can guarantee not to be pushed further back.' They were still keen for May 3, and some of them making clear they thought TB would be less visible in the campaign if he was still focused on FMD. I did most of the talking with GB pressing as devil's advocate, saying if we could not be sure when it was brought under control, why was June any more certain than May, and was there not a risk re jobs, tourism/economy, the continuing impact in the US and so on? I felt we could turn delay into a positive in many ways – country before party, TB on the right priorities, and then leading the process of getting it under control, using the time to strengthen campaign plans etc. If we delayed the locals, it would be seen as a clear signal the general election would be on the same day.

I could not quite work out if GB was thinking in self-interested terms or genuinely trying to work out the best for party and government. Philip felt they were pushing for May because it would lead to a good but reduced majority, with TB circumscribed in his role. We went on for some ninety minutes and by the end I was pretty isolated in saying June. Ed Miliband was the only GB person against May. GB was undecided. He took me aside again at the end and we had a calmer and friendlier version of our earlier exchange. The irony of his statement re Cabinet government was that his colleagues felt TB to be far more collegiate than he was.

Friday, March 30

TB was off to Dumfries for another FMD visit. Lucie [McNeil] was pretty much full-time advancing these visits and doing a good job. They were helping motivate and lead and also getting pretty good regional coverage, which was particularly important in a situation like this. TB was a bit alarmed when he was told he had to dress head to toe in yellow protective gear, but the pictures and words were strong. He had now totally settled on June and said he was convinced it was the right decision for him, and for the government. He was still being pressed by a few people but they were now wasting their breath. The Archbishop of York [Dr David Hope] had said there should be a delay, and that was leading the news.

I set off for Paddington to get the train down to Bevins' funeral, and bumped into JP and the usual chaos on the train. Joan [Hammell, special adviser] was flapping around trying to keep him calm, and Rosie [Winterton, Labour MP] had lost her ticket, and was turning everything upside down to find it, while JP was grumping and harrumphing before we settled down for quite a good chat about things. Like me, he was fonder of Bevins than of most of them, and we swapped a few daft stories about him. Then we turned to various electoral and political issues, though I was conscious we were being earwigged and kept trying to get him to talk more quietly. He was still pro May, but Rosie felt it would be madness. He was broadly onside at the moment, and knew TB had his plate full and was doing his best with FMD, with a lot of buggering around elsewhere in the government.

I'd always been surprised that Bevins was so friendly with [Robert] Kilroy-Silk [talk-show host, former Labour MP]. It was basically the Scouse connection, but I found Kilroy-Silk so unctuous, and Bevins so genuine, that it struck me as an odd one. As the coffin arrived, Kilroy-Silk shouted over to me that they needed someone else tall to carry it and could I help? We chatted amiably, mainly about Bevins, but also a bit about the political scene, on which his views were as off the wall as ever. The funeral was really moving, mainly because his kids were absolutely brilliant and because they captured the best of his character and personality. As the service went on, I remembered the Alan Howarth [defection] story, and the joy on Bevins' face when I dropped the story in his lap, and his immediate understanding of the political significance. I remembered too some of the times he'd phoned me when the shit was flying in my direction and he'd just say 'You all right love? If you need me, let me know.' And I remembered the times he did stories that drove me up the wall, and he'd just say 'Hey, it's not personal. It's only a story.' He was a great bloke, a big loss. I talked a bit to [Don] Macintyre, [Phil] Webster and [Trevor] Kavanagh re election timing, and they were still thinking May. I recalibrated and probably indicated too much it was looking like June. I went back with JP.

TB called and said Scotland felt better. We agreed to postpone Dr Strangelove's briefing till Tuesday. I waited for Fiona to come back from a visit with Cherie and we went to Philip's birthday party. I had a good chat with Bob Shrum re Clinton/Gore, which felt very TB/GB in some ways. Bob was very pro GB though, and clearly felt he could influence him. I said when they were working together, we were unbeatable but GB could be a nightmare to work with.

Saturday, March 31

My chat with Kavanagh had been written up hard as a June election, and the first call of the day was DB saying he was pissed off it came out in a newspaper like that. I explained the background, but everyone would think it was deliberate. It wasn't, but there we are. Of course nobody would point out it wasn't that long ago Kavanagh wrote definitively it was May 3, and I copped it for that as well. I had been hoping to steer Trevor off May and sixty-five per cent towards a delay, but he had gone with it one hundred per cent, and I knew I would have a price to pay with some of the other papers. TB seemed fairly unfazed, and was clear that the *Sun* staying on board was worth working for. Also Webster having chased it harder around 8pm last night, it looked like a News International favouritism job, and we would pay for it elsewhere.

I had an extraordinary call from GB, who said 'As you know I've always been in favour of May 3.' Unbelievable. He said were we confirming June 7? I said we are steering away from May. He said it would mean a nine-week campaign with every day effectively a referendum on the government. Well, there ain't much we can do about it now. TB chaired Cobra, we organised pictures as he left for Chequers and he felt things were better managed now. I tried to organise a bit of support for our position on delay, e.g. Trimble and Mallon, CBI, but it was pretty hopeless and in the end I had to do it myself because I wasn't confident the new system was capable. I did a conference call later with all the ministers due to be doing media tomorrow – RC, Byers, Reid, Nick B, Jack S – and the mood was very jolly. The papers were full of the usual rubbish and I said at one point obviously if you're asked about a reshuffle, just say where you want to go. John Reid said a conference call would actually be a good way of doing a reshuffle. Just pull the plug on people sacked, patch in the new boys and tell everyone what jobs they were doing. 'Would certainly save on emotional energy,' said RC. GB sent over a note on how to ensure we were not pushed beyond June to October, which was his new obsession. Andy Marr [BBC] called later on and, based on my chat, led the news with 'It's official – delayed till June' even though I had not gone beyond the line already out there.

Sunday, April 1

Yesterday and today TB and I were working on a statement for tomorrow re elections. At one stage we considered doing it today to give us an element of surprise, but that faded fairly quickly. Of course it was a problem in that we could not be certain re June if FMD remained as bad as it was, but TB felt we still had to do it this way. There was a big bad profile of Anji in the *Observer*, and it both upset Anji, because she was being targeted a bit, and it upset Cherie because there was lots of the 'other woman in his life' kind of thing. TB was furious, feeling Anji was being deliberately done in as a way of forcing her out. He said it was bad enough having to deal with Peter M and GB without this kind of stuff kicking off in the office. He said if he could not talk to his own key people without it spilling out to the press, what was he supposed to do? People were trying to thwart him re decisions he had made, and using the press to do so, and he was sick of it.

Sally called, said people would be fine if I was in overall charge of political strategy, but if Anji was his main political person, GB would exploit it in the party as part of a spiel that TB does not really care about the party, which he would not be able to do if it was me in charge. The phone was going all day, TB half a dozen times, Philip, Margaret McD, hacks galore, politicians galore, but we just about worked ourselves into the right position I think, and TB said he felt comfortable with what we were saying, and surer than ever there was no way we could call an election tomorrow. The best thing about the day was [Slobodan] Milosevic arrested [at his fortified villa in Belgrade]. The worst thing of all today was Blackburn hammering Burnley 5-0, prompting the usual rude messages from Jack Straw, 'Can we play you every week?' etc. We were terrible.

Monday, April 2

TB worked on a new draft statement, which I sent over to GB for his input, then we reworked it before signing it off. At my 8.30 FMD meeting, I totally lost it with Granatt and Lowson, said I was sick and tired of being told about all the things that could not be done, and we had to raise our game big time. Our job was not to cure the disease, because it was beyond this group. Our job was the words, the pictures, the visits, the arguments that gave some sense of confidence we were getting on top of things. Eventually I so lost it that I handed the media brief over to Godric, asked him to finish the meeting, and walked out. I went to see TB in the flat, where he was with GB, Jonathan and Bruce. GB was fretting about us being pushed even further, and said we had to get the balance right between a sensible delay and an indefinite delay. In the end, it went fine. TB did it well, the arguments felt right, and the lunchtime news bulletins were excellent. TB went off on another FMD visit, this time to Essex. He was finding these visits useful not just because it showed him leading from the front and what have you, but because every time he was being told things that he could get fixed. But so many of them were things that should have been sorted without us being involved, basic red-tape stuff. He said it was the third time he had felt no confidence in the MAFF operation.

I did a meeting of GB plus Group of 6, and we were now seeing things in three phases – FMD/Easter; early campaign; final phase. DM had the idea of setting up a series of speeches devoted to the big goals that would be in the manifesto. TB got back and we carried on the discussion. He said he wanted foreign visits stripped from the diary where possible. GB stated rather menacingly that he was clear TB should not go on holiday. TB said he needed a rest before the campaign, and was clear he would prefer to go somewhere hot. TB was very fired up after his visit to Essex, said he was moving to putting Hoon in charge of Cobra. He said his hair was curling at the levels of competence (not) he saw today. I sent round a note making clear nothing should be communicated that was not cleared through us. There were still too many people speaking without getting the full picture.

Tuesday, April 3

The press coverage of the election delay was not quite as good as yesterday's broadcast reports. The picture a lot of them had gone for was of me looking a bit steely and suspicious as TB announced it. Hague stole the overnight initiative with a call for the army to take over the fight against FMD from MAFF. It was not as daft as it sounded, and indeed TB and I had been talking about the MoD getting far more involved. But Hague overcooked it, some of the military already engaged, e.g. Brigadier [Alex] Birtwistle [officer overseeing culling and burial of sheep in Cumbria], who was emerging as very media-friendly, attacked the idea and it looked like another piece of Hague opportunism. The figures remained a problem and I now had Bill Bush and Catherine Rimmer [Number 10 research team] working pretty much full-time just trying to bring some sense to the statistical chaos we had. The latest figures given at Cobra suggested only thirty-one per cent of farms were culled within twenty-four hours, and that did not necessarily mean thirty-one per cent of animals. If the Tories got hold of that we were in real trouble. And why on earth, people would ask, were we doing all this, wiping out large parts of our tourism market, to protect such a small export market? Added to which, there were signs that some farmers were now deliberately spreading it to get full compensation, now rising to enormous sums. Of course if we went out on the front foot on that, watch the outcry backlash against us. My morning FMD meeting was a little better tempered, and Lowson even had a bit of a fightback, referring back to what he called 'your tirade yesterday', which had at least led to one or two of the things I asked for being done. Phil Bassett [special adviser] had done a terrific note on the weaknesses at MAFF and now we had to stop standing on ceremony and worrying about egos and get things sorted.

Wednesday, April 4

We finally agreed David King would do his presentation to TB and Nick, so he could frame it at PMQs, and then King see the media after that. He was clearly a clever bloke, and very keen to help, but both Jeremy and I had concerns the media would stitch him up, or at the least exaggerate and take out of context what he was saying, or verbal him into an over-interpretation that would scare the hell out of people. I told him not to imagine he was about to engage in a rational conversation with rational, intelligent people. They are intelligent but in the main they are out for trouble, and he needs to be very careful. In the end he probably came over as a bit too optimistic, and we had to recalibrate a little, as we did with Godric's briefing, which was a bit too negative re vaccination. I did the now routine morning round of FMD meetings, and we were finally getting decent service on figures. I had a meeting with Nick Brown and his special adviser, re Phil B's note. Nick accepted there were real problems. He was, he said, happy for more help from the centre, though that was not what he was saying elsewhere. At PMQs, TB did well, including a good answer to [Dennis] Skinner about the army taking over the Tories.

Thursday, April 5

There were more bloody pictures of me in the papers, this time re some crap story about special advisers' pay. I had a sense of foreboding about the profile getting too high as we entered the campaign stage. Yesterday was in part about trying to make out it was as much about me (and therefore issues of spin) as TB making the decision to delay, and if the Tories thought they were on to something, it would pick up as the campaign went on. We were now stepping up the message work re tourism, and got Chris Smith engaged in a few events. We had a broader election planning meeting, but it was dispiriting. TB was not really focused, his mind currently dominated by FMD, GB was not engaging, and JP chipped in with a few random comments. I was pushing for them to see how much we could get out of the agency's *Economic Disaster 2* posters if we really put some weight behind them, but I sensed resistance from GB, and JP was the first to admit he didn't really get this 'clever adman stuff'. I wanted to start selling them in movie shops and getting film ads done etc. It was one of those posters that worked OK on its own but would really break through if we built properly around it.

At Cabinet, they went through FMD in some detail, and there was definitely a feeling of it slowly coming under control. TB did a strong no-complacency message, and was back at them about making big-picture speeches. TB asked me to go through to his room at the end and we had yet another discussion re the office, this time re Anji. I said he had to think through whether the political links job was her strength. I told him Sally Morgan's view, that if it was possible with the Civil Service, I could head up communications and politics, and have different people working to me, possibly Sally and Anji on the politics front. I said both Anji and I were not exactly job-title people. Was this just about trying to keep Anji? Yes it was, he said. The longer I am in this job, he said, the more I realise how few people you can trust totally. You are one of them, and she is one of them. She is also someone who brings a dimension others don't. I said well, I think it is better you keep her, and if that means a better salary and a bigger job, give it to her, but does it have to mean structures that will upset others, including his missus? I said Fiona might agree to me staying if we could genuinely say there were ways of cutting the workload and the pressure but I did not think what he was proposing would do that. *Au contraire.*

Re his own future, he said he didn't know how long he wanted to stay in the job, but he felt GB was imagining he would go halfway through the second term. The look on his face made it clear GB had no chance of that. TB seemed genuinely unsure re a third election, but I suspected he would go for it if we had a decent majority second time around. Jack Straw came to see me, really hacked off at what he believed was Blunkett's deliberate strategy to talk himself up as next Home Secretary. He said was it true, and I said it's not fair to ask what TB may or may not have said to me re reshuffles post-election. Jack said if he was to be moved, he would be interested in DETR, if it became a proper, big department not there purely to keep JP happy. He felt David B was wrong to be doing what he was doing and hoped I could get him back in check. The reshuffle was going to be tough. Chris Smith had actually been improving, and it was not easy to spot obvious sackings. TB, DM and I had a meeting on the manifesto, and the need to drive a political message through it. It was definitely coming on though as a solid piece of work. We then had a meeting on the Lords where Charlie and DM were keen on a major elected element and TB and I were not. I felt we were falling too much for the line being run against us that we were all-powerful.

Friday, April 6

We got big hits on tourism today, with TB, JP and other ministers out and about beating the drum for tourism. TB was out on the road and called in several times, to discuss whether we should get more political on the subject of footpaths, where he was beginning to think some Tory councils were deliberately going OTT on restrictions as a way of maximising problems for the government. Nick [Brown] had clearly lost confidence in the MAFF operation and we now just had to take over. Mike G was still maintaining it was all fine, and it wasn't. RW asked me earlier how I felt the machine was handling things. I said poor to average, which was polite, and he seemed taken aback even at that. We agreed we needed message work, storyline development, a visits team, proper wordsmiths. Four years on, the culture and the general calibre was pretty much unchanged.

Saturday, April 7

Not as busy as it might have been. Three or four conference calls on FMD to agree a plan and then a script for the Sundays and overnight broadcasters based on Nick B's letter to farmers saying they must

April '01: TB unsure about a third election

co-operate with the 48-hour neighbouring farm cull policy. Then, when the letter went out, it didn't have the lines we would agree to brief in it. Comical if it wasn't so serious. I persuaded Mo M to do a visit to a pub in Hampshire, and got other ministers out in the regions doing visits to say the countryside is open, just stay off farmland. We were also building the pressure on councils we suspected of being politically driven in keeping all footpaths shut to the public. There was a diversionary media frenzy though, the *News of the World* having stitched up Sophie Wessex in a series of conversations with a fake Arab sheik.[1] It was a good news sponge, though we erred into it, first with Byers making a few critical remarks, and then Kim Howells [trade and industry minister] saying the Royals were a bit bonkers. I love him dearly, but this was one to let run without giving the media any excuse to put us at the heart of it.

Sunday, April 8

On the Royals, we agreed one hundred per cent supportive and politically stay out of it as best we can. TB asked me to speak to the Palace and assure them we were one hundred per cent supportive and I spoke to [Sir] Robin Janvrin [private secretary to the Queen] to let him know what we were saying. The Palace switchboard put me through to him as 'Sir Alastair on the line, Sir Robin,' at which we both had a laugh. 'Can't see it myself,' I said. I read through the latest manifesto draft, which was definitely getting there, and made a few suggestions for tightening and also for making the storylines come out more clearly. Sophie was running very big, and there was some bollocks running about how TB/CB pulled out of a dinner because she was meant to be there. But they were never intended to go in the first place, but it didn't stop a mini frenzy. Following Kim and one or two others, there was a bit of 'Is Labour republican?' kicking off, and TB called to say he wanted it killed stone dead.

Monday, April 9

Sophie was still running big, with new FMD outbreaks, and Nick doing a Commons statement, there was no media respite on that front. GB was on *GMTV* and I felt looked very uncomfortable, but Fiona thought he was very cleverly building a profile outwith the obvious economic issues. I went in with Philip, who felt that Hague

[1] The wife of Prince Edward, Earl of Wessex, criticised certain members of the government and appeared to suggest she used her royal status to gain clients for her PR business.

was being prevented from going into mega-attack mode because TB was so focused on FMD. My worry was that TB was using it to avoid facing up to some of the campaign decisions we had to make. At his morning meeting, we peremptorily skipped through the political situation, and he was totally focused on FMD. Fine, so long as he didn't go into denial. I had a session with Godric re my future. I put to him the idea of him and Tom Kelly being joint PMOS, and he thought there was something in it. He was a very good guy to have around, and someone I could talk to very frankly. He seemed nervous of the thought at first, but then as he came back to it during the day, he was warming to it. After the eleven o'clock, I went to TBWA and had a brainstorm with Trevor [Beattie] et al. re how to build out from the *Economic Disaster* poster, and build around it an argument about the Tories' past, present and future. Trevor was so not your average political hack, yet was really committed to what we were doing, and clever, with a good team. I was enjoying the work with the agency as a release from some of the madness elsewhere.

Tuesday, April 10

Though I had been one hundred per cent down the line on it yesterday, the *Mail* and the *Sun* had pieces on me as a 'Roundhead', leading the anti-monarchy charge, along with CB. PG had done some groups last night and said there was a definite sense we were doing better, but it could flare up again very quickly. We had to maintain competence above all. I told GB at his meeting that I felt the more we forced the Tories into the FMD situation, the better re the coming campaign, because we could prevent them laying some of their attack messages. We had established the idea of Hague bandwagoning and being opportunistic and we had to make him worried that every time he moved from FMD, he was nervous. The idea so that some of the farmers were responsible for spreading the disease was out there, and we were not copping it, as the trading standards people were making clear their disquiet. But this was always on a knife-edge, partly because emotions were at play here. We had a meeting on the manifesto. TB was happy it was getting there but felt we needed a phrase in the area of aspiration, success, ambition. Bruce was arguing that we should not be rewriting the Sermon on the Mount, in other words we knew what we wanted Labour governments to do, and we should shout it out. I had a separate meeting with GB and his crew, which in some ways was more interesting. TB had been focusing very much on the final presentation of an agreed plan; GB was trying to reopen some of the bigger strategic questions, including – his latest wheeze – whether we could go for an election earlier than June 7. He also felt rather than go for a pledge card as before, we should have a 'choice card'. I felt we could do both in the same card, but he was looking for ways the whole time to emphasise the choice so that it was not just about us. It was the right approach but the pledge card was too well established for us to change the format too much. TB saw Jack S to discuss asylum. TB felt the Home Office had not gripped the politics of this, and wanted a proper political strategy worked up. Calum came in to meet me on the way to Wimbledon vs Burnley. We won 2-0. The play-offs were back in sight again.

Wednesday, April 11

Devon NFU were leading the news with a call of support for farmers ignoring movement restrictions on welfare grounds. TB called, said he was getting irritated at how we got all the blame for this, when it was negligence that started it, and when some of the farmers were being totally unreasonable now. We had a visit planned for Devon and on the plane down, he said he was worried re demos. We went to the MAFF offices, where the reception was not quite as friendly as last time. These guys were under pressure but they seemed more on top of things than before. I had dinner at the hotel with TB and Anji, in his room. He was piling the pressure on both of us now. Neither of us really believed the stuff about it becoming easier in the second term, but he said surely we have to give it a try, surely we don't want to leave when there remains so much to do, loaded on top with flattery galore re how he couldn't have done it without us etc.

He said on Monday, GB had started a conversation with him straight out with the words 'You betrayed me. You said you would never challenge me and you took that job away from me.' TB said GB was still very sore, and operated on the basis there was a genuine grievance, which TB did not accept. I said it might have been better if there had been a contest, because TB would have won it by a mile. GB was back to saying TB had an operation ready to roll in 1994. TB told him again he was happy to support him in becoming the next leader, but not if he sought to remove him. Then all bets were off. GB said to him 'You cannot lay down conditions.' TB told him he had to accept who the leader was. After Anji left, TB said you have to understand how important it is that both of you stay. I cannot lose the people I really trust. He said he didn't care whether

I dealt with the press or not, but he wanted me for politics and judgement, and he wanted Anji because she gave him an angle nobody else did, which was the upper end of the middle-class market, and they were important to New Labour.

Thursday, April 12

Breakfast with TB. We discussed some of the names we might want to bring in post-election. I felt whatever the attacks, we had to get more power not less at the centre, which as FMD showed once more was still far too much at the mercy of departments with their own systems, personnel and outmoded ways. I worked on a new organogram, taking in some of his ideas, and adding some of my own. I said to him also that he needed to sharpen up his own managerial and motivational skills. There were still too many people in the government, including in Number 10, who didn't get what he was on about half the time, and who felt he took too much for granted. The *Indy* splashed on a story about me [saying AC would quit after the election] and it was running on the BBC. I stayed out of sight all day, which itself was ludicrous. I had a chat with Anji, who said she still felt she ought to go. I said I wanted to go, but it was very hard when he set it out as he did, and he was clearly genuinely worried re GB. I suggested to him he do the reshuffle consulting only JP and the chief whip, treat GB like any other minister. He filled me in more on his conversation with GB on Monday, said he told him he always overplayed his hand, and fucked up the big moments. TB felt when Neil [Kinnock] went GB should have gone for deputy leader, but Gordon did a deal with John Smith [previous Labour Party leader] to be Shadow Chancellor and now he worried he missed his moment.

The media were trying to film me all day and Godric said there was endless blah about me on the airwaves all day. I used it to say later to TB that it showed why it might be an idea to go. He said it showed that I was too big a figure to be doing all the day-to-day, but also too big a figure to lose. He went over some of the campaign issues and was also working through e.g. party chair, general secretary, chief whip. I chaired a conference call to plan the next few days on FMD. We needed to move to another level on the tourism message, and keep a sense of doing whatever it takes to knock out the disease. Julian [Braithwaite, speech-writer] did an excellent piece of work on the 1967 outbreak. The biggest difference of all in my mind was that in those days the media hoped the authorities succeeded; today they are willing us to fail.

Friday, April 13

Loads more crap re me in the press, a lot of it hostile, after an apparently fairly negative – and far too large – piece on *Newsnight* last night. I told Granatt there was nothing in the story about me taking over the GICS. Last thing I wanted. At Cobra, there was a pretty alarming report from the Chief Medical Officer. TB was talking to Prince Charles re vaccination. Nick Brown was still not oozing confidence and had the look of a man being driven by events rather than controlling them. Fiona and I had a very nice evening out for dinner with Melanne [Verveer, chief of staff to Hillary Clinton] and her husband Phil, a lawyer. They were both genuinely bemused by the level of focus in the media on me, and the way I was treated like a politician rather than an aide. He said there had been a fair bit of stuff about me and Peter M in the US press too, but here it was 'crazy'.

Saturday, April 14

In media terms, FMD was going backwards, showing once again that if we did not keep our eye on every aspect of the communications, and bear down on them the whole time, it didn't happen. TB, easier said than done, said we had to get back on the front foot quickly, rightly observing that actual operations seemed to improve when we were driving the comms agenda. As ever, MAFF seemed intent on strangling good ideas, e.g. RSPCA getting more involved in the animal welfare cases, which would at least show we understood the concerns and the emotions here. We were led to believe yesterday Nick B was visiting farmers in Cumbria today but then it emerged he hadn't gone. Also, there was no grip to the vaccination debate which was going on without any real explanation for people of the pros and cons, and was being talked of as a 'why did nobody think of that before?' miracle cure. Finally, yesterday's briefing had gone a bit awry in that figures designed to show the scale of the operation now underway to eradicate the disease were seized on to show the size of the backlog. David North, who had been pushing for vaccination for weeks, and Jeremy were really pushing to get out the King report on vaccination. The Sundays arrived and were not great re FMD. Also, there was loads of stuff re me in the papers, which was annoying. [Film-maker] Michael Cockerell in the *Indy*, [Kevin] Maguire in the *Observer* saying I should go, [Peter] Dobbie [*Mail On Sunday*] saying Hague needed someone like me, [Peter] Oborne saying I was probably on the way out. Working it all out will be harder if it is surrounded by all this bollocks.

Sunday, April 15

TB called, wanted a concerted effort to get up the issue of vaccination in the next couple of days. Anji said she was still minded to go. I felt I had to stay for a while post-election to see whether things got any better. I didn't think TB was being unreasonable in saying give it a few months. I had a really nice run over the Heath with Rory who was telling me again I would be mad to give it up, that it was an amazing thing to be closer to a historic figure like TB than anyone. He saw things incredibly clearly for someone of his age.

Monday, April 16

Easter Monday, but TB was busy for large parts of the day on FMD and calling fairly regularly re things he had seen in his papers, ideas for the week ahead. I went out for a run and bumped into [Baroness] Helene Hayman [Lords MAFF minister] who looked really tired and a bit edgy. I think sometimes we were so used to dealing with the high-octane stuff that we underestimated the impact on people suddenly pitched into real crisis management at this level. She clearly shared our exasperation with MAFF and was also beginning to lose it with some of the farmers. We were getting hit a bit on dithering re vaccination. Liz [AC's sister] had organised a joint birthday party for Mum and Dad so we went up there pm. Mum was pretty moved by the whole thing.

Tuesday, April 17

I went to see Robert Templeton [relative who has serious long-term illness and is bedridden]. I always find it humbling, and also slightly shaming, that I see him so infrequently. He is in amazing humour considering. He couldn't get the words out very well today, but he said Tony was the best PM we had ever had, and I had to stick with him to the end! I spoke to TB several times as we sought to resolve the vaccination issue. We ended up after a TB, NB, AC etc. conference call agreeing a line that we accepted it in principle but the nearer a decision got, the clearer it became the farmers wouldn't wear it at all. TB was clearly getting irritated now re the me/Anji situation, said it was discombobulating him at the worst possible time. He was also moving from irritation to rage re GB ducking for cover on FMD. TB had been working pretty flat out over the Easter weekend but said he felt rested. I had done very little work by comparison but I felt anything but.

Wednesday, April 18

We were still being hit by a sense of dithering on the vaccination issue. The line we had agreed was about as well as we could do, but it underlined weakness in the face of a massive crisis. The *Mail* splashed on petrol prices after Shell put up petrol by 1p. The BBC led on it at lunchtime, another classic case of the BBC mindset that if it led the *Mail* it must be news, and I called [Richard] Sambrook [director of BBC news] to complain. He was in some ways easier to deal with than [Tony] Hall, but they all believed they would combust and die if they ever admitted the BBC got something wrong. I went in to see TB before he left for Durham. Meanwhile, JP's note re whether he should become Minister for the Cabinet Office set out what kind of areas he felt he should cover – Europe, regions, crisis management and sport!!! It was a bit of a kitchen-sink list and TB just looked at it, shaking his head. JP was in any event involved in a mini PR disaster, having briefed he would be in Kyoto but in fact going to the US. TB said he had been trying to reach GB over the past forty-eight hours but he had literally gone AWOL. TB called several times pre his doorstep in Durham, which was fine. DM came to see me, said he was worried TB had lost his sense of project, and that focusing on FMD was a kind of displacement. I got really fed up through the day with TB's incessant calls, his constantly saying he was right on this and right on that, which was usually a sign he was looking for reassurance.

Thursday, April 19

FMD was looking really ragged again, not just because of vaccination dither, but also because of some of the operational side seeming less under control. Also, we had got so used to the sight of these pyres on TV – I wish to God they didn't show them twenty-four hours a day though – that we maybe underestimated the growing impact they were having. There was something a bit medieval about the whole scene at the moment. We agreed to get King up again to try to get the focus on the figures showing the cases coming down. He did a 4pm briefing where he said things were broadly under control. After TB spoke to Ben Gill, he asked me to call him to try to get the farmers on to a less hostile line re vaccination. TB wanted to get them to ask for more time to look into vaccination, and we would then agree to that, but in a way it was too complex and sophisticated a line to get through a difficult organisation with its own processes and structures. The truth was they were not really up for it. The day's unexpected story was RC's heavily briefed speech on race, really going for the

Tories.[1] None of us knew it was coming but we decided to pile in and turn to our advantage. Hague and Portillo did a dreadful double act out on a farm visit somewhere, and it did nothing to end the rift story. TB said 'the Tories really are our greatest gift'.

Friday, April 20

I went down to Chequers with David M. We went through my draft organogram. Anji and I both felt TB was diddling us around, piling on the pressure but not actually thinking through changes that would make a difference to the operation. She said he told her that any new job she was being offered would be a joke compared to what he was asking her to do. I think he underestimated how freaked she was by some of the media attention recently. I wasn't convinced, and nor was Anji, that he was actually fighting to keep her for a specific job, it was more talismanic, but I think Anji was closer to the exit door than I was. DM had also pretty much decided he wanted to leave, and find a seat. TB wanted to keep Sally. We had a pretty average internal meeting then Douglas A joined a discussion on the election, where finally you felt there was a plan falling into shape. GB missed the meeting because he was doing a reading at [former Scottish footballer] Jim Baxter's funeral. I didn't know they knew each other, let alone that he might have been close. The Tories were in a bad way. TB asked me to do a note on meritocracy and how we could get that theme running through the campaign. He was keen to have at least one plank that deliberately resonated with Thatcherites and thought the whole meritocracy/aspiration field was the place. He finally came to the decision that he wanted me out on the road with him, which pleased Bruce. He was worried though that Peter M was really gunning for me at the moment, and responsible for some of the negative briefing.

Saturday, April 21

I set off for Burnley vs Birmingham with Calum, en route speaking to Hoon re FMD, putting together a note on TB's upcoming speech on yobbery, and endlessly trying to deal with the office jobs front. Anji seemed pretty much settled on leaving, and TB seemed to be making it worse not better by the way he was treating both of us, coming close to telling her she was being disloyal, and telling me I

[1] Cook argued in a speech to the Social Market Foundation that the British were not a race, but a gathering of countless different races and communities. He attacked a William Hague speech that asserted that a second Labour term would turn the UK into a 'foreign land'.

April '01: David Miliband seeks a Commons seat

was not trying to persuade her to stay as a way of easing my own situation with Fiona. FMD was more under control but the media was now relentlessly negative about it. We changed at Preston and on to the train piled a load of Birmingham fans, the worst sort, effing and blinding and generally offensive and abusive. I kept my head down but after a while got recognised and really sensed trouble as one or two of the gobbier ones started mouthing off. I ignored them at first, then told one of them to keep quiet, and they started to come our way, before one of the older ones stepped in and just said 'Leave it, he's all right.' They went back, and he said to me he may be a hooligan but he supports Labour. Fuck me, saved by a Labour-supporting Brummie hooligan. Calum had said on the train to Preston that he noticed how many more people recognised me when we were out and about, which was a bit weird considering I didn't do telly and stuff, but there was so much in the papers now, and so much blather on the radio and telly, that it was probably inevitable.

Sunday, April 22

Rory was running in the mini marathon so I ran early and later we all set off by Tube. Really nice day, and a fantastic event. I would love to do the real thing myself. TB came over for a while and got a good reception down the Mall. I met Tanni Grey-Thompson [Paralympic athlete] who agreed to take part in one of our PEBs. He had done a note on the next stages for New Labour, and on the campaign, building on some of the discussions yesterday, which was a good piece of work.

Monday, April 23

FMD still our biggest problem. Also thanks to RC's speech, the race issue had become a Tory–Labour row rather than a straight internal problem for them. GB said he had a speech tomorrow but no matter how many times I asked, I could not establish what it was about or how big it would go. TB was trying to get the office issues sorted and saw a number of people individually before he had a dinner for his key people. We went through his weekend note and tried to work through the planned changes in the areas he wanted us to focus on – delivery, operations, beefed-up strategy operation, international, possibly splitting out Europe as a separate job. He was a lot clearer than of late but the mood was still a bit tense because so many people were unsure about their future. Anji was very subdued. Fiona seemed happier and said later she thought it might work but she reserved judgement. CB said she felt the need at least to know what was going on, and feel involved in the planning of his time. We also went through some of the Civil Service problems, particularly the whole problem of departmentalitis. But we also had to take a different look at our own way of operating. Ministers needed to be entrusted far more to drive their departments, and not get captured. There was a danger TB just created an ever-expanding cadre close to him without the capacity strengthened elsewhere.

Tuesday, April 24

GB was in a foul mood, raging at JP in the *Guardian* saying we intended to review the Barnett Formula [for public expenditure]. Whenever these things happened GB always seemed to direct his comments at me. 'You have to stamp out this ill discipline,' like I had somehow created it. I pointed out that JP was not the only one to be doing stuff today we were not exactly a hundred per cent across. 'I told you about my speech.' Mmmm. TB was doing a speech on the yob culture and the need for a proper agenda driven locally to address it, which was going fine. I met Jack S to go over the plans on his asylum speech tomorrow. He was having a laugh at Robin's expense re chicken tikka masala [Cook had pointed out in his speech that this was now the national dish in the UK], but RC had definitely got us into the wrong place on race. FMD was all ragged again. We just couldn't seem to maintain and hold momentum on this. Just when it felt like we were getting on top, it would slip away again. GB sent over a draft line re JP which if we had delivered it would have produced screaming 'Blair condemns Prescott' headlines, so I ignored it. I saw JP who said he was simply talking about the existence of a local government review and it was no big deal.

Wednesday, April 25

GB was full of angst at the *FT* which splashed, as I suspected they would, on the tax pledge from their lunch with TB yesterday, and also at Andy Grice's piece [in the *Independent*], probably from Peter M, that the manifesto was deemed boring and had to be rewritten. TB said GB had said to him he was worried Peter M and I would form an alliance against him. Christ, Peter was barely speaking to me at the moment, and thought I single-handedly 'defenestrated' him. But GB had been banging on again at TB saying we had to 'deal with Peter'. What more could we do? He had been kicked out and some would argue unfairly. We were taking a big hit on asylum at the moment and desperately needed to get back on to a positive agenda. When I suggested a big TB speech on the choice next Monday,

GB changed tack again. He was also having a big downer on the pledges at the moment, saying they were not an effective vehicle for 'the choice', but they were if we shaped them along with proper clear dividing lines. If we wanted the pledges to be part of the choice, it was not that difficult. He just had to stick at it. It would come right. The BBC did a big number on the cost of government ad campaigns, which ran all day. A lot of it was public sector recruitment and benefit ads but it was hard to defend some of them. I had a series of meetings post-PMQs, the best of which was a brainstorm on the nature of the election campaign. I also had a good meeting with PG, DA, PH, Stan Greenberg and Bob Shrum re TB's note saying he wanted 'Britain breaking from Thatcherism' to be a key election theme. I liked it, because it would allow us to say what we were, not just what we weren't, and it would help TB generate a bit more zeal and inspiration, but Bob and Stan both thought it was dangerous and unnecessary, that we could alienate people whose support we still needed to win. I liked having Bob around and Douglas was developing a lot, particularly when he was away from GB.

The big unexpected issue of the day was a calf called Phoenix which should have been culled five days ago, had not been, and now the family were trying to save it. It was one of those classic ultimately silly stories that would grip the media's imagination and be a screaming pain in the ass for us. MAFF were saying it had to die. After a lot of toing and froing we got them to agree it could be part of the softened contiguous cull policy. In other words, the policy was not being changed to reprieve it, but a reprieve would be the effect of a change of policy happening anyway. I suspect many members of the public felt it was a sentimental load of bollocks given how many thousands had already gone up in flames, but it became that thing most loved by our wretched media – a symbol – so we had to play along.

At 7pm, TB called me round for a chat. He felt PMQs had gone fine, that though we still had problems on FMD, it was broadly under control and he sensed the Tories were a bit worried about over-exploiting. He felt he could begin to concentrate on the election. He said GB was brilliant, but flawed, and at the moment the flaw was outweighing the brilliance. But he felt it would come back provided we stuck with him and tolerated some of the madness. He said I had to keep trying to maintain good working relations. He said earlier today GB virtually said I [TB] am a crap PM, and it was time I moved over and let someone better do the job. 'I laughed out loud, then it got even more comic when GB told me that he would be better placed to do it because "it was time to return to Cabinet government".' TB told him he may be a control freak, but he was a mere beginner compared with GB. He said GB went on yet again about my interview on *Newsnight* on the day John Smith died, convinced to this day that it was part of some heinous plot to deprive him of his rightful inheritance.[1] He also asked him why, if he knew I was doing a diary, he didn't stop me, to which TB said why shouldn't he, and why should any of us worry what he says provided he sets things out as he sees them? TB said he continued despite it all to have residual reserves of loyalty to GB and the upsides still outweighed the down-sides, though he was sorely tested from time to time. He said he had just about had enough of Ed Balls talking to him like something on his shoe.

Thursday, April 26

Phoenix was a bit of a fiasco, because of course having spoiled their 'Save Phoenix' campaigns, now they wanted to say the contiguous cull policy had been changed because of one calf in the news, and the whole spin thing was back up in lights. It was balls but it was just one of those media frenzies that came along from time to time, and we were going to have to just get through it. TB was doing a press briefing, and GB came over to see him. I was hanging round the outer office and not for the first time we could hear raised voices, GB's the louder, and TB told us later he asked straight out, again, when was he leaving? TB said he was like a raging bull. Cabinet was very scratchy. TB didn't do the planned pre-campaign pep talk, instead they just meandered round a few issues, obviously mainly FMD. He talked of the need for maximum discipline as the election neared. GB gave an update re Millbank as though he was spending lots of time there. He warned against every day being a referendum on us.

Chris Smith complained re all the stuff in the media speculating what would happen to them all post-election. Nick B complained at the stuff against him. TB pointed out there was nothing we could do to stop this, other than make clear we never ever talked about reshuffles, which was true. He stopped short of saying the truth – the media tended to pick on the ones they could see for themselves were not that good. Nick's protest was made in such violent terms that TB called him over with me at the end and said 'I hope you

[1] On the day John Smith died, Campbell said on *Newsnight* that Blair would be Smith's successor.

don't think these stories are coming from here.' 'I didn't say that.' 'No, but that is what anyone listening will have taken from what you said.' 'Could they really be so cynical as to believe that is what I was saying?' He was very offside at the moment, then muttered something about 'Who appointed them in the first place?' and stalked off. I could see GB clocking the whole exchange from the other side of the room. It was a bad meeting. I didn't like the feeling of it at all. Next thing we heard MAFF were briefing that the first Nick knew of Phoenix being saved was when he heard it on the news.

Friday, April 27

I travelled down to Chequers with David Miliband. Traffic dire. We arrived and I was surprised to see Peter M there. Nobody had said he was going, but I guess TB was concerned he was causing trouble and was better in than out in his current frame of mind. We were perfectly civil to each other but it didn't take much for the bruises to show, and he said after lunch that it was 'dreadful' he had to be smuggled in there as though he were some kind of non-person. I suspected he would brief fairly soon the fact of the meeting, and his presence at it, which would inflame JP and GB. We had a discussion on TB's own campaign. He stressed three areas where he had to up his game – the vision and the big argument; basic explanation of the government narrative; personal reconnection. He was worried that there would be protests of one sort or another dogging every step. I said I felt we had to be more relaxed and he had to stop the frightened-rabbit look whenever anything unexpected happened. We were strong on all the main arguments and that was much more important. He was building up the nerves and tension in himself deliberately as the campaign neared. We had another discussion about whether to kick things off with a speech burying Thatcherism, but he was worried it would be misrepresented à la forces of conservatism, and get the campaign off on the wrong foot. Peter M made clear he didn't think we were where we needed to be in terms of story development, and that was certainly right. We went over various big-ticket possibilities – sentencing review, a specific crime-fighting department, deregulation, sport, a new department of the working age, a separate pensions department, a reshaped education department, local taxes for education, reform of LEAs [local education authorities]. But the shape of a campaign was there. What we really needed now was the off. TB was warming to the idea of a tax on oil companies specifically to be spent on expanded university education. TB said he reckoned our first year of the second term could be the toughest yet because we would be making reforms that would take on doctors, teachers, police, 'the mother of all battles with the judges on rules of evidence, sentencing, weekend courts, changes to bail'. There would be two education bills, big changes to the NHS, big changes on criminal justice. Three crime bills, assets recovery, police reform in the second session, Civil Service reform, incapacity benefit reform, on and on he went. 'Then you do the euro,' I said. He laughed, but went on to say he would also be vulnerable internally to an argument that he 'wasn't really Labour', because internally opponents would say he was destroying the public service ethos when the goal was to modernise it for today's world.

On the one hand, we were desperate to get going. On the other, as TB unhelpfully reminded me once or twice, the campaign would be ghastly and tough and we would be working flat out round the clock to keep the show on the road. We agreed we should use six set-piece speeches as the policy spine of his campaign, that the key driving themes and dividing lines should be around the economy, investment, the civic society, engagement on the world stage, optimism. We should start with one big speech in Sedgefield laying out those themes, and making it clear this will be a New Labour campaign and a New Labour second term. It had to be about defining clearly the next phase of New Labour. On the economy, the focus had to be productivity, skills, developing regional economies. On investment, money for modernisation. On the civic society, rights and responsibilities. On the world stage, leadership so that we could reform the institutions. He felt that though we recovered OK, Robin's chicken tikka masala speech was a 'catastrophic intervention' because it seemed to want to dump our history. He felt Thatcherism was part of the context for the campaign but not its story. The 60s gave us a period of social democracy. Thatcherism was a reaction. New Labour is neither old left nor new right but builds on the best of both. We are a party of aspiration and compassion.

I didn't feel we were yet in proper shape, but then it struck me that if it had not been for FMD we would now be entering the last week of the campaign for a May 3 poll. Truth is you are never ready until you go, and then you find if you are ready or not. We probably were and as we drove home, I felt confident that despite all our problems, we could win and win well. I had a surreal moment in the cab home with Kate [Garvey] when I looked out of the window and saw a huge poster 'Alastair Campbell, watch and

April '01: Defining next phase of New Labour

learn!' It was an ad for a new TV series, *Spin City*, but it was a bit alarming to see it up there.

Saturday, April 28

TB went to the Rugby League Cup Final at Twickenham. He was booed a little bit, and was alarmed. I said it was inevitable. There were bound to be at least some Tories there and in any event, he was no longer a new kid on the block, he was a high-profile controversial figure and all in all it was still worth doing. He called me two or three times after the Burnley–Sheffield United game so he was clearly a bit concerned about it all. I said there was definitely a sullen mood out there but that was because we had been through a fairly long hard time. It would come back on our terms once the campaign proper was under way and we got legitimacy for political attack again. The general view on FMD was settling around the notion that we had handled it badly at the start, and never really recovered from that though we made a lot of improvements once we took it over and TB led from the front. We were never going to win this one, but we had done not a bad job coming from behind. He was now moving away from the idea of a big 'break from Thatcherism' speech at the start of the campaign. I did a really good hills session in the morning then set off for Doncaster en route for the match.

Sunday, April 29

I spoke to Tom Kelly re the idea of him and Godric as joint PMOS and he seemed pretty keen. Bob Shrum had done an excellent outline for the Sedgefield speech to kick off the campaign and I got Philip to bring him round for a cup of tea. Philip said GB was taking amiss to Bob helping us, so we had to be ultra nice. GB was still being difficult. Yet he was still operating OK. His speech to the staff at Millbank had gone down well, and PG felt it was time TB did the same. Bob was in mellow and optimistic form, said he felt it was even possible we would get a bigger majority. Don't say that, I said. I felt we had to keep everyone focused on the idea we were starting from 0-0 with everything to lose. TB called after the Mandela concert. He said it was impossible to be with Mandela without feeling that you were an inferior political being, because of the aura that surrounded him. TB was also coming to terms with the fact that there were people on the right and on the left who actually hated him – on the right because he was a successful Labour politician likely to win again; and on the left because he didn't do all the things they believed Labour leaders should do, even if it meant losing ad infinitum. I said you are not confident at the moment, are you? He said you read me too well but no, I'm not. It was the thought of the next few weeks that was getting him down a bit. He said he went through these phases. He felt confident on the arguments, and confident he could do anything required of him, but he sometimes got fazed when so much of the focus would fall on him personally, and on his personality, and he just needed to steel himself. 'I'll be fine. I have to go down to come up again, but I will bounce back, don't worry.' He said he needed a lot of support at the moment. It made me more confident he would peak at the right time again, which happened in 1997. He said he was feeling more than usually vulnerable and he wanted someone to know that. I said I should be honoured to be that someone but please don't pile all the pressure on like you sometimes do. I won't, he said, but I do feel particularly vulnerable at the moment. I felt this must just be nerves, allowing the tension to build so that he could bring out the best in himself, a bigger version of what happens every year at conference. He was coming up to a period of enormous pressure and scrutiny and it would be odd not to have the odd moment of self-doubt.

Monday, April 30

TB's office meeting was really poor. After Chequers I thought he was getting it together but the conversation yesterday indicated a bad period to come. He was unfocused, a bit panicky, and people left the room unclear what they were meant to be doing. I stayed back and said shit, that was bad. Don't worry, he said, I'll get there. I was worried enough to go and see CB later. She said he was pretty down over the weekend. She said he was anxious about the campaign, and felt sure there would be real aggro out on the road. She was going to be important to keeping his spirits in the right place, and she said I was going to have to work on keeping his confidence up. I felt once we were under way, things would improve. This was all just the nerves in the dressing room before you got out on to the pitch.

Tuesday, May 1

TB told me openly he was feeling really spooked re GB at the moment. They were due to have dinner next Tuesday and he intended to say to him he would help him take over but only if the nonsense stopped. I persuaded TB he should do an FMD press conference before the campaign kicked off, because when he went up on it, we at least gave a sense of authority and everything being done. King agreed we should be out there on the front foot with TB again. Nick wasn't so sure. He said it was important at some point that TB withdrew and it became another departmental issue, but we were nowhere near that. I felt that a big set-piece press conference showing the thing basically under control was necessary to begin the process of withdrawal and the normalisation of TB's diary as we neared the campaign. Like drawing a line before we could move on. Meeting with TB, AH, Jonathan, DM, SM, PH, Peter M and me. We agreed TB should do asylum on Friday in the form of an article followed by a doorstep. I suggested on Monday he chair a political Cabinet, dominate the news on our terms, let expectations run that he will call an election on Wednesday, then do it on the Tuesday. Also he not GB should do the main strategic presentation and he should make it clear he was in overall charge of the campaign at all times. He said again he was not feeling on form but he did feel he was psyching himself up at the right time. He said he hoped I realised how much support he was going to need in the next few weeks. I said as long as there was leadership, it was all there ready to happen. I met Godric and Tom to go over the joint PMOS idea. It was in a way entirely dependent on them and their personalities and I was sure it could work. I had a good meeting with Mark Lucas [Labour film-maker] re the PEB. Matthew Freud [PR expert] had delivered Geri Halliwell [singer] as promised and though she and the other celebs were kind of fleeting in the overall scheme of things, I liked that. TB called after I had gone to bed, said he was really worried about how low his confidence was.

Wednesday, May 2

Bush on NMD was going to be the main thing for the day, and TB wanted us to stay neutral leaning to positive but by the end of the day it was up big time because I answered 'yes' to the question whether we supported it in principle. I hated fucking up, and this was another fuck-up, and another reason why it was time to give up these wretched fucking briefings. Godric thought I was beating myself up too much, that it was one of those situations where fence-sitting was hard because too far the other way and we would have had screaming headlines about Blair condemning Bush. But I wasn't happy with how I handled it. We were continuing to make good preparations for the FMD press conference. I had a Group of 6 on the shape of the campaign, which was better than before. But I was still struggling with words and the strategy paper he had asked me to work on was weak. Thankfully Peter H was motoring at the moment, and Bob Shrum was making a difference. Ann Taylor [chief whip] came to see me re Geoffrey Robinson. [Elizabeth] Filkin [parliamentary commissioner for standards] was due to report and she felt it would be pretty bad. I thought the sooner out the better.

The *Sun* had a poll saying we were heading for an even bigger majority, which gave me the heebie-jeebies because it would just get the complacency juices flowing in certain parts. PMQs was OK and TB got through it fine, which is why I was doubly pissed off I screwed up at the briefing. The Tories were straight out on the line – who decides the policy, me or TB? I suppose I should take it as a compliment that neither they nor the media liked to go for the idea I just screwed up. There was always meant to be some deeper plot at play. It led to endless blah-ology on the airwaves, especially on *Newsnight*. I had reached the stage where I hated hearing about myself on the news. To be fair to him, TB was fairly relaxed, said don't let it worry you. Of course Jonathan was totally in favour because it is what he thought we should be saying anyway. But these briefings were now a menace. Anyone else could say things and get away with it. I couldn't any longer. Following on from the 'bog-standard' frenzy, it was definitely time to give them up. The diary meeting actually became a good discussion about how to improve TB's modus operandi. John Sawers and Jeremy in particular were arguing that he couldn't just sail through a second term as he had the first, that we needed much clearer systems, and we had to get more strategic re the use of his time. It got quite heated, and after a while I closed it down because there were things being said about TB that were a bit much from people meant to be working for him.

Thursday, May 3

The news was leading on the build-up to the FMD press conference, but there was still too much on re me and NMD. We had a touch of last-minute-itis re the press conference because TB wasn't totally on top of the report. GB was still playing on his mind. He said at their dinner tonight he intended to say he would go at a time of his choosing, and that if he felt he was being forced out, he would not help him take over. He had put up with more than any prime minister he could think of and he could not let it carry on through a second term. Anji and I had a chat pre the press conference. She was clearly going to miss it all. I was trying to kick him out of this bad period. TB wondered whether Fiona couldn't take over Anji's role in schmoozing the right-wing press. But she basically loathed them and she was a bit like me in her inability to hide that sometimes. The press conference was OK though it lacked the impact we'd been hoping for. I wondered afterwards whether it hadn't been a waste of time. TB spoke to Schroeder about not going to Berlin on Monday and in no time *The Times* knew about it. We briefed on it which sparked a bit of election fever. I worked on the *Times* article on asylum while TB was seeing Rebekah Wade [now editor of the *News of the World*]. I later learned GB was seeing Murdoch. The Filkin report on Robinson was difficult and he could be forced to quit.[1] TB felt not. We agreed on the plan for a bank holiday Cabinet. Later TB called me out to the garden, and we strolled around. He asked if we were ready for this election. I said as much as we ever will be, it will be fine. He said he felt it would be liberating because he would not feel the same pressure to fight a third term.

Friday, May 4

TB's asylum piece was running fine, but we were still getting problems re Robinson. DB called, first asking what GB was up to seeing Murdoch, and also saying the Cabinet would be very angry having to come down on a bank holiday. He could be a bit whiney when he wanted to, and I pointed out that we were about to launch an election campaign and it might be an idea for the Cabinet to meet. I was speaking at a Jim Rodger [Scottish sports journalist] memorial event in Glasgow so set off for Heathrow. TB asked me to speak to JP re the possible deal on the Tube [part-privatisation], and I did a conference call from the airport with him, Jeremy, Gus [Macdonald] and others, and said if they were going to go for it we needed a simple explanation and they should get it to the *Standard*. Jeremy said GB was still not totally happy with it. JP said as far as he was concerned, GB had signed it off with TB and that was that. Kiley was keen for TB's involvement to be part of the briefing, but there was no need for that. In the Glasgow speech I mainly told funny stories, then just a shortish serious bit at the end, and it seemed to go fine. I played the pipes at the end and they raised £1,400 for that. Douglas Alexander said the SNP contingent looked gutted when they saw the pipes come out. He felt the event went really well, that they had all expected a monstering and I was charm itself. TB called and I sensed his dinner with GB had gone badly.

Saturday, May 5

I did a conference call with DA, PH, GS, re the Sundays and I worked up a script around mandate for change, continuing reform, no complacency. They were all going to be writing up elections so we did not

---

[1] The cross-party Standards and Privileges Committee found that Robinson had failed to declare a deal he struck with the late newspaper tycoon Robert Maxwell.

need that much. Then I did a conference call for all the Sundays which went on too long. The *Observer* had a leaked Jeremy H memo re public service problems, which was a pain. Also Ronnie Biggs[1] was coming to Britain on Monday with the *Sun* which would be a big hoo-ha and cut across the message out of the Cabinet. TB called from Chequers, he was still very cagey about his dinner with GB, though Cherie had told Fiona it had been a bit of a disaster, that GB had said that TB, Peter M and I had been plotting against him back in 1990!

Sunday, May 6

Peter M was back in fairly regular contact with TB, who said it gave him a different dimension, and it's true that when he is on song, he is worth having around. My main worry was whether we were setting ourselves up for a GB/Peter M fault line through the campaign. Peter was liable to brief off his own back without keeping us fully in the picture, and there was always a danger GB would shut down an engine or two if he thought Peter was too involved. Went in for a meeting with GB and the TBWA people, plus key people from Millbank. GB was the only one not dressed casually. He looked tired. We were still arguing about the nature and the timing of the pledges. I wanted us to get going sooner rather than later and build them up big as we went. They were one of the key planks and there was a danger we wasted the potential. Re the first few days we agreed Monday Cabinet, Tuesday launch, Wednesday GB 'goals' speech plus PMQs/PLP, then TB to St Albans for a Q&A with pledges as the backdrop, Thursday we start to unpick the Tories' policy platform, Friday waiting lists and pensions, trail the PEB into the Sundays.

Monday, May 7

Peter H picked me up and we went in to see TB. He had been sent various notes and pieces of advice about his opening words for the campaign, and was sitting at the table in the corner of the sitting room, penning a few thoughts of his own. He said he was still a bit low on confidence but was psyching himself up and just wanted the thing to get under way. PH and I both argued that we needed a real sense of challenge out there, that there are big challenges for us and for the country and there had to be a sense of joint mission to meet them. We needed to be hitting the no-complacency buttons as hard as ever and we needed to be laying out the kind of storylines we

[1] Great Train Robber who escaped from prison in 1965 was voluntarily returning to the UK from Brazil.

wanted to drive through the campaign. It was actually fairly straightforward but of the three of us, only PH had been on form on the
words front in the last week or so. We had agreed that there should
be a tone of humility – as in the 'Thank you' campaign, and in the
admission a lot remained undone – but TB warned this must not
become an admission we had done nothing, which is how our opponents would present it. The foundations we had laid were strong.
Now we had to build upon them. He wanted to reform the public
sector with the same kind of zeal Thatcher sought to reform the private
sector, and show up the difference in values in so doing. I put together
a briefing note that was about 'schools and hospitals first', plus a big
reform message for the second term. We had a desperate need to
excite and enthuse given the walls of cynicism which now surrounded
so much of the coverage, and I think it was that that was getting to
him a bit, because so much of it would fall to him.

We had a meeting of TB's key people, GB and his main people,
plus some from the party, and it was a bit depressing. They were so
clearly singing a different song. Also, GB kept pushing himself, AD
and DA as the main voices for the campaign after TB. All male, all
Scottish. In a way the worst thing about the meeting was not that
there were big arguments – at least we knew where we were with
those – but that they pretended to be saying the same things when
in fact they weren't. Every time we thought we had an agreement on
a line or a strategy, GB would sum it up slightly differently to how
we saw it, and we just went round in circles most of the time. The
Cabinet meeting wasn't that much better. TB did an OK presentation,
started by saying he would go to the Palace tomorrow. On the tracking
poll we were eighteen points ahead. In all the main policy areas we
were ahead. But we were not just fighting the Tories. We were fighting
cynicism, and the Tories were exploiting it. They positively want a
low turnout because that is their only hope, that our support stays
away and theirs comes out. The right-wing media were trying to turn
it into a referendum on us. We had to remind people it was a choice.
He felt on delivery, 'a lot done, a lot to do' was the best way to frame
it. At every stage we have to remind people of the Tory alternative
– back to instability, underinvestment, social weakening, isolationism.
'A lot done, a lot to do, a lot to lose if we go back to the Tories.' GB
said the real challenge was to establish and maintain our own agenda.
DB said people were sick of knockabout and wanted more serious
debate. Jack S talked about the importance of getting to young people
but then made a dreadful presentation of our argument on asylum,
so that at one point TB stepped in and said he disagreed, that we had

to come at this from the point of acknowledging there were genuine concerns, and the system was not dealing with them adequately, whereas JS mainly wanted to highlight the contribution immigrants and asylum seekers had made down the years. Most of the others chipped in with contributions of varying quality. TB did an OK summing up, not exactly Agincourt but enough to put a bit of fight in them I think. I did a briefing, a big anti-complacency number and said it was the Tories' strategy not ours to talk up a Labour landslide. I left for home with DB who was coming round for dinner. He seemed very down. He was also even more down on GB than ever, said his recent exchanges with him had been terrible.

Tuesday, May 8

The *Today* programme's sneering tone was even more pronounced than usual and there was a cynicism in the Beeb's coverage all day. I went up to the flat when I got in, where TB was going through his words for the campaign launch at the school. It was a bit long and repetitive in parts so we went through it trying to hone it a bit, and both of us were worried whether a school audience would happily sit through a fairly long speech, even one that was kicking off the election. The reform message was strong now. TB said he still wasn't properly psyched. Maybe once we were out on the road he would get into it. We had a big media turnout in the street, and the BBC had a helicopter to track him to the Palace and back, but somehow managed to lose him. Despite that the full hype machine was in full swing, with the TV and radio guys outside babbling away the whole time. TB got back after seeing the Queen, and now we were set for the off. Blunkett was waiting in the hall. TB helped him into the car and off we set. They got a fantastic reception from the kids as we arrived. I sensed the head teacher was a bit nervous and maybe it was only now the scale of what was going on struck her, with all the crews and hacks and the satellite trucks and the rest of it. She asked me if TB was as nervous as she was.

I wanted a bit of time with TB to go through a marked copy of the speech and to try to psyche him up a bit, but I was buttonholed by one of the governors, who was the first ear-bending bore of the campaign. It was a good school though, and the kids were brilliant considering they had to sit through it all, and content-wise I think we had the right message. I was a bit worried by how much of a God element there was to the whole thing, the backdrop, the choir singing a religious song, a hymn at the end, and it was a bit odd that he was doing a big number on the importance of voting to a group of people who couldn't vote. There was a bit of a scrum outside and the media were pretty cynical about the whole event, but I thought it was just about OK. Mind you, how we kept this cynical bunch of wankers interested for four weeks of this was a question I didn't like to think about too often. We were going to have to stick to our strategy as best we could, but also be tactical where possible to maintain media interest and try to get the basic messages pumping through to the public. The story they wanted was plucky unspun Hague up against the mighty Labour machine. I thought Hague looked ridiculous on his visit to Watford, but he came across fine on the bulletins. I thought TB would be a bit jumpy about the St Olave's [school] event, as it was clear the press were focusing on the God side of things, but he was pretty relaxed.

Wednesday, May 9

Anji called, said Kate [Garvey] was upset at the press coverage of the launch at the school, which as expected focused on the God side of things, making TB look very preachy. I called her and told her not to worry, said she was doing a good job and we had to keep taking risks on visits and pictures. The truth was it was just one gear over the top. We could have got away with the choir, the song, the cross or the hymn, but not all of them. What I was worried about was the blame game opening up right at the start of the campaign. I went into Millbank with Philip. It was the first time I was there 'legitimately' as it were, having resigned as a civil servant for the duration of the campaign. I was glad to be there, but nervous, knowing as I did, reminded by Philip as we arrived, that a lot of them were looking to me to lift things and to hold it together when things got rocky. When GB came back from his economic speech, which was OK if a bit dull and heavy, I sat down with him, Ed Balls, Bob Shrum, PG and DA and talked over the next few days. We were working together fine but it was a real problem that GB prevaricated over some of the little decisions. We agreed that if we established the Tories were doing their manifesto tomorrow, we would do the pledges. I went back to Number 10 to see TB before he left for his meeting with the PLP over at the House. He got a great reception before he even started, did a big thanks to the PLP, said unity and discipline had been good and now we had to work together at this important time for party and country. He went through the big arguments, the policy areas to focus on, the dividing lines, the cynicism 'back door' strategy that would be run against us, but in all the main policy areas, we were strong. Nothing was more important than stability vs boom and bust. He felt the Tories were vulnerable above all on tax and spend because they were promising to tax less while spending more and we had to pick that apart day by day. He felt re delivery that we did not make enough of progress on equality and social division, and how the Tories tried to stop measures like the New Deal, the minimum wage, the winter allowance and so on. On Europe, we had to make sure people understood the inherent danger of their policy, which would take us to the exit door of the EU with catastrophic effect on jobs and investment and our standing in the world.

We had the last PMQs which would get a fair bit of coverage. I felt we shaded it on the arguments but Hague had the best one-liners which meant the media would give it to him. We finally agreed with GB that we should do the pledge card, and AD came over so that I could brief him. GB was keen we set it in the context of the broader economic message, which was easy enough. AD was straightforward enough to work with, though he could do with a lighter touch from time to time. GB was in a better mood, cracked a joke about the TB hymn-book pictures, and was properly engaged in the discussion re the next few days. I then left with TB for St Albans, where we would be formally unveiling the new pledge card. I went through it all with TB in the car to the train station. He was still lacking in basic confidence and was a bit edgy when people just came up to us. He said he would get there but he was struggling to find his rhythm. PG said the groups were not bad, and they were a disaster for Hague, though asylum still had the potential to do us a lot of harm.

Thursday, May 10

As expected the media gave PMQs to Hague. Philip said on the way in it showed how out of touch the media were. They played the entire exchanges to the focus groups last night and TB was the clear winner in every one of them. TB was still in fretful nervous mode. He arrived for the 7am meeting at Millbank, but he looked a bit out of sorts and after a few words let GB and me take it over. The problem with both of them was that they wanted everything too easy. GB was scared of being asked about tax, and overcomplicated the lines of defence. All he had to do was point to our record in keeping the pledge, and say he could not write every Budget years in advance. TB and I both wanted to build up health in advance of tomorrow's good waiting-list figures, but there was some resistance to be overcome, because they wanted to keep motoring on the economy without getting pinned on tax. It was perfectly possible to do both and it was a bit of a non-argument. TB saw GB privately at the end, and he felt GB was a bit

May '01: Formal unveiling of election pledges

put out at TB's interview in the *Standard* in which he said there was no 'gentlemen's agreement' to hand over the leadership during the second term. They did the press conference which was average, with TB not yet motoring and GB's answers too complex and monotone. There was a lack of passion and drive at the moment and we had to find it soon.

We then got on to the campaign bus, which was dire. We had asked for the best, most modern, hi-tech and all that stuff and it was just another campaign bus with no legroom, drinks spilling, the same as '97. It had a pretty negative effect on both of us and the only response was to turn it into a running joke. The papers were laid out on the table at the back and TB made the mistake of reading them. He said he hadn't realised Hague was getting such an easy ride. But Philip was adamant the public were seeing through it. TB still felt we were weak on storylines for the next four weeks, and he was in one sense right. But we had the lines basically sorted and now we need to inject the creativity and the passion. A lot of that was down to him. I said to him afterwards he was giving the impression of someone who saw the election campaign as a bit of an inconvenience getting in the way of being prime minister. When was campaigning ever easy? He was talking about Hague as though he was some great statesman getting a great press, but he was neither really, and the public were seeing him as a wally. I said he was underestimating the strength of signals he sent out to others – like at the morning meeting today where he didn't show balls or leadership, and we were going to need loads of both. He had to get less buttoned up. The aim was to generate serious and meaningful dialogue, not just fight day to day around the headlines. We set off for Leamington. We were stopping at various points to pick up local media and do onboard interviews. I popped outside to make a couple of phone calls and was harangued by some red-faced old Tory whose bottom lip was trembling with rage, and who got more and more steamed up the more I wound him up. I was sometimes a bit taken aback by the emotions I aroused in some people, mainly hacks and Tories. We got a helicopter back to London. We were both making clear to Anji we wanted to minimise time spent on the bus. Philip was really stepping up the focus-group work, and did a couple at lunchtime which he said were better for Hague.

I went into the agency who had worked up a nice ad campaign on the theme of last-minute 'must vote' Post-it reminders. It was a clever idea and it lent itself to positive or negative messages. My only worry was whether it was too twee, and whether on a poster site you would actually notice the writing on the Post-it. We also discussed what slogan to put on the poster of Hague with Thatcher's hair. The ad guys seemed to prefer 'Be afraid, be very afraid.' I preferred 'Vote Labour – or this gets in.' It was tough, in your face, but the humour of the poster meant we could get away with it. Later, I softened it to 'or they get in'. We agreed to do overnight a 'Just William hasn't done his homework' poster on Hague. Blunkett called to say he felt the rebuttal material being sent to ministers was too heavy. I said I would look at it personally before it went out. We had a good meeting – TB, AC, Jonathan, PH, Bob S – on TB's Sunday speech in Sedgefield. We agreed it should be very personal, show he believed the same things now as he always had done but that what he offered was the ability to make those things happen. His defining belief was the potential of all people, given the chance, to make a difference, and how if a country tapped into that it could be successful. We also went back to the idea that the big political argument to put over was that we were leaving behind the false choice of 70s socialism and 80s Thatcherism and instead building a new progressive consensus. TB was not himself though, lacking confidence, tired-looking, still a bit nervy, and it was draining having to try to pump him up the whole time, using sometimes humour, sometimes sympathy, sometimes probably being a bit brutal. We had a policy-rich manifesto and maybe that would help him shape the campaign better once it was out there.

Friday, May 11

The press were still trying to ramp up Hague, but considering yesterday they launched their manifesto, the papers were nothing like as good for them as TB seemed to think. The media had just decided to mark us down a bit for being slow and sluggish. It was not the end of the world. The tax pledge [not to increase income tax rates], which we had held back from St Albans, was leaked to the *Guardian* after last night's meeting to agree the manifesto, and was set to be the story for the day, and I felt we might as well run with it. It wasn't ideal but I still felt it was better that it was out on its own before the manifesto launch. Also, though tax gave us difficulties, it did at least mean the debate went to the economy. I went to Number 10 to meet TB and head for *GMTV*, which was always a culture shock because they always seemed to have an odd assortment of human interest and showbiz stories when we went in there. He got a fairly hard time on the phone-in but did fine, was beginning to engage a bit better. He said he had had a decent night's sleep and he had felt more confident. At last, I said. Don't lose it. I worked on a briefing note for the Sundays based on trailing TB's Sunday speech. One good line

May '01: Pledge to hold tax rates leaked

came out of some of PG's groups, in which several people said they felt he had started the job and should be given the chance to finish. We started to use that in some of our language. I did the Sundays by phone and sensed they felt it was a substantial briefing. I could usually tell from briefing a speech in advance whether the speech would work, and I felt this one would. I also liked the feel of a campaign that said it had a strategy and intended to hammer it out day after day. I did a conference call with GB and co re the TV debates being planned among senior ministers and Shadows. GB was not keen on doing one with Portillo. TB was much better out on the road today, did some good relaxed walkabouts in Kent and Essex. He always did them better when Cherie was around.

Saturday, May 12

The papers were still not too bad, but the broadcasters were pretty much following the Tory agenda the whole time, and they were put under nothing like the pressure we were. GB was discombobulated by a piece in the *FT* which indicated someone was briefing against the campaign and needless to say he believed it was Peter M. He spoke to TB who suggested we just ignore it. GB said 'It's OK for you, you're not the one being criticised,' which was not wholly accurate as we were still getting flak for the school launch. We had to get more life into the campaign. I met Derry and Charlie F to work up a strategy. In general, I felt we had to be more energetic about getting into the big arguments but he was more keen on going policy area by policy area. I also called together all the press people and said we had to get more disciplined on agreeing and circulating written lines to take on any of the difficult issues that came up. There were too many people seemingly talking to the press as commentators rather than spokesmen. Relations with the media were getting fractious already. John Pienaar [BBC] complained that Ed Miliband had accused him of invention. David Hill and Hilary C were angry at Marr for reporting that the Tories were doing a good job at avoiding questions – had it been us there would have been no 'good job' about it, but it didn't add up to much and we had a long way to go. We hit the road and TB did the best off-the-cuff speech of the day to a smallish crowd in Kettering, big message and dividing lines, lot to lose etc. Back on the bus, he was a lot happier re the nature of the campaign, felt comfortable with the idea that we were trying to get up serious argument in the face of cynical media and opportunistic Opposition. PG also felt the combination of TB's charisma and GB's solidity was working well.

TB still felt neither he nor GB were operating that well yet. CB wondered whether I shouldn't be back in Millbank full-time 'to keep an eye on him'. But I felt happier as we reached the first weekend than I thought I would. He did a couple of stops in Gedling, then Rotherham, and he was definitely finding his voice in the stump speeches he was doing. He was definitely better when CB was there. Likewise, I liked it when Fiona came out with us, and felt calmer, though neither of us liked it when we were both away from the kids. Bruce and I went through the speech for tomorrow, which was now pretty strong. TB rewrote it later, made it more personal and a bit quirky in parts, which I liked. The office faxed up the Sundays, which were full of splits over campaign tactics, largely based on the *FT*, but clearly too many people were talking and stirring. There were a few suggesting I should take over at Millbank, which is what DB had also been suggesting. Robert Harris had another vile piece about me and New Labour, which Peter denied having helped.

Sunday, May 13

We were up early to prepare for *Frost*. TB had no problem getting up the messages we wanted. We did a conference call with GB who was pretty angst-ridden, asking 'When is the briefing against me going to stop?' TB and I were on separate phones in the study at Myrobella and he just shook his head. Sally, Jonathan, DH and PG all now thought I should be based in Millbank. Philip felt GB was a bit lost when I wasn't there, and there was also the sense developing of two operations. Jonathan said that when I was not there, there was no oomph whenever the Tories screwed up. GB and DA were too cautious about attack. Fraser Kemp was not being used properly yet and so was doing his own thing, pretty effectively. I spoke to a few journalists post-*Frost* and the general feeling was that we were in OK shape. The Sedgefield speech, after all the rewrites, effectively became a marriage of Bob's basic draft and TB's more personal bits. TB was more interested in it being seen as a very New Labour speech. I always liked it when he did things in Sedgefield because the mood and the atmosphere were good. He delivered it well and I felt the combination of speech plus *Frost* gave us a good day. We got back to the house and word came through that Shaun Woodward had got St Helens [constituency], which was another New Labour signal if ever there was one. David Miliband got selected in South Shields, which was great news and we had a chat later on. I was really pleased for him and I had no doubt it was the right thing. I had dinner with Bruce [Grocott], Mark [Bennett] and some of the staff. The mood was definitely better. I loved having Bruce around because he constantly

May '01: Shaun Woodward adopted at St Helens

reminded us of how divorced the media bubble was from the real world. He was the one relentlessly Old Labour voice that TB had no trouble listening to, because he did it without side and with humour, but he also knew New Labour/TB were the key to another big win.

Monday, May 14

The reaction to TB's speech had been pretty good and we were in OK shape. The *FT* had a big story about a Shadow Cabinet minister saying they would go for £20bn tax cuts and David Hill and I really wanted to go for it and drive it up the agenda, define 'Hague-onomics' as spend more, tax less, sums don't add up. But GB didn't want to move off the business story and the New Deal. It was pretty hopeless, and there was a real churlishness to him at the moment. I was working well with all of his people, but with GB things seemed to have moved backwards. Philip said I had to spend more time in Millbank because anything that required risk was just being strangled down there. TB was doing the *Today* programme down the line with [John] Humphrys, who just droned on and on about Keith Vaz. Humphrys was a parody of himself. So as TB headed for Inverness, Mark B and I flew south. By the time we landed, the Tories had had their press conference, which was seemingly a shambles, nine minutes long and with no answers on tax. Also, the £20bn story was taking off and GB agreed to put something on it into his speech in Swindon, while I got a bit on 'Hague-onomics' into TB's words. Oliver Letwin [Shadow chief secretary to the Treasury] was widely thought to be the Shadow Cabinet member responsible for £20bn, so we commissioned 'Wanted' posters. Letwin was a bit of a liability, and the more we could keep the argument on matters economic, the better. A bit of humour would also help set up the *Economic Disaster II* campaign. I felt we were motoring and I was enjoying going for the Tories again. I met GB when he came back and he was still looking around for policy stories that were not really what we needed right now. Letwin had given us an open goal and we had to hammer into it – what did £20bn mean in terms of schools and hospital cuts? TB called in, said the mood up north was good and he felt strong with the arguments.

I complained to Carolyn Quinn [BBC journalist] who was obsessed with the idea of everything being stage-managed, and whose bulletin report was really shallow. The travelling press were complaining re lack of access so TB went to see them and Hilary [Coffman] seemed to think it worked. But the truth was the campaign media entourage was becoming outdated because the main guys could follow it all on TV anyway. We had an asylum meeting, where Margaret McD was very forcible, said we really had to understand how dangerous this was. There was even a case for making it one of the main headlines out of the launch. TB's concern was that if we were not careful, it would become the main thing. I was sent a Good Luck card from Britney [Spears] – presumably from her PR – which I gave to the *Star*, who loved it. Hugh Whittow [deputy editor] said they might even get the election on the front for once. Asylum still had the potential to give the Tories traction and a way back in. It was all part of his own way of getting himself mentally in the right place for what was to come.

Tuesday, May 15

The Tory tax shambles was OK, but it hadn't quite reached meltdown proportions and the media were keen to move on. The 'Wanted' posters on Letwin had worked and now we got Adrian McMenamin [press officer] dressed up as Sherlock Holmes with a couple of Great Danes with 'Looking for Letwin' covers on them. Even if these things didn't break through to the public – and I think this one could, depending on how the Tories handle it – sometimes these things are worth doing just for internal morale anyway. The mood was a lot better now we were laying into the Tories a bit as well as doing the positive policy stuff. The *Mail* had set out some questions for TB and I wrote to [Paul] Dacre [editor] to say we would reply to them. He said he would only do it as an interview with [Lynda] Lee-Potter, so I did up the replies anyway and gave it to the *Express* as the piece the *Mail* wouldn't run. TB called, felt we were in OK shape. He was being pressed re the Libs and we agreed the best way to deal with them was to say we agreed on the need for increased investment, but could they be trusted with the economy? We had to bring everything back to the economy at the moment.

I went over to see GB in his office over by the far wall, and he was banging away at his computer. He had a pile of papers to the right and on the top had written 75 pence, and below it, in large black letters, 'Who will silence Mandelson?' It was clear Peter was at it again in the *Telegraph* today. I pointed to his 'silence' writing and tried to make a joke of it, but he was having none of it, went on a great tirade, said we were letting him destroy the campaign, undermine him, be ill-disciplined, on and on he went and eventually I lost it, said Peter was nothing to do with me and I did not like the implications that I could be held responsible one way or the other for what he was or was not up to. 'Well it has to stop,' he said. 'Telling ME it has to stop suggests that in some way I might be responsible and I fucking resent that, given I am the one Peter blames for him not being in the fucking government.' I said we all had jobs to do and we should get on and do them instead of wallowing in this crap. Let Peter do whatever he is doing. We should have better things to do than worry about it and if he ever suggests I am encouraging him or helping him to undermine the campaign, that will be the last time we work together. I could feel the gorge rising and I was suddenly conscious that I was jabbing my finger at him and thought it would be better to leave. Also the raised voices had been heard and there were people looking in. But I was really angry, less at the veiled accusation than at the fact he was allowing this stuff to stop him doing what he should be doing – driving the bloody campaign.

I went back to my desk, really steamed up. Bob Shrum came over, having heard it all, and said he backed what I had said, I was right to be angry. He said GB thought Peter was trying to destabilise the campaign. If that was true, the only thing we could do was work together, so I must not let one row get in the way of me and Gordon working together. I said I wouldn't, but I was sick of coming in to see GB and his people obsessing over some piece of rubbish in this paper or that when what we should be doing is getting above it. I said I was fed up being expected to sort out all these feuds and personality clashes when it was time we just pulled together. I calmed down pretty quickly and had loads to do, and was hoping GB would not go further into his shell. After the press conference, he made no effort even to paint on a smile when he saw me, just glared and glowered and walked by. I had a chat with JP who was also furious with Peter and said if one more thing appeared he would go for him publicly. He thought that in speaking to Peter, TB was giving him licence. He wanted me to speak to TB and warn him if Peter was not brought under control, he would speak out. We also discussed respective roles after the election. He wanted his own move to be seen as part of the strengthening of the centre. Yelland called and I totally fucked up by letting slip Blunkett was likely to move, and given we had been talking about asylum, he put two and two together, made four, and the *Sun* decided to splash on it. It was one of those stories that would be OK for the public, but bad for the Cabinet and I would cop the blame, not unreasonably.

We had a meeting on posters and went for a 3-1 negative to positive balance in the last five days. We also reviewed the election broadcasts, which weren't great. The first one had got really good figures and reaction, and we needed to maintain the high level. TB was up in Leeds and we were trying to do his speech by phone as well as working through the script for tomorrow's manifesto launch. After the usual endless circular conversations, he, GB and JP were fine with Birmingham [manifesto launch], but there was a fair bit of last-minute logistics to sort. We got into a bit of confusion when we heard some Tory candidates were saying withdraw from Europe, which we stirred up until we heard that there were Labour candidates on there too. The Tories played out a Willie Horton[1] type broadcast on early-release prisoners who went on to commit crimes, and we decided not to play it up, just to say we go positive, they go negative, but then someone stuck a microphone in front of Paul Boateng [Home office minister] who went way over the top, it became a huge row and knocked tax off the news. GB and I were united in our anger. He called me over for a chat re things, neither of us mentioning the row earlier, and seemed OK. TB's Leeds speech went well, but Boateng had got the Tory broadcast to the top of the news and they would get some purchase on it.

Wednesday, May 16

The pre-manifesto briefing went fine and we were well set up. The *Star* splashed on 'Britney backs Blair', which we hung up around the office, and the *Express* used the *Mail* piece fine. The *Sun* was a problem for various reasons – it pissed off GB because it was so pro Blunkett; it annoyed Jack because it suggested he was being moved out, and David claimed not to like it because it presumed victory. It was annoying but would hopefully blow over quickly. We left for Euston and waited for GB and Blunkett on the train. There were good crowds, loads of hacks and the mood was fine. We worked on TB's script on the journey up, GB redoing the tax section, Pat McF working on achievements. I got one of the Garden Room Girls [Civil Service secretaries in Number 10] into trouble by getting her to type it up, which was irritating. TB was a bit jumpy and nervy, GB growling a lot less since our altercation yesterday. The bus from the station in Birmingham seemed to take an age but we used it to go over tough questions and he was pretty fired up by the time we got there. We had another ten minutes or so with GB going over the hard questions again, tax, euro, usual stuff, then we were pretty much set. We briefed

[1] Horton, a murderer serving two life sentences plus eighty-five years in Massachusetts, had been the beneficiary of weekend release programme. Failing to return to prison, he committed assault, armed robbery and rape. Horton's case was the subject of a 1988 television advertisement from the George Bush presidential campaign, attacking Democratic candidate Michael Dukakis – governor of Massachusetts at the time of Horton's release.

the Cabinet, most of whom would not be required to speak until they went on their own visits and media rounds. Clare [Short] had a little whinge about being 'over-directed'. God, does she turn my stomach.

The venue had been done out well and it looked stylish and professional. TB did well, both in terms of the opening remarks and the Q&A. He got the tone and mood right, and it felt confident and strong. There was the usual whining from the media about there not being much new, as if the launch of a party's manifesto was not a big event in itself. Also I got into a bit of a muddle afterwards on the exact role of the private sector in the public services and I felt I may have hit the private sector buttons too hard, and the press would go off and wind up everyone they could find. TB went off ahead on a visit as I did the media rounds and we were due to link up again at the QE2 hospital. I got there ahead of him and was taken up to a holding room, where I lay down on a sideboard, and tried to steal a nap.

He came in about an hour later, looking really shaken. I asked what was wrong, and he just shook his head. There were hospital staff around so he didn't want to talk about it, or complain, but it seems he was confronted on arrival by a woman complaining about her partner's treatment.[1] As the cops and the staff followed in behind him, I could see from the looks on their faces too that it was not good. She had laid into him big style, and while Anji et al. were trying to move him on, he just had to stand there and take it. I caught up with some of the hacks but of course they hadn't seen it as they were arriving at the same time as he did. But then the TV boys told me what had happened and said they were 'fantastic pictures' – for them, that is, not us. I asked TB how bad it was – bad, he said. Bad enough to blow out the manifesto launch? Definitely, he said. All that fucking work, and we will be lucky if most people see or read a bloody word of it, because one woman has a pop in front of the cameras. It also meant we had to put people on checking out all the facts. The tragedy was this was one of the best hospitals in the country but nobody was going to know that now. The visit went on in a rather surreal atmosphere. I did my best to talk things down but when I finally saw the exchanges I realised we had no chance. Sharron Storer had entered the political lexicon in an instant.

We tried to keep his spirits up and by the time we got to Watford, we were able to laugh about it, but things then got worse, when we heard Jack Straw had been slow-handclapped at the Police Federation

---

[1] Sharron Storer had harangued Blair in front of the media, complaining that there was no bed in the bone-marrow unit for her partner, a cancer patient.

[annual conference in Blackpool]. Then even worse when we got a phone call saying JP had thumped a guy in Wales who whacked an egg into him.[1] TB was about to pre-record BBC *Question Time* with David Dimbleby and we had to decide whether to tell him before he went on. Hilary and I were worried Dimbleby would get a message about it and ask him cold. But he had enough on his plate, and he was in the zone so we left him to it. He did a good job, though there was too much sleaze and too much Dimbleby. I was in and out of the green room where we were watching it, talking to JP, who was now holed up down in Wales. It had all been caught on camera and I spoke to Charlie F and Derry, who were waiting to see the pictures. I felt instinctively there would be a lot of support for JP, but also that he should say he wished he hadn't responded like that. He was not up for it one bit, said the guy was a total twat and 'Anyway, you never apologised when you hit Michael White.' I pointed out that I was then a Mirror hack.[2] He is the deputy prime minister, but he wasn't having it. He said it was bloody ridiculous that we had to take all this shit from people just because we were politicians and he would not be apologising. I admired him for it, but I knew TB would want something to defuse things.

When he came out from the studio, he was pleased with how it had gone, but I quickly brought him down to earth, said the good news was Sharron Storer was no longer leading the news; the bad news was that JP had thumped someone and that had taken over. He did one of his gobsmacked looks, and as I filled him in on every last detail, we ended up laughing about it. What else could you do? But there would be calls on him to sack him and we had to deal with that pretty quickly. No way, he said, no way. He felt there were people out there trying to recreate a sense of the fuel protest, and unless JP had provoked the whole thing, he was not even going to contemplate action against him. He felt there would be a lot of sympathy for him if he was just belted out of the blue with an egg. Also Hague had had a spot of bother in Wolverhampton [heckled and surrounded by a hostile crowd on a walkabout] and there may be a case for making a general defence of politicians. The manifesto was disappearing down

[1] Craig Evans, a countryside protester, had attacked Prescott with an egg as the deputy prime minister walked into a Labour rally in Rhyl, North Wales. Prescott retaliated. The 'Prescott punch' became a memorable image of the election campaign.

[2] When *Mirror* proprietor Robert Maxwell drowned off the side of his yacht in 1991, White (*Guardian*) entered the *Mirror* office in the Commons joking about 'Cap'n Bob, bob, bob'. Campbell eventually punched him. White hit him back.

a plughole. We agreed that we should do health and education tomorrow to try to recover some of the ground inevitably lost from today's series of unexpected disasters.

Charlie F described the pictures to me and it was clearly going to be a major media thing. JP was now talking me through it second by second, and having a laugh about it. 'Well you said we needed a bit of life in the campaign.' What a bloody day. We started thinking it would be the usual clean hit the media usually give you for the manifesto launch. Instead we had three totally unexpected human situations that would totally wipe out everything else. Peter M sent me a message, 'Pity about today, but eventually people will come back to the manifesto, which is strong.' That was going to depend on us, and how we got them to come back to it. Carol Linforth [Labour official] texted me, 'Spirits up'.

Thursday, May 17

JP was big in the papers and massive on the broadcasts. Sky were playing the punch and the scrum afterwards on a continuous loop, again and again and again. [Adam] Boulton was working himself into a total 'Prescott must go' lather. In all the vox pops, men seemed to be fine, women less so. It was the same internally. Having watched the incident, TB and I both felt instinctively that there would be more sympathy than anger, and we should back him to the hilt, but Fiona, Sally and Anji all thought it was pretty bad, and damaging, and I sensed a feeling of mild panic when I went into Millbank. I worked on TB's lines to take pre-press conference on all the various incidents from yesterday, but the hardest thing would be getting the tone right re JP. At GB's meeting, we went through the positive plans for the day and then discussed how to handle JP. We agreed Charlie F, Derry, Joe Irvin [Prescott adviser] and I should do a conference call with him to agree how best to handle it. JP was adamant he would not apologise but was happy for us to say the whole incident was regrettable, but he was also clear if he was interviewed himself he would say he had no idea what it was, and his first instinct was that it was more serious than an egg, and he was actually frightened by what was going on.

We discussed it with TB who felt he should just make light of it, and in the end he used the line 'John's John' pretty effectively. He said he would not have done it himself, but then defended JP's character. Alex F called me having heard it on the news and said he thought people would be really impressed by how he handled it. Boulton was the only one getting overly antsy about the whole thing.

The manifesto coverage was OK, but limited. Letwin had conceded he was responsible for the £20bn line and GB and I agreed we now had to try to keep the focus on it. Blunkett and Milburn were not going to get much of a look-in with their announcements, but we had a fairly strong overall package by the end of it. It was maybe a bit too jovial, and I didn't like DB hitting his fist into his hand, but overall the tone was fine and again we looked confident and in charge despite it all. TB spoke to JP afterwards, said he felt he had to say he would not have responded in the same way, in an attempt to take the sting out of it, but assured him it was a strong defence.

JP was still resisting making any kind of concession on it, but TB and I both felt he had to say something today or else it would just run on. He was up in Scotland and after several calls we persuaded him to do a pooled telly interview and I called Fiona Ross [STV] to ask if she could interview him when he reached Edinburgh. I told her the score, namely that he was reluctant but I felt sure she would win him round. I advised him to be a bit softer and more emollient than usual. He said he was embarrassed at how much attention it was getting but he felt anyone would have reacted the same way. Fiona said he did fine. When I spoke to him afterwards we agreed he should now just make a joke of it whenever it was raised, and use the current attention to keep going on about policy and dividing lines as the things that mattered.

Hague weighed in with a really silly and over-convoluted clip about me and Britney [Spears] and how the campaign song was not 'Hit me baby one more time'. I did three or four pretty full-scale briefings through the day and felt by the end of it we were about as well placed as we could be considering. We went by helicopter to Loughborough, Bruce and I writing random jokes on the way. TB did a school visit, and I saw the press there and briefed on the nature of the campaign, trying to get up the dividing line as us as serious and desperate to focus on policy, Tories on anything but.

Then Halifax, and the Ridings school, and even on the bus TB was now getting into his stride. He did a few local papers, and in between we were joking about having a daily punch to enliven the campaign, and going through who we would most like to punch. There was a fair bit of interest in TB's Manchester speech in the evening, and we worked up a direct appeal to One Nation Tories to come over as a new way of getting up Letwin's £20bn, which I briefed in advance after we got over from Halifax. We were in the Lowry hotel, which was fantastic, and I had time for a run in the gym before we left. GB and I were speaking a lot on the phone and the row had cleared the

May '01: JP says anyone would have done the same

air and got us working together better again. We had a good celeb turnout for the rally – Alex F, Mick Hucknall [singer], Sir John Mills [veteran actor] – 'the oldest switcher in town'. It was a good night. I got driven back with Mark Bennett to be at Millbank for the morning.

Friday, May 18

Asylum was dominating the news, and was clearly seen by the media as the Tories' last big shot, and they were determined to try to give them a lift. I went in with PG, and both of us thought our politicians were still too defensive on our so-called negatives, didn't pick it up and turn it into a bigger argument. We had tried to get up the idea of the mini manifesto going to loads of homes as a way of generating policy but they didn't really bite. We had GB, Milburn, Estelle [Morris] and Barbara Roche [Home Office minister] to deal with asylum at the press conference. Barbara did OK, but not great, while earlier Jack had not been on his best form, and we agreed TB would have to go up on asylum at some point during the day. The Tories were getting pretty uncritical free-hit coverage and we had to get our line out more clearly.

I spoke to TB after the morning meeting, then put him on to GB. GB was a bit spooked by the issue, whereas TB felt we could take it from them, provided we displayed real confidence – there were weaknesses in the system which had to be tackled but we would never turn our backs on genuine cases. He felt the issue, and understood people's anger, whereas GB just thought it was a bit of a nightmare. To be fair, GB was good at the press conference and TB, who was calling the whole time before he did his clips, was fine too. I spent all day at Millbank, and the day was like a rolling meeting with a few breaks to catch breath and try to sort the things agreed from the meeting before. TB ended up in Norwich doing a Q&A with Ross Kemp [actor and Labour supporter] which went fine. He was picking up his pace all the time. We had a meeting on our plans to use it to hit the basic economic messages again. I did the Sunday lobby, focusing mainly on private polls, pensioner rallies and our determination to keep going on Letwin. Douglas was very keen to do the briefing with me and I think was a bit taken aback by how rude I was to them. I just couldn't help myself with the Sundays because of the drivel most of them churned out week after week.

Saturday, May 19

It was pensions day and we pretty much dominated the bulletins. Also, asylum had not flown for them as much as I feared. There were a few campaign pieces saying I was spending more time in

Millbank to keep an eye on GB, which we would have to iron out for the Sundays. Since our argument we had been getting on a lot better. He was in Scotland today but kept in touch and was not in the usual 'The problem is' mode the whole time. We had Margaret B, Alistair D and Gus for the press conference, which went fine, three grown-ups. We got a cake in to celebrate Letwin's birthday, Margaret cutting it to illustrate £20bn cuts. The Letwin sub-campaign was going well. I took a meeting on the Shadow Budget, which would help us keep it going. TB was in Wales, worried that his campaign on the road was not really zinging, but I felt we were getting most of the arguments in the right place most of the time, and when he did come in on stuff, he was on pretty good form. Hague was not doing that well at the moment, and I felt they were ending the first full week pretty demoralised. We had hurt them on £20bn and there was plenty left in it yet.

Sunday, May 20

The Sundays weren't too bad and the polls were still strong for us. I went in about 10 and worked up a TB piece the *Sun* wanted on public services. I worked a bit on the Shadow Budget preparations. We had to make this, and the Tories' £20bn cuts problem, as big as anything else in the campaign. There was a case for TB presenting it, but GB was not keen. TB was down at Chequers for Leo's birthday. GB was in a bit of a state about another 'GB wings clipped' story, this time in *Sunday Business*. I hadn't seen it, in common with 99.9 per cent of the population, but by the time I got in, all his people were walking around with copies of it, yellow marker pens having gone over the offending sections. He also raised it with TB. I got the *Sun* piece done by lunchtime, then worked on a script for tomorrow and the final version of the pledge card.

I had a good meeting with Douglas and Philip to go over my note on how to make TB's tour more people-friendly and less prone to the charge of stage-management. But I suspected we were on a no-win situation on this. Whatever we did, they say it is stage managed, unless it is anarchy or a disaster for us. We were going to struggle to keep them interested for three more weeks of this though. I had my first big 'I wish to God this was over' moment. Jack Straw was doing [new regulations to prevent] Internet paedophilia today, still sore about the Blunkett story in the *Sun*. But Jack is a grown-up and once I admitted it was more cock-up than conspiracy, he was fine. Andrew Smith [chief secretary to the Treasury] did fine with Portillo on *On the Record*. There were no real

May '01: GB hates another 'wings clipped' story

problems out of the Sundays, but TB was concerned about the dynamic of the campaign.

Monday, May 21

The Tories did an OK job getting up our refusal to rule out a rise in NICs [National Insurance contributions], while we did OK getting up the Shadow Budget, but we lacked the real killer instinct, and we still didn't have the feel of TB's own campaign quite right. I said to him I sensed he needed to 'break out of the box' a little more, that he was still very controlled and buttoned up. The groups were showing real irritation at the media coverage, and the tit-for-tat, and we had to break through it somehow. We were still getting some mileage out of Letwin who was still being kept under wraps. We had the idea of a human rights 'Free Letwin' march outside Central Office. I wanted to do a parachute drop of missing person leaflets into his constituency, but GB was cautious. The BBC eventually tracked him down so we had to change tack a little, but I was in no doubt the more people saw and heard of Letwin, the better for us. I did the morning meetings then over to see TB with Bill Bush pre his Nicky Campbell [BBC Radio 5] interview, which was as good a chance as any to start being a bit more people-friendly in use of language. He was sure he should not be seen as the main negative campaigner but he was still missing a few free hits. We also needed far more spontaneity, and I was suggesting more unscheduled stops, phone-ins from the bus, anything to give a sense of interaction and reaching out. I went back for a series of planning meetings on the next few days.

TB, GB and I had quite a good discussion on the dynamic of the campaign. GB felt we underestimated the problems we were getting through tax. Alistair Darling had real problems at the launch of the Shadow Budget re NICs. GB felt it would dominate tomorrow as well. He seemed a bit down but did at least say, and I was glad to hear it, that there were bound to be some days when the media would let the Tories take the news with a specific attack on this or that tax – we just had to maintain a bigger argument about the economy. TB was concerned it was coming over too much as an old-fashioned tax and spend argument, that meant the public were hearing Tories for tax cuts, us for spending, that we had not yet demolished their credibility on tax cuts. We also discussed Europe, which was likely to be their next phase of attack, and whether we should get out on the front foot. GB was still, though more gently and with less angst, going on about Peter M, saying he was at it and it was unacceptable to have this undermining of the campaign going on.

Tuesday, May 22

The Tories were still going on NICs – three days of it now – and GB was putting out such anxious vibes that people could sense we were worried. TB felt GB's caution allied to his obsessive nature meant he wasn't handling this with the tactical guile it needed. GB's argument was that we may have to lift the NI ceiling to raise necessary funding for the NHS, but TB was adamant we had to stick to the line that we did not write a parliament's worth of Budgets in advance. TB did the press conference on health and was on good form, confident and strong and there was no question that left him fazed. Thatcher was out and about in the *Mail* today and he was fine on that. We had a problem in that the broadcasters' lead story was Margaret McD's letter of complaint re collusion between the media and protesters.[1] There was some evidence of it but of course the media couldn't resist making the story about themselves, and it was one of those that had little or no relevance to the public's attempts to follow the campaign. TB called me just after 6, and said we had to shut it down. I prepared a statement for the morning meeting and we rang round to try to kill it, having agreed with Margaret there had to be a bit of a climbdown.

TB came to the meeting but he tended to sit back and let GB chair and GB and me do most of the talking, coming in when he felt we were missing a point or taking too long to decide. GB said there were three competing stories – the one the media wanted, i.e. Margaret's letter; the one the Tories wanted, NICs; and the one we wanted – Letwin. I pointed out that we were trying to get up health today. I suppose on one level it was good that he wanted to focus all the time on tax and the economy, but it was an odd thing to say to a roomful of people when we were about to have TB fronting a press conference on health. I felt we just had to keep going on schools and hospitals as the best way of emphasising the dividing line on investment and values, with the economy underpinning all the arguments. Then he said he thought we should do Europe tomorrow rather than education, which was ridiculous. We argued about it on and off all day.

After the press conference, TB had to go back to Number 10 to see the Crown Prince of Japan [Naruhito]. TB and I went for a walk round the garden afterwards. He said he was worried about GB's demeanour at the press conferences, felt it was too samey and lacking in touch. He

[1] In a letter to the BBC, ITN and Sky, McDonagh wrote 'I have been provided with growing evidence that broadcasters have been inciting and colluding with protesters at campaign visits . . . I am sure that like me, you will want to ensure that this behaviour ceases immediately. It crosses the line between creating and reporting the news.'

May '01: Margaret McDonagh's collusion complaint

also felt he hadn't handled NICs well. He felt we lacked a really good public attack dog against the Tories that the press would be interested in and take seriously. He even at one point suggested I do it, which would have been a pretty odd development during the middle of the campaign. We had a hospital visit, then *JY Prog* [Jimmy Young, BBC Radio 2], loads on NICs. As we left, he called GB and said he felt we had a real problem on this. It was being taken as read that we were going to raise NICs or impose new so-called stealth taxes, or even 50p top rate. He felt we had to develop a better body language on this. I spoke to GB when we got back and said we should make this part of the attack on the Tory Lie Machine. He wanted to say it was all a smear, which to me sounded odd. His clips were not that great.

TB felt we were missing Peter's mind on this kind of thing, and also that we did not have enough good politicians who were visible and making an impact. Milburn was around a lot in Millbank and I felt we needed to integrate him more. TB had a few interviews to do before he left for a Q&A in Wimbledon. He said he was feeling the need to let rip, that he felt it would be down to him to get some life into the campaign. We were shrouded in media cynicism, but we had not really made it an issue, so it was going to take something different to break through it.

Thatcher said something on EMU – never – that went beyond Tory policy, so we had a quick conference call on how to react. Robin was desperate to go up but GB didn't really want him up on it, which was ludicrous. TB called after I'd gone to bed. He had had a bad conversation with GB. He had told him he found him too defensive and that he needed a lighter touch with the media. GB said 'You can do all the press conferences then.' TB felt we were a few days away from a real problem with him, either internally or possibly publicly. We were both moving to the idea that we had to get the focus more on him and more out on the road, and that probably meant letting rip sometime soon.

Wednesday, May 23

The polls were still showing us way ahead and yet there was still a lot of anxiety around. PG and I drove in together, and agreed we needed to crank up a gear, and break through the current mood inside and outside the campaign. I was trying to persuade TB that it was time to have a real go at the broadcasters for the nature of the coverage, which was personality- and process-driven, and anything but the real dialogue on the issues they had promised. Stan Greenberg had a new poll which he went through at the morning meeting. TB said afterwards he was horrified that a wide-ranging poll like that was presented to such a large meeting. It was pretty much as before, though we had taken a big fall on tax which was a real worry.

GB was not in a good way. After the meeting, TB said he 'wanted a word'. GB said 'What about?' The campaign. 'What's wrong with it?' I want to discuss it. 'I know you think I've fucked up on NICs. I know there are people briefing against me. If you wanted someone else to do it, fine, just appoint them and I'll move over.' Gordon, I just want to discuss it, and work out how we can raise it a gear or two. If we cannot have a conversation about this we have real problems, he said. Afterwards, he said he felt we had a real problem. GB only really engages when it is his area, tax and the economy, and even then he does it so defensively that people assume we have something to hide. He had got worse since Balls was around more. These guys just saw everything through a GB prism and they missed the bigger picture. TB was pretty exasperated. So was Robin, who called me and said he was doing stacks of media on Europe and it was going fine, but we had started on the back foot because the campaign was being overly influenced by the character of the person nominally in charge – dour, dull, anxious on good days, paranoid on bad days. He also felt the people around him were a bad influence.

The Tories had a bad press conference on tax so we went for a second one, ostensibly on Europe, to keep the Tory problem areas running, then briefed hard on health for tomorrow to show we were sticking to our agenda whatever happened. On the train down to Southampton, TB said he sometimes genuinely worried about GB. He said he had an alarming conversation yesterday, and another one today. He really does believe we are trying to do him in the whole time. I pointed out that I spent a good deal of my time telling the press how marvellous he was. TB said there was a real flaw – he could not see beyond his own interests and as a result he often miscalculated how to meet them. He did an interview with the *Independent* on the train, mainly Europe but also starting to talk about his frustration with the campaign. On the [Itchen] college visit, a young girl dressed in a Union Jack T-shirt ruffled his hair and the snappers loved it.[1] I did a briefing on how £20bn cuts would impact constituency by constituency and they quite liked it.

[1] A student, Jo Balchin, had asked Blair if he was worried some young people might resort to drug dealing or prostitution to pay their way through university. Blair responded 'There's no need for you to do that; you won't have to pay anything back until you earn £10,000', after which Balchin hugged him and patted his head.

We had another school visit in Dorset [Royal Manor School, Portland] and arrived a bit early and had a bit of time to kill. We stopped at a little cafe on a stunning spot overlooking the sea. It was warm, sunny, with a nice breeze and although the people in the cafe were gobsmacked to see TB, the entourage and a stack of security arrive on the scene, it was as near as we'd had to a normal moment for ages. We walked around for a bit, and he said 'Don't you some-times wish we just had a normal life like the people who live over there?' Sometimes, I said, but the moment passes quite quickly. 'It's a weird life though, isn't it? I mean if you stand back a bit and analyse how we live during these campaigns, and then the things we have to do, it's all a bit abnormal.' It was nice to have a little break, and a decent cup of tea which the cops brought over from the cafe, and which we were able to drink without spilling half of it over papers and floor as was generally the case on the bus. He was tired and a bit dispirited, still feeling there was something not quite right with the campaign. It wasn't exactly off track but nor was it brilliant. Philip and Peter H were calling constantly from Millbank, worried either about the state of the election broadcasts, or just complaining that we weren't hitting the Tories hard enough. When the BBC did tax again, plus some paranoid rubbish from [Norman] Tebbit [former Conservative Party chairman] about UKIP and MI5 [Tebbit claimed that people with MI5 links had 'infiltrated' the UK Independence Party], I thought enough was enough and put out a statement really whacking them for being as keen as the Tories were to avoid proper policy discussions.

Thursday, May 24

We did a bit better today getting up our agenda. Health ran pretty well from the press conference and the idea was certainly out there that the Tories were not really focusing on the big policy issues. The *Independent* interview did loads on TB's frustration at the nature of the debate. TB was still worried about GB, sufficient to say he wanted me to stay at Millbank all day rather than go to Bristol. He wasn't happy with the way the morning meetings were going. TB came to the meeting this morning, but let GB chair them so that he didn't feel in any way undermined, but it was odd to have him there, sometimes sitting at the back while we sorted out the day ahead. I could tell he was worried. Then later the GB lot went demented when Douglas was being interviewed by Andrew Neil [broadcaster and journalist] and was asked about TB taking over the campaign. In any normal, rational world, nobody would bat an eyelid and, according to David

Hill, in the [Commons Press] Gallery nobody did. But GB's lot were convinced this was going to be the story of the day. Douglas and Ed Miliband asked me to call [Andrew] Marr and make clear GB's role was unchanged. It revealed their defensiveness once more. Marr wasn't even planning to touch upon it, said it was Andrew Neil making mischief. But it put them in a strop for the whole day. There was also something a bit weird about any suggestion that the leader of the party wasn't actually in overall charge anyway.

The press conference was OK if a bit flat but he did one particularly good answer to Mike White which ought to carry. On the way out I was harangued by some of the sisters – Jackie Ashley [*New Statesman*], Jo Andrews [ITN], Catherine MacLeod [*Herald*] among them – because we had Tessa [Jowell] on the platform but GB had not referred any of the questions to her. I could see why they found it irritating, but we were now at the stage of the campaign where people were disappearing inside their own bubbles, overreacting to the slightest thing. My defence – that if it hadn't been for me we wouldn't even have had a woman up there – seemed to make things worse not better because it underlined the idea that it was tokenism. I suggested not a single vote would be swung one way or the other by it, and they were overreacting. Then I went over the top, started doing a bit of 'there, there darling' and knickers really started to get twisted.

TB did an interview with the *FT* on the bus while I stayed back to do a note on the next few days and a briefing note on his speech for tomorrow. We had a brainstorm on how to push the idea of what we now believed were serious Tory divisions, and which the media weren't currently really going for. TB called in a few times and was still desperate to get the campaign into a different gear. Milburn was around Millbank more and more, which I found helpful but GB was resisting giving him a broader public profile. Blunkett wasn't enjoying it and wasn't keen to come down for a press conference. Robin had become less visible and was pretty disgruntled when I called him for a chat. They didn't find the campaign interesting or inspiring. They blamed GB as much as anyone and agreed that TB needed to find his own voice more and let rip.

Friday, May 25

The *FT* interview was way overspun by them. They had always wanted to go on the euro and led on the line of TB saying he could win the euro referendum. It was a bit of a problem, in that we didn't really want euro up in lights again, added to which him saying – hardly earth-shattering – that he would have to discuss the [five economic] tests with GB, served this up as GB's big funk of the day. I guess we had to do most of these interviews, but they did always carry this danger, that they take us on to their agenda and off ours. We were helped today in that the Tories were going on schools.

TB was still down in Bristol. He and I, then he and GB, and then our 7am meeting, discussed how to deal with it. GB's demeanour was so defensive that he gave out worried vibes the whole time to people we then expected to help turn things around. He, Ed Balls and I met afterwards, and he kept saying why had TB moved it on, why didn't he just stick to the line of the 1997 statement, five tests etc.? I said if a paper like the *FT* asks perfectly reasonable questions about a subject as important as the euro, you can't just recite a mantra. The question is how do we get the focus on to Europe not the euro, and sufficiently low-key so that it doesn't take over from public services. I felt we would be able to do it provided we showed no worries and no divisions. He said it was a green light to Cook, Byers and Mandelson to ventilate it, push on on Europe. I said I would speak to them and make clear that is not what TB wanted. The other worry was the *Sun* and *The Times*, but I think I persuaded them the *FT* had overspun it. GB got far too wound up about these things.

TB flew up to Scotland and we had the usual last-minute pre-speech nightmares. This was the worst attack of lastminutitis. Bruce, about as technophobic as I am, was up with TB in Scotland. Pat [McFadden] was down with me. We had the telly on in the background with a blank screen and the Sky reporter saying TB would be appearing any second to make the speech. I was at the time talking to TB on one phone while dictating some changes to Bruce who was taking them down in longhand, then to take them to Tom Dibble [intern] to type up, whilst simultaneously Pat was re-editing the press-release version. Tony was losing it with Bruce and Tom and shouting 'Where's the fucking speech?' You have to hand it to him, he came on a couple of minutes later, calm itself, and delivered it perfectly well.[1] But we really had to change the way we did these

---

[1] Blair told the audience in Edinburgh 'True patriotism is standing up for the British national interest first and, in the twenty-first century, that patriotism demands that in a world moving ever closer together, we do not turn our back on Europe . . . in which we do sixty per cent of our trade. Neither can it mean ruling out even the option of joining a single currency, should people vote for it in a referendum.'

speeches. I did the Sundays and tried to get up Tory divisions on Europe. They seemed to think Hague was going to put all his eggs in the basket marked Europe. GB was up in Newcastle and phoned in complaining that someone was briefing the Sundays against the campaign. In fact, the general feeling in the media was that things had picked up.

Saturday, May 26

Philip and Stan both felt we would lose a couple of points on the back of Hague really concentrating on Europe. He was unveiling a countdown clock to the end of the pound today. Milburn was doing our press conference and though we rehearsed all the difficult questions on Europe, none came. Alan was very confident, totally non-defensive, communicated a good mood. TB was doing a Michael Winner [film director and Police Federation supporter] police memorial event and then the NHS rally [in Rochdale]. It was interesting that when he came on for these events being covered live on Sky, the GB people tended not to watch, whereas anything to do with GB was an 'everything stops' situation. I dared to suggest to Bob Shrum and Ed Miliband that the press conference went better because GB hadn't been there, and therefore it wasn't as defensive as usual. Ed in particular seemed shocked, but it wasn't simply a criticism of GB, more an observation that we hadn't been imaginative enough about developing a horses-for-courses strategy.

Finally, after days of discussion and dithering, we had the Trojan Horse I had been asking for, a device to keep the attack on the Tories' public service cuts going. I'm not sure it was worth ten grand, but it was an impressive piece of work [custom-made by carpenters]. We also had some good people on the new-technology side, who were getting some good games going via the website. DB called to say he hoped a story in the *Sun* was right and that Estelle would be Education Secretary because if not, it would be a very cruel blow. TB called about 8 after *Newsnight* flashed up the *Sunday Times* splash 'Blair snubs Brown on euro'. I had tried to get Michael Prescott [political editor] to dump the story but clearly failed. GB needless to say believed it came from Peter M, which it may well have done. GB was on at him, saying when was it going to stop, why had we not dealt with him? TB listened for a while and eventually said 'Do I rage at you every time one of your media cronies says something about me? No. I had nothing to do with this story, so let's just stop talking about it.'

May '01: Sun tips Estelle Morris for education

The Oldham race riots were obviously the big overnight story.[1] Simon Hughes [Liberal Democrat home affairs spokesman] was up attacking the Tories over it, but we had a discussion and decided best to stay out of it, or at least make it as unpolitical as possible. TB agreed there was little to be gained from him going up on it. He was still banging on about the dynamic of the campaign not being right. He was pretty much losing faith with GB, felt he was currently over-influenced by Balls, and also perhaps worrying about stepping up to the leadership role. He had become much more open in his assessment of GB's shortcomings. I went for a run, then we did a conference call on the next few days which needed to encapsulate our key issues, economy, preferably through mortgages and living standards, investment in public services, schools and hospitals first. We were just going to have to make a virtue of banging the same drum again and again. TB wanted a bigger argument, but this was surely the time to get more simple, not more complicated. It was also the week in which the focus on the leaders would intensify further, which again was to our advantage.

GB suddenly claimed he had never seen the wig poster [Hague with Margaret Thatcher's hair], which I found hard to believe given how long it had been around. It had certainly been through his key people, but now he got on to TB and said he was against using it, because it would be seen as a personal attack. It was classic too-late-ism. He would know that the sites were already booked, so we had to assume it meant he was setting himself up to distance himself from it if it went wrong. His basic problem in this campaign was that he focused too much on problems rather than opportunities, didn't want to take risks, didn't want to get involved in anything too difficult or to do with TB.

We had a meeting on the last five days, which was OK, but again not much more than that. GB was really grumpy today. I wanted to dump the business manifesto launch being done as a press event, instead do a proper press conference on living standards with the business launch as an event outside, with endorsers. We had twenty or so ministers and MPs lined up to take calls after the PEB, which turned into a total disaster at the start because BT totally fucked up and so the calls weren't coming through. But we had the cameras in

[1] The short but violent rioting, following interracial tension in the Lancashire town, was the worst in the UK for fifteen years. Similar riots in Bradford, Leeds and Burnley were to follow.

there and at one point we had to get staff to call the ministers on internal phones so that at one point Phil Bassett was quizzing Robin Cook about Europe. We just about got away with it, and it gave us the best laugh of the day, but it was quite a contrast to when we first did one of these in 1997.

Monday, May 28

Europe was still far too dominant and with the Tories going on it again, there was a case for GB not doing the press conference but of course the moment I suggested that, they sensed another motive, that I was somehow moving against him. They took it amiss, but the truth was the lottery story we had planned for the day was not really going to dominate so we were yet again going to be driven by the Tory/ media agenda. It may be that with [Lionel] Jospin's speech [supporting a vision of the European Union as a federation of nation states], and the Tories going on the cost of changeover to the euro, it was inevitable. But if GB was up there, it becomes certain. TB called on his way to the airport and said the most important thing today was his Trimdon [Labour Club] speech in the afternoon, that we really have to lift it up on the Europe front.

GB was smouldering as he came into the morning meeting. I was arguing to be dismissive on Europe, paint the Tories as obsessives, which is what the Libs were doing. At one point, GB thumped the table and said this whole thing was a self-inflicted wound. Derry at one point said to me 'Why is he so angry? He's absolutely smouldering.' Even if it was the case that TB had got a few words out of place in the *FT*, so what? It was four days ago. And even if it was the case that he had done it deliberately, which I doubted, was it really worth this kind of mood? We had to move on.

These full days inside Millbank were now long and pretty tough, meeting after meeting, the mood not quite right, but nobody had the real fear of defeat. I had a brainstorm with David Hill, Philip and some of the press people on storylines for the last five days, which sparked silly recriminations when Douglas complained to GB he was being excluded. Ridiculous. He had not been there when I had the idea of the meeting, simple as that. I also told GB it was good to involve the press office more because they had good ideas. 'Like what?' I said it was always good to find out. It was hard work and I agreed with TB that GB had been worse since Ed Balls was more on the scene. TB was out on the road, interviews went fine, speech OK later. I did a briefing on the polling, focusing on the economy and leadership. GB was arguing against getting up leadership, which was ludicrous. Also Ed Balls was suggesting we pitch the wig poster as being about Thatcherism rather than about leadership. Just as ridiculous.

Europe was coming through more as an issue on the phone banks. I spoke to Clare Short who had agreed to do a speech on leadership. I thought we would get more out of it if someone not normally seen as a Blairite loyalist was to do it. David H was worried about it. Anji told me that my name was currently mud with GB's lot. I ran home and we went to Tessa's for dinner. Margaret McD called to say the blame game was already starting on the posters. I was still confident the wig poster would work.

Tuesday, May 29

Philip was worried about the euro, said it was coming up through the groups much more than before. Ed Balls had suggested to me yesterday that TB do an article for the *Sun*, which I sent over today with a few additions from Jospin and [Romano] Prodi's speech on EU integration [political, legal and economic integration of states wholly or partly in Europe]. Philip felt TB had to take the line over, but GB was so defensive he didn't even want to say there would be a referendum, but that is what the public wanted to hear. I drafted a line that there would be no referendum until the tests were met and there could be no single currency without a referendum. The morning meeting was a long ramble round the block, going over pretty much everything, apart from the fact that TB had a big speech on crime tomorrow. David Hill made the point that the press would only generate coverage about us on the Tories when we made big attacks and accusations and yet GB didn't even want to say that they would scrap the minimum wage, have a lower inflation target, stop the child benefit rises. TB came in, sat there pretty impassive. Fuming a bit.

Afterwards, he, Philip and I were talking and GB quietly walked out. I got him to come round to TB's office. TB said we couldn't not talk about a referendum, we just had to emphasise the tests. The body language between them was worse than ever. TB could barely disguise the fact he was fed up with it. GB was more defensive and everyone noticed it. A combination of TB's irritation and GB's smouldering made for a pretty tense pre-meeting before the press conference. Chilly. We didn't really even go through the tricky questions. TB dealt fine with questions on Jospin and Prodi, GB OK on the economy.

I worked on Clare Short's speech, and wrote a briefing on the wig poster. I had a better chat with Douglas after the nonsense over my meeting with the press office. Philip told me that Douglas felt unable to talk to me properly because he thought I was too big a figure in the campaign. I said I didn't think anybody had reason to find it difficult to talk to me, and be honest. Once TB was out on the road, I had several sessions with GB. I did the briefing on the wig poster. They neither loved it nor hated it, but they knew it was a moment, and with Thatcher out on the campaign trail again and Major doing a big attack, it was a good day to do it. I did the briefing with Douglas, but there was no real heat coming back. They got the argument.

Major's speech was absolutely pathetic. I put out a line to one or two of them that it was the revenge of the underpants.[1] Philip said we just weren't hitting the Tories hard enough, that the theme of risk wasn't out there enough. He said the groups were pretty dodgy on Europe. I went back to Millbank afterwards, to a new problem. JP and GB were doing an event tomorrow on regional government for England. TB had given JP the go-ahead on the White Paper, but this was going to cut across what we had already planned on mortgages and crime. As DH said, we needed more TB in the campaign, not less.

Wednesday, May 30

We got exactly the right pitch on the poster, several front pages but without it being a real firestorm. The *Sun* said it was brilliant and my idea, which it wasn't. It was Trevor Beattie's, or at least the agency's. But media-wise it was a good hit. The Tim Franks [political correspondent] two-way on the *Today* programme was largely about me and John Major's underpants. Get over it. We were leading the news on mortgages plus TB's article in the *Sun*. So everything was pretty well set with a week to go, added to which we had TB's crime speech set to go big later in the day. Ed Balls was baulking, saying it cut across the message of the morning. I said we needed two big hits a day now. JP and GB were doing a mortgage street visit in Yorkshire. There was definitely space for a crime speech. I reviewed the PEBs. The groups, particularly working-class women, had liked the TB one. We had a choice though, and went for the unsung heroes for the

[1] As a journalist, Campbell had claimed that the then Conservative prime minister, John Major, habitually tucked his shirt into his underpants. The claim, seized on by cartoonists and others, served to weaken Major's authority as he was portrayed on an almost daily basis wearing his underpants outside his trousers. Campbell would later concede it was 'not a great piece of journalism'.

pledges PEB, TB rerecording the voiceover after another press conference at which his body language with GB was poor. But on the substance, they, Margaret B and Byers were all pretty good. As David Hill and I watched it, he said you had the feeling that we were motoring, and the media were waking up to the idea that it was all over. The feeling was beginning to develop of a potential Tory meltdown, with people coming out critical of their strategy banging on so much about the euro.

Hague had done an interview in *The Times* retreating on the idea this was the last chance to save the pound and they felt pretty close to meltdown. GB was still very dour though. Philip said some of his people seriously thought I was doing him in. I set off for Euston with TB, we finished the speech on the train, pointing out the tougher sentences for attacks on nurses and teachers, and exclusion orders for parents who were abusive at school. It was a strong speech. I did a briefing at Newport in Shropshire. There were a few [Countryside Alliance] demonstrators around yelling abuse but it all went fine. The speech was strong. TB said afterwards you could always tell when an audience was listening, and this one was. We got a helicopter to Milton Keynes. I did a couple of conference calls to plan tomorrow. We were also planning the rebranding of all our materials. I also felt we needed to see more of Milburn and Blunkett, with TB, to hammer 'schools and hospitals first'.

We had a couple of hours' downtime at the hotel to prepare for *Question Time*. TB was pretty nervous. We were trying to keep his sprits up by exaggerating how ghastly the audience would be, suggesting they had been placing ads in local papers: 'Do you hate Tony Blair?' I really got him going at one point when I said Sharron Storer would be in the front row with six other women complaining about the NHS. In fact, the *Sun* had run a piece about someone who said they intended to confront him on the programme. He did well though, showing once more that he was always better when he forced himself to be nervous in advance. I had a stack of pager messages immediately afterwards from people saying they thought it was his best yet. The message that was really getting through now was investment vs cuts. We flew back to Battersea. I felt we were moving ahead now, at the right time. Now we needed to raise another gear. The woman at *Question Time* had said she thought we could get a bigger majority. TB thought we would be lucky to get more than seventy. I still felt it could be small or huge, but I was moving towards the latter. Today had gone well. Good events. Good speech. Good interviews. Tories in trouble, TB on form.

There was a real sense of the Tories unravelling. The polls were good for us but the story was now apathy and low turnout. Philip was getting more and more exasperated with GB and his people. He said they were totally paranoid about me, felt I was briefing against them, which I wasn't, though I accepted I probably gave out too many vibes internally. We had good feedback on *Question Time*. In to do schools and hospitals poster launch press conference. TB and I both felt we had to acknowledge apathy, before we could enunciate properly a clear 'must vote' strategy. GB was against. TB was on good form at the press conference. We looked strong whereas the Tory press conference was really poor. The Tories were going on taxation and child benefit which put GB in a lather. He just could not see that he wasn't the centre of attention. His mood seemed to dive a bit more every time TB did better or got more energetic. TB also echoed Philip's view that GB was paranoid about me at the moment. David H and I were both at a loss to understand why he wouldn't do more Tory-attack stuff, or encourage others to do it properly.

I went to Victoria to meet Mark B and drove to Croydon. TB was back fretting about the dynamic of the campaign, also worried about the Brighton open-top bus, partly because he thought it looked triumphalist but more probably because his hair would get blown all over the place. At Croydon I did a good strong briefing on the PEBs then went to the gym. TB spoke to Clinton later who said the key now was to show real hunger, really look like you want it, make it clear that it matters even more now than it did the first time round. He felt that no matter how much the media thought the game was over, we had to fight like our lives depended on it. Richard Wilson [actor and Labour supporter] was at the rally in Croydon. Milburn didn't quite do it. The nurses were good. TB OK. I felt we were now doing OK, in third gear, but we still had to lift it, and in particular try to win over more of the apathetic and disengaged DEs.[1] GB did a meeting at the *Guardian*, which I only found out about by chance although he seemingly was really hitting some of the Old Labour buttons, starting to try to shape the post-campaign narrative about who did well and who did badly.

[1] People in demographic grades D, semi- and unskilled manual workers, and E, casual or lowest grade workers, and others who depend on the welfare state for income.

The focus was clearly shifting out to the road and to be fair to GB, he admitted we should now be trying to shift the focus away from Millbank. TB called just after 6am, worried about two things: the negative reaction to the schools and hospitals agenda by people like David Hart [general secretary, National Association of Head Teachers] and the BMA [British Medical Association], said we needed to get up more people in the services who were supportive; second, all the talk on landslides. It was now part of the Tory strategy to talk up a landslide, signal the contest was over so that our vote stayed at home and theirs came out. TB was convinced we had to move up a gear, admit there was a problem with apathy and be seen to address it. GB wasn't so sure.

I felt TB should be directly addressing the issue of apathy with big statements about democracy, values, and also use it as a way of communicating delivery. We should go back to the theme of the 'Thank you' campaign. We also needed to start making attacks on the Tories that really hurt, but whenever I said that, GB thought I wanted to go over the top. Both of them were anxious again. God knows what they would be like if we suddenly went into a slide. The press conference was flat, OK but flat. TB and I went out to Battersea, met CB, off to Stansted, plane up to Liverpool. He did the *News of the World* on the plane. Usual mix – policy hobby horses, Leo, and a little joke at the end about the Mile High Club.[1] It took up pretty much the whole journey, annoying Andy Marr who had wanted to do an interview. We had a whole series of interviews and articles planned for the Sundays. GPs' ballot [on renegotiation of contracts] was a big story. Hague went up on it so we got TB to revise the stump speech at the Wirral. He was beginning to get his voice. This was his best yet. I had another row with Marr who wanted a clip on the BMA. I said take it from the speech, because all that happens when we do clips is they go into over-mediated packages the whole time. I called [Richard] Sambrook [BBC] and said I felt the media were not really explaining campaigning issues at all, just reporting process.

We did a visit at Everton FC, had a nice chat with Walter Smith [Everton manager], who said I ought to hire a PR man to get a better press for myself. Alex F and he had agreed to joint articles for us. We got to the hotel for a meeting with [Swedish Prime Minister] Göran

---

[1] *News of the World* journalist Andy Coulson asked the Blairs if they were members of the 'club'. He would later become director of communications to Conservative prime minister David Cameron.

Persson. I did a call with GB who agreed we should start doing press conferences outside London, starting with DB and TB in Salford tomorrow. TB and Persson did a little doorstep in which he dished the Tory policy on the Nice Treaty. There was a real scouse wedding going on and TB popped in, got a great welcome. He had a Q&A on the ['Bev's Bar'] set of *Brookside* [long-running Liverpool-based soap opera] which was a bit surreal but he did well. I did the Sunday lobby on the squawk box from somebody's fictional bedroom, usual crap. We set off for Manchester, got to the [Lowry] hotel, long run, dinner with Bruce, Mark and the girls to plan tomorrow's press conference. I got to bed early, which felt a bit weird. S Club 7 [pop group] were at the hotel and I was under instruction from Grace to get autographs.

Saturday, June 2

Between them Millbank and the North-West region had put together a good press conference at Salford Community Centre with two excellent local heads. I worked on TB words then had breakfast with him. He was in twittering mood again. I called David Frost to take him through the £20 billion cuts arguments pre his interview with Hague. TB spoke to him, said he felt the Tories were close to losing it. Blunkett came over. More discussion on apathy. The head teachers were excellent at the press conference. The questions to TB were instructive – lots on landslide, and what did he think of the Tories' strategy. We were going to have to work hard not to let this run ahead of itself. After Shipley, then Leeds, two good working-class venues. We had to do a lot more of these, really connect with the heartland base, working-class estates. I was struck by how well Hilary Benn [Labour MP for Leeds Central] seemed to go down with people. TB got a good reception and again was finding his voice. Cherie was on form, doing really well with the kids. I did an article for Alex for the *Sunday Mail*, then TB on his mum [Hazel, who had died of cancer in 1975] for the *News of the World*, drugs for the *Sunday Mirror*. The papers were pretty much falling into place.

The conference call was all about PR, tactical voting which had suddenly taken off for obvious reasons. GB really wanted us to kill it but TB said he didn't want a full frontal attack on the Libs. I kipped on the plane back and got home. Good day, really straightforward, real sense of things moving our way now. I went for a walk on the Heath with Rory, who had a pretty astute view about politics and the election. He reckoned we would win big again but the Libs would do better than we thought. The papers arrived. Only the *Mail* and the *Telegraph* were backing the Tories. The *Observer* was good. The red tops were OK though there was a lot of sniffiness around. It was going to be hard to drive up the vote.

Sunday, June 3

I had a bit of a cold and was worried I was losing my voice. Philip felt we still had a problem with working-class women, and in some areas tuition fees was really hurting us. The more they saw of TB, the better. He had to go flat out now. The Tories had briefed their latest poster, 'Time to burst Blair's bubble'. It was the latest evidence they were effectively admitting defeat, suggesting the best they could do was bring him down to size. I felt TB was over-complicating things by calling it a back-door strategy. We should simply be saying they don't want people to vote and we have positive reasons to vote for us and against them. GB's morning meeting went quickly over the next few days, and how we deal with apathy and all the landslide talk. They had obviously been talking to each other all weekend, working themselves into little frenzies, and today's buzzword was complacency.

Back for a meeting on the last four days. I wanted TB out and about in as many council estates, shopping centres etc. as we could. I wondered if we shouldn't just keep peeling off by helicopter. We had to find ways of showing we were going flat out for every vote. Fiona and I went to Number 10 for lunch. TB was out in the garden working on his boxes and had fallen asleep. I left him and worked on his speech for the youth event at Watford this evening. After lunch, I had a kip myself before the four of us left in the people carrier for Hemel Hempstead Hospital, good visit, though Anji had to see off a potential Sharron Storer. I briefed the press on the youth vote. TB did a teleconference for candidates. June Sarpong [television presenter] was the MC for the evening, did a great job. TB got really pumped up and passionate, if a bit long in his opening remarks. PG called to say GB et al. were planning to make tomorrow's press conference a big attack on Thatcherism, which TB wouldn't want and I didn't think we needed. There was no real story out of the evening but there was a sense of momentum with us. Andrew Lansley [Conservative Party vice chairman] said on Radio 5 that I had an obsessive desire to destroy the Conservative Party.

Monday, June 4

Landslide/apathy still our main problem, and how do we connect in the way that reaches the disconnected? There was a bit of an eerie feeling out there today, so few posters, no sense at all that the whole country was talking or thinking about the election. I drove in with Philip who felt we needed to motor on Thatcherism, but I felt we needed to be focused on a personal offer to voters. I watched the latest PEB, which was terrific. GB wanted to make today an appeal to One Nation Tories to come over, which was fine, but I still felt we had a problem with some of our own core, and that was best addressed as much by activity on core messages as by a political pitch. TB arrived a bit late and we set off in the bus for Harlow. Rory Bremner was there drawing as much attention to himself as possible. TB did another press conference with head teachers. The questions had all moved on to post-election, size of majority, and TB was passionate in saying the British people are the boss and it's the British people who will decide it. I had to deal with the ridiculous Will Self [author and columnist] complaining he had not been allowed on the bus, so I got him on the bus and did an interview telling him to stop whingeing.

We had a long drive round to Gillingham, picked up CB on the way, who was with Mark B at a Little Chef. TB's little stump speeches were getting good, today focusing on why it mattered to vote. Then to Enfield Southgate, Dermot O'Leary [television presenter] chairing a pretty tough Q&A, then back to Number 10. I went for a run before going with TB to do *Newsnight*. This was a really weird one because both I and Euan [Blair], who came along for the ride to watch it being pre-recorded, thought TB was poor and that [Jeremy] Paxman slaughtered him. I said to TB afterwards I thought it was the worst interview he had done, and he looked surprised. But when I watched it on TV, as opposed to hearing it in the room, it was absolutely fine, quite strong. That was the general view too. Weird. I always got the feeling Paxman quite liked him. Then we were off on the road again doing a joint TB/GB event. GB was pretty grumpy but we had a bit of a laugh when I asked him not to shine too much tonight because Tony had been so bad on *Newsnight*. In the end they both did fine.

Tuesday, June 5

In early for what would be the last morning meeting of the campaign. GB seemed to me to be worrying more now about how people were seen at the end of the campaign than on getting the foot on the accelerator to win it. Later he visited the *Sun*, and did an interview with *The Times*. Alan Milburn said to me there ought to be an inquest into the campaign. We had been saved because the Tories and Hague were so useless, because TB had been OK on the road, and because we just about gripped the centre. But we were kidding ourselves if we thought it was a good campaign. He was right. We had done a lot of planning, and where we had planned, e.g. advertising, visits, speeches, we had done better. But storyline development not great. Purpose and unity poor, and at times it really had felt like pushing stones up hills. GB had played more to his weaknesses than his strengths.

According to Philip, TB was definitely breaking through at the right time. I went to see him in the flat, agreed his press conference words which were about the NHS but also trailing his 'end of Thatcherism' speech. The *Today* programme were doing more stuff on Vaz and I felt we should go for them over it, but he thought not. In the car, he kept asking if people were going to come out and vote. The papers were coming out for us one by one, other than the obvious ones, but without much enthusiasm. We drove to St Pancras, reworked the speech on the train, press conference went fine, not that many up from London, but so what, the feeling of momentum was there and Hague was in trouble.

On to Rugby, bit of a scene with a few UKIP headbangers, Burton, another little speech, then [Birmingham] Yardley the main speech of the day on the end of Thatcherism. It was strong. We had a little incident with the photographers, who went 'on strike' because we couldn't fit them on the helicopters tomorrow. They looked a pathetic bunch, downing tools, standing around with their cameras at their feet. I left Anji to sort them out. TB was doing stacks of interviews, local and national, being pushed hard, but in his stride. I talked to Godric and Julian about Friday, which we would do much lower key than '97.

We had a bit of downtime in the hotel. He was starting to think about the reshuffle. He said he knew he couldn't sack GB but it had really worried him this campaign to see just how driven by fear and loathing he was. He shook his head and said he couldn't really believe that it had got as bad as it had. Philip called to say that our message that it was the people not the pollsters and the media who decided this election was beginning to get through and hurt the Tories so we had to keep going with it. Off to Derby and a rally with Margaret B, Heather Small [singer] providing a bit of music and glamour, though she had to sing 'Proud' twice because of a problem with the sound system. She struck me as really quiet and shy when I first met her but when the sound failed, she had quite a temper on her. TB did a good speech, nice atmosphere, then an interview with Bill Neely [ITN] on the bus. TB was now saying he didn't want to be killed charging round the country all day tomorrow. I called [Sir] Victor Blank [chairman of Trinity Mirror] to say I really thought the *Mirror* coverage had been a joke, just not serious. At least the *Sun* tried to be serious in some of its coverage, then we were pissed off that they splashed on a story about one of the *Hollyoaks* stars [Terri Dwyer] we used in the PEB not voting. Just one full day to go. We were all getting tired, but just one day and it was over. Staying in a not nice hotel, overlooking a not nice nightclub.

Wednesday, June 6

Last day, packed. I was up early to go in and meet him and prepare for *GMTV*. He was a bit subdued and down, as was I. There had been racial troubles in Leeds overnight which we thought would take over the news but didn't really. He did well on *GMTV*, pushing the basic message, vote for schools and hospitals. Through the day we worked up the line that not voting was dishonouring the dead. He did fine on *Election Call*. The *Mirror* led on [TB's] Calvin Klein underpants plus a piece on page 5 about my campaign diet for fuck's sake. We came out of BBC Nottingham, and it was interesting the reaction on the building site nearby, very warm and positive. Then to the press conference with GB and Margaret B. I drafted some strong words with PH and the overall effect was pretty good. GB was resisting Margaret chairing the press conference, which was irritating. TB was on great form. It was clear, talking to some of the hacks, that GB was already setting up the briefings about his own role. I couldn't be bothered with it really, and was losing the appetite for a briefing war, and maybe it didn't matter. But I decided to write, and circulate, a long note suggesting we emphasise the team effort, TB's leadership, GB's strategy, JP's motivational work, professionalism at Millbank etc.

We were flown down to Wales, TB and I passing notes backwards and forwards on possible words for the final message stuff. We got to Colwyn Bay where he did a good little stump speech. We visited a school and were there for what seemed like an age because the helicopter had gone off to refuel. TB was shown round the school and it became almost comic, an eve of poll visit which went on so long that the entirety of the media had left. But they were at least saying there was a sense of urgency, no complacency, a mood of quiet determination. Up to Dumfries, raining a bit. The feel was pretty good, Labour posters everywhere, though there were a couple of women outside with placards which said 'Blair, you are a cunt', and 'Blair, wanker'. He could now do these stump speeches on autopilot. He asked Russell Brown [Labour MP for Dumfries] if he could win. No doubt, he said, and looked like he meant it. There was an ICM poll narrowing at the right time, helping us with the no-complacency message.

Then down to Castleford [West Yorkshire], on the way writing a letter to Piers Morgan about his pathetic coverage, and to Charles Moore [*Telegraph* editor] thanking him for the honour of calling me the most pointlessly combative person in human history. The clips being used on the news were all the right ones. There was an astonishing moment of TB selfishness as we arrived in the rain, Jess Tyrell [events team] standing there holding a brolly which TB just took out of her hands and walked on, leaving her to get wet. TB went live into the *Six O'Clock News*, which was OK but probably not worth doing because I much prefer coverage of him out with people rather than talking to yet another interviewer. Then back on the bus and off to Sedgefield, a real sense of last-lap time.

TB, CB and I discussed Gordon. Cherie had pretty much always been of the view, then I came to it, that a large part of GB was basically working against him. TB said that sadly, very sadly, he had reached that conclusion too, but it wasn't possible to sack him or to move him, and in the event it wouldn't be the right thing because for all his flaws, he does have real talent, it's just that we saw the wrong side of him in this campaign. But that's us, he said. Neither the party nor the public would remotely understand if they thought I wanted to get rid of him. They would think it was just a leader trying to dispose of a rival. It would be wrong. He didn't believe GB would strike necessarily, though he might try over Europe, but he felt the party would see through it pretty quickly. There was definitely a big flaw there, and it would become a big problem. We got to Trimdon [Labour Club] about 8 and after watching the match [England 2, Greece 0] TB did a speech at half-time, which was pretty good and got to the top of the later bulletins. Philip called, said we definitely broke through today, but turnout was still the big problem. We stayed in the bar for a bit. TB wanted to go home. I had a few notes to do and scribbled away listening to Radio 1. Philip believed the worst-case scenario was a majority of seventy-five, best was 200, but it was all about turnout. TB and I both felt tired, and a bit depressed. I had the same feeling I had in 1997 after the results came through, so I was hoping that this time I was getting the depression out of the way early and would actually enjoy it tomorrow.

Thursday, June 7

I didn't sleep well, woke up feeling really tired and thinking how crazy it was that we helter-skelter round the country for weeks, work round the clock, then have one day – the election – to start getting your mind in shape for what follows if and when we win. The papers weren't bad, though the *Sun* was still slightly playing it both ways, and the *Mirror* was hopeless. I went for a run, found a nice hilly area, and loved the feeling of being out on my own, with the wind gusting every now and then, and feeling I had done all I could and though it had not been perfect, we were definitely going to win. Myrobella was the usual mild chaos as TB, CB got ready to go over and vote. It wasn't as exciting as 1997, but there was still that special feeling you get knowing that it is now all down to millions of different people in all sorts of weird and wonderful places making up their own minds for their own reasons. Jonathan had come up and he, Bruce, Sally and I were chatting away. It was clear Richard Wilson was up to a few tricks – e.g. wanting to reverse the Order in Council that allowed Jonathan and me to instruct civil servants. Jonathan and I were now down as 'advisers' on his list. We would have to sort that.

TB came back at 1 after a tour of some of the polling stations and we got going on the Cabinet. JP arrived by helicopter, which TB thought a bit OTT, and they had a session to go over some of the changes, though JP was still pressing re his own responsibilities. TB told me earlier we would all see a difference in his modus operandi second term, that he would be more confident because a second mandate is in some ways more powerful than the first, plus he had learned, and had experience of how to work the system. He said he alone would decide the Cabinet and unless there were genuine reasons for any objections from JP and GB, he would press ahead.

Things were slightly complicated by the message that Estelle Morris may lose her seat [Birmingham Yardley]. Robin C would not be pleased to be moved, but TB felt there had to be some change in the top jobs. He was keen on Blunkett for the Home Office, was worried about whether Estelle had the depth and the toughness but thought it worth giving her a go at Education, Byers taking on Transport and the Regions, Pat Hewitt Trade and Industry, Tessa to Culture, Media and Sport, Charles Clarke as party chairman, another one who may not like it. He said he wanted to put the right people in the right jobs, regardless of all the usual personality stuff. That being said, he was keen for me to get the briefing re JP in the right place for JP.

He spoke to GB and afterwards said it was classic – not only did he want Alistair Darling to DTI, and Andrew Smith to Work and Pensions, but he felt Douglas [Alexander] should go straight into Cabinet at Scotland. Bruce said it would be the worst thing that ever happened to him. He would be eaten alive. But it showed once more that GB was looking down a very narrow telescope. GB was also pushing for Michael Wills to be minister for employment. Bruce in hysterics. Bruce was also warning loudly that Nick Brown would be a real problem on the back benches.

The day was peppered with calls giving us information on how things were going, a lot of it anecdotal, but the general picture seemed to be good result but turnout low. The Libs seemed to be doing better than we thought, which sparked a bit more fretting about Estelle. Losing her would be a blow. I was pressing for Dick Caborn [Minister of State, Department of Transport, Local Government and the Regions] for sport. TB was keen on promoting Pat H, felt she had the brain but was worried about how good she was in the House. Bruce, though not necessarily her biggest fan, thought she'd be fine. The sackings as ever would be the hardest thing, particularly if he put Derry straight out. He was also thinking about moving out Andrew Smith, to create more space, but the Derry situation was the one clearly worrying him. We were sitting in the front room/office and TB was in a low, small armchair, wearing a rugby shirt, tracksuit bottoms and a pair of ridiculous-looking slippers with a badge of Australia on them.

After he got his list more or less settled, we went for a little stroll round the garden, which felt a bit like a prison exercise, just walking round in circles and chatting. He kept emphasising it was all going to be different second term, that he was older, wiser, more experienced, would deal with the crap better, would be more focused on the things that he needed to focus on. He went off for a kip. The word was that the BBC exit poll was narrowing. Philip was calling the whole time to witter and blather. This was the eerie period – nothing to do but wait, lots of people calling assuming you knew things that they didn't, but the reality is we knew no more than anyone, we just had instinct, rumour and anecdote to go on. The Estelle rumour was fuelling a lot of calls.

I had a long chat with Bruce, who is such a lovely bloke and always so supportive of me, telling me TB could not have done it without me, and I had to stay with him to the end. Around 8, TB wanted another run through the Cabinet. Re JP, we were talking about a new Deputy Prime Minister's Office from where he oversaw the Cabinet Office. TB was OK on him having more Cabinet committees, but not QFL [Cabinet committee on future legislation], or civil contingencies. But this had to be seen as a Heseltine [former Conservative Deputy Prime Minister] role, not Mo. He would be TB's rep on Kyoto [climate change protocol], chair the committee on the regions and so on. At one point, as the jigsaw pieces slid around, even RC was talked of as a possible leaver, though he accepted that was over-brutal. I wondered whether he might walk anyway if he felt Leader of the House was being over-demoted, but TB, Sal and Bruce all thought he would stay. Re Derry, TB felt he should stay for another year or so. Margaret B was set for the new Rural Affairs job, with the Environment.[1] He was troubled by Bruce saying people worried about Pat H in the House.

I tried to raise the issue of Number 10 operations but he wasn't really wanting to know. Then afterwards he said let's go outside for a minute, and asked me to run through all the things I thought should be changed, in my and others' roles. I had done a note setting out how I thought I could use my time to be more strategic, but it meant other people picking up the slack in different places. Then he said he intended to have one more go at persuading Anji to stay. I said I agreed with him that she had showed her worth on the campaign again, but did he really want another explosion from CB, Sally and Fiona? I said I'm not sure if I have the will to start back after what everyone is saying is a historic win by being plunged into a new wave of *Peyton Place* [soap opera]. I had a word with him about Richard W, said I felt he was up to a few tricks and we had to watch it.

Come ten o'clock, and both BBC and ITN were predicting another landslide. For a few minutes, there was a genuinely happy atmosphere in there. Cherie and the kids, Leo and Olwen [TB's father and step-mother], Bill and Katy [TB's brother and sister-in-law], Cherie's sister [Lyndsey Booth], Carole [Caplin], they were all laughing and having a good time, and for a while I felt pretty up about things. But before long we were back into the office and between us we were talking things down and starting to worry about other things. There was something odd about this inability just to enjoy the moment of winning, him because he was straight off focusing on the next thing that could go wrong, me because of some general dourness defect that kicked in when everyone else was enjoying themselves. Weird. Then the media were straight on to the story being the low turnout and we had to get over the line that we suffered because of the sense of it being a foregone conclusion the whole way through. We were due to leave for the count around 12 and we agreed TB should maybe have a written text for one of his speeches tonight so that we had a core script on a lot of the obvious points coming our way – apathy, turnout chief among them. I did an interview with [Jon] Sopel [BBC] pre the count, to get up a few pro-TB messages, and also to say I would not be doing nearly as many briefings.

[1] Secretary of State at the Department for Environment, Food and Rural Affairs [DEFRA], replacing the Ministry of Agriculture, Fisheries and Food.

We watched the results coming in in the same room as in 1997. Peter M's acceptance speech – 'I'm a fighter not a quitter' – was a bit gut-wrenching.[1] Bloody hell, TB said, what's he up to here? Estelle won, which gave everyone a lift. Newbury was held by the Libs after another strong rumour to the contrary. By and large it was all going to plan. TB's speech after the Sedgefield result was fine, maybe a bit too long, then we piled into the cars and set off for Trimdon, where he did a more emotional version of the same speech. The crowd was terrific, and he was up for it now, and people finally felt a bit of emotional release.

TB was in some ways now a lot more emotional than '97, felt this was more his mandate in a way. We got back to Myrobella and he and Cherie had a glass of champagne. He was totally wired now, really buzzing and up and full of what we had to do tomorrow. Cherie was very nice to me, said thanks for everything, and TB said 'It is an amazing thing we have done. In a relatively short period of time, we have totally taken the centre ground.' I said we seemed to have destroyed the Tories in the process. They looked absolutely shell-shocked tonight. TB and I went through to the dining room, and he said once more that he wanted to do all he could to keep the old team together. He was going to have another go at Anji, and he wanted me to persuade Fiona that I should stay and so should she.

We set off for the airport but were hanging around for ages before taking off. The mood was pretty good, though obviously lacked the excitement of four years ago. It was incredible really, that we looked to be on course for a majority as big as the first one, and it was almost taken for granted.

On the plane down, he and I went down the plane for a bit of a chat with some of the hacks. They seemed happy enough to be with the winning side. I was feeling a bit flat again, and the feeling only lifted when we arrived at Millbank, and I caught sight of Rory and Georgia [Gould, daughter of Philip Gould and Gail Rebuck] on the ropeline as we jumped out of the cars. 'Lifted' [song by the Lighthouse Family, the campaign theme] was playing, it was daylight now, and I was really pleased he had waited there. He was with Neil [Kinnock], who gave him a big hug and when I got over there, both Rory and Georgia said well done, and for the first time I felt really moved, and enjoyed the last hour or so.

[1] In a highly emotional speech at the Hartlepool count, Mandelson said 'Before this campaign started it was said I was facing political oblivion – my career in tatters never to be part of the political living again. Well, they underestimated me because I am a fighter . . . and a fighter not a quitter.'

TB did the same little speech as up north, thanks, now the future etc., and then it was just people milling around and chatting and swapping stories. I started to worry about not having any sleep and having to be back in Number 10 by the morning. I collected Rory, shared a car with Philip and Georgia and got home for a couple of hours' sleep. In some ways, I had enjoyed the night more than in 1997, but I still didn't feel the kind of exhilaration others seemed to. It was also because I knew there would be no let-up, and in all sorts of ways the future was unclear. Maybe it was just my nature.

Friday, June 8

There were hundreds of media in the street shouting at me as I walked in. The Number 10 staff seemed genuinely pleased to see us back. I had a quick walk round the press office to say hello to everyone, then up to the flat to see TB and work out what we needed to do for the day. The start of the election felt a long time ago, it was also odd how quickly it was back to an almost 'business as usual' feel. He was due to leave at 10.50. Again he and I were working on finding the right words. Jeremy said that Richard W was bracing himself for a real drive for change, and I don't think he meant the changes in the Civil Service that TB had been talking about, but trying to retrench, push back on some of the changes we had made. Jonathan was pretty sure Richard wanted to clip our and my wings in particular. TB went off to see the Queen, which I followed on TV while talking to Godric etc. We waited for him to come back, got the kids out there in the street, and he did his words. The line that the result was a mandate for investment and reform, and an instruction to deliver carried pretty well.

We had one final go on the reshuffle.[1] Robin and Nick Brown were likely to be the stumbling blocks. He then got into it, Jack S happy, David B happy, Margaret B absolutely thrilled. She was wearing a green trouser suit and I said when she arrived 'You've come in the right colour,' which seemed to perplex her. When she came out, she

[1] In the Cabinet reshuffle, Robin Cook became Lord President of the Council and Leader of the House of Commons; Jack Straw, Foreign Secretary; David Blunkett, Home Secretary; Margaret Beckett, Secretary of State for Environment, Food and Rural Affairs; Alistair Darling, Secretary of State for Work and Pensions; Patricia Hewitt, Secretary of State for Trade and Industry and minister for women and equality; Tessa Jowell, Secretary of State for Culture, Media and Sport; Estelle Morris, Secretary of State for Education and Skills; Charles Clarke, Minister without Portfolio and party chairman. Nick Brown was appointed Minister of State for Work.

was positively beaming, which made something of a mockery of the worries we had had that she might see it as demotion from Leader of the House. She popped round after she had seen TB, and said she was stunned, that there was always a part of her that thought TB didn't see her in one of the big jobs, but she saw this as a huge job and was thrilled.

Robin's reaction, unsurprisingly, was different. There was no way of pretending it wasn't a demotion to Leader of the House, and I think he had been shocked when TB put it to him. He came round, sat down at the table in my office and said he really thought he deserved better given the support he had given TB in difficult times. He feared he would come out of this badly in the media and he needed a little time to think whether it might not be better going to the back benches. I said I wasn't going to pretend it would be hard for him not to take something of a hit, but we would be stressing two things in any briefing – his reputation as a great House of Commons man, and also the benefit to the government as a whole that he would be back at the centre of domestic politics, close to the heart of everything. He was very subdued, said he and I had always got on and he was confident if he did this job, I would do what I could for a soft landing, but he really did need time to think it through. He went back to the Foreign Office, doubtless phoned a few friends, spoke to Gaynor [his wife] and after a while said he would do it.

After all the to-ing and fro-ing, Nick Brown was finally minister for work below Alistair [Darling] as Secretary of State, but able to attend Cabinet. John Spellar, who had really impressed TB at the Cobra meetings on FMD, was to be minister for transport, not attending Cabinet. All odd. By 8, we pretty much had the whole thing done and Godric was able to brief at 8.30. The main media focus was Jack, Robin and the new women. Patricia [Hewitt], Tessa [Jowell] and Estelle [Morris] all popped round for a little chat, all seemingly very happy. Charles Clarke, party chairman, clearly thought he was going to get something different. He didn't seem overwhelmed, but TB felt it was the right appointment.

Meanwhile Fiona had discovered that Anji was staying [in the new role of director of government relations], there was still confusion over who was doing what, she had been to see CB and told her she was leaving. We were straight back into *Peyton* fucking *Place*. Just won a second landslide and I have got Fiona in tears because TB wanted to keep someone working for him who has worked for him for years. TB had clearly indicated that Cherie was happy about it all, when she wasn't. In fact Cherie told me she would grin and bear it because she had little choice. It meant after working round the clock for a few weeks, going the last few days without sleep, I was now straight back on the treadmill and in circumstances where, because I was staying, Fiona and I were barely speaking, and when we did it was to argue. She said that what made me good for him – driven and single-track and obsessive – is what made it difficult for her. I felt between a rock and a hard place, that there were consequences to staying, but there were consequences to leaving too. And I felt for TB, who had just won again and was having to deal with this too.

Saturday, June 9

I didn't read the papers but the reshuffle seemed to have come out fine, my changed role [director of communications and strategy rather than chief press secretary and Prime Minister's official spokesman] was a very small thing in the scheme of things, so all in all not bad. There was a dreadful atmosphere at home. TB called, and both of us were reflecting how bad things were at home considering we had just won a second three-figure majority. Fiona said later it was about not being valued, but for both of them they had a neuralgia about Anji that I didn't quite get. She said TB was driven by the fear of losing me and Anji and it was as though nobody else mattered. She felt we had given them enough and got back a lot of grief and misery, which again in the context of winning a couple of days ago, seemed over the top. Any pleasure in Thursday and Friday had pretty much gone.

Sunday, June 10

Things were now getting totally ridiculous. Cherie sent Tony a fax, and she sent a copy through after speaking to Fiona at 7. Her note to him said her views had been misrepresented, that it wasn't true she was happy about a new role for Anji but she would grin and bear it. Fiona showed it to me and said to CB that it was sad it got to this. I couldn't bear all this *Peyton Place* stuff any more and was losing the appetite for going back at all. TB had effectively told Cherie that he would not allow her to dictate who worked for him. The papers were full of TB/GB, RC demotion, speculation about Keith Vaz being sacked [as minister for Europe]. I went out for a run and quite a few people were saying congratulations. Yet by now I was completely down about things. I went into Number 10 later for a discussion on the second part of the reshuffle. Real jigsaw time. Vaz out. [Kate] Hoey out [as minister for sport]. Should Charlie [Falconer] go to Europe minister? Lots of moving round the Ministers of State. Bruce [Grocott] successfully lobbied for the Africa job as a PUS [parliamentary undersecretary at FCO]. Sally [Morgan] was pushing for Harriet [Harman] as Solicitor General. Douglas [Alexander] in as Minister of State [for e-commerce and competitiveness, DTI]. TB and I had another discussion about Anji, Fiona etc. He said he had to be able to appoint the people he wanted. He said Anji had shown in the last four weeks how capable she was and he did not want to lose her. He had to be allowed to appoint the people he wanted. I supported that, but said equally he had to understand the need to be open with people, and honest with them, and deal with concerns they had too.

Monday, June 11

Peyton Place day with knobs on. I woke up after next to no sleep, really anxious about things. Fiona really upset, said she wasn't even going in. All very grim. Anji called me on the way in and said if her staying was causing all this chaos, she didn't want to stay. TB had told her that Cherie was happy with her staying on. Fiona meanwhile felt that TB had effectively taken a large part of the job she had agreed from her. Anji said she wanted me to go and see TB and tell him she was not going to stay if that's what it took to please CB. TB went into 'shoot the messenger' mode, clearly thought I had talked her into it when I hadn't. He asked what I had said. I had said there was confusion about who exactly was doing what, and who thought what about it. TB had led people to believe everyone else was reasonably happy, when the slightest discussion around the place revealed that not to be so. I said to him we had to sort it out and he had to understand I was in a difficult position.

He was going completely over the top now, said if he can't have the people he thinks he needs to do the job, then he won't do it. I said don't be ridiculous. He said he would not put up with being blackmailed. I suggested that if he had got everyone into the same room and worked this out, it could have been sorted, but it was different people being told different things. He went to get CB who came in, seemed pretty calm, said she was OK with Anji staying, provided Fiona had proper status and recognition. Later, Fiona having refused to come in, we had a meeting, TB, CB, AC, Jonathan, Anji.

Cherie did most of the talking, mainly addressed to Anji, admitted they had had very bad times before but in recent weeks she felt it was a lot better, that Fiona felt she had a decent job worked out and that TB, without realising, had upset her effectively by taking the job away. She felt we ought to be able to work together but there were people who had doubts about Anji's politics and felt uncomfortable with her having a bigger political role. She was emotional but held it together and was reasonably nice to Anji. The basic position we tried to reach was Fiona in charge of a new unit dealing with visits and events, Anji doing what she does for TB but not directly in charge of politics.

TB sat there as first CB, and then Anji, both said he had misrepresented the situation. He was angry we even had to discuss all this. I said we had to sort it. I felt it was doubly difficult for me because I was trying to sort it out for the office, but also for Fiona when deep down, I think she probably wanted out whatever, and me out too. But I could not have a situation either where she felt she was being misled, which she had, or where she felt undervalued. Anji said she was bewildered and would need time to think.

I went home for a bit for Grace's sports day and on the way TB called, said he knew he had handled it badly but felt the whole thing was being got completely out of proportion. He said he rated Fiona but he could not have her or anyone else telling him who he employed where. He had GB breathing down his neck – he asked for a departure date again today – he had some difficult issues coming up and he knew he needed a strong central operation. He said there were not many people that GB feared but he feared me because of guile and toughness and he feared Anji because of her links into the right-wing press.

He had plenty of good people, but exceptional people who gave him things nobody else could or would were hard to find. He had GB and Peter M who were of real top quality but flawed. I said that's all fine, but it doesn't help much with Fiona. And he was having to deal with the ministerial reshuffle. How we would be lacerated if people knew how much time was being spent on this other stuff. I did see his point about having to be able to exercise his own judgement about personnel but boy had he fucked up the management of it. He said he was willing to apologise to Fiona and said he was really keen to keep her. She didn't buy it, said his real concern was that if he upset her too much he was worried he would lose me.

I called Neil [Kinnock] to get his advice, and he felt we just had to try to keep going till the summer, and repair damage done. We got the reshuffle finished around 6. I went to Lance Price's farewell, and it was nice to see all the party people again, then home. Sally, Cherie and Fiona were never off the phone. Cherie was desperate for Fiona to stay. It really did feel at the moment like living in a soap opera. I had a real sense of foreboding that if Fiona left and I stayed, it would end up in tears. Equally, if we both stayed, and she felt there under duress it could be just as bad. But I also felt that if left with conditions where I felt I was being forced to leave unreasonably, that was a bad and dangerous scenario too.

Tuesday, June 12

There was a fair build-up of TB/GBery, likely to be exacerbated given that I spotted [Rupert] Murdoch and Irwin Stelzer coming in to see GB. I felt drained after the last couple of days trying to resolve Fiona's situation. She still wasn't happy, far from it, but Cherie had persuaded her to stay and give it a go and TB later saw her to try to repair some of the damage. Maybe working together had never been the right thing, but at the moment I was more worried about the alternative. TB was starting to recover some of his strategic grip. He felt we had to keep the Liberals to our left on some issues and hope that the Tories try to come towards the centre on Europe but right on other issues. He felt Portillo was probably the best bet for us as Hague's successor.[1]

The euro was becoming more problematic, presumably as a result of briefing. It was just becoming a given that TB was keen, and GB was against. We had a series of meetings on the Queen's Speech, then the first of several meetings about personnel for the Policy Unit. TB was moving against the merger of the Private Office and the Policy Unit. Wilson was clearly moving to block some of this. I had meetings over the MMU [Media Monitoring Unit], where Chris McShane and Carl Shoben [special advisers] still felt they were being blocked from doing what needed to be done for a proper media monitoring operation. Mike Granatt told me he was moving on to some national resilience unit and he thought Brian Butler [Home Office] should be his successor. He said a lot of people out there wanted to be more involved but they were scared of me. I said I was at a loss to know what more I could do to make them realise that far from being scared, they should welcome our openness to ideas.

This was turning into a horrible period because virtually everyone who had been working for me in the first term was looking either for reassurance or advance. Even Godric came to complain that he didn't feel centrally involved enough to follow me on the briefing front. I saw Fiona with Lucie [McNeil] to discuss the idea of Lucie and Kate [Garvey] job sharing between visits and press. Then it was a stream of people wanting new roles, bigger roles, better offices, all the personnel rubbish that I couldn't be bothered with. Bill Bush told

[1] William Hague had announced his resignation as Conservative leader the day after the election.

me he was going to go as a special adviser for Tessa. I said why do you want to leave Manchester United to play for Blackburn? He said he would rather play regularly for Blackburn than be on the bench for Man United. I fear he was another one who didn't feel valued enough. Then in the middle of it all, Calum called from a school trip saying I had to go and pick him up.

Wednesday, June 13

TB was off to Brussels for the NATO summit, Tom [Kelly] and Godric with him, and I stayed in the office mainly doing management stuff. We had a good meeting on how to make the diary and the Grid more strategic. We had to fill his time better. I still felt he was seeing far too many journalists. Peter H seemed very pissed off with things, probably felt frustrated at having been much more central during the campaign, now less so back in government. I got together press, SCU and Research people, tried to give them a sense of the next stages, but I could tell they were becoming affected by all the discombobulation elsewhere. Gus Macdonald [now Minister for the Cabinet Office] came in for a chat about his role. Interestingly, he felt we should try to get some proper research done at to whether the BBC are routinely breaking the rules of their charter in their political coverage. Gus was a good thing to have around the centre.

Jeremy popped round having discovered GB was doing a big number on the euro on Wednesday. This was going to be a running sore, as I told Ian Austin. I had a very good chat with Charles Clarke who said he was frankly bemused when TB first asked him to be party chairman, but was now totally up for it. When they got back from Brussels, I had a chat with Godric and Tom about how their new roles would pan out. The idea was that they share the briefings between them, that I did as little hands-on briefing as possible, and tried to focus much more on strategy. I had confidence in both of them, though it was one of those arrangements that did depend on their personalities, them being able to get on with me and each other.

I still wasn't convinced the new role was entirely me. Though I hated the briefings, in a way they were what disciplined me to stay on top of everything. I was growing a bit alarmed about how much time was currently going on personnel and just listening to people's worries about their own roles or the direction of the government. What with all the *Peyton Place* stuff going on too, less than a week after what should have been a great victory and a great feeling of victory, I was already feeling tired and depressed.

Thursday, June 14

People were beginning to ask me what the new job entailed, and I was beginning to wonder. I was also wishing I had taken a break, because the tiredness was beginning to hurt. I woke up tired and that feeling stayed pretty much all day. The changes to my operation led to a rather ludicrous scene at Cabinet with not just me, but Godric and Tom, Peter Hyman, Phil Bassett and Paul Brown all there. We were going to have to sort it.

Cabinet lapsed pretty quickly into political analysis, day-to-day, a bit of Grid clearing. TB was hitting the reform message for the Queen's Speech pretty hard. Robin was impressive, really pumped up and making clear he was up for the job. He gave them all a little lecture about the importance of bills being ready, echoed by TB. TB said we need to get the difficult things done at the beginning. He said in the first term we came close to disaster in the third session because of lack of preparation of some of the bills. We won't get away with it again and we have to learn the lessons from that. Some of the new ministers dutifully spoke up for their bills, and there was palpable excitement amongst the new people in particular. Milburn said we could not keep pushing back the mental health legislation. JP said we are now in our fifth year and if we make a mess of the bills, it's our fault because we know how to work the system. TB did a little spiel at the end, said the two questions for the parliament were could the Tories revive themselves, and will we get through radical change without the Labour Party reverting to type? He said the political role of ministers was more important than ever. But we were in a strong position and now was the time to make the difficult decisions. We are a government of change and we must not rest on our laurels, even at the risk of losing short-term popularity.

GB said nothing, just sat there, fuming, about what in particular I don't know. Robin on the other hand was looking happy and confident, and talking about the parliamentary process as if to the manner born. Thabo Mbeki [President of South Africa] was in seeing TB while I had a separate meeting with his press team who wanted advice on the operation they were setting up. Then briefing TB before the press conference in the garden. There were still all sorts of office accommodation issues being sorted. TB called on his way to the airport, felt Cabinet had been OK but he said GB's behaviour had been a bit odd.

Friday, June 15

I felt like I had some kind of post-natal depression. We'd won the election, which ought to have been great, but virtually every day since it had felt like swimming through shit. The only good thing to be said for it was that the only way was up.

Saturday, June 16

Pretty much a total day off. I said to Fiona that a large part of me wished that we packed it in. Rory was training on the Heath extension and I went for a long run in the pouring rain which was fantastic. We went for lunch with Neil, Glenys and [their daughter] Rachel [Kinnock]. Neil seemed a lot more relaxed. He shared some of my concern about GB. He said he's about the only man in history who is about as guaranteed as it's possible to be to be the next leader and PM, establishing a record as being a great Chancellor, but somehow it's not enough. The [anti-EU, anti-capitalist and anti-US] riots in Gothenburg [EU summit] were the main story. TB did his summit press conference wearing an extraordinary tie.

Monday, June 18

GB was leading the news with his enterprise agenda. As ever, he had set it up well, and was managing to look substantial and powerful, whereas TB out on a health visit was rather playing into the idea of him being the frontman. TB said he was more than happy for GB to be seen as a big figure because that was good for the government. But at the office meeting, the first one to be attended by Robert Hill [now Blair's political secretary] and David Hanson [Labour MP, Blair's new PPS], I said we had to really watch the potential fault line running through everything as a result of GB putting himself in slightly different positions. It was definitely the case on public service reform, and on the euro. Afterwards, TB said we really needed to think through how we handled Gordon this term.

TB asked if I was depressed and I said I was. The last few days had got me down with all the rows going on. Also, if you think of it in horse-racing terms, we had trained ourselves to the peak for the big race, and now all I felt was flatness, so I felt ready for the knacker's yard. He said my problem was having to make a transition from full-on, round the clock, day to day, but I had to do it. You're in the paddock, too keen to get back on the track. But he agreed I would need new direction to keep me fully motivated. It was different for him, because he faced real challenges and real issues, and in the end, no matter how much advice he might have, he took the real decisions. I felt in some ways that I had done what I was best at, during the period it was most needed, and he now needed those skills less than he used to, and less than others did. He didn't really buy it, said virtually every major leader that he met was aware of me and saw my value to him, which he described as indispensable. He felt that once people had recharged after the election, things would feel very different.

We discussed Peter M and whether he could appoint him to the Belgian presidency's Future of Europe group under Guy Verhofstadt, which would include some pretty big hitters. TB was in no doubt Peter was the best person for the job but accepted there were serious presentational and political downsides. It would be seen as Peter back with a licence to meddle in all things European. It would give him platforms galore that he would use. GB would go mental. The media would go mental, and it would unleash a wave of speculation about him coming back to government. Even Jonathan and Anji seemed reluctant. It would be one thing if he just got on and did the job quietly, but we all knew that wouldn't happen. TB kept coming back to it, saying who else? TB said he wanted someone who could build an alliance with [former European Commission president Jacques] Delors and [Italian Prime Minister Giuliano] Amato to isolate [Belgian Prime Minister Jean-Luc] Dehaene. He believed Peter could do that. Sally said he overestimated the esteem in which Peter was held overseas, and as a result of his election acceptance speech, which was the last some people would have seen of him, people would have big doubts. But TB was definitely going to push for it.

I was working on TB's speech for Wednesday, and trying to mug up on the main bills to try to link them strategically. Anji agreed with the post-natal depression analysis. She said she felt exactly the same, that we had all worked hard for a big win and since it had happened, there had been nothing but grief. She felt surer than ever that she wanted and needed to leave and that we had to make him less dependent on us. She also believed he would not stay the full term and would hand over to GB in exchange for his help and support in winning a euro referendum. I think that was wishful thinking. The Northern Ireland talks were going badly.

Tuesday, June 19
TB called several times, at one point saying GB's problem was that the longer he went on, the more his weaknesses were accentuated. He still believed the upsides far outweighed the downsides. But he felt there was an ambivalence about GB in the top job. He was happy to be seen as the giant of the government but he thought there was a lack of self-confidence about the final step. I said the TB/GB tension risked being the dynamic of the government from now till the end,

and it was dangerous for all of us. I felt it was demeaning for TB if GB was seen as the giant figure and he was Mr public services, Mr crisis management, Mr international tootling-along-behind. TB said I was right to be concerned about GB but wrong if we let it dominate our thinking. He wanted me working on longer-term strategy, planning where the government needed to get to, and helping him make sure it happened. We could not stop GB being ambitious and difficult, even if we wanted to. It's politics, and we have to manage it.

He had a bilateral later with GB who showed him the draft of his Mansion House speech tomorrow. There was a big focus on Europe with a long passage on the euro and though it didn't change the policy, it said that the pre-assessment was being done, and it was very pro in tone. TB read it that way, so did Jonathan. Jeremy read it the opposite way, felt it was designed to be pro in tone so that it could be spun as sceptic on substance. Whatever, it was going to be the big story and we couldn't quite work out what he was up to. I felt he was covering his business flank. The charitable interpretation was that he was falling in behind TB. In any event, however, TB felt it was too pro.

GB and Ed Balls came over to discuss it and I said I thought the story out of it would be that we were going in tomorrow. GB cracked a joke about how he was keeping back a line about going to Brussels to tell them to print notes and coins. Eddie George [Governor of the Bank of England] was making a speech tomorrow saying sterling was not ready. I couldn't really understand why GB wanted to be into this right now. TB said he didn't mind what he was saying, or the timing, or the fact he would be upstaging him again, provided it was the right thing. But GB was deliberately leaving a bit of ambiguity in there, presumably so he could spin it either way.

Verhofstadt wanted to announce his Future of Europe group today but we couldn't get it together on time. TB said Peter M would have to be clear he could not grandstand. It was ridiculous to imagine he wouldn't. He clearly wanted Peter to do it, and again, I sensed, was diddling us a bit. He claimed Verhofstadt had suggested Peter but John Sawers said that wasn't true. At one point, TB seemed to suggest Peter knew what was going on but then at another suggested he didn't realise he was being considered. It was perfectly obvious he had told him and probably promised him it already.

Wednesday, June 20
The press briefing on the Queen's Speech was going OK though there was too much focus on the private sector, and that was almost the

June '01: We can't stop Gordon being difficult, says TB

whole focus of JP on *Today*. I was in fairly early, up to see TB to discuss his speech in the Commons. As ever, we spent a disproportionate time trying to work up a few jokes and funny lines. The serious stuff was well set up, but there was a chance that by the end of the day GB on the euro would have taken over.

Peter M's name had appeared in a Belgian paper in relation to the Verhofstadt group. TB was still minded to do it, though Jack S and GB were both now warning him against. We moved over to the office at the Commons, where I said we had to have an answer. We agreed it should be Peter, Robin, [former Conservative Foreign Secretary Douglas] Hurd or Jack Cunningham [now a Labour backbencher]. Chris Smith was ruled out. TB felt strongly Peter would be the best but he accepted it would be very difficult. He finally agreed to go for Robin. We got Jack S in, who said he could live with Robin. Then TB was about to see Robin when word came from the Belgians that they did not want us to appoint a government minister.

TB saw Peter, and told him he wouldn't be appointing him. Peter asked if he was acceptable to the Belgians. TB said he was but it was his decision and he was not going to appoint him. Peter really lost it and stormed out. He said we had done nothing for him. I asked TB if long term he wanted him back, and he said he didn't mind but it would become impossible unless he cures himself of this egocentric view that makes him think he's a law unto himself. I watched the [post-Queen's Speech] debate with Bruce. TB and Hague both did OK.

I spoke to Balls a few times re GB's [Mansion House] speech. They had taken TB's words and the assessment, and they had accepted our view that the tone was very pro but in rectifying it, they had gone way too far the other way, so it looked like he was being very sceptic. Ed was fine about it, and GB was fine with TB, and I think was genuinely trying to get the words right. Jeremy said that yesterday they had had a good and friendly discussion. He clearly felt he was currently in the ascendant, which perhaps explained today's ultra co-operation. In the end my fears it would knock the Queen's Speech off the top of the news were unfounded. The speech led and GB was the second story.

Fiona, Kate, Magi [Cleaver, press officer] and I had a meeting with TB and CB on their summer holiday. TB was pretty two-fingerish about it all, felt he had worked bloody hard and should be allowed a holiday without having to be so defensive about it. It was a pain for them but after the pay-rise story we had to be careful. We definitely all needed a break though, but there were still a few weeks to go.

The GB speech probably ended up in the right place but I guess it was an indication of the suspicions around that I couldn't work out whether they had outmanoeuvred us by putting in such a pro-EU draft which we made them tone down, possibly to the more sceptic position they wanted in the first place, and around which they briefed that GB had won the day. Seemingly GB felt we had outmanoeuvred him. What was clear was that it was going to be a little off the front burner for a while. GB blanked everyone as he walked in at Cabinet, very dour and surly today, didn't look at the cameraman who was in to do pictures of the new Cabinet.

TB picked up from the Queen's Speech, emphasised the need for improvements in public service delivery to go alongside the new reforms. Clare was chipping in the whole time, said at one point that we had said the spin was stopping so why are we picking all these fights with the public sector? TB looked really irritated, slapped her down, said she was tumbling into the trap being set for us, that nobody was picking fights. But there was an argument to be had about how we deliver better public services. Picking fights was the press agenda not ours. Jack warned of UNISON going into unholy alliance with the Libs.

Clare came back, said our rhetoric would push away good decent people in the public services. She was having one of her 'intervene every few minutes' days, including when DB briefed on the release of [Robert] Thompson and [Jon] Venables, the [James] Bulger killers. TB said afterwards he thought the discussion was interesting because it showed up the problems we would have if we didn't get the shape of this parliament right. In an ideal world, we would do the tough stuff on reform of public services, then the euro if things work out right, then work out TB/GB.

I had a meeting with Mike Granatt and was trying to get people into their operation to improve on the regional media side. I felt listening to Mike that I was hearing the same things as four years ago. John Spellar called, said the SWP [far-left Socialist Workers Party] were taking over UNISON at branch level, which was why we were getting such grief from them. I spoke to Piers who said they [*Mirror*] had moved from eighty per cent support to fifty per cent support because there is no opposition to us. He claimed they would support us when it came to the reform agenda.

TB and I went upstairs to the flat and he said these are the three questions we have to think through – can we deliver on public services? Can we get into the euro? Will GB make a challenge at any point? Cherie was in the next room and could hear us and she shouted out 'No, no, yes.' TB laughed out loud. I was still thinking the new job was not quite me. Fiona thought I had only stayed because it was her idea that we should leave. Godric clearly had a lot of anxiety about stepping up. Peter H was constantly nagging me about his own role, the need for him to be given a proper big project job.

Friday, June 22

TB called early en route to Sedgefield. Labour MPs were putting down critical EDMs [Early Day Motions] on a number of issues like National Missile Defense, hunting, EMU. Phil Stephens had done a piece in the *FT* which troubled TB. It suggested he had been outsmarted by GB on the euro and did he want to go down in history as the prime minister who sorted the plumbing? It was only a problem really if it was a line being promoted by GB. I spent a good deal of the day talking to various members of staff, the bulk of whom seemed pretty fed up. I think the basic problem was uncertainty about how my new role would pan out for them, but other than with one or two of them, it was hard to confess that I shared a lot of the uncertainty, and maybe that's what they were picking up on. TB was right back into regular calling whenever he had a break in his programme, usually to have the same conversation and his big issues were still public services, delivery, euro, GB.

Saturday, June 23

TB called early, was working on a note, as was I. He had asked me to set out his strategic note on public services, and the shape of the next twelve months. He felt the course of the parliament was fairly clear, but worried about our organisational capability. He felt we needed something akin to the debate on organisation generated by Clause 4 to win a big argument on public service reform. He felt it would give us the definition we lacked for parts of the first term.

Sunday, June 24

GB's people were clearly briefing that TB and I changed his speech on the euro to make it less pro. [The *Observer*'s Andrew] Rawnsley had a line that I had described GB as a colossus out of control. I finished the strategy note after a couple of calls from TB, briefed DB before *Frost* and then went for a long run. The Milibands were round for dinner and I helped David with his [House of Commons maiden] speech for tomorrow. He had clearly done the right thing in becoming an MP [in South Shields], was not unhappy to be gone from Number

10, but worried about political direction with Andrew [Adonis, new head of the Policy Unit] and Jeremy the main policy drivers.

Monday, June 25

The IPPR [Institute for Public Policy Research] report on PPP [public-private partnerships] was going quite big. Martin Sheehan [press officer] got Milburn on to *Today* and I briefed him on the way, but we didn't have a clear enough line which meant anyone wanting to cause trouble at the moment could do so. On the one hand, TB was wanting these public sector reform issues to give us definition, but on the other he did not want us constantly diverted by unnecessary rows and divisions.

At TB's office meeting, we went through his and my notes, which he wanted to distil into a forward political strategy for the next six months. He also liked some of Charles Clarke's ideas for doing conference differently. He didn't really engage on the section of my note dealing with apathy/heartlands. I felt this needed specific thought-through strategies, which would require a lot of his time and which he felt at the moment he wasn't there to give. Sally, David Hanson and I all made the point that we had to be clearer about the public service arguments and be careful we were not just pushing reform for the sake of it, but constantly have improvement and delivery to show. But TB was pretty gung-ho about it. My worries were confirmed a bit later when Leslie Butterfield [advertising executive] came in to do a presentation on focus groups on Europe, when he said that saying the euro was good for business was seen by many as a negative because people did not automatically think that business was good for them. That point had been lost on TB, who also believed the reform message per se had to be made a positive.

I had a meeting with Charles Clarke and Hilary Armstrong [now chief whip]. Charles had clearly got over his initial disappointment and seemed to be buzzing, although he did have a habit of starting a point and then moving on to another one before finishing the first. But he would be good to have around on the political front, and he would make waves, hopefully in an interesting way. I then saw Gus Macdonald and eight junior ministers trying to engage them more in communication of the general message from the centre. Riots in Burnley was the main story of the day,[1] which was pretty depressing,

---

[1] A fight between two gangs, one white, one Asian, had escalated into a riot. Around 200 white and Asian youths were involved in violence and destruction of property.

as was Leslie's presentation on Europe. We were kidding ourselves that we were winning the argument.

DB, unbeknownst to us, had written to Sussex Police Authority seemingly putting on pressure for the chief constable [Paul Whitehouse] quitting and by 8am he had quit, so another news sponge.[1] Burnley riots were still going on. Some of my people were beginning to complain about lack of clarity re the Number 10 organisational changes. People really did find change hard.

Gavyn Davies[2] came in to see TB for a discussion on the euro. TB was clear that whilst the economic conditions were key, he did favour going in early, that there was a lot to be gained politically through driving structural change in Europe, and more to be gained through changes at the ECB [European Central Bank] if we went in early. Gavyn said we shouldn't go in any higher than exchange rate 2.80 and that we could not direct policy towards that because it would mean higher inflation, taxes going up and at the wrong time, so we had to wait for the dollar to fall and the euro to rise and that was in the lap of the gods. He, Stephen Wall and I all said in different ways there was no point going for a referendum if we thought we would lose.

TB said this was an issue where he felt he had a duty to recommend entry if he thought it was the right thing to do. He was dismissive and contemptuous of the pro-euros who wanted to have the fight now when it was clear we weren't ready to get in the ring. But he passionately believed if we went in, we would change the European Union quickly and for the better. There was a lot we could do out, but a lot more we could do in. The Franco-German motor was weakening, enlargement would unleash enormous change on that front and Schroeder was keen to work with us. Instinctively he felt everyone apart from the French wanted us in. If we wait four to five years we will not be able to extract as good a deal and we will have less influence. So while there is a political case for delaying, the national interest may be best served by joining early if the economic conditions are favourable.

A lot of this was about the British character. There were two sides

[1] Whitehouse and other senior officers had been criticised over the fatal shooting of a naked and unarmed man, James Ashley, in a botched drugs raid in St Leonards, East Sussex, in 1998.
[2] Goldman Sachs economist, unofficial policy adviser to Blair, and husband of Sue Nye, adviser to Gordon Brown.

June '01: TB keen on early entry into euro   651

to it relevant here. Part of the British character was conservative, but just as powerful a part was adventurous. I said there was a third, bloody-minded and anti-establishment and that might combine with the conservative part to resist change advocated by government and business. He felt that once more and more British people got used to dealing with real euro notes and coins, perceptions would change. There was an outside possibility of a referendum in June 2003, even autumn 2002. It would all depend on the economics but we were likely to have to take a decision early next year on whether to stoke up the temperature. He really believed we could turn the debate. Gavyn said he thought it better to be eighty per cent certain in five years than sixty per cent certain in two years.

TB had an education stocktake and he thought Estelle [Morris] was a bit unfocused, and maybe lacking in confidence. I saw Charles Clarke who said he was exasperated at Richard Wilson and his efforts to obstruct him and make his life more difficult. He said he intended to make every effort to get on and work well with GB, but he knew it was difficult. I had lunch with Trevor Kavanagh, who was all sweetness and light, and clearly believed the TB/GB dynamic was the big political story.

Wednesday, June 27

First PMQs after the election, but there was also a lot of focus on TB's dinner with union leaders [to discuss public sector reform]. TB was unaware it had been building as a story and was so angered by it, the impression of them coming in to lay down the law, that he suggested calling it off. I said do not be so mad. He did need to see them, and even if they did a bit of grandstanding, so what. [The GMB's John] Edmonds particularly annoyed him because he felt he deliberately and constantly misrepresented what we were trying to do, especially in his use of the word privatisation. I felt that if people thought greater use of the private sector represented the totality of our reforms, it was not a great position and we had to get a better exposition.

He was pissed off at the way quite a few of the PLP seemed to think we could go back to the old ways of win followed by ill discipline. He came back from his address to the PLP a bit troubled, said there was not a good mood and if you added together the discontented and the disappointed, those who always disagreed with us and those who saw no future personally for themselves, it was quite a number. He also sensed 'a lot of Gordon out there', the argument being fed to them that they could have victory but an easier politics after it. He felt some of GB's people fed the line almost that it would be possible to run as New Labour but govern in a different way. He was really troubled by it, mentioned several times that he didn't like the feel of it one bit.

I was in this ridiculous position where attending the PLP was one of the things I was supposed not to do, so I phoned around a bit to see if others thought it was as bad as TB did. Most of them, including David Hanson, didn't. TB said 'Well maybe their antennae are not as sharp as mine, which are twitching badly.' PMQs was OK but Hague was on to one of the points we thought he would be, namely how do you have private management of public services, and we didn't really have all the answers, e.g. on clinical units. Godric came back from the four o'clock saying they sensed that we were not on top of all of the arguments. I bumped into GB, who looked exhausted. Just how I felt. TB said I needed a long rest over the summer then needed to come back all guns blazing. I was still sorting personnel and office space and all the rest of it, trying to fit the people we had to the jobs we needed done.

Thursday, June 28

TB got a pretty crap press from PMQs and they picked up that he was a bit defensive. The dinner with the unions was running in different directions, the *Guardian* saying no backbone, *Telegraph* saying he was in full retreat.[1] The PLP meeting had really spooked him. He called me up to the flat after my morning meeting and said he felt a real sullen mood, and a lot of GB-ery. He said he felt some of them reverting to type. They had by and large behaved because they knew we had to win a second term, but now they felt that argument didn't apply. We carried on the discussion when JP came in for a bilateral. He and I both felt he was arguing too narrow a definition of public service reform so that people heard reform without the values and the commitment to a public service ethos. Throw in all the jockeying and competing for attention of the unions and it was difficult. But interestingly, JP did not think the PLP was that bad, and he felt it was better after TB had spoken.

At Cabinet, TB actually looked worried and was sending out very

[1] Dave Prentis, the general secretary of UNISON, said after the dinner 'I don't believe that this government will want to spend the next two years in conflict with the trade unions about the role of the private company when the clear agenda is that we have got to improve public services.' An unnamed union leader was quoted as saying 'The only thing we agreed on was not to disclose the menu.'

unconfident vibes. GB just sat there, silent as the grave but also with a slight look of smugness. Before, he was locked in really intense discussion with Clare. When Charles set in train a discussion about the party, again GB just sat there. Charles had clearly thought a lot and was making a broader argument about political engagement, as well as the process. He was also keen to go out and make the case for politics in public life. Clare had chipped in that there was a heartland problem, because we focused so much of our energies on marginals.

JP gave her one of his withering looks, but agreed we weren't winning hearts and minds. But part of that was because we keep going round talking ourselves down as if we have something to apologise for. Too many of our MPs think they can be commentators. He cited Jim Murphy [Labour MP for Eastwood] as someone who just kept putting across the case day in day out in his own constituency, and increased his majority [from 3,236 in 1997 – a Labour gain from the Conservatives – to 9,141 in 2001]. He said that MPs didn't work hard enough. By now Clare was looking sullen and resentful. Anji was suspicious that GB had put her up to it. He was saying nothing.

Patricia [Hewitt] did a really good job explaining how she had turned round her local party organisation, rebuilding her local party [in Leicester West]. Jack and Robin both made interesting contributions but GB just sat there. Milburn came to see me afterwards, said GB was enjoying that because he could feel TB was jumpy. He said he was worried that we were sounding too managerial, non-political, non-ideological. We had to give a sense not just that we care about public services, but we do care who runs them and why. He felt the PLP was really sullen and difficult. The irony was that TB was the person who could settle this down. But don't underestimate how many malcontents there are who feel they have been overlooked, and don't underestimate how GB could exploit it.

Before TB left for Northern Ireland, I went to see him and told him I thought he had looked weak and nervous and they had left with bad vibes out of that. He said Anji had already told him the same. There had been a funny moment during Cabinet when Jack was briefing about Macedonia[1] and had said the president [Boris Trajkovski] was good but weak, and the prime minister [Ljubčo Georgievski] bad but strong, and Robin chipped in 'There must be a third way.' It took

[1] There had been fighting in the former Yugoslav republic between government troops and ethnic Albanian rebels demanding greater constitutional rights.

John Reid to say we had it, a prime minister who was good and strong. TB tapped Richard Wilson's arm and said 'It should be recorded that that was John Reid.' TB said he knew he had been off form, but he was not unreasonably pissed off that three weeks after delivering another massive majority, he was surrounded by so much anger and sullenness.

He said it underlined more than ever why I had to work on political strategy and engage MPs and ministers more in it. He said he thought I sometimes underestimated how big a player I was in the eyes of ministers and MPs and I needed to do a lot more politics for him. He called again after he got back from Belfast and sounded a bit more chipper. He said we just had to accept there wasn't much we could do to change GB's ways. We just have to make sure we have a strong political strategy and were able to deliver it. He said the best thing to be said for the meetings in Northern Ireland was that they were short. And he had a lot of work to do. [Slobodan] Milosevic was taken to The Hague [International Criminal Tribunal]. It was a huge story but, as Fiona pointed out, TB seemed to be getting none of the credit that he deserved for the fact it was happening at all.

Friday, June 29

Milosevic, waiting for [murdered TV presenter Jill] Dando and [Jeffrey] Archer verdicts,[1] Trimble resignation [as Northern Ireland's First Minister] due soon, there were an awful lot of big stories around. TB called a few times, emphasising what he wanted me to work up by way of strategy. I felt I was maybe still being drawn too much into the day-to-day, but it was going to take time before Tom and Godric could do most of their jobs without constantly calling on me. Also, he had to understand that it wasn't just the usual suspects who were worrying about the politics being in the wrong place, or too narrowly defined. If public service reform just became an argument about the private sector, that was not good. This had to be about delivering real change that improved the services, the focus on ends not means. He was confident we could win the arguments and show the improvements, but I was also worried 'radical' was being defined in right-wing terms and we needed more balance. I played the bagpipes at Gospel Oak's [primary school] international evening and

[1] Barry George was found guilty of Dando's murder, though after three appeals the conviction would be quashed in 2007. After a retrial George was acquitted. Former Conservative candidate for mayor of London Lord Archer was found guilty of perjury and perverting the course of justice and jailed for four years, serving half his sentence.

though I don't think anyone noticed, played really badly because I was so out of practice.

Saturday, June 30

TB called a couple of times and he had got a lot of his confidence back. But the themes were the same at the moment – public service delivery and reform; Europe; whether GB was 'limbering up'. He felt GB was waiting for things to go wrong, for mistakes to be made, for the TB lustre to fade. I had meanwhile plunged back down into a fairly deep gloom. I had a kip in the afternoon, then after dinner with the kids, went to bed and had another heart-to-heart with Fiona.

She felt my depressions were cyclical, and followed a pattern, and when I was down got down about everything, but had to put on a face at work, then got home and crashed. Her basic take was that I had made the wrong decision in staying, but that because it was her pushing me to leave, I had dug my heels in. But she said she knew me long enough to know I would rediscover my energy and enthusiasm and in the end want to stay. But she still felt that though I might be helping TB and the government, the downsides for her were heavy.

I said it was hard to leave, because I felt for the first time that what I did really mattered and made a difference. She said fine, but she didn't think we would be genuinely happy until I was out of it. I felt under huge pressure all the time, but she felt a different sort of pressure, born of the struggle just to cope with it all. She felt that considering how much she wanted to leave, she had accepted the decision to stay, and my demand on her to stay, with considerable good grace and I should respect that more. I had to understand also that her heart was not in it, she was basically there because I wanted her to be, and she felt as ever I made the big decisions and she followed on. I said I did appreciate it but I also knew I was not great at showing it.

Sunday, July 1

Trimble quit at midnight.[1] TB called to go over his weekend note, back on the same themes. I ran for an hour or so and felt a lot better.

---

[1] Trimble, the Ulster Unionist leader, resigned as First Minister of the power-sharing executive in protest against the IRA's failure to redeem its pledge to decommission all weapons.

There was a definite growing offsideness about the commentariat, lots of 'running out of steam' around the place. We were still drifting on PPP, and I spent much of the day working through a note with Robert Hill to circulate to the PLP, trying to get it into a broader context and give a simple explanation as to what we were trying to do. I got into my stride on it, and after Robert and I completed it, I did one on the broader public service reform issues too. It always made sense to write these arguments through, expose the holes in our own arguments, try to work through the answers to the difficult questions. I was pleased with both notes, though I was on and off still agonising about whether to stay or go. I talked things over with Peter H, who was very warm and human about it all, said he felt TB would really miss me, and also that I would really miss the job. Kate [Garvey] said much the same. John Kerr [FCO permanent secretary] was offering me more FCO help on the personnel front, felt it had been good for the FCO to have people working in my office and was looking to expand the arrangement.

Anji told me Kate Hoey [former minister] had received a fulsome letter from GB after her departure from the government. I guess he was writing to all the sacked people to win them over if he could. TB felt it was just too obvious and would be counterproductive. TB had had dinner over the weekend with Peter M and John Birt [former BBC director general] and told Peter he would not make it back until 1. he accepted a lot of his fate had been of his own making, and 2. he changed. TB said Birt had been shocked at Peter's demeanour, still very much the victim, and speaking to TB in a very offhand kind of manner.

I went with Fiona and Godric to [the late *Express* political editor Tony] Bevins' memorial service. GB was a couple of rows in front, looking exhausted. Peter M barely acknowledged us. I didn't think much of the speeches. Andy Marr was really poor. Mo and [Labour MP Bob] Marshall-Andrews spoke but I felt they were talking about themselves as much as about him.

TB was due to have dinner with all the main delivery ministers. He asked why I wasn't on the list for the dinner. I said I had to get home. The truth was I couldn't face it at the moment. He said he wanted me and Charles C totally locked in to the delivery ministers, shaping the strategy with them the whole time. He needed me totally engaged on this. He said he felt tired and needed a holiday. So did I, to think through what we were going to do. I didn't confide I was back to thinking about leaving. The Dando trial ended, guilty verdict.

Tuesday, July 3

Peter H was doing a lot of good work at the moment, really motoring, which was a good job because I wasn't. TB called me round to brief me on last night's dinner. He was pretty fired up, said he felt he had a good team of people in the key departments, but it was important we were alongside them every step of the way. He said this was the kind of thing he wanted me focused on, not the day-to-day ins and outs in the media.

I was working on an overall forward strategy note in between a stack of meetings, mainly on Europe. Peter Hain [newly appointed Europe minister] seemed to be settling in well, and seemed to be clear he wanted to stay off the euro for now, focus on economic reform arguments, and networking around the EU. Then, after a crap diary meeting, a good though overlong meeting on the Post Office, where GB was for whatever reason keen that I should be in charge of putting together the overall communications and political strategy.

Wednesday, July 4

[Alistair] Darling's speech on incapacity benefit reform suddenly popped up and gave us another problem with the party, leading to TB getting whacked at PMQs.[1] I was still down at the bottom of the depressive ladder, and Fiona and I had another couple of long chats re whether to stay or go. I was so low today I was wondering whether staying would drive us apart for good, and lead to us splitting up, but that leaving the job could also lead to a similar outcome, either if I ended up feeling forced out, or if we found that we'd just drifted apart anyway but the job had meant we were too busy to notice. She was perfectly reasonable and rational but had such a negative view of the impact the job had had on me, and on us, that I kind of wondered whether it wasn't just hopeless.

There was more rumbling in the media re PPP and IB [incapacity benefit] and TB seemed to accept now GB had quite an operation going on. He felt he was working the PLP, the unions, the party, the media, and not always on a shared agenda. TB said this was going to be a rocky phase and we just had to ride it. 'This is politics. It happens. Name me a prime minister who has not had to deal with this to greater or lesser degrees. You will never change it,' he said.

[1] The Work and Pensions Secretary had made a speech to a think tank announcing more rigorous checks on incapacity benefit claimants, to be included in the Welfare Reform Bill. Darling said 'Being out of work should be something temporary, not permanent. There should be a change in the culture of the benefit system.'

He had picked up on my mood, said he thought the problem was I had gone from obsessive management of day-to-day to now being a bit disengaged, almost deciding no communication was better than one that got attacked.

I did feel we had to go into a downspin mode but I was equally conscious I was not motoring, and maybe looking for reasons not to have to. I didn't actually tell him I was thinking of leaving, as he was preparing for PMQs, but he knew I was not in the right frame of mind. He got a mauling from our side at PMQs, but he felt it at least gave definition that what we were trying to do was difficult and was about real change. He also clearly wanted room for manoeuvre because I reckon he was up for doing more on this than he was letting on even to us. He said I know the storms are coming on this, but the party needs to know there are plenty more difficult decisions to face up to.

TB reckoned it was 'not impossible I will be gone in a couple of years – it depends how much change they will take'. I left with Fiona and Anji for David Frost's party, usually pretty stunning turnout. [Sir Angus] Ogilvy [husband of Princess Alexandra] took me aside at one point and asked me straight out what advice I would give to the Royals at the moment. He said I want you to be honest – do you think they're in trouble? I said I thought while the Queen was there, no, but post her and the Queen Mum, things might change fast. I suspected not, but I felt they needed a more connecting strategy. That didn't mean slimmed down and bicycling dukes and all the usual bollocks, but just a sense of them moving more into the modern world, less extravagant and wasteful, more rooted. I felt Charles prided himself on his old-fashionedness but he needed a different dimension. Charles Clarke was on *Newsnight* re his job, and was excellent. I liked his tone, very different to what people expect of a party chairman.

Thursday, July 5
As soon as I walked into Number 10, just after 7, the security guy said the PM wanted to see me in the flat. He'd got a bit of a mauling in the papers re PMQs and I thought it might be for a bit of a moan. But the thing worrying him was the line in *The Times* saying he would spend 'half' of his summer holiday in the UK, when what we had actually said was 'part'. I wound him up about the planned itinerary – five days in Butlins at Ayr, five days in a Falmouth farmhouse B&B, five days in a caravan touring Norfolk.

On matters general, he said he was worried that I was confusing downspin – the right thing – with non-communication – the wrong thing. Spin is not the same as communication, he said. Clinton had told him 'never stop communicating', and 'he was right'. I said I was not going to motor again till after a holiday. He wasn't happy, felt we were not getting over the big-picture messages about what the government was all about. I did him a speaking note for Cabinet, re how it was no good willing the ends without the means. I had a couple of good meetings with women ministers on women's media, first the Cabinet women, then others, and felt they got more than most of the men the importance of the non-news media. Hilary Armstrong told me the PLP got a bit of a fright yesterday and was coming back to us. Cabinet was the same, much better. TB was a lot more relaxed than of late and it was a good discussion. Byers went through the Tube detail and the three preferred bidders. Alistair Darling said re incapacity benefit 'The Queen read it out [Queen's Speech] but nobody noticed.' Alan Milburn said we needed a bit of a fight with the BMA to emphasise reform. Ditto Reid. TB did the Police Bravery awards for the *Sun* afterwards, a good event, and I had a long chat with [editor David] Yelland.

Lunch with Phil Stephens [*Financial Times*] who was a bit down because he'd just heard he wasn't getting the editorship. He felt GB bounced us on the EMU speech. I was probably a bit loose re TB/GB, said I thought TB in a different league re leadership. I had a good meeting with the Treasury team re the Post Office plans. This was going to be a huge thing and we had to get the presentation right. This was effectively a privatisation, and we needed to lay the ground carefully. It was good to be working with Douglas [Alexander] again [now a DTI minister]. He made a very good crack about how he missed the camaraderie of the morning meetings pre-election. This was a tough job for him, and potentially career-breaking, but he struck me as on top of things. We agreed we had to use this to get up the bigger argument about the world of change, and its impact on public services we take for granted. I sensed from Ed Balls they were pushing this our way, and in particular my way for the strategic communications, because they didn't really want it to be seen as their thing.

Friday, July 6

Worked at home. TB called, joking re my three-day week, and whether I was getting enough time to fit my work around my sporting commitments. I went up to Highgate Cemetery to visit John's [Merritt, friend of AC] grave and stayed there for an hour or so, just pondering and wondering what he would think about whether I stay or go. Trouble is, he would be so amazed I was there in the first place. Probably go.

But I was really torn now. Peter H came round pm and we worked up a draft of TB's next public services speech. Good job.

I called Alex [Ferguson] to go over my current situation. He felt strongly I should stay. Only leave if you are genuinely unhappy, or if you feel the situation with Fiona is so bad you won't survive. 'You are the best there is at your job, and if you are really good at something, and it is important, you shouldn't give it up.' He said I should sit down, ignore everything anyone was saying to me, and just ask myself 'is it the right thing to stay or go?' I think you'll end up saying it's right to stay, he said. We went for dinner at Philip and Gail's. PG said much the same, said it might look like an easy option to make Fiona happy, but I would hate it and we would end up more unhappy, not less.

Saturday, July 7

We went to Tessa's [Jowell] house in the Cotswolds, and work-wise had a fairly quiet time. GB was in Italy for the meeting of the G7 finance ministers which led to a couple of calls, and there was a bit of the usual bollocks from the Sundays, but it was as near to a day off as I had had for ages. Tessa was sounding me out re whether I wanted to be chief executive of Sport England [government agency]. Tempting but no. She said she felt I should be able to do any job I wanted, that I had given more to them all than anyone, and she wasn't sure I would enjoy the new role. TB called after I had been for a run. Both of us had seen the brilliant Clinton interview on a rain-sodden Centre Court at Wimbledon.[1] He was a brilliant communicator, and had become even more popular here since leaving. He'd had a meeting with GB yesterday and said it was 'full and frank', and he felt things would be difficult for a while.

Sunday, July 8

The Sundays were the usual crap. The *Sunday Express* did some story about the guy playing me in Rory Bremner's show [actor Andrew Dunn] being too fat and facing the sack. I had a really nice run with Rory, but he was soon going to be way too fast for me. Nice chat with Tessa, David [Mills, her huband] and Jessie [their daughter]. Jessie was adamant I should leave, said I'd done my bit, made my mark, taken loads of shit for everyone else and I should get a life of my own. She was a brilliant kid, really smart and attractive, and very

---

[1] To the delight of the Wimbledon crowd, Clinton gave an impromptu interview when torrential rain held up tennis.

plain-spoken. Both she and [her brother] Matthew are great kids, and a credit to them, and to state schools in North London. Tessa was really serious re Sport England, felt it was what they and I needed.

TB called, worried that there was a real build-up of negative NHS stuff around and we had to challenge it better. The Tube [opposition to the public-private partnership to modernise London's Underground network] was also pretty bad in the media. GB came on, and asked why we hadn't got a grip of it yet, as if it had nothing to do with him at all. He was constantly referring to me on this because he didn't want to be too identified with it.

Monday, July 9

Bradford riots[1] were dominating the news, and also David B appeared to be softening the line on cannabis/criminalisation. I called him. He said he was trying not to sound out of touch whilst at the same time not really opening up the debate. Yet we were getting the message from [officials at] the Home Office that David *did* want to open up the debate, and shift the policy at some point. I sensed that DB was starting to inhale his own propaganda at the moment, and thinking he could push things more than was maybe reasonable or realistic. There was definitely a new tone to the way he spoke now, saw himself as a big player. TB asked me if I thought the cannabis line was a problem. I did.

TB had been having breakfast with Clinton before heading on to Weston Park [Staffordshire stately home, location for Northern Ireland peace talks]. He had a weird new theory today, saying that [British tennis hope] Tim Henman's failure [at Wimbledon] was another reason to go deeper into Europe! Unbundle that one for me, I said. He said it is about confidence, that we currently lack confidence because we have not seized our future where it really lies. I said I didn't know about Henman but his parents looked like Tories to me.

I had a very nice lunch with Don Macintyre [*Independent*] who thought the longer I stayed the harder I would ever find it to leave. But equally he felt I shouldn't rush into leaving. He reckoned when I did, I should be the next [Michael] Parkinson [chat show host], but I was getting more and more jaundiced about the whole telly thing anyway. I had a session with Jeremy, Anji and Peter H to plan the awayday, and decide what we wanted from it. Charles Clarke came

[1] Following riots in Burnley, tensions between Bradford's growing ethnic minority community and the white majority were exacerbated by the confrontation of far right-wing groups by the Anti-Nazi League, resulting in a riot involving an estimated 1,000 people.

to see me about the unions. He said even the moderate unions were getting really angry and confused about PPP. I suggested he do a note to TB setting out honestly where they all were on some of these issues. Peter H wrote a good note setting out his concerns on the education White Paper [on schools reform]. TB hadn't really focused on it, and it was not that good. We had a whole stack of these kinds of problems building – PPP, unions, [London] Tube, schools, lack of clarity.

Tuesday, July 10

I got in late. TB called, asking for an update on the Bradford riots. I felt we were looking a bit out of touch on it all. The NI talks at Weston Park were going nowhere, and there was a feeling it was going belly up. I told Bruce [Grocott] I was thinking of leaving, and he said it was not possible. The place will collapse, he said. That is OTT, I said, none of us are irreplaceable. He said he would be really worried because it was not just what I did with the politicians and the media, but above all what I did to keep TB in touch and with his feet on the ground. I also told [AC's GP, Dr Tom] Bostock later and he said straight out 'You'll regret it. You'll be severely depressed in no time.'

The German ambassador [Hans-Friedrich von Ploetz] came in again, and was basically trying to be helpful. He made a little crack about how 'you must know from all my telegrams', clearly trying to indicate he assumed he was spied upon. But he was a nice guy, very intelligent and had a good feel for what was happening in our politics.

I had a long meeting with Estelle Morris and the education people and we agreed to delay the White Paper. Estelle was OK but a bit flaky and I wasn't convinced she was on top of it all. She was keen to wait till September. There were issues re the public/private relationship that I felt we just didn't need up in lights at the moment. There was an expectation this was coming sooner, but I felt we could manage a delay without too many problems. It was clear there were problems between her and Andrew Adonis, who spoke down to her most of the time, and it was obvious she was going to have to assert herself a bit more. She also needed a much more political hand in there and I suggested David Miliband. AA was opposed, but I was worrying the combination of an unsure Secretary of State and an oversure but politically inexperienced AA was potentially a real problem for us. She was unsure of herself, and was going to need a lot of support. It was crazy that TB had spent so little time on this. Surely this was a priority?

I left to listen to the Tory leadership ballot. [Michael] Portillo forty-nine, IDS [Iain Duncan Smith] thirty-nine, [Kenneth] Clarke thirty-six,

[David] Davis and [Michael] Ancram twenty-one. Chaos. Absolute chaos. Just about the best result for us. I went for an appointment re my asthma, and he wanted me to go for X-rays.

Wednesday, July 11

TB being tied up with NI, Robin was doing PMQs and he came over for a meeting with TB's usual team. He was comic in his pomposity. He would regularly get up and stroll around the table, rehearsing lines and arguments. He came in carrying a clean suit and shirt in a suit carrier. I suggested he sit in TB's chair at the Cabinet table, and his chest puffed out and he did a little chirrup of delight. He really was beyond parody today. I had sent him over a note about the Tories/ *Big Brother* [TV programme] and he was up for using some of the lines. As we worked out a few different options and lines of attack, he was off wandering up and down the room again, loving it. I suggested we get someone in to take notes of what he was saying. A secretary came up from the Garden Room and tried to make sense of what he was reciting as he marched around with his head up, his chest out and his belly breathing in and out. He was fine on all the policy stuff but spent ages worrying about how to handle the Tory leadership.

He asked me what sort of state JP got into at this stage. 'Oh far worse,' I said. 'What about Tony?' 'Cool as a cucumber.' Humph. I went over to the House with Robin and he was on much better form. I had David Hanson [Blair's PPS] trying hard not to laugh when I slipped him a note saying a Rory Bremner researcher would have an immediate multiple orgasm if he walked in and saw Robin right now. He was so puffed up I thought he might explode. But he did well. He had a real presence in the House and he got into his stride quickly. I had TB in hysterics later describing the scene. It was interesting how even though he and JP had been in the House for years, they found the step up to PMQs such a big thing. TB said it took him ages before he was basically confident about it.

I got back for the Grid meeting and I was pretty clear now we needed to postpone the schools White Paper. Sally [Morgan] called after the PLP, said it was the worst she had been to, dreadful. There was real anger that Gwyneth Dunwoody and Donald Anderson [senior Labour backbenchers] had been kicked off their select committees [transport and foreign affairs respectively]. I told TB later and he said Gwyneth had no support. I was not so sure about that. Even if there were not that many who actively liked her, they would not like this. 'These people need to get a grip and grow up,' he said. 'The idea that select committee chairmanships are a job for life is ridiculous.' Mike

Granatt's new emergencies unit [Civil Contingencies Secretariat, Cabinet Office] was on the front of the *Telegraph*. A hundred fucking people in it!

Thursday, July 12

We were entering a phase of the commentariat being very down on us. We were getting a bad press re NI and there was a feeling around that we were not really motoring. I got a lift in with Philip who said the latest groups were pretty grumpy, with people getting more and more impatient for change. TB called me in first thing for what turned out to be a bit of a heart-to-heart. We kicked off on the Tories, and he felt they were heading for the worst of all worlds. He was sure they wouldn't go for Portillo or Clarke. The problem was a fundamentally divided party, with the right still in basic command. He then said re me that politics was a mix of intellect and instinct, and that if you had both in good measure, you generally had good judgement, and he said he felt I had good judgement and he needed it around.

He and Clinton had had long discussions re Al Gore and GB, and felt both were strong on intellect, stronger in their own ways than BC and TB, but they were not so great on instinct. That was why they tended to rely overly on pollsters. TB and BC would listen to pollsters, but use it to inform rather than to lead their decisions. BC felt Gore and GB were slightly poll-reliant, reluctant to take risks if the polls were saying don't do it. He said Bill was very down on some of the pollsters.

He asked me how I was, and I said bored, demotivated and depressed. I was not sure I was up for it any more. He asked if I was missing the front line and the daily battle. I said maybe a bit, but actually it was more that I had more time to think and when I thought too much, I was always liable to get myself down. I felt that the grip I had over events in the first term came from the fact that I had to be on top of everything myself because I was being asked about everything on a daily basis, so there was buy-in from the Cabinet at pretty much every stage. But now they had less of an interest in the centre being all-knowing, all-commanding, and I feared that meant we were slightly losing our grip. It was easy to devise and agree a strategy at the centre, a lot harder to impose it across government. I also felt the structures in Number 10 were vaguer and less effective, and the political operation was not motoring as it should.

We had a good meeting with Estelle and agreed to delay the White Paper. TB had gone through it properly and agreed it wasn't strong enough. He also felt that though it was good for teachers, we needed to show far more clearly why it was good for parents and kids. He was really pushing the diversity [of schools] agenda, but I still could not really see the link with improvements in all schools.

At Cabinet, Hilary [Armstrong] went over the select committee business, and it was clear there would be a rebellion and it was not clear we had the support. Clare said we should be relaxed about the Commons overturning us on it. Eyes rolling all over the place. Hilary said we should not be relaxed at all. Northern Ireland was the only other big issue being discussed, and things were a bit bleak at the moment.

GB was doodling madly with a big thick pencil, covering page after page with odd scribbles. He left his pad at the end and I went to have a look. Really thick black lines, up and down, a drawing of what looked like a dustbin, with the lid on the ground, and then the single word HARD written with real force on the page so that the impression went through several pages of the pad. There was a lot of anger and frustration there, even in his doodles. I had a very good meeting afterwards with Charles Clarke, who was keen to start going for the BBC re its coverage of politics. I had a session with Margaret B re the FMD inquiry but I was very conscious at the moment that I was kind of treading water. I also felt that people were beginning to notice. Jonathan said there was real lassitude around the place and I was conscious of the fact it was normally me and him that would generate most of the energy. There was just no drive just now. Tory leadership second ballot – IDS on the move, Portillo waning, Ancram out.

Friday, July 13

TB called me up in the morning and we went over all the same old problems. He was really pissed off with the party at the moment, felt the mood was over-rebellious and that we didn't deserve the reaction we were getting. 'This is the old Labour Party at its worst, thinks we have won two elections so now let's go back to the old divisive and self-indulgent ways.' He was also worried re GB, said at their one-on-one yesterday he had said in terms he wanted more money for schools and hospitals and less for GB's tax credit schemes. GB had originally assured him we would be spending £500 million on tax credits. It was more than £2 billion! 'They basically lied to me about it, to get it through me.' At another meeting, he had said we had a manifesto commitment to raise investment and standards in schools and hospitals. Ed Balls said we also had a manifesto commitment to lift one million children out of poverty. 'He talks as though he is a minister, and I am a junior official,' said TB, laughing.

He said GB is a big figure, and a formidable politician but because he knows he is weak on the instinct side of things, he relies too much on advisers and he doesn't always get good advice, because they think too narrowly about GB's interests. I told him about the doodle I had taken off the table. TB said he was really worried about GB at the moment. He was also worried about me, said I had to find my motivation again, had to understand how important I was to him and to the whole operation. I said I was finding it hard, and I wasn't convinced I could get myself up for it. He said we would both be better after a holiday, but he really needed me on my best form. I said I felt more Unibond [sponsors of the Northern Premier] League than European Cup at the moment. He felt that our anti-spin strategy was not working, because too many in the government had taken it to mean we should not be communicating. Our opponents, internal and external, were mounting arguments against us and we were failing to put over the right counter-arguments.

He had a series of meetings on public services delivery and I popped in and out of those. Michael Barber [head of Blair's Number 10 Delivery Unit] was impressive and seemed like a really good bloke. Wendy Thompson [head of the Office of Public Service Reform] looked a bit worried by the scale of what she had taken on, and I sensed she was having trouble finding her way around the Civil Service jungle. She said we had too many targets. They needed to be simplified and then the professionals encouraged to be innovative in how they met them. In the NHS in particular she felt there was just too much being expected of them. Also GB, who up till now had shown next to no interest in the PSA [Public Service Agreements] process, was now calling in ministers who were getting conflicting messages from Numbers 10 and 11. Richard Wilson sent a note to TB saying the sense of a split between them was also causing difficulties for the management of public services. Too many targets, too much interference from the centre, differing signals.

TB, PH and I had a session on his [public service reform] speech. I said I was not at all clear what we were saying about the private sector stuff, or that it was really a fight worth winning. All that mattered in the end was that we improved public services and that people benefited from those improvements, but he wanted this to provide definition. TB and Jonathan etc. set off for Weston Park again around 3. He called me up again before he set off, said he was sure things would be fine after a holiday. He said he would rather have me for two hours a day than most people for twelve, though he would prefer me to be motoring full-time. The *Guardian* got hold of the fact we were postponing the [schools] White Paper and were putting their own spin on it – fear of unions etc. There were riots in Belfast [as a result of the re-routing by the Parades Commission of a number of Orange Order parades] so the backdrop to the talks was worse than ever.

Saturday, July 14

The Tory leadership contest was still the main political story. TB called from Weston Park, clearly a bit agitato. Peter M had had dinner with Roy Jenkins [former Labour Cabinet minister] and there seemed to be three things winding up the chatterers – lack of clear direction; TB/GB division; lack of progress on Europe. He had said they were losing faith with TB and becoming contemptuous. This was classic Peter, going a couple of gears over the odds to provoke him into a reaction, and hopefully doing something about it. There was no doubt we had been drifting a bit.

He said Bertie had a different take, that the Tories seemed to be in self-destruct mode and people would instinctively understand that was because of the changes we had made to get into the centre ground. He seemed to think I needed to be out there with the media more, that the one big downside of the changed role was that my voice was not out there clearly heard speaking for the government. Remember Clinton's edict, he said – never stop communicating. He was a bit worried we had.

He was very down re GB who seemed to be hibernating. I was sorely tempted to get out the line that GB had not made a single meaningful contribution to Cabinet since the election; and that he was accusing us of building up Blunkett as a foil to him. I resisted the temptation.

Sunday, July 15

TB called a couple of times after I sent over a briefing note to try to get our minds focused on the arguments in the [public service] speech. He wanted to hammer the reform buttons. I had two long runs today, and was feeling a lot fitter. The main political event today was Amanda Platell's video diary.[1] I watched it and in between wondering why

---

[1] Platell, spokeswoman for William Hague, had kept a private video diary throughout the general election campaign, which was broadcast by Channel 4.

on earth she did it, I really enjoyed it from a personal perspective because I could feel the disintegration of their campaign day by day.

Monday, July 16

In early to get the speech finished. Hoping it would do the business for us, but it was to be an odd day at the end of which TB's authority would be severely diminished. We got enough of the speech done and signed off by him to give out extracts at the eleven o'clock and Milburn was up doing bids. TB was still pushing the private sector too hard for my taste. [John] Edmonds was getting wound up, and there was a feeling that people like him and plenty of our MPs just wanted to give us a bit of a whack. TB's morning meeting was a bit subdued. Charles was moving towards David Triesman [general secretary of the Association of University Teachers] as general secretary [of the Labour Party]. TB was worried about the fallout if Maggie Jones [senior UNISON official] didn't get it. Hilary A felt it was possible we would be OK in the vote on select committees tonight. TB seemed a bit detached while I was feeling more and more fed up. We had settled on the Royal Free Hospital as the venue for the speech. Bostock [AC's GP] was in the audience and like quite a few of them, not wholly impressed. It didn't help that he read it like it was the first time he had ever seen the words. The immediate reaction from unions and others was pretty negative.[1]

When we got back to Number 10, TB took me out to the garden and we walked around a bit. GB had again asked him yesterday when he was planning to go. TB insisted it depended upon him working properly with him in the meantime. GB complained he never consulted about anything. TB said he had been trying to consult e.g. over the general secretary's appointment. GB's reaction was that if he made a suggestion, TB would do the opposite. And so on and so on. 'He seems to think he can just intimidate me into going.' TB wanted to know why I was not going on so many foreign trips. He also wanted me to speak more regularly to Peter M. We had a meeting later on the George Bush visit and in particular how to deal with problems on Kyoto and NMD. Later there was a little party for the Labour

[1] In the speech, which was widely criticised by trade unions in particular, Blair promoted choice in access to public services, saying 'If we who believe in public services don't change them for the better there is an alternative political position that will seize on our weakness and use it to dismantle the very notion of public services as we know them. It really is, I believe, reform or bust.' GMB general secretary John Edmonds responded 'We are . . . facing the prospect of ministers kicking down the front door and hurling privatisation on to the mat.'

Party in the garden, where TB did an off-the-cuff speech saying how important it was that they were so professional and disciplined.

Then came a massive bloody nose from the Commons with a huge vote in support of Donald Anderson and Gwyneth Dunwoody [more than a hundred Labour MPs voted against removing them as select committee chairs]. I said to TB if we were going to end up reinstating them, we should do it tonight. TB said the party was going through a spasm, somehow believed the election had been gifted to us. We had to challenge the party, face them up to the role discipline and leadership had played in getting us to where we were. I said there was nonetheless a feeling amongst a lot of people that they were irrelevant and unwanted and he had to be more careful. He thought the problem was being exaggerated, but warned the party would go back to its old ways unless we challenged them constantly. He was beginning to sound a bit more arrogant, potentially out of touch.

Tuesday, July 17

The papers were a bit of a war zone. Massive on the select committee rebellion. The BBC in particular were giving total blowjob interviews to any of the critics. Speech coverage wasn't as bad as it might have been though lower key, plus we had John Edmonds about to announce the GMB planned to pay less to the party [withdrawing £250,000]. TB and I had a bit of a spiky conversation about the general scene. He was definitely developing a kind of 'I'm always right' tone. When he saw Jack S to discuss the Bush visit, he spoke of NMD as though it were barely a problem. Jack had obviously thought about it a lot, while TB seemed to be operating on a pretty superficial level on it. I was also pissed off that he constantly defined himself against the left and not the right. I was generally pretty down because on the one hand I was spending half my time demotivated and thinking about leaving and on the other I knew that people inside the operation were looking to me to lift it and to get a grip on issues like PPP, and I just wasn't up for it. I told Jeremy Heywood I was still thinking of going and he seemed genuinely shocked. He felt if the judgement was a purely personal one for me, I should probably go, but he felt that for TB it would be bad because he felt there was nobody else he trusted constantly to be developing the arguments and the lines for the public, the media, Cabinet, etc.

I got *The Times* wound up to start going for Edmonds a bit, not least pointing out the relation of all this to the inter-union [membership] recruitment war. The Tory leadership third ballot was a bit surprising, with Clarke winning, IDS second and Portillo out. We had another meeting on Bush. TB agreed that Kyoto was the one area where he felt we could openly express clear disagreement, but he wanted to park NMD, and he wanted the warm personal stuff to be evident. I had lunch with David Frost. I let him in on my current dilemma and he felt I should stay to the bitter end and then after that become the next Des Lynam [sports broadcaster]. Felt the Tories were done for, that TB was popular with the public but we had a real problem with the chattering classes in several London postcode areas.

Jack Straw said he had had a difficult conversation with Robert Hill, said he didn't like being told what to do. He said he could just about take it from me on media stuff but not from Robert Hill on policy. Jack felt TB was not listening to people and needed to be more inclusive of his supporters.

Wednesday, July 18

TB wanted to know why I wasn't going to Genoa [G8 summit], said he needed me there on these big trips and that I ought to go. I said I couldn't see a real role. He said he disagreed. He felt there was a general problem of depoliticisation and I needed to be around to make sure ministers and the Number 10 people did not lose sight of politics. He had had a word with Andrew Adonis to be more political and Jack S having taken up his conversation with Robert Hill with TB himself, TB told Robert to be more respectful of ministers. Portillo was the big story of the day.

I took advantage to call a few meetings on domestic policy to try to iron out some of the communications problems that were flying as a result of policy not being sorted. Tube first of all. The truth is we had lost the argument over the last two years, partly because we and the Treasury and DTLR [newly realigned Department of Transport, Local Government and the Regions] were all on different pitches. It was an OK meeting but I found it alarming how much people who knew the policy detail inside out looked to me to make decisions they were more qualified to make. It was an OK meeting though and we had something to work on. I spoke to Derek Smith [managing director] at London Underground to get his agreement to do major advertising on the Tube. I felt we should be really going for [Bob] Kiley.

It was Hague's last PMQs. I came up with a line 'It's goodbye from Mr Boom and goodbye from Mr Bust' which TB did bang on 3.30. PMQs generally was fine. Later we went for another walk round the garden and he was in very boisterous mood, telling the story of Clinton at Chequers when Bill told Carole [Caplin] about his bad back and she showed Bill how to stretch by bending over the piano. Clinton said to him afterwards that he could not believe that Cherie let her anywhere near him. Ian Austin called but I was tied up and then five minutes later it broke on PA that Sarah [Brown] was pregnant. We had to go along with the pretence that TB had known about it for some time. It didn't exactly engender a lot of warmth around the place. Bush arrived [in the UK]. Magi [Cleaver] said she was absolutely at the end of her tether with the Yanks [White House visits team].

Thursday, July 19

There was a fair bit of positive coverage for GB on the pregnancy. TB said a few nice words at Cabinet. On the Bush visit, TB said that on Kyoto, he would simply agree to disagree. On NMD, it would be years before we have to do this, before it comes to fruition. The line we need to get to is that if it comes to it, they do it in consultation not just with allies but also Russia, but it must not become a huge source of division. Robin C agreed, said it would be daft to allow this to become a big problem now. Clare chipped in as ever, said she didn't buy the argument about rogue states and that the party was worried about it. TB said if the technology exists to defend yourself, then nobody can stop the Americans developing it. In the end we will be their allies, and that is the truth, and in so being, we can shape it. There was a good discussion on globalisation, GB saying that this was not just about America but how we develop better systems of global co-operation. TB said it was a real problem, e.g. pre-Genoa, that the easy way to get a case heard now for protesters was through violence. GB said it was our job to make sense of globalisation or else these people were going to fill the gap and people would stop believing in elected politicians. I was impressed by Charles C.

Early afternoon, we travelled down to Chequers to wait for Bush and go through the difficult stuff, Kyoto and NMD in particular. TB seemed pretty nervous, and was repeating the same arguments again and again. There had been a total fuck-up earlier re the reception we had planned for the White House press corps because someone at the White House had cancelled the visit to Number 10 and Buckingham Palace. Tanya Joseph [press officer] just about rescued it. Magi said Bush's advance people were even worse than Clinton's. Total nightmare. Bush arrived by helicopter, and we were surprised to see him not wearing a tie, his advance people having said that he would be. He and TB had a very long chat one-on-one, mainly going over the tricky stuff before they came through for a session with the rest of us in the room upstairs with the Cabinet table. Bush seemed a bit more on top of detail, though had to ask at one point whether Trimble had resigned. He said he had been very tough with Putin, claimed he had told him 'If you carry on arming rogue states, you're going to end up eating your own metal.' Putin had insisted they were only selling conventional weapons and Bush claimed he had said 'No you're not.' He said the good news was Putin looked a bit scared. Balkans, Russia.

On the Middle East, Bush was very down on [Palestinian leader Yasser] Arafat, but also wondered how on earth [Israeli Prime Minister Ariel] Sharon could do a deal with someone he had called a lying pig. He had told Sharon he believed they were planning to go in and eliminate Arafat and if they did so, it would be impossible to stand by them. The one-on-one having been so long, the rest of us had long chats with his people, particularly Karen Hughes [White House counsellor], Ari Fleischer [press secretary], Andy Card [chief of staff], Karl Rove [senior adviser to Bush] and the guy who had been appointed ambassador [William S. Farish III], who was a close friend of the Queen. They had enjoyed their session with the Queen. Chris Meyer said they had all been very nervous, including Bush. They were very right wing but they had a wit and a charm that took them a long way.

In Karl Rove, I sensed a bit of a kindred spirit. He didn't take himself too seriously but he took what he did seriously and more than most advisers admit, understood strategy and understood the media realities you had to take into account in shaping it.

Over dinner, he, Karen and I talked at length about how the media was impacting for the worse on politics, how in the end this was a power struggle and elected politicians were going to have to reassert themselves, get more power and control not less, if they were not to be swept aside by the relentless cynicism most of the media now pumped.

We had a good discussion too about our respective campaigns. I said I thought Gore fucked it up and that Clinton would have beaten them. They disagreed needless to say, though Rove did say that neither TB nor GWB had faced the toughest opponents in the world. I gave them ironic thanks for all the help and advice they had given to Hague.

The press conference was OK. Bush put TB in a bit of a difficult position by being so warm about him in the context of NMD which the press took as TB backing Bush. TB, needless to say, didn't seem to mind too much. TB and Bush went back for their own dinner while the rest of us went off to some fancy hotel nearby. The mood was pretty good and I think both sides were determined to get on. Andy

Card had a quiet authority about him, Condi [Condoleezza Rice, National Security Advisor] was clearly growing into the job. I drove back to town with Chris Meyer who felt they were feeling their way a bit but determined to get on with us.

Friday, July 20

The Bush stuff was low-key [in the media] and in any event the story was moving to Genoa riots [around the G8 summit] which were bound to be self-fulfilling. TB wanted to get up on it, make the case for summits as an important part of economic progress for the whole world. Rebekah Wade threw a dinner party for [her partner, actor] Ross Kemp's birthday at a dining club near the German Embassy. I was sitting next to David Liddiment [director of programmes and channels, ITV] who was much brighter than most media people and we had a good discussion on politics, the media, globalisation. He felt these people protested at summits because they felt so remote from political decision-making.

Saturday, July 21

I was up early to go for a long run before heading for Wales for Rachel Kinnock's wedding [to Stuart Bentham]. TB called a couple of times to say we had to get a better media strategy vis-à-vis the rioters. I think Godric was beginning to get a feel for his [TB's] circular conversation style, called and asked me what was the best way to deal with him when he kept saying the same thing. I said, just keep saying the same answer, unless you end up being persuaded that you're wrong. Fiona and I had a massive row in the car park of a service station on the M4 because she suddenly realised she hadn't packed her shoes. And of course it all turned out to be my fault because I work for Tony Blair and that meant she didn't have time to think because she had so much to do for me and the kids. She didn't take kindly to my suggestion of going into Swindon and finding an ordinary person's shoe shop and buying a pair that didn't cost a fortune.

We got down to Neil and Glenys' and left Grace, who was mega excited about being Rachel's bridesmaid, up to the hotel before setting off for the wedding. It was a nice enough do. Rachel looked great and Gracie was loving every minute of it. Fiona and I weren't speaking at all. Neil gave a good speech. The best man was probably a bit near the knuckle for some of them and his piss-taking of Wales didn't go down a bundle. He said the National Museum of Wales was nearby and 'worth a visit if you've got five minutes to spare'. A protester got killed in Genoa.[1] TB called before going up to do interviews on it.

Sunday, July 22

I was up early for a swim in the hotel gym, Fiona and I still not speaking. We went round to Neil's to collect Grace's stuff. Godric told me TB had given him a talking to about how I seemed to have given up and had decided on an anti-spin strategy that actually meant we weren't communicating at all. We drove back home and got changed before heading for Crystal Palace and the athletics. I had a nice chat with Seb Coe [Lord Coe, former Olympic runner and Conservative politician] and [Nicky] his wife. He thought we were simply better than them pretty much every day during the campaign. Loads of the big stars were racing and the kids enjoyed it. Brendan Foster and Steve Cram [former Olympic runners, now BBC commentators] lobbied me again on Pickett's Lock.[2] They were really against it. Rory had a session with David Moorcroft [former Olympic runner] who told him his personal best was faster than his had been. Grace was full of it about the wedding and the pictures there were of her in some of the papers.

Monday, July 23

The news was leading with a follow-up to the *Telegraph* story on TB ordering a halt to the foot-and-mouth disinfection programme. TB said he had had another one-on-one with GB which was a 'collector's item'. GB had talked about the Tube policy as though it had nothing to do with the Treasury. In his view, this was all about the relationship between local and central government. TB was gently pressing me to raise a few gears, saying we needed a proper communications strategy for August/September focused on public service reform. He was really getting worried, I could tell, that I was taking the anti-spin stance too far, that because I saw the media as the real spin merchants, I had decided just to cut off the communication. There was something in it, though it was more that I was just feeling generally tired and down, and couldn't be much bothered with any of it at the moment. Fiona thought I should see the doctor to see

[1] In the protests against the G8 summit, 23-year-old Carlo Giuliani was shot dead by a Carabinieri officer after Giuliani threw a fire extinguisher at a police Land Rover. The vehicle ran over Giuliani twice.
[2] Pickett's Lock, North London, had been announced in March 2000 as the location of the planned National Athletics Stadium, a project that would later be abandoned due to the high cost and poor transport links.

whether I wasn't actually depressed again, but I knew in myself I was but I didn't want to go down the medication route. I think the election took more out of me than I felt at the time.

I said to TB I felt he needed to focus more on the really big moments and events that we knew broke through to the public, and less on the day-to-day. I went to a long meeting chaired by GB, a kind of election post-mortem with party and polling people. GB was very nice to everyone, said congratulations were in order, but always good to work out what we could have done better. I didn't actually feel the discussion did that. It was like a more polite version of a grumpy Cabinet meeting, people making random points but I'm not sure we vowed to do anything different as a result. Greg Cook [Labour staff, polling expert] went through the post-election polling, then Margaret [McDonagh] reviewed organisation, and then we just kind of kicked things around the block. I suppose having won another big landslide, it would be judged a success, but I felt as a campaign we could have done better and I don't think the discussion took us there. The reality is that WE found the campaign dull, so why should we have expected the public to find it interesting? And also, WE were complaining the whole time that the language being used in political discourse was disconnecting and disengaging, so what were we going to do to change it? GB's basic point was that political engagement was now a real problem. Incumbency made it harder, and we had fought in the foothills not on the mountaintops.

Stan Greenberg said that even though the Tories fought a bad campaign, they had the makings of recovery there. He felt New Labour had come over as a bit of an orphan, that it wasn't clear who owned it. In the end, we did better with the working-class vote, but fewer and fewer were feeling engaged. Greg said that among young people the Tories did proportionately better than with other groups, which was a worry. It was also a myth that the euro was more popular with the young. He felt we needed to think carefully about racial politics, that there were the makings of real problems, particularly in the Pennine belt [following the riots in Burnley and Bradford]. Margaret felt the problem of disengagement had built up through the parliament because too many of our politicians never linked government to politics and politics to values. TB took a meeting on conference strategy, and he and I were becoming stuck records in the argument about communication. He said we needed more communication. I said he meant more spin, which is what we were trying to cut out. I think Charles [Clarke] was more on my side of the fence, felt that there had to be real as well as symbolic change and also that we needed to focus our minds on the big moments and events, e.g. TB's conference speech, and worry less about the piddling in-between stuff. I also felt we were lacking clarity on the basic policy approach and felt until that was resolved it would be difficult to communicate coherently across the piece.

TB was clearly getting irritated with my stance. I still felt though our problem was lack of policy clarity. He felt it was lack of communications strategy. He insisted the argument on the private sector was clear. I tested that in the meeting, asked everyone there if they felt it was clear, and none did apart from him. The truth was there was a lot of unease about it. He was also concerned we were vacating the *Mirror/Guardian* field to GB, who was really working on them. My problem was I was beyond caring what these newspapers thought or said. They were superficial tossers in the main and I had had enough of talking to them, or trying to win them round. I genuinely felt if we worried more about what we were doing and saying, less about what they thought, and always stayed ahead of their arguments, we would change the terms of the debate more quickly than he realised. Fiona apologised for the shoes outburst [last Saturday] and I apologised for my mood.

Tuesday, July 24

I was working on the Chequers awayday presentation and also my speech to heads of information tonight. I was keen to get a real discussion going with them but I wasn't hopeful. Apart from a few of them, I still felt most did not get it. TB was meeting the parents [Carol and Dean Maddocks] of a girl [eight-year-old Alice] looking for a bone-marrow match who had challenged him during [BBC] *Question Time* in the election campaign. We agreed it would not be sensible to change policy or offer more money but in the end he pretty much did so. I felt for him sometimes in these situations where people in difficulties felt that he ought to have the answer to all their problems. He was hugely empathetic though, and what he said came over really powerfully on the bulletins.

TB had a long session with Prince Charles on rural issues, and came back with the view he was well-meaning but misguided, and once they got into argument, not so well meaning. JP got done for speeding – at 36 mph for God's sake – but we agreed best to get it out today. The heads of information meeting was actually rather good. They for once had some constructive points amid the complaints. I tried a much more open and discursive style and they responded. One or two made the point that people in the public services didn't feel the government liked or respected them. Others were buying in to the notion of more cross-departmental groups.

Wednesday, July 25

Peter Hyman picked me up and we left for Chequers and the internal awayday. On arrival, TB took me through to the study and said it was really important that I lifted people, that I didn't allow my current mood to affect them. I said fine, as long as we went through the tough questions and got some clarity. He said OK, but it was important I lifted them. I put a lot of work into the opening presentation which I based around the ten policy and communications questions I felt most urgently needed answering.

Andrew Adonis went through where we were going on policy. He felt we had only laid the foundations and a lot of the big questions were still being ducked. Then Jeremy on some of the big spending issues coming up, where he gave full vent to his and TB's concerns over the money going on tax credits. He said the Treasury basically misled us about the cost of the tax credit schemes. He felt that if we were really serious about investment delivering world-class public services we would need a 10p rise on the basic rate to deliver £17 billion for health, £10bn for education, £4bn for transport, £2bn for crime. If anything these were conservative assessments, he said.

Michael Barber went through how his Delivery Unit intended to work, and was impressive. Robert [Hill] did party management, then Anji his diary. The nub of the discussion that followed showed up that both in terms of investment and reform, we didn't have a strong enough forward narrative. TB felt even if we did the things we planned to, he was not convinced it was sufficient to deliver what we wanted, but even with what we were talking about he would find it hard to take the party with him.

Andrew A felt on higher education, we did have the right programme but shared TB's assessment that on schools and hospitals, what we were doing was necessary but insufficient. Geoff Mulgan [policy and strategy adviser] said we had not yet squared the circle of how to make step changes without higher taxation. Barber said he was confident we would have significantly higher results for fourteen-year-olds and far more successful schools. Jeremy kept coming back to earth by saying just how much money we needed. TB said there was insufficient sense of the consumer coming first. Reform had to be based around national standards, accountability in the system, competition in provision. The money alone was not going to transform public services in the way we wanted and TB in particular felt the reform programme wasn't radical enough. He would only be happy with a genuine transformation of public services.

We had a long argument on education and there was a clear divide between me, Sally, Fiona, David Hanson and RH in what I described as the Labour camp while TB, Andrew A, Jonathan and Jeremy were on a very different agenda. Jeremy was at one point arguing for vouchers. I asked TB and AA to persuade me that choice would drive up standards for all, said that for most people it was meaningless and for some meant exclusion. TB said at one point I was beginning to sound like [former Labour deputy leader] Roy Hattersley.

The other thing that was apparent through the day was that on virtually all of these issues – Europe, public services, tax credits – TB felt GB to be in a different place. He said we were going to go through some very choppy waters. On the PPP row, he felt we had to reshape it to be about social justice and opportunity. At least it had been a proper discussion and at the end TB commissioned maybe ten different papers and various projects. He said he intended to do his own strategy paper while he also wanted Number 10 to do an audit of public service spending. He said he had underestimated the ability of the Labour Party not to be happy about winning, to want to take victory and from it sow the seeds of defeat. There was enough in the discussion to make me fear that the [Labour] conference speech would be a bigger nightmare than usual.

After lunch, TB said there were a lot of people in the party who basically don't like New Labour. But we cannot run the second term like the first. He felt we had to recast public service reform as a social justice agenda. Sally felt the language was still them and us. Fiona, Robert and I all argued that it wasn't clear what we were saying. TB felt the party and the unions were going to be very difficult, economic circumstances were going to be difficult and we could easily be fifteen points behind within a year. But he said there was no point being in government unless we used it to make real change and the two most important areas were public services and Europe. He felt we had to change the terms of debate on Europe.

He said he wasn't interested in cautious government. He wanted more radical thinking on public services. He wanted a better assessment on where to get savings. He wanted us to think about how we remade the New Labour argument again. He wanted to lead personally on Africa and the environment. And he wanted a new approach on diversity, work/life balance and sport. I got back to Number 10 for a session with all my staff to go through some of the arguments.

Peter H asked if today had pushed me further out or pulled me further in. I didn't know the answer.

TB called later to say he wanted me to go with him to Hull tomorrow and for the meeting with Bertie on Friday, but I had fixed all my August planning meetings for the next forty-eight hours. He said there was a fair chance he would be fighting for his political life quite soon, and GB was limbering up. He felt our discussions had shown where the divides would come but he felt this was the time to go more New Labour, not less.

Thursday, July 26

In for a meeting on Europe with Jack S, which he chaired really well. He seemed to be settling in well. He and I had a chat about his speech tomorrow, where I know TB was worried he would go over the top in backing Jospin or in saying he was relaxed about the EU constitution. Ian McCartney [pensions minister] popped in to tell me about a session he had had with GB, who was clearly chatting him up, and after a while Ian asked him what he wanted and whether he was asking him to join 'your little group that John Healey [newly appointed minister, previously Brown's parliamentary private secretary] chairs to boost your operation', to which GB replied 'I don't know what you're talking about.' Ian said it was all too obvious.

Robert Lacey [historian and author] came in for a chat on his book on the Royals [*Royal: Her Majesty Queen Elizabeth II*], which [Sir] Robin Janvrin [private secretary to the Queen] had asked me to help with. I had lunch at the Savoy with Phil Webster [*Times*] and Charles Reiss [*Evening Standard*]. Charles was adamant we'd had it on the Tube. Phil was probing mainly on the euro and on my role. I got back for a meeting with the education team on the [schools] White Paper which was going to be difficult, and I didn't feel they had a proper handle on it yet.

Friday, July 27

Meeting with Sue Jenkins [deputy head, GICS], who said that to a lot of people in the system I was this huge mythological figure and we had to do more to break that down for people. She said it was ironic the people who ended up working for me seemed to like it and yet out there there was still quite a fear about coming to Number 10. She said that when her office had taken a call this morning for her to come over, there was a palpable sense of fear around the place. It may be bizarre to me, she said, but I had to understand that. She was keen to bring on the next generation and wanted me out there talking to them more.

July '01: Time for more New Labour, not less

Saturday, July 28

The kids had been up seeing Dad and felt he had been looking worse. They thought I should go up to see him. My only worry was if he took the message from that that we basically thought he was on the way out. In the end I went up, and was glad I did. He was shaky on his legs, found it hard to keep his eyes open and his upper arms were wasting. But he was totally compos mentis. TB called just as I arrived, was totally frank re GB, said it had all the feel of a Greek tragedy, and it was getting worse and worse. We agreed that TB and GB united could be a pretty formidable narrative for the second term, but he said there were moments recently when he had been really worried about him, and there was something ridiculous about his demands that he step aside and let him take over. It wasn't just that it was so unreasonable, given we had just won the election, but it made him worry if in fact he was suited to the top job.

TB had just done the National Policy Forum and said there was definitely a different mood and that some of it was orchestrated and deliberate. He said it was clear a lot of the angst and the anger was about him. I said it's because people feel that you feel you somehow own the party and can do whatever you want and if they don't like it, tough. That's why GB has such a purchase, because they feel he can be a check. If you go back to our awayday discussion, it's extraordinary how many of our problems go back to that same thing – TB/GB. Europe, public services, general positioning, his image. TB felt he put us slightly in the wrong place all the time. When I told Fiona, she said it was all part of TB's emotional blackmail, trying to give me things to motivate me. But it was the first time he had been so absolutely frank, and on a mobile phone. He felt GB was undermining him at every turn, and it was going to have to be brought to a head. We had a very nice party for Calum's birthday, most of it out on the street.

Sunday, July 29

TB and CB both called on the way to the airport [for official visits to Brazil and Argentina, before holidaying in Mexico]. TB was really seized of the GB situation, said it was ugly and he needed to reflect very carefully. He said it was important I had a proper rest. Cherie spoke to Fiona and said TB was worried about me, and Fiona told her I had been having second thoughts. Fiona had picked up that [BBC journalist James] Naughtie's book [*The Rivals: The Intimate Story of a Political Marriage*, on the relationship between Blair and Brown] was going to say that Cherie was the real anti-Gordon force in Number 10. It was incredibly hot and I had a terrific run with Rory. The *Sunday Telegraph* was chasing some story about my salary.

Monday, July 30

TB called from Brazil, said he had been thinking really hard about GB, felt that there was a case for sacking him at some point. It had to be brought to a head, because a prime minister could not and should not tolerate the constant undermining. He wasn't sure what GB would do if he was out in the cold, and how he would handle it. He said Sue Nye told Anji that GB had a few drinks one night and had said TB was never going to hand over so he would have to make him. TB was doing a speech out in São Paolo with quite a tough economic reform message, which would get a fair bit of play here as well.[1]

I had a session with JP on August. He clearly had doubts about Charles [Clarke], felt he was too much of a TB shadow. I felt Charles had brought a breath of fresh air to things and although he sometimes talked a good game, he was generally a good thing. JP was as ever raging at the press. I felt he needed to make a couple of serious speeches on the [public service] reform agenda before the TUC. He said the unions were really getting ready to give TB a bloody nose.

Tuesday, July 31, and August holiday

The holiday started in the Alps where we stayed with Terri Taverner [friend] for a day or two on the way down to Puyméras. Neil and Glenys had taken the house at the end of our road, along with Steve [Kinnock] and Helle [his wife] and the kids. Chris Meyer and his wife [Catherine] popped over one day and I felt they were a bit over-probing on the TB/GB situation, and that she in particular was far too indiscreet. He was raging about Michael Levy, felt it was embarrassing to have him anywhere near foreign policy. Neil and Glenys were in much better form than previous years, perhaps in part because I had made it clear I didn't want to spend the whole time talking about politics. I wanted to have a couple of weeks to think about things and then a third week to decide. I went on a few runs with Steve who was

[1] Blair drew comparisons between the British and Brazilian governments, saying both were 'tackling many of the same challenges. Promoting both economic dynamism and social justice. Reforming the education system so that all children have the same chances in life. Modernising the health care system so that it provides choice and high quality care to everyone . . . progressive governments in Europe and Latin America are responding to the challenges of globalisation not by resisting change, but by pushing ahead with economic reform.'

fascinating on what it had been like when his dad had been leader and getting all the stick that he did, and Steve had often felt Neil had never really been there, and only now had he come to terms with the fact that he had had one of those jobs where it was difficult just to be there. He felt it was the same for me, but was amazed how well I seemed to get on with the kids, particularly the boys who had at least known something else, whereas Grace never had.

It was incredibly hot part of the time and we had the World Athletics Championships [in Edmonton, Canada] on TV to keep me and the boys occupied during the day and we were out pretty much every night. I was out running most days but just couldn't get my head straight as to what I wanted to do. Fiona was convinced that I was clinically depressed again. The kids were brilliant but I was definitely worried about the old demons coming back, and about my falling off the wagon.

I'd never drunk enough to be 'drunk' but I had been testing myself with it a bit. Interesting that this is the first time I've actually put anything in here about it. Maybe denial, don't know. Fiona seemed to think it was no real problem, provided she knew, and provided I drank no more than she did, which was never more than a glass or two at dinner. I had a chat with Neil about it. He felt it was OK too but I had to watch out. I can't remember the first time I actually had a drink. I can remember having a couple on the boat coming back from the Dome on Millennium night. But that wasn't the first time, I know that. As I went so long without – thirteen, fourteen years – you'd think I would remember. I can't. I remember having a drink on one of the EU trips, Germany I think, I remember being worried about it, so stopped again. But this holiday I was drinking more, not every day, far from it, and never a lot. But I must be worried, or else I would have recorded it before, I think.

It must be part related to the mood too, so I knew I needed to watch it. Funnily enough, on one of the calls, when I was at the bar, TB was asking how I was feeling, and I said OK but he could tell not, and he said 'Thank God there's no danger of you hitting the bottle – now that really would freak me out.' I said to Fiona partly it was a desire to feel 'normal' but I really did not want to get into the habit. I said she would have to keep an eye on it, as would I. Only she and the kids, and now Neil and Glenys, Philip and Gail, knew that I'd had these mild falls off the wagon. It wasn't a great sign, and yet it was interesting that I had no sense I was going to go off on a great bender.

There was a paradox in Fiona's position on the job. On the one hand, she was desperate for us to leave, but on the other she said it wasn't possible for me to leave straight away because it would leave them in such difficulties. I had a couple of long conversations with TB and said there were really three bottom lines for me. First, I had to get a better work/family balance. Second, there had to be a recalibration of the politics in the building, in particular on policy where David M had gone and Andrew A had moved things to the right. And third, the GB situation had to be sorted because a big part of the nightmare was constantly having to pick up the pieces from that. On the politics, he clearly had decided he wanted Sally M back in a central position and was prepared to let Anji go. On the conference speech, he felt it had to be US enterprise plus European social justice, but I felt it could be simpler than that, economy the rock, public service investment and reform what sets us apart from the Tories, big and positive on Europe. It was the same old thing really, and probably explained why I was demotivated.

Neil and Glenys were both adamant I couldn't leave, that it would be too powerful a political signal and damaging. Philip and Gail felt the same, though Philip was honest enough to admit his big worry was that he would have nobody there to work through. TB said he felt we had both been a bit distracted after the election, him because he felt GB had been terrorising, me because of all the *Peyton Place* stuff. He said I had not helped by being so down, that I was one of the few people in the building who could lead people and get them up and when I was down, the building went down.

By the end of the holiday, I felt I was in a better place. We had the Goulds there for a while and the kids were having a great time. On the drive back, it was pretty clear that Fiona had basically had it with TB, she had been pretty alarmed by the [Chequers awayday] discussion on public services. She also felt that I still never really involved or consulted her, and that the whole political process was making me depressed and harder to get to. She said it was fine if I stayed, but she couldn't pretend her heart was in it.

Thursday, August 20

I went in to catch up on things. Our new offices in Number 12 were up and running and things seemed to be fine there.[1] TB called as he was leaving France [second leg of his holiday] to say we should have dinner tonight. He had spoken to Anji and seemed to have told her

[1] Campbell's team had moved into offices on the ground floor of 12 Downing Street, traditionally the offices of the government chief whip.

that maybe she could go. She had every right to be angry in that she had wanted to go and he had made her stay. I was beginning to feel the same way. He went over the problems – 1. public services, whether we could find the extra money that was needed, whether we could develop a more radical approach; 2. Europe, where he felt the economics were difficult and GB making them more so; 3. the office and our political operation; 4. GB.

He still believed there was a lot of good in GB, and that the best thing was if they worked together. But he was in no doubt he had been responsible for a lot of the malign stuff after the election. And most reasonable people would think it extraordinary that he had basically been asking for a date for TB's departure as soon as the election was over. TB insisted GB was not working with him properly, had told him that when they worked together, GB was never off the phone, but all that had stopped. TB had directly accused him of building up an operation designed to undermine him. GB had said 'Well give me a date,' to which TB had said he would not be bullied out of the job. He got back later and was on very good form after his holiday, said he was clearer about what we needed to do. We went in for dinner and Fiona gave him a very hard time, said he didn't get the party, and they basically felt he had no time for them at all. She told me later she felt she didn't have a serious job and it would be better if she left and I stayed.

TB felt he needed to bring the GB situation to a head within six months to a year. If things didn't improve, he would ask him to move and if he refused, he would have to go. But he said a wounded GB on the back benches would be very, very dangerous. Meanwhile, we would have to build up the other contenders. He said GB had gone totally ballistic about a briefing I did during the election to the effect that Blunkett had been a real hit. He said he still went on, on a regular basis, about 'psychological flaws'. I said can you tell me why you are asking me to work flat out again to get to a position where you hand the premiership on a plate to someone you are describing in these terms? Cherie said if the party and the public knew how GB treated TB, they would be horrified. I felt that eventually TB would end up in a position of not wanting to endorse GB.

TB was clearly worried about just how aggressive Fiona was with him. It was obviously personal now as well as political. She admitted as much on the way home, said she felt they had taken so much out of us and still didn't actually appreciate what we did. I think they did, or at least he did, but what she really didn't like was the job she was doing. TB was clear he was not going to let the Labour Party lapse back to some kind of 60s' old-style social democracy. He said he was a progressive, centre-left politician but he felt that left to its own devices, the party would not make enough change, would think it was all about money, didn't like the difficult reforms that went with it. He said he had a lot of experience of the Labour Party and too often its instincts would go to a lowest common denominator. He said people in the party talked about Neil as having done a great job and in many ways he did, but I'm not sure he would have done some of the really difficult things that we need to do. He was very tanned, and pretty relaxed, but there was definitely a greater steeliness than in the weeks leading up to the holiday.

Cherie asked me as we left whether I was up for it and would see it through and I said probably, but I had to have those three bottom lines met. TB said at one point that it could be some people don't want to see it through to the end because the end is always inevitable. He said this was a good government and he felt he was a good prime minister. That we had the chance for this to be a great government and the next term would decide it. I felt that unless he sorted the GB situation, and unless we started defining ourselves more clearly against our own values rather than through the prism of our opponents, it would be a struggle.

Friday, August 31

Cherie called for Fiona and asked me how I felt yesterday had gone. I said fine but he did have to listen. Fiona was very out of sorts and I felt in part had taken years of anger and frustration with me out on him. I was a bit down that I had taken a month to decide once and for all whether to stay or go, and I was still unsettled.

Saturday, September 1

I took the boys up to Mum and Dad's. Dad was looking a bit better but said that the bits were beginning to fall off. TB called half a dozen times or so, mainly about the public service agenda but also about how to play the Tories in the pre-conference season. I was conscious of the fact that when the phone went, and it was the Number 10 switchboard, I felt my spirits fall a bit. I was pretty clear in my own mind that I wanted more time with family and was not convinced that was compatible with the job. England beat Germany 5-1 in Munich, which would really lift the national mood, which currently was driven with endless crap in the media on teacher shortages, NHS in crisis, asylum.

Sunday, September 2

TB called after *Frost* and was much more interested in how IDS had got on than Estelle [Morris]. He was still identifying himself far too much vis-à-vis the Tories, rather than his own vision and plans. He was sorting out Sally M's return and it was ridiculous really, everything that we had gone through to end up pretty much where everyone had wanted to start. Sally called and told me she couldn't get TB to see why the party felt like it did about Andrew A, compared to David M. I took the boys to Bradford vs Burnley, 3-2 to us, great win.

Monday, September 3

I had a sleepless night, which felt a little bit more than first-day-back blues. At his morning meeting, TB was focusing on the Lib Dems, saying how they positioned themselves after the Tory leadership would present an opportunity for us. If they rejected co-operation, he felt that would be a mistake on their part, and if they ended up positioning themselves to the left of us, he felt long term that would help us too. But I was worried they would successfully position themselves as the public service investment party ahead of us.

He seemed to be more open to an argument about part election of the Lords. He was seized about our seeming inability to get decent coverage for the good things happening in public services. Tom Kelly did the 11, and was savaged on asylum. I spoke to DB about going up. I had lunch with Max Hastings [editor, *Evening Standard*] at Wiltons but was conscious of not being on form at all. I think maybe I'd just had enough of talking to these people. I bumped into Gordon coming down the corridor to the Cabinet Room. 'Hello Gordon, how are you?' 'Fine.' And on he went.

Tuesday, September 4

Asylum was grim but Blunkett did pretty well on the media. We had a big problem on public services more generally with no real buy-in for the idea of improvement. TB wanted to do an article in *The Times*. Peter H and I rewrote Andrew's draft but I was still lacking energy and drive. I chaired the morning meeting, mainly asylum and schools. I had a session with TB on the article. He was very up, in part because Jack had indicated he was pro euro. I had a good meeting with David Triesman. He seemed to know what he was talking about, and I thought he had a good political feel. He had been having real problems with attacks by anti-Semites on his home near us. I felt basically he would be a good thing.

Cherie called wanting me to demand a correction and apology

from the *Sun* re [columnist Richard] Littlejohn's piece on the Oratory [school attended by Euan and Nicholas Blair], which was pretty vicious. I had a meeting with Gus Macdonald, who seemed a bit dislocated, struggling to work out exactly what he was meant to be doing. I said he needed to build up his public profile, which would help with internal clout at the centre. He was excellent in many ways, but obviously wanted clear understanding of what he was meant to be about. TB saw Charles Kennedy who was muttering more loudly about pulling out of the JCC [Joint Consultative Committee on policy, set up by Blair and Paddy Ashdown in 1997].

Wednesday, September 5

The *Sun* apologised and agreed to a donation to charity. The education White Paper coverage was all in the wrong place, too much focus on the private sector, not enough on standards. TB was pleased with the *Times* article in the end but that was a fairly solitary view. Most people thought it was crap, and I wished we hadn't done it at all. I spoke to Estelle before her interviews, suggested she park private sector stuff. I was working on preparation for the Cabinet awayday. TB had produced a note that was pretty tired, just reheating the old Third Way stuff, not the fresh intellectual stimulus he usually brings after a long holiday. I had a session with Steve Byers who said GB was making both the Tube and Railtrack more difficult. I was also having to resolve one of those awful 'who sits where' disputes between some of the staff.

Thursday, September 6

Another internal awayday at Chequers, this time with Charles C. Fiona, PH and I drove down together and it was an odd feeling in that we were basically arguing against TB. I still felt his note was rather tired and I had written a response about the need for reassertion of basic beliefs and values, that we had lost the sense of mission and conviction. We needed to bring out more the different parts to his leadership and personality – strong party leader, strong international leader, courageous moderniser, family man, Christian socialist. We weren't really motoring on any of these with the exception of moderniser. His main fear was whether we really had the structures and the changes planned that would actually deliver the better public services. He was still worried that even if Michael Barber's changes went through, and even if all the targets were met, would that actually deliver the first-class public services we had talked of. His approach though was still very top down. Wendy Thompson was

September '01: Sun apologises over vicious piece

there for her first meeting of this sort and I sensed that was her basic feeling.

We had a pretty desultory discussion on Europe, Stephen Wall made clear he wasn't that confident about us getting our way. He was very down on Schroeder and Jospin. I felt that the conviction I talked about required that he did something to take us forward on the euro and he was not sure he wanted to fight on that front as well as public services right now. Stephen said the euro was 'condemned to succeed'. TB felt sure Schroeder wanted us in and would in many ways prefer to be dealing with us, but he was convinced the French basically saw us as a rival. Jeremy was pretty sure the economics wouldn't work out anyway. Jeremy had done a very interesting paper on tax and spend. Nearly all of the plans we were talking of would require big money, maybe £13bn or more, so it was pretty clear we would have to raise taxes. GB as ever was hanging over the conversation. TB asked us all to hand back the Jeremy paper. Geoff Mulgan felt there was a big gap between rhetoric and policy on the public services. TB felt in the first term we were very bureaucratic and interventionist and we now had to open up the system.

Over lunch, I had a read of [Andrew] Rawnsley's latest TB/GB split stuff. Also *The Times* had done a piece on my [office] move to Number 12, which was OK. Then a discussion of the party and policy, Andrew Adonis setting out the big decisions ahead, Charles C on his ideas for revitalising the party, Robert Hill on what he called 'quick wins'. It was an OK discussion but didn't exactly leave you with fire in your belly. Peter H and I left to work on the TUC speech. Both of us felt TB had looked a bit out of touch and isolated. Charles had said a lot of ministers didn't really know where he was. He said there was no clarity on the public/private question. Sally felt we needed a clearer definition of why we were in government. First term was about undoing. What is the big forward positive message? Both TB and Charles were pretty down on the Civil Service but Andrew said they were only as good as their ministers. Geoff Mulgan said the problem was the Civil Service didn't understand the basic principles of reform. Jeremy H said it was two years into Thatcher's second term before the Civil Service got it. Fiona felt we weren't doing enough on family/work balance.

Friday, September 7

TB was up north. I took Grace to school, then in to spend God knows how many hours listening to people whingeing about where their fucking desks were. There were a few stories about the office move, including the *Telegraph* implying I lived in Number 12. Charles Moore agreed to take a letter correcting it. We got the Oakington verdict[1] which was a bit of a disaster, and with [asylum seeker] figures coming next week it would be worse than ever. Asylum was really becoming a big problem again.

TB did a visit in Hartlepool where he played the guitar, which got loads of coverage through the day. I did a note for him on the TUC speech, the need to do more serious stuff on the economy and address their worries on [the decline of the] manufacturing industry. I felt a speech that set out the economic fundamentals, the contours on public service reform and with a strong section on Europe would be fine.

Saturday, September 8

There was a real sense of build-up to the TUC, the media wanting to crank it up as a big drama. There was a bit of interest in Naughtie's book on TB and GB, *The Rivals*. It was pretty poor and not very revelatory. I took Rory up to Manchester for the Everton match, worked on the TUC speech on the way up. Had lunch with [Manchester United chairman Sir] Roland Smith and chatted at half-time to Ulrika Jonsson, Angus Deayton and Richard Wilson [celebrities]. TB was really focused now on the TUC and the *Guardian* interview we were planning. Roland and his wife Joan said they thought we were basically in forever if the Tories went for Duncan Smith as leader. I briefly saw Alex afterwards who said he hoped Fiona had forgiven him for telling me I'd be mad to leave. I was home as the papers arrived. Total shit as usual. Did a bit more on the speech.

Sunday, September 9

I did a conference call with Godric et al. but the only thing to worry about was getting the TUC speech in the right place. They were really building it up now to be a bad day for him. He sent through a new version which had taken in a lot of the stuff I put through on Friday.

Monday, September 10

The unions were really cranking things up in advance of tomorrow. Added to which, there was a bit of bad news on the economy around, problems on asylum, transport, teacher shortages. TB was a bit on

---

[1] The High Court had found in favour of four Iraqi Kurds who had complained that their detention at the Oakington Reception Centre for up to ten days was a breach of Article Five of the Human Rights Convention.

the back foot in his *Guardian* interview. Both Charles C and I said to him that we felt he needed much greater clarity on some of the questions that were causing neuralgia. He said he didn't want to be ruling out things prematurely. On asylum, we seemed pretty hopeless at the moment. I had a meeting with Charles and Hilary Armstrong about party conference and also how to get the dividing lines in the right place.

I left with TB for the *Guardian*. He did OK, though he couldn't hide his irritation at points, e.g. when they tried to get him going about McDonald's [fast-food chain] sponsoring a reception [at Labour Party conference]. On most of the difficult stuff, he stuck to his guns without being too provocative. We got back to the office for a meeting on Wembley [being redeveloped as a national stadium]. TB's basic view was that we probably did need a national stadium but we should be careful about financing it beyond vital infrastructure and transport links.

Tuesday, September 11

I woke up to the usual blah on the radio about TB and the TUC speech, all the old BBC clichés about us and the unions, the only new thing GMB ads asking if you trust TB not to privatise the NHS. Peter H and I went up to the flat. TB had done a good section on public-private, an effective hit back at the John Edmonds line. With the economy, public services, Europe/euro and a bit on asylum which was really worrying, we had a proper speech. We sharpened it and honed it a bit. He was furious at the GMB ads, said he intended to give Edmonds a real hammering. We finished it on the train, were met and driven to the hotel. We were there, up at the top of the hotel putting the finishing touches to the speech, when the attacks on the New York Twin Towers began.

Godric was watching in the little room where the Garden Room girl had set up, came up to the top of the little staircase leading to the bit where TB and I were working, and signalled for me to go down. It was all a bit chaotic, with the TV people going into their usual breathless breaking-news mode, but it was clearly something way out of the ordinary. I went upstairs, turned on the TV and said to TB he ought to watch it. It was now even clearer than just a few moments ago just how massive an event this was. It was also one that was going to have pretty immediate implications for us too. We didn't watch the TV that long, but long enough for TB to reach the judgement about just how massive an event this was in its impact and implications. It's possible we were talking about thousands dead.

We would also have to make immediate judgements about buildings and institutions to protect here. TB was straight on to the diplomatic side as well, said that we had to help the US, that they could not go it all on their own, that they felt beleaguered and that this would be tantamount to a military attack in their minds. We had to decide whether we should cancel the speech.

There was always a moment in these terrorist outrages where governments said we must not let the terrorists change what we do, but it was meaningless. Of course they changed what we did. At first, we felt it best to go ahead with the speech but by the time we were leaving for the venue, the Towers were actually collapsing. The scale of the horror and the damage was increasing all the time and it was perfectly obvious he couldn't do the speech. We went over to the conference centre, where TB broke the news to [John] Monks [TUC general secretary] and Brendan Barber [Monks' deputy] that he intended to go on, say a few words, but then we would have to head back to London. We would issue the text but he would not deliver the speech. John Monks said to me that it's on days like this that you realise just how big his job is. TB's mind was whirring with it. His brief statement to the TUC went down well, far better than his speech would have done.[1] We walked back to the hotel, both of us conscious there seemed to be a lot more security around. We arranged a series of conference calls through Jonathan with Jack S, Geoff Hoon, David B. We asked Richard Wilson to fix a Cobra meeting as soon as we got back.

We set off for Brighton station. He said the consequences of this were enormous. On the train he was subdued, though we did raise a smile when someone said it was the first and last time he would get a standing ovation from the TUC. Robert Hill was listening to the radio on his earpiece and filling us in every now and then. TB asked for a pad and started to write down some of the issues we would have to address when we got back. He said the big fear was terrorists capable of this getting in league with rogue states that would help them. He'd been going on about [Osama] Bin Laden for a while because there had been so much intelligence about him and al-Qaeda. He wanted to commission proper reports on OBL and all the other terror groups. He made a note of the need to reach out to the British

[1] Blair told trade union delegates 'This mass terrorism is the new evil in our world today. It is perpetrated by fanatics who are utterly indifferent to the sanctity of human life and we, the democracies of this world, are going to have to come together to fight it together and eradicate this evil completely from our world.'

Muslim community who would fear a backlash if this was Bin Laden. Everyone seemed convinced it couldn't be anyone else.

We got back and before Cobra he was briefed by Stephen Lander [director general of MI5], John Scarlett [chair of the Joint Intelligence Committee], RW. DTLR [Department of Transport, Local Government and the Regions] had closed airspace over London. There had been special security put around the Stock Exchange and Canary Wharf. The general security alert had been raised to Amber. Three hundred companies were being contacted to be given advice. Scarlett said OBL and his people were the only ones with the capability to do this. Neither he nor Lander believed other governments were involved. TB said we needed a command paper of who they are, why they are, what they do, how they do it. He said at the diplomatic level he felt the US would feel beleaguered and angry because there was so much anti-Americanism around. Lander felt the pressure on the Americans to respond quickly, even immediately, would be enormous. Afghanistan was the obvious place. Iraq, Libya, Iran, the Americans will be trying to find out if they helped in this. He said there were a lot of people sympathetic to Bin Laden, more than we realised. TB said they will move straight away to the international community and their response. If I were Bush, I would demand the Taliban deliver him up.

Scarlett and Lander were both pretty impressive, didn't mess about, thought about what they said, and said what they thought. Scarlett said this was less about technology than it was about skill and nerve. Lander said this was a logical step up from the car bomb. Turning a plane into a bomb and destroying one of the great symbols of America takes some doing but they have done it and they have been able to do it because they have any number of terrorists prepared to kill themselves. TB's immediate concern, apart from the obvious logistical steps we had to take, was that Bush would be put under enormous pressure to do something irresponsible. If America heard the general world view develop that this happened because Bush was more isolationist, there would be a reaction. He felt we had to take a lead in mobilising diplomatic solidarity in the rest of the G8 and the EU. We had to start shaping an international agenda to fill the vacuum. He spoke to Schroeder, who wanted a G8 meeting, Chirac and Jospin, who were not so sure, and then Putin, who had a real 'I told you so' tone, said he had been warning us about Islamic fundamentalism.

TB and I both pressed Scarlett and Lander on why they were so sure there were no rogue governments involved in this. They said because Bin Laden was able to do it himself and that suited his purposes better. We all trooped over to the Cobra meeting, which was a bit ragged, but that was to be expected given what people were having to deal with. There were contingency measures that had gone into effect. Private flights had been stopped. There were no commercial flights to go over the centre of London. All small-plane flights were being grounded unless they had specific clearance. Security was being stepped up around financial centres and major computer sites. The Met [police] were raising numbers on visible patrols, particularly at Canary Wharf, Heathrow and in the North London Jewish areas. We had upped protection on our premises in the Middle East. There was talk of moving some of the planes based at RAF Leuchars to London in the event of a hijack. Jack S said the EU GAC [European General Affairs and External Relations Council] was planning to meet. Geoff Hoon gave a briefing on what troops were where in the Middle East.

TB did a very good summing-up, first going through all the different measures that I should brief, then on the specific reports he wanted to commission, then on the importance of a diplomatic strategy to support the US. He said they would feel beleaguered and all the tensions that had been apparent before would now become more open, whatever the warm words around the world. He asked Jack and Geoff to come through to Number 10, said it was vital that we worked up an international agenda that went beyond the US just hitting Afghanistan. He felt NMD would quickly rise up the agenda.

He intended to say to Bush that he should deliver an ultimatum to the Taliban to hand over Bin Laden and his people and then hit them if it didn't happen. He had been reading the Koran over the summer. [The Prophet] Mohammed had lost battles but there was a belief that if you died in the cause that you believed in then you went straight to heaven. That was a very, very powerful thing to work against. TB's public words were very much in total support of the US. He said this was going to be a nightmare, as big and as bad as any we had endured. It was interesting that he had not asked GB to come back for the smaller meeting. I asked him why and he said because in their recent discussions he had been monosyllabic. The Israelis were making massive attacks on the terror groups. TB said we were going to have to work exceptionally hard on the international response. Bush was getting it in the neck for not being in Washington.

Everyone was in bed when I finally got home, and Fiona had fallen asleep watching it all on the TV. I did a call with Jonathan to go over how much we would need to kick out of the diary in the coming days. Pretty much all of it, at least for a while. Jonathan said the Americans would be unlikely to let Bush travel – it was a bit much that he couldn't even go to his own capital – but the fallout from this

September '01: TB talks of worst nightmare

was going to need an awful lot of diplomatic activity. I think we're going to be seeing a lot of the insides of planes, he said.

I turned off the TV in the bedroom and went downstairs to channel-hop while writing it all up. The TUC felt a bloody age ago. Some of the footage of the aftermath, clouds of dust and debris literally rolling down streets, was extraordinary. So were the eyewitness accounts. Gut-wrenching. What was amazing about this was that people like Bush, TB, Chirac and the rest were having to react and respond in exactly the same time frame, and with pretty much only the same knowledge of the incident as people watching on TV. The difference was they were going to have to take some huge decisions about it too.

To be continued.

Index

128, 129–30, 152; and Ladbroke Grove rail crash 126, 129; would like to have been Jesus! 128; a further Cabinet reshuffle 128–9, 130, 131–2; at Tampere summit 136–8, 147–8; meets Jiang Zemin 142; strained relations with Prince Charles 143–4, 151–2; and beef ban 136–7, 145, 152, 153, 157, 158, 180–81; at CHOGM in South Africa 158–60; criticised by AC 158–9, 160, 167–8; and NI 159; and Mugabe 159, 160; clashes with GB over public spending 164, 167, 174; and publicity over baby 163, 164, 165; at Florence seminar 165–7; PMQs 167–8, 174; at Anglo-French summit 168–9; hosts dinner for General Clark 171; opposes withholding tax 172, 178, 179, 180, 182; and Woodward's defection 175, 176–7, 186, 188, 190; tours the North West 176, 178–80; and Cockerell's filming 180 (see Cockerell, Michael); at Helsinki summit 181–4; visits the homeless 187; and first public handshake with Sinn Fein 188; furious at GB's writing off of Third World debt 189, 190, 191; and 'Operation Myopia' 113 and n, 179, 191; his pre-Millennium speech 193; and problems with London Eye 193, 194; Millennium Eve 195–6, 197

January–August 2000
worries about Dome 199–200; Portuguese holiday 200, 201–2, 204; worried about GB and the flat 200, 201, 202, 203; wants to push for reform 204–5; dinner with GB 205–6, 208; speaks to Winston re NHS remarks 209, 210; *Frost* interview 207, 210, 212; heckled at Institute of Education 213; has minor car-crash 217; 'very down' 217; compared with Thatcher 217, 218; tells Hague to get a grip on his party 219; at Davos 221; in BBC documentary 222; NFU speech 223, 224–5; website and webcasts 225, 232, 234, 240, 251; and NI 225, 226, 228, 232, 233–4, 237, 293, 301, 302–4, 310–11; visits West Country and Wales 225–7; Blackpool speech 228; and Stansted hijackers 231; and Mo Mowlam (q.v.) 231, 232, 235; has ministers meeting 235; disastrous dinner with GB 237; furious with JS and Mo 237–8; at Windsor banquet 238; PMQs 238, 295; and bad polls 243–4; GM food article seen as U-turn 246, 247; gives Labour Party centenary speech 245–7; heckled at road safety event 249–50; and Clare Short (q.v.) 252–3; and ex-nanny's revelations 253–5, 257, 259, 260; caves in to Schroeder re IMF post 257; and Scottish Labour Party 257, 258–9; in Russia with Putin (q.v.) 260–62; and BMW/Rover 265, 266, 281, 282; and NHS 265, 266, 267, 268, 269, 274, 275, 284–5; waffly on *Today* 270; at Lisbon European Council 271, 272–3, 275; with Schroeder at Königswinter Conference

274; and GB and 'Britishness' speech 274, 275; complacent and remote 280–81; and Hague 281–2; in Wales 284–5; plays football with AC and the boys 298; and London riots 299; and local elections 289, 300, 301, 302; argues with GB over reform 303, 304; speaks to Livingstone 304; and Mo Mowlam 305, 306, 310, 360; and Rover deal 307–8; in front of the camera 306–7; satirised by Bremner 308; at PMQs 309; irritates AC 312, 313, 315; and 'the bigger picture' 316; on TBWA brainstorming sessions 318; and Leo's birth 318, 319, 320; on lack of communication 320, 339; sets out washing-line theory 322, 380; never wrong 322, 324 ; policy differences with GB 323–5, 31; Women's Institute speech 323, 332–4, 335, 336–7, 338–9, 340; worn out 345, 346; is compared to Major 346; at Feira European Council meeting 346, 347, 348–9; and GB/PM relations 345, 347, 356; clashes with JS 345–6; tries to get CSR discussion with GB 349–50; human genome speech 354; at *Sun* lunch 355; and PM's AV speech 355, 356; fails to back AC 356, 358; plans for reshuffle 357, 362; Tübingen speech 356, 357, 358; bad at PMQs 363; and Euan's arrest 363, 364, 365, 366, 374; at black churches conference in Brighton 364; on *Question Time* 364–5; stops for a pint 365; on the economy 368; dinner with *Mail* 369; his notes leaked 369, 370, 371; at Tokyo G8 372–6; and Leo's christening 378, 379, 380; and GB's wedding 381; on holiday 382, 383, 384; and Euan and the press 382

August–December 2000
'in a different position' in politics 385; backs Scottish Labour MP over exams crisis 386; at Balmoral 387; further problems with Mo Mowlam 387–8, 390; in USA 389–92; at UN and P5 meeting 391–2; and freeing of Sierra Leone hostages 393; and fuel crisis 393–401 *passim*, 404; at GB's post-wedding party 403; and Ecclestone 403, 405; worried about GB 405, 406; felt to be arrogant and out of touch 406; at Brighton conference 406–11; his conference speech 382–3, 384–5, 401, 402, 403, 406–8; and the fall of Milosevic 414; his speech to Polish Stock Exchange 412–13, 414, 415–16; and pictures of Leo 422; at Biarritz European Council 422, 423–4; tired and grey at Police Federation event 428; at DD's funeral 428–9; press interview on plane to Korea 429–30; ASEM speech 430; 'becalmed' 433; environment speech 433 *and n*; and AC's note on campaign and communications problems 434–5, 436; distracted at Cabinet 435; on political strategy 435; and Corbett 436–7; on fuel tax cuts 437, 442; and Spanish protests over HMS

677 ; has session with Prince Charles on rural issues 677; and discussions at Chequers 678–80; worried about JS's speech on Europe 680; worried about GB 681, 682, 684, 685; and National Policy Forum 681; on official visits in South America 681, 682; holidays in Mexico 681; phonecalls to AC 683, 684; wants to keep Sally Morgan and let Anji Hunter go 684, 687; and FM's antagonism towards him 685, 686; interested in Tories 686, and Lib Dems 687; pleased with *Times* article 687, 688; at another Chequers awayday 688–9; plays guitar 690; and TUC speech 690, 691; and 9/11 691–2

views and policies on: asylum 286, 289, 293, 294–5; 'Britishness' 224, 274, 275; GB 60, 101, 116–17, 168, 183, 194–5, 229, 230, 236, 239, 278, 298, 304, 342, 362, 363, 375, 384, 401, 405, 406, 408–9, 420, 449, 466, 511, 529, 552, 529, 558, 631, 640, 645–6, 667, 679, 681; AC's role and relationship 106, 139, 140, 156–7, 173, 270–71, 280, 281, 293–4, 297, 298, 322–3, 339–40, 361, 362, 376, 377, 378, 384, 385, 431, 445, 448, 449, 482–3, 488, 520; Prince Charles 145, 151–2, 552; euro and EMU 58, 61–2, 91, 127, 132–3, 273, 342, 344, 355, 357, 378, 389, 414, 415, 429, 430, 448, 515, 616–17, 618, 641, 645, 649, 651–2, 689; Europe 90, 91, 236, 244 *and n*, 275, 413–14; 'forces of conservatism' 140–46 *passim*, 149; GM foods 38–9; Hague 272, 542; heartlands/ Middle England 263, 278, 279, 283, 284, 323, 329, 331, 332, 334, 337; Tim Henman 662; hunting 81, 341, 342, 357, 361, 418, 445, 482, 490, 493, 496; Iran 86; Lib Dems 15, 687; the Lords 113, 687; PM 362, 384, 410, 417, 420, 425, 427, 449; the media/ press 182–3, 210, 223, 263, 271, 272, 274–5, 276, 284, 297–8, 331, 338, 362, 370, 373, 379, 380, 381, 417, 449–50, 491, 513; NHS 210, 211, 213–14, 215, 223; New Labour 277, 278, 279, 286, 305, 313, 320, 324, 448, 516*n*, 581; North–South divide 177–8; One Nation 225; PLP 652, 653; politicians 449; PMQs 664; public service reform 100, 650, 653, 655, 678–9; religion: schools 385, 665–6; Section 28 258, 277, 378; Speakers 432–3; Third Way 390, 688; Tories 102, 107, 108, 154–5; unions 652; washing-line theory 322, 380

Blair, William (Bill) 393, 634
Blank, Sir Victor 462–3, 629
Blumenthal, Sidney 390
Blunkett, David (DB): does 'freelance initiatives' 106; and North–South divide 176, 178; low-key 212; 217, 219, 259, 268, 269–70; meets Delia Smith 269, 270; and GB's meetings 287; and Romsey by-election 302; 'hitting the right notes' 314; and longer-term planning 321, 328; and Oxbridge row 325; complains about GB 334; impresses AC 336, 339; in Cabinet 350, 368; loses case against NUT

369 *and n*; mentions 'mole' 372; gets a great press 377–8; and fuel crisis 395–6, 450; and Woodhead's departure 417, 419, 423, 425, 428, 434, 443; and GB 420, 514, 548; critical of Robinson's book 425; at DD's funeral 428; criticises *Who Wants to Be a Millionaire?* 465 *and n*, and rail companies 466; angry at Guthrie's speech 482; and GB's New Deal speeches 466, 491; at political Cabinet 510; annoyed by AC's 'bog-standard comprehensive' comment 519–20, 521, 524; upset by GB's Budget 544; and New Deal next steps 549; on effects of FMD 551, 559; annoyed with AC over election date 567; questions GB's meeting with Murdoch 591; 'a bit whiney' 591; and election campaign 593, 594, 604, 608, 616; and *Sun* article 604, 610; and reshuffle 632, 636 *and n*; on *Frost* 649; pressurises chief constable to quit 651; and cannabis/ criminalisation 662; does well 686; and 9/11 692

BMW/Rover *see* Rover
BNFL *see* British Nuclear Fuels
Boateng, Paul 604
Boffey, Chris 305, 310
Bognor Regis: tornado (2000) 438 *and n*
Bolland, Mark 483
Bonfield, Sir Peter 238
Bono 60, 499
Booth, Gale 320
Booth, Lyndsey 634
Booth, Tony 165
Boothroyd, Betty 174, 367–8, 378, 461*n*
Bosnian War (1992–95) 416 *and n*
Bosnich, Mark 147
Bostock, David 136, 249, 348
Bostock, Dr Tom 125, 663, 669
Botham, Ian 343 *and n*
Bouchard, Lucien 532
Boulton, Adam 60, 121, 160, 210, 219, 347, 375, 380, 437–8, 607
Bourne, Robert 491
Bower, Tom 553; *The Paymaster* 555
Boycott, Rosie 167
BP 397–8
Bradford riots (2001) 662 *and n*, 663, 676
Bradshaw, Ben 352
Bradshaw, David 47, 343
Brahimi, Lakhdar: report 391 *and n*
Braithwaite, Julian (JB): and Kosovo 3, 5, 6, 8, 9, 11, 12, 13, 14, 15, 17, 21, 22, 34–5, 42, 44, 55, 56–7; drafts TB speech 90, 91; on Portillo 107; drafts TB article 133; at Helsinki summit 181, 184; with TB in Ghent 244; at meeting re EU presentation unit 249; reports media coverage 272, 275; and IRA statement 305; and TB's WI speech 336; and EU defence rebuttal 460; on 1967 FMD outbreak 576
Branson, Richard 191
Bremner, Rory 306, 438, 628; show 138 *and n*, 308, 369, 376, 456, 459, 542, 554, 661
Brighton: Labour Conference (2000) 406–11

Bristol (2001) 493, 615, 616, 617
Britain in Europe group 62, 81, 82, 85, 127–8, 132–5, 136, 138, 140, 213, 215, 218
British Airways 193–4
British Chamber of Commerce 276, 439
British-Irish Council 188
British-Irish Intergovernmental Conference 188
British Journalism Review 229, 341
British Legion 447
British Medical Association 625, 660
British Nuclear Fuels (BNFL)/Sellafield 240 *and n*, 274, 275, 276, 373
British Society of Magazine Editors 311
British Venture Capital Association 80
Britton, Paul 175, 176
Brookside 626
Brown, Gordon (GB)
May 1999–March 2000
TB's views on *see* Blair, Tony: *views and policies*; agrees with TB on reshuffle 24; in Cabinet 30; and Europe 40; appoints special adviser 49; and EMU 58, 132; 'flawed' 60; suspected by Anji Hunter of being up to no good 63; and Britain in Europe campaign 81, 82, 85, 127–8, 132–3, 134, 135, 136; meets with PG re poll 90; accuses PM of being behind stories on euro referendum 91; 'onside' 93; and RC's euro speech 104; tax credit campaign 104, 105; good on *Today* 105; on Richard and Judy show 105; gives views on future strategy 106–7; OK with PM 107; understates economic success 108; at Chequers 111, 112; delivers upbeat speech in New York 112; furious at TB backing Diana memorial 114; and public spending 115; and press reports on his relations with TB 118, 119, 120; conference speech discombobulates TB 120; undermines TB 121; and TB's reshuffle 131, 132; critical of Milburn 144; and euro 144, 217; more engaged 144; relaunches computers in school 149; 'in a sulk' 149; and Livingstone 154, 158, 161, 162, 163, 164; on the Tories 155; and PBR 155, 156, 157, 158; and CB's baby 164; clashes with TB over public spending 164, 167, 168, 171; backs Glenda Jackson 167; uncooperative at strategy meeting 168; sets up own strategy meetings 171; and North–South divide 171–2, 173; in 'foul mood' 174; and Ashdown's diaries 176; causes mayhem in Helsinki 180, 181, 182, 183; and IMF post 183, 200; announces writing off of Third World debt 189, 190, 191; offers flat to Blairs 193, 200, 201, 202, 203, 204, 230, 231; advice to TB re Dome leaked 204; policies differ from TB's 204, 206; embarrassing behaviour 208, 209; and mayoral contest 210, 212; angry at TB's *Frost* interview 210, 211, 212, 213; thinks AC responsible for 'psychological flaws' briefing 212, 329; heckled 213; opposed to TB 215;

'smouldering' 215; a serious problem 217, 218; and 'Britishness' campaign 218, 224, 231, 232; further differences in policy 229; and EU match funding 229 *and n*; and minimum wage 229, 236, 238; announces pre-Budget issues in the press 230, 238, 239; further undermines TB 234, 239–40; his attempt to set up two-government system angers AC 236, 239; rows with TB 237; wipes a fortune off BT share price 238, 239, 240; becomes co-operative 240; and TB's weak response 243, 244; angry at enterprise speech being overshadowed 247, 248; strategy paper discussed 251; and mayoral contest 256, 263; advises caution on Section 28 259; pushes for Amato in IMF post 259; nice about AC's gaffe on tax burden 263, 264; dislikes TB talking about health spending 165; and the Budget 264, 266, 267–9, 270
March–November 2000
on Tories and the media 271; and NHS reform 274, 310, 321; discombobulates TB 275; in 'killer driller' mode 277; on strategy 277, 278, 301; and local elections 283, 301; chairs morning meetings 286–7, 300–1; and unemployment figures 294; against AC's briefings dominating agenda 298; and Hague 299, 301; wants Callaghan involved 299; on 'need for goals' 304, 307, 312; and pensioners 306, 309, 324; relations with PM 311, 331, 335, 338, 353; rages about his euro speech 314, 315, 316; and police numbers 313; works on TBWA mission statements with AC 316, 317, 318; further differences with TB 321, 322, 323–6, 331; and Oxbridge row 323–33 *passim*; and CSR 326, 330, 341, 350, 357, 368; and Lampl report on NHS 334; supportive at Cabinet 338; and Alexander 341; and Byers' euro speech 341; and euro row 342, 344, 345; false bonhomie with RC 346; clashes with TB in Feira 346, 347, 348, 349, 350; 'in a sulk' 349; shocks Ed Miliband with his behaviour 349; against One Nation politics 350, 353; gives party 351; discusses party discipline 353, 365; and Europe 353, 355, 365; rages about leaked memo 361; goes to Japan 365; and Milburn's NHS paper 366–7; in Scotland 368; CSR presentation 370–71, 373, 376, 377; excellent in the House 371; and health 377, 380; on the economy 378; secretive and difficult 379; sees Grid notes for the first time 379–80; and conference slogan 381; wedding 381; Kinnock's views on 382; his mood post-honeymoon 387; at OPEC 393; and fuel crisis 394, 395, 397, 398, 399–400, 401, 402, 403; again brings up subject of 'psychological flaws' 401; has post-wedding party 403; and Ecclestone donation 403–5, 407; causes problems with interviews 404, 405–6; conference

Handley, David 440, 441, 442, 444, 445, 448, 450, 451, 553
Hannay, David 39
Hanson, David 644, 650, 653, 664, 679
Hardy, James 441, 445
Harman, Harriet 403, 639
Harman, Sir John 558
Harrington, Illtyd 508 *and n*
Harris, Chris 269
Harris, Jonathan 254
Harris, Robert 503, 505, 510
Hart, David 625
Hartpury Agricultural College (2001) 540
Harvey, Nick 350
Hastilow, Nigel 493
Hastings, Max 101, 136, 249, 389, 687
Hatfield rail crash (2000) 426, 427, 428, 464*n*
Hattersley, Roy 337, 679
Hayman, Baroness Helene 578
Healey, John 680
Heathcoat-Amory, Edward 520
Hellawell, Keith 104, 230, 237, 258
Helm, Sarah 349, 351
Helsinki European Council (1999) 172, 178, 180, 181–4, 458*n*
Hemel Hempstead Hospital (2001) 627
Henman, Tim 662
Hennessy, Professor Peter 222
Herald 258, 262, 263, 616
Herald Tribune 57, 59, 62, 375
Heseltine, Michael (MH) 62, 86, 128, 133–4, 321, 463, 482, 485
Hester, Laura 454
Hewitt, Gavin 433
Hewitt, Patricia 93 *and n*, 191, 277; in Cabinet 632, 633, 634, 636*n*, 654
Heye, Uwe-Karsten 17
Heywood, Jeremy: at EMU meeting 58; on cost of TB's bathroom 98; on public spending 115; and Mo Mowlam 157; dinner with AC 183; at meeting on EU presentation unit 249; backs AC over local elections 288, 290, 291; not happy with new set-up 308–9; and CSR 345–6; in Feira 348; critical of TB 352; in Japan 373; and fuel protests 398, 436, 443; and Corbett 437; and criminal record checks 514; worries about Budget 538; surprised at CB's and FM's anger at planned changes 549; and FMD 556, 564, 570, 577; on improving TB's modus operandi 590; says GB is not happy with Tube deal 591; memo on public service problems leaked 592; on RW 636; on GB 642, 647; shocked that AC is thinking of leaving 670; on tax credits 678; and education 679; does paper on tax and spend 689
Hill, David 441, 539, 599, 601, 615–16, 620, 621, 623, 624
Hill, Peter 549
Hill, Robert 203, 209, 285, 287, 315, 329, 378, 644, 657, 671, 678, 679, 689, 692
Hince, Vernon 242, 243
Hinduja, Srichand: passport application affair 499 *and n*, 500–1, 502–8, 509, 510

Hinton, Les 378, 540
Hodges, Dan 151
Hoey, Kate 93–4, 638, 657
Hoge, Warren 351
Hollick, Lord Clive 167, 464, 468
Holmes, John 271, 281, 346, 348
Hombach, Bodo 272
homosexuality *see* Section 28
Hong Kong 142, 393
Honours lists 35, 191, 192, 440
Hoon, Geoff 128, 132, 158, 235; and Guthrie 145, 462; attacked by Clare Short 250, 252; and Sierra Leone hostages 393; at DD's funeral 428; and bombing of Iraq 523; as campaigner 538; and FMD 558, 569, 580; and 9/11 692, 694
Hope, Dr David, Archbishop of York 566
Hornby, Johnny 318
Horton, Willie 604 *and n*
House of Lords 113, 191, 214, 229, 232*n*, 257
Howard, Michael 17
Howarth, Alan 175 *and n*, 176, 188, 566
Howarth, George 93
Howe, Kevin 307*n*
Howell, Paul 190
Howells, Kim 130, 133, 573
Hucknall, Mick 280, 609
Hudson, Hugh: *My Life So Far* 114
Hughes, David 184, 374
Hughes, Karen 673
Hughes, Simon 286, 368, 619
Hume, Cardinal Basil: funeral 64–5
Hume, John 83, 477
Humphrys, John 13, 79, 270, 403, 424, 601
Hunter, Anji: organises TB's visits to refugee camps 4, 6; on lack of focus 34; tries to set up new media systems in Skopje 44, 45; and GB 63, 106; and Cabinet reshuffle 91, 92, 93; and CB's pregnancy 120; warns of alienating people 125; and Geoffrey Robinson 142, 143, 146; and mayoral contest 154, 180; and the Millennium 193, 194; works with AC on strategy re the press 223; and GB/TB battle 235; warns AC not to run GB down 239; plays down problems 239; critical of TB 274, 275; at Chequers discussions 278; on need for reform 284; worried about Cockerell's film 287; on TB/AC relations 313; offers to help AC 322; on Oxbridge row 329, 332; and TB's WI speech 333, 334, 336, 339; as possible Millbank/Number 10 liaison 340; emails leaked 369–70; annoys AC over crowded diary 372; sees him lose it with TB 376, 377; says she will leave after election 386, 393; reports on PM's meeting 419; reports on TB's flood visits 443; wants to leave 489, 495, 511, 578, 580; argues for AC to go to Millbank 490; and PM/ Hinduja affair 503; stops GB from seeing AC's letter 511; and TB's planned changes 516, 549, 571, 575, 576, 580; and the press 563, 568; and the 'Prescott punch' 607; tells AC his name's mud with GB people 621; saves TB from

heckler 627; sorts out photographers 629; TB wants her to stay 634, 635; becomes director of government relations 637, 638, 639–40; feared by GB 640; depressed 645; suspicious of GB and Clare Short 654; at David Frost's party 659; angry with TB at being told she can leave 684–5

hunting, ban on 81, 89, 103, 106, 122, 151, 154, 340, 341, 342, 357, 418, 425, 445, 482, 483; vote on 495, 496

Hurd, Douglas 647

Hussein, Saddam 532, 533

Hutchison, Ian 325, 329

Hutt, Jane 285

Hutton, Will 403

Hyman, Peter (PH) 99, 100; on Dobson 100; works on TB's conference speech (1999) 106, 112, 113, 115, 116, 119–20, 121–2; feels Labour has sense of project back again 125; works with Dobson 131; briefs on TB's education speech 142; at GB's first strategy meeting 171; and TB's North-West tour 178; works on TB's pre-millennium speech 193; wants TB to focus on education 225; works on Budget and health statement 266; suspicious of GB's motives 268, 286; writes note on New Labour 311, 313; at meeting on NHS 315; at meeting with AD 316; and TB's WI speech 332, 333, 334, 335; drafts TB's health statement 378; lack of motivation 383; disillusioned by TB 385; works on conference speech (2000) 407; does papers on strategy 417, 419, 426; at DD's funeral 428; on GB/ PM relations 431–2; on TB 505; compares GB with TB 513; dispirited by PG 523; on Hammond Inquiry 539; critical of TB's planned changes 549; and election timing 565; at meeting on election issues 583; and TB's opening speech 592–3; thinks AC should be at Millbank 600; states need for more TB in campaign 622; 'pissed off' 642, 649; 'warm and human' 657; doing good work 658, 661, 663; at Chequers 678, 680

IMF see International Monetary Fund

immigration 594, see also asylum issues

incapacity benefit 24, 155n, 658, 660

Independent 8, 40, 94, 117, 118, 133, 140, 276, 289, 340, 351, 359, 368, 469, 576, 577, 615; see also Grice, Andy; Macintyre, Don

Independent International Commission on Decommissioning 22, 78n

Independent on Sunday 44, 122, 246, 254n, 246, 406

Ingham, Bernard 362

Ingram, Adam 93

Institute for Public Policy Research: report 650

Institute of Education: Labour Party meeting (2000) 213

interest rates 106, 207, 208, 215, 284, 437, 439, 444, 445, 446, 525n, 544

International Criminal Tribunal for the former Yugoslavia 35

International Monetary Fund (IMF) 183 *and* n, 256

IRA: and decommissioning 31, 67, 69–79 *passim*, 83, 86–8, 163, 226, 233, 234, 237, 293, 296, 301, 302, 303, 304, 305, 310, 354, 434, 436, 545, 656n; threatens death for local crimes 99

Iraq: US–UK attacks (2001) 523–4; TB/ Cheney discussions on 532; TB/Bush discussions on 533, 535

Irvin, Joe 93, 151, 524, 607

Irvine, Alison 428

Irvine, Derry, Lord Chancellor 60, 126, 282, 283, 405, 428; and PM/Hinduja affair 503, 506, 507; and 'cash for wigs' row 526 *and* n, 527, 530; wound up by GB 547; and campaign strategy 599; and the 'Prescott punch' 606, 607; questions why GB is so angry 620; and reshuffle 633, 634

Irwin, General Sir Alistair 477, 498

Itchen College, Southampton 614 *and* n

ITN 101, 192, 214, 249, 343, 358, 408; *see also* Brunson, Mike

ITV: *This Morning* 105; *Ask the Prime Minister* 476, 480–81

Ivanov, Igor 51, 291, 460

Jackson, Glenda 92, 151, 162, 487

Jackson, Jesse 3–4

Jackson, General Sir Michael (Mike) 5, 6, 42, 43–4; sick of spin doctors 45; announces agreement with Milosevic 46; and Russian movements 49, 50, 52, 53; and AC's trip to Priština 56, 57, 58; meets TB at KFOR HQ 95; and Wes Clark 96, 97, 171

Jackson, Michael 61

Jackson, Sarah 171

Janvrin, Sir Robin 202, 573, 680

Jay, Baroness Margaret 142, 214, 221, 428, 511

Jay, Sir Michael 148, 281, 433, 473, 517

Jeffrey, Bill 300

Jelley, Monica 336

Jenkin, Bernard 127

Jenkins, Roy 240, 299, 668

Jenkins, Simon 202

Jenkins, Sue 680

Jertz, Major General Walter 4, 6, 13, 19, 34–5

Jiang Zemin, President of China 141–2, 143, 145, 152, 391, 392

Johnson, Boris 28, 330, 343

Johnson, Donald C. 78

Johnson, Paul 301, 335

Johnston, Assistant Commissioner Ian 364

Joint Consultative Committee 688

Jones, George 94, 143, 262, 263, 271, 424

Jones, Jack 447

Jones, Maggie 669

Jones, Nick 91, 119; *The Control Freaks* 548 *and* n

Joseph, Tanya 123, 260, 284, 351, 376, 672

MEPP *see* Middle East peace process
Merritt, Ellie 49
Merritt, John 660
Meyer, Catherine 682
Meyer, Sir Christopher 5, 308, 389, 493, 535, 673, 674, 682
MI5 110, 242–3, 296, 615, 693
MI6 42, 110, 243, 358*n*, 405 *and n*, 510
Michael, Alun 12, 23, 229 *and n*, 230–31 *and n*, 235
Middle East peace process (MEPP) 372, 374, 389–90, 416, 418, 421–5 *passim*, 532, 534, 673
Mihailova, Nadezhda 25
Milburn, Alan: becomes Health Secretary 128, 131, 132; has bad press 138; worries GB 144; refuses to do radio and TV 145; and Winston's attack on NHS 209; and Shipman 221, 223; at ministers' meeting 235; and NHS plan 268, 269, 275, 277, 288, 289, 315, 328, 329, 341, 354, 378; liaises with Lib Dems 345, 350, 361; on private sector 344; launches plan 380–81; and fuel blockades 398, 399; as a reformer 409; on GB/PM relations 427; at DD's funeral 428; in North-East 444; at Chequers 458; and nurses' pay 481; and BSE 462, 463; on *Dimbleby* 468; agrees to Marr interview 492; and organ transplants 512; and GB 514, 544, 545, 565, 654; and election campaign 538, 608, 609, 613, 616; gives confident press conference 618; suggests an inquest on campaign 628; on *Today* on PPPs 650; wants to fight BMA on reform 660
Miles, Alice 201, 377
Miliband, David (DM): dinner with AC 4–5; does double act with AC at *Express* 91; at Conference 120, 121; feels Labour's losing the plot 156; at Queen's Speech meeting 201; and MB 201; and Russians 262; at *Express* with AC 287; unhappy with new set-up 309; and GB 349; unmotivated 383; on TB 385; gatecrashes TB's meeting with BC 390; senses tensions between Clinton people and Gore people 392; conference speech 409; feels TB is 'becalmed' 433; with AC at *Observer* 462; breakfast at *Express* 476; defends policy process 527; thinks AC should be at Millbank 539; wonders whether to become an MP 484, 545, 580; and election manifesto 572; on the Lords 572; worried about TB 579; at Chequers 585; becomes an MP 600, 649–50
Miliband, Ed 105, 288; mission statement 318; and Tory pension promises 322; 'leftish' 325; defensive 350, 616; at GB's wedding 381; and PM 410, 419; and GB's refusal to launch poster 548; and election timing 565; accuses Pienaar of invention 599; shocked at AC's observation re GB 618
Millar, Audrey 383, 508, 541
Millar, Fiona 3; on Kosovo 22, 30; fed up with broken nights 51, 53; quarrels with

AC 106, 116; at Blairs' Christmas card photographic session 110; and unpleasant article in *Mail* 114; and CB's pregnancy 118, 120–21, 123, 163–4; dinner with *Independent* 122; approves of Oborne's book on AC 123; lack of emotional support for AC 155–6; out and about with CB 164–5; at dinner with American ambassador 169; on Prince Charles 170; 'pissed off' 178; on Millennium Eve 195, 196, 197; birthday celebrations 200; calls Oborne 209; on GB and TB 230; at first football match *en famille* 246; and Blair's ex-nanny 254, 259, 276; and Rory's behaviour 273; with AC at Ferguson's testimonial 279, 280; concerned at TB's lack of conviction 281; with AC at Irvine dinner 282; and Cockerell's film 287; at media reception 292; thinks AC should sue over smear 305; speaks to Bharti Vyas 307; with AC at Delia Smith's 315; and Leo Blair's birth 316, 318, 319, 320; wants AC to leave job 351, 362, 377, 383, 488–9, 490, 512, 527, 537, 538, 541, 543, 544, 545, 551, 553, 555; and Euan Blair's arrest 364; suspects PM of stirring 366, 367; on Cockerell film 369; on leaks 369; on GB 410; sides with CB over pictures of Leo 422; at Rory's birthday dinner 433; with AC at Blairs' 448, 449; annoyed at articles on AC and Britney Spears 458; angry with CB 469; at the Dome on New Year's Eve 485; at film *en famille* 488; dinner with Rubin 489; unlikely to want to stay in job 522; hostile towards TB 528–9, 538–9, 549; and Ferguson's advice 538, 539; angry at planned changes 549, 551; talking properly to AC again 557, 560, 658; at PG's birthday party 567; on GB's *GMTV* appearance 573; dinner with Melanne Verveer 577; happier 581; as Anji Hunter's replacement 590; and the 'Prescott punch' 607; angry at Anji's new role 637, 638, 639, 640; persuaded by CB to stay 640, 641; at meeting re TB's summer holiday 647; feels TB should get credit for Milosevic 655; on AC's depressions 656; at Bevins' memorial service 657; at Frost's party 659; forgets to pack shoes 674; not speaking to AC at Kinnock wedding 674, 675; thinks AC should see doctor 675–6; mutual apologies 677; at Chequers discussions 679, 684; accuses TB of emotional blackmail 681; tells CB AC is having second thoughts 681; on Naughtie's book 681–2; and AC's drink problem 683; in paradoxical position re AC's job 683–4; and TB 684, 685, 686; at Chequers awayday 688, 689
Millar, Gavin 204, 305, 431, 463, 541, 560
Millar, Oscar 204, 463
millennium bug 187 *and n*
Millennium Dome 106, 110, 149, 185, 190, 191–2, 194, 195–6, 197, 199–201, 202,

203, 204, 205, 216, 223, 236, 320, 321, 322, 324, 326, 389, 390, 391; Nomura pulls out of purchase 395; Clare Short on 405; and legacy 412, 417, 451; foiled diamond robbery 447 *and n*; and Cabinet minutes leak 452, 453; TB's visit 482

Mills, David 325, 512, 560, 661

Mills, Jessie 560, 661–2

Mills, Sir John 609

Mills, Matthew 662

Milosevic, Slobodan: and Jesse Jackson's visit 4; TB's views on 7, 8, 11, 26, 36; and NATO conditions 12 *and n*, 28, 40; and the media 14, 34; orders partial troop withdrawal 16, 17, 18; and fears re his survival 25, 27; indicted as war criminal 35; Jospin on 36; negotiates conditions 40–41, 42, 43, 44, 45, 46, 47, 53; hangs on to power 59, 60, 64; tries to get money to China 91; fall of 414–15; arrested 568; at Hague Tribunal 655

minimum wage 236, 238

Mitchell, Senator George 85, 86, 87, 103, 153, 161, 163

MMU *see* Media Monitoring Unit

mobile phones: and safety 309, 310

Molloy, Mike and Sandy 315

Monks, John 111*n*, 396, 409, 692

Montgomery, David 464

Montgomery, Robbie 320

Moody-Stuart, Mark 400

Moorcroft, David 675

Moore, Charles 169, 329, 352, 386, 631, 690

Morgan, Piers 105, 114–15, 163, 164, 165, 190, 201, 211, 214, 427, 441, 631, 648

Morgan, Rhodri 231, 232, 284, 285

Morgan, Sally 91; on TB/GB relations 100; and mayoral contest 180, 219; and CB's pregnancy 120, 123; on GB 229, 377; on Livingstone 240; at TBWA brainstorming session 318; and TB's WI speech 333; and Anji Hunter 340, 569; on 'Sell Blair' feeling 343; and Hain's article 368; lack of motivation 383; at DD's funeral 428; argues for AC to go to Millbank 490, 600; TB unlikely to retain 516; with TB in Gloucester 540; going to the Lords 543; and the 'Prescott punch' 607; pushes for Harriet Harman as Solicitor General 639; on PM in Europe 645; on public sector reform 650; at dreadful PLP 664; and education discussion 679; on Adonis 687

Mori, Yoshiro 373

Morley, Elliot 443, 451

Morris, Bill 111, 289, 396, 409

Morris, Estelle 235, 538, 609, 618; wins seat 632, 633, 635; and Cabinet reshuffle 632, 636*n*, 637; 'a bit unfocused' 652; and postponement of White Paper 663, 665; advised by AC 688

Morris, John 92

Morris, Steve 465

Moss, Vincent 89

Motion, Andrew: 'In a Perfect World' 110, 111

Mountbatten, Lord Louis 169

Mowlam, Mo 30–31, attacked by Trimble 62; on GB 63; chirpy 64; and NI Executive suspension bill 83; and reshuffle 86, 87, 90, 92; behaves oddly 86; nasty press story about 99; defended by AC 99; as Minister for the Cabinet Office 129, 130, 131–2, 143, 150, 152, 158; admits to taking cannabis 148, 150, 156, 157; gives bad interview 162; and mayoral contest 162, 178–9, 180, 186, 200, 205, 214, 216, 217, 219, 220; and the press 185; overestimates abilities 186; speech on Tories 205; on TB's unpopularity 215; and whispering campaign 221, 223, 224; feels excluded from Dome discussions 227–8; joins mayoral contest 231, 234, 235, 241, 242, 243; and drugs meeting 237–8; at Chequers 277; and Falconer 298; and McDougall's documentary and article 302, 304, 305, 306; upset by TB 310; 'all over the shop' 314; in need of a role 323; sulking 324; 'spin campaign' against 326 *and n*; critical of spin 338; on Levy 352; Royal gaffe 354, 356; attacked by AC 360; dreadful on *Today* 367, 368; does photocall with Massow 381; discusses resignation with TB 387–8; and Kofi Annan 390; at DD's funeral 428; wants new role 450; feels snubbed at Chequers meeting 458; speaks at Bevins' memorial service 657

Mozambique: floods (2000) 248 *and n*, 249, 250, 251–2

Mugabe, Robert 159 *and n*, 160, 283, 294, 295, 296

Muirhead, Oona 62

Mulgan, Geoff 678, 689

Mullally, Sarah 247

Mullin, Chris 94

Murdoch, Elisabeth 123

Murdoch, Rupert 31, 123, 142, 194, 240, 271, 401, 417, 439–40, 641

Murphy, Darren 378

Murphy, Jim 654

Murphy, Joe 310, 366, 459

Murphy, Paul 68, 428

Murphy, Phil 241

Murray, Denis 84, 87, 233–4

Musharraf, General Pervez 132*n*

NAC *see* North Atlantic Council

Naish, Liz (*née* Campbell) 431, 578

Naruhito, Crown Prince of Japan 612

National Air Traffic Services (NATS) 141, 307, 309

National Association of Head Teachers 625

National Executive Council (NEC) 114, 132, 133, 161, 162, 163, 242, 279, 409

National Farmers' Union (NFU) 223, 224–5, 537, 549, 554, 556, 564, 575

National Health Service (NHS): 'winter crises' 190, 203, 204, 468, 453, 464; and flu epidemic 205; Winston's attack on 208–10; and private sector involvement 212; criticism of 213, 217, 236, 263, 284–5,

307; spending on 213–14, 265, 266, 267, 269; Audit Commission report on 276; nurses' pay and recruitment 210, 211, 246, 247, 248, 275, 451, 481 *and n*; plan for reform 274, 287, 314, 345, 350, 373, 376, 378, 380–81; *see also* Milburn, Alan
National Insurance contributions (NICs) 451, 611, 612, 613
National Missile Defence (NMD) 291, 374, 517, 518, 532, 533, 534, 536, 589, 649, 669, 670, 671, 672, 673, 694
National Union of Teachers 369
NATO: and Kosovo 3, 8, 9, 10, 12–14, 15, 17, 19–20, 21, 22–3, 32, 33; conditions demanded of Milosevic 12 *and n*, 28, 40; and Schroeder 29; exposed as ineffective 55; and EU defence 470 *and n*; different interpretations of role 517; commitment to 532, 533–4; Brussels summit (2001) 642; *see also* Robertson, George; Solana, Javier
Naughtie, James 347, 351, 388; *The Rivals...* 681–2, 690
NEC *see* National Executive Council
Neely, Bill 629
neighbourhood renewal 482, 484–5, 494, 495
Neil, Andrew 615, 616
Neill, Lord Patrick 405; Committee report 207 *and n*
'New Deal' 62
New Millennium Experience Company (NMEC) 192, 196, 200, 321
New Statesman 200, 205, 208, 616
New York Times 31, 32, 351, 377
Newby, Lord Dick 257
Newcastle: airport terminal 443
Newport, Shropshire (2001) 623
News Corporation 31
News International 122
News of the World 128, 165n, 359, 360, 387, 402, 5 73, 591, 625 *and n*, 626
Newsweek 24, 453
next-steps agenda 278, 325, 454, 466, 479, 492, 498, 500, 510, 513, 514, 515, 516, 520, 526, 549
NFU *see* National Farmers' Union
NHS *see* National Health Service
NHS Direct 179, 210
Nice: European summit (2000) 464, 468, 469, 470–76, 480
NICs *see* National Insurance contributions
Nieminen, Brigadier Tauno 78n
Nissan car plant, Sunderland 498
NMD *see* National Missile Defence
NMEC *see* New Millennium Experience Company
Nomura (Japanese bank) 395
Noonan, Peggy xvii
Norman, Archie 295 *and n*
Norris, Geoffrey 265
Norris, Steven 165, 235, 241, 242, 250, 305
North, David 150, 347, 412, 553, 556, 564
North, Oliver 296 *and n*
North American Free Trade Agreement (NAFTA) 355
North Atlantic Council (NAC) 17, 34, 46

North–South divide, report on 171–2, 173, 175–6, 177–8, 180, 182, 294
Northern Echo 359
Northern Ireland *see* Adams, Gerry; Blair, Tony; IRA; McGuinness, Martin; Social Democratic and Labour Party; Trimble, David; Ulster Unionist Party
Northumbria, University of 443–4 *and n*
Norton, Jon 156, 157, 186, 388
Norwich (2001) 609
Norwood, Melita 108 *and n*, 109, 110, 218
nurses *see* National Health Service
Nye, Sue 212, 511, 565, 651n, 682

Oakington Reception Centre 690 *and n*
Oakley, Robin 61, 121, 160, 219, 271, 311–12
Oborne, Peter: book on AC 114, 116, 118, 123, 124; on AC 117, 207, 209, 343, 577; on TB 146
O'Brien, Mike 485; and PM/Hinduja affair 501, 502, 503, 507, 509, 512, 539, 543
Observer 49, 102, 103, 146, 165, 210, 212, 262, 276, 310, 319, 351, 360, 403, 431, 462, 499, 518, 568, 577, 592, 627
O'Donnell, Gus 215, 343
OECD (Organisation for Economic Co-operation and Development) 154, 443
Ogilvy, Sir Angus 169, 659
oil companies 394, 397–8, 400, 423
OK! magazine 462
Oldham: race riots (2001) 619 *and n*
O'Leary, Dermot 628
Olympic Games 345, 411, 494
Oman, Sultan of 87
Omand, David 349, 396
on-the-spot fines 357, 358, 359, 361, 363, 364
Ondaatje, Sir Christopher 488
'O'Neill, P.' (IRA spokesman pseudonym) 237
O'Neill, Terry 110
OPEC (Organisation of the Petroleum Exporting Countries) 393, 400
Orange Order 57, 66, 67, 71, 668
Oxford University/Oxbridge row 323 *and n*, 324, 325–6, 327–8, 329, 330, 331, 359

PA *see* Press Association
Page, Jennie 196, 200, 202, 203, 227, 228, 229
Paisley, Ian 74, 293, 497
Pakenham, Michael 53, 351
Pallas, Omar 359
Parades Commission (NI) 67n, 68, 668
Parker-Bowles, Camilla 169
Parkinson, Jo 255
Parkinson, Michael 438, 444
Parliamentary Labour Party (PLP): and TB 61, 63, 349; and AC 342; and Cockerell film 371; up in arms re 'bog-standard comprehensives' 521; and GB's charm offensive 562; TB's campaign speech 595–6; 'spooks' TB 652–3; gets a fright 660
Parris, Matthew 222n
Parry, Emyr Jones 470
Party election broadcasts (PEBs) 37, 581, 589, 592, 619–20, 622–3, 624, 628, 630

364; new role 366; friendly to AC 366;
angry with Hain 368; Transport Plan
goes well 372; his carpet gets in the
press 379; chairs final morning meeting
383; and French ferry blockades 386; and
fuel blockades 395, 400; angry with GB
405, 417, 420; at Conference 409, 410,
411; and Hatfield rail crash 427, 430, 435,
464; on TB 430; and Robinson's book
431; votes for new Speaker 432; angry
with TB 436, 438, 440; rows with AC
440; dinner with PM and GB 441; and
floods 440, 442, 444; in York 444;
complains about PM 456; on
campaigning structures 457; blames
French minister for collapse of Hague
talks 464 *and n*; and mystery donors 487;
on TB/GB relations 514 *and* n; and
bombing of Iraq 523, 524; accuses AC of
trying to run his department 548; and
Green Paper on jobs 550; and Bevins
566; against 'clever adman stuff' 571;
sets out jobs he could do 579; has mini
PR disaster 579; annoys GB 582; and
Tube deal 591; at manifesto launch 604;
punches protester 606 *and n*, 607, 608;
campaigns with GB 622; arrives in
Sedgefield by helicopter 632; discussions
on possible posts 633; on *Today* 647; and
public service reform 653; and Clare
Short 654; had up for speeding 677; has
doubts about Charles Clarke 682; rages
at press 682; on the unions 682
Prescott, Michael (Mike) 303, 618
Prescott, Pauline 96, 97, 123, 124
Press Association (PA) 95, 191, 228, 237, 241,
250, 256, 307, 360, 420, 427, 465, 672
Press Complaints Commission (PCC) 115,
191, 379, 380, 412, 449
Preston, John 297
Preston, Roz 297
Preston by-election (2000) 461*n*, 463
Price, Jack 547
Price, Lance 34; reports to AC 98, 152, 163;
at GB's first strategy meeting 171; and
Shaun Woodward's defection 175, 176,
185, 187, 191; briefed on his
responsibilities by AC 235; moves to
Millbank 313; at meeting on NHS 315;
and Massow's defection 381; and
Alexander 433; briefs on party donors
489, 491; lacks authority in Millbank 513;
at *Express* 519; his farewell 640
Primakov, Yevgeny 19
Prince, Jonathan 3, 5, 9, 20, 26, 27, 45, 46, 47
Prodi, Romano: and Levi 80; and French
beef ban 136, 147, 181; bemused by AC
137–8; bilateral with TB in Japan 373; on
Britain and Europe 413, 414, 415; at Nice
summit 472, 476; at Stockholm European
Council 559; visits London 521; speech
on EU integration 621
Progress 368
proportional representation (PR) 63, 138,
204, 556, 626; AV 354, 355, 356
Public Accounts Committee 98

public-private partnerships (PPPs) 141, 161,
162, 561*n*, 650, 657, 658, 662, 663, 670,
679
public service reform 100, 490, 644, 649, 650,
652, 653, 655, 657, 661, 667, 668, 669, 675,
679, 682, 690
Punch magazine 342
Purnell, James 406
Putin, Vladimir, President of Russia 252,
260–62; London visit 286, 287, 288, 289,
290; in Japan 374, 375; at P5 392; and
TB's visit to Moscow 459, 460–61;
Chrétien on 531; and NMD 533, 559;
Bush on 534, 535; TB fills him in on
Bush 559; Bush tough with 673; and
9/11 693
Puyméras, France 381–2

QMV (qualified majority voting) 423, 462,
472
Queen's Speeches/debates: 1999 126, 129,
145, 146, 159, 160, 162, 163; 2000 454*n*,
459, 464, 467, 468, 469–70; 2001 641, 646,
647, 648, 660
Quin, Joyce 93, 152
Quinn, Caroline 601

Radio Free Europe 30
Railtrack 129, 172, 173, 428, 434, 464*n*, 688
railways 126, 438, 466; crashes *see* Hatfield;
Ladbroke Grove; Selby; Southall; *see also*
Railtrack
Ramaphosa, Cyril 303, 313, 353
Rambouillet Agreement 12*n*
Rawnsley, Andrew 102, 212, 312, 346;
Servants of the People 276 *and n*, 392–3,
402, 403, 404, 406, 407, 410; misquotes
AC 649
Rayner, Terry 438
Raynsford, Nick 93 *and n*, 112, 136, 548
Raznatovic, Zeljko (Arkan) 9, 11, 14
Read, Rob 276
Real IRA 477
Rebuck (Gould), Gail 90, 281, 306, 335, 492,
661
Redwood, John 127
Reedie, Craig 345
Reid, John 24, 94, 96; and DD 102; has
conspiratorial chat with AC 191; at
ministers' meeting 235; and PPB film
258; and the media 321, 337, 341;
excellent in Cabinet 338; and fuel
blockades 394; on GB 422; at DD's
funeral 428; in Cabinet 442; investigated
by Standards Committee 464 *and n*, 483;
at AC's conference call on TV debates
495; and PM/Hinduja story 503; as
Secretary of State for NI 505, 545; as
possible campaigner 538; on reshuffles
by conference call 568; on TB 655
Reiss, Charles 159, 374–5, 680
Reith, General John 26
Reuters 95
Rex Features 191
Rice, Condoleezza 493, 532, 533, 535, 674
Richard, Cliff 201, 202

Richards, Ed 349
Richards, Steve 205, 363
Richardson, Bryan 204
Riddell, Peter 100, 122, 403
Ridgeway, General Andrew 49
Rifkind, Sir Malcolm 452n
Rimmer, Catherine 570
Robbins, James 463
Roberts, Sir Ivor 82, 301
Robertson, George (GR): and Kosovo 16, 33,
  44, 46, 47, 52; becomes NATO Secretary
  General 87, 94, 95, 97; last Cabinet
  meeting 112; hands over to Hoon 132;
  wants Special Branch protection 171, 221
Robertson, Sandra 87
Robinson, Anne 211
Robinson, Geoffrey (Coventry City
  president) 204
Robinson, Geoffrey (Labour MP): in the
  press 140, 142–3, 145–6; Mail interview
  424; and serialisation of The
  Unconventional Minister 425, 429, 500;
  makes government look ridiculous
  426–7; Bower book on 555; and
  Standards and Privileges Committee
  589–90, 591 and n
Robinson, Mary 21
Robinson, Matthew 188
Robinson, Nick 480, 506
Rochdale (2001) 618
Roche, Barbara 609
Rodger, Jim 591
Rodgers, Lord Bill 257
Rollo, Brigadier Hamish 5
Romsey by-election (2000) 299 and n, 301–2,
  303
Rooker, Jeff 93 and n, 337
Rosenthal, Jim 33
Ross, Fiona 608
Rotherham (2001) 600
Rothermere, Lord 369
Rough Sleepers Unit 186
Routledge, Paul 19, 114, 217, 500
Rove, Karl 673
Rover Group 264, 265, 266, 268, 271, 274,
  276–7, 280, 281, 282, 284, 298; bought by
  Phoenix 307–8, 309
Royal Free Hospital: TB's speech (2001) 669
  and n
Royal Manor School, Portland (2001) 615
Royal Ulster Constabulary (RUC) 277, 303,
  304, 478–9
Royal United Services Institute: AC's speech
  (1999) 62, 81–2
Rozenberg, Joshua 530
RSPCA: and FMD 577
Rubin, Jamie (JR) 9, 30, 39, 40, 351, 368–9,
  489
RUC see Royal Ulster Constabulary
Rugby (2001) 629
Rugby League Cup Final (2001) 587
Rugby World Cup Final (1999) 156
Rugova, Ibrahim, President of Kosovo 96
Rumsfeld, Donald 493
Rusbridger, Alan 111
Russell, Tony 351, 352

Russia: and Kosovo 15, 40, 41, 43, 48–9,
  50–52, 53, 54, 55, 59; see also Putin,
  Vladimir; Yeltsin, Boris

Saatchi, Maurice 169, 256
SACEUR see Clark, General Wesley
Saga magazine: poll 484 and n
Sagar, Jez 149, 191, 192, 203
Sainsbury's 398
St Olave's school, London 594–5
St Thomas's Hospital, London 248
Salford Community Centre (2001) 626
Salt Grammar School, Yorkshire 466
Sambrook, Richard 579, 625
Saudi Arabian Airlines: hijack (2000) 425 and n
Saunders, Brigadier Stephen 338 and n
Sawers, John (John S): with AC in Kosovo 5;
  needs an office 12; reports to AC on BC/
  TB phonecall 28; passes TB's views on
  GM foods to Prince Charles' office 39;
  and Kosovo 40, 42, 46, 50–51, 52, 53, 54,
  57, 59; and NI Executive suspension bill
  82–3, 84; and IRA statement 87; sets up
  support for Robertson 95; and spy story
  110; and MoD lobbying re JC 128; at
  Tampere summit 136; on beef 157; at
  CHOGM 160; at Helsinki summit 181;
  and NI 225, 226; and Putin 291; and
  Cockerell's filming 291; critical of TB
  335, 373; at Biarritz summit 424; in
  Moscow 459; and Bush 468; at Nice
  summit 471, 473, 476; and bombing of
  Iraq 523; fills TB in on Chrétien 530; on
  improving TB's modus operandi 590; on
  PM and Future of Europe post 646
Sawyer, Diane 389
Sawyer, Lord Tom 333
Scarlett, John 218, 693
Scholar, Michael 142, 143
schools see education
Schroeder, Gerhard 17; and Kosovo 12, 25,
  26, 28, 29, 32; dismissive of socialist
  leaders' meeting 37; and CFSP post 39;
  at Cologne summit 41; more friendly in
  Bonn 45–6; and Robertson's NATO
  appointment 94, 95; at Tampere summit
  136, 137, 138; speaks at Congress of the
  Socialist International 156; on CB's baby
  165, 166; at Helsinki summit 183; and
  IMF post 256, 257; at Lisbon 272, 273;
  with TB at Königswinter Conference 274;
  at Feira 348; jokes with AC 357–8; in
  Japan 372, 375; at Biarritz summit 422,
  424; at Nice summit 470, 471, 472, 473–4,
  475; relations with TB 510; at Cahors
  summit 517, 518; TB speaks up for 534;
  steals the show at Stockholm 559; on PM
  and Future of Europe post 646; keen to
  work with Britain 651; and 9/11 693
Schüssel, Wolfgang 272, 273, 424
Scientific Steering Committee, EU (SSC) 149,
  150 and n
Scotland: cashmere industry 389, 390;
  devolution 524–5
Scotland, Patricia 94
Scotsman 258

722   Index

Illustration
Acknowledgements

Picture research: Amanda Russell

Section 1

p. 1   top right: Steve Back/Daily Mail/Rex Features; centre right: Murray Sanders/Daily Mail/Rex Features; below left: PA Photos/TopFoto; below right: Author's private collection

p. 2   top: TopFoto/UPP; centre: Author's private collection; below: Rex Features

p. 3   top: PA Photos/TopFoto; below left: PA Photos/Topfoto; below right: PA Photos/Topfoto

p. 4   top: TopFoto.co.uk; centre above: Paul Faith/PA Archive/Press Association Images; centre below: PA Photos/Topfoto; below: PA Photos/Topfoto

p. 5   top: Ken Towner/Evening Standard/Rex Features; below left: Hugo Philpott/AFP/Getty Images; below right: TopFoto

p. 6   top: Martin Rowson; below left: PA Photos/TopFoto; below right: Toby Melville/PA Archive/Press Association Images

p. 7   top left: PA Photos/TopFoto; top right: Peter Lomas/Rex Features; below: Reuters/CORBIS

p. 8   top right: Author's private collection; centre left: Author's private collection; below right: Punch Ltd

Section 2

p. 1   top left: Jeroen Oerlemans/Rex Features; centre right: PA Photos/TopFoto; below left: Words and pictures Woman's Own/Rex Features

p. 2   top left: James Fraser/Rex Features; top right: PA Photos/TopFoto; below left: Raoul Dixon/TopFoto.co.uk; below right: PA Photos/TopFoto

p. 3   top left: Author's private collection; top right: Darren McCollester/Rex Features; centre: Getty Images; below: Ron Sachs/Rex Features

p. 4   top: Reuters/CORBIS; centre: Author's private collection; below: © Press Association Images

p. 5   top: Martin Rowson; below left: TopFoto.co.uk; below right: Author's private collection

p. 6   top: PA Photos/TopFoto; centre left: Brian Harris/Rex Features; below left: PA/PA Archive/Press Association Images; bottom right: PA Photos/TopFoto

p. 7   top right: Reuters/CORBIS; centre left: Author's private collection; bottom left: Rex Features; bottom right: William Conran/PA Archive/Press Association Images

p. 8   top left: TopFoto/ImageWorks; top right inset: Sipa Press/Rex Features; centre: Sipa Press/Rex Features; bottom: PA Photos/TopFoto

Illustration Acknowledgements